THE OXFORD HANDBOOK OF
ÉMILE DURKHEIM

THE OXFORD HANDBOOK OF
ÉMILE DURKHEIM

Edited by
HANS JOAS
and
ANDREAS PETTENKOFER

OXFORD
UNIVERSITY PRESS

Oxford University Press is a department of the University of Oxford. It furthers
the University's objective of excellence in research, scholarship, and education
by publishing worldwide. Oxford is a registered trade mark of Oxford University
Press in the UK and certain other countries.

Published in the United States of America by Oxford University Press
198 Madison Avenue, New York, NY 10016, United States of America.

© Oxford University Press 2024

All rights reserved. No part of this publication may be reproduced, stored in
a retrieval system, or transmitted, in any form or by any means, without the
prior permission in writing of Oxford University Press, or as expressly permitted
by law, by license, or under terms agreed with the appropriate reproduction
rights organization. Inquiries concerning reproduction outside the scope of the
above should be sent to the Rights Department, Oxford University Press, at the
address above.

You must not circulate this work in any other form
and you must impose this same condition on any acquirer.

Library of Congress Cataloging-in-Publication Data
Names: Joas, Hans, 1948– editor. | Pettenkofer, Andreas, editor.
Title: The Oxford handbook of Émile Durkheim / edited by Hans Joas and Andreas Pettenkofer.
Description: New York, NY : Oxford University Press, [2024]. | Series: Oxford handbooks series |
Includes bibliographical references. | Identifiers: LCCN 2023051651 (print) |
LCCN 2023051652 (ebook) | ISBN 9780190679354 (hardback) |
ISBN 9780190680374 (epub) | ISBN 9780190679378
Subjects: LCSH: Durkheim, Émile, 1858–1917. | Durkheimian school of sociology. | Sociology—Philosophy.
Classification: LCC HM465 .O946 2024 (print) | LCC HM465 (ebook) | DDC 301.092—dc23/eng/20231218
LC record available at https://lccn.loc.gov/2023051651
LC ebook record available at https://lccn.loc.gov/2023051652

DOI: 10.1093/oxfordhb/9780190679354.001.0001

Printed by Sheridan Books, Inc., United States of America

Contents

Acknowledgments ix
About the Volume Editors xi
List of Contributors xiii

1. Introduction: Some Reasons for (Re)reading Durkheim Today   1
   HANS JOAS AND ANDREAS PETTENKOFER

SECTION I: KEY CONCEPTS

2. Durkheim's Signature Project: The Science of Morality as Rational Moral Art   21
   MARK S. CLADIS

3. Solidarity and Attachment in Durkheim's Sociological Thought   39
   SERGE PAUGAM

4. The Sociality of Mind: Key Arguments, Inner Tensions, and Divergent Appropriations of Durkheim's Sociology of Knowledge   57
   FRITHJOF NUNGESSER

5. In Defense of Collective Consciousness: Reassessing Durkheim's Argument   82
   FRANCESCO CALLEGARO

6. Religious Rituals and Logical Thought in Durkheim: The Level of Existence of Social Things   102
   BRUNO KARSENTI

SECTION II: CONTEXTS

7. The Dreyfus Affair and Durkheim's Experience of Anti-Semitism   116
   PIERRE BIRNBAUM

8. Durkheim and the Philosophy of His Time   129
   JEAN-LOUIS FABIANI

9. Durkheim's Team: L'Année sociologique   145
   MARCEL FOURNIER AND PAUL CARLS

10. Durkheim and Bergson, Durkheimians and Bergsonians   164
    HEIKE DELITZ

11. Durkheim, Pragmatism, and Sociology   182
    ROMAIN PUDAL

12. Émile Durkheim's Germany   195
    WOLF FEUERHAHN

SECTION III: THEMES

13. The Modern Individual   213
    W. WATTS MILLER

14. Durkheim and Economic Sociology   228
    PHILIPPE STEINER

15. Reflecting on Durkheim and His Studies on Law through Cancellation of British Citizenship   245
    DEVYANI PRABHAT

16. Émile Durkheim and the Sociology of Religion   264
    MATTHIAS KOENIG

17. Durkheim's Ambivalence toward Art   283
    EDWARD A. TIRYAKIAN AND JOSEFINA CINTRON TIRYAKIAN

18. Durkheim and Social Movements   299
    KERSTIN JACOBSSON

19. Durkheim and the Sociology of Human–Animal Relations   316
    ROBERT SEYFERT

20. Durkheim and the Sociality of Space   333
    MARKUS SCHROER

21. Émile Durkheim and the Modern Family 350
    François de Singly

SECTION IV: APPROPRIATIONS AND DEBATES

22. Durkheim, Tarde, Latour 364
    Bjørn Schiermer

23. Sociology of the Sacred: The Revitalization of the Durkheim School at the Collège de Sociologie and the Renewal of a Sociology of Sacralization by Hans Joas 382
    Stephan Moebius

24. Lévi-Strauss's Critique of Durkheim 404
    Jing Xie

25. Ordinary Rituals: Durkheim, Mead, Goffman 424
    Frédéric Keck

26. Durkheim and the New Sociology of Morality 438
    Steven Lukes

Index 461

Acknowledgments

We would like to thank Christian Scherer for his outstanding support in copy-editing the manuscripts, checking and correcting quotations, and proofreading the text.

About the Volume Editors

Hans Joas is Ernst Troeltsch Professor for the Sociology of Religion at Humboldt University Berlin. For more than twenty years, he was a Visiting Professor of Sociology and in the Committee on Social Thought at the University of Chicago. He received his PhD from Freie Universität Berlin in 1979 (*G. H. Mead: A Contemporary Re-Examination of His Thought*, MIT Press, 1985, 1997). Among his numerous prizes are the Max Planck Research Award in 2015; the Prix Paul Ricœur in 2017; and the Distinguished Lifetime Achievement Award of the German Sociological Association in 2022. His last book in English is *Under the Spell of Freedom: Theory of Religion after Hegel and Nietzsche* (Oxford University Press, 2024).

Andreas Pettenkofer studied sociology at Freie Universität Berlin, the École des Hautes Études en Sciences Sociales, and the University of Bielefeld and received his PhD at the Max-Weber-Kolleg, University of Erfurt. After positions at the University of Göttingen and at the Fernuniversität in Hagen, he is now a fellow at the Max-Weber-Kolleg, University of Erfurt, where he heads the group "The Local Politicization of Global Norms."

Contributors

Pierre Birnbaum, Professor Emeritus of Political Sociology, University of Paris 1 Panthéon-Sorbonne

Francesco Callegaro, Professor of Sociology and Philosophy, National University of San Martín, Argentina

Paul Carls, Fellow, Luxembourg Institute for Socio-Economic Research

Mark S. Cladis, The Brooke Russell Astor Professor of the Humanities, Department of Religious Studies, Brown University

Heike Delitz, Chair of Collective and Cultural Studies, University of Regensburg

Jean-Louis Fabiani, Professor Emeritus, Department of Sociology and Social Anthropology, Central European University

Wolf Feuerhahn, Senior Research Fellow, CNRS

Marcel Fournier, Professor Emeritus of Sociology, University of Montreal

Kerstin Jacobsson, Professor of Sociology, University of Gothenburg

Hans Joas, Ernst Troeltsch Professor, Theological Faculty, Humboldt University of Berlin

Bruno Karsenti, Researcher in Philosophy, EHESS

Frédéric Keck, Senior Researcher, CNRS

Matthias Koenig, Professor of Sociology, University of Heidelberg

Steven Lukes, Professor Emeritus of Sociology, New York University

Stephan Moebius, Full Professor for Sociological Theory and Intellectual History, Karl Franzens University of Graz, and Full Member of the Austrian Academy of Sciences

Frithjof Nungesser, Postdoc Researcher, Department of Sociology, University of Graz

Serge Paugam, Professor of Sociology (EHESS); Director of Research (CNRS)

Andreas Pettenkofer, Fellow, Max-Weber-Kolleg, University of Erfurt

Devyani Prabhat, Professor of Law, University of Bristol Law School

Romain Pudal, Research Fellow, CNRS

Bjørn Schiermer, Professor, Department of Sociology and Human Geography, Oslo University

Markus Schroer, Professor of Sociology, The Philipps University of Marburg

Robert Seyfert, Professor of Sociology, Kiel University

François de Singly, Professor Emeritus of Sociology, University Paris Cité

Philippe Steiner, Professor Emeritus of Sociology, Sorbonne University, Paris

Edward A. Tiryakian, Professor Emeritus of Sociology, Duke University

Josefina Cintron Tiryakian, Independent Researcher, Duke University

W. Watts Miller, Independent Scholar, British Centre for Durkheimian Studies, Oxford

Jing Xie, Faculty of Philosophy, Fudan University

CHAPTER 1

INTRODUCTION
Some Reasons for (Re)reading Durkheim Today

HANS JOAS AND ANDREAS PETTENKOFER

THE PROVOCATIONS OF A DURKHEIMIAN SOCIOLOGY

MORE than a hundred years after his death, Émile Durkheim remains one of the most controversial and most deeply misunderstood classics of social theory. To see more clearly why there are reasons for (re)reading his writings today, it seems useful to discuss at least briefly why Durkheim still has to be seen as a highly provocative theorist.

The first provocation of Durkheim's sociology is a more uncompromising version of the general provocation caused by sociology as a discipline. Durkheim defends a particularly strong version of the claim that the social should be treated as a real object in its own right. According to Durkheim, "societies" should be seen as self-sustaining entities that cannot be reduced to by-products of agents' individual decisions; even many of the *mental* phenomena we really care about are, as Durkheim argues, actually constituted by "society"; the "inner" states of individual agents should, therefore, be seen as elements of the recursive processes through which such structures of cooperation sustain or transform themselves. On the one hand, this is a claim about what is sometimes called the "cognitive" dimension—first of all, about the classifications that enable agents to make sense of their environments (Durkheim/Mauss [1903] 2010). Durkheim tried to show that these mental phenomena are part of what he called, with an often-misunderstood term, a "common or collective consciousness": not only are the relevant beliefs shared, and understood to be shared, by the members of a given collective; according to Durkheim, they even owe their stability and their efficacy to this shared awareness of their being shared; explaining their stability and efficacy requires, therefore, grasping the social processes that create and sustain this type of shared awareness (Durkheim [1893] 2013: 63–84; [1912] 1915: 212).

On the other hand, this is also a claim about the sociality of deeply held evaluative attitudes. Durkheim tried to show that one misunderstands such attitudes by treating them simply as something that is internal to the individual agent. A central idea of his sociology is that such attitudes owe their action-guiding effects to recurrent interaction situations that, by proving the reality of a set of shared evaluations, create euphoric experiences that are essentially social in character (Durkheim [1893] 2013: 75–84; [1912] 1915: 226–232). Indeed, Durkheim's claim is that, through shared experiences of this type, such attitudes or, rather, the objects to which they refer become quite literally *sacred* to the members of a given collective. This does not mean that such attitudes necessarily presuppose the kinds of ideas that are traditionally associated with the term "religion"— for instance, ideas about a deity or deities, roles that are explicitly designated as priestly, organizations that are explicitly designated as churches, and so on (Durkheim [1912] 1915: 206–210, 220). Rather, Durkheim's argument points to the importance of attitudes that, while not linked to religious ideas in the ordinary sense of the term, nevertheless for those who share them take precedence over almost anything else, in a way that seems nonnegotiable or close to nonnegotiable, because their objects are seen as categorically different from other objects (which, in contrast to them, appear as merely profane), and as fundamental for the way in which those who share these attitudes understand themselves: for their ideas about how they should live their lives, and their ideas of what is valuable about themselves. Likewise, the practices through which such attitudes are being sustained—continually repeated situations where participants, by their participation, prove to each other that their convictions are still being shared—need not be designated by their participants as religious rituals; nevertheless, Durkheim claimed, they do *function* like religious rituals. In order to make sense of such attitudes, Durkheim introduced a conceptual distinction between the "sacred" and the "religious"; from the vantage point offered by his sociology, the religious is just a particularly easy-to-observe version of the sacred.[1]

This is the second provocation of Durkheim's sociology. Here, he does not simply articulate a more radical version of a familiar sociological perspective; instead, he breaks with a preunderstanding that has shaped the dominant version of sociology which has essentially accepted the modernist self-description of contemporary societies. While Durkheim's first book on *The Division of Labour in Society* ([1893] 2013) can easily be read as assuming the kind of distinction between "traditional" and "modern" societies that has become commonplace in the social sciences (and remains so even after explicit versions of "modernization theory" have lost much of their appeal), already his *Suicide* (Durkheim [1897] 2002) loosens this distinction. In *The Elementary Forms of the Religious Life* ([1912] 1915), Durkheim breaks with the assumption that presupposing a fundamental difference between "traditional" and "modern" social orders is helpful for understanding contemporary social processes. Within Durkheim's argument, this is not just one additional hypothesis, but a central claim about how social cooperation becomes possible; in this sense, Durkheim tried to show that "modern," apparently secular societies are in fact deeply structured by sacralizations; his claim is not that such attitudes necessarily exist in every social context, but that some of the more demanding forms of cooperation will be impossible without such socially supported attitudes (Durkheim [1912] 1915: 427–428). This is also linked to a fundamental methodological shift; *The Elementary Forms* marks the beginnings of a rupture with a kind of evolutionism that remains common in the social sciences. Starting from a reinterpretation of then-recent ethnographies about the Arunta (a society of Australian desert dwellers), Durkheim practiced a new strategy for dealing with "non-Western" empirical observations: looking at what anthropology, at that time, used to call a "primitive" society, Durkheim's strategy of comparison does not focus on contrasts (as, during the following decades, theories about "modernity" and "modernization" would suggest to do), but on commonalities. The book's methodological premise is that observing apparently "nonmodern" social order helps to uncover social mechanisms that also operate under "modern" conditions but are often hidden by modernist self-descriptions. This strategy had a deep impact on the practice of social research;[2] at the same time, it received a very muted reception in mainstream sociology, including the mainstream teaching of sociology.[3]

Problems of Finding an Audience

From the outset, Durkheim's radical theory was incompatible with many of the approaches that dominated the social sciences. During the last decades, finding a receptive audience became even more difficult.

On the one hand, Durkheim's claim that one can find out something important about contemporary societies by looking at sequences of religious rites seemed to go against the theories of secularization that, for quite some time, have been treated as self-evidently true. Of course, Durkheim's theory—which, as discussed earlier, rests on a distinction between the religious and the sacred—is, in principle, quite consistent with the kind of empirical observations that these theories of secularization use in order to make their case. Nevertheless, Durkheim's conclusions do not really support the deeper intuition behind these theories. An implication of Durkheim's argument would be that, while theories of secularization might be superficially true in the sense that in some parts of the world, religion has lost much of its influence, these theories' descriptions of such cases may be flawed on a more fundamental level, because the sacred-profane distinction that is characteristic of religion can also shape so-called secular contexts.

On the other hand, Durkheimian perspectives are difficult to reconcile with the theoretical individualism that has come to dominate the social sciences, and that is by now so much taken for granted, particularly in the English-speaking world, that it often no longer seems to be a conscious choice; an individualism that informs several influential theoretical positions which, at first, might seem to be directly opposed to each other—not only all the current "rational actor" explanations (including "opportunity structure" theories according to which all effects of social institutions are mediated by rational decisions made by individual actors) but also those versions of "interpretive" sociology that assume all social processes to be mediated by *individual* interpretations. Moreover, these academic theories were lent additional plausibility by a massive political success of individualist models of cooperation.[4]

But this has changed. Criticizing Durkheim's work in the name of a theory of secularization has become even less convincing. The claim that religion has been losing its social influence has turned out to be quite exaggerated. In particular, with the exception of some parts of Western Europe, organized religion—in a quite traditional sense of the term—has remained a crucial *political* force. Indeed, the obvious continuing relevance of religion within contemporary societies would be one reason for rereading Durkheim today.

Durkheim's Sociology as an Inspiration for Nonindividualist Social Theories

Also, the type of individualist social theory that, for many readers, seemed to offer good reasons for rejecting a Durkheimian approach has lost much of its plausibility. The notion that individualist modes of cooperation constitute the natural basis of a well-functioning society is no longer as credible as it once seemed to be. The difficulties of the "neoliberal" program—which may have found their most visible expression yet in the 2008 banking crisis—have contributed a lot to the weakening of this intellectual agenda.

Here, Durkheim's sociology becomes interesting again. It offers not just a "metatheoretical" critique (which, in itself, would be of limited interest), but a set of heterodox strategies of explanation. Therefore, not only because of the solutions it suggests, but already because of the questions it asks, and because of the perspectives it opens up, it can be an important source of inspiration for everybody who is interested in constructing theoretical alternatives to explanations that see egoism and interest as the main motives of action (or as the main framework that agents use to make sense of their situations), and the market and the contract as the dominant modes of institutionalization. Crucially, for Durkheim, the alternative to atomistic theories neither amounts to the mere appeal that individuals should act in ways that can be morally justified, nor to a hope for a stricter bureaucratic control that might help to implement morally justifiable ways of acting (Lemieux 2017). Indeed, this seems to have been Durkheim's reason for, having studied philosophy, turning to the new precarious discipline of sociology. In his work, the sociological perspective appears as an instrument for identifying mechanisms through which patterns of cooperation can stabilize themselves even without centralized control.[5] In this context, Durkheim always also tried to demonstrate that, contrary to what conventional liberal theories may suggest, a "strong" concept of the social does not, as such, necessarily result in a theory of how individuals are being oppressed. Durkheim certainly appropriated ideas from deeply conservative theorists.[6] Nevertheless, there can no longer be any doubt about the fact that Durkheim's work is not intended as a critique of the modernist value of protecting individuality, but as an attempt to grasp the social phenomena which make it more likely that the dignity of every individual remains a socially recognized value.[7]

Here, Durkheim's central arguments are as follows. Stable large-scale social structures enhance individual capacities because they offer infrastructures, resources, and opportunities for cooperation which create possibilities of action that, in an atomistic social order, would simply be unavailable (Durkheim [1912] 1915: 212). Also, the kinds of cognitive categories that are sufficiently clear-cut for creating a capacity to reflect on, and guiding, individual action can only emerge through social processes, and not through individual efforts alone; hence, it would be erroneous to see "mind" as an inner domain on which "the social" could only have contaminating effects. Moreover, such social structures also heighten individuality because they require a type of division of labor that allows for, and probably has to rely on, a high degree of heterogeneity among individual members (Durkheim [1893] 2013: 102, 143–144).[8] Most importantly, the idea that individual persons as such—and not only specific types of individuals—are owed protection can only become plausible through a specific type of sacralization: it requires that the human person in its inviolability is, for all practical purposes, treated as sacred (Durkheim [1898] 1973; Joas (2013); such a sacralization can only be sustained collectively through institutions, practices and shared values, and only within certain types of social structures. This is a core claim of Durkheim's sociology: when collective processes generate new moral attitudes, they do not necessarily create collectivist beliefs; they can also create beliefs that are able to sustain different types of *individualist* practices.

DURKHEIM'S SOCIOLOGY AS AN INSPIRATION FOR THEORIES OF NORMALITY AND EXCLUSION

There is yet another context where an issue that was central for the Durkheim school presently returns to the front stage, namely, the question of how notions of what constitutes normal behavior, or what constitutes a normal member of society (and, therefore, which beings are not seen as members, or at least not as full members), acquire their plausibility and are being stabilized or transformed. During the last decades, this question has often been discussed outside of sociology, in areas like, for example, gender studies, Black studies, or disability studies. Nevertheless, it is also one of the core questions of Durkheimian sociology, and Durkheim's writings are shaped by an antiessentialist impulse that is quite close to that of these more recent research programs;[9] if one reads Durkheim's work in the context of the French academic debates of his time, one sees that it is also directed against contemporary essentialisms of "race" and "soil" (cf. Noiriel 2013: 239–243).

Paying attention to this conceptual affinity would be helpful. Let us briefly illustrate this with an example from one of the most influential theorists of this field. A core idea of Judith Butler's approach is that the question of gender is a question about social categories and about the practices that sustain them; her claim is that gender categories are, most of the time, continually being restabilized through situations where specific "performances" reaffirm their plausibility. This is very much the type of process that Durkheim describes—all the more so since it is hardly possible to doubt that, in many contexts, the gender binary actually has a sacred status in the Durkheimian sense.[10] And indeed, in her early writings, Butler explicitly presents her argument as an application of a theory of ritual to the phenomenon of gender. Her starting point is the work of Victor Turner: "In what senses, then, is gender an act? As anthropologist Victor Turner suggests in his studies of ritual social drama, social action requires a performance which is *repeated*. This repetition is at once a reenactment and reexperiencing of a set of meanings already socially established; it is the mundane and ritualized form of their legitimation" (Butler 1988: 526). Now certainly, some of the rites on which Turner focused are rites of passage including gender rituals (e.g., rituals of "becoming a man"); and the fact that, within a given social context, versions of such a rite keep being repeated will usually contribute to the social plausibility of the categories on which this rite is based. Nevertheless, Butler's analysis of gender practices also highlights different, less formally institutionalized sequences of repetitions, like continually recurring everyday small-scale celebrations of traditional gender categories. In this sense, Durkheim's less narrow theory of rituals fits better than Turner's to what Butler is trying to achieve.

This example also suggests that building bridges between these debates can be useful for sociology because it helps see how analyses from the various "studies" offer additional answers to genuinely sociological questions. For example, Butler offers a new analysis that shows in detail how *specific* types of social categories are being stabilized—and also, for instance in her analysis of drag (Butler 1990), how disruptions of such rites can also destabilize the categories on which a given structure of cooperation relies (an issue to which Durkheim and his disciples hardly devoted any attention, even though it is crucial for a Durkheimian sociology). At the same time, building such conceptual bridges could be useful for the "studies" because it helps create explanatory linkages to analyses of social processes. Reconstructing these debates from the vantage point of Durkheimian sociology would also make it easier to integrate explanatory elements that contribute to answering the questions asked by the "studies" but do not fit well into a culturalist framework. For example, a Durkheimian perspective can also account for the importance of what Durkheim calls *morphological* effects, for instance, processes of spatial segregation that need not be primarily driven by "cultural" differences, but nevertheless change existing patterns of interaction, and therefore generate new locally relevant ideas about who is normal and who can be trusted (Uslaner 2012). A Durkheimian perspective also makes it easier to accommodate the observation that a relevant part of "racial" inequalities seems to be caused less by a primary revulsion against those perceived as different than by an attraction to those perceived as similar: Such an attraction can, for instance, sustain opportunity-hoarding "white" networks through chains of interaction that affirm, and celebrate, such perceptions of similarity, while at the same time sustaining attitudes of *relative* indifference toward those who do not belong to these networks. This can then nevertheless enable the members of these networks to think that they have no racist feelings toward "black" persons (DiTomaso 2013).

Making Use of the Theoretical Possibilities Offered by the Durkheimian Tradition Requires Going beyond the Dominant Appropriations

The statement in this headline obviously applies to those early appropriations which created an influential image of Durkheim as a theorist of immobile consensus-based order, and which continue to shape the ways in which his work is being understood.[11] Remarkably, this reading was not created by Durkheim's critics alone; it owes its influence to the fact that it was also shared among many of Durkheim's early adherents, and it has been articulated within quite different national traditions and with quite different theoretical starting points. Within British anthropology, Alfred Radcliffe-Brown developed a highly consequential version of such an interpretation.[12] These general ideas about Durkheim's sociology were essentially repeated, in a conceptually more sophisticated guise, by Talcott Parsons. His reading of Durkheim was all the more influential since those theoretical developments in sociology that were directed against Parsons's approach often tried to make their point by attacking Durkheim *as understood by Parsons* (e.g., Tilly 1981)—and thereby unintentionally helped to spread the Parsonian interpretation of Durkheim. An appropriation that uses Durkheim's ideas for sociological purposes which are quite different from Parsons's, but nevertheless rests on rather similar interpretive premises, was articulated by Theodor W. Adorno (1967), an influential early representative of the "Frankfurt School" of critical theory. While fiercely critical of Parsonian sociology, Adorno—in a preface to the German translation of Durkheim's *Sociology and Philosophy* (Durkheim [1924] 2010) that strongly influenced the way in which Durkheim's work has been understood within the German-language social theory debate—also presented Durkheim as a theorist of stable consensus; the main difference being that Adorno saw this as a building block for a theory of ideology, with Durkheim as a theorist of social oppression.[13] This kind of appropriation, too, had a lasting influence; in current empirical research, too, concepts from Durkheim's *Elementary Forms* are often used exclusively for the purpose of describing forms of cooperation that the respective author sees as pathological.[14]

But this also applies to those dominant appropriations that strongly influenced the ways in which Durkheimian ideas have been used in sociology and its neighboring disciplines during the last decades. While they critically react to these earlier appropriations, they often retain some of their core premises; therefore, they do not fully show how much can be done with Durkheim's concepts. We will very briefly illustrate this with three examples that, at least in the Anglosphere, probably constituted the most influential appropriations of Durkheimian sociology during the last decades.[15]

We'll start with Pierre Bourdieu, who used Durkheim's sociology of sacralizations—in particular, his concept of totemic objects—in an attempt to solve central problems of inequality research. Bourdieu's claim is that even in "modern" societies, sacralized objects lend plausibility to social boundaries. Because, as he tried to show, aesthetic judgments are closely linked to deep evaluative attitudes about what constitutes a good person, the aesthetic objects which are part of the fabric of ordinary life, and more generally the aesthetic dimension of everyday activities, play a crucial role in the genesis and maintenance of symbolic boundaries; through this, they significantly contribute to maintaining the stable differences which establish entities like "social classes" (cf., e.g., Bourdieu [1979] 1984: 479).[16] Therefore, "highbrow" cultural events function as ascetic rituals in the Durkheimian sense (Bourdieu [1979] 1984: 7).[17]

However, Bourdieu could retain only certain aspects of a Durkheimian approach, because he linked these ideas to a model of highly stable social structures. Therefore, some central explanatory strategies of a Durkheimian sociology were no longer available to him. This led him, on the one hand, to give up important explanatory possibilities of a Durkheimian sociology: the Durkheimian idea that the existence of given social structure depends on an ongoing sequence of rituals does not support strong stability assumptions (because a chain of interaction situations can easily be disrupted). Bourdieu, therefore, had to downplay the explanatory relevance of interactions (e.g., Bourdieu [1980] 1990: 58–59). This does not only mean that in most of his writings, Bourdieu defended the view that such situations enact preexisting rules, but only very rarely contribute to a transformation of such rules. Since he could no longer attribute a strong causal role to such situations, he also could no longer rely on the idea that rituals often *stabilize* preexisting action orientations. So, while Durkheim tried to explain the stability of a given rule as an effect of sequences of interaction situations, Bourdieu treated such "ritual" interaction situations mostly as mere *expressions* of preexisting structures, that is, as occasions for *observing* these structures (by their effects); therefore, he also could no longer use Durkheimian ideas about the explanatory importance of emotions. To compensate for the explanatory elements he had given up, Bourdieu introduced some strong anthropological assumptions (that, notoriously, very much restrict the range of possible observations). First, he assumed that the stability of a given social structure should be explained by rules that agents have internalized, that is, by what he called their "habitus" (Bourdieu [1980] 1990: chap. 3). To derive concrete predictions from the available evidence, Bourdieu added a second anthropological assumption: all actions follow a logic of maximizing power (e.g., Bourdieu [1979] 1984: 310); therefore, the meanings of the totemic objects that help stabilize a given structure of cooperation are also tacitly shaped by this logic of power, for example, by an agent's desire to distinguish oneself from others. Hence, Bourdieu used Durkheim's approach mostly as a theory of *illusionary* distinctions, and therefore, almost exclusively as a theory of ideology.

Jeffrey Alexander—who, as a cofounder of the Yale Center for Cultural Sociology, has instigated one of the most influential Durkheimian research programs within current Anglophone sociology—offers what is, in the end, a surprisingly similar way of selectively appropriating Durkheim's work. Certainly, Alexander is highly critical of Bourdieu's approach, particularly of its relentless emphasis on processes of reproduction (see Alexander 1995); more generally, he stresses the poverty of those appropriations of Durkheim's theory that discount its arguments on the role of emotions (Alexander 1988a). Also, Alexander focuses much more explicitly, and much more extensively, on public rituals. A central goal of his research program is to show how "secular" political events can acquire the function of Durkheimian rituals. He develops this view in a series of case studies that demonstrate how, for example, election campaign assemblies (Alexander 2010), and televised meetings of congressional committees (Alexander 1988b) continually evoke, and reaffirm, a set of political rules that almost everybody who enters a political competition in the United States has to treat as sacred. Thus, Alexander uses Durkheimian concepts in order to develop a new perspective on classical questions of comparative political sociology. However, while he takes Durkheim's arguments about the role of interaction processes much more seriously than Bourdieu, he, too, links his analyses to strong assumptions about highly stable structures, his paradigmatic case being the (purportedly) long-term stability of a political culture that he calls the American "civil society" (Alexander 2006). In that sense, his appropriation is not so different from Bourdieu's. Here, too, rituals are almost exclusively treated as mere enactments of preexisting rules. And here, too, accommodating this rearticulation makes it necessary to adopt a theory about agents and activities that is quite different from Durkheim's own: defending claims like those about a long-term continuity of an overarching political culture of the United States makes it necessary to see this culture in terms of a relatively thin consensus that almost everybody is at least paying lip service to. Therefore, Alexander's substantive analyses of political rituals put a strong accent on practices of *strategic* adaptation to what a given ritual requires and, more generally, to these (purportedly) stable rules (e.g., Alexander 2010). In this sense, this appropriation leads back to a rather conventional theory of instrumental action.

Randall Collins takes a different point of departure. While Durkheim's exposition of his argument, in the *Elementary Forms*, focuses on easy-to-observe cases of highly visible public rituals, he already mentioned the crucial role of situations of cooperation that can be observed in unspectacular everyday sequences of interactions (Durkheim [1912] 1915: 211). These situations, too, can function as Durkheimian rituals because they tacitly celebrate the rules and evaluations that sustain a given structure of cooperation. Still, even though this is an essential element of Durkheim's argument, he himself discussed it only very briefly. It was later taken up by Erving Goffman (1967), but it is only with Collins (2004) that its full relevance for a social theory has been made explicit. Also paying attention to the ritual aspect of small-scale interactions makes it possible to see social order as an effect of what Collins calls interaction ritual chains. Through this change of focus, Durkheim's sociology becomes a genuinely processual theory of order-building "from below"; such a theory is also much better suited to capture processes of social change and does not have to invest in strong assumptions about structural stability. Collins's monumental comparative study of philosophical "schools" (Collins 1998) also offers sufficient proof that, in principle, such an approach is able to grasp *institutional* phenomena as well. However, through the specific way in which he elaborates this approach, Collins, too, uses Durkheim's explanatory strategy only selectively and compensates for this by introducing concepts that severely restrict the range of possible observations. In Durkheim's own strategy of explanation, preexisting structures of meaning play a rather important role.[18] He sees situations where a preexisting sacralization is being reconfirmed as one crucial type of occasion where "collective effervescence" can happen. Collins, in his attempt to focus strictly on effects that could be attributed to interaction situations as such, very much downplays the role of such meaning structures. Therefore, in order to explain why, in some types of situations, the strong emotions evoked by Durkheim actually do occur, he has to resort to a different solution. On the one hand, he claims that such shared emotions directly result from situational features that have to be described in a strictly objective way, like close physical proximity of the participants, and the emergence of shared rhythms of movement (e.g., Collins 2004: 52). On the other hand, Collins, too, introduces a strong anthropological assumption: the fact that ritual situations are (sometimes) being repeated in a way that creates an "interaction ritual chain" should, according to Collins, be explained by a universal, culture-independent human desire to maximize what he calls "emotional energy" (Collins 2004: chap. 3). This is quite close to a conventional rational-actor model (Greve 2012); in this sense, Collins returns to the kind of individualist ontology that Durkheim wanted to leave behind.

Rereading Durkheim's original writings helps go beyond the problematic preunderstandings that shape these appropriations and see more clearly what one can do with Durkheim's concepts. Indeed, during recent years, the state of the debate has changed markedly. There are deeper, more subtle reconstructions of Durkheim's theoretical arguments, supported by historical work that situates these arguments in their original academic and political contexts;[19] there is new empirical research that uses Durkheim's ideas and shows how much can be achieved with them; and there is research showing that important strands of postwar social theory in fact build upon, and newly conceptualize, ideas from Durkheim's works. So this is a good moment for taking stock of these Durkheimian debates. In its four sections, this handbook is an attempt to give a comprehensive overview of these more recent developments.

Overview of the Handbook

Key Concepts

Each of the five chapters in this first section approaches Durkheim's sociology through one of the concepts that constitute Durkheim's central contribution to sociology, and that remain controversial, concepts like morality, solidarity, collective consciousness, ritual, and the social.

In "Durkheim's Signature Project: The Science of Morality as Rational Moral Art," Mark S. Cladis discusses Durkheim's goal to develop a science of morality, or what he called rational moral art. The idea of a *rational art* will strike many as an oxymoron. Yet as Cladis argues, it is at the intersection, and within the tension, of these two terms that we find Durkheim's most mature efforts at establishing a science of morality. This science is *rational* insofar as it is attentive to the actual, lived social practices and institutions in various cultures at various times. It is a form of *art* insofar as it employs practical judgment when it seeks to move from the studies of the social scientist to the reformist critique of social institutions and practices.

Serge Paugam's chapter, "Solidarity and Attachment in Durkheim's Sociological Thought," seeks to identify the reasons why Durkheim abandoned the concepts of mechanical and organic solidarity. Paugam shows that Durkheim's shift from a theory of the evolution of solidarity to a theory of social attachment does not mean that Durkheim in any way renounced the ambitious program he had originally developed in Bordeaux. On the contrary, he sought to extend this program by carrying out a more complete analysis of the plurality of social bonds that attach individuals to society, at a time when the concept of solidarity began a new career.

In "The Sociality of Mind: Key Arguments, Inner Tensions, and Divergent Appropriations of Durkheim's Sociology of Knowledge," Frithjof Nungesser examines the Durkheimian contribution to the sociology of knowledge. Drawing on Durkheim and Mauss's "Primitive Classification" essay and Durkheim's *The Elementary Forms of Religious Life*, he distinguishes two key arguments that result in two different lines of reception, one focusing on classificatory homologies and one on ritual, the sacred, and the emergence of nonordinary realities. Systematizing the tensions within Durkheim's arguments as well as within and between its appropriations, the chapter explains the continuing provocative force of Durkheim's sociology of knowledge.

Francesco Callegaro's chapter, "In Defense of Collective Consciousness: Reassessing Durkheim's Argument," addresses a key concept that has been accused of being at the same time absurd, inadequate, and dangerous. Having clarified to what extent the issue at stake concerns the social philosophy underlying sociology, the chapter reconstructs Durkheim's perspective, in order to assess his central thesis: that there is no collective or social life without a collective or social consciousness. After clarifying the meaning of "collective," the chapter elucidates the nature of "collective representations" through an examination of Durkheim's criticism of "consciousness." The chapter concludes that the concept of collective consciousness has a definite sociological meaning.

Bruno Karsenti's chapter, "Religious Rituals and Logical Thought in Durkheim: The Level of Existence of Social Things," examines the central function of ritual within Durkheim's argument in *The Elementary Forms of Religious Life*. It is on its redefinition that the constitution of sacred things rests, in relation to the constitution of the group itself and to the formation of categories of thought. In this chapter, Karsenti restores the basis of this conception: the interpretation of the ritual of the *intichiuma*, and more particularly its mimetic dimension, which prevails over its sacrificial dimension. The relationship between practice and objective thought turns out to be the touchstone of the concept of the sacred as developed by Durkheim.

Contexts

The six chapters in this second section situate the concepts of Durkheimian sociology within the contemporary political and theoretical debates they are responding to.

In "The Dreyfus Affair and Durkheim's Experience of Anti-Semitism," Pierre Birnbaum emphasizes the importance of the Affair for the manner in which Durkheim approached the subject of anti-Semitism. In a series of articles and letters, Durkheim reflected on the causes of anti-Semitism and proposed an interpretation of Jews as scapegoats; in his view, society's suffering was resolved by ostracizing Jews as pariahs. Birnbaum argues, however, that Durkheim's interpretation of anti-Semitism is unsatisfactory: his analysis of explanatory variables is not convincing; it remains focused on psychological considerations rarely seen elsewhere in his work.

Jean-Louis Fabiani's chapter on "Durkheim and the Philosophy of His Time" reminds us that Durkheim was trained as a philosopher, taught philosophy, and never left the philosophical field, starting his career with the standard philosophical equipment but also with a growing disenchantment about the eclectic and metaphysical mainstream of the discipline. Durkheim simultaneously pursued two goals. He established a firm demarcation line between philosophy and sociology, guaranteeing the full autonomy of the latter. At the same time, rationalism, largely based on a French version of neo-Kantianism, remained his lifetime affiliation.

In "Durkheim's Team: L'Année sociologique," Marcel Fournier and Paul Carls examine the team of sociologists that, since 1896, collaborated with Émile Durkheim to create the journal *L'Année sociologique*. The chapter follows the development of this Durkheimian school and its historical legacy after Durkheim's death in 1917: its maintenance of a prominent position in the 1920s and 1930s, its relative post–World War II obscurity, and its rebirth, beginning in the 1970s and 1980s, through renewed academic interest in the work of members of the team. Special attention is given to collaborators such as Célestin Bouglé, Henri Hubert, François Simiand, Maurice Halbwachs, and Robert Hertz.

Heike Delitz's chapter, "Durkheim and Bergson, Durkheimians and Bergsonians," begins with a review of the state of research on Durkheim versus Bergson. It sketches the relationship between the Durkheim school of sociology and Henri Bergson as a discipline-constituting aversion. It then reconstructs Bergson's own sociological theory (as articulated in *The Two Sources of Religion and Morality*) and the ways in which it follows, and contradicts, Durkheimian sociology. A final section traces the elective affinities between Bergson's philosophy and later theories of the social by authors such as Georges Canguilhem, Claude Lévi-Strauss, Gilbert Simondon, Gilles Deleuze, and Cornelius Castoriadis.

Romain Pudal's chapter, "Durkheim, Pragmatism, and Sociology," discusses Durkheim's critical reading of pragmatism. In spite of the similarities that, according to Durkheim, exist between sociology and pragmatism, he develops a series of theoretical objections against this philosophy, especially concerning the concept of truth. This chapter examines these objections and discusses their political and ideological context: Durkheim's reading can also be understood in the context of a French appropriation of pragmatism that used it as an intellectual weapon against the dominant rationalism of the French university of the time, of which Durkheim was a prominent figure.

In "Émile Durkheim's Germany," Wolf Feuerhahn starts from the dilemma that, while the importance German scholarship had for Durkheim seems indubitable, writing about his relationship with Germany is not easy because, in the tense political context of his time, this relationship became a main reason for attacks against him. Even saying that Durkheim was "influenced" by German thought reiterates the language of these attacks. This chapter therefore does not talk about "influence"; instead, it focuses on the question of what exactly Durkheim describes as "German," in order to understand how his perception evolved between the 1880s and World War I.

Themes

The nine chapters in this third section of the handbook offer surveys of empirical research that uses Durkheimian concepts; they address fields of research that were already central for Durkheim's own work—the development of the Durkheimian approach was not just driven by internal theoretical considerations but also, and quite importantly, by the empirical topics the Durkheimians were confronted with—as well as topics that Durkheim hardly touched upon. These strands of research show what can be done with Durkheim's concepts; they also show (better than mere theoretical reflection) where Durkheim's sociology suffers from conceptual tensions, contradictions, or blind spots.

In "The Modern Individual," Willie Watts Miller tracks key changes and continuities in Durkheim's approach to the modern individual, beginning with his thesis on the division of labor. The chapter shows that, despite Durkheim's increasing belief in the dynamics of creative effervescence, both as a foundation of an irreducibly social realm and as a way to get going processes of reform, he never abandoned his commitment to the importance of social structures, as in his call for a web of new intermediate groups or in his view of the division of labor as a source of modern ideals.

Philippe Steiner discusses "Durkheim and Economic Sociology." Durkheim's doctoral dissertation on the division of labor had an economic dimension, and his study on suicide rates put a strong emphasis on the professional group for the social reform he had in mind. Beyond Durkheim's own achievements, this chapter considers the work of François Simiand and Maurice Halbwachs, and Marcel Mauss's work on gift-giving. Finally, the strengths of the Durkheimian approach to economic sociology are illustrated through some contemporary inquiries.

Devyani Prabhat's chapter, "Reflecting on Durkheim and His Studies on Law through Cancellation of British Citizenship," argues that Durkheim's studies on law offer rich insights for contemporary sociolegal research. She emphasizes, however, that Durkheim is overoptimistic in his view that a modern morality has emerged which venerates the sacredness of the individual. An analysis of nationality deprivation cases in the United Kingdom reveals a breakdown of social solidarity and a failure to protect individuals from statelessness. It appears that, contrary to Durkheim's views, solidarity of the kind that supports human rights is not always a matter of seamless moral and legal progression.

Matthias Koenig's chapter, "Émile Durkheim and the Sociology of Religion," revisits Émile Durkheim's *sociologie religieuse* and explores its potentials and limitations for analyzing contemporary religious reconfigurations. He discusses the inherent tensions in Durkheim's theory of the sacred, its relation to society, and its impact on morality and knowledge. The chapter shows that this theory of the sacred, while failing to grasp religio-political power configurations so central to the Weberian tradition, helps discern the persistence and production of collective religious forms in a global age, ranging from nationalisms to human rights.

In "Durkheim's Ambivalence toward Art," Edward A. Tiryakian and Josefina Cintron Tiryakian trace Durkheim's views on art from his early career at Bordeaux to his "cultural turn" in Paris, manifested in *The Elementary Forms*. Before this turn, Durkheim had discussed art's contributions to society: as a facilitator for teaching morality, and as leisure and recreation. But it is while reading about tribal sacred rituals that he discovered art's role in enhancing solidarity and group identity. Additionally, the chapter explores transgressive approaches to Durkheim's views on art, as well as contemporary authors who have probed Durkheim's perspectives on art.

In "Durkheim and Social Movements," Kerstin Jacobsson points out that the dominant Durkheimian approaches to social movements have been social disintegration approaches, and collective effervescence and ritual life-inspired analyses. She suggests that there are *other* openings in Durkheim's works that can be made productive for social movement theorizing, particularly his sociology of morality as developed in *Moral Education*. The chapter argues that Durkheim's reflections on morality allow for a theoretical perspective which is able to reconcile structure and agency, encompass a parallel focus on conflict and consensus, and allow for the theorization of emotional intensity as well as moral reflexivity in the analysis of movements.

In "Durkheim and the Sociology of Human–Animal Relations," Robert Seyfert presents Durkheim as a nonanthropocentric theorist. Through a reading of Durkheim's work on totemism, the chapter shows how Durkheim generated a dynamic social theory that can explain how relations between humans and nonhumans vary according to history and culture. According to Seyfert, Durkheim's work can show us how the preoccupations and practices of totemic societies have the capacity to speak to us about our own present struggles with how to treat nonhuman others.

Markus Schroer's chapter on "Durkheim and the Sociality of Space" shows that spatial formations play a key role in Durkheim's theory of modernity. He assigns to *social morphology* the task of systematically investigating the material substratum of societies. This makes it possible to examine how different types of societies relate to space in distinctive ways. At the same time, Durkheim emphasizes that physical space is inherently shaped by social practices of classification and division. In light of the renewed attention given to materiality and space by proponents of the "material" and the "spatial turn," this makes his work seem surprisingly contemporary.

François de Singly writes on "Émile Durkheim and the Modern Family." Indeed, Durkheim's first specialized course in Bordeaux was on the sociology of the family. Although his work on the topic is not his best known, and is often rather misunderstood, it is still quite interesting. Durkheim was able to perceive what were the two leading characteristics of change in the European family from the 1850s through the 1960s: the personalization of ties, and the increasing intervention of the state in family affairs. Understanding this change, however, did not lead Durkheim to approve of it.

Appropriations and Debates

Some of the five chapters in the final section bring out the divergent, and competing, ways in which Durkheimian ideas have been appropriated and reformulated within more recent theoretical developments, thus showing yet more of what can be done with Durkheim's approach. Other chapters offer surveys of the most important critical debates on Durkheim's approach and critically analyze some of the common objections.

Bjørn Schiermer's chapter, "Durkheim, Tarde, Latour," is motivated by the recent reappraisal of the debate between Gabriel Tarde and Durkheim, sparked by Bruno Latour's attempt to repatriate Tarde as the true classic of (French) sociology. The chapter delves into the young Durkheim's programmatic ideas for his new science of sociology and seeks to make Tarde's (and Latour's) objections understandable. It discusses some ambivalences in Tarde's work that are of great significance for the debate. Finally, it delves into Latour's critique of Durkheim, assesses the merits of this critique, and intimates a possible compromise between Latour and Durkheim.

In "Sociology of the Sacred: The Revitalization of the Durkheim School at the Collège de Sociologie and the Renewal of a Sociology of Sacralization by Hans Joas," Stephan Moebius analyzes three stages in the development of the sociology of the sacred: the Durkheim school, the Collège de Sociologie, and the work of Hans Joas. It shows that the Collège de Sociologie was deeply influenced by the Durkheimians' studies on religion and the gift but interpreted them in a very specific way, disagreeing on important theoretical, methodological, and political issues. Then, it compares Joas's studies on sacralization processes to the Durkheimian sociology of religion and the sacred sociology of the Collège.

Jing Xie discusses "Lévi-Strauss's Critique of Durkheim." This critique is considered important because it raises questions about the philosophical foundations of Durkheimian sociology, and because it is regarded as a turning point in French social anthropology, offering structuralism as a solution to Durkheimian difficulties. The chapter outlines Lévi-Strauss's core arguments and shows that the orthodox view on this debate oversimplifies Durkheim's account of social reality. The author demonstrates that Lévi-Strauss's structuralist turn is in fact a cognitivist one which, instead of offering solutions to Durkheimian questions, dismisses those questions.

Frédéric Keck's chapter, "Ordinary Rituals: Durkheim, Mead, Goffman," establishes a more complex sociological genealogy from Durkheim to Goffman, by bringing G. H. Mead's work into the picture. Goffman transformed the Durkheimian conception of ritual by linking extraordinary ceremonies of primitive groups to ordinary interactions between urban individuals. The concepts of the sacred and the symbolic that are at the heart of Durkheim's sociology are thus challenged through Goffman's concept of ordinary ritual.

In "Durkheim and the New Sociology of Morality," Steven Lukes, together with Edward A. Tiryakian doyen of Durkheim studies, examines Durkheim's writings on morality, distinguishing his earlier, more familiar account from later developments that advance new ideas relevant to present-day debates. He asks to which extent familiar criticisms of Durkheim's sociology of morality are justified, and he suggests ways in which sociologists and anthropologists can gain from reconsidering Durkheim on morality. Lukes considers Durkheim's influence on current work by sociologists of morality and shows that apparently non-Durkheimian studies of trust, collective action, and the evolution of social norms are nonetheless Durkheimian in their object of inquiry.

All in all, the four sections of this handbook, the diverse character of the contributors, and the originality of the contributions may be considered a confirmation of the intuition we had when we started this editorial project, namely that Durkheim's work in its surprising boldness remains a crucial source of inspiration for sociology in the twenty-first century.

Notes

1. See Joas (2001: 54–68) on why one should take this distinction seriously, and Joas (2021) for a comprehensive theoretical elaboration.
2. For example, it was taken up by Marcel Mauss, most prominently in his essay on *The Gift* (Mauss [1925] 2016); by Pierre Bourdieu, who used his ethnography of Kabyle life as a starting point for analyzing contemporary French society (Bourdieu [1972] 1977, [1980] 1990); and also by theorists who are highly critical of many of Durkheim's substantive ideas—see, for instance, Bruno Latour's programmatically titled *We Have Never Been Modern* ([1991] 1993).
3. For example, even in French-language sociology textbooks, the core ideas of Durkheim's *Elementary Forms* hardly appear (Béra 2014).
4. For a general account of the close interaction between dominant ideas about what constitutes a good polity, and the "social science" theories members of a given polity draw on in order to describe, and to criticize, what happens within that polity, see Boltanski and Thévenot ([1991] 2006).
5. See also Karsenti (2013) on the emergence of sociology as a science of self-organization. It is obvious that in this sense the writings of Parsons and his school and of the older Chicago School have an affinity with this orientation.

6. In his account of Louis de Bonald as a theorist of processes of societal mediation, Karsenti (2003) suggests how much Durkheim owes to his work.
7. On this point, see Cladis (1992), Joas (2013), and Callegaro (2015). On Durkheim's engagement in the Dreyfus Affair—a key context for his articulation of the claim that contemporary societies need to rely on the idea that there is such a thing as human rights—see also Fournier ([2007] 2013: 285–308); more generally on Durkheim's (largely implicit) treatment of anti-Semitism: Birnbaum ([2004] 2008) and Goldberg (2017). See also Tiryakian (1988) on Durkheim's *Elementary Forms* as a book on how to save the legacy of the French Revolution.
8. For a recent defense of Durkheim's theses on what he called organic solidarity, see Herzog (2018).
9. Garfinkel (1967) offers a pioneering Durkheimian take on the practice of gender categorization. (On Garfinkel as a Durkheimian, see Garfinkel 2002.)
10. The sacralization of gender roles sometimes happens within an explicitly religious framework that treats them as, for instance, God-given. (For an example, see Riesebrodt [1993] on the patriarchal origins of what is today being discussed under the label "right-wing populism.") But it does not depend on such a framework: Even in contexts that their participants see as secular, gender can be understood as a category which is so fundamental that it overrides all others, and becomes linked to nonnegotiable convictions about legitimate ways of living one's life.
11. Against this misunderstanding of reading Durkheim as a theorist of highly stable structures, see Plouviez (2012) and Hausner (2016).
12. On the long-term influence of this appropriation within anthropology, cf. Stedman Jones (2013); see also Watts Miller (2017).
13. For an application, see Horkheimer and Adorno ([1944] 1987: 37–38, 44).
14. See, for instance, Hochschild (2016) on collective effervescence during a "Tea Party" rally.
15. For a general discussion of the theoretical approaches of Bourdieu, Alexander, and Collins, see Joas and Knöbl (2009: 371–400, 309–338, 174–198), see also Joas and Knöbl (2009: 453–462) on Butler. For a comprehensive overview of the Durkheim reception, with a certain bias in favor of the Yale school, see Philip Smith (2020).
16. Bourdieu's idea that cultural processes are crucial for structuring social inequality because they create categorical distinctions where, otherwise, one would observe only continuous distributions, see Weininger (2005).
17. For more on Bourdieu's use of Durkheimian concepts, see also Witte (2014).
18. On this point, see Pettenkofer (2010: 220–243), starting from the problem how to explain social protest, and Pettenkofer (2017) for a more general discussion.
19. There are even new primary materials, namely Durkheim's "Philosophy Lectures" based on notes from his classes in 1883/1884 and his "Lecons de sociologie criminelle," a course he taught in 1892/1893.

References

Adorno, Theodor W. 1967. "Einleitung." In *Émile Durkheim: Soziologie und Philosophie*, 7–44. Frankfurt am Main: Suhrkamp.
Alexander, Jeffrey C. 1988a. "Durkheimian Sociology and Cultural Studies Today." In *Durkheimian Sociology: Cultural Studies*, edited by Jeffrey C. Alexander, 1–21. Cambridge: Cambridge University Press.

Alexander, Jeffrey C. 1988b. "Culture and Political Crisis: 'Watergate' and Durkheimian Sociology." In *Durkheimian Sociology: Cultural Studies*, edited by Jeffrey C. Alexander, 187–224. Cambridge: Cambridge University Press.

Alexander, Jeffrey C. 1995. "The Reality of Reduction: The Failed Synthesis of Pierre Bourdieu." In *Fin-de-siècle Social Theory*, 128–217. London: Verso.

Alexander, Jeffrey C. 2006. *The Civil Sphere*. Oxford: Oxford University Press.

Alexander, Jeffrey C. 2010. *The Performance of Politics: Obama's Victory and the Democratic Struggle for Power*. Oxford: Oxford University Press.

Béra, Matthieu. 2014. "Le traitement des *Formes élémentaires* dans les manuels de sociologie: de l'occultation aux rejets." *Cahiers de recherche sociologique* 56: 13–32.

Birnbaum, Pierre (2004) 2008. *Geography of Hope: Exile, the Enlightenment, Disassimilation*. Stanford, CA: Stanford University Press.

Boltanski, Luc, and Laurent Thévenot. (1991) 2006. *On Justification*. Princeton, NJ: Princeton University Press.

Bourdieu, Pierre. (1972) 1977. *Outline of a Theory of Practice*. Cambridge: Cambridge University Press.

Bourdieu, Pierre. (1979) 1984. *Distinction: A Social Critique of the Judgement of Taste*. Cambridge, MA: Harvard University Press.

Bourdieu, Pierre. (1980) 1990. *The Logic of Practice*. Stanford, CA: Stanford University Press.

Butler, Judith. 1988. "Performative Acts and Gender Constitution." *Theatre Journal* 40 (4): 519–553.

Butler, Judith. 1990. *Gender Trouble: Feminism and the Subversion of Identity*. London: Routledge.

Callegaro, Francesco. 2015. *La science politique des modernes. Durkheim, la sociologie et le projet d'autonomie*. Paris: Economica.

Cladis, Mark S. 1992. *A Communitarian Defense of Liberalism: Emile Durkheim and Contemporary Social Theory*. Stanford, CA: Stanford University Press.

Collins, Randall. 1998. *The Sociology of Philosophies*. Cambridge, MA: Harvard University Press.

Collins, Randall. 2004. *Interaction Ritual Chains*. Princeton, NJ: Princeton University Press.

DiTomaso, Nancy. 2013. *The American Non-Dilemma: Racial Inequality without Racism*. New York: Russell Sage.

Durkheim, Émile. (1893) 2013. *The Division of Labour in Society*. Translated by W. D. Hall. Basingstoke, UK: Palgrave Macmillan.

Durkheim, Émile. (1897) 2002. *Suicide*. Translated by John A. Spaulding and George Simpson. London: Routledge.

Durkheim, Émile. (1898) 1973. "Individualism and the Intellectuals." In *Durkheim on Morality and Society*, edited and with an introduction by Robert N. Bellah, 43–57. Chicago: University of Chicago Press.

Durkheim, Émile. (1912) 1915. *The Elementary Forms of the Religious Life*. Translated by Joseph Ward Swain. London: Allen & Unwin.

Durkheim, Émile. (1924) 2010. *Sociology and Philosophy*. London: Routledge.

Durkheim, Émile, and Marcel Mauss. (1903) 2010. *Primitive Classification*. London: Routledge.

Fournier, Marcel. (2007) 2013. *Émile Durkheim: A Biography*. Cambridge: Polity.

Garfinkel, Harold. 1967. "Passing and the Managed Achievement of Sex Status in an 'Intersexed' Person." In *Studies in Ethnomethodology*, 116–185. Englewood Cliffs, NJ: Prentice Hall.

Garfinkel, Harold. 2002. *Ethnomethodology's Program: Working Out Durkheim's Aphorism*. Edited and with an introduction by Anne W. Rawls. Lanham, MD: Rowman & Littlefield.
Goffman, Erving. 1967. "The Nature of Deference and Demeanor." In *Interaction Ritual*, 47–95. New York: Anchor.
Goldberg, Chad Alan. 2017. *Modernity and the Jews in Western Social Thought*. Chicago: University of Chicago Press.
Greve, Jens. 2012. "Emotionen, Handlungen und Ordnungen. Überlegungen zu Randall Collins." In *Emotionen, Sozialstruktur und Moderne*, edited by Annette Schnabel and Rainer Schützeichel, 181–200. Wiesbaden: VS.
Hausner, Sondra L. 2016. *The Spirits of Crossbone Graveyard: Time, Ritual, and Sexual Commerce in London*. Bloomington: Indiana University Press.
Herzog, Lisa. 2018. "Durkheim on Social Justice: The Argument from 'Organic Solidarity.'" *American Political Science Review* 112 (1): 112–124.
Hochschild, Arlie. 2016: *Strangers in Their Own Land: Anger and Mourning on the American Right*. New York: The New Press.
Horkheimer, Max, and Theodor W. Adorno. (1944) 1987. "Dialektik der Aufklärung." In *Gesammelte Schriften* 5, edited by M. Horkheimer, 11–290. Frankfurt am Main: Fischer.
Joas, Hans. 2001. *The Genesis of Values*. Chicago: University of Chicago Press.
Joas, Hans. 2013. *The Sacredness of the Person: A New Genealogy of Human Rights*. Washington, DC: Georgetown University Press.
Joas, Hans. 2021. *The Power of the Sacred: An Alternative to the Narrative of Disenchantment*. New York: Oxford University Press.
Joas, Hans, and Wolfgang Knöbl. 2009: *Social Theory: Twenty Introductory Lectures*. Cambridge: Cambridge University Press.
Karsenti, Bruno. 2003. "Autorité, société, pouvoir. La science sociale selon Bonald." In *L'invention de la société*, edited by Laurence Kaufmann and Jacques Guilhaumou, 261–286. Paris: Éd. de l'EHESS.
Karsenti, Bruno. 2013. "Le dialogue des modernes." In *D'une philosophie à l'autre. Les sciences sociales et la politique des modernes*, 9–32. Paris: Gallimard.
Latour, Bruno. (1991) 1993: *We Have Never Been Modern*. Cambridge, MA: Harvard University Press.
Lemieux, Cyril. 2017. "La politique sociologique selon Durkheim." In *Socialisme et sociologie*, edited by Bruno Karsenti and Cyril Lemieux, 123–150. Paris: Éd. de l'EHESS.
Mauss, Marcel. (1925) 2016. *The Gift*. Translated by Jane I. Guyer. Chicago: HAU Books.
Noiriel, Gérard. 2013. *Les origines républicaines de Vichy*. Paris: Fayard.
Pettenkofer, Andreas. 2010. *Radikaler Protest. Zur soziologischen Theorie politischer Bewegungen*. Frankfurt am Main: Campus.
Pettenkofer, Andreas. 2017. "Beweissituationen. Zur Rekonstruktion des Konzepts sozialer Praktiken." In *Pragmatismus und Theorien sozialer Praktiken. Vom Nutzen einer Theoriedifferenz*, edited by Hella Dietz, Frithjof Nungesser, and Andreas Pettenkofer, 119–160. Frankfurt am Main: Campus.
Plouviez, Mélanie. 2012. "Sociology as Subversion: Discussing the Reproductive Interpretations of Durkheim." *Journal of Classical Sociology* 12 (3–4): 428–448.
Riesebrodt, Martin. 1993. *Pious Passion: The Emergence of Fundamentalism in the United States and Iran*. Berkeley: University of California Press.
Smith, Philip. 2020. *Durkheim and After: The Durkheimian Tradition, 1883–2020*. Hoboken, NJ: Wiley.

Stedman-Jones, Susan. 2013. "Durkheim, Anthropology and the Question of the Categories in *Les formes élémentaires de la vie religieuse*." In *Durkheim in Dialogue: A Centenary Celebration of the Elementary Forms of Religious Life*, edited by Sondra L. Hausner, 143–164. New York: Berghahn Books.

Tilly, Charles. 1981. "Useless Durkheim." In *As Sociology Meets History*, 95–108. New York: Academic Press.

Tiryakian, Edward E. 1988. "Durkheim, Mathiez, and the French Revolution: The Political Context of a Sociological Classic." *Archives européennes de sociologie* 29: 373–396.

Uslaner, Eric M. 2012. *Segregation and Mistrust: Diversity, Isolation, and Social Cohesion.* Cambridge: Cambridge University Press.

Watts Miller, William. 2017. "The Anthropological Roots of Émile Durkheim's British Career." *Sociologie* 8 (3): 309–314.

Weininger, Elliot B. 2005. "Foundations of Pierre Bourdieu's Class Analysis." In *Approaches to Class Analysis*, edited by Erik Olin Wright, 82–118. Cambridge: Cambridge University Press.

Witte, Daniel. 2014. *Auf den Spuren der Klassiker. Pierre Bourdieus Feldtheorie und die Soziologie*. Konstanz: UVK.

CHAPTER 2

DURKHEIM'S SIGNATURE PROJECT

The Science of Morality as Rational Moral Art

MARK S. CLADIS

Rational Moral Art

"Moral facts" is one of Durkheim's most famous concepts and the development of a science of morality is one of his most ambitious endeavors. For some, these represent what is best in Durkheim; for others, what is most problematic. What accounts for such widely divergent assessments of Durkheim's signature project, the science of morality? All agree that Durkheim sought to bring ethical inquiry, broadly construed, into the domain of the social sciences (especially history, economics, anthropology, "history of religion" or religious studies, and—of course—sociology). Those who applaud Durkheim's attempt maintain that ethical inquiry should entail more empirical investigations and less speculative, metaphysical ones. Those that oppose the attempt frequently interpret Durkheim's empiricism as akin to positivism or, at the very least, to a reductive approach that is not sufficiently wary of the very idea of a social or moral *fact*. Much, then, hangs on what "empiricism" or "the empirical" meant for Durkheim. Unfortunately, Durkheim himself was not always sufficiently clear on the matter. Still, I will argue that when we situate his work in the context of his intellectual and social milieu, carefully unpack his arguments, and note their development over the course of his career, we are not likely to interpret his work on *la morale* as being that of a positivist or a naive empiricist but rather as the work of an interpretive sociologist who takes the empirical world seriously—that is, the world of history, law, economics, institutions, statistics, customs, social practices, and ideals.

Labels such as empiricism, positivism, rationalism, and pragmatism often do more harm than good when interpreting a complex thinker like Durkheim. If, however, I had to assign one label to describe his project for the development of a science of morals,

I would employ his own term, *rational moral art* (*l'art moral rationnel*) (Durkheim [1904] 1979: 32). The very idea of rational art will strike many as an oxymoron. What could the creativity and practical judgment of art have to do with the facts and logical inquiry of the rational? Yet it is precisely at the intersection, and within the tension, of these two terms—art and the rational—that we find Durkheim's most mature efforts at establishing a science of morality.

On the one hand, this science is *rational* insofar as it is attentive to the *actual, lived social practices and institutions* of humans in various cultures at various times. It honors and depends on the detailed work of historians, economists, anthropologists, scholars of religion, and sociologists, especially insofar as this work is comparative. On the other hand, this science is a form of *art* insofar as it employs practical judgment and creativity as it seeks to move from the detailed studies of the social scientists to the reformist critique of social institutions and practices. It is a science, then, that places a premium not only on *describing* but also *reforming* normative practices and institutions. The practical and reformist aspect of Durkheim's science of morality acknowledges and embraces *risk*. All our knowledge is "partial," as Durkheim noted ([1904] 1979: 32). And when we attempt to apply science to practical problems, we are confronted not only with the limits of our empirical research but also with an additional set of uncertainties and challenges as we attempt to make specific proposals for change. As Durkheim put it, when one engages in reformist efforts, "one runs a risk, try as one might, which no method can automatically eliminate" ([1904] 1979: 32). The risk of uncertainty, then, is fundamental to Durkheim's most cherished project, *rational moral art*. In light of such risk, Durkheim counsels us to begin "setting resolutely to work"—reflecting on our common involvements, traditions, and ideals, investigating our institutions, practices, and structural arrangements—without waiting for "a plan anticipating everything" ([1897] 1951: 392). In short, he recommends that we join *sociohistorical skill to moral commitment and imagination*.

Later in this chapter I will argue that Durkheim, especially in his early work, failed to adequately grasp the level of risk and uncertainty in the *first part* of rational moral art, that is, in the detailed social scientific studies of human institutions and practices. But if he was at times naive about the very idea of a "social fact," we can excuse him somewhat by noting the intellectual current against which he struggled. Many of the topics central to Durkheim's new science, sociology and its science of morals, had for some time belonged to the work of "the philosophers." While Durkheim had much respect for many philosophers, he complained that most of them neglected to concern themselves with how real humans live, instead constructing speculative theories based on conceptions of an "abstract human," or an "abstract creation of their own minds." In contrast to this abstract creature, "the real human—the one whom we all know and whom we all are—is more complex; he is of a time and of a country, he has a family, a city, a fatherland, a religious and political faith, and all these factors and many others merge, combine in a thousand ways, their influence crossing and crisscrossing such that it is impossible to say at first glance where one begins and the other ends" (Durkheim

1888: 29, my translation). My point here is that while Durkheim at times failed to register the interpretive dimensions of his "empirical data"; he was compensating for what he took to be the philosopher's wholesale dismissal of "thick descriptions," that is, of empirical investigations that pertain to "real" and not "abstract" humans.

Although Durkheim highlighted the need for empirical studies in an attempt to discover "real" humans and their practices, he did not think that ethical inquiry should confine itself to simply representing or reflecting the status quo. Habits, customs, population densities, institutional arrangements, economic relations, and ideals: such sociohistorical material was central to the investigative work of rational moral art. Yet this work also entailed critique, that is, deliberation on the means *and* ends of moral practices. Such critique, in Durkheim's view, often involved making *implicit* moral practices and understandings more *explicit*, that is, more manifest, so that they could be more subject to judicious scrutiny. The critique of rational moral art, in any case, remains rooted in "real" humans and their actual social situations, and it therefore tends to work on a case-by-case basis, shunning abstract absolutisms that have no anchor in lived experience. To shun abstract absolutisms, however, does not entail rejecting general moral ideals rooted in time and place. In the case of modern, European societies, Durkheim's moral critiques were often guided by the progressive ideals of the Third Republic—equality, liberty, solidarity, and the sanctity of the human person.

Unfortunately, for some time now Durkheim has been interpreted as a conservative sociologist preoccupied with understanding and maintaining social order and the status quo (Coser 1960; Levitas 1974: 31; Lukes 1985: 131; Nisbet 1965: 23; Nizan [1932] 1967: 191–192). No doubt, many have attributed conservatism to Durkheim precisely because of his commitment to viewing humans and their moral principles and practices as ineluctably rooted in their social institutions and histories. The logic here goes something like this: social theorists who begin and end with human situatedness can never rise above present (or past) social ideals, customs, and institutions. These alleged conservative theorists are bound to the status quo, unlike, say, "rational" theorists who discover moral universal truths outside present or past social worlds. Yet Durkheim's rational moral art investigated the webs and patterns of social order for the sake of critique and the establishment of greater social justice. Indeed, it is precisely Durkheim's commitment to the sociohistorical stuff of human existence that enabled him to be a radical critic. Why radical? He went to the root of many problems of modern social life by exposing their sociohistorical development and present social circumstances.

Throughout his career, Durkheim wore the hat of the social critic. His work was normative through and through. It is impossible to separate his efforts to found sociology from his hope and belief that the new science would do its part to promote such aims as social and economic justice. And the subfield within sociology that was most focused on this normative endeavor, and that was perhaps dearest to his heart, was the science of morals. We find it from his first publications to his last unfinished work, *Introduction à la morale*. And it is to that last work that we will now turn.

To Begin at the End:
Introduction à la morale

In the final months of his life in 1917, Durkheim wrote his last text: the *Introduction* to what he had hoped would have been his greatest accomplishment, the science or sociology of morals. And so we begin with Durkheim's mature thought on the topic.

"The word *morale* is normally construed in two different ways" (Durkheim [1920] 1979: 79). With this opening line, Durkheim began the *Introduction à la morale* by bringing attention to the complex and even ambiguous meanings associated with the word *moral*. On the one hand, it refers to the lived, day-to-day moral experience of individuals and their communities; on the other hand, it refers to scholarly "systematic, methodical speculation" on *les choses de la morale* (80). Most of the *Introduction* is an elaboration on what Durkheim meant by systematic, methodical approaches to *les choses de la morale*. As it turns out, Durkheim was doubtful about most of these approaches unless we count among them his own favored approach, "the science of morality" (92). But before turning to his lengthy discussion of systematic approaches to *les choses de la morale*, it is worth lingering on the first and supposedly more straightforward construal of the word *morale*, namely, lived moral experience.

Our everyday lived moral experience, according to Durkheim, is made up of tacit moral judgments. These judgments, he claimed, "are imprinted on the *conscience* of the normal adult. We find them ready-made within us, and in most cases without our being aware of having actually formed them in a conscious, let alone scientific or methodical way" (79). If we didn't know better, we might suppose that Durkheim belonged to a Natural Law tradition or some such school of thought subscribing to the view that humans contain within them a universal moral code. But we do know better. From the start of his career, Durkheim maintained that our moral life is fundamentally shaped by sociohistorical circumstance. If Durkheim subscribed to a natural law, it was this one: humans are creatures *naturally in need of the social* and are radically shaped by the social in diverse ways in time and place. And so Durkheim began the *Introduction* with what he took to be a fundamental fact about human existence: humans are naturally social and our moral life is rooted in our second nature.

By "second nature," I refer to the process and condition of acquiring dispositions, habits, practices, beliefs, and perspectives and of so thoroughly internalizing them that they become "natural"—that is, innate—to us. Our first nature, then, can be understood as a set of potential capacities that we are born with; our second nature, in contrast, is a formative process and product of our experience of living in time under specific sociohistorical circumstances. By means of this formative process, our capacities develop and our habits, practices, and beliefs are forged. Without explicitly employing the name, "second nature," Durkheim employed the concept, and right at the start of his *Introduction*. It was imperative that, early on, he captured the way in which our moral judgments feel immediate, "spontaneous," and "ready-made within us," so much so that they seem to stem "from the very depths of [our] nature" (79). Durkheim chose to begin his last work with one of his first and foremost commitments: *humans are naturally social creatures.*

In sum, then, the first construal of the word *morale* refers to the spontaneous, immediate moral judgments of sociohistorically habituated individuals. The second construal, in contrast, refers to "all systematic, methodical speculation" on *les choses de la morale.* Think of this meaning of *morale* as referring to a second-order discourse that critically engages with and reflects on the first order, that is, on everyday lived moral experience. Unlike the typical moral agent who lacks systematic thought about his or her moral perception and action, the practitioner of this second-order discourse (whom Durkheim usually calls "the philosopher" or "the moralist") is in the business of "giving reasons" for prescribed moral ideals and practices (80). The reasons given are not, for the most part, the result of carefully observing actual, lived ethical practice and then articulating the reasons implicit in such practice. Rather, the reasons given are usually derived from assumed principles that are systematized and variously justified. The philosophers and moralists are therefore not bound by the moral perspectives and practices of "general opinion," since their moral principles are deduced not from actual lived moral experience but rather from a preconceived, a priori "view of man":

> He is envisaged as a rational or sentient being, as an individual; or, on the other hand, as essentially sociable, as seeking general, impersonal ends or else pursuing quite particular goals, etc. And it is this view which serves as a basis for advocating that he should follow one precept for action rather than another. (80)

Durkheim then proceeded to offer examples of how the philosopher or moralist often proposes moral practices that indeed contradict prevailing views. Philosophers championing socialism, for example, propose moral practices that greatly differ from dominant notions of property rights.

Thus far, in the first pages of the *Introduction*, Durkheim has subtly criticized the philosophers and moralists (including some socialist philosophers) for paying more attention to abstract moral principles than to actual lived moral experience. He wrote, for example, the "philosophers are *a long way* from having determined with any precision" the object or method of systematic moral inquiry (80, emphasis added). We might be led to think, then, that the philosophers and moralists are judging society based on their own favorite set of abstract principles that have no grounding in the actual society in which they live. And that would be largely correct. But then, without any warning, Durkheim segued from his claim about socialist philosophers and others contradicting the "general opinion" to the following claim:

> Every morality, no matter what it is, has its ideal. Therefore, the morality to which men subscribe at each moment of history has its ideal which is embodied in the institutions, traditions and precepts which generally govern behaviour. But above and beyond this ideal, there are always others in the process of being formed. For the

moral ideal is not immutable: despite the respect with which it is vested, it is alive, constantly changing and evolving. (81)

How are we to account for this transition? Durkheim claimed that even the abstract principles of philosophers (including those principles that contradict general moral practice) are in fact grounded in sociohistorical processes. However, the philosopher, unlike the sociologist, is not sufficiently aware of such grounding. And that, as it turns out, is the fundamental difference between the moral philosopher and the sociologist of morals. Moral philosophers, according to Durkheim, are largely oblivious to the sociohistorical sources and dynamics of moral thought and practice, including that of their own systematic, methodical speculation on *les choses de la morale*.

What, then, has Durkheim claimed thus far? The word *morale* can refer to the everyday lived moral experience, on the one hand, and to the philosopher's systematic reflection on the moral life, on the other. The philosophers, deducing their moral claims from particular first principles or foundational assumptions about the nature of humanity, may issue moral prescriptions that diverge from common, everyday moral practice. And while this would seem to imply a wedge or chasm between the two senses of the word *morale*, Durkheim in fact insisted that both the lived moral experience and the philosopher's moral abstract principles emerge from and manifest sociohistorical currents—institutions, laws, practices, habits, and ideals. Moral philosophers, unwittingly, may help to articulate the contradictions and potential future directions of sociohistorical moral forces; they can play an important role in indicating where society (morally speaking) has been and where it is heading. Yet their work is limited because they are not sufficiently aware of the various ways in which individuals, society, and even their own research is in fact shaped by sociohistorical matter and manners. They have helped along the science of morals by making the implicit moral practices and ideals of everyday moral life a bit more explicit. But it will take the work of the sociologists, those equipped to analyze the social, historical, and institutional aspects of the moral life, to make the implicit more fully explicit. And so while Durkheim, in this final piece, struck a more conciliatory note with the philosophers and at times suggested a respectful division of labor, in the end he made it clear that the sociologist of morals takes over well before the moral philosopher leaves off.

Let's now turn to Durkheim's account of a robust, systematic approach to *les choses de la morale*. Durkheim began the second section of the *Introduction* with the claim that "there is no science worthy of the name which does not ultimately become an art, otherwise it would be no more than a game, an intellectual pastime, erudition pure and simple" (82). That's quite a claim coming from someone who is often labeled as a narrow positivist. One might have thought that Durkheim would insist that sociology in general and the sociology of morals in particular are purely descriptive and explanatory enterprises. Why burden this new science, one desperate for legitimacy, with art? Yet Durkheim held the deep conviction that the science of morals has potentially much to offer to society as it wrestles with pressing moral issues and problems. Furthermore, not wanting to suggest that sociology was an anomalous science in this regard, Durkheim boldly stated that *all* science has normative aims. As we will see, Durkheim did not collapse relevant distinctions between science and art. Rather, he held that the scientist should be willing to practice art, that is, to embrace risk and attempt to extend one's research to apply to practical concerns. On this, Durkheim stood closer to Marx and further from Weber.

Early on in the second section of the *Introduction*, Durkheim turned to his central question: By what manner and method is the scholar to contribute to the art of the moral life? He started by showing how it is *not* to be done. Scholars of "all schools" generally proceed as follows:

> They postulate that the complete system of moral rules is subsumed within one cardinal notion, of which it [the system] is merely the development. They strive to discover this notion and, once they believe they have been successful, all they need [to] do is to deduce the particular precepts it implies and they will have attained the ideal, perfect morality. (82)

From this "cardinal notion," the seed of all morality, the scholar then *deduces* the moral ends and practices appropriate for humanity. Durkheim rejected this approach for various reasons. It cannot satisfactorily account for the diversity of moral aims and practices found in different regions and in different periods. And its deductive method generates moral perspectives that follow from the theorist's (abstract and simple) starting point, not from society's (concrete and complex) past and present. In contrast to the abstract, deductive approach, Durkheim championed an empirical, inductive approach. The science of morals investigates a broad range of what Durkheim called "moral facts," a subset of social facts. Unlike, say, the Kantian's noumenal and its moral postulates that cannot be investigated in time and space, moral facts are "a category of natural things" (90) and are therefore subject to empirical inquiry. Only via an investigation of society's moral facts, that is, its past and present moral institutions, ideals, and lived practices, can the scholar make empirically justified claims about a society's complex moral life.

Later I will say more about the nature of social and moral facts. For now, it is important to register the radical historicism and dynamism that characterizes Durkheim's science of morals. To the ears of some, a science that focuses on "moral facts" might sound static and fixed. Through empirical observation, you observe and analyze static facts and then deduce human moral nature—once and for all. Yet in contrast to static approaches, of which Durkheim accused the philosophers and economists, he claimed:

> *All life is change and is alien to that which is static.* [...] It is always premature to say that a living creature is intended for one single type of existence and to lay down in advance a set type of existence from which it cannot diverge. *Such fixedness is the negation of life.* (86, emphasis added)

You can imagine the radical challenge that Durkheimian dynamism posed to the universal, colonial claims of hegemonic Christianity and European morality. Cultures outside the Christian West, in Durkheim's view, have their own legitimate, changing forms of moral life. Moreover, Durkheim's social dynamism applies not only to place but also to time: "Not only is history the natural context of human life, but man is a product of history. If, disregarding his historical context, we attempt to see him as fixed, static, and outside time, we only denature him" (86). Here, in Durkheim's last writing, we find his strongest statements about *the flow of life as the natural condition of humans*. Any serious moral inquiry, he insisted, must take such dynamism as its point of departure. The first step of Durkheim's science of morals may be the empirical investigations of moral facts, but those facts can only be grasped and suitably analyzed when located in the flow of life.

What of the second step in the science of morals, the step that follows an investigation of moral facts? Moral art is the applied or practical aspects of the science of morals. Moral art and science, in Durkheim's view, are closely linked: "the art of morality and the construction of the moral ideal presuppose an entire science which is positive and inductive and encompasses all the details of moral facts" (90). Science and art are not the same, but they pull together to produce *rational moral art*. In this two-step method, the empirical investigation of moral facts (the historically fashioned institutions, laws, customs, and ideals) provides solid grounding from which to engage in the indeterminate work of moral art and to discern a society's best interpretations of its moral perspectives, ideals, and practices. Rational moral art is an empirically rich and far-reaching form of *immanent critique*. From society one crafts—via research and art—the very means by which to critique society.

A starting point for Durkheim's science of morals, we have seen, is the fluidity of human nature. Viewing human nature as dynamic can safeguard against spurning other, alien ways of life simply because they are not one's own. Moreover, it can make one more receptive to moral innovation within one's own society. Durkheim's empirical work, grounded as it is in comparative and historical inquiry, was not only about making accurate sociological statements. He was staking out a normative position: the moral life of a society is enriched by sensitivity to its historical nature.

Some might want to call Durkheim a relativist, since he rejected the idea of universal, ahistorical moral truth. Yet out of that rejection he mounted a powerful argument for a form of moral realism. We discover much about our moral identity as we investigate our moral traditions and practices. We acquire objective, rational viewpoints as we scrutinize and evaluate the very social sources that support our rationality. It is not my intent here to supply a full defense of a moral realism based on Durkheim's work (for a discussion of Durkheim's moral realism, see Cladis 1992: 248–250). I only want to note that it can be misleading to label him a relativist. And it would be a mistake to label him a political and moral conservative due to his practice of immanent critique (judging society by its own moral resources). Only within the (implausible) framework of *external criticism* would the charge of conservatism make sense. The external critic, especially if she has "revolutionary" sensibilities, may claim that modern societies are fraught with false ideologies and contradictions, and that therefore there are no moral resources within these societies, at least none sufficient for the required drastic transformation. Durkheim, however, would want to know how she identifies what changes need to be made. If she appeals to universal moral or economic laws, Durkheim would likely be interested in her specific positions, and would try to show how these, in fact, have emerged from some portion of her society's values and institutions. Her dissent, he would argue, is a sign that she is morally implicated in society. If she appeals, on the other hand, to a foreign culture's moral resources, Durkheim would point out that her initial appreciation of these alien ways was, at least to some extent, grounded in her own cultural experience.

Given an adequate grasp of the notion of rational moral art, Durkheim looks like an interesting and helpful social reformer. Rational moral art is based on the view that the best way to reform society is to study it scientifically; identify its most promising moral traditions, perspectives, and ideals; and then seek to reform society accordingly. Science (systematic, empirical inquiry) provides the detailed accounts of society's moral life; art, in contrast, seeks to transform society, not from scratch, not from a priori first principles, but from situated moral ideals and practices that highlight social ills and emancipatory change. Durkheim sought neither to merge nor radically separate science and art. Moral art is informed by empirical, scientific investigations, but its practical propositions cannot be guaranteed by science. Art involves risk and uncertainty. Of course, science entails its own risks and the possibility of getting things wrong, and facts are both found and made. The extent to which Durkheim understood as much will briefly be addressed in my conclusion.

Moral Facts and the Science of Morality

In the *Introduction*, Durkheim promised to elaborate on the nature of moral facts, but he did not live long enough to complete that promise. He did, however, extensively discuss moral facts in some relatively late publications, especially in "The Determination of Moral Facts" (1906). Durkheim began "The Determination of Moral Facts" by asserting that the moral life can be studied with two different approaches: "One can set out to explore and understand it and one can set out to evaluate it" (Durkheim [1906] 1974: 35). As we have seen, Durkheim considered both approaches as part of a two-step process in the enterprise of rational moral art. In "The Determination of Moral Facts," Durkheim mainly focused on the first step, that is, on the empirical investigations of moral facts or what he called "the theoretical study of moral reality." The chief question that he addressed is, "What are the distinctive characteristics of a moral fact?" (35). Moral facts are a subset of social facts, the fabric of society—patterned relations, practices, customs, habits, institutions, laws, and ideals. For the purpose of this chapter, I'll focus on *ideals*—which may not intuitively strike many as *facts*. A brief examination of Durkheim's account of ideals will help to illustrate his complex epistemology, and that in turn will supply the necessary context for appropriately understanding his notion of social and moral facts.

When Durkheim wrote, "to love one's society is to love this ideal [the dignity of the human person]," he was appealing to a *concrete* ideal—to a social fact (59). Ideals, in Durkheim's view, are not the result of private speculation. Nor are ideals innate features of the mind or of Nature. They are, as Durkheim put it, subject to time and space. They are natural but only insofar as they are produced by sociohistorical forces, and these forces are basic to human existence. Durkheim challenged not only the materialist/idealist dualism but also the nature/culture dualism. Social and cultural phenomena—language, texts, customs, beliefs, means of production, any and all social institutions—are, in principle, no more or less mysterious than other material aspects of our lives. Social ideals, Durkheim wrote, are "subject to examination like the rest of the [...] physical universe" (Durkheim [1911] 1974: 94). They are real. They are tangible. Durkheim's social epistemology, which sought to do away with the empiricism/apriorism dichotomy, is a middle way, or put better, a different way. It portrayed an inextricable, transactional relation between the material world and the conceptual world. To speak of two worlds, in fact, is misleading. Durkheim materialized ideals and idealized matter—and he historicized both. In the process, he attempted to overcome a set of tyrannous dualisms—empiricism and apriorism, materialism and idealism, nature and culture. The resulting position, I believe, appropriately describes the materiality of beliefs, values, and customs, as well as the sociality of knowledge, facts, and logic. It is in the context of this sophisticated epistemology that we need to interpret Durkheim's concept of social and moral facts.

What is distinctive about that special subset of social facts—*moral facts*? Moral facts are marked by two salient characteristics: *obligation* and *desirability*. On the one hand, moral facts (moral rules and practices) "are invested with a special authority by virtue of which they are obeyed simply because they command" (Durkheim [1906] 1974: 35–36). On the other hand, "it is impossible for us to carry out an act simply because we are ordered to do so and without consideration of its content. For us to become the agents of an act it must interest our sensibility to a certain extent and appear to us as, in some way, *desirable*." All moral rules and practices have these two aspects, "even though they may be combined in different proportions" (36). This is an extraordinary account of moral rules and practices. Essentially, Durkheim brought together Kant's notion of duty and obligation with the virtue theorist's notion of a habituated love of the good. And in the process, he mounted a powerful challenge to those such as Kant or Freud who portrayed human nature as sharply divided against itself. Durkheim complained that "Kant's hypothesis, according to which the sentiment of obligation was due to the heterogeneity of reason and sensibility, is not easy to reconcile with the fact that moral ends are in one aspect objects of desire" (45–46). If Durkheim objected to positing an absolute antagonism between individual desire and social obligation, it is because he did not conceive of human nature as fatally divided against itself. From the publication of *Suicide* in 1897 until his death, Durkheim increasingly employed the voluntaristic vocabulary of love, respect, and desire—in addition to that of duty, command, and obligation—to describe the individual's relation to society and, not coincidentally, the nature of moral facts.

If duty and desirability mark moral facts (the subject matter for empirical investigations of moral reality), then cultivating the capacity for discipline and attachment are twin goals for the applied ethical work of moral education. Discipline is central in those moral traditions that emphasize duty and self-control. Attachment is central in those moral traditions that celebrate the desirability and loveliness of the good. Discipline characterizes Kant and *Moralität*; attachment characterizes Hegel and *Sittlichkeit*. Durkheim was eager to keep these two aspects in a harmonious tension. Law and grace, duty and love—these are dual, alternative descriptions of the moral life. Some personalities may tend more toward one than the other, as may some cultures. The point, however, is that both aspects spring from our twofold relation to moral traditions, beliefs, and practices: we are both governed by them and attracted to them.

The sacred, in Durkheim's view, has the same duality as moral facts: it is that which is forbidden and must not be violated, yet it is also "good, loved and sought after" (36). The shared duality between the moral and the religious life was of paramount importance to Durkheim; he stated emphatically that

> If I compare the idea of the sacred with that of the moral, it is not merely in order to draw an interesting analogy. It is because it is very difficult to understand moral life if we do not relate it to religious life. For centuries morals and religion have been intimately linked and even completely fused. [...] There must, then, be morality in religion and elements of the religious in morality. In fact, present moral life abounds in the religious. (48)

In "The Determination of Moral Facts," Durkheim's principal example of the sacred in contemporary moral life was *the dignity of the human person*. This ideal is "a sacred thing." On the one hand, "one dare not violate it nor infringe its bounds," while on the other hand, our "greatest good is in communion with others" (37) as we cherish and uphold this sacred moral ideal, the sanctity of the human person. The connection between the moral and religious life and how it manifests itself in modern democracies had been a topic for Durkheim at least since the Dreyfus Affair. In his Dreyfusard article, "Individualism and the Intellectuals" (1898), Durkheim argued that moral individualism—the beliefs and practices associated with progressive, social democracy—"appears to those who aspire to it to be completely stamped with religiosity. [...] Whoever makes an attempt on a person's life, on a person's liberty [...] inspires in us a feeling of horror analogous in every way to that which the believer experiences when he sees his idol profaned" (Durkheim [1898] 1973: 46, translation modified).

With this new understanding of the connection between the sacred and the moral, Durkheim would go on to develop a social theory that articulated and promoted the sacred rights of the human person in the moral idiom of democratic social traditions and commitment to a common good. A fundamental feature of democratic solidarity, in this view, is its commitment to the dignity of the person. As France confronted the "otherness" of Dreyfus the Jew, Durkheim argued that his nation needed to realize more fully its commitment to the dignity of all individuals, regardless of their racial, ethnic, or religious identities. This was his argument and hope, and with it he challenged the intense nationalism of various Roman Catholic and royalist reactionaries. In contrast to their nationalistic vision of French solidarity, Durkheim held that normative French solidarity depended on, and contributed to, upholding the protection of human rights and the defense of diversity. He had come to believe that the elementary forms of religious life permeate not only traditional but modern societies as well. Although its tenets and rites have changed, its basic forms have not. Robust collective beliefs, practices, and institutions still shape, move, and enliven us, though perhaps not in domains traditionally associated with religion. The political, economic, and even scientific realms are infused with the religious. Individual rights, notions of economic fair play, and the spirit of free inquiry, for example, are charged with the sacred. Durkheim now had a powerful vocabulary for articulating the normative, communal aspects of progressive, modern democracies—the vocabulary of *sacred values* and *moral religion*.[1]

In "The Determination of Moral Facts," Durkheim anticipated a standard objection to the very idea of immanent critique: "If morality is the product of the collective," claims Durkheim's critic, "it necessarily imposes itself upon the individual, who is in no position to question it whatever form it may take, and must accept it passively" (Durkheim [1906] 1974: 59–60). In reply to this charge of conservatism, Durkheim argued that "the science of reality puts us in a position to modify the real and to direct it. [...] The science [...] furnishes us with the means of judging it and the need of rectifying it" (60). "Rectifying" the status quo may entail bringing attention to moral crises in which worthy ideals and practices are suppressed (think of the Dreyfus Affair, for example). It may also entail helping society to navigate among competing moral traditions and claims, especially in the face of new moral developments. In either case, Durkheimian rational moral art, a form of immanent critique, seeks to reform society by self-consciously working within its situated, socially produced inheritance, that is, sociohistorical ideals, customs, beliefs, institutions, and practices.

Durkheim's moral art and its immanent critique addressed such fundamental questions as, What kind of normative criteria do we possess for evaluating our shared understandings? Are tradition-bound reasons all we have to draw from? In Durkheim's view, there is no universal reason, no moral law, residing outside history or inside human nature. Our only objective (that is, reason giving) evaluation of morality is one that empirically discovers what is in place and then proceeds, in an artful fashion, to dialectically scrutinize one portion of collective life while relying on another portion (66). Durkheimian moral art does not have the sure warrants of something like Natural Law or Universal Reason. Uncertainty is inherent in it (67). But acknowledging such ostensible limits is an honest recognition of human finitude, the complexity of the moral life, and the challenging task of social reform.

To End at the Beginning: The Early Work on *La science positive de la morale*

Having given much attention to Durkheim's mature thought on the science of morals, we are now in a position to consider expeditiously his early thought on the subject, noting continuities and discontinuities.

In 1885, Durkheim received a fellowship to visit German universities and learn about their current work in philosophy and the social sciences. In "La science positive de la morale en Allemagne" (1887), Durkheim presented not only a report on trends in German scholarship but also a clear and passionate declaration for a new approach to moral inquiry: the science of morals. Unlike philosophy's abstract ethical reflections, the new science of morals conducted its investigations by analyzing such sociohistorical facts as practices, customs, law, and economic arrangements. This new empirical approach that he saw in the work of Wilhelm Wundt, among others in Germany, was a refreshing development for Durkheim, given his education in Paris. But he must already have had an elective affinity for just such a sociohistorical method before ever studying in Germany. Although the work of such French scholars as Auguste Comte and Charles Renouvier was not as empirically rich as, say, that of Wundt or Gustav von Schmoller, it still suggested to Durkheim the promise of a scientific approach to morals. When he arrived in Germany, then, he was receptive to what he found. And what did he find?

Durkheim found a young science committed to observing and analyzing a society's lived moral life; considering moral phenomena as social facts (and not just a matter of individual psychology) that are subject to socioscientific investigation; and regarding moral facts as interwoven with other kinds of social facts (legal, economic, historical, and so on). Durkheim was passionate about the promise of this new science and about what it required of scholars:

> We cannot construct morality out of nothing in order to impose it subsequently upon reality; rather, we must observe reality in order to induce morality from it. We must examine it in its multiple relations with the unending number of phenomena in terms of which it is shaped, and which, in turn, it regulates. [...] When it [ethics] loses contact with the very source of life, it becomes arid to the point of being reduced to nothing more than an abstract conception, entirely limited to a dry and empty formula.
>
> (Durkheim 1972: 95)[2]

In this remarkable passage from 1887, we see that Durkheim's ardent commitment to the sociohistorical investigation of morals is found at the very beginning of his career. And his attempt to capture the strengths (and to identify the limits) of Kant and "the utilitarians" can also be found at the beginning. He noted that the Kantians rightly see the moral life as a distinctive subject matter for inquiry, but they declare (erroneously) that it is outside the scope of science. The utilitarians, in contrast, rightly "treat morality as an empirical fact, but one which has no specific properties of its own. They reduce it to this highly confused notion of 'utility'" (91). Throughout his career, Durkheim would pursue and develop an engaged critique of Kantian and utilitarian approaches to ethics.

What of the practical side of the science of morals? Is that, too, found in Durkheim's earliest work? Durkheim cautiously alluded to the future potential of an applied science of morals. In his view, many more preliminary sociohistorical investigations needed to take place before such art could robustly proceed. Indeed, his main criticism of "the German school" was its rush to establish a "general formula of morality" and then seek to apply it (Durkheim [1887] 1993: 129). Like other sciences, the science of morals, according to Durkheim, needed to study a "multitude of particular problems" (129), moving case by case, and not hurrying to discover "a formula which will encompass them all" (130). Yet in spite of this critique of the German school, Durkheim did, over the course of his career, increasingly join Wundt in the aspiration to join the sociological study of morals with the normative art of social critique and reform. While Durkheim always insisted that science and art not be conflated, he developed nuanced accounts of the very nature of science, accounts in which the imagination played a larger role in science and served as a bridge between science and art.

At the same time, his philosophical anthropology underwent important changes. The early Durkheim, for example, frequently endorsed theories about natural moral sentiments (social inclinations), whereas the later Durkheim emphasized the formative role of collective representations and social ideals. Of course, even the early Durkheim understood natural sentiments to account for only a rudimentary human sociability. As Durkheim's philosophical anthropology underwent changes, so did his sociological approaches and methods. Increasingly, he moved away from describing society in terms of morphological social facts in favor of socially generated representations and ideals. In *The Division of Labor* and in *The Rules of Sociological Method*, social beliefs and ideals (usually called collective sentiments, not collective representations) appear as external constraints imposed on individuals. The social substratum, comprised of morphological facts, produces collective sentiments. These sentiments, having little life of their own, are an expression of the social substratum. In *Suicide*, Durkheim revised this position. Shared beliefs, ends, norms, practices, and ideals (now called collective representations, but still understood as social facts as well) take on a somewhat autonomous nature as they themselves become agents of social change. It would be a mistake, however, to make too much of this discontinuity between an early and late Durkheim. From *Suicide* on, material structures (morphology) and social ideals (collective representations) are two sides of a rapidly spinning coin.

Joining Sociohistorical Analysis to the Moral Imagination

The overall trajectory of Durkheim's science of morals is one of enhanced complexity and sophistication. In order to avoid the "naturalistic fallacy," that is, the identification of "what is" with "what ought to be," he separated the science of empirical inquiry from the art of applied ethics and social critique. This is why I have described rational moral art as a two-step process: only after performing empirical investigations is one in a position to generate normative judgments. These judgments are based on reasons and, unlike those of "the philosopher," they are connected to and spring from rich comparative sociohistorical accounts. Yet increasingly Durkheim acknowledged the presence of art in the science. The Durkheim of *The Elementary Forms of Religious Life*, *Pragmatism and Sociology*, and *Primitive Classification* developed a complex epistemology that highlighted the sociohistorical dimensions of reason and science. In *Pragmatism and Sociology*, for example, Durkheim claimed that

> Man is a product of history [...]; there is nothing in him that is either given or defined in advance. [...] Consequently, if truth is human, it too is a human product. Sociology applies the same conception to reason. All that constitutes reason, its principles and categories, has been made in the course of history.
>
> (Durkheim 1983: 67)

And as Durkheim increasingly understood the role of art in science, he also maintained the role of science in art, that is, the role of the empirical studies in assisting normative critique. Durkheim ultimately never conflated the two steps, but he did increasingly mitigate the rigid science–art polarity. This mitigation is, in part, what I have in mind when I refer to the "enhanced complexity and sophistication" of Durkheim's mature vision for rational moral art. Increasingly, he came to understand the uncertainty that adheres to science as well as the confidence that can be assigned to art, that is, to practical judgments. Had he lived longer, perhaps Durkheim would have departed from the two-step science-to-art process altogether, and instead would have simply mounted detailed sociological investigations with explicit normative aims, thereby bringing science and art still closer together. In fact, just such an approach is found in Durkheim's mature work. In some ways, his *theory* about moral science had yet to catch up with the actual *practice* of rational moral art in his later work. Perhaps, in time, the theory and the practice would have become better aligned. While it may not be useful to imagine the future development of Durkheim's work on moral art had he lived longer, it is helpful to reflect on what has become of his vision. There are important trends in philosophy, anthropology, history, religious studies, economics, and sociology, among other fields, that are very much in line with the spirit of Durkheim's rational moral art. Increasingly, scholars in the social sciences and humanities seek to wed empirical, sociohistorical investigation with normative social critique. While Durkheim would applaud these new trends, he would no doubt lament that an institutional home in the social sciences for systematic normative work has yet to develop.

Due to his early death, Durkheim was only able to draft the introduction to the book that he most wanted to write—a book on ethics and rational moral art. However, he did produce a large body of work that could justifiably be called rational moral art. This is not surprising, given the deep normative commitments that implicitly and explicitly motivated many of his sociological studies. I wish to conclude this chapter by providing one example of Durkheim's mature work that exemplifies the spirit of rational moral art.

In *Professional Ethics and Civic Morals*, Durkheim brought together sociohistorical skill and moral imagination. He offered a compelling account of democratic solidarity that entailed moral pluralism and a plurality of morals. "A plurality of morals" refers to the diverse goals, ideals, and practices that characterize groups in the domestic, occupational, civic, and global spheres. "Moral pluralism," in contrast, pertains to the relation between the goals, ideals, and practices of the political community and those of such voluntary associations or groups as churches and synagogues, ethnic organizations and activist alliances. This can include associations that are said to rest upon comprehensive religious, moral, or philosophical doctrines. In Durkheim's view, the solidarity of the political community does not require broad agreement from these associations on every issue; in other words, democratic solidary does not require social homogeneity. On some issues, however, such as the protection of diversity, widespread agreement is needed. Moral pluralism, then, refers to a plurality of communities and associations that promote distinctive practices and beliefs, and yet also contribute to—or at least do not threaten—common public projects and goals.

Moral pluralism, as Durkheim conceived it, supports and requires the solidarity of a political community, a community that encompasses all others. This social realm aims for inclusion and open, agonistic critical reflection and engagement. Potential agreement rests on the fact that diverse citizens share a common history or future or both, and they often care about the problems and promises that are germane, not only to a particular community, but to the broader political community in which all participate. Solidarity, in Durkheim's account, is not the result of state-sponsored coercion or of a natural harmony among secondary groups. Rather, it emerges from, and contributes to, the various interactions between the democratic state and its various secondary groups. The solidarity of the political community, then, does not work against pluralism, but rather is constitutive of its very existence. And the health of the political community requires a rich variety of diverse secondary groups.

Durkheim's commitment to enhancing a democratic solidarity was fueled by his worry over a private economy that put the maximization of profit above human social welfare. His multifaceted study on professional and civic ethics was motivated by his belief that economic institutions should be accountable to a society's civic, public life. His worry was that as modern societies become increasingly fragmented, shared aims and ideals lack the strength to guide the economic life in light of democratic conceptions of justice. The economy, in his view, should not be understood as a discrete, amoral, private realm, but rather as an integral moral component of the public life. Hence, Durkheim claimed that a stable and just economic sphere "cannot follow of itself from any entirely material causes, from any blind mechanism, however scientific it may be. *It is a moral task*" (Durkheim 1957: 12, emphasis added). Why a moral task? Because we should not expect just economic social practices to emerge spontaneously from private contracts or "supply and demand" or from any other liberal market devices. A moral task is at hand because people, equipped with sociohistorical understanding and moral imagination, must *do something* to bring justice to the economic sphere. Yet without a sense of ourselves as a people with shared perspectives, problems, and goals, we will not be able to tackle such a pressing and massive problem as an economic sphere unaccountable to democratic institutions.

Durkheim's empirically informed work on democratic solidarity and pluralism reflects normative commitments that motivated much of his work, including his lifelong aspiration to establish a science of morals and the craft of rational moral art. It would be a shame if we relegated this aspiration to an antiquated, positivist quest for certainty in the realm of values. The aspiration that Durkheim set for himself should become our own, as we wrestle with the challenge of joining sociohistorical analysis to the moral imagination.

Notes

1. Unfortunately, Durkheim systematically refused to grasp women's rights as being among such "sacred values." Marcela Cristi, for example, argues that Durkheim's "reputation as defender of human rights is undermined by his theoretical treatment of the female sex. Durkheim refers to the 'individual' in generic terms, but his approach to a just social order and rights is essentially formulated in terms of the 'social' male individual" (Cristi 2012: 409).
2. This is an excellent but abridged translation of Durkheim's article.

References

Cladis, Mark S. 1992. *A Communitarian Defense of Liberalism: Emile Durkheim and Contemporary Social Theory*. Stanford, CA: Stanford University Press.

Coser, Lewis A. 1960. "Durkheim's Conservatism and Its Implications for His Sociological Theory." In *Emile Durkheim, 1858–1917*, edited by Kurt H. Wolff, 211–232. Columbus: Ohio State University Press.

Cristi, Marcela. 2012. "Durkheim on Moral Individualism, Social Justice, and Rights: A Gendered Construction of Rights." *Canadian Journal of Sociology* 37 (4): 409–438.

Durkheim, Émile. 1888. "Cours de science sociale: Leçon d'ouverture." *Revue internationale de l'enseignement* 15: 23–48.

Durkheim, Émile. (1897) 1951. *Suicide: A Study in Sociology*. Translated by John A. Spaulding and George Simpson. Glencoe: The Free Press. Originally published as *Le suicide. Etude de sociologie*. Paris: Alcan.

Durkheim, Émile. 1957. *Professional Ethics and Civic Morals*. Translated by Cornelia Brookfield. London: Routledge & Kegan Paul.

Durkheim, Émile. 1972. "The Science of Morality." In Émile Durkheim, *Selected Writings*, edited and translated by Anthony Giddens, 89–107. Cambridge: Cambridge University Press.

Durkheim, Émile. (1898) 1973. "Individualism and the Intellectuals." In *Emile Durkheim: On Morality and Society*, edited by Robert N. Bellah, 43–57. Chicago: University of Chicago Press. Originally published as "L'individualisme et les intellectuels" in *Revue bleue*, 4e série 10: 7–13.

Durkheim, Émile. (1906) 1974. "The Determination of Moral Facts." In Émile Durkheim, *Sociology and Philosophy*, edited and translated by D. F. Pocock. New York: Macmillan, 35–62. Originally published as "La détermination du fait moral" in *Bulletin de la Société française de philosophie* 6 (4): 169–212.

Durkheim, Émile. (1911) 1974. "Value Judgments and Judgments of Reality." In Émile Durkheim, *Sociology and Philosophy*, edited and translated by D. F. Pocock. New York: Macmillan, 80–97. Originally published as "Jugements de valeur et jugements de réalité" in *Revue de métaphysique et de morale* 19: 437–453.

Durkheim, Émile. (1904) 1979. Review "Lévy-Bruhl, *La Morale et la science des moeurs*." In Émile Durkheim, *Essays on Morals and Education*, edited by W. S. F. Pickering, 29–33. London: Routledge & Kegan Paul. Originally published in *Année sociologique* 7: 380–384.

Durkheim, Émile. (1920) 1979. "Introduction to Ethics." In Émile Durkheim, *Essays on Morals and Education*, edited by W. S. F. Pickering, 77–96. London: Routledge & Kegan Paul. Originally published as "Introduction à la morale" in *Revue philosophique* 89: 79–97.

Durkheim, Émile. 1983. *Pragmatism and Sociology*. Edited by John B. Allcock. Cambridge: Cambridge University Press.

Durkheim, Émile. (1887) 1993. *Ethics and the Sociology of Morals*. Edited and translated by Robert T. Hall. Buffalo, NY: Prometheus Books. Originally published as "La science positive de la morale en Allemagne" in *Revue philosophique* 24: 33–58, 113–142, 275–284.

Levitas, Maurice. 1974. *Marxist Perspectives in the Sociology of Education*. London: Routledge & Kegan Paul.

Lukes, Steven. 1985. *Emile Durkheim: His Life and Work*. Stanford, CA: Stanford University Press.

Nisbet, Robert A. 1965. *Émile Durkheim: With Selected Essays*. Englewood Cliffs, NJ: Prentice Hall.

Nizan, Paul. (1932) 1967. *Les Chiens de garde*. Paris: F. Maspero.

CHAPTER 3

SOLIDARITY AND ATTACHMENT IN DURKHEIM'S SOCIOLOGICAL THOUGHT

SERGE PAUGAM

The Division of Labour in Society represents Durkheim's main dissertation, which he defended on March 3, 1893, at the Faculty of Letters at Bordeaux; its French subtitle can be translated as "A Study of the Organization of Superior Societies." This was Durkheim's first book, in which he tried to establish the foundations of sociology. In a way it is the cornerstone of the new edifice of sociology. Through the metamorphoses of the idea of solidarity, Durkheim looks at the question of social relationships. He provides an analytical framework to analyze both the process of differentiation between individuals and the cohesiveness of modern societies. For over a century, research in the social sciences has constantly referred to *mechanical solidarity* and *organic solidarity*; these are key concepts that form the basis of our understanding of the social world. But curiously enough, while these two concepts are central to Durkheim's argument and, to this day, remain a subject of stimulating interpretations and discussions, Durkheim himself never referred to them again in the works published after his thesis. This disappearance is an enigma. Although we cannot completely solve it, we would like to suggest some elements of an interpretation of his choice to abandon these terms.

We can posit no less than three hypotheses. The first is based on Durkheim's reaction to the criticism he received, and on the misunderstanding these two concepts inevitably provoke. This is particularly true of the highly controversial theory of organicism, which the term *organic solidarity* inescapably evokes. It could be that Durkheim finally decided that these two concepts were too abstract to explain the diversity of human forms of solidarity. The second hypothesis is related to the fact that Durkheim's dissertation falls within the trend of Republican thought that gave birth to the doctrine of solidarism. This concept gained considerable popularity at the end of the nineteenth and the beginning of the twentieth century in France, as well as elsewhere in Europe, and this political and ideological usage of the concept of solidarity certainly detracted from the strictly sociological interpretation Durkheim had envisaged. Finally, we can suggest the hypothesis that, having enriched his analytical framework, particularly after his study of *Suicide*, Durkheim preferred to replace the concept of solidarity, which had become too ideologically charged, with the idea of the attachment to a group. He developed this idea further in his lectures on *Moral Education*, emphasizing the link between multiple forms of attachment and the different types of morality that prevail in each society. In this chapter we will first outline the main arguments of Durkheim's dissertation and then look successively at the three hypotheses previously described.

Mechanical Solidarity and Organic Solidarity

In order to understand the origins of his dissertation, we should look at the years preceding the writing of this work, when Durkheim taught a number of sociology classes at the Faculty of Letters at the University of Bordeaux. He became professor of pedagogy and social science in 1887 and, until he was appointed to the chair of education at the Sorbonne in 1902, the University of Bordeaux served as his sociology laboratory. His first "Public Lectures on Social Science" (that in the second year went on to become "Public Lectures on Sociology") deal with *social solidarity* and, in a way, represent the bedrock of his dissertation. The only article available, "Cours de science sociale: Leçon d'ouverture," published in 1888, presents his opening lecture and reveals Durkheim's intellectual ambition while announcing the direction of his work. What is particularly striking in this introductory text is the fundamental mission the founder of French sociology attributes to the new discipline. He envisages its role as that of giving society a stronger awareness of its representations of itself and its unity, and reinforcing the bonds that attach individuals to each other while making them more visible, in order to stave off the selfishness they are susceptible to. In other words, it serves to avert the risk of disaggregation and anomie that society, taken as a whole, faces. He ends his lecture with this declaration:

> Our society must regain the consciousness of its organic unity; the individual must feel the presence and influence of that social mass which surrounds and penetrates him. This feeling must continually govern his behavior because to experience it only in particularly critical circumstances is not enough. [...] I believe that sociology, more than any other science, is suited to restoring these ideas. It is sociology which will enable the individual to understand what society is, how it completes him and what a small thing he is when reduced to his own powers. It will teach him that he is not an empire enclosed within another empire, but the organ of an organism and it will show him what is valuable in the conscientious performance of his organic role.

> Sociology will make the individual feel that solidarity and dependence on someone else does not diminish him. He will learn not to be self-centered. No doubt these ideas will become truly efficacious only if they are spread throughout the deepest levels of population. But to do that, it is first necessary to elaborate them scientifically at the University. My principal concern will be to contribute to the attainment of this goal to the best of my ability, and nothing will make me happier than to succeed in some small measure.
>
> (Durkheim [1888] 2008: 203–204)

Scientifically developing ideas of solidarity at the University is clearly the objective Durkheim sets out to achieve in his thesis. His ambition is to study moral facts and their transformation. He does not intend to deduce morality from science, but to constitute a science of morality. Like other sociologists, particularly Tönnies and Weber in Germany (Jones 1993, 1999: ch. 4), he questions the basis of social relationships in modern societies,[1] looking specifically at morality. The question underpinning his thesis can be formulated in the following manner: "Why does the individual, while becoming more autonomous, depend more upon society?" (Durkheim [1893] 1933: 37). Durkheim notes that these two movements of autonomy and dependency run parallel to each other, and at the end of the preface to the first edition he states: "It appeared to us that what resolves this apparent antinomy is a transformation of social solidarity due to the steadily growing development of the division of labor. That is how we have been led to make this the object of our study" (37–38). This project leads him to provide explanations for the shift from traditional to modern society, based on an analysis of the conditions of long-term social change.

Let us first look at the distinction he makes between the two types of solidarity he identifies. *Mechanical solidarity* is a solidarity based on common values and beliefs. This concept refers to traditional societies in which individuals differ little from each other, share the same feelings, obey the same beliefs, and adhere to the same values. *Organic solidarity*, characteristic of modern society, is the opposite. This means that social relationships in these societies are essentially based on an interdependency of occupations. They give every individual, regardless of their differences, a specific social position. Durkheim also uses the term "segment" to describe a social group into which individuals are closely integrated. He sees mechanical solidarity as corresponding to a social structure marked by a system of homogenous segments that resemble each other. Organic solidarity, on the contrary, is not sustained by this type of segments, but "by a system of different organs each of which has a special role, and which are themselves formed of differentiated parts" (Durkheim [1893] 1933: 181). Durkheim arrived at this opposition by first elaborating other concepts. To start with, that of collective consciousness, which he defines in the following manner:

> The totality of beliefs and sentiments common to average citizens of the same society forms a determinate system which has its own life; one may call it the *collective* or *common conscience*. [...] It is, thus, an entirely different thing from particular

consciences, although it can be realized only through them. It is the psychical type of society, a type which has its properties, its conditions of existence, its mode of development, just as individual types, although in a different way.

(Durkheim [1893] 1933: 79–80)

Using this definition, we can examine the variations between traditional and modern societies. In the former, collective consciousness covers most individual existences, as feelings are so strongly shared, and the rituals that characterize social life are so clearly defined. The significance of each act and each belief is obvious to everyone. In a way, the individual is absorbed into the group. In the latter, collective consciousness is weakened. There is greater room for an individual interpretation of social taboos, and social control is less effective. This reduction of collective consciousness is particularly evident in the fact that there is clearly less unity within society. This weakening is not only an aspect of organic solidarity, it is also a condition of the division of labor. It is only possible if individuals are free and capable of acting independently of their groups. But at the same time, the individuals who make up society can lose sight of their sense of complementarity and withdraw into themselves. Durkheim was aware of this. This is why he so strongly emphasized secular morality as a factor of unification.

Durkheim did not limit himself to this concept. To develop his argument, in the first chapter of Book I, he emphasises the relationship between solidarity and the law. The stronger the ties between the members of a society, the more likely they are to share an intense solidarity. He underscores that "the number of these relations is necessarily proportional to that of the juridical rules which determine them" (Durkheim [1893] 1933: 64–65). This statement leads him to distinguish between two types of legal rules, depending on the different sanctions they entail. These rules are those of *repressive* law, which sanctions misdemeanors and crimes, and of *restitutive* law, which does not necessarily involve inflicting suffering on the agent but is more focused on restoring the situation to its original state and organizing cooperation between individuals. The former affects the individual in terms of his honor, fortune, or freedom, and hence leads to depriving him of all or a part of his goods and pleasures. It is based on penal law. The second seeks to restore the relationships that existed prior to the incriminating act, or in other words, what is considered the normal functioning of society. It thus fights deviation and can be based either on civil or commercial law, or on administrative and constitutional law. Although repressive law exists in every society, according to Durkheim it is more characteristic of societies based on mechanical solidarity, as the multiplication of sanctions reveals the strength of the collective consciousness and the obligation to ensure that social taboos are respected. Restitutive law hence corresponds to societies based on organic solidarity. It reflects the need for an organization capable of ensuring a coordinated existence between the different members of the same society. It is essentially *cooperative*, another term Durkheim used to define it.

Thus, for Durkheim, the division of labor we see in modern societies is not an obstacle to solidarity. On the contrary, it is the very basis of this solidarity. The most remarkable of its effects is not to increase the productivity of separate occupations but to make them supportive of each other. The results are most visible not in the field of economic interests but in the establishment of a *sui generis* social and moral order. Individuals are not independent; they have to work together. Rather than dividing people, the division of labor reinforces their complementarity by forcing them to cooperate. Thus, each one gains a sense of being useful to the group through their work. Hence, it is in the work relationship itself that an employee can experience satisfaction, which is largely based on the recognition, by other employees, of his contribution to the productive activity. This process is based on the principle of the complementarity of occupations that involves each participant internalizing a role that corresponds to a type of participation in the social system as a whole.

When solidarity is based on the uniformity imposed by beliefs and practices, the internal organization of society is not disturbed by the departure of certain members or by the arrival of additional individuals, as long as there are positions to be occupied. However, when division of labor is the founding principle of social life, the integration of new elements can alter the existing relationships of interdependency, create perturbations between the members of society, and lead to forms of social rejection. Thus, at least implicitly, Durkheim underscores potential forms of discrimination that exist in modern society. When each person's usefulness is defined on the basis of his or her participation in the functioning of the whole, the other, who comes from a foreign country and has a different culture, can be seen as a threat. Mutual complementarity does not occur naturally; it is fragile, which can be expressed in racist reactions. In the same way, losing one's place in a strong system of interdependency represents a particularly painful experience for the individual for whom it signifies the loss of social usefulness.

Another of Durkheim's observations deserves particular attention. Chapter II of Book II, dedicated to the causes of the division of labor, ends with a long footnote in which he describes the possibility that there might be exceptions to the general law of the progressive evolution of the division of labor. The question is whether homogenous and similar segments, characteristic of those found in societies that are based on mechanical solidarity, can exist in a society organized on the basis of organic solidarity. The fact that this question only appears in a footnote says a lot about the problem Durkheim faces. If a general law is contradicted by facts, it loses its pertinence as a general law. Durkheim nonetheless approaches the problem through the case of England.

> But it may very well happen that in a particular society a certain division of labor, and notably the division of economic labor, may be greatly developed, although the segmental type may be strongly pronounced there. This seems to be the case with England. Great industry and commerce appear to be as developed there as on the continent, although the cellular system is still very marked, as both the autonomy of local life and the authority of tradition serve to prove.
>
> (Durkheim [1893] 1933: 282)

How should we interpret this contradiction? To start with, in this case, Durkheim does not emphasize the social nature of this division of labor, but its economic nature which, according to him, only occurs at the surface of social life.

> It is sufficient, then, that some sort of circumstance excite an urgent need of material well-being with a people for the division of economic labor to be developed without the social structure sensibly changing. The spirit of imitation, the contact of a more refined civilization can produce this result. It is thus that understanding, being the culminating part and, consequently, the most superficial part of conscience, can rather easily be modified by external influences, as education, without the seat of psychical life being changed.
>
> (Durkheim [1893] 1933: 282)

Thus, the division of labor would be nothing more than an outer layer, characteristic of economic society; nevertheless, it contains an inferior type of social structure. Durkheim specifies that occurrences of this type are exceptional. Nonetheless, it is clear today that Durkheim's observations are not as exceptional as he envisaged during his time. Contemporary sociologists are more sensitive to the intertwining, within modern societies, of different types of social relationships. Some of these represent organic solidarity, others mechanical solidarity. In other words, relationships developed on the basis of a complementarity of occupations have not completely dissolved the older relationships that developed out of a system of homogenous beliefs and practices. One could even say that the weakening of the collective consciousness and the risk of the dissolution of values has, in certain cases, engendered forms of resistance to a generalized interdependency, expressed through community groupings.

THE DIFFICULTY OF MUTUAL UNDERSTANDING BETWEEN DURKHEIM AND TÖNNIES

Before his thesis was published, Durkheim was aware of Ferdinand Tönnies's book, titled *Gemeinschaft und Gesellschaft*, that appeared in 1887 (Tönnies 2001), and he published a critical commentary on it in the *Revue philosophique* in 1889. Tönnies's response to this was to publish a fairly severe critique of *The Division of Labour* (Tönnies [1896] 1972).

At first glance, there seems to be a striking similarity between these two authors. Both are studying the same question, and they attempt to answer it through a large-scale analysis dealing with the historical transformation of human societies. Tönnies explains the growing individualization of human relationships by contrasting two key concepts: *Gemeinschaft* and *Gesellschaft*.

Durkheim found it deeply unfortunate that the words *Gemeinschaft* and *Gesellschaft*, which Tönnies uses to qualify two types of society, are untranslatable; nonetheless, they recall the two types of solidarity that Durkheim describes. Mechanical solidarity is similar to a *Gemeinschaft* nation, and organic solidarity recalls a *Gesellschaft* nation. In reality, a closer study of this comparison reveals deeper complexities. Indeed, Tönnies distinguishes between *organic will* and *reflective will*. The former is expressed in pleasure, habit, and memory; it envelops and determines thought and constitutes the source of any undertaking or creation. In short, it is characteristic of *Gemeinschaft*. The latter is the product of thought that serves to guide and direct the energies and impulses which emerge from organic will. This can be seen as *Gesellschaft*. Thought makes it possible to distinguish, and oppose, goals and means. For Tönnies, capitalism is primarily the result of the disappearance of community and its replacement by modes of organization, laws, and principles of government no longer based on the idea of community. In other words, Tönnies sees the composition of *Gemeinschaft* as organic, while the composition of *Gesellschaft* is mechanical.

Durkheim considers that Tönnies should have discovered that the *Gesellschaft* social type is just as natural as smaller community aggregates. He reproaches him for an insufficient observation of the facts and having stopped at abstract conceptual constructs. In Tönnies he sees the illustration of a neo-romantic type of preference for the intimate and warm unity of traditional communities and considers that the method he uses to define collective *Gesellschaft* type life is "altogether ideological." In other words, Durkheim is against Tönnies's dialectical and classificatory approach which, according to him, is characteristic of the methods employed by German "logicians." With this he states the need to proceed "inductively," which, for example, means "to study *Gesellschaft* through the laws and mores which are associated with it and which reveal its structure" (Durkheim [1889] 1978: 121–122).

For his part, in his explanation of the differences that set him against Durkheim, Tönnies states:

> This doctrine of mine is basically indifferent toward the theory that the *esse formale* of the social life or that of *Gesellschaft* is organic. I have never had any doubt about the possibility of comparing the mutual effects in the developed political economy with organic mutual effects. My conceptions do not exclude in any way the fact that ruling and other active corporations or individuals in a big nation as well as in a village or town community take an attitude toward their entirety as organs do toward an organism. However, I do not find very instructive the way in which Mr. Durkheim presents the social types and their mutual relations. He deals with the division of labor pedantically without the critical analysis which many times was praised in Bücher's work.
>
> (Tönnies [1896] 1972: 1200)

At a more general level, this debate echoes the difficulties in the exchanges between German and French sociologists. Beyond a shared sensitivity to the transformations of social relationships, Tönnies and Durkheim represent two divergent approaches that we can only fully understand if we resituate them in the specific sociocultural contexts of Germany and France of the end of the nineteenth century. In any event, we cannot ignore the hypothesis that Durkheim himself tired of the debate, given the difficulties in understanding each other and the inevitably fragile nature of these conceptual conflicts. For this reason, he may have preferred not to pursue the quarrel, while sticking to his analyses.

The Controversies around the Organicist Theory

However, this was probably not the only reason why Durkheim did not return to the central concepts presented in his thesis. The discomfort he must have felt may have been reinforced by the growing usage of the concept of a social organism, and by the development of organicism as a means of representing society. René Worms was a key organizer within the world of sociology at the end of the nineteenth century, and he strongly influenced the spread of organicism. In 1893, he founded the *Revue internationale de sociologie* and then, in 1895, the Paris Sociological Society. He soon became one of Durkheim's competitors, possibly even an adversary. In 1896, Worms published his thesis, titled *Organisme et société*, which he defended at the Sorbonne. This thesis sought to provide a complete theory of organicism. However, it provoked certain reservations due to what was seen as an untimely use of biological metaphors and syllogisms in an attempt to demonstrate that society functioned just like any organism.

The relationship between Durkheim and Worms was never cordial. Durkheim never participated in any of Worms's initiatives (review, society, conferences), and he asked his nephew Marcel Mauss to spread the word that his distant attitude was primarily motivated by the low intellectual esteem in which he held the director of the *Revue internationale de sociologie*.[2] Organicism went on to become the object of numerous controversies, including within the Paris Sociological Society, and it was discredited at the Congress of the International Institute of Sociology in July 1897 (see Geiger 1981). As is well known, Durkheim liked using metaphors, or making comparisons between the way society is organized and the organization of living things (see Filloux 1979). He also spoke of society as an organism, but avoided developing this viewpoint into a general theory as Worms and several collaborators with the *Revue internationale de sociologie* did. But is it not true that the concept of organic solidarity lent itself to confusion? We cannot ignore the hypothesis that Durkheim, a posteriori, believed that this concept was becoming somewhat equivocal because of the direction that the theory of organicism took and, above all, because of the questioning it was subjected to in the years following the publication of his dissertation.

Avoiding this concept was, without a doubt, the most efficient means of avoiding the semantic confusion between the exclusively metaphorical and methodological usage Durkheim made of it and the global theoretical interpretation it was likely to suggest. In the preface to the second edition of the *Division of Labour*, Durkheim no longer uses this concept and prefers to focus on occupational groups and their impact on society. It was as if, without mentioning the concept of organic solidarity, he was providing more specific content for it by confronting it with empirical examples that were related to real and desired transformations in the world of work. We should also note that in this 1902 edition, the subtitle of Durkheim's thesis—"A Study of the Organization of Superior Societies"—no longer exists. There is no doubt that the organicist connotation had become an embarrassment.[3]

While the concept of organic solidarity could be confusing, its opposite—the concept of mechanical solidarity—was not exempt from criticism either. In the decade following the publication of Durkheim's dissertation, ethnographic knowledge grew. It is likely that Durkheim gradually became aware of the fragility of his analyses. His nephew Marcel Mauss was later forced to look anew at the hypothesis of the absence of differentiation between individuals in the simplest societies, which are marked by a division of labor on the basis of gender, age, generation, and clan. He was to respectfully underscore that Durkheim's false hypothesis was nonetheless necessary (Mauss [1931] 1969: 221).

Thus, the fact that Durkheim did not return to these concepts is at least partially due to the misunderstandings and controversies they gave rise to in the years following the publication of his dissertation. Instead of wasting time by responding directly, he preferred to continue his work and dedicate his energy to another project—the study of suicide. But it is also likely that he realized that beyond the distinction between the two forms of solidarity he had identified, the concept of solidarity had escaped him as it had taken a different path.

Solidarism, or, the Solidarity Concept's New Career

Durkheim's dissertation met with a certain success in bookshops (Fournier 2007: 192). In a letter addressed to Marcel Mauss on May 28, 1894, Durkheim declares himself satisfied with the sales: of the 1,330 copies printed, only 500 were left unsold. However, when *The Division of Labour in Society* was released, the concept of solidarity had already embarked on a new career. Jean Izoulet's thesis appeared first, in 1895, titled *La cité moderne*. Some of the reflections it contained were a priori quite close to Durkheim's, at least as far as the analysis of solidarity and its rootedness in the organicist thinking of the time are concerned. But his diagnosis is quite different from Durkheim's. For Izoulet, hierarchical differentiation is at least as important as the principle of association: "Without a doubt, an organism is essentially a form of solidarity. But it is also, and to the same degree, a division of labor, a differentiation between the managed and the managers, the crowd and the elite, the trunk and the head. A physical organism that remains undivided in terms of work, and in a non-hierarchical state, is nothing more than an inferior animal" (Izoulet 1895: 646). It hence turns out to be essential to maintain the principle of subordination and not give in to a sort of reductive idealization of solidarity as the basis of social relationships. This young philosophy professor was highly appreciated in Republican circles, and his thesis was to have a great impact. He even went on to be appointed to the chair of social philosophy at the Collège de France in 1897 (see Blais 2007: 217ff.). Although *La cité moderne* was not handed down to posterity, at the time it had a far greater impact in the media than Durkheim's *Division of Labour*.

The concept of solidarity was also being developed outside of the field of sociology and the academic world. We owe the doctrine of solidarism to Léon Bourgeois, a member of the radical-socialist party and President of the Council of the League of Nations. He gave a framework for action and some kind of an official philosophy to the Republican state that was facing numerous difficulties at the end of the nineteenth century. Three years after the publication of Durkheim's thesis, Bourgeois published a book called *Solidarité* (Bourgeois [1896] 1998) that went on to become a reference work in terms of thinking on the social reforms to be accomplished. Now, Bourgeois makes no reference to Durkheim, but rather to the philosopher Alfred Fouillée, who had published a work titled *La science sociale contemporaine* in 1880. In it, he defends the principle of a "reparative" justice based on fraternity. For Bourgeois there is no part that is not part of a whole, the whole is greater than the sum of its parts, and human beings owe what they are as individuals to human association. Starting from this fundamental idea, he develops the idea of social debt. The following passage is now a classic quote:

> As soon as the child has finished breastfeeding, is completely separated from its mother, and becomes a separate individual receiving the food necessary for its existence, he becomes a debtor. He will not take a step, make a gesture, enjoy the satisfaction of a need, or exercise any of his nascent faculties, without drawing from the vast reservoir of utilities accumulated by humanity.
>
> (Bourgeois [1896] 1998: 44–45)

This debt to the ancestors is vast. It refers not to a few exceptional individuals or a few superior groups, but indeed to all human beings who, as a result of their interdependency in terms of work, contributed to the progress of humanity. Hence, the doctrine of solidarism is based on the principle that a debt exists between different generations. Human beings, however, are not only indebted to their ancestors. A large share of their activity, their property, their freedom, and their person is the result of an exchange of services with other human beings. This part is social and has to be pooled. In other words, Bourgeois clearly sees solidarity as the foundation of social relationships. It has to correspond to a rational acceptance resulting from a tacit contract that connects the individual to society as a whole. According to Bourgeois, as each living individual has a debt toward all the other living individuals, a general contract, binding every individual to the others, should be formulated, and replace contracts voluntarily established between individuals. The continuity between private and public law should be guaranteed in this manner. This exchange of services constitutes what Bourgeois calls an *associative* "quasi-contract" that connects all people to each other.[4]

This doctrine leads us to question the role of the State. Léon Bourgeois took his thinking to a deeper level in the context of several conferences that followed the publication of his book. The evolution of this doctrine, and specifically its translation into the legal context, were commented upon by several authors, particularly by Célestin Bouglé, one of Durkheim's disciples. The latter recalls how solidarism managed to extend State control without personifying the State or lending it a will of its own, superior virtues, or special rights. Thanks to the theory of quasi-contract, he says, "the law of the State becomes the translation of pre-existing wills of its members" (Bouglé 1907: 78).[5]

Solidarism thus defines one of the State's essential missions, that of ensuring social progress without becoming an oppressive tutelary power. This doctrine is expressed as a form of Guaranteeism. Justice would only exist among men if they become solidary associates by neutralizing, for each other, the risks they have to face. This doctrine thus establishes an intermediate path between liberalism and collectivism. In a way, solidarism is the prelude to the national welfare state. The rise of social insurance, completely in keeping with the doctrine of solidarism, takes us to a state of planned social organization based on risk technology, and henceforth nothing seems to hamper the progress of this movement.

It is striking that Durkheim never discusses these debates on social policy. While Bourgeois did not quote Durkheim, the latter made no reference to the doctrine of solidarism. A few years after he defended his dissertation, he began to look anew at the reforms required. He supported the idea that the constitution of occupational groups should be reinforced, but he did not talk about social insurance. He seemed to favor the themes of recognition through work, and of occupational integration, over the theme of social protection. The protection system of social insurance was, however, to affect all the relationships binding the individual to society. But Durkheim does not seem to anticipate this development and does not discuss it in his publications (unlike Mauss who discusses it in his essay on the gift). The inevitable association between the concept of solidarity and the doctrine of solidarism may have irritated Durkheim, who probably saw it as a potential threat, likely to modify the initial definition of solidarity that he had formulated.

From Solidarity to the Attachment to Groups

Although Durkheim no longer refers to the two concepts of mechanical and organic solidarity, he does not completely abandon references to feelings of solidarity. He associates the latter with the plurality of types of attachment that individuals experience among themselves and toward society (Paugam 2017). He persists in trying to answer the question he formulated in his dissertation: How do autonomous individuals organize themselves as a society, and how do they manage to connect to society? We find some elements of an answer in the conclusion to this work, but on their own, they are not conclusive (Besnard et al. 1993). We find other answers in the later texts that he published during the last decade of the nineteenth century. Beyond his dissertation, they include *The Rules of Sociological Method* ([1895] 1982), *Suicide: A Study in Sociology* ([1897] 1951), and the lectures that he gave at the University of Bordeaux,[6] and that were later published in the form of books. These include *Moral Education* ([1925] 1961)—a set of lectures that he probably gave in the year after the publication of *Suicide* and modified when he taught his first course at the Sorbonne in 1902–1903—and the lectures, written between November 1898 and June 1899, that were later published as *Leçons de sociologie: Physique des mœurs et du droit*, translated as *Professional Ethics and Civic Morals* ([1950] 1957). These different texts address a common set of questions, and a partial reading of them does not provide a clear understanding of the issue.

Progressively, Durkheim discovered a source of morality in the attachment to groups. He dedicated a number of pages in *Moral Education* to this theme; in this course, he tried to draw lessons from his empirical work, particularly his study of suicide. Durkheim now developed a stronger sensitivity to the plurality of relationships that connect individuals to society. He saw this as a means of recognizing the complete social texture of the individual, by distinguishing what connects an individual to his or her family, to social groups that are constituted during secondary socialization, and more generally, to the institutions governing all societies.

Let us start with the definition of morality that Durkheim provides in the conclusion to *The Division of Labour*: "Everything which is a source of solidarity is moral, everything which forces man to take account of other men is moral, everything which forces him to regulate his conduct through something other than the striving of his ego is moral, and morality is as solid as these ties are numerous and strong" (Durkheim [1893] 1933: 398). According to him, society is the precondition for these plural moralities: "It is not a simple juxtaposition of individuals who bring an intrinsic morality with them, but rather man is a moral being only because he lives in society, since morality consists in being solidary with a group and varying with this solidarity" (399). In other words, the basis of this morality is the individual's attachment to society.[7] It is not freedom but the state of dependency that contributes to making the individual an integral part of the social whole, and, from the outset, a moral being. Hence, says Durkheim, "Let all social life disappear, and moral life will disappear with it, since it would no longer have any objective" (399).

Since individuals define themselves through plural attachments to society, plural moral rules can exist. One of the aims of *Professional Ethics and Civic Morals* was to show in which ways these rules can intersect. Durkheim distinguishes three main types of morality that result from a belonging to a specific group: attachments to the family and the kinship system form the basis of domestic morality, attachments to the world of work, particularly to guilds, are the basis of occupational morality, while attachments to the homeland are the basis of civic morality. What distinguishes these three types of morality? Domestic and civic duties a priori concern all the members of a society, while occupational duties, by definition, vary from one occupational group to another. Durkheim emphasizes that there are multiple organs of occupational morality, indeed as many as there are professions.

At this point, Durkheim introduces a distinction between two types of professions: there are those that are strongly regulated by moral rules; they are directly linked to the state (army, teaching, magistrature, administration, etc.) and have a defined corps, a unity, and special regulations. Then there are the economic professions, both in industry and trade. Here, the lack of organization is a reflection of a lack of occupational morality, or at least of its rudimentary nature. In his opinion, the crisis European societies were going through was precisely due to the lack of a moral regulation of economic life and of the professions involved in it: at a time when the whole society is being industrialized, nothing exists to regulate the inevitably infinite and insatiable human appetite.

This is why, in *Professional Ethics and Civic Morals*, Durkheim launches into a sociohistorical analysis of the guilds. He actually uses numerous passages from these lectures in his preface to the second edition of *The Division of Labour*, published in 1902. Although in the first edition he is aware of the need for regulations to govern economic life, his thinking had developed over the following years. He believes the guild system is essential, not for economic but rather for moral reasons, as it is the only institution that Durkheim believes to be capable of moralizing economic life. In the guild reforms, he invites us to identify a process that is all the more legitimate as it is based on a knowledge of the economic dysfunction of his time and its social effects.

But although Durkheim ardently emphasizes the role of occupational groups, and hence of the type of relationship that is being woven between actors in the occupational world, this in no way signifies that he underestimates other types of relationships. Several times he explicitly returns to the results he arrived at in *Suicide*, in order to enrich his argumentation on different types of relationships and the key principles of moral education. He specifically looks at *egoistic* suicide and *anomic* suicide, because he is obsessed by the risk of disintegration modern societies face, and by the weakness of the links connecting the individual to the group.

But beyond the distinction between egoistic suicide and anomic suicide, we should remember the distinction between *integration* and *regulation*, which was very important to Durkheim. Throughout his work, these two concepts represent the cornerstones of the social relationship. Hence, it is unsurprising to find them articulated in a very similar manner in *Moral Education*. Durkheim believes that the first two elements of morality are the spirit of discipline and an attachment to groups, and it is easy to identify the concepts of regulation and integration as a translation of these elements. While it is the spirit of discipline that makes regulation possible, attachment to groups is the translation of the need for integration. At the beginning of the fifth lesson, he reminds his audience "that we are moral beings only to the extent that we are social beings" and that "Egoism has been universally classified among the amoral traits" ([1925] 1961:

64–65). From this he deduces, on the one hand, that "if there is such a thing as morality, it must necessarily link man to goals that go beyond the circle of individual interests" and, on the other hand, that "beyond the individual there is only a single psychic entity, one empirically observable moral being to which our wills can be linked: this is society" (65). Moral rules cannot be invented out of nothing; they are strongly determined by the prevailing social conditions, and it is necessary to start by carefully studying the latter. A moral education cannot be transmitted independently of a reflexive review of what constitutes social life in general, or in other words, a precise knowledge of the foundations of social relationships, to which sociology makes a clear contribution. This reasoning leads him to emphasize that which, beyond the cultural differences between social groups or societies, constitutes the universal in human existence. This is how we should understand expressions like: "Individual and society are certainly beings with different natures. But far from there being some inexpressible kind of antagonism between the two, far from its being the case that the individual can identify himself with society only at the risk of renouncing his own nature either wholly or in part, the fact is that he is not truly himself, he does not fully realize his own nature, except on the condition that he is involved in society" (67–68). Or: "Man possesses all the less of himself when he possesses only himself" (69).

An essential question remains: *Which* groups do individuals attach themselves to in order to satisfy their vital functions and express their integration to society? And this immediately gives rise to another question: If there are several types of group, can they be organized into a hierarchy? Just as, in order to appreciate the nature of social relationships, it is easier to discuss the different connections that bind the individual to the social system, it is also easier to deal with the multiple groups in which the individual lives, in order to understand what society as a whole could be. Now, while Durkheim in published writings often describes society in general, as if it were a single entity, in *Moral Education* we find an analysis of the multiplicity of attachments. He chooses three of them: the family, the homeland, and humanity. These three groups correspond to different phases of our social and moral existence, but today, they can be superposed without being exclusive. At this point, one can only be surprised by the fact that Durkheim does not mention the guild or the occupational group as fundamental social groups, even though elsewhere, particularly in the preface to the second edition of *Division of Labour*, he describes them as solutions to the threats presented by the world of work. In reality, he does not completely ignore them. At the beginning of the sixth lecture, he organizes and enumerates the different societies that we are engaged in, and here, instead of three groups, we have five: the family, the guild, political association, the homeland, and humanity. In the second part of the book, Durkheim only describes four groups, and political association is no longer mentioned, although he gives no reason for this. As we saw, it is also likely that these lectures were mainly written just after the publication of *Suicide*, at a time when Durkheim had not finished writing his *Professional Ethics and Civic Morals* and had not yet written the second edition of *The Division of Labour in Society*. In addition, although he does mention occupational groups, he notes—and deplores—that in France, unlike in Germany, the national temperament shows a weakness where the spirit of association is concerned, and there are no consistent intermediary corps between the individual and the State. Thus, he sees the guild as a nascent group that was extremely important in the past but needs to be reconstructed. According to him, the school should fulfil this mission, by showing the pupils on a daily basis that in the classroom, they belong to a group that is different from their families.

Durkheim's answer to the question of the hierarchy of these social groups is interesting. He has no doubt that while the family, the homeland, and humanity—to restrict ourselves to these three main groups—are all vital, "The evidence suggests that familial goals are and should be subordinated to national objectives, if for no other reason than that the nation is a social group at a higher level" (Durkheim [1925] 1961: 74). Because it constitutes a less impersonal goal than the homeland, the family is often confused with personal interest. At least in part, the child leaves the home to receive a public education. For Durkheim, who remains faithful in this to the emancipating ideals of the Third Republic, the State should take precedence over the family. As for humanity, it would be easy to imagine its superiority over the homeland, since humanity-level goals seem so much more elevated than national goals. But this supremacy remains equivocal, as it does not refer to a constituted society and does not have its own organization.[8] "Humanity" is too abstract a term for us to be able to give it precedence over a more limited group that actually exists. This is how Durkheim manages to place the homeland at the summit of the hierarchy of groups of attachments.

Durkheim returns to the homeland in *Professional Ethics*, particularly in the sixth lecture:

> Now, patriotism is precisely the ideas and feelings as a whole which bind the individual to a certain State. If we suppose it to have weakened or to have ceased to exist, where is an individual to find this moral authority, whose curb is to this extent salutary? If there is no clearly defined society there with a consciousness of itself to remind him continually of his duties and to make him realize the need for rules, how should he be aware of all this?
>
> (Durkheim [1950] 1957: 73)

The question of the hierarchy of these groups is fundamental. The normative system regulating every society provides a more or less precise version of this hierarchy. European societies, for example, do not all attribute the same importance to the role of the family, as we can see in numerous recent comparative works. In the same manner, the role that intermediate corps like associations play is very different from one society to the next. In some, this bond is called upon to regulate most social problems or dysfunctions, while in other societies, it remains almost nonexistent, or subordinate to state action. Durkheim's response to this point is more normative than sociological; but the hierarchy he establishes between the different types of bonds is coherent with his representation of the State and the homeland. What we today call the bond of citizenship is similar to the way in which Durkheim defined civic morality.

Conclusion

In this chapter, we have tried to identify the reasons why Durkheim abandoned the two key concepts of solidarity that he had developed in his dissertation to the benefit of a fuller analysis of the plurality of social bonds that attach individuals to society. He thus shifted from a theory of the evolution of solidarity to a theory of social attachment. This does not mean that Durkheim in any way renounced the ambitious program he had developed in the first years of his life in Bordeaux. Although he no longer refers to these two concepts of mechanical and organic solidarity in the works written after his thesis, he does not abandon the theoretical framework he constructed. On the contrary, he seeks to amplify it by carrying out his sociological study of suicide at a time when the concept of solidarity begins a new career. And it is in fact just after the publication of *Suicide* that he uses the concept of attachment to groups to refer to the plurality of social bonds and the morality associated with them. A closer look shows that this theoretical perspective already existed in *The Division of Labour*, but it seemed to be somewhat submerged by the conceptual base that overshadowed the two contrasting types of solidarity. Although the latter have been handed down to posterity, it does not mean that Durkheim found them completely satisfying. All the more so as, at the time, they contributed to confining him to controversial theoretical debates around organicism and ideological issues that seemed to him far removed from his vision of sociology.

Does this mean that the concept of social attachment conforms to the sociological definition of solidarity as Durkheim envisaged it before it was twisted in this way to serve political and ideological ends? What is certain is that if we follow the global analytical framework Durkheim defined, we can easily define solidarity on the basis of all the bonds that attach individuals to each other. We can also see in this one of the anthropological foundations of social life: individuals cannot live without attachments; they spend their lives developing bonds or recreating attachments after a rupture. The individual is an anthropologically interdependent being who cannot live without the multiple attachments that guarantee both protection from the hazards of daily life and a recognition of identity and of one's existence as a human being (Paugam 2008). But what does attachment really signify in a society of autonomous individuals, or of people who see themselves as such? How, and to what extent, can and should one be interdependent on the family, on the various groups one belongs to, and on the nation? The answers to this universal question will differ according to the social background and, mainly, the type of society. Hence, the main question is how to understand the anthropological underpinnings of human solidarity when carrying out a sociological analysis of its varying forms in the contemporary world.

Translated from the French by R. George.

Notes

1. According to Mauss, it was in 1884 that Durkheim clearly defined the project for his thesis. This was the year preceding his sabbatical to study the social sciences in Paris and then in Germany (Mauss [1928] 1969: 505).
2. Letter from Émile Durkheim to Marcel Mauss, Bordeaux, July 8, 1894 (Durkheim 1998: 35–36).
3. This point is emphasized in the introduction in Besnard et al. (1993: 6).
4. On this question Durkheim put forward a different analysis. In Chapter VII of *The Division of Labour* titled "Organic Solidarity and Contractual Solidarity," he had clearly wanted to differentiate himself from Spencer's conception, according to which association was based on contract. Durkheim believed that human beings associate naturally, and that contracts can only be born out of this association.
5. The English translation is taken from Mallard (2011: 230).
6. The original title Durkheim gave this course in 1896–1897 was "La physique générale des mœurs et du droit," and he retained the same title for four years. The theme of civic and occupational morality that he deals with in *Leçons de sociologie* seems to be a subsection of his course for the year 1899–1900. He had already used a very similar title—"Physiologie du droit et des mœurs (la famille)"—in 1890–1891. On this point, see Fournier (2007: 125).
7. The theme of attachment to groups is also very much present in Durkheim's analysis of collective effervescence. He emphasizes that collective excitement is produced by mutual attachment between individuals when they share social values and hence, a moral life (Durkheim [1912] 1995).
8. This bond of attachment to humanity could nonetheless also be envisaged from the dual perspective of protection (in reference to the promulgation of human rights, for example) and recognition, in that it promotes equal dignity for all men (which the 1949 Universal Declaration of Human Rights explicitly recognizes).

References

Besnard, Philippe, Borlandi, Massimo, and Vogt, Paul, eds. 1993. *Division du travail et lien social. La thèse de Durkheim un siècle après*. Paris: Presses universitaires de France.
Blais, Marie-Claude. 2007. *La solidarité. Histoire d'une idée*. Paris: Gallimard.
Bouglé, Célestin. 1907. *Le solidarisme*. Paris: Giard & Brière.
Bourgeois, Léon. (1896) 1998. *Solidarité*. Villeneuve-d'Ascq: Presses universitaires du Septentrion.
Durkheim, Émile. (1893/1902) 1933. *The Division of Labor in Society*. Glencoe: Free Press.
Durkheim, Émile. (1897) 1951. *Suicide: A Study in Sociology*. Translated by John A. Spaulding and George Simpson. New York: Free Press. Originally published as *Le suicide. Etude de sociologie*. Paris: Alcan.
Durkheim, Émile. (1950) 1957. *Professional Ethics and Civic Morals*. Translated by Cornelia Brookfield. London: Routledge & Kegan Paul. Originally published as *Leçons de sociologie. Physique des mœurs et du droit*. Paris: Presses universitaires de France.
Durkheim, Émile. (1925/1902–1903) 1961. *Moral Education: A Study in the Theory and Application of the Sociology of Education*. Translated by E. K. Wilson and H. Schnurer. New York: Free Press. Originally published as *L'éducation morale*, edited by Paul Fauconnet. Paris: Alcan.
Durkheim, Émile. (1889) 1978. "Review of 'Ferdinand Tönnies, *Gemeinschaft und Gesellschaft*.'" In *Emile Durkheim on Institutional Analysis*, edited and translated by Mark Traugott, 115–122.

Chicago: University of Chicago Press. Originally published in *Revue philosophique de la France et de l'étranger* 27: 416–422. Reprinted as "Communauté et société selon Tönnies." *Sociologie* 4, no. 2 (2013): 213–216.

Durkheim, Émile. (1895) 1982. *The Rules of Sociological Method and Selected Texts on Sociology and Its Method*. Translated by W. D. Halls. New York: Free Press. Originally published as *Les règles de la méthode sociologique*. Paris: Alcan.

Durkheim, Émile. (1912) 1995. *The Elementary Forms of Religious Life*. Translated by Karen E. Fields. New York: Free Press. Originally published as *Les formes élémentaires de la vie religieuse. Le système totémique en Australie*. Paris: Alcan.

Durkheim, Émile. 1998. *Lettres à Marcel Mauss*. Edited by Philippe Besnard and Marcel Fournier. Paris: Presses universitaires de France.

Durkheim, Émile. (1888) 2008. "Course in Social Science—Inaugural Lecture." *Organization & Environment* 21, no. 2: 188–204. Originally published as "Cours de science sociale: Leçon d'ouverture." *Revue internationale de l'enseignement* 15: 23–48. Republished in *La science sociale et l'action*. Paris: Presses universitaires de France, 1970, 85–117.

Filloux, Jean-Claude. 1979. "Durkheim et l'organicisme. L'influence de Spencer et d'Espinas dans l'élaboration du fonctionnalisme durkheimien." *Revue européenne de sciences sociales* 17, no. 47: 135–148.

Fournier, Marcel. 2007. *Emile Durkheim (1858–1917)*. Paris: Fayard

Geiger, Roger. 1981. "René Worms, l'organicisme et l'organisation de la sociologie." *Revue française de sociologie* 22, no. 3: 345–360.

Izoulet, Jean. 1895. *La cité moderne. Métaphysique de la sociologie*. Paris: Alcan.

Jones, Robert Alun. 1993. "La science positive de la morale en France. Les sources allemandes de la division du travail social." In *Division du travail et lien social. La thèse de Durkheim un siècle après*, edited by Philippe Besnard, Massimo Borlandi, and Paul Vogt, 11–41. Paris: Presses universitaires de France.

Jones, Robert Alun. 1999. *The Development of Durkheim's Social Realism*. Cambridge: Cambridge University Press.

Mallard, Grégoire. 2011. "*The Gift* Revisited: Marcel Mauss on War, Debt, and the Politics of Reparations." *Sociological Theory* 29, no. 4: 225–247.

Mauss, Marcel. (1928) 1969. "Introduction to: Émile Durkheim, Le socialisme." In *Œuvres*, vol. 3: *Cohésion sociale et divisions de la sociologie*. Paris: Les Éditions de Minuit, 505–509.

Mauss, Marcel. (1931) 1969. "La cohésion sociale dans les sociétés polysegmentaires." In *Œuvres*, vol. 3: *Cohésion sociale et divisions de la sociologie*. Paris: Les Éditions de Minuit, 11–27. Originally published in *Bulletin de l'Institut français de sociologie* 1: 49–68.

Paugam, Serge. 2008. *Le lien social*. Paris: Presses universitaires de France.

Paugam, Serge. 2017. "S'attacher à la société. Durkheim et la théorie des liens sociaux." *Revue internationale de philosophie* 280, no. 2: 89–115.

Tönnies, Ferdinand. (1896) 1972. "A Review of Émile Durkheim's *De la division du travail social*." *American Journal of Sociology* 7, no. 6: 1199–1200. Originally published in *Archiv für systematische Philosophie* 2: 497–499.

Tönnies, Ferdinand. (1887) 2001. *Community and Civil Society*. Edited by Jose Harris and translated by Margaret Hollis. Cambridge: Cambridge University Press. Originally published as *Gemeinschaft und Gesellschaft. Abhandlung des Communismus und des Socialismus als empirischer Culturformen*. Leipzig: Fues.

Worms, René. 1896. *Organisme et société*. Paris: Giard & Brière.

CHAPTER 4

THE SOCIALITY OF MIND

Key Arguments, Inner Tensions, and Divergent Appropriations of Durkheim's Sociology of Knowledge

FRITHJOF NUNGESSER

MORE than one hundred years ago, Émile Durkheim and Marcel Mauss ([1903] 1963) argued that the way we order and classify the world around us is shaped by the structures of our social groups. A few years later, in *The Elementary Forms of Religious Life*, Durkheim ([1912] 1995) even claimed that the fundamental dichotomy between the sacred and the profane as well as the very categories of mind (such as space, time, or causality) are formed by the dynamics of social life. Since then, these radical socio-epistemological claims have been a bone of contention not only within social theory but also between the social sciences and the natural sciences.

Just as Durkheim's other major works, his studies in the sociology of knowledge have to be understood as an attempt to demarcate a field of phenomena that can only be studied by sociological means. According to Durkheim, the structures of mind are not "simple," nor are they "innate" or "powers of the individual alone" (Durkheim and Mauss [1903] 1963: 4). This is why, for Durkheim, it does not suffice to refer to "individual representations." Instead, we must consider "collective representations" in order to explain why all the members of a social group perceive and classify their environment in the same (or at least similar) way, why the worldviews of different groups differ so drastically, or why these group-specific perspectives are experienced by the individuals as self-evident (Durkheim [1898] 2010). Hence, Durkheim curtails the explanatory claims of both philosophy and psychology by positing the fundamental sociality of mind.

Ever since Durkheim, the question of the sociality of mind has remained both contentious and fruitful. On the one hand, Durkheim's studies provoked numerous and strong objections—both within and outside the social sciences; on the other hand, they facilitated the development of crucial innovations in social theory. Against this background, the chapter discusses the main arguments, appropriations, and prospects of the Durkheimian sociology of knowledge in three steps. First, Durkheim's two key contributions to the sociology of knowledge as well as their similarities and differences will be outlined. Second, by drawing on the works of such diverse thinkers as Claude Lévi-Strauss, Pierre Bourdieu, Luc Boltanski, Laurent Thévenot, Robert Bellah, and Hans Joas, two quite different lines of reception of Durkheim's arguments will be distinguished. Finally, by systematizing the various tensions within Durkheim's sociology of knowledge as well as within and between its different appropriations, it will become possible to understand why the Durkheimian sociology of knowledge continues to exert such a provocative force—not only on the social sciences but also on approaches such as evolutionary psychology.

"Primitive Classification" and *The Elementary Forms*: The Two Key Contributions to the Durkheimian Sociology of Knowledge

Most authors agree that there are two main contributions to the Durkheimian sociology of knowledge: first, the long article "Primitive Classification," coauthored by Marcel Mauss and published in 1903 in the sixth volume of *L'Année sociologique* (Durkheim and Mauss [1903] 1963);[1] second, Durkheim's last major work, *The Elementary Forms of Religious Life*, which was published in 1912 (Durkheim [1912] 1995).[2]

Apart from their preoccupation with questions of the sociology of knowledge, the two studies share other important characteristics. What is perhaps most noticeable is the fact that they do not—like, for example, Durkheim's monograph on *Suicide* ([1897] 1951)—focus on modern Western societies. Instead, both studies are primarily based on ethnographic literature. "Primitive Classification" looks at the Australian Aborigines, the Zuñi, and the Sioux as well as at the traditional Chinese art of divination, while the *Elementary Forms* almost exclusively focuses on Australian cultures—especially the Arunta.[3] This focus results from a general development in Durkheim's work that increasingly turns to findings in ethnology[4] and religious studies.[5] One of the crucial reasons for this is Durkheim's methodological assumption according to which the basic mechanisms of the social can be best analyzed with respect to "simple societies" which underwent little historical change. This methodological assumption, in turn, is linked to Durkheim's evolutionary scheme according to which the Aboriginal societies of Australia "stand as close as possible to the origins of evolution" (Durkheim [1912] 1995: 93).

The relationship between the 1903 article and *The Elementary Forms* is described in various ways in the literature. In some publications the claims and arguments included in these two works are not separated explicitly but are presented as one major argument (e.g., Lukes 1973: ch. 22); in others the article on "Primitive Classification" is understood as a preparatory work that paved the way for the "more refined" theory developed in Durkheim's late masterpiece (Joas [1992] 1993: 63, 132); still others emphasize the differences between the two studies and highlight the importance and originality of Durkheim and Mauss's article (Needham 1979: 25; Pickering 1993: 53; Šuber 2012: ch. 4). Therefore, it seems advisable to present the two contributions separately in order to get a clear picture of the respective key claims and arguments. In the next section of this chapter, it will be shown that the similarities and differences between the two key contributions were of crucial importance for the reception of the Durkheimian sociology of knowledge.

"Primitive Classification"

In line with their evolutionist assumptions, Durkheim and Mauss begin their article on "Primitive Classification" with the analysis of Australian Aboriginal classificatory systems, which they interpret to be the "most rudimentary" and "most simple systems of classification" (Durkheim and Mauss [1903] 1963: 9–10). Despite their alleged simplicity, the Australian classifications have the same basic structure as those of other indigenous or modern societies. By means of classifications, the indigenous Australians not only arrange entities in their environment into separate groups but also create a certain hierarchy between these groups. Thus, their classifications do make the environment intelligible by dividing it into distinct classes and by establishing certain relations between these classes. In other words: they use taxonomies.[6]

In their article, Durkheim and Mauss strive to answer the question why classificatory systems around the world exhibit this structure. According to the authors, this question can only be answered by looking at the social structure of the most "primitive" indigenous societies. The social structure of Aboriginal societies—what Durkheim calls their "social morphology"[7]—is tightly coupled to their kinship systems. The basic elements of these kinship systems are not—as, for example, in Inuit or modern Western societies—nuclear families but moieties, which split the whole society into two exogamous halves (Durkheim and Mauss use the Old Greek kinship term "phratries" to refer to these moieties). In the course of social evolution, Durkheim and Mauss argue, these moieties developed subgroups, which the Aborigines call "skins" or "skin groups" (Durkheim and Mauss use the term "clan"). Each of the moieties and subgroups is linked to a totem—usually an animal, a plant, or a natural element. In many cases, these totems are considered to be (real or mythical) ancestors of the groups they are assigned to. Since the kinship system is constitutive for the social structure of Australian Aboriginal societies—as it is in all indigenous cultures (Kohl 2012: ch. II.2)—the importance of the kinship-based classificatory system "extends to all the facts of life" (Durkheim and Mauss [1903] 1963: 14). Rituals and myths, judicial, political, and economic processes—all dimensions of society are structured by the same kinship-based mental order.

The focus of Durkheim and Mauss's study is not, however, on the interrelations between the morphology and the social practices of indigenous societies. Rather, Durkheim and Mauss emphasize that there is a far more surprising structural congruence between the social morphology of the groups and their classifications of the natural and physical environment. Plants and animals, planets and regions—everything in nature is ordered according to the morphological pattern of society. As a result, there exist various structural congruences—also known as "isomorphies" or "homologies"—between the different classifications, which shape the perceptions, beliefs, and practices of the group. For example, during a certain ritual, a sorcerer may only use those plants that are assigned to his own kinship group and he may only be accompanied by members of this group (15).

Durkheim and Mauss do not content themselves with establishing the correspondences between morphological and classificatory structures but posit a *causal* connection. The "classification of things," they claim, "reproduces this classification of men" (11, italics removed). In other words: the indigenous Australians divide the natural world by means of taxonomic classifications because this is the way their social morphology is organized. Just as their society is divided into moieties and subgroups, so the natural world is divided into genera and species. This is why human thinking is structured by a kind of "sociocentrism" (86).

Whereas classificatory systems owe their original structure to the social morphology of "simple societies," this sociocentric determinism becomes weaker in the course of social evolution. Thus, Durkheim and Mauss argue, classifications can obtain a certain autonomy from the social structure (32). As Robert Bellah (1959: 457) notes, at this point in their narrative, human culture becomes an independent historical factor. Accordingly, in the later sections of their article, Durkheim and Mauss draw on ethnographic material on the Pueblo culture of the Zuñi, the Sioux, and the traditional Chinese art of divination to demonstrate how, over time, classifications became more and more independent of the morphological features of society—although the basic taxonomic structure still bears witness to their social origin. Hence, in the course of social evolution, the classifications also became increasingly complex and flexible. Also, due to the structural decoupling, the social and affective bonds between the mental classes vanish, which allows for a more rational and detached way of thinking. It does not come as a surprise, then, that in the closing pages of their evolutionary narrative Durkheim and Mauss return to Europe. Just as Chinese philosophy, they argue, ancient Greek philosophy was characterized by "the abstract and relatively rational types" of classification (Durkheim and Mauss [1903] 1963: 79). Hence, at the very end of Durkheim and Mauss's study, we arrive at the cradle of modern scientific thought.

The Elementary Forms of Religious Life

The Elementary Forms of Religious Life is the second major source of Durkheim's sociology of knowledge. In this book, Durkheim presents an in-depth analysis of the totemic society of the Australian Arunta. Again, the selection of this somewhat surprising research subject can only be understood against the background of Durkheim's evolutionist assumptions. From Durkheim's perspective, Australian totemism is a kind of "strategic research material"—to use a phrase of Merton's[8]—since it typifies the most primordial type of society, the most elementary form of religion, and the most "primitive" system of classification. This is why *The Elementary Forms* is a seminal study both in the sociology of religion and the sociology of knowledge.[9]

In part, *The Elementary Forms* continues the analysis of "Primitive Classification." Accordingly, Durkheim emphasizes the correspondences between the kinship system of the Arunta and their classifications of the plants, animals, and objects in their environment (Durkheim [1912] 1995: 141–145, 444–445). Yet this reconstruction of homologies is only a small part of a more extensive and more radical analysis. With respect to the sociology of knowledge, two innovations are of special importance: (1) the dualism between the sacred and the profane and (2) the claim of the social constitution of categories.

(1) As in Durkheim's other major studies, morphological arguments play a crucial role in *The Elementary Forms*. However, in contrast to "Primitive Classification," in *The Elementary Forms*, Durkheim focuses neither on diachronic developments nor on kinship structures. Rather, he highlights the rhythmic morphological changes in Arunta society (216–225). While most of the time Arunta society remains in a state of dispersion that "makes life monotonous, slack, and humdrum" (217), ordinary life is interrupted by religious festivals at regular intervals. According to Durkheim, in the course of these events the physical concentration of the group as well as their dances and songs generates "a sort of electricity" (217) that unleashes the passions and eventually leads to an ecstatic group experience—the well-known collective "effervescence" (218).[10] The individuals involved in the ritual are overwhelmed by the social dynamic and easily lose not only their self-control but also their very sense of self. This is why the individuals often do not recognize themselves in retrospect. According to Durkheim, the ritually induced collective emotions are so strong that they can only be understood by interpreting them as the result of external forces that exist beyond the familiar world of daily life. Therefore, for Durkheim, it is through these rituals that the fundamental classificatory distinction between "two heterogeneous and incommensurable worlds" (220), that is, between the sacred and the profane, emerges. With this distinction, Durkheim argues, religion is born.[11]

After the "delirium," Durkheim argues (228), the individuals associate their ecstatic experiences with familiar objects, movements, or expressions which, as a result, become symbols charged with religious and emotional significance (231–236). They help to conserve, stabilize, and even revitalize the otherwise ephemeral sacred experiences and become representations of the group and the moral unity of its members. "It is by shouting the same cry, saying the same words, and performing the same action in regard to the same object that they arrive at and experience agreement" (232). Hence, a "vast symbolism" (233) of physical, bodily, and expressive signs is created that constitutes a kind of second layer of reality. This layer refers to forces and entities beyond the world of ordinary life but is interwoven with the texture of concrete everyday reality. In accordance with Durkheim's definition of religion, this nonordinary layer of reality is important in two fundamental respects. First, in the words of Karen Fields (1995: xviii), it provides for "shared mental constructs with the help of which [...] human beings collectively view themselves, each other, and the natural world." Second, it serves as a guiding force that structures and motivates the practices of the collective. Some elements of the nonordinary layer of reality—the "left sacred"—are repulsive, evil, and impure; hence, they are put under a taboo and are avoided. Other parts of this layer—the "right sacred"—are attractive, benevolent, and pure; accordingly, they direct and drive the individuals to follow the aims and ideals of the group (Durkheim [1912] 1995: 412–417).[12]

Crucially, according to Durkheim, the dynamics described are not limited to indigenous cultures but can also be found in feudal and modern societies. Durkheim himself refers to the Crusades or the French Revolution to illustrate how ecstatic violence or mass protest can trigger situations of collective effervescence which give birth to new sacred practices and objects such as crosses or flags (213–216). Thus, it becomes clear that Durkheim's understanding of religion also encompasses the secular sacred, which plays such an important role in social movements and political history.

(2) In *The Elementary Forms*, Durkheim argues not only for the social origin of the basic religious distinction between the sacred and the profane but also for the social origin of the very categories of thought, that is, the fundamental principles which render the world intelligible. Already in "Primitive Classification," Durkheim and Mauss maintained that the specific way in which a society divides space and time is socially constituted. For example, according to this argument, the Sioux conception of space is a reflection of the physical layout of their settlements (which, again, traces back to the social structure of Sioux society) (Durkheim and Mauss [1903] 1963: 57–59). In *The Elementary Forms*, Durkheim goes a step further by arguing for the social origin of the category of space itself—and the same applies to other categories such as time, force, or causality. Importantly, Durkheim does not claim that nonhuman animals or imaginary isolated individuals could not orient themselves in space and time (Durkheim [1912] 1995: 443–444). Instead, he maintains that with the genesis of human society and religion the possibility arose to recognize and to make explicit abstract categories beyond the immediately perceptible reality.[13]

For example, with regard to the category of force, Durkheim points out that in many indigenous societies there exists an abstract principle of force—such as the *orenda* of the Iroquois or the Melanesian *mana*—that circulates between inanimate as well as animate objects and that is used to make sense of processes in the environment (193–200). The modern understanding of physical force, Durkheim claims, shares its essential characteristics—such as "impersonality" or "communicability"—with these indigenous notions (368). Both the indigenous and the modern concepts of force, Durkheim maintains, have their roots in the primordial understanding of religious and, hence, social forces: "When I run against an obstacle, I have a sensation of confinement and discomfort; however, the force causing that sensation is not in me but in the obstacle and thus beyond the range of my perception. [. . .] This is not the case with social forces.

Since they are part of our interior life, we not only know the results of their action but see them in action" (369).

The discussion of "Primitive Classification" and *The Elementary Forms* illustrates that Durkheim's two key contributions to the sociology of knowledge show important methodological similarities and some substantial overlap. However, it also becomes clear that there are marked differences in focus and argumentation.[14] Five differences are of special importance: (1) While in *The Elementary Forms* the question of the social origin of categories plays a major role, Durkheim and Mauss's article focuses on the social constitution and increasing autonomy of classificatory systems (Pickering 1993: 53; Schmaus 2004: 3); (2) while *The Elementary Forms* center on the importance of religion in society, it plays only a minor role in "Primitive Classification" (Pickering 1993: 58); (3) while emotions are a crucial explanatory factor in *The Elementary Forms*, in "Primitive Classification" "the emotional/religious/sacred element seems tangential to his [Durkheim's] main argument and is added as an appendix to demonstrate why he has not been more successful in making a thoroughly rational analysis of classification" (Pickering 1993: 58); (4) while in *The Elementary Forms* ritual dynamics do not only take center stage but are interpreted as a formative force of social life, in "Primitive Classification" ritual practices only serve as proof for the formative force of socially constituted classifications; (5) finally, while in *The Elementary Forms* the focus is on one indigenous society, which serves as a kind of magnifying glass that helps to reveal the elementary processes of all societies, "Primitive Classification" outlines a multistage narrative of social evolution.[15]

Divergent Appropriations: Two Traditions in the Durkheimian Sociology of Knowledge

Durkheim's studies in the sociology of knowledge develop innovative and exceedingly ambitious claims. These claims have given rise to numerous and sometimes fundamental objections. In part, these objections refer to the deficiencies of the ethnographic data that Durkheim used or to the way he made use of them.[16] The bulk of the criticisms, however, aim at the gaps and contradictions within Durkheim's arguments as well as at the disparities between "Primitive Classification" and *The Elementary Forms*.[17] Yet, despite—or perhaps because of—their controversial status, Durkheim's contributions have laid the foundations for an important and diverse tradition of social thought. Like the classical works, the appropriations of Durkheim's studies are often situated at the boundaries between sociology, ethnology, history, and philosophy.

In the following, I will focus on two strands of social thought that can be characterized as critical appropriations of Durkheim's sociology of knowledge. The first and in a way "structuralist" line of reception is quite obvious and may, arguably, be characterized as the classical continuation of the Durkheimian theory of classification. The second line of reception that will be outlined can be found in the works of Robert Bellah and Hans Joas. Compared with the first line of reception, Bellah and Joas focus more on Durkheim's sociology of religion. I argue, first, that either of these lines refines some of the basic concepts of Durkheim's sociology of knowledge and, second, that these two lines of reception—at least to a certain degree—mirror the differences between Durkheim's two major contributions to the sociology of knowledge.[18]

Classifications, Homologies, and Social Structure

The "structuralist" reception of the Durkheimian sociology of knowledge starts with the groundbreaking works of (1) Claude Lévi-Strauss, continues with (2) Pierre Bourdieu, and leads to contemporary authors such as (3) Luc Boltanski and Laurent Thévenot. As will become clear, these authors do not constitute a homogenous group. Instead, important differences can be identified between their respective approaches and severe debates were (and are) waged between different "camps" within this group. Still, by contrasting this theoretical strand to the second one, some important similarities in the general orientation will become perceivable.

(1) In his seminal book *Tristes Tropiques*, published in 1955, Claude Lévi-Strauss writes ([1955] 1976: 73), "at this moment, I am probably more faithful than anyone else to the Durkheimian tradition." From his perspective, this holds true with respect to his work in the anthropology of kinship which draws heavily on Marcel Mauss's classic study *The Gift* ([1925] 2002), which—in Lévi-Strauss's words ([1950] 1987: 41)—"inaugurates a new era for the social sciences."[19] Moreover, it does also hold true with respect to Lévi-Strauss's work on classification, which is deeply influenced by Durkheim and Mauss's "famous essay" (Lévi-Strauss [1962] 1973: 39).[20] The influence of the Durkheimian theory of classification can be identified already in Lévi-Strauss's earliest writings that were published between the mid-1930s and the early 1940s, that is, before the famous "revelation" of structuralism (Lévi-Strauss [1958] 1963: 33). For example, in his very first ethnographic publication, he analyzes the morphological structure of the Bororo village Kejara as a direct translation of their social organization—an interpretation which is clearly reminiscent of Durkheim and Mauss's interpretation of the settlements of the Zuñi or Sioux.[21] From the early 1940s on, Lévi-Strauss combined this Durkheimian impulse with the innovations of linguistic structuralism, thereby creating his structural anthropology, which in the 1950s and 1960s became a formative intellectual influence on the following generations of philosophers as well as social and cultural scientists.

Of course, there are important differences between Lévi-Strauss's structural anthropology and the Durkheimian approach. With respect to the topic at hand, two are of special importance. First, while Lévi-Strauss certainly agrees that there are enormous differences between the classificatory systems of different societies that can only be addressed by the social sciences, he argues that the basic structure of classifications and the fundamental categories of thought are not of social origin but universal features of the human mind. Hence, social morphology does not constitute the foundation of human thought; instead, the universal structures of human thought find their expression in various social structures (Kauppert 2008: 8, 42). Second, because of his universalistic anthropological stance, Lévi-Strauss ([1958] 1963: 230) claims "that man has always been thinking equally well." Lévi-Strauss criticizes evolutionist and ethnocentric interpretations of indigenous thought and therefore disagrees with Durkheim and Mauss who, for example, impute "mental confusion" to "the least evolved societies" (Durkheim and Mauss [1903] 1963: 6).[22]

Why, one may ask, does Lévi-Strauss underscore his faithfulness to the *durkheimiens*, if he rejects their evolutionism, ethnocentrism, and sociologism? In order to answer this question, two important facts need to be kept in mind. First, the Durkheim school allows him to reject two other influential anthropological perspectives: Lévy-Bruhl's claim of the "pre-logical" character of indigenous thinking and Malinowski's claim of the functional character of primitive classifications.[23] In contrast to Lévy-Bruhl, Durkheim and Mauss (81) claim that there is "no break in continuity" between "primitive" and modern thinking. Despite their "simplicity" and "confusion," the Durkheimians argue, indigenous classifications share all "essential characteristics" with "the first scientific classifications" (81). In contrast to Malinowski, Durkheim and Mauss highlight that classifications in indigenous cultures do not focus on the useful but strive to encompass the "totality of things," "all details," and "all the facts of life" (83, 67, 14).

Second, Durkheim and Mauss's sociology of classification is of such importance for Lévi-Strauss because it helps anthropology to understand (1) that the meaning of a cultural element is constituted by its position in a relational classificatory network, (2) that structural homologies exist between different classifications, and (3) that "primitive" thought operates by the use of "global classifications" (Lévi-Strauss [1962] 1973: 57). Hence, despite important differences, the *durkheimiens* and Lévi-Strauss share a belief in the classificatory elegance and the "totalitarian ambition of the savage mind" (Lévi-Strauss 1978: 17) that allow for the establishment of intricate connections even between the most specific attributes of plants and animals, weather phenomena and landscapes, personality traits and causes of death. Only by considering these features does it become possible to make sense of the practices and beliefs of indigenous societies.

(2) The influence of Lévi-Strauss can clearly be seen in the work of Pierre Bourdieu, which also incorporates philosophical, anthropological, and sociological perspectives. Early studies of Bourdieu such as the famous paper "The Kabyle House or the World Reversed" can even be characterized as typical structuralist analyses.[24] However, already in the 1960s, Bourdieu began to distance himself from Lévi-Strauss's structuralism because it conceptualizes the human individual only as a kind of passive medium of structures which itself does not contribute anything to the generation and reproduction of sociocultural patterns (Bourdieu [1980] 1990: ch. I.1). In contrast, Bourdieu seeks to understand classifications both as the basis and outcome of the individuals' activities. Indispensable in this context is Bourdieu's core concept of "habitus."

As is well known, according to Bourdieu, the habitus is characterized by a passive as well as an active side. On the one hand, the habitus is an "opus operatum" (Bourdieu [1979] 1984: 168), that is, the product of the specific living conditions of the individual. Due to its socialization in a specific social class, the individual adopts certain schemes of perception, thought, and action but also the corresponding dispositions and motivations (esp. Bourdieu [1980] 1990: ch. I.3). Hence, the habitus also has an active and generative side. As "modus operandi," it produces a unified set of "classifiable practices" (Bourdieu [1979] 1984: 169). Moreover, the habitus also structures how the practices of others are perceived and judged. The habitus, in short, produces both "classifiable" and "classifying" practices.

In his pivotal study *Distinction*, published in 1979, Bourdieu refers to the concept of habitus to explain why individuals produce a coherent pattern of everyday practices, that is, a specific "life-style" (Bourdieu [1979] 1984: ch. II.3). What and how a person eats, what cultural events and institutions she visits, or what clothes she wears and how she wears them is, according to Bourdieu, not the result of random or innate individual predispositions but results from a certain habitus that corresponds to a specific position in social space. This position, in turn, is a function of the volume and structure of capital that the individuals have at their disposal (ch. II.2). Although there are no functional or intrinsic connections between culinary preferences, leisure activities, and aesthetic preferences, due to the workings of the habitus, certain practices become "metaphors" (168) for each other and constitute a coherent unity.

By demonstrating the fruitfulness of the relational mode of thinking and the search for homologies between seemingly independent sociocultural practices, Bourdieu puts himself in the tradition of Durkheim, Mauss, and Lévi-Strauss (Bourdieu [1980] 1990: 4–5). Against this background, Loïc Wacquant argues that Bourdieu's theory of classification can be interpreted as a "reformulation and generalization" of Durkheim and Mauss's study, which refines the original approach in four respects (Bourdieu and Wacquant [1992] 2008: 12–13): first, Bourdieu does not limit the analysis of social homologies to indigenous societies but also applies it to modern societies; second, by developing his concept of habitus, Bourdieu provides a causal mechanism that explains the homologies between classifications (an explanation that was missing in Durkheim and Mauss's approach); third, Bourdieu reveals how systems of classification contribute to the maintenance of social order through their connections to power relations and the mechanisms of symbolic dominance; finally, Bourdieu describes that there is a constant struggle over classifications within politics and the different fields of cultural production.

(3) Another important contribution to the first line of reception can be found in the works of Luc Boltanski and Laurent Thévenot. In their major study *On Justification*, the authors ([1991] 2006: 34) argue that individuals involved in critical moments are subject to an "imperative of justification"—at least as long as a contentious situation is not resolved by violence or the need of justification does not arise because of affective bonds or the force of personal routines.[25] In order to arrive at a better understanding of how people justify themselves, Boltanski and Thévenot compare three quite different types

of materials: classical texts of political philosophy, contemporary guides for managerial practices, and descriptions of everyday conflicts. By means of this "very disrespectful operation" (Boltanski and Thévenot 1999: 369), they identify six regimes of justification that emerged in the course of social and cultural history and that are used in contemporary societies. These six regimes of justification, in turn, correspond to six "common worlds": the world of inspiration, the domestic world, the world of renown, the civic world, the market world, and the industrial world (Boltanski and Thévenot [1991] 2006: ch. 2 and 6; 1999: 369–373).[26]

Depending on the world a certain situation is assigned to, different classifications apply. According to Boltanski and Thévenot, each world features a different kind of worth, different kinds of subjects and objects, and different kinds of relations and examinations (Boltanski and Thévenot [1991] 2006: 140–144; 1999: 368). The different worlds and regimes of justification do not constitute separate social fields or (sub-) systems but coexist in the same social domains or institutions—as, for example, in the modern company. Hence, Boltanski and Thévenot do not present a theory of functional differentiation in the classical sense. Otherwise a crucial requirement of their theory would not be fulfilled, namely, the possibility to refer to different regimes within one and the same contentious situation. For example, if an artist who was only known to experts rises to fame and wealth, she becomes vulnerable to criticism. In the past, the critics may complain, she only lived for her art and did not care about the public's opinion, but now she is not an artist anymore because "in reality" everything is about the money and the fame. In this situation, elements of the market world and the world of renown are mobilized to call into question the artist's prestige in the world of inspiration. However, Boltanski and Thévenot do not only analyze conflicts and critiques (Boltanski and Thévenot [1991] 2006: ch. 7 and 8) but also compromises between the different worlds (ch. 9 and 10). For example, they interpret the emergence of "worker's rights" as a compromise between the civic world (in which rights and duties play a crucial role) and the industrial world (which focuses on work, expertise, and effectiveness).

Boltanski and Thévenot's "pragmatic theory" can be understood as an important, albeit often implicit, criticism of Bourdieu who, until the mid-1980s, was a decisive influence on both authors. Three differences are critical for an understanding of Boltanski and Thévenot's perspective as well as of the debates that followed. (1) While Bourdieu emphasizes the unconscious and quasi-automatic functioning of the habitus, Boltanski and Thévenot highlight the "critical capacity" of the actors and their reflexive use of the sociocultural regimes of critique. (2) While Bourdieu claims that sociology has a privileged epistemic perspective that can reveal what is "really" going on in everyday social interactions, Boltanski and Thévenot revoke this privilege. Within their theoretical framework, Bourdieu's theory constitutes a relativist position that is unable to do justice to the criticisms formulated in everyday life (Boltanski and Thévenot [1991] 2006: ch. 11). (3) While Bourdieu focuses on the homologies between social structure and classifications, Boltanski and Thévenot refer to the relative cultural autonomy of classifications.

Ritual, the Sacred, and the Emergence of Nonordinary Realities in Human Evolution

Another important, yet quite different way to build on Durkheim's sociology of knowledge can be found in the works of the American sociologist of religion Robert Bellah and the German sociologist and social philosopher Hans Joas. In contrast to the first line of reception, these two authors focus on the importance of ritual, the sacred, and the emergence of nonordinary realities in the course of human evolution and social history. In the following, I will describe (1) how Bellah integrates Durkheim's account of Aboriginal Australian societies into his broader scheme of religious evolution. Against this background, it can be shown how Bellah and Joas revise the Durkheimian narrative—(2) both with reference to the evolutionary prehistory of religion and (3) with reference to the historical transformation of religion. Finally, (4) arguments used by Bellah and Joas to refine Durkheim's conceptualization of religious experience and articulation will be presented.

(1) In Durkheim's account of religious evolution there is a peculiar combination of continuity and discontinuity. On the one hand, Durkheim posits a deep gulf between the "primitive" societies of the Aboriginal Australians with their "elementary" forms of religious life and the "higher" and increasingly secular societies of Western modernity. On the other hand, Durkheim claims that the insights of his analyses of Australian religious practices can be transferred directly to phenomena in contemporary France (Joas 2017: 128, 284–285, 432–433). Bellah and Joas address this problem by means of substantive empirical insights into evolutionary theory, anthropology, history, and comparative religious studies accumulated in the last decades. By drawing on this research, they distance themselves from Durkheim's ethnocentrism and evolutionism and aim at a revision of his evolutionary narrative that gives an empirically tenable account of religious development and considers both the internal complexity of all societies and religions and the contingency of historical changes (Bellah [1964] 2006: 23–28; 2011: 156).

From Bellah's perspective, Durkheim's study of the Aboriginal Australians provides an analysis of what he calls "tribal societies" and "tribal religion,"[27] which is—despite all its deficiencies—still important and acceptable in important respects.[28] Tribal societies, in Bellah's view, are made up of small face-to-face groups. These groups are rather egalitarian with flexible and low hierarchies based on age, gender, and specific abilities. Religious practices consist in various rituals in which all or most members of the group are involved and which aim at the (re-)establishment of cosmic harmony, the revitalization of solidarity, and the initiation of the young. Religious beliefs are not differentiated from other areas of knowledge but interwoven with a comprehensive network of mythic narratives.

(2) Whereas this account of tribal societies shows marked similarities to Durkheim's description of indigenous cultures, Bellah's evolutionary scheme differs from Durkheim's narrative in two essential respects. First, in contrast to Durkheim, Bellah

does not present tribal societies as "the elementary form" of social development. Instead, by drawing on diverse findings in evolutionary theory, primatology, and paleoanthropology, Bellah outlines the complex evolutionary and historical processes that paved the way to tribal forms of human cooperation, religious practices, and cultural cognition. For example, he presents an evolutionary account of the gradual emergence of nonteleological forms of action that eventually would lead to the first forms of ritual (Bellah 2011: 66–97). In the course of anthropogenesis, Bellah argues, the size of groups increased, the dominance structures changed, and empathic capacities became refined. With reference to Sarah Hrdy (2011), he claims that these changes led to an increase in cooperative practices such as collaborative childcare. Within such highly cooperative groups individuals more often entered what Bellah, following Gordon Burghardt (2006: 77–78), calls a "relaxed field," that is, a situation in which the essential needs such as food, childcare, or security are fulfilled. According to Burghardt and Bellah, such a "relaxed field" is a crucial precondition for the emergence of nonteleological actions such as play, that is, actions that are done for their own sakes. In the course of human evolution, increasingly complex cultural formats of cognition—episodic, mimetic, and mythic[29]—become integrated in these nonteleological interactions, thus giving rise not only to more complex forms of play but also to the first forms of ritual.

(3) While the first chapters of Bellah's major study *Religion in Human Evolution* describe some of the biological and cultural developments that resulted in the emergence of tribal societies, the bulk of the book analyzes the formation of larger societies that began rather late in human history. In other words, relative to Durkheim's understanding of Australian religion, these chapters describe later changes in social history.[30] The second phase in Bellah's evolutionary scheme is characterized by the rise of the archaic state (Bellah [1964] 2006: 33–36; 2011: ch. 4 and 5). In stark contrast to tribal societies, archaic societies are territorially extensive, organized in a strictly hierarchical way, and ruled by divine or quasi-divine kings. During rituals only the king, priests, and selected others play an active role. New forms of ritual such as worship and (human) sacrifice emerge that function as a communication system between gods and men. Ritual and myth are still predominant in archaic religion, and the profane reality and the sacred world continue to be merged in "a single cosmos" (Bellah 2005: 70).

It is exactly this concept of "a single cosmos" that changed dramatically in the Axial Age in the first millennium BCE—the third phase in Bellah's evolutionary scheme.[31] Within a relatively short period of time, the Axial Age witnessed the deep intellectual and religious innovations articulated by such figures as Confucius, Buddha, Zoroaster, the Hebrew prophets, and the Greek philosophers. These innovations, Bellah argues, also paved the way for our present worldview (Bellah 2005: 73). Just as other major developments in intellectual and religious history, the revolutionary consequences of the Axial Age cannot be understood without considering the underlying macrohistorical changes.[32] Bellah (e.g., 2005: 72–75) refers to different social, economic, and cultural innovations in the first millennium BCE such as a further increase in population, metallurgical improvements (especially iron), the widespread use of coinage, and intensified trade. Also, the widening circle of literacy allowed an increasing number of people access to the growing external cultural memory. However, as Bellah (74–75) emphasizes, these changes occurred in a period characterized by "incessant warfare between small states" and "the rise of large territorial states militarily more efficient than their Bronze Age predecessors, especially in the Middle East. These impinged on and acted to destabilize the incipient axial societies." Thus, in certain social strata in the Axial Age, cultural and technical progress and economic prosperity rendered possible something like a "relaxed intellectual field" that allowed for a systematic consideration of the deep conflicts, tensions, changes, and fears of the age.

According to Bellah, the Axial Age saw the emergence of a genuinely "theoretic culture" (the fourth stage in Merlin Donald's account of cultural and cognitive development). This does not mean that conscious and rational reflection did not occur in the stages before the Axial Age. Rather, what characterizes theoretic culture is reflection on reflection that is performed for its own sake (80).[33] Such a systematic form of reflection, Bellah maintains, made possible a radical form of "symbolic transcendence," that is, the possibility to understand ordinary reality in terms of another realm beyond the world of daily life. Joas, in turn, focuses on the fundamental changes in the notion of the sacred, namely, the emergence of an elaborate concept of religious transcendence. Thus, in the Axial Age, the "single cosmos" typical of tribal and archaic worldviews was broken up and the tensions between the profane reality and the sacred became intensified. The profane and the sacred layers of reality that are merged in Durkheim's account of religion were torn apart, thereby giving rise to fundamentally new forms of social and political criticism and religious self-reflection.[34]

(4) In their writings, both Bellah and Joas draw on alternative theoretical traditions in order to deal with the "hermeneutic" or "semiotic deficit" in Durkheim's sociology of knowledge (Joas 2017: 435). In *Religion in Human Evolution*, Bellah combines Durkheim's definition of religion with Alfred Schütz's concept of "multiple realities" and Clifford Geertz's notions of "cultural spheres" and "symbolic systems" (esp. Bellah 2011: xiv–xviii, ch. 1). Within the framework of Bellah's argument, this connection of Durkheim's notion of religion with other prominent and more general concepts in the sociology of knowledge fulfills three functions. First, Bellah tries to lend plausibility to Durkheim's idea of religion as something set apart from ordinary life by showing that there is nothing odd about living in and referring to other realities—even in modern societies. According to Bellah, Schütz and Geertz show that different nonordinary realities such as science and religion share crucial characteristics. In all of them "the brackets that the commonsense world of daily life puts on the idea that anything could be other than it appears have come off. In these other worlds, taken-for-granted assumptions no longer rule" (Bellah 2011: xv). Second, by referring to Schütz's and Geertz's concepts, Bellah strives for a better understanding of the relations between these different realities. He emphasizes that "other realities that human culture gives rise to cannot fail but overlap with the world of daily life" and the ordinary world will "never [be] quite the same again" after another world has been entered (xv, xvii). Third, Schütz's and Geertz's concepts make it possible for Bellah to outline a continuous evolutionary

sequence that starts with the earliest forms of play and continues with mimetic, mythic, and theoretic forms of nonordinary reality. From Bellah's standpoint (96), play is a "fundamental form of life," a clearly delineated nonordinary realm of action—just as religion or science.[35]

Joas criticizes Durkheim because he does not complement his account of ritual practice and collective effervescence with a plausible theory of the interpretation and articulation of these experiences. In Durkheim's account, Joas argues, it seems as if the ecstatic experiences speak for themselves (Joas [1997] 2000: 67–68; 2017: 435–436). To be sure, Durkheim has a rudimentary theory of signs. In *The Elementary Forms*, he describes how the ritually induced emotions become attached to certain objects, actions, and words. This ad-hoc process of symbolization, however, is not situated within the general social context. Therefore, Durkheim is unable to grasp the interpretative situatedness of religious experiences in an appropriate way. As a consequence, Durkheim can neither analyze struggles over the interpretation of religious experiences nor can he take into account that every such interpretation takes place in a field of power in which certain groups and institutions try to monopolize the right of religious interpretation (Joas [1997] 2000: 67–68; 2017: 439–446). Finally, Durkheim is also unable to consider the historical situatedness of religious articulation. Only by means of such a contextualization is it possible to understand why certain forms of religion only became conceivable in and after the Axial Age or why religious articulation became more individual in modernity. In order to solve these problems, Joas argues, Durkheim's theory of experience needs to be supplemented with a theory of signs and articulation as can be found in the works of Josiah Royce and Charles Taylor (Joas [1997] 2000: ch. 8; 2017: 84–109, 435–438).

A Taxonomy of Tensions: Understanding the Provocative and Productive Force of the Durkheimian Sociology of Knowledge

Apart from its radical claims and profound originality, the productive force of Durkheim's approach seems to result from its inherent tensions which reverberate in its various appropriations up to this day. Against the background of the preceding sections, it is possible to construct a kind of "taxonomy of tensions" that helps to understand why Durkheim's sociology of knowledge—even after more than one hundred years—continues to exert a stimulating force on social theory. Four "taxonomic levels" can be distinguished.

(1) As could be seen in the first section of the chapter, various tensions can be identified within Durkheim's writings. The comparison between "Primitive Classification" and *The*

Elementary Forms unearthed significant differences between the two key contributions to the Durkheimian sociology of knowledge. Put schematically, the two studies differ with regard to the basic explanatory level (social morphology vs. religion), the main explanandum (classifications vs. the profane/sacred distinction and categories), the role of emotions and rituals (expressions vs. causes of classifications/categories), and the general narrative structure (multistage evolution vs. focus on one methodologically privileged case).

(2) Important tensions could also be identified between Durkheim's studies and the two lines of reception as well as within these two lines. As could be seen in the second section, each of the appropriations disagrees with Durkheim in important respects. All of the approaches presented reject Durkheim's evolutionist and ethnocentric presuppositions. Lévi-Strauss, in addition, criticizes Durkheim's sociologism, while Bourdieu adopts Durkheim's focus on social morphology but calls for a stronger focus on the links between classifications, social conflicts, and symbolic dominance in modern societies. Boltanski and Thévenot, in turn, emphasize the relative cultural autonomy of classifications and criticize Bourdieu for his fixation on questions of power and dominance and the neglect of the reflexive and critical capacity of individuals.[36] Within the other line of reception, we can observe a more convergent development. Originally, Bellah and Joas drew on Durkheimian concepts in different contexts and with reference to different questions. Bellah's "Durkheimian path" led him from questions of comparative religious studies and questions of religious history to questions of the sociology of knowledge, while Joas's "Durkheimian path" began with the problem of the creativity of action and the genesis of values and later led more and more to large-scale historical questions. Overall, due to the differences and debates within the two lines of reception, empirical problems, systematic tensions, and analytical potentials hidden within the Durkheimian sociology of knowledge were made explicit and became crucial aspects of sociological thinking.

(3) Important differences can be identified not only within but also between the two main lines of reception. To a certain degree, these differences mirror the tensions between Durkheim's key contributions to the sociology of knowledge. While the first line of reception focuses on the nature and variability of classifications, on the homologies between different classifications, and on the interconnections between classifications and social structures, the second line of reception highlights the importance of rituals, collective emotions, the sacred, and nonordinary realities for the history of human knowledge and thought. Hence, although the two lines of reception agree in their rejection of Durkheim's evolutionism and ethnocentrism, they draw different conclusions from this. While the "structuralist" line of reception prefers a synchronic comparison of different systems of classification, the second line aims at a cautious, empirically tenable, and nonethnocentric reformulation of Durkheim's historical narrative which connects the development of ritual practices and collective experiences with the history of social and political structures. Against this background, it is instructive that Bellah (2011: 33, 134, 568) and Joas ([1997] 2000: 198; 2017: 125) concur with Lévi-Strauss's description of mythic thought and his criticism of Durkheim's understanding of totemism,

but criticize Lévi-Strauss's rejection of Durkheim's theory of rituals and emotions (Joas [1992] 1993: 64).[37] From Bellah's and Joas's perspective, Lévi-Strauss's studies provide valuable insights into the classificatory complexity and general logic of "tribal" societies. However, from their standpoint, he shuns the problem of religious evolution and he fails to recognize the constitutive role of rituals and emotions as well as the importance of the sacred for the structuring of experience and knowledge.

(4) Finally, there is a fourth level of tension that has not been discussed so far. For more than twenty years advocates of evolutionary psychology have singled out Durkheim as the prototypical representative of what they term the "standard social science model" (SSSM) (Tooby and Cosmides 1995). The SSSM, John Tooby and Leda Cosmides maintain, rests on the claim that "'human nature' (the evolved structure of the human mind) cannot be the cause of the mental organization of adult humans, their social systems, their culture, historical change, and so on" (25–26). Tooby and Cosmides (23) interpret this model as the result of an "isolationism" of the social sciences. Instead of subscribing to the "modern denial of human nature"[38] that goes along with this "isolationism," evolutionary psychologists argue, we have to accept that the human mind is made up of highly specialized modules that developed in the course of evolution and that are hard-wired in the brain.

Warren Schmaus (2003: 26) is certainly right when characterizing the SSSM as a "straw man position." Nevertheless, it would be a mistake to ignore this challenge since it touches on the very basis of the (Durkheimian) sociology of knowledge. What is more, even though the criticism of evolutionary psychology is misguided in several respects, the dialogue with recent findings in the biological sciences is nevertheless important in order to arrive at a better understanding of the sociality of mind. Although I cannot go into details here, the discussion in this article points to two aspects that are of substantial importance for this debate. First, it became clear that Durkheim does not advance a tabula rasa view of the human mind. He does not claim that a basic and preconscious understanding of space and time is constituted by society. Rather, society constitutes categories in the sense that they become "conscious relationships" that have a specific cultural form (Durkheim [1912] 1995: 444; see also 9–10).[39] Second, Bellah's arguments regarding the evolution of play and ritual suggest that it would be worthwhile to systematically look into the prehistory of the sociality of the human mind. Against the background of recent findings in cognitive ethology and primatology, it seems plausible to "stretch" the logic of Durkheim's sociology of knowledge. The sociality of mind, it seems, does not start with humans. Rather, already in nonhuman animals we find practices that involve an elaborate use of different kinds of classifications that seem, at least in part, to be due to processes of social learning.[40] However, this does not change the fact that only in humans we find a highly complex, flexible, and cumulative transmission of classificatory systems, the explicit reflection of categories, and the fundamental distinction between the sacred and the profane. Hence, by integrating the findings from the biological sciences and the (Durkheimian) sociology of knowledge, it might be possible to arrive at a better understanding of the gradual evolution of the sociality of mind.

Notes

1. Because the basic claim and argumentative structure of the article seems to be Durkheim's merit (Šuber 2012: 98), I speak of "Durkheim and Mauss's article" and of "Durkheim's (or the Durkheimian) sociology of knowledge."
2. Already in Durkheim's earlier writings one can find arguments that are relevant for the sociology of knowledge (e.g., Durkheim [1898] 2010). For a detailed analysis of Durkheim's early contributions to the sociology of knowledge, see Šuber (2012: ch. 3). Durkheim's late lectures on pragmatism (1983), which were only published posthumously, do also contain arguments that are of interest from a sociology of knowledge perspective.
3. For the sake of clarity, I will refer to the different indigenous cultures by the same names used by Durkheim (and Mauss). However, it needs to be noted that many of these names are exonyms, that is, external names usually coined by neighboring cultures or/and European colonizers, which are often imprecise and pejorative.
4. The close link between ethnology and sociology is a characteristic feature of the Durkheimian tradition (and French social thought in general). Already in his first major work, *The Division of Labor in Society*, published in 1893, Durkheim uses "lower societies" as a foil in order to understand how "higher societies" are organized. His famous distinction between "mechanical" and "organic solidarity" and the comparative analysis of repressive and penal law, on the one hand, and cooperative and restitutive law, on the other hand, not only draws on biblical and Roman material but also on early ethnographic reports about Iroquois and Australian societies (esp. Durkheim [1893] 2014: ch. I.2, I.5, I.6).
5. As is well known, Durkheim himself attributed his increased focus on religious phenomena to the reading of the Scottish theologian and religious scholar Robertson Smith in the mid-1890s. Smith's studies on ancient Jewish and pre-Islamic Arabic religious culture were among the first works that not only took a genuinely sociological perspective on religious phenomena but also claimed that rituals are of crucial importance for the emergence of religion and that totemism is the most elementary form of religion. Other influences such as Durkheim's former teacher Fustel de Coulanges and, probably, the Indologist Sylvain Lévi (who was also a teacher of Mauss) also contributed to this turn toward religion (Lukes 1973: 237–244; Joas 2017: 136–153).
6. As Rodney Needham (1979: 66–67) notes, Durkheim and Mauss confine themselves to *taxonomic* classifications. Other forms of classifications and their possible origins are not discussed.
7. Already in his earlier studies, Durkheim used the concept of "social morphology" to raise the question whether and (if yes) how the size, density, spatial distribution, and intensity of interaction of a certain population influence the characteristics of social life (see Andrews 1993). Such morphological arguments play a crucial role in all of Durkheim's major works.
8. According to Merton (1987: 1–2), "strategic research materials" are "strategic research sites, objects, or events that exhibit the phenomena to be explained or interpreted to such advantage and in such accessible form that they enable the fruitful investigation of previously stubborn problems and the discovery of new problems for further inquiry."
9. As Steven Lukes (1973: 407, 459) mentions, Durkheim originally intended to entitle the book *Les Formes élémentaires de la pensée et de la pratique religieuse*. This (perhaps rather bulky) title would have highlighted the double focus on the "elemental forms of thought" and on "religious practice."

10. Already in 1906, Marcel Mauss described this rhythmic alternation between social concentration and dispersion in his famous study on the *Seasonal Variations of the Eskimo* ([1906] 2004). The crucial importance of the dynamics and consequences of "social rhythms" is also emphasized in later anthropological research on religion and ritual—as can be seen, for example, in Victor Turner's ([1969] 2017) seminal book *The Ritual Process* (on the link between Durkheim and Turner, see Olaveson 2001). Anthropological studies such as Turner's, in turn, became a crucial influence on sociological interpretations of Durkheim that emphasized the central role of ritual in society—as, for example, Robert Bellah's (which will be discussed in the next section of this chapter).

11. As is well known, Durkheim does not define religion as the belief in god(s), spirits, or saints but as a "unified system of beliefs and practices relative to sacred things, that is to say, things set apart and forbidden—beliefs and practices which unite into one single moral community called a Church, all those who adhere to them" (Durkheim [1912] 1995: 44, italics deleted). With respect to the concept of the sacred, it is again important to note that key aspects of Durkheim's perspective on religious phenomena can already be found in earlier studies of other *durkheimiens* such as Marcel Mauss (Tarot 2009: 12–13; Moebius 2012: 638–651).

12. Already before *The Elementary Forms* the ambiguity of the sacred was an important topic in the studies of the Durkheimians—as can be seen in the work of Robert Hertz (esp. [1909] 1973). Later, it became an essential impulse for the members of the *Collège de Sociologie* (for details on this, see Stephan Moebius's chapter in this volume).

13. In this context, the question arises to what extent Durkheim's *Elementary Forms* aim at a "sociologization" of Kant's epistemological analysis of categories (Pickering 1993: 56–57, 66). With regard to this question, divergent answers can be found in the literature. Some authors maintain that "Durkheim's sociology of knowledge stems directly from problems set by Kant" (64). Others hold that the influence of (Neo-)Kantianism on Durkheim should not be exaggerated and that other philosophical perspectives such as Bergson's were of greater importance for the development of Durkheim's thought (Joas [1992] 1993: 194). Still others argue that there is "no reason to assume, however, that Durkheim had Kant's concept of a category in mind" (Schmaus 1998: 177) and that his project can only be properly understood if the development of contemporary French philosophy and its influence on Durkheim's thought is considered (Schmaus 1998, 2004). This is not only a historical or philological but also a systematically important question. What is at stake here is what Durkheim actually means when using the term "category."

14. As some authors criticize, in many publications on Durkheim's sociology of knowledge, these differences are largely ignored (Pickering 1993; Šuber 2012: 102–103).

15. For example, the Zuñi—which play such an important role for the multistage evolution described in "Primitive Classification"—are only referred to in passing in *The Elementary Forms* (Durkheim [1912] 1995: 11, 145, 148).

16. For different (and in part divergent) assessments of the ethnological reception of Durkheim's work, see, e.g., Pickering (1984: 86–90, 109–114), Hahn (2012), and Delitz (2013: 156–160). On Durkheim's treatment of ethnographic material, see Morphy (1998).

17. For criticisms that aim at the cogency of Durkheim's arguments, see esp. Needham (1963: xii–xxix; 1979: 27, 56–57), Lukes (1973: 445–449), Joas ([1992] 1993: 63–67), and Pickering (1993: 61–66).

18. Of course, I do not claim that this chapter presents a comprehensive account of the appropriations of Durkheim's sociology of knowledge. Instead, I focus on two major

appropriations that differ in theoretically important and instructive respects. A more comprehensive presentation would have to include various other contributions such as the ones by Mary Douglas, Jeffrey Alexander, or Harold Garfinkel (to name just a few). Different accounts of the reception of Durkheim's sociology of knowledge can be found in Schmaus (2004: 2–12), Šuber (2012: ch. 5), and Ogien (2016).

19. For details on Mauss's influence on Lévi-Strauss's anthropology of kinship, see Hénaff (1998: 36–39) and Moebius and Nungesser (2013a: 236–245; 2014: 4–8).
20. Also in other works such as *Structural Anthropology* Lévi-Strauss refers approvingly to Durkheim and Mauss's essay (e.g., Lévi-Strauss [1958] 1963: 290–291).
21. In the original article, Lévi-Strauss (1936: 271) writes: "La structure morphologique du village traduit immédiatement l'organisation sociale." Morphological arguments also play an important role in *Structural Anthropology* (e.g., Lévi-Strauss [1958] 1963: ch. 7 and 8). An in-depth analysis of the impact of Durkheim's sociology of knowledge on Lévi-Strauss's thought can be found in Moebius and Nungesser (2013b).
22. In this context, it is quite fitting that Durkheim and Mauss ([1903] 1963: 6) refer to the Bororo as a typical example of the "indifferentiation" of "primitive" thinking, while Lévi-Strauss makes use of Durkheim and Mauss's approach to demonstrate the complexity of Bororo classifications and practices (Lévi-Strauss 1936; see also Lévi-Strauss [1958] 1963: esp. ch. 6 and 8).
23. For this double demarcation of structural anthropology, see Moebius and Nungesser (2013b: 187–190).
24. Bourdieu's study on the Kabyle House was already written in the mid-1960s. Later, it found its way into the Festschrift that was published on the occasion of Lévi-Strauss's sixtieth birthday in 1969. An English translation of this article can be found in *The Logic of Practice* (Bourdieu [1980] 1990: 271–283).
25. For more details on these alternatives to the regime of justification, see esp. Boltanski ([1990] 2012) and Thévenot (2001).
26. A concise summary of their theory of justification can be found in Boltanski and Thévenot (1999). In *The New Spirit of Capitalism*, Luc Boltanski and Eve Chiapello ([1999] 2007) identify "the project" as a seventh regime of justification that emerged in the wake of certain criticisms of capitalism in the decades after 1968.
27. For Bellah's view on "tribal societies," see esp. Bellah ([1964] 2006: 28–33; 2011: ch. 3 and 4). In his 1964 paper "Religious Evolution," Bellah used the term "primitive religion." Due to the "pejorative implication" (Bellah 2005: 69) of the word "primitive," he later preferred the term "tribal"—although it also has "treacherous" (Bellah 2011: xix) implications.
28. For Joas, *The Elementary Forms* is a study of "epochal importance" (2017: 113); Bellah even praises the book as "the greatest work of sociology ever written"—this quote can be found on the book jacket of the new English translation of *The Elementary Forms* (Durkheim [1912] 1995). Nevertheless, the authors emphasize the shortcomings of *The Elementary Forms*. Especially Joas points out empirical, methodological, and theoretical problems of Durkheim's study (Joas 2017: 123–136, 432–433).
29. Bellah makes use of Merlin Donald's distinction of four stages in the evolution of cultural cognition. In *Origins of the Modern Mind*, Donald (1993) distinguishes an episodic, mimetic, mythic, and, finally, a theoretic phase in cultural development. While the first two stages precede (and become integrated into) mythic culture, theoretic culture develops after (and based on) the mythic stage.

30. Of course, one needs to keep in mind that Durkheim's assumption that the Australian societies at the end of the nineteenth century resemble the tribal societies that once gave rise to more complex forms of social organization is problematic—even more so considering that Durkheim himself, especially in "Primitive Classification," refers to substantial social changes in Australian societies (Durkheim and Mauss [1903] 1963: ch. 2).
31. For Bellah's perspective on the Axial Age, see esp. Bellah (2005; 2011: ch. 5–9). Already in his 1964 article on "Religious Evolution," Bellah ([1964] 2006: 25–26) referred to the revolutionary changes in the first millennium BCE without using the term "Axial Age." For a review of the debate that followed the publication of Bellah's magnum opus, see Stausberg (2014). For Joas's view on the Axial Age, see esp. Joas (2012; 2017: ch. 5 and 7). In 2012, Joas and Bellah coedited an important volume on this topic (Bellah and Joas 2012).
32. For a concise overview of Axial Age research in history and historical sociology, see Wittrock (2015).
33. It is important to note that, according to Bellah, "nothing is ever lost" (Bellah 2005: 72; 2011: 13, 267). That is to say, earlier stages of social evolution "are not lost, but only reorganized under new conditions" (Bellah 2011: xviii). This credo applies to cognitive developments, religious practices, and social structures alike. For example, mimetic or mythic elements continue to play a role after the emergence of theoretic culture (Bellah 2005: 81) and rituals remain an integral part of more rationalized forms of religious practices (Bellah [1964] 2006: 32; [2005] 2006: 151).
34. Although many scholars agree that seminal changes occurred in the Axial Age, there is far less agreement on which innovation exactly provoked the profound social, intellectual, and religious changes. Bellah's claim of the emergence of a theoretic culture and Joas's claim of an increasingly elaborate and reflexive concept of the sacred are two of a whole group of positions on the Axial Age. Also, it is important to see that Bellah's and Joas's interpretations of the Axial Age are not mutually exclusive but may complement each other. For details on the development of and the different positions in the Axial Age debate, see Joas (2012; 2017: ch. 5).
35. Since his main focus is on the emergence and historical development of religion as a "nonordinary reality," Bellah does not provide a detailed discussion of the similarities and differences of the theories of Durkheim, Schütz, and Geertz. Instead, his argument seems to assume the general compatibility of their theoretical perspectives. This assumption needs to be reviewed critically, however. For example, in his theory of "multiple realities," Schütz (1945: 553–554) emphasizes that the different "provinces of meaning" (such as the world of religion, play, dreams, or science) are "finite," that their "cognitive style" is "not compatible with the meaning of everyday life," that "there is no possibility of referring one of these provinces to the other by introducing a formula of transformation," and that the "world of working in daily life is the archetype of our experience of reality. All the other provinces of meaning may be considered as its modifications." In contrast, both Durkheim's and Bellah's arguments require that the nonordinary world of religion can modify the world of daily life and that nonordinary experiences can be "translated" into ordinary practices. This suggests that a more detailed discussion of the compatibility of these different traditions in the sociology of knowledge—especially of their conceptualizations of the relation between ordinary and nonordinary life—is needed.
36. Additional contributions and tensions within the "structuralist" line of reception could be added. For example, in his seminal anthropological studies, Philippe Descola (esp. [2005] 2014) argues that the distinction between nature and culture is not known in

many indigenous societies. With this claim, Descola questions a fundamental premise of his former teacher Lévi-Strauss. Moreover, this position poses a radical challenge to Durkheim's and Mauss's arguments since the sociocentrism thesis presupposes the distinction between society and culture, on the one hand, and nature, on the other (Joas [1992] 1993: 66).

37. For a more detailed account of the discussion on Lévi-Strauss's criticism of Durkheim's sociology of religion, see Jing Xie's chapter in this volume.
38. This is the subtitle of Steven Pinker's influential 2002 book *The Blank Slate* which also attacks the social sciences for their (alleged) tabula rasa view of human nature and mind. Just as Tooby and Cosmides, Pinker (2002: 23–24) criticizes Durkheim and with him the whole "*sociological* tradition" of which he has an extremely broad and undifferentiated understanding: "the tradition of Plato, Hegel, Marx, Durkheim, Weber, Kroeber, the sociologist Talcott Parsons, the anthropologist Claude Lévi-Strauss, and postmodernism in the humanities and social sciences" (284–285).
39. See Schmaus (2003) for an important discussion of this question.
40. On the question of social learning and culture in primates, see, e.g., Boesch (2012). For an impressive example of the combination of temporal and spatial cognition and botanical classification in chimpanzees, see Janmaat et al. (2014).

References

Andrews, Howard F. 1993. "Durkheim and Social Morphology." In *Emile Durkheim: Sociologist and Moralist*, edited by Stephen P. Turner, 111–135. London: Routledge.
Bellah, Robert N. 1959. "Durkheim and History." *American Sociological Review* 24 (4): 447–461.
Bellah, Robert N. 2005. "What Is Axial about the Axial Age?" *European Journal of Sociology* 46 (1): 69–89.
Bellah, Robert N. (1964) 2006. "Religious Evolution." In Robert N. Bellah and Steven M. Tipton, *The Robert Bellah Reader*, 23–50. Durham, NC: Duke University Press.
Bellah, Robert N. (2005) 2006. "Durkheim and Ritual." In Robert N. Bellah and Steven M. Tipton, *The Robert Bellah Reader*, 150–180. Durham, NC: Duke University Press.
Bellah, Robert N. 2011. *Religion in Human Evolution: From the Paleolithic to the Axial Age*. Cambridge, MA: Harvard University Press.
Bellah, Robert N., and Hans Joas, eds. 2012. *The Axial Age and Its Consequences*. Cambridge, MA: Harvard University Press.
Boesch, Christophe. 2012. *Wild Cultures: A Comparison between Chimpanzee and Human Cultures*. Cambridge: Cambridge University Press.
Boltanski, Luc. (1990) 2012. *Love and Justice as Competences: Three Essays on the Sociology of Action*. Cambridge, MA: Polity.
Boltanski, Luc, and Eve Chiapello. (1999) 2007. *The New Spirit of Capitalism*. London: Verso.
Boltanski, Luc, and Laurent Thévenot. 1999. "The Sociology of Critical Capacity." *European Journal of Social Theory* 2 (3): 359–377.
Boltanski, Luc, and Laurent Thévenot. (1991) 2006. *On Justification: Economies of Worth*. Princeton, NJ: Princeton University Press.
Bourdieu, Pierre. (1979) 1984. *Distinction: A Social Critique of the Judgement of Taste*. London: Routledge.
Bourdieu, Pierre. (1980) 1990. *The Logic of Practice*. Stanford, CA: Stanford University Press.

Bourdieu, Pierre, and Loïc J. D. Wacquant. (1992) 2008. *An Invitation to Reflexive Sociology*. Chicago: University of Chicago Press.
Burghardt, Gordon M. 2006. *The Genesis of Animal Play: Testing the Limits*. Cambridge, MA: MIT Press.
Delitz, Heike. 2013. *Émile Durkheim zur Einführung*. Hamburg: Junius.
Descola, Philippe. (2005) 2014. *Beyond Nature and Culture*. Chicago: University of Chicago Press.
Donald, Merlin. 1993. *Origins of the Modern Mind: Three Stages in the Evolution of Culture and Cognition*. Cambridge, MA: Harvard University Press.
Durkheim, Émile. (1897) 1951. *Suicide: A Study in Sociology*. Translated by John A. Spaulding and George Simpson. New York: Free Press.
Durkheim, Émile. 1983. *Pragmatism and Sociology*. Edited by John B. Allcock. Cambridge: Cambridge University Press.
Durkheim, Émile. (1912) 1995. *The Elementary Forms of Religious Life*. Translated by Karen E. Fields. New York: Free Press.
Durkheim, Émile. (1898) 2010. "Individual and Collective Representations." In Émile Durkheim, *Sociology and Philosophy*, translated by D. F. Pocock, 1–34. London: Routledge.
Durkheim, Émile. (1893) 2014. *The Division of Labor in Society*. Edited by Steven Lukes and translated by W. D. Halls. New York: Free Press.
Durkheim, Émile, and Marcel Mauss. (1903) 1963. *Primitive Classification*. Translated and edited by Rodney Needham. London: Cohen & West.
Fields, Karen E. 1995. "Translator's Introduction. Religion as an Eminently Social Thing." In Émile Durkheim, *The Elementary Forms of Religious Life*, xvii–lxxiii. New York: Free Press.
Hahn, Hans Peter. 2012. "Durkheim und die Ethnologie. Schlaglichter auf ein schwieriges Verhältnis." *Paideuma. Mitteilungen zur Kulturkunde* 58: 261–282.
Hénaff, Marcel. 1998. *Claude Lévi-Strauss and the Making of Structural Anthropology*. Minneapolis: University of Minnesota Press.
Hertz, Robert. (1909) 1973. "The Pre-Eminence of the Right Hand: A Study in Religious Polarity." In *Right and Left: Essays on Dual Symbolic Classification*, edited by Rodney Needham, 3–31. Chicago: University of Chicago Press.
Hrdy, Sarah Blaffer. 2011. *Mothers and Others: The Evolutionary Origins of Mutual Understanding*. Cambridge, MA: Harvard University Press.
Janmaat, Karline R. L., Leo Polansky, Simone Dagui Ban, and Christophe Boesch. 2014. "Wild Chimpanzees Plan Their Breakfast Time, Type, and Location." *Proceedings of the National Academy of Sciences of the United States of America* 111 (46): 16343–16348.
Joas, Hans. (1992) 1993. *Pragmatism and Social Theory*. Chicago: University of Chicago Press.
Joas, Hans. (1997) 2000. *The Genesis of Values*. Chicago: University of Chicago Press.
Joas, Hans. 2012. "The Axial Age Debate as Religious Discourse." In *The Axial Age and Its Consequences*, edited by Robert N. Bellah and Hans Joas, 9–29. Cambridge, MA: Harvard University Press.
Joas, Hans. 2017. *Die Macht des Heiligen. Eine Alternative zur Geschichte von der Entzauberung*. Berlin: Suhrkamp.
Kauppert, Michael. 2008. *Claude Lévi-Strauss*. Konstanz: UVK.
Kohl, Karl-Heinz. 2012. *Ethnologie—die Wissenschaft vom kulturell Fremden. Eine Einführung*. 3rd ed. Munich: C.H. Beck.
Lévi-Strauss, Claude. 1936. "Contribution à l'étude de l'organisation sociale des Indiens Bororo." *Journal de la société des américanistes* 28 (2): 269–304.

Lévi-Strauss, Claude. (1958) 1963. *Structural Anthropology*. Vol. 1. New York: Basic Books.
Lévi-Strauss, Claude. (1962) 1973. *The Savage Mind*. Chicago: University of Chicago Press.
Lévi-Strauss, Claude. (1955) 1976. *Tristes Tropiques*. Translated by John and Doreen Weightman. Harmondsworth, UK: Penguin.
Lévi-Strauss, Claude. 1978. *Myth and Meaning: Five Talks for Radio*. Toronto: University of Toronto Press.
Lévi-Strauss, Claude. (1950) 1987. *Introduction to the Work of Marcel Mauss*. London: Routledge.
Lukes, Steven. 1973. *Emile Durkheim: His Life and Work*. London: Allen Lane.
Mauss, Marcel. (1925) 2002. *The Gift: The Form and Reason for Exchange in Archaic Societies*. Translated by W. D. Halls. London: Routledge.
Mauss, Marcel. (1906) 2004. *Seasonal Variations of the Eskimo: A Study in Social Morphology*. London: Routledge & Kegan Paul.
Merton, Robert K. 1987. "Three Fragments from a Sociologist's Notebooks: Establishing the Phenomenon, Specified Ignorance, and Strategic Research Materials." *Annual Review of Sociology* 13: 1–28.
Moebius, Stephan. 2012. "Die Religionssoziologie von Marcel Mauss." In Marcel Mauss, *Schriften zur Religionssoziologie*, edited by Stephan Moebius, Frithjof Nungesser, and Christian Papilloud, 617–682. Berlin: Suhrkamp.
Moebius, Stephan, and Frithjof Nungesser. 2013a. "'La filiation est directe': Der Einfluss von Marcel Mauss auf das Werk von Claude Lévi-Strauss." *European Journal of Sociology* 54 (2): 231–263.
Moebius, Stephan, and Frithjof Nungesser. 2013b. "Total Art: The Influence of the Durkheim School on Claude Lévi-Strauss's Reflections on Art and Classification." In *Durkheim, the Durkheimians, and the Arts*, edited by Alexander Riley, W. S. F. Pickering, and William Watts Miller, 178–201. Oxford: Berghahn Books.
Moebius, Stephan, and Frithjof Nungesser. 2014. "'La filiation est directe': L'influence de Marcel Mauss sur l'œuvre de Claude Lévi-Strauss." *Trivium. Revue franco-allemande de sciences humaines et sociales / Deutsch-französische Zeitschrift für Geistes- und Sozialwissenschaften* 17 (*Relire Mauss / Relektüren von Marcel Mauss*); http://trivium.revues.org/4836.
Morphy, Howard. 1998. "Spencer and Gillen in Durkheim: The Theoretical Construction of Ethnography." In *On Durkheim's Elementary Forms of Religious Life*, edited by N. J. Allen, W. S. F. Pickering, and William Watts Miller, 13–28. London: Routledge.
Needham, Rodney. 1963. "Introduction." In Émile Durkheim and Marcel Mauss, *Primitive Classification*, translated and edited by Rodney Needham, vii–xlviii. London: Cohen & West.
Needham, Rodney. 1979. *Symbolic Classification*. Santa Monica, CA: Goodyear.
Ogien, Albert. 2016. "Durkheim as a Sociologist of Knowledge: Rudiments of a Reflexive Theory of the Concept." *Journal of Classical Sociology* 16 (1): 7–20.
Olaveson, Tim. 2001. "Collective Effervescence and Communitas: Processual Models of Ritual and Society in Emile Durkheim and Victor Turner." *Dialectical Anthropology* 26 (2): 89–124.
Pickering, W. S. F. 1984. *Durkheim's Sociology of Religion: Themes and Theories*. London: Routledge & Kegan Paul.
Pickering, W. S. F. 1993. "The Origins of Conceptual Thinking in Durkheim: Social or Religious?" In *Emile Durkheim: Sociologist and Moralist*, edited by Stephen P. Turner, 52–70. London: Routledge.
Pinker, Steven. 2002. *The Blank Slate: The Modern Denial of Human Nature*. London: Penguin.

Schmaus, Warren. 1998. "Durkheim on the Causes and Functions of the Categories." In *On Durkheim's Elementary Forms of Religious Life*, edited by N. J. Allen, W. S. F. Pickering, and William Watts Miller, 176–188. London: Routledge.

Schmaus, Warren. 2003. "Is Durkheim the Enemy of Evolutionary Psychology?" *Philosophy of the Social Sciences* 33 (1): 25–52.

Schmaus, Warren. 2004. *Rethinking Durkheim and His Tradition*. Cambridge: Cambridge University Press.

Schütz, Alfred. 1945. "On Multiple Realities." *Philosophy and Phenomenological Research* 5 (4): 533–576.

Stausberg, Michael. 2014. "Bellah's *Religion in Human Evolution*: A Post-Review." *Numen* 61 (2–3): 281–299.

Šuber, Daniel. 2012. *Émile Durkheim*. Konstanz: UVK.

Tarot, Camille. 2009. "Emile Durkheim and After: The War over the Sacred in French Sociology in the 20th Century." *Distinktion. Scandinavian Journal of Social Theory* 10 (2): 11–30.

Thévenot, Laurent. 2001. "Pragmatic Regimes Governing the Engagement with the World." In *The Practice Turn in Contemporary Theory*, edited by Theodore R. Schatzki, Karin Knorr Cetina, and Eike von Savigny, 56–73. London: Routledge.

Tooby, John, and Leda Cosmides. 1995. "The Psychological Foundations of Culture." In *The Adapted Mind: Evolutionary Psychology and the Generation of Culture*, edited by Jerome H. Barkow, Leda Cosmides, and John Tooby, 19–136. Oxford: Oxford University Press.

Turner, Victor. (1969) 2017. *The Ritual Process: Structure and Anti-Structure*. London: Routledge.

Wittrock, Björn. 2015. "The Axial Age in World History." In *The Cambridge World History*, vol. 4: *A World with States, Empires, and Networks, 1200 BCE–900 CE*, edited by Craig Benjamin, 101–119. Cambridge: Cambridge University Press.

CHAPTER 5

IN DEFENSE OF COLLECTIVE CONSCIOUSNESS

Reassessing Durkheim's Argument

FRANCESCO CALLEGARO

WITHIN the vast repertoire of concepts that Émile Durkheim has forged to introduce a sociological point of view, none has attracted as much criticism or provoked more controversy as "collective consciousness." Early denounced, by his opponents, as a mere chimera (Tarde [1901] 1989), this fundamental concept ended up being questioned even by those who were supposed to revive his research program (Gurvitch 1950). After the postwar years, marked by an insurrection against Durkheim's sociology (Lévi-Strauss 1943; Merleau-Ponty [1960] 1964), "collective consciousness" was finally abandoned as a useless scientific myth. Today, most theoretical works, even when they invoke Durkheim's legacy, emphasize from the outset that it is an unacceptable notion, which should be substituted with a more objective alternative, like "institution," seen as a demystified translation of the original yet mysterious idea of "collective consciousness" (Descombes 2000; Bloor 2014).

Why is this idea so disputed? In fact, the indictment against "collective consciousness" consists of several charges. While philosophers criticize it as an absurd theoretical hypothesis, inducing us to see the collective as a subject on a large scale (Habermas [1981] 1987), sociologists denounce it as being an inadequate epistemological tool, incapable of making enough room for the free agency of individuals (Hinkle 1960). Concerned about its normative implications, philosophers and sociologists together finally impugn it as the basis of a dangerous political project, promoting an illiberal, conservative consensus of values, constructed to legitimize a constraining social order (Coser 1960; Adorno 1967). Collective consciousness seems then to condemn Durkheim's sociology as such, insofar as it rests on an abusive dichotomy of the individual and the collective, according to a vision formerly criticized in light of Marx's dialectics, as today with Tarde's imitation (Deleuze 1986; Latour 2002).

These objections reproduce an unshakable *doxa* about Durkheim's sociology (Stedman Jones 2001a). If there is one reason to doubt that they can go so easily together, it is the fact that the problem posed by the relation between the individual and the collective is not the same at each level. While the last two criticisms emphasize the empirical and normative problems of an idea of collective consciousness that would tend to obscure and even repress individual initiatives, the former highlights what is conceptually inadmissible in the theoretical premises of a sociology that transforms the collective *itself* into an individual. Different in scope, these accusations are also distinct in their significance. Indeed, one cannot reject such a fundamental concept for being both absurd in itself as inadequate and dangerous for us as moderns. If the idea of collective consciousness were to prove meaningless, it would be necessary to get rid of it before putting it to test in a sociological investigation, since nothing could correspond to it in reality; conversely, in order to be able to measure the limits of this concept, concerning its empirical application in history and its normative consequences for modernity, it is first necessary to understand its meaning.

We have to give priority, therefore, to the most radical of these standard objections: the one that questions the meaning and validity of the very idea of "collective consciousness" from a conceptual point of view. It is a necessary precondition of any further attempt to assess its potential relevance, both empirical and normative. Undoubtedly, trying to decipher the enigma of the collective consciousness would be a vain undertaking if it were not, contrary to what has been written (Nemedi 1995), the key concept of Durkheim's sociology, constantly mentioned throughout his work. A reference to "collective consciousness" is already present, indeed, in Durkheim's first important essay, devoted to the German sociologist Albert Schäffle (Durkheim [1885] 1994), while a final one can be found in the last pages of his *Elementary Forms of Religious Life* (Durkheim [1912] 1995). While the permanence of the term does not imply the continuity of a same conception, it suggests that a few reasons led Durkheim to constantly resort to this idea. In fact, Durkheim saw the idea of "collective consciousness" as resuming the "great problem of sociology" (Durkheim 1908, [1975] 2001).

To understand this thesis, it is first necessary to distinguish "collective consciousness" as such from that "common consciousness" which is generally associated with it, because of the terminology used in *La division du travail social*. By referring to a *collective or common* consciousness, Durkheim sought to account for the social foundations of criminal law and to identify the specific kind of solidarity that characterizes nonmodern societies, standing in the background of modern ones. Following this view, the few contemporary analytical discussions and empirical uses of this concept have been confined to the field of criminal sociology (Smith 2014), when they have not used it in cultural anthropology (Bohannan 1960). The existence of another level of analysis was, however, already evident in another passage of the *Division of Social Labor*: Durkheim distinguished there the collective or common consciousness from the "social consciousness" understood as the broader horizon of "the psychic life of society" (Durkheim [1893] 2013: 64, transl. mod.).

From *Suicide* on, Durkheim started referring to this constitutive mental horizon of social life as such by speaking also of "collective consciousness." The "collective" and the "social" thus ended up being identified, on a general theoretical level aiming to single out a distinctive characteristic of the domain of reality explored by sociology, regardless of the difference introduced in history by modernity. It is this *collective or social* consciousness that will be discussed here, since the conceptual objection is directed against it. Focusing on those theoretical-methodological texts in which it has been developed at the required level of abstraction, we will try to clarify Durkheim's key sociological category and assess his central thesis: that there is no collective or social life without a collective or social consciousness.

First, we will clarify the meaning of the "*collective*" itself. By analyzing the criteria of "constraint," we will bring to light Durkheim's reference to those obligations that give access to an irreducible collective being. This will enable us to characterize the real subject of collective consciousness, while answering to the objection that points out the risk of an ontological hypostasis. We will then elucidate the nature of "collective representations." Examining Durkheim's criticism of "consciousness" as supported by an ego or a self, we will reconstruct the lineaments of his social conception of mind, developed in order to embed the normative "representations" making up the collective into the dispositional "unconscious" of the acting subjects composing it. This will allow us to specify the content of collective consciousness, while answering to the objection that highlights the danger of a psychological hypostasis. In order to reach the conclusion, we will finally have to clarify the meaning of "reflexive consciousness." By going deeper into Durkheim's social conception of mind, we will make room for those practical situations that require a rise in the level of reflexivity, triggering a dynamic process that allows the members of a group to make their implicitly shared normative dispositions explicit. Our conclusion will be that the concept of collective consciousness allows grasping those crucial effervescent social phenomena that produce a *conscious collective being*, made of subjects able to knowingly say "we."

THE SOCIAL AND THE COLLECTIVE: THINKING THE GROUP

The starting point of Durkheim's reflection about the social is difficult to dispute. If sociology must have a method of its own, it cannot fix the rules of its inquiries without first *thinking the object* to which they must be applied. Thus, far from having yielded at the outset to objectivism (Lukes 1982), Durkheim has sought to help sociology to achieve a higher consciousness of its proper object, by articulating the meaning of the "social" from the ground of shared experience, as given in ordinary language and common practices. In this context, he proposed an operative definition allowing sociologists to fix the criteria for using their fundamental concept, in order to classify facts as social or nonsocial. From the perspective of sociology, this general "delimitation" problem resulted in a specific question, the one addressed in the first chapter of *The Rules*: how to mark the *threshold* that separates the social from the individual, seen as the generic human being that modern forms of knowledge, such as biology and psychology, already isolated in its intrinsic natural properties.

When Durkheim said of "generality" that it is a necessary yet insufficient condition for a sociological regulated use of the concept of the social, it is of the general character of anthropological facts that he was thinking first. Sticking to this level would imply to consider as "social" the fact that all individuals drink, sleep, and eat. It is in this sense that the social differs from the individual: it can only go beyond the *life cycle* in which every human being is caught, by the fact of having an organism caught in the loop of sensations and impulses. To go beyond this *simple* generality and cross the threshold of the social, Durkheim gave some ordinary examples. The intention was to confront us with phenomena that seem "social" in that they cannot be derived from the individual as such, taken in isolation and considered in its intrinsic constitution. If we consider the first example, we see quite clearly why a given individual, identified by his body, cannot fulfill his role as a "brother," "husband," or "citizen," if he does not understand what these concepts convey, with their internal relations to complementary positions, and what the normative status adopted implies, for himself and others (Durkheim [1895] 2001: 50; Winch [1958] 2014).

In all the cases described, individuals can participate in the practice in question only if it already exists outside their organisms and the reduced kind of consciousness they support, made up of sensations and impulses. They must then have access to the concepts and norms on which the positions adopted in these practices depend. Durkheim thus tried to extract from these ordinary examples the two main criteria that manifest the social origin and nature of the mentioned common practices. Fixing the conditions of use of the "social" as a classification of given facts, he focused his perspective on their "exterior" and "constrained" character (Gane 2010). With regard to exteriority, Durkheim referred explicitly to a "characteristic experience": *education* (Durkheim [1895] 2001: 53, transl. mod.). Any education in a given practice shows indeed the efforts that must be made to give access to the concepts and norms that define this practice, so that new entrants can participate in it. Yet education in a given practice also manifests the other sign of the social: *sanction*, insofar as it presents itself first as report of a fault (Lemieux 2009).

Whether the deviation is a senseless mistake, a prejudicial technical error, or a serious moral and juridical misdemeanor, the other's sanction reveals that the given practice is not only present in the outside world, but that it also has a distinctive *normative* character. In the flow of action, one can thus locate the social when a deviation is signaled as a fault. It is on the level of normativity as such that the social emerges. This is the basic criterion of use: a fact can be classified as "social" if the action in which it consists can be traced back to some given *rules*, knowing that they cannot be separated from the ideas which order their field of application. This is what Durkheim will retain from the first chapter of *The Rules* in a later text, where he will make of "impersonal norms" the "sociological phenomenon par excellence" (Durkheim [1900] 1975).

We must ask ourselves, however, to what extent this normative understanding of the social already implies the demanding idea of a "collective" contemplated by Durkheim, when he speaks of individuals as belonging to "partial groups" and to an integral "political society" (Durkheim [1895] 2001: 52). While the chosen example goes in this direction, since the individuals in question seem to be members of a partial or total group, a family (brother, husband) and a city or nation (citizens), the collective has not been yet introduced. It is enough to change the example to realize that the "constraint" of the rules does not imply, as such, going beyond the level of a *pair of actors*, interacting with one another in the context of a given *normative system*. A speaker and interlocutor, communicating on the basis of a "system of signs," as well as a buyer and seller, exchanging through a "system of currencies" (Durkheim [1895] 2001: 51, transl. mod.) are not *necessarily* part of a collective being, partial or total, even if these two systems are governed by impersonal norms. In order to grasp what justifies the conceptual transition from the social to the collective, it is necessary to make explicit what is implicitly contained in the key notion of "constraint."

Compelled by the reactions aroused by his initial reference to a "power of coercion" (Durkheim [1895] 2001: 52, transl. mod.; Tarde [1894] 1898), Durkheim endeavored to clarify the narrow meaning that he gave to his criteria. Excluding that the transmission of social practices is always done through "violence" or "coercion," he insisted on the fact that the "force" which supports social practices is not *necessarily* "material": in general, it is "moral authority" that invests the "products of social activity" (Durkheim [1900] 1975). Constraint is not the same as coercion, because the rule is not always based on physical force: its *authority* can be marked by both symbolic and material sanctions, positive as well as negative. Yet in saying that the authority of social rules is above all "moral," Durkheim not only distinguished between normative commitments and physical impositions, he also traced "constraint" back to *prescriptive* rules. It is in the very fact of "obligation" that we have to look for the "proof" that certain "ways of acting and thinking" are not the "work of the individual" but emanate from a "moral power above him"(Durkheim [1898] 2009: 10). The ways of acting and thinking to which Durkheim refers to here are those which make this properly social feature manifest in our practical experience, inasmuch as prescriptive rules emerge in them more clearly than in others: religion, morals, and law (Callegaro 2015).

Within the vast and varied field of normativity, including those constitutive and strategic rules that we now distinguish, after Ludwig Wittgenstein and John Rawls, from prescriptive rules (Wittgenstein 1953; Rawls 1955; Descombes 2009) Durkheim granted such a seemingly undue privilege to obligation, only because this reference to "morality" could help better understanding what "social" means. Indeed, obligatory rules make immediately visible, for an external observer such as a sociologist, the presence of a collective *within* shared social practices. This thesis was already present in *The Rules*. It is on the fact of obligation that Durkheim based the inferential move to the collective as the proper object of a distinctively sociological thinking: "A phenomenon can only be collective if it is common to all members of society or, at the very least, to most of them, and hence if it is general. Certainly, but if it is general, this is because it is collective (*that is to say, more or less obligatory*), far from being collective because it is general. It is a state of the group" (Durkheim [1895] 2001: 56, transl. mod., my emphasis).

We see here what "collective" means. This term refers to a defined group, more or less ample, whose members are linked together by their implicit acceptance of some obligations (Durkheim [1906] 2009, [1911] 2009). The "collective" thus conceived can be distinguished from other kinds of associations by the presence of a specific kind of internal relations, those that Durkheim tried to clarify by resorting to the principles of a *holistic logic* (Descombes 2014). Obligation makes it possible to say, indeed, of a relatively general phenomenon that "it is in each part because it is in the whole, far from being in the whole because it is in the parts" (Durkheim [1895] 2001: 56, transl. mod.). Through obligation, individuals think of themselves and others as parts of a whole. The reference to impersonal norms as they are currently being followed in practice therefore does not exhaust the meaning of the *social stance* implied in this change of position. Far from being only interacting actors within an impersonal system, individuals are now caught in the normative network making up the practices of the group to which they reciprocally see themselves as belonging. It is this kind of belonging that is expressed explicitly when one of them says "we" for all.

From this properly Durkheimian point of view, an external observer can say of a practice that it is social only if the group implicitly endorses the rules that organize the interactions between individuals. Therefore, it is always an open question whether the rules are really "ours," that is, whether the group can appropriate them or not. This explicit appropriation, which is at the center of Durkheim's sociology, marks the passage from practices to institutions. For such is the task of an institution: to make explicit, in the form of endorsed rules, the norms implicitly accepted in practices.

This is a demanding conception of the social: the concept refers to real and concrete groups, likely to last in time through the renewed use of shared endorsed rules, distributed between practices and institutions. It does not, however, rely on the dichotomy of the individual and the collective, which Durkheim's critics claim to see. Indeed, if the group is certainly distinct from the present members composing it, it is in the same way as the rules constituting it, as Durkheim noted already in a telling passage of *The Rules* (Durkheim [1895] 2001). Animating practices in the implicit form of norms or deposited in institutions in the explicit form of codes, rules cannot be reduced to the current applications that are made of them, since they can stand despite the fact that they are not actually used. Different from the present list of members composing it, the collective is not yet separated from the whole of individuals of which it is made, for it comes down to them to apply the rules constituting it, following these rules in practice and making them explicit when they cannot avoid doing so. The collective is thus the level of reality corresponding to the social stance the individuals adopt when, reciprocally thinking of each other as parts of a whole, they transmit, preserve, or transform the rules that make up the group of which they consider themselves members. This appears clearly when the rules in question express more or less definite obligations—religious, moral, and legal—in which the group itself is at stake.

Durkheim strongly opposed the accusation of *ontological* hypostasis raised against him by Tarde and others because of the thesis that a social practice can exist independently of its individual expressions. Rejecting the "obvious absurdity" according to which a global political society would be possible without the existence of individuals, he always claimed what he tried to put forward in *The Rules*. The collective must have a *different* substratum than the given individuals, for it can exist without *each* of them: the group cannot be reduced to the current list of its members, because it precedes and survives them, thanks to its rules. Yet this substratum is not different in nature from the associated individuals, since the collective could not exist without *all* of them: the group is nothing but the whole of its members, linked to each other in solidarity through the use of the obligatory rules that constitute it. This is Durkheim's sociological truism: "The group formed by associated individuals is a reality of a different kind than each individual taken apart" (Durkheim [1897] 2005: 284, transl. mod.). Different from each individual, the group is identical to the whole formed by all the normatively associated members. We can then read Durkheim's central thesis about the social as an answer to the philosophical question concerning the identity of a group (Descombes 2016). What allows a collective to be *one and the same* in time is the transmission and transformation of those obligations that constitute the group itself. In short, it is *its own morality*, to use Durkheim's synthetic albeit equivocal term.

It remains to be seen whether in order to think the collective, we must also resort to the controversial idea of collective *consciousness*. It is this further step that puts Durkheim's sociology in a difficult position. Indeed, it seems impossible to understand "collective consciousness" otherwise than as a duplicate on a large scale of the individual conscious minds of which it is composed: the collective designated by the actors in the form of a "we" would thus become the support of a consciousness belonging to *itself* and not to *them*. In fact, while trying to resist the accusation of a *psychological* hypostasis, Durkheim used a language that seemed to make this interpretation inevitable. In the fifth chapter of *The Rules*, he answered this already widespread objection by introducing a collective being which seemed to come down to the psychological macro-subject denounced by his critics: "By aggregating, interpenetrating and fusing together, individual souls give birth to a being, psychic if one wishes, but which constitutes a psychic individuality of a new kind" (Durkheim [1895] 2001: 129, transl. mod.). This specter will return in Durkheim's work, as in the pages of *Suicide* devoted to the same defense of the collective or social consciousness (Durkheim [1897] 2005: 275).

How can we understand these passages without attributing to Durkheim the idea that the collective is a higher-order subject of whom we should speak in the third person of the singular, saying, "he thinks and wants," as we do with another person? This *personalization* of the collective seems all the more inevitable as Durkheim indulged in this rhetoric more than once in his work: of the collective, he often said that it "thinks, feels, wishes" (Durkheim [1898] 2009: 11).

The prevailing strategy to save Durkheim's sociology on this crucial point consisted in seeing the fusion of the individuals, illustrated by the metaphor of a "chemical synthesis," as alluding to the dynamics supposedly discovered in *crowds* by social psychologists

(Borch 2012). Several scholars have thus tried to extricate ourselves from the intellectual discomfort in which the reference to a psychic being of a new kind puts us by using the resources of social psychology: collective consciousness would be the emerging effect of those encounters which originally constituted the collective itself, in analogy with what happens in crowds. Embarking on this path, one comes, however, to the paradoxical conclusion of saving the controversial idea of collective consciousness at the price of the more fundamental reference to the collective. According to the demanding conception implied by the normative criterion of obligation, the collective contemplated by Durkheim *is not* and *cannot be* the contingent result of interindividual encounters: the whole that must be already introduced in order to understand and explain the interaction of the parts, at least when the members reciprocally commit to the use of the constitutive norms of the group to which they see themselves as belonging.

Thus, Durkheim criticized social psychology for blurring the boundary between "unorganized crowds," where only present individuals act together, and a "regular society," in which "to the action of contemporaries that of the previous generations is added" (Durkheim [1895] 2001: 131, transl. mod.). We must look therefore for another strategy, keeping faith with the grounding distinctive character of the social. In this perspective, collective consciousness can only be understood as the *consciousness of a collective*: it must be linked to concrete lasting groups, like a clan or a tribe, a class or a professional association, a city or a nation, a sect or a church, even an international organization.

What is at stake here is the internal connection between the *social* and the *historical*, as they can be joined together through the reference to a given collective: a definite group including the present and the absent, stretching from the past to the future, because of its historical nature, which is assumed as such by the individuals belonging to it when they say "we" without referring *exclusively* to themselves. How did Durkheim manage to make room for the peculiar "mental" contents of a collective being thus considered, without transforming it in a subject writ large, living a life of its own? His most developed answer is contained in his essay on "Individual and Collective Representations."

The Collective and the Individual: Exploring the Unconscious

To bring out the main thesis in Durkheim's 1898 essay, we have to introduce a twofold modification in relation to current readings (Nemedi 1995). While scholars tend to focus mainly on the formal "ontological" analysis of the relations between the different strata of reality—inorganic, organic, conscious, social—based on the existence of the same type of "relative autonomy," we must rather take into account in particular the specific incursion into the realm of the mind (Karsenti 2011). Moreover, while the emphasis has been put on Durkheim's use of a specific empirical approach, especially the one advanced by Pierre Janet in his *L'automatisme psychologique* (Pickering 2014), we have instead to take into account that Durkheim came to take up the idea of a "psychological automatism" only after having questioned the implicit philosophy of mind that supported empirical psychology as such. From the empirically based defense of the relative autonomy of individual consciousness, seen as a preliminary step to the questionable introduction of a supra-individual collective consciousness, we have to move to the philosophical dismantling of the very idea of individual "consciousness," as the conceptual prelude enabling Durkheim to embed the "representations" of the collective in the minds of the individuals associated within it, and thus to avoid the psychological hypostasis of a macro-subject.

If we read Durkheim's article as a philosophical criticism of psychology's background presuppositions, we see the intellectual space he was trying to open: he aimed to show that the "limits of consciousness are not those of psychic activity," for "representative life extends beyond our actual consciousness" (Durkheim [1898] 2009: 8–9, transl. mod.). Thus, far from having carried out a defense of individual consciousness in order to justify an objectified conception of collective consciousness, Durkheim sought to introduce a *categorical change* likely to dethrone the "ego" or "self" ("moi") as such, seen by the modern psychologists of the French School as the control center of our thoughts and intentions, defining our own status as persons: "All that we wish to say is that certain phenomena occur in us which are of a psychic order and which are nevertheless not known by the self/ego that we are" (*le moi que nous sommes*) (Durkheim [1898] 2009: 9, transl. mod.). In putting forward the idea of "psychic states without consciousness," where "consciousness" means the "apprehension of a given state by a given subject," Durkheim encouraged a *conceptual* innovation concerning ourselves, as it is shown by the main obstacle that he had to overcome.

This obstacle was indeed conceptual. It concerned the logical identity between "representation" and "consciousness," implied by the mentalist language currently used in the modern psychological framework, as it focused, since John Locke and through his heirs, on the reduction of the person to a punctual ego (Taylor 1989; Descombes 2016). The *tautology of psychology* could only consider the notion of "unconscious representation" that Durkheim wanted to introduce as inherently "contradictory" (Durkheim [1898] 2009: 6, transl. mod.). By crossing the bounds of sense, Durkheim therefore launched a philosophical challenge to empirical psychology as a precondition for the very existence of sociology. Questioning the a priori logical identity, he tried to widen the scope of mental life, beyond the narrow perspective of the punctual ego, in order to reveal the existence of bedrock representations escaping consciousness without being part of the reflexes of the given organism. It is in the place left *empty* by the actual consciousness of the ego that Durkheim will locate collective representations.

The justification of this conceptual change was not a matter of experimental findings. It was based on the testimonies of our *experience of action*, put forward by Durkheim at the outset of his confrontation with empirical psychologists such as William James: "What directs us is not the few ideas that are currently occupying our attention; but all the residues left by our past life; the habits contracted, the prejudices, the tendencies which move us without our realizing it" (Durkheim [1898] 2009: 4, transl. mod.). The conceptual change required moving from the focus on the internal *states* of the ego, given through introspection or projected by experimentation, toward the agent's *dispositions*—habits, tendencies—directly observable in publicly accessible action. We are here in the context of a depsychologization of psychology analogous to the one further carried out by the philosophy of mind in the second half of the twentieth century, in the wake of Gilbert Ryle and Ludwig Wittgenstein (Ryle [1949] 2000; Wittgenstein 1953; Cavell 1969).

Thus, while scholars used the logic of "representation" to point out the paradoxes in which Durkheim supposedly locked himself up as a consequence of his thoughtless acceptance of the predominantly mentalist philosophical outlook of his time (Schmaus 2014), we must use the representationalist paradigm to identify the three cornerstones of the *empiricist philosophy of mind* that he tried to dismantle, in order to develop a coherent alternative outlook resulting from its reversal. Forged in the context of modern epistemological reflections on the knowledge of the external world, the paradigm of mental representation requires positing at once a *subject* that represents, a set of *cognitive* states that represent, as well as a world of *natural* objects represented. Now, the category change advocated by Durkheim led him to challenge these three bulwarks of the ego, to the point of transforming our spontaneous psychological self-understanding.

First, acquired dispositions do not need to be attributed to a conscious individual, synthetizing his manifold experience thanks to the active control of an ego seen as the unifying pole of current mental states. Once acquired, habits and tendencies can be activated, in a given circumstance, without the individual having to exercise effective control over his action, in the sense of an actual vigilance experienced by the internal states corresponding to it. In the context of action, the only criterion for the attribution of a mental life to an individual comes down to the visible presence of signs indicating a *virtual* control, proving that the agent is not an automaton. Thus, according to Durkheim, we say of some phenomena that they are "psychic without being apprehended," intentional without being presently conscious, when we see, in action, the "characteristic signs of mental activity": these are, for instance, the "hesitations," the "trials and errors" which express the search for the "adjustment of movements to a preconceived end" (Durkheim [1898] 2009: 7, transl. mod.) Durkheim anticipated here what the philosophy of action calls today, following Elisabeth Anscombe, the *intentional structure of action*: to be attributed, this structure does not need to be actualized in consciousness, nor to be projected into the brain, as if the individual were to contain at any price a trace of it, beyond its manifest presence in action (Anscombe 1957; Descombes 2011).

Durkheim thus sought to free the mental life of the individual from the government of the ego, by referring to habits and tendencies putting it out of play, as the meaning they are carrying is immanent in an action that does not require actual control. In this sense, the question was not to free the self or ego from the brain, but the mind as such from both, by introducing a certain "unconscious" reality constituted by acquired dispositions. The ego and the brain are, for that matter, closely associated by Durkheim, since actual consciousness, once isolated from the rest, only amounts to an epiphenomenon of the nervous states, being no more than a purely *organic-psychical* sensation

(Durkheim [1898] 2009: 4). Conversely, as soon as one goes beyond the already given sensations and impulses, a "whole of representations" appears which is precisely *not* conscious, in the sense of being attached to an ego: the mind is thus freed from the brain only because it is also detached from the self, as the dispositions which constitute it are not synthesized by any actual consciousness, being deposited instead in a memory that is "properly mental" insofar as it is made of "unconscious phenomena" (Durkheim [1898] 2009: 6).

It is only after clearing the space for this *properly mental because unconscious memory* that the crossing point of the individual and the collective could be highlighted. The field of unconscious memory represented indeed, for Durkheim, the place where a connection between the body and the social could be established: dispositions are the individual counterpart of the rules which constitute the group, the place where the capacities to understand and apply them are stored. In this way, it is also the link between the social and the historical that Durkheim tied at the individual level, insofar as unconscious memory is nothing but what assures the link between the present and the past. The attribution of an acquired disposition, far from enclosing us in the interiority of the actual mental states of an ego, opens us to the way in which the agent deals with the social-historical world where he is called to deploy his habits and tendencies. If one looks for the mind in dispositions, it must be said, with Durkheim, that the "*soul is in the world*" and that "*its life is involved with that of things*" (Durkheim [1898] 2009: 12, transl. mod., my emphasis). It is enough to develop this externalist pragmatic thesis about the mental to bring down the other two foundations of the ego-logic of representation.

The introduction of dispositions entails indeed ridding oneself of the mentalist conception of "representations," insofar as this conception refers to an internal cognitive state that a contemplative subject would recognize in itself as a copy of a given reality, on the model of sensations. This is not at all the *meaning* that Durkheim gave to this notion, despite his use of the *term*. On the contrary, he referred to "representation" in order to single out the contents of the dispositions of an agent actively involved with the world, transforming it to add to brute facts those irreducible social properties that it does not present, as he will explain in his essay on "Value Judgments and Judgments of Reality" (Durkheim [1911] 2009). This intellectual content, while detached from organic determinations, is no less invested in action: we are in the sphere of that thinking-for-acting that Durkheim will describe in *The Elementary Forms* (Durkheim [1912] 1995; Karsenti 2012). We must conclude that, by referring to "collective representations," Durkheim was less concerned with mentalizing the social than with *socializing the mind*, distributing it across the bodies interacting within a collectively shared world. While individual representations as such are reduced to given organic sensations and impulses, the collective ones refer to what social agents are required to use in order to make sense of their common world, thus recognizing each other as persons (Callegaro 2012).

The last pillar of the philosophy of consciousness could not remain intact then. Once the cognitive states of the ego have been replaced by the practical tendencies of the agent, the world facing the individual can no longer be reduced to the totality of natural objects that would confront a knowing subject. Instead, it must be configured as the set of *symbolic* objects that allow the agent to activate his dispositions, in the context of his interaction with others. In a passage of *Suicide*, Durkheim clarified his thesis about the pragmatic significance of objects, focusing in particular on the "definite formulas" of religion or law. While the formulas "would remain a dead letter if there was no one to represent them and put them into practice," they nevertheless have a "mode of action of their own": they are not "mere verbal combinations without effectiveness," but "active realities, since they produce effects that would not take place if they did not exist" (Durkheim [1897] 2005: 279, transl. mod.) Expressing the same "representations" embodied in individual dispositions, these objects produce social effects, acting as a *dispositive* that makes agents do what they could not otherwise do. Durkheim even came to give a relative priority to the outside on the inside, to a dispositive over a disposition, at least in the order of knowledge, since his objective was to grasp the social mind of which they favor the production: "We start from the outside because it is only immediately given, but it is to reach inside" (Durkheim [1897] 2005: 280n12, transl. mod.).

Undoubtedly, social-historical collectives, insofar as they are made of "representations," do not always materialize in symbolic objects. The reality in which these *immaterial* representations become manifest is not, however, inner in any sense: it is no less that of a visible action in the world, exercising certain effects in it. Thus, the diffuse "aspirations" to which Durkheim often referred in his work, pointing out that they can circulate freely without affecting the "cardinal precepts of law and morals," are not more intimate or inaccessible than the consolidated tendencies that they undermine. These aspirations aim at realizing in practice a "higher" ideal: involved in a transformative social dynamic, they are manifested externally by all the phenomena that characterize a "great collective movement." It is the presence of an observable intensification of interactions that constituted, for Durkheim, the sociological criterion for identifying those "creative periods" during which an encompassing collective makes its rules explicit, in order to reaffirm or create a new morality (Durkheim [1911] 2009; Joas [1992] 1996).

We have here a coherent social conception of the individual mind, based on a pragmatic reading of "collective representations." If we have not been able to grasp it, it is because we have projected into Durkheim's texts the mentalist paradigm that he criticized in order to develop his alternative account. We have thus read the distinction between the external "sign" and the internal "thing" with the lens of the traditional philosophy of consciousness, believing that it came down to locate the latent meaning of an explicit formula in the internal mental states of a mysterious collective subject, different and separate from the individuals composing it (Tarot 1999). Yet if Durkheim preserved a significant gap between the mind and the symbol, he did not consider their relationship according to the predominant paradigm of *mental* representation, where the external sign serves to present to others an inner and private idea.

It is strange to have imagined that a sociologist such as Durkheim could have endorsed such as perspective, knowing that he was trying to establish *empirical* investigations on firm grounds. To this end, he argued rather from the alternative paradigm based on the model of *expression* in action of a disposition, already developed by such philosophers as Hegel (Taylor 1979, 1985). In this context, the function of a sign is not to present to the outside world an already constituted internal state, but to bring to a more clearly articulated expression what would otherwise remain *indefinite*, in a relation of mind to symbol where the implicit "state" is better understood by becoming an explicit "action" or "claim" (Brandom 2000). In this framework, action is the first expressive means whose inner potentialities can be further explained by the use of ordinary-language speech acts, before the technical tools made available by some meta-languages, like the one used by law, make the content of collective representations even more explicit.

Thus, the fundamental concept of "collective consciousness" refers to the dynamic system of dispositions and dispositives, joined in an action having different degrees of reflexivity according to the level at which "collective representations" are expressed. Far from having substituted the concept of "collective consciousness" with that of "collective representations," Durkheim actually identified them, as shown by the conclusion of his 1898 essay: the collective is constituted by the same "representations" of which the consciousness in question is made of. Under the term "collective consciousness," taken as an equivalent of "social consciousness," Durkheim tried then to better understand the "system of representations" which other early sociologists had already placed at the heart of the social (Stedman Jones 2001b). In order to avoid the psychological hypostasis, Durkheim had to develop a social philosophy of mind likely to embed collective representations in the *unconscious dispositions* of individuals interacting within their groups. Collective consciousness, thus understood, has nothing so mysterious about it. We have not been able to see that Durkheim was speaking of the same social reality he had already brought to light in the first chapter of *The Rules*: the social-historical collective, the group constituted by those embodied rules that are transmitted in education and perpetuated or transformed in action.

There is, however, one last difficulty. One may wonder, indeed, why Durkheim insisted on speaking of a "collective consciousness" when his overall account showed that its fabric consists of *unconscious* shared normative dispositions. While some of his critical followers have encouraged a further conceptual change, moving toward the idea of an inaccessible collective unconscious (Lévi-Strauss [1950] 1987), the fact that Durkheim resisted the reduction of collective consciousness to a set of unconscious causes invites us to have a closer look at those reflexive dynamics which we have already pointed out as lying at the heart of his social conception of mind.

The Unconscious and the Conscious: Understanding Reflexivity

The dethronement of the "ego" does not preclude, it even requires a sociological reformulation of the nature and role of the "control center" of mental life. If there are many hints of an alternative account of consciousness in Durkheim's work, developing such a view was one of the major theoretical achievements gained from his confrontation with classical American pragmatism (Durkheim [1913–1914] 1983; Joas 1993; Rawls 1997; Karsenti 2012). Attracted by the epistemological questions that occupy the center stage, interpreters have left this dimension in the background. Yet, throughout the debate about knowledge and truth, it is the general question of *thought* that Durkheim wished to pose. Radicalizing the Kantian displacement (Brandom 2002), he thus came to explore the social conditions of possibility of "reflective consciousness," seen as the distinguishing feature of human persons, considered as subjects able to think and act through concepts. Durkheim's sociological perspective required explaining to what extent the social-historical collective was involved in the production of this characteristically human conceptual reflexivity.

Once the question of thought was raised, the encounter between sociology and pragmatism took the form of a dispute about what Durkheim recognized as a common problem, resulting from shared premises. This is what emerges in his critical analysis of John Dewey's perspective. Far from calling into question the "facts" used by the American pragmatist to draw his picture of mind and rationality, Durkheim considered them as "undeniable" (Durkheim [1913–1914] 1983: 79). This acceptance of the descriptive premises of the pragmatist conception of mind is not surprising, once we see that they concern the same *experience of action* that Durkheim took up, in his 1898 essay, in order to extend mental life beyond the exclusive actual consciousness of the punctual ego. Therefore the theoretical difference between sociology and pragmatism did not concern the facts themselves, but rather their interpretation: the confrontation turned around the reading of practical experience, as it involves a general lesson about the sources of our distinctive conceptual abilities in their relation with social-historical reality.

The first fact lies at the heart of practical experience: it concerns the presence within it of those *habits* that govern intentional movements without needing any actual consciousness. Durkheim did not question this first phenomenological fact. In his discussion with Dewey, he even radicalized his position, pushing further the one he found in *Human Nature and Conduct*. Consciousness has so little to do with action, according to Durkheim, that it can hinder it, even paralyze it: in the flow of action, it exercises no function, except that of an obstacle of which the agent has to get rid. Thus, far from retiring as an "actor who would have finished playing his role," usually consciousness does not even enter the stage, since the "conditions of its existence are not realized": "When there is an equilibrium between our dispositions and the milieu, vital movements occur automatically" (Durkheim [1913–1914] 1983: 80–81, transl. mod.). Durkheim concluded from this manifest fact that only the "experience of action" can teach us what we have to do in a given situation: "We must act in order to know how we should act" (Durkheim [1913–1914] 1983: 83, transl. mod.).

The agreement between Durkheim and Dewey concerns also the second main fact about the phenomenology of action. Reflective consciousness enters the scene only as a result of a practical necessity: the original equilibrium between the disposition and the milieu must somehow have been disturbed for an explicit thought to emerge. The primary source of reflexivity is thus the presence of an "uncertainty," a "malaise," an "uneasiness," as Dewey says in the quoted passages of the French translation of *How We Think*. In his own work, Durkheim had already emphasized this pragmatic circle, well before his direct confrontation with pragmatism: he saw practical reflection as an answer to the "necessities of life," having no other end than to restore the troubled "vital equilibrium" (Durkheim [1900] 1975). Durkheim came to say in his lectures that in order for reflective consciousness to arise "there must be some holes (*trous*), some shortcomings (*lacunes*) in action" (Durkheim [1913–1914] 1983: 83, transl. mod.). These gaps impose a shift to a higher degree of reflexivity.

Thus, Durkheim did not criticize Dewey for having given primacy to dispositions in the understanding of action, or for having anchored reflection in practical necessities. In this sense, he shared a first conclusion, namely that when the "automatism" of spontaneous action is disorganized by some trouble, practical reflection must arise in order to overcome it: "It is only too natural for thought to intervene to arouse the movements that are lacking" (Durkheim [1913–1914] 1983: 83, transl. mod.). It is rather Dewey's more general conclusion concerning human conceptual capacities that, for Durkheim, raised a serious philosophical and sociological problem. In fact, reasoning from the practical roots of thought, the pragmatist American philosopher tended to endorse a reduction of thought to practice which obscured, according to Durkheim, significant differences between irreducible expressive levels *internal* to the sphere of thought.

The question thus raised concerned what characterizes the "conscious being" that we are, *beyond* our pressing need for practical reflection in order to live. Here, Durkheim's objection to Dewey touched the heart of the classical pragmatist conception of mind insofar as it was based on an assimilationist overall vision of the conceptual, accentuating the continuities between discursive and nondiscursive creatures, opposed as such to the rationalist philosophical tradition which emphasized instead the discontinuity between us, concept-mongering beings, and them, merely living creatures (Brandom 2011).

Thus, the main problem of classical pragmatism, according to Durkheim, was that, because of its implicit empiricism, it could not draw a sufficiently clear boundary between the reflective consciousness that characterizes us as persons and the instinctive consciousness of a living organism. The criterion of the mental, as far as *we* are concerned, cannot be sought *only* in the external signs attesting practical intentionality, since this would also apply to merely living beings: "When equilibrium has been broken, the animal itself seeks, gropes, tries out other movements appropriate to the situation" (Durkheim [1913–1914] 1983: 55, transl. mod.). While agreeing with this description of "instinctive consciousness," Durkheim put in inverted commas the reflection aroused by the *physical obstacles* encountered by the living organism on the way of satisfying its given needs: if "the animal does not find what it needs […] it has to 'reflect' to wonder where it will find it" (Durkheim [1913–1914] 1983: 37). Action itself expressively displays intentionality, yet the conclusion that must be drawn is not that there is no other kind of mental activity, but only that "doubt and uncertainty" are not the "privileges of reflective thought" (Durkheim [1913–1914] 1983: 55, transl. mod.).

By criticizing the reduction of thought to useful practice, Durkheim aimed at clarifying the *kind of thought* produced by our reflective consciousness, without detaching it from the practice from which it results and into which it fits. If one wishes to trace the boundary between the person and the living organism without departing from a pragmatic horizon, it is necessary to consider the practical tests that force the passage to proper conceptual thinking. The disagreements between sociology and pragmatism thus concerned nothing but the interpretation of the *gaps* of action that thought is called to fill. The instrumental language that pragmatists adopted because of their acceptance of evolutionary biology reduced the "malaise" to a form of "maladjustment": thinking was thus conceived as being oriented toward the vital adaptation to the given milieu. It is this *naturalization of the mind* that Durkheim intended to contest, insofar as it did not make a proper place for the exception constituted by our conceptual capacities and therefore for the peculiar social nature of the troubles we encounter in action.

In Durkheim's perspective, the exception of our own mind was the main consequence of the very *exception of the social*, insofar as social-historical collectives cannot be reduced to a natural milieu: a group is a "moral" milieu constituted by changing normative dispositions, not by fixed natural structures. It followed that the relationship between the individual and the collective cannot be grasped in terms of adaptation without disregarding what is at stake in social relations, as they are based on implicit normative commitments. Only the disruption of the organic-psychic order by the social, in that it refers to *unnatural norms*, makes it possible to explain a phenomenon as paradoxical for the logic of the living, as that to which Durkheim drew attention: the *suspension of action*. Indeed, if it does not refer to the mere absence of movements imposed by physical obstacles, the fact of action coming to a standstill points to the presence of a *normative* impediment, required by the obligations that structure implicitly a given situation. This is already shown by the elementary phenomenon of sanction: action is stopped in its spontaneous unfolding, even though nothing in the organism or in the vital milieu seems to justify or explain this halt. Reflexivity is therefore an internal consequence of normativity, as rules presuppose and imply a capacity of stepping back from the given situation that the living organism does not display. The necessity of thinking is therefore practical only insofar as it is normative, obligatory, and not merely useful. We are obliged to think by our very social belonging.

Such is Durkheim's pragmatic yet antipragmatist thesis. If the "conscious being" we are observing can be considered to be a person, this is because it is first an agent who can constitute himself as such in and through action, by stepping back when normatively required, thus opening the void filled by conceptual thinking: the role of reflective consciousness is not so much to "direct behavior," but rather consists in "*constituting a being that would not exist without it*" (Durkheim [1913–1914] 1983: 82, transl. mod.). The difference between the mind and the organism is once again traced back then to the difference between the collective and the individual, when considered as such: acquired dispositions have the function of making possible the experience of action, in which the agent can and even has to do without reflection, only because, being normative dispositions, they also make it possible, under specific troubling circumstances, to grasp the same act in a reflective mode, through the suspension of action imposed by the collective obligations they embodied.

It is on the basis of this pragmatic conception of reflective consciousness that the last difficulty of the "collective consciousness" can be solved. Far from referring to the irrational processes that would transform a plurality of beings who already are human individuals into a crowd of inhuman automats, the concept of collective consciousness makes it possible to grasp those peculiar social situations that trigger the reflexive dynamics through which a whole of individuals, already bound together within defined groups, come to be aware of the collective foundations of their own minds. The move, contemplated by social psychology, from a given individual consciousness to a collective unconsciousness is thus reversed by Durkheim's sociological perspective: in effervescent social situations, what happens is the conscious reflexive taking by present associated individuals of their whole shared unconscious past.

As Durkheim pointed out, the sociological concept of collective consciousness would be pointless without this reflexive dimension: "If there is a collective consciousness, it must include and account for conscious facts as well as unconscious facts. For, finally, since it is a consciousness (assuming it exists), it must be conscious in some place" (Durkheim [1908] 2001: 220, transl. mod.). Thus, using the concept required asking "where" the collective consciousness is indeed conscious; that is, in which practical situations a given group takes a reflexive grasp on itself, as long as its members come to see themselves explicitly as parts of a whole. Thinking about what allows the group to show the same reflective consciousness that it makes possible in individuals is the same as thinking about what allows members to bring to light the contents of their own dispositions: the process by which the group becomes conscious of itself is the one that leads its members to become more self-conscious, making rules explicit that already stand in the background of their spontaneous interactions. In short, it is the process that allows them to knowingly say "we," thus constituting a new kind of being, analogous to their own condition as persons because resulting from the same social source.

In his sociological investigations, Durkheim tried to grasp the explicit manifestation of the collective—the very object of his sociology—in concrete historical experience. He used the idea of collective consciousness in order to understand and explain those phenomena that were marked by both a collective *and* conscious character, the situations in which a group becomes a *conscious collective* because of a reflexive process. In analyzing crime, ritual, and conflict in *The Division of Labor, The Elementary Forms of Religious Life*, and *Professional Ethics and Civil Morals*, Durkheim has shown how law, religion, and morals, thanks to their dispositives and meta-languages, can create a conscious collective, resulting from the effervescent dynamics triggered by the affects circulating in practices, as a consequence of a common reaction to a moral malaise, before being handled by some specific institutions, such as the Tribunal, the Church, or the State. Delving into these sociological analyses allowed him to discover what kind of specific obligations required a cessation of spontaneous interaction and a rise in reflexivity capable of engendering a *reflexive collective consciousness*, engaging the group in explicating its relation to past, present, and future, that is, to history.

What is at stake in these specific social situations is always a fundamental *political* process, ensuring the perpetuation or transformation of that common normative core—morality—that constitutes the collective as a large and lasting group. It is thanks to these situations that Durkheim was able to found his own sociology on firm grounds, as a new political science, since within them the object of social sciences is no longer constructed but effectively given: the group manifests itself by itself, by constituting a collective endowed with the reflexivity that it enables in the subjects who bring it to light as the reality to which they belong.

It is on this ground that we should test the empirical and normative relevance of the idea of collective consciousness of which we have sought here to elucidate the meaning and validity, on a purely theoretical level, in order to grasp the conceptual foundation of Durkheim's sociology.

References

Adorno, T. W. 1967. "Einleitung zu Emile Durkheim, *Soziologie und Philosophie*." In *Gesammelte Schriften*, vol. 8, 245–279. Frankfurt am Main: Suhrkamp.
Anscombe, E. 1957. *Intention*. Oxford: Blackwell.
Bloor, D. 2014. "Collective Representations as Social Institutions." In *Durkheim and Representations*, edited by W. S. F. Pickering, 157–166. London: Routledge.
Bohannan, P. 1960. "Conscience Collective and Culture." In *Emile Durkheim et al.: Essays on Sociology and Philosophy*, edited by K. H. Wolff, 77–96. New York: Harper Torchbooks.
Borch, C. 2012. *The Politics of Crowds: An Alternative History of Sociology*. Cambridge: Cambridge University Press.
Brandom, R. 2000. *Articulating Reasons*. Cambridge, MA: Harvard University Press.
Brandom, R. 2002. *Tales of the Mighty Dead: Historical Essays in the Metaphysics of Intentionality*. Cambridge, MA: Harvard University Press.
Brandom, R. 2011. *Perspectives on Pragmatism: Classical, Recent, and Contemporary*. Cambridge, MA: Harvard University Press.
Callegaro, F. 2012. "The Ideal of the Person: Recovering the Novelty of Durkheim's Sociology. Part I: The Idea of Society and Its Relation to the Individual." *Journal of Classical Sociology* 12, no. 3–4: 449–478.
Callegaro, F. 2015. *La science politique des modernes. Durkheim, la sociologie et le projet d'autonomie*. Paris: Economica.
Cavell, S. 1969. *Must We Mean What We Say?* Cambridge: Cambridge University Press.
Coser, L. 1960. "Durkheim's Conservatism and Its Implications for His Sociological Theory." In *Emile Durkheim et al.: Essays on Sociology and Philosophy*, edited by K. H. Wolff, 211–232. New York: Harper Torchbooks.
Deleuze, G. 1986. *Foucault—Le Pouvoir*. "Cours du 7/1/1986." Année universitaire 1985–1986. Transcription by Annabelle Dufourcq, with the aid of College of Liberal Arts, Purdue University.
Descombes, V. 2000. "Philosophie des représentations collectives." *History of the Human Sciences* 13, no. 1: 37–49.
Descombes, V. 2009. "L'impossible et l'interdit." In *Le raisonnement de l'ours, et autres essais de philosophie pratique*, 394–408. Paris: Seuil.

Descombes, V. 2011. *The Mind's Provisions: A Critique of Cognitivism*. Princeton, NJ: Princeton University Press.

Descombes, V. 2014. *The Institutions of Meaning: A Defense of Anthropological Holism*. Cambridge, MA: Harvard University Press.

Descombe, V. 2016. *Puzzling Identities*. Cambridge, MA: Harvard University Press.

Durkheim, E. (1885) 1994. "Review of Albert Schaeffle, *Bau und Leben des sozialen Körpers: Erster Band*." In *Emile Durkheim on Institutional Analysis*, edited by M. Traugott, 93–114. Chicago: University of Chicago Press. French version: "Organisation et vie du corps social selon Schaeffle." In *Textes*, vol. 1, 355–377. Paris: Minuit, 1975.

Durkheim, E. (1893) 2013. *The Division of Labour in Society*. Basingstoke, UK: Palgrave Macmillan.

Durkheim, E. (1895) 2001. *The Rules of Sociological Method and Selected Texts on Sociology and Its Method*. London: Macmillan.

Durkheim, E. (1897) 2005. *Suicide*. London: Routledge.

Durkheim, E. (1898) 2009. "Individual and Collective Representations." In *Sociology and Philosophy*, 1–34. London: Routledge.

Durkheim, E. (1900) 1975. "La sociologie et son domaine scientifique." In *Textes*, vol. 1, 13–36. Paris: Minuit.

Durkheim, E. (1906) 2009. "The Determination of Moral Facts." In *Sociology and Philosophy*, 35–62. London: Routledge.

Durkheim, E. (1908) 2001. "Debate on Explanation in History and Sociology." In *The Rules of Sociological Method and Selected Texts on Sociology and Its Method*, 211–228. Basingstoke, UK: Macmillan. French version: "Débat sur l'explication en histoire et en sociologie," *Textes*, vol. 1, 199–217. Paris: Minuit, 1975.

Durkheim, E. (1911) 2009. "Value Judgments and Judgments of Reality." In *Sociology and Philosophy*, 80–97. London: Routledge.

Durkheim, E. (1912) 1995. *The Elementary Forms of Religious Life*. New York: The Free Press.

Durkheim, E. (1913–1914) 1983. *Pragmatism and Sociology*. Cambridge: Cambridge University Press.

Gane, M. 2010. *On Durkheim's Rules of Sociological Method*. London: Routledge.

Gurvitch, G. 1950. "Le problème de la conscience collective dans la sociologie de Durkheim." In G. Gurvitch, *La vocation actuelle de la sociologie*, 351–408. Paris: PUF.

Habermas, J. (1981) 1987. *The Theory of Communicative Action*, vol. 2: *Lifeworld and System: A Critique of Functionalist Reason*. Boston: Beacon Press.

Hinkle, R. C. 1960. "Durkheim in American Sociology." In *Emile Durkheim et al.: Essays on Sociology and Philosophy*, edited by K. H. Wolff, 267–295. New York: Harper Torchbooks.

Joas, H. (1992) 1996. "The Problem of the Emergence of a New Morality as the Underlying Theme in Durkheim's Work." In H. Joas, *The Creativity of Action*, 49–64. Cambridge: Polity.

Joas, H. 1993. "Durkheim and Pragmatism: The Psychology of Consciousness and the Social Constitution of Categories." In H. Joas, *Pragmatism and Social Theory*, 55–78. Chicago: University of Chicago Press.

Karsenti, B. 2011. *L'homme total. Sociologie, anthropologie et philosophie chez Marcel Mauss*. Paris: PUF.

Karsenti, B. 2012. "Sociology Face to Face with Pragmatism: Action, Concept, and Person." *Journal of Classical Sociology* 12, no. 3–4: 398–427.

Latour, B. 2002. "Gabriel Tarde and the End of the Social." In *The Social in Question: New Bearings in History and the Social Sciences*, edited by Patrick Joyce, 117–132. London: Routledge.

Lemieux, C. 2009. *Le devoir et la grâce*. Paris: Economica.
Lévi-Strauss, C. 1943. "French Sociology." In G. Gurvitch and W. E. Moore, *Twentieth Century Sociology*, 513–545. New York: Philosophical Library.
Lévi-Strauss, C. (1950) 1987. *Introduction to the Work of Marcel Mauss*. London: Routledge.
Lukes, S. 1982. "Introduction." In *The Rules of Sociological Method and Selected Texts on Sociology and Its Method*, 1–30. London: Macmillan.
Merleau-Ponty, M. (1960) 1964. "From Mauss to Claude Lévi-Strauss." In *Signs*, 114–125. Evanston, IL: Northwestern University Press.
Nemedi, D. 1995. "Collective Consciousness, Morphology, and Collective Representations: Durkheim's Sociology of Knowledge, 1894–1900." *Sociological Perspectives* 38, no. 1: 41–56.
Pickering, W. S. F., ed. 2014. *Durkheim and Representations*. London: Routledge.
Rawls, A. W. 1997. "Durkheim and Pragmatism: An Old Twist on a Contemporary Debate." *Sociological Theory* 15, no. 1: 5–29.
Rawls, J. 1955. "Two Concepts of Rules." *The Philosophical Review* 64, no. 1: 3–32.
Ryle, G. (1949) 2000. *The Concept of Mind*. Chicago: University of Chicago Press.
Schmaus, W. 2014. "Meaning and Representation in the Social Sciences." In *Durkheim and Representations*, edited by W. S. F. Pickering, 139–156. London: Routledge.
Smith, K. 2014. *Émile Durkheim and the Collective Consciousness of Society: A Study in Criminology*. London: Anthem Press.
Stedman Jones. S. 2001a. "General Introduction: Reflections on the Interpretation of Durkheim in the Sociological Tradition." In *Emile Durkheim: Critical Assessments of Leading Sociologists*, edited by W. S. F. Pickering, vol. 1, 1–18. London: Routledge.
Stedman Jones, S. 2001b. *Durkheim Reconsidered*. Cambridge: Polity Press.
Tarde, G. (1894) 1898. "Les deux éléments de la sociologie." In *Etudes de psychologie sociale*, 63–94. Paris: Giard et Brière.
Tarde, G. (1901) 1989. *L'opinion et la foule*. Paris: PUF.
Tarot, C. 1999. *De Durkheim à Mauss. L'invention du symbolique*. Paris: La Découverte.
Taylor, C. 1979. "Action as Expression." In *Intention and Intentionality*, edited by C. Diamond and J. Teichmann, 73–89. Ithaca, NY: Cornell University Press.
Taylor, C. 1985. "Hegel's Philosophy of Mind." In C. Taylor, *Human Agency and Language*, 77–96. Cambridge: Cambridge University Press.
Taylor, C. 1989. *Sources of the Self: The Making of Modern Identity*. Cambridge: Cambridge University Press.
Winch, P. (1958) 2014. *The Idea of a Social Science and Its Relation to Philosophy*. London: Routledge.
Wittgenstein, L. 1953. *Philosophical Investigations*. Oxford: Basil Blackwell.

CHAPTER 6

RELIGIOUS RITUALS AND LOGICAL THOUGHT IN DURKHEIM
The Level of Existence of Social Things

BRUNO KARSENTI

IN the first of *The Rules of Sociological Method*, which requires us to "treat social facts as things," Durkheim didn't simply suggest a method. He also laid the foundation for a certain realism and kept working on its coherence, even in *The Elementary Forms of the Religious Life*. A notably equivocal sentence in the second preface to *The Rules* shows this: "[W]e do not say that social facts are material things, but that they are things just as are material things, although in a different way" (Durkheim [1895] 1982: 35).

The turn of phrase is confusing. They are things *just as* are material things, although *in a different way*? Resolving the consistency of social things in a purely representative—that is, mental—reality certainly involves the risk of introducing an idealism incompatible with the empirical method meant to attach weight to social facts and, above all, restore their irreducible exteriority. Thus, it would be commonplace for the philosophers, anthropologists, and sociologists condemning Durkheimianism—and later on for dawning structuralism as well as phenomenology (see Lévi-Strauss 1947; Merleau-Ponty 1964)—to criticize this ambiguous "thing-ism" ("*chosisme*"). According to them, Durkheim was a prisoner of an insoluble antinomy, who strove to reconcile the irreconcilable, namely, things and representations. And this impossibility supposedly appears nowhere better than in his interpretation of totemism. The latter shows the inadequacies of a sociology still too imbued with positivism, albeit a moderate positivism, filled with a guilty conscience and doomed to go to the opposite extreme.

Let us take a closer look at the quote, though. It doesn't so much link things with representations as *social* things with things in general. In other words, the link stems from this very particular "thing-ism" sociology reconstitutes. Yet it is certain that Durkheim didn't really tackle this issue until his very late work: when, as a sociologist of religion, he looked into the status of ultimate social things, such as sacred things and objects of worship, that is, the realities determining certain *rituals*. This is what I would like to study here. To what extent is it possible—by examining as closely as possible the way in which Durkheim refers to Australian ethnography, by focusing on the objects of worship of so-called primitive religions—to shed light on the foundations of the sociological realism his entire work contributes to? We will see that this realism ultimately depends on an unprecedented link established between the strictly ritual phenomenon and the activity of thought.

Churinga

In *The Elementary Forms*, Durkheim draws essentially on Spencer and Gillen's ethnography of the Arunta of Australia (Spencer and Gillen 1899, 1904; see also Strehlow 1907–1921). In this corpus, he identifies the "sacred thing" type, on which his analysis will be based: the *churinga*, that is, pieces of wood or bits of polished stone varying in shape. Each group owns a collection of them and scrupulously regulates the handling of these objects.

So what is the relation between the group, these particular things, and the other beings in the world, namely the animals or plants the totemic logic—whose operator is the *churinga* according to Durkheim—refers to? Here the sociologist straightaway inflects the meaning of the work he draws on. Spencer and Gillen had insisted on the mythical narrative that defines the *churinga* as the place where the ancestor's soul resides, even as an image or a part of the ancestor's real body. By contrast, Durkheim views it merely as the after-the-fact justification of a feeling of respect based on something else. The myth clarifies nothing since it only relates a sacred being to another. It doesn't account for the fact that certain *churinga*, not less sacred than others, are artificially made to the knowledge and before the eyes of all. These objects are preserved in the same manner and endowed with the same ritual efficiency as the others. To understand the *churinga*'s sacredness, we must pay close attention to the thing it is, instead of getting misled by the false alternative of its naturalness or artificiality. We must focus on the mark drawn or engraved on it. And this isn't even enough. We must also refrain from projecting onto this mark a representation based on something else than its own order.

> Although the Australian may show himself sufficiently capable of imitating the forms of things in a rudimentary way, sacred representations generally seem to show no ambitions in this line: they consist essentially in geometrical designs drawn upon the *churinga* [...] or the human body. They are either straight or curved lines, painted in different ways, and the whole having only a conventional meaning. [...] These facts prove that if the Australian is so strongly inclined to represent his totem, it is in order not to have a portrait of it before his eyes which would constantly renew the sensation of it; it is merely because he feels the need of representing the idea

which he forms of it by means of material and external signs, no matter what these signs may be.

(Durkheim [1912] 1964: 126–127)

Totemism is rooted in the need to represent the idea of the totem by a sign. It is therefore a need for a so-called abstract representation. The latter is essentially the *representation of an idea*—as opposed to the representation of an exterior reality. The totemic sign imposes itself by virtue of a certain lack of thought: the idea isn't enough; it must necessarily be represented by a sign. Only then does the sign actually relate to things in the world and to established facts. Hence the confusing turn of phrase in *The Rules of Sociological Method* we mentioned earlier: lines, curves, drawings, and dots are things "just as" are other physical things, "although in a different way." The way in which these things exist and are distinguished is supposedly due to their link with other things in the world—this link coming second in relation to their institution as sacred things. This is evidenced by the fact that, in such circumstances, the sign doesn't follow a purely and simply imitative logic that would make it reproduce an object or a state of the world.

Let us summarize Durkheim's first step. What is at work in the experience of the sacred is the decentered mental experience the group has of itself in certain things imposing themselves on it. The members of the clan certainly get a sense of the totem. But they can't access this idea mentally—only *materially*, through things. Because they can't picture it directly, in their inner selves, they must manufacture the object, thanks to which they will become aware of the idea and of what they are in relation to it. We can speak of *collective consciousness* at this level, but not in the full, reflexive form of the group's self-presence. On the whole, it seems that the totem, in its materiality, is rather like a substitute for consciousness. It is not so much a thought-made thing, through a linear process of qualification of reality, as a "thought-thing": a certain thought deposited in a thing. Speaking about consciousness therefore seems inadequate for the kind of experience we aim to describe.

This is why, going against all other anthropological theories existing at the time, Durkheim says that the images of totemic beings are "more sacred than the beings themselves" ([1912] 1964: 133), and that, as such, they form a register of experience that should be considered autonomous. In Durkheim's intellectual context, this meant departing from any form of deduction of totemism based on zoolatry and, more generally, on any worship of natural beings. Above all, at a primordial level, this meant introducing a breaking point in human experience: the perception of sacred things doesn't amount to the perception the subjects are likely to have in the profane register, in their ordinary sensible experience.

But Durkheim tackles this breaking point again in another way, correlative to the gap we've just mentioned in relation to sensible perception and imitation. Considered in its generality, totemism involves a conception of the whole universe, a real "cosmological system" encompassing the entire knowable reality. How can we understand this extension as a totalization? Totemism is characterized by the fact that it constitutes an autonomous level of experience, distinct from that of profane experience. Separating itself from the things in the world, the totem opens onto *another world*. It doesn't just mark out an empirical sphere, by restriction or by outlining itself against a broader ordinary area. On the contrary, not only does it totalize the things it includes in its systematics, but it also endeavors to integrate "all known things" ([1912] 1964: 142) by requalifying them in its frameworks. The original connection between religion and knowledge has its deepest root there.

Through the higher sacredness of the *churinga* emblem, the universality of things can be embraced by the group. Precisely, it can be embraced in a horizon of *knowledge*: not as a series of disjointed perceptions, to which each being is subjected, but as a conceptual or categorical totalization. Based on his essay "On Some Primitive Forms of Classification" written with Mauss, Durkheim points out that, while the notions of gender and class do originate in the religious way of thinking that underlies totemism, social things are characterized by the fact that they appear in a framework of a knowledge of the world, disconnected from the immediate sensible experience of each individual isolated and considered separately. Thus, the distinctiveness of the experience of the sacred takes on a completely different meaning: it is not so much an affective determination, a test of sensibility, as a manifestation of *human thought* in its ability to surpass sensible perception as such. This surpassing, this passing from the generic image to the very concept, is therefore inseparably religious and cognitive. In other words, the *concept* is the ultimate logical framework whose access is reserved for Men, as social beings, which mainly means for them to live *religiously*, that is, to experience the sacred.

MANA

By linking up human groupings and real groupings, and by integrating them into a single system where their relations are regulated, totemism shows us that conceptual thought can only be social. Hence the question: What do sacred things substantially have in common? And what is the link between this substantial sharing and the fact of thinking conceptually? The answer lies in the role Durkheim assigns to the Melanesian *mana*, raised to the status of "totemic principle." Here the analysis is no longer based on Australian ethnography—not directly at least. Instead, the facts Durkheim mentions come from Melanesia as well as from northwestern America (the Sioux *Wakan* and the Iroquois *Orenda*). However, this isn't far from what the study of Australian *churinga* has shed light on—since, as Spencer and Gillen point out, the latter applies "both to an object and to the quality it possesses" (Durkheim [1912] 1964: 198). What matters is indeed the degree of abstraction conferred on a certain quality, independently of its particular material substratum:

> What we find at the origin and basis of religious thought are not determined and distinct objects and beings possessing a sacred character of themselves; they are

indefinite powers, anonymous forces, more or less numerous in different societies, and sometimes even reduced to a unity, and whose impersonality is strictly comparable to that of the physical forces whose manifestations the sciences of nature study. As for particular sacred things, they are only individualized forms of this essential principle. [...] Perhaps there is not a single religion in which the original *mana*, whether unique or multiform, has been resolved entirely into a clearly defined number of beings who are distinct and separate from each other: each of them always retains a touch of impersonality, as it were, which enables it to enter into new combinations, not as the result of a simple survival but because it is the nature of religious forces to be unable to individualize themselves completely.

(Durkheim [1912] 1964: 200–201)

So sacred things retain "a touch of impersonality": this is the lever of the Durkheimian interpretation of ethnography. Belief in the sacred, the matrix of all beliefs, focuses on anonymous forces rather than determined beings (which explains that, from this perspective, the idea of a personal god is necessarily secondary or derived). Things are sacred only if they exceed their dimension as particularized things, experienced one by one as discrete entities, separate from one another and withdrawn into their individuality. Their impersonality is actually what characterizes them. It is a power that invests them by linking them together, by letting them get out of their mode of empirical donation to make up certain relations, which thought must precisely establish and stabilize.

Mana sheds lights on the continuity between religious thought and logical thought—such is the peculiarity of Durkheim's reading of this topic, popular in early twentieth-century humanities and philosophy. The "touch of impersonality" surrounding sacred things and generally indicating their contagious nature isn't an indeterminate fluid. On the contrary, it must be viewed as a linking resource, not as a factor of indistinction. *Mana* is not a substance. It is a logical operator in the strongest sense of the term. Indeed, it precisely designates the breaking point no generic or conceptual thought can develop without: the break with the personality of beings, considered in their sensible particularity, as things perceived by an isolated individual. Analytically reduced to its active principle, totemism supposedly has the merit of showing this. In this particular conception of *mana*, it can thus be viewed as the forgotten first chapter of the sociology of religions as well as of the theory of knowledge.

Intichiuma

This is also what widens the gap between *The Elementary Forms* and the commonplaces of British anthropology. Robertson Smith's thesis of the contagiousness of the sacred had considerable influence at the time, even over works in the orbit of Durkheimian thought, especially over Lucien Lévy-Bruhl's work centered on participation and the prelogical mentality. The thesis rests on the idea that the separation of the sacred and the profane provides sacred things with their own expansion power passed on by contact—a power either destructive or saving, depending on how it is used. Hence a very obvious "ambivalence," not only due to the contradictory values assigned to these forces but also due to the way in which they emerge: by instituting itself, the separated tends to cross its own borders, thus abolishing itself as it institutes itself. Separation and confusion come from the same source. And the ritual system, at least on its negative side, can be viewed as the fact of keeping separate what should be, that is, reinforcing the separation partly against itself—against its expansive consequences at least. The explanation of contagion distinguishes Durkheim from Robertson Smith on this topic:

> But if religious forces have a place of their own nowhere, their mobility is easily explained. Since nothing attaches them to the things in which we localize them, it is natural that they should escape on the slightest contact, in spite of themselves, so to speak, and that they should spread afar. [...] So the contagion is not a sort of secondary process by which sacredness is propagated, after it has once been acquired; it is the very process by which it is acquired. It is by contagion that it establishes itself: we should not be surprised, therefore, if it transmits itself contagiously."
>
> (Durkheim [1912] 1964: 323–324)

The contagion doesn't stem from the intrinsic properties of a substance, only from the break with any substantial particularity, which starts off a positive movement of impersonality. This break is only actualized by the links it allows and by the specific level of experience these links structure. In this sense, the contagion is precisely the relation through which the sacred is made. It only designates its mode of production. Far from being an escape that makes the sacred elusive, it designates its *fixation process*, the way in which it is determined, the specific relations established between beings who, without it, would remain withdrawn, lost in the darkness of sensible experience.

However, this appears only when viewing the ritual system in a sufficiently comprehensive way, when the analysis isn't exclusively focused on the negative rites and when it relates them to their counterparts: the positive rites. The prohibited act of handling—or even coming close to—the sacred without caution can be equated with the enforcement of a separation that is constantly at the risk of collapsing, on the brink of being transgressed. It thus implicitly gives access to the contagion. But while the contagion is indeed the suspected process, while it serves first and foremost to "bind together things which sensation leaves apart from one another" (325), we mustn't stop there. We must examine the positive rites, where the contagion is much less passive than controlled and activated, that is, perceived as the opening of a certain regime of relation social subjects are actively engaged in.

Moreover, it should be emphasized that the element of "respect," on the negative side of the ritual, has actually already indicated this: paradoxically, the individual derives a principle of self-elevation from his duties toward sacred things. Now this principle asserts itself even more directly in the positive relations to the sacred things the individual must maintain, in a certain way and following certain rules. These rituals reveal the core of a purely social action. The general framework is provided by a positive ritual in particular: the *Intichiuma* of the Arunta, where Durkheim sees a decisive change in the conceptions relating to the sacrificial institution.

The *Intichiuma* is a ritual that takes place toward the end of the rainy season, when wildlife is blooming. Ethnography generally describes it as a "ritual of multiplication" (for a more recent analysis, see Testart 1985: 275–276). Again based on Spencer and Gillen's data, Durkheim distinguishes two very clear stages within the *Intichiuma*. First, the individuals trigger or help trigger the multiplication of the totemic species. Thus, they participate in the fecundating work of nature in the particular sector they view as kin. In the *Intichiuma*, the power of the *churinga* is for instance spread by rubbing it on a stone from the place where it is stored, so as to scatter dust all around it. In certain clans, individuals let streams of blood flow onto rocks since in that blood supposedly lies the same "principle of life" that "assure[s] the regular reproduction of the totemic species" (Durkheim [1912] 1964: 330–331).

It is worth noting that the belief underlying this first phase of the ritual isn't submitted to a factual refutation procedure. If the multiplication is visible before the celebration of the *Intichiuma*, the phenomenon is explained by assuming that the ancestors performed a subterranean action. And if the *Intichiuma* deceives the group's hopes, it was supposedly counteracted by evil spirits. The essential lies elsewhere: in the effective contribution the group thinks it brings to a natural process that imperatively requires it. Based on that, the ritual continues in two phases Durkheim carefully distinguishes from one another. First, there is a reinforcement of the ordinary system of interdictions whose objects are the sacred beings. The alimentary interdictions are stricter. It is even prohibited to touch the sacred beings, as if this might result in neutralizing the multiplication that has been triggered. Then, a final ceremony puts an end to this period of aggravated interdictions. According to Durkheim, during this ceremony, one is allowed to see the very *sacrifice*: members of the clan gather or hunt the species that has reproduced, and a ritual consumption is organized. Although the conditions of this consumption vary from clan to clan, they generally show a communion through commensality that is worth highlighting. The meal is collective, which is for Durkheim the culmination of the ritual. The latter confirms Robertson Smith's "intuition of genius," which can be considered to be the touchstone of the modern interpretation of the sacrificial institution.

Pars pro toto

We know that the *Lectures on the Religion of Semites* (Robertson Smith 1889) have had an extraordinary impact on turn-of-the-century thought—in particular on Freud's shift in his work on cultural phenomena. Durkheim didn't escape this general tendency. As regards anthropology, Robertson Smith's contribution consisted not so much in clarifying the general meaning of sacrifice as in shifting the approach to the problem. More precisely, he started from commensality and then examined propitiatory and expiatory sacrifices, doing the opposite of what had been done until then. But audacity has its price. By 1899, Hubert and Mauss's *Sacrifice: Its Nature and Function* had thus highlighted the weakness of Smith's deduction, and it seems that Durkheim largely agreed with his disciples' reservations.[1] Yet the tribute remains powerful in *The Elementary Forms*, and rightly so. The hypothesis of commensality as evidence of a common origin can indeed be viewed as indicative of an internal regeneration of the totemic principle, within each member assigned to take part in the meal. Some elements of totemism, in particular tattoos and scarifications, have already pointed to the fact that the totem could lie in everyone and be constituted by the individuals' bodies. However, ingestion clarifies something different: partial consumption can serve as a replenishment of the principle in its entirety. In short, the consecration of the food eaten during the shared meal presupposes that the part is considered to be *the whole*.

Highlighting the *pars pro toto* principle is crucial for Durkheim. Indeed, this principle helps redefine the problem of the relation between the social thing—the consecrated thing, that is, the food—and the *actual* animal or plant, which exists as a thing in the world each individual can ordinarily experience, independently of any process of consecration. We can see here, from a different perspective, the issue of the representativeness of the totemic drawing or engraving. The *pars pro toto* principle sheds light on the fact that representation doesn't amount to imitation. The fact that the sacred thing can lie entirely in each of its parts isn't sufficiently explained by an internal expressive quality. It stems from a symbolization understood only in this expressive sense. Indeed, in this case, it would still be necessary to account for the way in which this kind of quality formed. This is precisely what Durkheim manages to do, in a purely logical mode, exclusively based on the independence of the property of the social thing with respect to the properties of the material thing serving as its substratum:

> This conception would be inexplicable if the sacredness of something were due to the constituent properties of the thing itself; for in that case, it should vary with this thing, increasing and decreasing with it. But if the virtues it is believed to possess are not intrinsic in it, and if they come from certain sentiments which it brings to mind and symbolizes, though these originate outside of it, then, since it has no need of determined dimensions to play this role of reminder, it will have the same value whether it is entire or not.
>
> (Durkheim [1912] 1964: 229)

The independence of value with respect to the physical integrity of the substratum clarifies what is meant by *symbolic property*, defined as a distinctive feature of a properly social thing. Let us not forget the ambiguous phrase we started from: "just as" material things, social things do exist, although "in a different way." It is precisely this "different way" that is conceived here, based on the kind of perceptive alteration the processes of sacralization seem to involve. In short, the symbolic gap, an affirmation of the irreducibility of the social thing to the substratum, manifests itself as a departure from the fundamental physical property of spatial divisibility, according to which the part is unequal and inferior to the whole.

In this sense, the *pars pro toto* principle has a logical—not physical—meaning. Rather than interpreting it as a supernatural quality affecting certain kinds of beings, it should be viewed in the light of a certain requirement of intelligibility. Through it, the "social thing" manifests itself in its irreducibility and needs to be grasped as such. Thus, the cornerstone of the principle lies elsewhere than where we are inclined to see it: the fact that, regarding sacred things, the part is equal to the whole doesn't mean that the whole can be found in each of its parts, in the sense that it would physically be contained in them; it simply means that the way the *whole* is given is different from the way the parts in which each physical thing is decomposed are given. This corresponds to the perceptive gap imposed by the mode of donation of the sacred, even though it exists only in incarnate, objectified form. Thus, *without ceasing to be things*, sacred things go beyond the requirements of the perception of things in their strict materiality. Far from any imitative derivation, it is again the process of impersonalization at the root of contagiousness that asserts itself, a sign that social reality forms an autonomous level of existence, calling for an independent approach.

Oblation and Communion

The hypothesis of a communion meal thus clarifies the analysis of the *Intichiuma*, at least as far as the sacrificial part of the ritual is concerned. Nevertheless, it doesn't come without difficulty: merged into communion, the oblation it conveys turns out to be affected by some contradiction. Smith engages in contortions that haven't escaped Durkheimians' attention: Smith was unable to find an explanation for these gifts and offerings that started from the experience of the sacrificial community. This is why he had to resort to an extrinsic factor: the notion of property, which in itself has nothing religious about it, and which is supposed to explain the fact that the victim is offered as a tribute to the gods, considered as "kings of the earth." The problem with this genealogy is that, in order to solve the question of the sacrifice, it discounts the religious lineage. With this nonreligious adjuvant, the sacrificial logic is diverted from its natural course and reduced to a transaction between men and gods. But the construction only gives away the circularity Smith struggles with from the start: oblation is initially poorly conceived of, because we can't grasp that the divinity is primitively a principle of life, devoted as such to providing human beings with their food, and that these same human beings are simultaneously compelled to give it what it gives them. Durkheim's objection raises a question: why should the gods expect from Man what they give him already? "Why should they have need of his aid in order to deduct beforehand their just share of the things which he receives from their hands?" (Durkheim [1912] 1964: 341).

As we can see, there is a circle here. The totem is what gives life to Man, but for that Man has to help it. The ultimate question posed by the *Intichiuma*, considering its entire cycle, from the rituals of multiplication to the sacrifices, is: How exactly are communion and oblation connected with each other? In this ritual system, Durkheim actually gives two explanations nested in the same text. Their compatibility isn't obvious, even though they aren't presented as alternatives.

The first aims to show that oblation is in fact an offering from the subjects to their very nature as social beings, objectified as a totem. The meaning of the gesture therefore consists in highlighting that the gods are immortal. Indeed, the one stage of the *Intichiuma* ritual which helps fertilization indicates more or less implicitly that the subjects would die weren't the rite performed. In keeping with this idea, Durkheim endeavors to stress the fact that their existence depends on their regeneration in thought, that is, on the symbolization operation itself, viewed as a mental transfer in things:

> The things which the worshipper really gives his gods are not the foods which he places upon the altars, nor the blood which he lets flow from his veins: it is his thought. Nevertheless, it is true that there is an exchange of services, which are mutually demanded, between the divinity and its worshippers. The rule *do ut des*, by which the principle of sacrifice has sometimes been defined, is not a late invention of utilitarian theorists: it only expresses in an explicit way the very mechanism of the sacrificial system and, more generally, of the whole positive cult. So the circle pointed out by Smith is very real; but it contains nothing humiliating for the reason. It comes from the fact that the sacred beings, though superior to men, can live only in the human consciousness.
>
> (Durkheim [1912] 1964: 346–347)

However, we can clearly see that this insistence on thought, and even more on the "gift of thought" only deepens the mystery Durkheim's critics kept pointing out. If social things are thusly produced, how can we describe their constitution process as indissolubly "mental" and "thing-like"? Here comes again the nagging question: by invoking anew the twofold face of social things, by saying it holds the individuals only to the extent that it is held by them, by assuming that man and the objectified society belong to a same entity, and by highlighting its mental nature, we haven't broken Smith's circle, we haven't even made it intelligible, we have merely illustrated it. And, sure enough, the difficulties stemming from the hypothesis of a pure projection—according to which what can be found outside is constituted inside in advance—arise again.

Yet Durkheim provided another explanation. By exploring the first part of the ritual, its multiplication phase, he revealed an additional and more fruitful aspect of his own thought. As we will see later, this effort lies in his analysis of a particular category of positive rites, the imitative rites, in the light of which the *Intichiuma* must ultimately be evaluated.

Nonimitative Mimesis

Durkheim describes the ritual as closely as possible. How do clan members help assure the fecundity of the totemic species? In the *Intichiuma*, there are not only oblations but also imitations of cries and of movements of animals of the totemic species. From Durkheim's perspective, the fact is worth noting since he initially firmly rejected the idea that the sacralization of totems was based on any imitative process. What is it, then? The question must actually be asked the other way round: if, in this case, imitation isn't the reproduction of an exterior given, how can it correspond to a *production*, viewed as a multiplication of the species? How can one multiply without reproducing, but by producing, and thus by introducing something new into reality?

The classical British anthropological school hasn't ignored the problem and has attempted to solve it with the notion of sympathetic magic. In a clearly evolutionary framework, Frazer has defined it as the origin of religious rituals. But he then aimed to explain the reproduction of a model based on the muddled idea consisting in "assuming that things which resemble each other are the same" (Durkheim [1912] 1964: 357). It is above all the contagiousness of the sacred that occupies Frazer's attention. He explains it as an effect of magical practices that implement associations of ideas resulting from contiguity and similarity, an associative process which, according to him, is fundamental to the human mind, individually considered. But this method isn't appropriate to what we are trying to understand here. Here, insofar as we can't resort to such a derivation from an animal viewed as an objective reference—since the representation comes first, not second—this can't be the case. On the contrary, we must turn again to the totem to understand that the mimetic ritual can truly be productive.

> The men who assemble on the occasion of these rites believe that they are really animals or plants of the species whose name they bear. They feel within them an animal or vegetable nature, and in their eyes, this is what constitutes whatever is the most essential and the most excellent in them. So when they assemble, their first movement ought to be to show each other this quality which they attribute to themselves and by which they are defined. The totem is their rallying sign; for this reason, as we have seen, they design it upon their bodies; but it is no less natural that they should seek to resemble it in their gestures, their cries, their attitude. Since they are emus or kangaroos, they comport themselves like the animals of the same name. By this means, they mutually show one another that they are all members of the same moral community and they become conscious of the kinship uniting them. The rite does not limit itself to expressing this kinship; it makes it or remakes it.
>
> (Durkheim [1912] 1964: 357–358)

In short, the imitative rite doesn't so much *express* as *create*. It produces kinship. Thus, we can say that the principle invoked here by Durkheim, by which "like *produces* like" ([1912] 1964: 358), must be taken literally. Indeed, it doesn't point to a mechanism of imitative reproduction, but rather to the generation of a kinship internally experienced by the subjects of the ritual—a ritual that should be regarded as a process of mental self-affection, a condition for a constructed kinship. *To experience oneself as* a kangaroo or an emu, in these circumstances, doesn't mean living like an actual kangaroo or emu. It means producing in oneself a belonging to the group of kangaroos or emus. In this case, resemblance would be at work on a level that is neither a resemblance between disjointed identities nor a resemblance between differences: rather, it would be the vector of an alteration internal to the subject, through which the latter's membership of a collective occurs. This explains the centrality of imitative rituals. This is how, according to Durkheim, they shed light on a secret motivation of any kind of religious conduct, including the modern one, which the rationalistic arguments rightly challenging the object of faith don't undermine. Indeed, the meaning of religious rituals lies first and foremost in the way in which "they affect our mental status" (Durkheim [1912] 1964: 360), which deserves then the name of *faith* and must be related to this psychological modification that ritual mimesis makes visible. Independently of the rational operations based on perceptual experience, faith refers to a distinct mental experience.

The imperviousness of primitive thought to experience, far from being the sign of its resistance to logical thought, as Lévy-Bruhl had wrongly believed, is indicative of a surpassing of experience both among the primitive and the civilized. Yet logical thought constantly draws on this surpassing, wherever it occurs. In this respect, the *Intichiuma* has indeed been the starting point for a completely renewed inquiry into the conditions of thought.

In this case, the inquiry stems from questions on causal thought. And we understand why. In fact, the reverse mimetic question—whose principle is "like produces like" rather than "like reproduces its model"—only expresses the law of causality. In short, there is no causality without a sort of faith—not a belief based on habit, according to the empirical thesis, but the constitution of a mental status where the surpassing of experience develops logically. What exactly is this logic at the heart of mimetic rituals? First, causality involves a theory of real change. A thing acts on another thing, and this action produces an effect. But where does this idea that a thing can, literally, *act* come from? A classic answer is provided by Comte's category of fetishism, which, as Canguilhem (1983) has shown, draws on Anglo-Scottish thought, more precisely on Hume and on Adam Smith. Fetishism could appear as the first stage of human thought because it contained the original hypothesis of an action by things analogous to ours, by the projection of the subjects' feeling of being at the source of their own actions.

By contrast, we can see what Durkheim's totemic shift consists in: under the totem, and insofar as the latter precisely isn't the totemic animal or plant, as a thing in the world, a force is put inside things; this force isn't to be found in any of them in particular and can only link them on account of this extraction. This force is essentially characterized by its impersonality. It is what enables reality to manifest itself to the subject as being linked from inside itself, by relations that, though they don't have the legibility of controllable relations of causation yet, are nevertheless already relations, mentally conceivable according to the "like produces like" causal proto-relation.

Conclusion

We know that one of the main goals of *The Elementary Forms* is to provide a sociological solution to the philosophical debate on the origin of categories—which, in the author's mind, means rejecting both the empiricist and transcendentalist solutions. As we can see now, this dismissal actually involves clarifying the imitative rituals manifested in the *Intichiuma*. We are finally brought back to the dimension of impersonality viewed as a resource truly intellectual, logical rather than affective. However, it must be emphasized that only a very curious conception of mimesis allows this conclusion. Indeed, far from relating mind to reality through a reproduction, mimesis is considered here to be a process of mental alteration forming a bond of kinship that contributes to an operation of surpassing *in thought*. This means that the subjects manage to position themselves on a level that isn't that of their experience as individual subjects perceiving certain things in the world.

It is worth noting that a certain concept of resemblance turns out to be the operator of this surpassing. This concept isn't to be confused with that mentioned by Lévi-Strauss in *The Savage Mind* as the key to his own explanation of totemism, namely a resemblance reduced to a homology of series, between, on the one hand, social groups and, on the other hand, natural species (Lévi-Strauss 1966: 227–233). In that case, the resemblance would only be a surface effect resulting from the formal relations between two ordered sets of elements. This is not what Durkheim is talking about. Here, resemblance is first at work within the various series—not between them. Involved in a multiplication dynamic, it retains a substantial nature and doesn't amount to a formal procedure of comparison. It underlies the mimetic operation, in each subject of each clan, in the act by which the subjects *experience themselves as* the totem of their clan and contribute to its growth by this ritual act. In short, resemblance underlies the mimetic operation in the act by which the subjects are involved in the ritual of multiplication or *Intichiuma*. Thus, insofar as mimesis is distinguished from the copy's imitation of its model, it shows the constitution in the subjects of a level of existence distinct from that implied by their pure individuality.

This level must be described as both social and intellectual. Accordingly, the "sociologic" that is sociology has its full validity there. But it does so only by following a path different from that opened up by structuralism. In this case, this involves granting that meaning forms in a strictly ritual order, insofar as this order relates the group members to sacred things, which are strictly social things. This relation is both material and intellectual. Its distinctive material nature lies in the fact that it is strictly speaking intellectual, that is, in the fact that it sets off a determined mental alteration, by which logical thought is essentially driven.

Finally, this construction is based on a paradoxical thesis on mimesis. Indeed, it uses a kind of resemblance the structural distinction doesn't grasp, when it only contrasts material contiguity with formal resemblance, identification with comparison, and sacrifice with totemism. On the contrary, from a perspective that remains strictly intellectual, Durkheimian thought requires us to reconnect each of these couples. Only then does Durkheim's conception of symbolism show its own rigor and true goal: to follow the convoluted paths of religious practice to shed light not on a remote phase of logical thought but on its most essential and permanent drive, namely its nonderivation from sensible experience. And to make the reality of social things depend on this religious and mental life in which any group, insofar as it constitutes a society, is actually immersed.

Note

1. Hubert and Mauss ([1899] 1964: 6) insist on a process of elimination of the sacrificial animal, a process that, in their eyes, constitutes a "primordial component of sacrifice, as primordial and irreducible as communion." According to this analysis, sacrifice is viewed as the opening of a passage between two irreducible worlds, and as the institution of mediations the ritual alternately covers in both ways. Still prevailing in Lévi-Strauss's work (see de Heusch 1985), this definition forms a paradigm in the anthropology of sacrifice: the latter amounts to a process by which a communication between the sacred world and the profane world is established through a victim, that is, a consecrated thing destroyed during the ceremony. Unlike Smith, Mauss does not only emphasize the double root of sacrifice, in both oblation and communion, but he also points out the importance of consecration. He thus shows that the victim doesn't have its religious nature from the start; the victim acquires it throughout an operation constitutive of the sacrifice.

References

Canguilhem, Georges. 1983. "Histoire des religions et histoire des sciences dans la théorie du fétichisme chez Auguste Comte." In Georges Canguilhem, *Etudes d'histoire et de philosophie des sciences*, 81–98. Paris: Vrin.
Durkheim, Émile. (1912) 1964. *The Elementary Forms of the Religious Life*. London: Allen & Unwin.
Durkheim, Émile. (1895) 1982. *The Rules of Sociological Method*. New York: The Free Press.
de Heusch, Luc. 1985. *Sacrifice in Africa: A Structuralist Approach*. Manchester: Manchester University Press.
Hubert, Henri, and Marcel Mauss. (1899) 1964. *Sacrifice: Its Nature and Functions*. Chicago: University of Chicago Press.
Lévi-Strauss, Claude. 1947. "La sociologie française." In *La sociologie au XXe siècle*, edited by Georges Gurvitch, vol. II, 513–545. Paris: PUF.
Lévi-Strauss, Claude. (1962) 1966. *The Savage Mind*. Letchworth: Garden City Press.
Merleau-Ponty, Maurice. (1959) 1964. "From Mauss to Claude Lévi-Strauss." In Maurice Merleau-Ponty, *Signs*, 114–125. Evanston, IL: Northwestern University Press.
Robertson Smith, William. 1889. *Lectures on the Religion of the Semites*. Edinburgh: Black.
Spencer, Baldwin, and F. J. Gillen. 1899. *The Native Tribes of Central Australia*. London: Macmillan.
Spencer, Baldwin, and F. J. Gillen. 1904. *The Northern Tribes of Central Australia*. London: Macmillan.
Strehlow, Carl. 1907–1921. *Die Aranda- und Loritja-Stämme in Zentral-Australien*. Frankfurt am Main: J. Baer & Co.
Testart, Alain. 1985. *Le Communisme primitif*. Vol. 1. Paris: Ed. de la Maison des sciences de l'homme.

CHAPTER 7

THE DREYFUS AFFAIR AND DURKHEIM'S EXPERIENCE OF ANTI-SEMITISM

PIERRE BIRNBAUM

The Dreyfus Affair began at the end of 1894 when Captain Alfred Dreyfus was arrested, imprisoned, and convicted of espionage on behalf of Germany. The case attracted little attention and gave rise to few public statements, either in support or in condemnation of the Jewish captain imprisoned and sent to Devil's Island and its deplorable conditions. Outside of Dreyfus's immediate entourage—his wife, his brother, and a few friends convinced of his innocence—silence reigned for more than three years, particularly in intellectual circles.

Before Taking a Position

During this time, Émile Durkheim, a sociology professor in Bordeaux, was quietly building his theories and publishing the major works that underlay his positivist science, opposed to preconceived notions and value judgments. The son and grandson of rabbis, Durkheim turned to the social sciences and patiently built a new scientific field with the publication of *The Division of Labor in Society* in 1893, *The Rules of Sociological Method* in 1895, and his most important work, *Suicide*, in 1897. In other words, while Captain Dreyfus was far away in his island prison, Durkheim, a fully assimilated Jew but one who adhered to Jewish tradition, kept his distance, as did all of his fellow citizens. Far from taking any political or societal position, he was working on a multivariate analysis that could explain specific social behavior. While researching the causes of suicide for his book of the same name in 1897 and emphasizing that social anomie was an important explanatory phenomenon, Durkheim encountered the specific example of Jews, who, paradoxically, had lower suicide rates than both Catholics and Protestants.

Here, he remarked that "the reproach to which the Jews have for so long been exposed by Christianity has created feelings of unusual solidarity among them. Their need of resisting a general hostility, the very impossibility of free communication with the rest of the population, has forced them to strict union among themselves." So if their suicide rate was lower than it was for people of other religions, "doubtless they owe this immunity in a sense to the hostility surrounding them" (Durkheim 1951: 159–160 / 1897: 159–160).

There is no allusion to the Dreyfus Affair in *Suicide*. We do not know whether Durkheim was sensitive to the hostility toward Jews that was raging in 1897, stoked by the incendiary writings of Edouard Drumont and his bestselling *La France juive*, which went through several printings, as well as by violent incidents involving Jews, particularly in the army. Durkheim returned to the Jewish question in *Suicide* when he examined the positive correlation between suicide rates and level of education. He observed that Jewish suicide rates were the lowest, even though they were highly educated. He said that "The Jew, therefore, seeks to learn, not in order to replace his collective prejudices by reflective thought, but merely to be better armed for the struggle" against the hate that he encounters as a member of a minority (Durkheim 1951:168 / 1897: 169–170). Education did not undermine Jews' collective beliefs but provided them with a way to deal with the hate they faced while strengthening their collective cohesion. While he also mentioned that the solidarity pervading the Jewish community is also linked to the "archaic" nature of their religion (159–160/159–160), he did not try to evaluate the relative importance of one or the other of these variables. If the hostility were to disappear, would solidarity subside with it and the suicide rate increase? If their "primitive" (168/170) beliefs were to evaporate, would their solidarity ebb with it and suicide rates likewise increase? Would they increase even if the hostility persisted? Durkheim did not answer these questions, but simply indicated the existence of distinct reasons for Jewish community solidarity and for the low Jewish suicide rates. Most commentators on this important work have neglected this aspect of Durkheim's demonstration. Formulated in 1897, it deserves an even more rigorous analysis given that Durkheim came from the same Jewish patriotic milieu in the occupied regions of eastern France to which Alfred Dreyfus also belonged. Strong ties bound him to those Alsatian families who, out of patriotism for France, left their home region after France was defeated in the Franco-Prussian war of 1870. Moreover, like Dreyfus, Durkheim was a "State Jew." One attended *l'Ecole normale supérieure*, the other *l'Ecole polytechnique*, two of the country's most prestigious schools. They were pure products of the republican meritocracy, public servants dedicated to the Republic that it would be impossible for them to betray. So it is legitimate to wonder whether *Suicide* "is not also a reflection, triggered and dramatized by the Dreyfus Affair, on the higher ethical requirements of the military officer and the university professor, a way of convincing himself that Dreyfus was not a coward when he let himself be accused" (Chamboredon 1984: 497). Notwithstanding these possible allusions, Durkheim continued his work as a sociologist, seemingly detached from outside events. In 1897/98, he published the first of his long series of thick volumes called *L'année sociologique*, in perfect harmony with his colleagues. In no article did they make the slightest reference to the Dreyfus Affair, which was taking a dramatic turn in the first few months of 1898.

Ardent Defense of Dreyfus

Durkheim, a dignified and austere university professor with his abiding respect for the law, a wise positivist and high-ranking civil servant who argued that the state's representatives must adhere to their obligations, suddenly entered the fray in favor of Captain Dreyfus at a critical moment. On January 13, 1898, Émile Zola published his scathing *J'accuse*. Zola's virulent attack on the army and the courts set off anti-Semitic riots and landed him in court. On February 23, he was convicted, to the great satisfaction of many. From January to March 1898, an anti-Semitic wave washed over the whole country. Crowds of several thousand marched in the major cities—in Paris, Rouen, Marseilles, Toulouse, and Bordeaux—to rallying cries of "Death to the Jews!," "Death to Dreyfus!," "Long live the army!," and "France for the French!." In Bordeaux, the violence was intense. Mounted police charged the demonstrators, many of whom were injured. The anti-Semitic movement reached even small cities and the countryside. Nationalist, anti-Semitic groups, such as the *Ligue antisémite française*, marched like military units and attracted hundreds of thousands of members. Virtually all newspapers, some of which had a circulation of several million, adopted an anti-Dreyfus point of view. *La Libre Parole* and *La Croix*, many national publications such as *Le Petit Parisien* and *Le Petit Journal*, and many local ones accused Jews of wanting to dominate France and replace the existing Christian society with a "Jewish republic." In reaction to this, with the Republic itself under threat, scholars and intellectuals now joined the fight on the side of Dreyfus. In the name of science and truth, the *Ligue des droits de l'homme et du citoyen* was created on February 20, 1898. Its most well-known founders were Parisian intellectuals such as Émile Duclaux and Edouard Grimaux. In the name of the law and respect for individuals, they intended to defend the ideals of the Republic by relying on scientific methods to demonstrate truth (Naquet 1999). As such, they stood in opposition to numerous members of the French Academy, nationalist intellectuals such as Charles Maurras, Maurice Barrès, and François Coppée, and partisans of *Action française*, which Auguste Renoir, Edgar Degas, and Paul Valéry had also joined.

In Bordeaux, Durkheim took up the pro-Dreyfus cause and played a little-known but essential role in the birth of the *Ligue*. In February 1898, he wrote to Marcel Mauss:

> Let's first talk about matters pertaining to France, which must be worrying you. The situation is serious, indeed. But it seems to me that anti-Semitism is only a superficial manifestation. What is serious is, firstly, that such an insignificant event—because in itself it is nothing—can produce such turmoil. There must be a profound moral disorganization beneath it all if an incident of so little importance can cause such

an upheaval. It is alarming that a reaction is developing against all sorts of principles that we thought had been agreed upon long ago. [...] We have never seen such moral disorder in France before. As you can see, I am not optimistic. But that does not mean we should let ourselves be discouraged [...] let's not give up the fight. I asked Hubert to suggest the idea of a permanent league for the respect of the law. He urged Herr to speak about it with Lavisse. We'll see what comes of it.

(Durkheim 1998: 110)

This letter reveals that Durkheim was present when the *Ligue* was formed, that he suggested its creation. He then became very active. He wrote to Mauss again in February to tell him that "we are looking to organize a league for the defense of the rights of the citizen, under the direction of Duclaux" and was disappointed by the lack of response he received in Bordeaux. He added, "I have so far received five signatures here. It is distressing to see all the cowardice we are up against. It's pathetic. I feel like an exile in my own country. I've withdrawn almost completely from the activities of my university department. What I see there is too painful to watch." Saddened by the lack of solidarity among his colleagues, Durkheim confessed to Mauss: "I am not jumping into the fray, but I am doing what I can to head off an intellectual and moral reaction movement that is very clearly developing" (Durkheim 1998: 110–115; see also Birnbaum 2011: 206–207). Also in February, with the anti-Semitism crisis reaching a fever pitch, Durkheim and two of his colleagues sent a letter to *Le Nouvelliste*, the Bordeaux-based nationalist newspaper, in which they declared,

During Dreyfus's trial, regardless of what one might think of it, there were undisputed illegal actions and procedural violations, and we believed it was important to protest against them. You blame us for doing so, but the expression "friends of the syndicate" that you use in your short piece goes too far, because we have absolutely no knowledge of the existence of a syndicate.

The paper's public response was scathing:

These gentlemen acknowledge that they have publicly protested against "illegal actions" and "procedural violations" in Dreyfus's trial. Their science is as remarkable as their ignorance [...] Whether they intended it or not, therefore, they are indeed "friends of the syndicate." They are civil servants revolting against the government and publicly proclaiming their sympathy for people who attack and insult the army [...] while foreign powers encourage and applaud them.

(Birnbaum 2000: 85)

In this context, it is difficult to understand how Durkheim could believe that the Dreyfus Affair was only an "incident," an "insignificant event" that revealed the depth of "moral disorganization" or "moral disorder." Although the situation was "serious," he believed anti-Semitism was a "superficial manifestation." And this when he was treated not even as an "exile in his own country," but rather, like Dreyfus, as an agent of a foreign power, probably Germany, which would applaud the stance he took. While hundreds of thousands of demonstrators across the country were crying "Death to the Jews!" in the streets, the Anti-Semitic Leagues' militants were blaring "France for the French!," and violent incidents were breaking out everywhere, Durkheim strangely persisted in believing that anti-Semitism was "superficial." What was important to the author of *The Division of Labor in Society*, which had just been published, was social disorganization, the anomie in French society, and he explained neither the causes nor the consequences of it. Why was this disorganization expressed through an outbreak of anti-Semitism? What link did he establish between anti-Semitism and the reaction against "principles that we thought had been agreed upon long ago," namely, the principles of 1789? Durkheim did not go into an historical analysis, nor did he mention the existence of a fiercely Catholic, reactionary Right that had never accepted the Revolution and that resurfaced intact during this time. He did not see this reactionary Right as launching a frontal attack on the universalist state that allowed Protestant and Jewish minorities to flourish and reach the highest levels of society. His diagnosis departed radically from the precepts of positivism, with its analysis of variables, correlations, and causality. These letters also show that Durkheim was so discouraged when he saw that his colleagues felt no urgency to defend Dreyfus, when he saw their "cowardice," that he came to see himself as an "exile in his own country." This is incredibly strong stuff for a republican patriot like Durkheim. A pure product of the Republic, a "State Jew" fully assimilated into the French nation, a senior civil servant mindful of his obligations, Durkheim nevertheless considered himself an "exile in his own country." Was it only as a French citizen that he felt this way? Or did the Jewish dimension of his personality also inform the feeling that he was being rejected by society when he saw the "cowardice" of his colleagues who were indifferent to the plight of a Jewish army captain mistreated by the courts? How can we distil Durkheim's Jewishness faced with anti-Semitism from the citizen actively defending society's morals?

Durkheim the theoretician then virtually transformed himself into a militant for the Dreyfus cause. He sent letters to several colleagues to encourage them to join the *Ligue*. He wrote to Célestin Bouglé almost in the same terms: "I have been a member of the Ligue since before it was formed [...] but it will be hard to recruit new members. The pettiness, the cowardice we see is unbelievable. [...] The sight of so much cowardice has discouraged me. Individualism must not be equated with selfishness, but with sympathy and pity of one man for another" (Durkheim 1975: 417–418). Once again, he spoke of his fellow citizens' "cowardice" and was unable to explain it. Durkheim could not explain how so many colleagues, who attended the country's elite *grandes écoles* and were steeped in republican ideals, reinforced by Jules Ferry's recent school legislation, were reluctant to commit themselves to science and truth, whereas they more than anyone should have been the ambassadors of these principles. He feared that this abandonment would spark other, possibly more dangerous moral crises and—without saying it outright—potentially other, more serious and equally inexplicable outbreaks of anti-Semitism in republican France. How much longer would he live with this feeling of being an "exile in his own country," forcing him to think about his condition as a marginalized Jewish citizen?

He never commented on the anti-Semitic demonstrations, which, far from being "superficial," were of an unprecedented scale, even in his home city of Bordeaux. There is no record in his correspondence of remarks about the nationalist processions he must have encountered, about the anti-Semitic insults he must have heard outside his window on the *Cours Pasteur*. From February to July 1898, we know nothing of his feelings or of his analysis of these nationalistic demonstrations, which were hardly as "superficial" as he suggested. We know only that he became the favorite target of the nationalist Right (Cazenave 1972) and that by virtue of his declarations in favor of Dreyfus, he attracted severe criticism from the rector of the University (Lukes 1973: 347, 349). Then, in July, the Paul Stapfer affair erupted. Paul Stapfer, dean of the University, gave the eulogy for Auguste Couat, the rector of the University of Bordeaux, taking a position implicitly in favor of the quest for justice and truth, and thus, in favor of Captain Dreyfus. Like many of those who defended Dreyfus, Stapfer was a Protestant who espoused the liberal values of the French Revolution. He attacked the "sectarian violence," denounced a "wave of unreasoned fury," and praised this great "intellectual," a term which, in its temporal context, meant the adversaries of the nationalist movements. He concluded unambiguously, "Gentlemen, justice is sometimes eclipsed by the clouds of passion." Confronted with the scandal, the minister of public education suspended Stapfer, and most of Durkheim's colleagues were hostile to Stapfer's pro-Dreyfus position, which was contrary to the verdict of the courts. On July 26, Durkheim sent a letter to the newspaper *Le Temps*, in which he declared that he shared the values espoused by Stapfer. The letter was reprinted in the anti-Dreyfus Bordeaux newspaper *Le Nouvelliste*, which commented on it as follows: "Mr Durkheim clearly wishes to make it known that he holds the same opinions as Mr. Stapfer on the Dreyfus question. We have no doubt that he is asking to share the dean's disgrace and that he wrote his letter expressly for this heroic purpose" (Birnbaum 2000: 86). Several of Durkheim's colleagues condemned his letter. Durkheim found himself isolated and was threatened by the unthinkable: resign from his University for supposedly not upholding his obligation as a civil servant to keep his personal opinions to himself, an obligation that he himself defended. He was once again demoralized by the abandonment, the "cowardice" which now affected him personally and reinforced his feeling of being an "exile in his own country," unbearable for one who so loved the Republic.

Also in July 1898, Durkheim answered his critics by publishing an essential article in *La Revue bleue* in which he intended to respond in the most straightforward manner to a text attacking intellectuals published by Ferdinand Brunetière, a Catholic, virulently anti-Dreyfus but not anti-Semitic writer. Durkheim did not mention Dreyfus's name nor the anti-Semitic fever gripping the country. Brunetière's article, entitled "After the Trial" and published on March 15, 1898 in the traditional *Revue des Deux Mondes*, attacked the intellectuals as "democracy's and the army's worst enemies, who invoke science so as to impose [...] the scientific method, an aristocracy of intelligence, respect for truth, all these grand principles that serve only to cover their penchant for *Individualism*, and *Individualism*, as we all know, is the great sickness of our time" (Brunetière 1898: 446). For Brunetière, this individualism had been disseminated in France by the supporters of Dreyfus who were attacking the army. "Free masons, Protestants, and Jews," he wrote,

> who all have that great advantage of freedom from commitment to the past, have come rushing in through the door left open for them. They have seized control of government offices, of the schools, and there they reign. Their legal, political, and administrative representation is not proportional to numbers in society that they are supposed to represent and this is certainly—along with being one of the causes of the current malaise and the government's weakness—one of the causes of anti-Semitism. Thirty-eight million French people are no more disposed today than they were a hundred years ago to constantly submit to the domination of a few hundred among them, the most recently arrived, the newest members of the family.
> (Brunetière 1898: 431; see also Duclert 1999)

Brunetière here embraced the views of Edouard Drumont, who was also hostile to the Protestant and Jewish minorities. His demonstration concluded with a particularly virulent statement: France was under the yoke of the "newcomers," that is, recently immigrated Jews, exactly what the nationalist Far Right had been claiming. Brunetière called for a revolution against them, an uprising similar to the one a hundred years earlier of the people against the aristocracy. In fact, anti-Semitic reasoning at the time often compared Jews to prerevolutionary aristocrats. The intellectuals, defenders of Dreyfus such as Durkheim, were thus singled out and accused of disseminating individualism which risked destroying the national cohesion safeguarded by the army. The accusation was all the more serious in that it was not formulated in the terms of the intransigent, Catholic nationalist Right. Rather, the intellectuals' individualism supposedly betrayed their indifference to the fate of the country and would tear apart the national fabric.

That Durkheim's sociology is often qualified as holistic, with emphasis on the specificity of social facts and the collective conscience, makes the charge that much more devastating. "Leaving aside the Dreyfus question," Durkheim wrote in a letter to Henri Hubert in 1898, "I would like to speak of the individualism that is held against us as a source of social disintegration and show that our accusers are playing with words, that individualism is not selfishness but sympathy and pity of one man for another," that the individualism of which intellectuals were being accused was the moral foundation of the individual and of his rights to truth and justice (Durkheim 1987: 491). Wanting to free himself from the events that nevertheless affected him personally, Durkheim started his article against Brunetière by writing, "Let us forget the Affair itself and the melancholy scenes we have witnessed. The problem confronting us goes infinitely beyond the current events and must be disengaged from them" (Durkheim 1969: 20 / 1898: 7). Even as he was the target of vindictive attacks, he persisted in his belief that the Affair and its consequences were just incidents that could be "forgotten" on the way to true analysis. He tried to demonstrate that individualism had nothing to do with utilitarianism, but that, following on from Rousseau, Kant, and the French Revolution's Declaration of the

Rights of Man, it had everything to do with our "moral catechism" that teaches us absolute respect for the individual and his rights against any national interest. It is the individual who is "sacred," and the justice to which he is entitled creates "the community of all men of good will" that an unjust court cannot infringe. For Durkheim it was the lack of respect for the individual that chips away at the community. Cutting against the grain of nationalistic writers and pamphleteers who felt it was important to defend an organic, national community and condemn individualism, Durkheim maintained that the national community was that much more vibrant as a "moral unit" when respect for each person was guaranteed (Durkheim 1969: 21–25 / 1898: 8–10; see also Cladis 1994: 271 and Jones 2001).

What Is Anti-Semitism?

This violent context threatened Durkheim's most deeply held values and saw him accused of being a foreigner in his own country. As a Dreyfusard but also, implicitly, as a Jew, Durkheim tried to take stock of the groundswell of anti-Semitism that constituted a "superficial manifestation" in his eyes. In 1899, he was asked to share his opinion as part of a study on anti-Semitism. This was certainly the only time in his career that he participated in such an undertaking. In the very first line of his response, Durkheim, the rigorous sociologist, confessed that serious research would be required before he could formulate a proper response. He was implicitly referring to his recent study of suicide and claimed that quantitative analysis based on independent variables would be essential. Any other response, he said, would be just "my impression," purely subjective and far removed from the work of a sociologist (Durkheim 2008: 321 / 1899: 59). But despite being conscious of this limitation, Durkheim suggested a few ideas:

> What distinguishes the two states of mind, it seems to me, is that German or Russian anti-Semitism is chronic, traditional, while ours constitutes an acute crisis, due to passing circumstances. The first [state of mind] has an aristocratic character; it springs from contempt and haughtiness. Ours is inspired by destructive, violent passions, which seek to assert themselves by all means.
>
> (Durkheim 2008: 322 / 1899: 60)

According to Durkheim, Germany and Russia, two societies that were as dissimilar as they could be at the time, whether in the type of division of labor, urbanization, educational levels, religion, or even the political system, had, oddly enough, the same type of anti-Semitism. Of course, Durkheim could not predict the Kishinev pogrom that would take place in Russia four years later, but at the end of the nineteenth century, he did not see that the situation of German Jews differed in every way from that of their Russian counterparts, virtually all of whom were marginalized, living in rural areas, and much less integrated into society. And in both cases, anti-Semitism in Germany and Russia could hardly be qualified simply as "aristocratic"; there was at least as much if not more bourgeois or mass anti-Semitism. French anti-Semitism, meanwhile, was produced by "violent passions, which seek to assert themselves by all means" and was the result of a "crisis" situation, an unclear term in Durkheim's lexicon. Durkheim was clearly referring here to the incredibly violent 1898 anti-Semitic demonstrations led by nationalistic leagues that wanted to take power by force. Indeed, that never happened during this period in Germany or Russia.

Durkheim then devoted the rest of his response to the case of France, whose anti-Semitic crises he explained by military defeats, as in 1870, and by economic crises, such as in 1848, following the severe economic crisis of 1847. He was able to "observe it closely" himself in Alsace in 1870, "being myself of Jewish origin" (Durkheim 2008: 322 / 1899: 60). The scion of several generations of rabbis on his father's side and several rabbinical ancestors on his mother's side, Durkheim said he was simply of "Jewish origin." Having "observed it closely," Durkheim attempted a sociological interpretation of a phenomenon caused by "passing circumstances," although these circumstances had also occurred in 1848, as well as in 1870 and 1898. In his view, "our current anti-Semitism is the consequence and the superficial symptom of a state of social malaise," and it was important to understand the reason behind the "social malaise" that expressed itself through a "crisis." Durkheim then proposed a functionalist explanation of anti-Semitism. For him, "When society suffers, it needs someone to blame, someone upon whom to avenge itself for its disappointments; and those persons whom opinion already disfavors are naturally singled out for this role. It is the pariahs who serve as expiatory victims" (Durkheim 2008: 322 / 1899: 61). So society's "suffering"—Durkheim does not analyze the source—arouses the need to find "someone to blame." The Jew, a "pariah," will thus serve as an "expiatory victim." This new psychological vocabulary in Durkheim's work is surprising. It departs radically from his usual sociological analyses and brings to mind Durkheim's more in-depth work on religious sacrifice (Graham 2007: 28). At best, one could read this as the claim that wherever there are pathological forms of division of labor that create pariah-like positions, those who hold these positions are, under appropriate circumstances, likely to fulfil the function of the criminal that Durkheim describes in his sociology of punishment.

It is also surprising that Durkheim saw these French Jews as "pariahs," since most of them had been perfectly well integrated into society as French citizens for more than a century and freely shared the public space. Why, moreover, would public opinion have already "disfavored" them? The record is silent on this. Here Durkheim used a timeless and relatively unsociological explanation for anti-Semitism—the scapegoat—which he then applied to the Dreyfus Affair itself. For him,

> What confirms my interpretation is the manner in which the trial of [Alfred] Dreyfus, in 1894, was greeted. There was a fervent joy in the streets. People celebrated as a success what they should have marked by public mourning. As a result of the

trial, people finally knew whom to blame for the economic troubles and the moral distress through which they lived. Evil came from the Jews.

(Durkheim 2008: 322 / 1899: 61)

In fact, it is difficult to understand why Jews would have served as "expiatory victims" for these "economic troubles," or to see the sociological link that Durkheim established this time between anti-Semitism and economic difficulties alone, which here took on new importance, rather than military defeats (Lukes 1973: 345). How is it that from one paragraph to another, Durkheim changed the principal causes for the outbreak of anti-Semitism that enabled society to feel "comforted," to find a form of solidarity in unity against the Jews?

As he did in *Suicide*, the major work he had just published, Durkheim tried to distinguish between the "principal" and "secondary" causes of anti-Semitism. But to advance his highly sophisticated, multivariate analysis of the causes of suicide, Durkheim used his abundant and varied quantitative data to isolate the variables and try to eliminate certain ones through rigorous analysis, so as to demonstrate the existence of a true, explanatory cause. This time, however, it was nothing of the sort. Durkheim himself said that he could rely only on "impressions," an almost untenable position for a positivist sociologist. He recognized the influence of his own position as a person "of Jewish origin" "observing" this phenomenon but not being able to quantify it or remain free of preconceived notions or personal values; that is, he was not able to observe it simply—as he wrote in *The Rules of Sociological Method*—as a "thing." Alongside the economic cause, which seemed to be the principal variable, Durkheim was quick to mention "secondary circumstances," constituting "secondary causes" (Durkheim 2008: 322 / 1899: 61). Faithful to his multivariate analysis, but now more metaphorical than quantitative and rigorous, Durkheim brings up "vaguely religious aspirations" that were expressed during the course of the Dreyfus Affair. Without specifying their nature, he was in all likelihood implicitly designating the emergence of radical Catholic elements that he preferred not to name. And he added, strangely, to these secondary causes "certain failings of the Jewish race [that] could be invoked to justify it," without specifying these surprising "failings" that could only exacerbate anti-Semitism. Using the same vocabulary, he went on to say that "the Jews lose their ethnic character [...] Only two generations and it was gone" (Durkheim 2008: 322 / 1899: 61). In his eyes, this rendered the criticism justifying anti-Semitism absurd. In other words, ethnic anti-Semitism was not in itself unreasonable; it was that Jews lose their ethnic character and so anti-Semitism loses its raison d'être. It remains to be understood how Durkheim the sociologist could reduce Jewishness to a biological characteristic reminiscent of classifications used by Jules Soury, for example. It is a view that ignores the history, values, and culture that have prompted Jews to remain Jews even in the absence of any ethnic component.

Durkheim's very subjective demonstration brings up many questions. As the many variables he enumerated proved to be disappointing, Durkheim changed his approach to anti-Semitism. Instead of having an incontrovertible cause, anti-Semitism was now "one of the numerous indications that reveals the serious moral disturbance from which we suffer" (Durkheim 2008: 322 / 1899: 62), an indication of a deeper moral decay. Did he intend to invoke his theory of social anomie, which he had just presented in *Suicide*, wherein the pathological division of labor leads to the disappearance of social norms, to explain the eruption of this "sickness," of this "evil"? All of these psychological notions were far removed from Durkheim's usual vocabulary and more akin to the writings of Gustave Le Bon. In this context, he confessed that "one cannot eradicate the evil at its source," but only try to combat its "symptom" (Durkheim 2008: 322 / 1899: 62). Indeed, his recommended solutions for doing away with anti-Semitism seem to lack potency. He proposed simply that the government take coercive measures to repress this hatred of certain citizens and that it "take responsibility for enlightening the masses" (Durkheim 2008: 323 / 1899: 62). Once again, this proposal is strange coming from Durkheim, who generally avoided speaking of "the masses." In France at that time, this notion belonged more to the vocabulary of Gabriel Tarde and Gustave Le Bon, from whom Durkheim differed sharply. Moreover, it is difficult to imagine how a government that had so aligned itself with the anti-Dreyfus cause and whose action Durkheim combatted in Bordeaux could successfully carry out such an educational task, which, in Durkheim's view, should be undertaken in the classroom.

Durkheim clearly had difficulty translating his "impression" into a convincing sociological explanation of the virulent, rampant anti-Semitism infecting all of French society before his eyes. As pointed out by Chad Alan Goldberg,

> Durkheim appears to violate his own sociological method by muddling together the cause and function of anti-Semitism. He seems to suggest that anti-Semitism arises in order to restore social solidarity and unite society around hatred of the Jew. To refine and complete Durkheim's analysis, one would need to provide a causal explanation of the origins of anti-Semitism and separate it clearly from Durkheim's analysis of the function it fulfils, in much the same way that he separated the causes and function of the division of labor.
>
> (Goldberg 2008: 315)

Durkheim was even less inclined to study the question according to the sociological canon for analyzing a societal phenomenon in that he considered anti-Semitism, as indicated earlier, to be a "superficial" phenomenon, caused by "passing" circumstances. In his view, it did not proceed from structural factors, be they economic, political, or founded on deeply held religious beliefs specific to a particular culture. Rather, the violent anti-Semitism convulsing the country was only a "passing" phenomenon. It was not rooted in an historical movement, a specific, French experience that saw the rise of Catholic counterrevolutionaries against the emancipating Enlightenment philosophers whom they accused of favoring Protestant and especially Jewish minorities. Durkheim offered nothing of an historical nature to explain this anti-Semitic flare-up, to connect it with the explosion of nationalism that was threatening the Republic, to compare it rigorously with manifestations of anti-Semitism in other societies that had other economic, political, or religious structures. His analysis remained strangely ahistorical and cut off from its specifically French context. In this regard, this short text, written in 1899, was almost a step backward from *Suicide*, published in 1897. In *Suicide*, in the margins of a quantitative analysis measuring the correlation between the suicide rate among Jews and their level of education, he did not hesitate to demonstrate that education helped them combat the hostility of Christian society, to strengthen their solidarity against the oppressive hate, the hostility they faced as a minority. All of these sociological notions were far removed from the dominant psychology of the period. It was not until 1902, in a letter to Eugène Fournière, that Durkheim revisited these events with a more fully formed political sociology and found "the idea that republicanism had itself paved the way for a rebirth of nationalism particularly compelling. One cannot use the desire for revenge and renewed military glory to forge the collective conscience of a people with impunity" (Durkheim 1979: 119). In recasting his view in this way, he assigned a central role in French political history to the stirrings of nationalism and anti-Semitism. He even posed a challenging question to his republican friends and developed a brilliant hypothesis that shed light on the ideological confusion of the Dreyfus Affair: Did the republicans unwittingly provoke unexpected consequences by advocating military revenge to such an extent that it became the essence of the "collective conscience," susceptible to all forms of xenophobia?

Translated from the French by Steven Sklar.[1]

Note

1. Translator's note: unless otherwise indicated in the References, all citations in quotation marks are my own translations from French.

References

Birnbaum, Pierre. 2000. *Jewish Destinies: Citizenship, State, and Community in Modern France*. New York: Hill and Wang.
Birnbaum, Pierre. 2011. "Durkheim, la communion républicaine et ses ennemis." In *Durkheim fut-il durkheimien?*, edited by Raymond Boudon, 205–232. Paris: Armand Colin.
Brunetière, Ferdinand. 1898. "Après le procès." *Revue des Deux Mondes* 146 (March): 428–446.
Cazenave, Elisabeth. 1972. "L'Affaire Dreyfus et l'opinion bordelaise. Essai de méthodologie." *Annales du Midi* 84 (106): 63–76.
Chamboredon, Jean-Claude. 1984. "Emile Durkheim: Le social, objet de science. Du moral au politique?" *Critique* 40 (445/446): 460–531.
Cladis, Mark S. 1994. *A Communitarian Defense of Liberalism: Emile Durkheim and Contemporary Social Theory*. Stanford, CA: Stanford University Press.
Duclert, Vincent. 1999. "Les intellectuels, l'antisémitisme et l'affaire Dreyfus en France." *Revue des études juives* 158 (1): 155–211.
Durkheim, Émile. (1897) 1951. *Suicide: A Study in Sociology*. Translated by John A. Spaulding and George Simpson. New York: Free Press. Originally published as *Le suicide. Etude de sociologie*. Paris: Alcan.

Durkheim, Émile. (1898) 1969. "Individualism and the Intellectuals." Translated by Steven Lukes. *Political Studies* 17 (1): 14–30. Originally published as "L'individualisme et les intellectuels" in *Revue bleue*, 4e série 10: 7–13. Republished in Émile Durkheim, *La science sociale et l'action*, edited by Jean-Claude Filloux, 261–278. Paris: Presses universitaires de France, 1970.

Durkheim, Émile. 1975. "Lettre à Célestin Bouglé, 18 mars 1898." In Émile Durkheim, *Textes*, vol. 2: *Religion, morale, anomie*, edited by Victor Karady, 417–418. Paris: Les Editions de Minuit.

Durkheim, Émile. 1979. "Autres lettres de Durkheim." *Revue française de sociologie* 20 (1): 118–121.

Durkheim, Émile. 1987. "Lettres de Emile Durkheim à Henri Hubert." *Revue française de sociologie* 28 (3): 483–534.

Durkheim, Émile. 1998. *Lettres à Marcel Mauss*. Edited by Philippe Besnard and Marcel Fournier. Paris: Presses universitaires de France.

Durkheim, Émile. (1899) 2008. "Anti-Semitism and Social Crisis." *Sociological Theory* 26 (4): 321–323. Originally published as a contribution to *Enquête sur l'antisémitisme*, edited by Henri Dagan, 59–63. Paris: Stock. Republished as "Antisémitisme et crise sociale." In Émile Durkheim, *Textes*, vol. 2: *Religion, morale, anomie*, edited by Victor Karady, 252–254. Paris: Les Editions de Minuit, 1975.

Goldberg, Chad Alan. 2008. "Introduction to Emile Durkheim's 'Anti-Semitism and Social Crisis.'" *Sociological Theory* 26 (4): 299–321.

Graham, E. Tyler. 2007. "The Danger of Durkheim: Ambiguity in the Theory of Social Effervescence." *Religion* 37 (1): 26–38.

Jones, Susan Stedman. 2001. *Durkheim Reconsidered*. London: Polity Press.

Lukes, Steven. 1973. *Emile Durkheim: His Life and Work*. London: Allen Lane.

Naquet, Emmanuel. 1999. "De la mystique à la politique? Intellectuels et édiles de la Ligue des Droits de l'Homme pendant l'affaire Dreyfus." *Cahiers Jean Jaurès* 154 (October–December): 65–83.

CHAPTER 8

DURKHEIM AND THE PHILOSOPHY OF HIS TIME

JEAN-LOUIS FABIANI

For a long time, Durkheim has been viewed as the herald of a coarse anti-philosophy. His fights against his fellow academic philosophers were often fierce. His aim to establish a new science that would include all forms of specialized knowledge on social issues was often considered as imperialist, positivist, scientistic, or conservative. Michel Foucault's evaluation of Durkheim seems to concentrate one century of philosophical common saying about the sociologist: "The old realism *à la* Durkheim, taking society as a substance that opposes the individual who is also a kind of substance integrated within society, this old realism seems unthinkable to me" (Foucault 2001: 469, my translation). Durkheim's work thus seems devoid of any theoretical potentiality. By saying that, Foucault situated himself in a long French philosophical tradition based on a strong anti-Durkheimism. Jean-Paul Sartre did not mean anything different when he proclaimed in 1943, targeting Georges Bataille's sociological project: "Durkheim's sociology is dead. Social facts are not things, they have meanings and, as such, they refer to the being by whom meanings come to the world, man, who could not be scientist and object of science in the meantime" (Sartre 1947: 186, my translation). The philosophical hostility against the founder of French sociology seems a little bit out of fashion: philosophers are reinvestigating his work, even in France (Karsenti 2006; Callegaro 2015). Its conceptual density is now fully acknowledged, particularly outside of France (Rawls 2005).

In order to understand the endurance of French philosophical hostility against Durkheim, one must reconsider his complex relationship to his native discipline. While nobody forgets today that he was the son of a rabbi, as he reminded us, many tend to forget that he was trained as a philosopher, taught philosophy, and never left the philosophical field during his lifetime. There is an ingrained retrospective illusion concerning a deadly fight between philosophy and sociology in France at the end of the nineteenth century, as if they were two comparable institutional entities. This is not the case. Sociological teaching in the time of Durkheim was nonexistent in universities.

The first mention of the term "sociology" in the title of a course appeared in 1913, in the famous lectures on pragmatism. This institutional fact has been largely unnoticed: Durkheim's lectures inaugurated the first official chair of Sociology in France and may be considered as a point of departure for a new development of the discipline and for its theoretical grounding (Baciocchi and Fabiani 2012). Ironically enough, the course was devoted to a topical philosophical issue, pragmatism. World War I interrupted the move: sociology remained an academic subfield of philosophy until a bachelor's degree in sociology was established in 1958, a fact that explains why so many French sociologists and anthropologists were trained as philosophers. This is particularly the case of Durkheim's first companions, Marcel Mauss, François Simiand, and Célestin Bouglé, among others, with the exception of Henri Hubert, who was a historian by training.

When he entered the *Ecole normale supérieure* in 1879, Durkheim studied philosophy. In 1882, he passed successfully the *agrégation de philosophie*, a national competitive examination intended to select the best teachers in secondary schools. His schoolmates were, among others, Jean Jaurès, Henri Bergson, and Octave Hamelin. His rank at the *agrégation* was not among the best: he came seventh out of eight, a result that may indicate some uneasiness with the academic philosophy of his time.

After his success, he engaged into a doctoral philosophical work on the division of labor, which he defended successfully in 1893. He worked on his dissertation while he was teaching philosophy in provincial high schools (*lycées*) in Sens and Troyes and during a yearlong stay in German universities. This implies that his foundational gesture took place within the academic field. When he got a job in higher education, he taught the science of education in Bordeaux (first in 1887), then at the Sorbonne (starting in 1902). His interest in pedagogical issues was largely the consequence of his peculiar conditions of accession to university teaching. The University of Bordeaux needed replacement for Alfred Espinas's course on pedagogy. Sociology entered university "through the narrow door of pedagogy," as Maurice Halbwachs reminded us in his foreword to *The Evolution of Educational Thought* (Durkheim [1938] 2009: xi, translation modified). What does that mean concerning the relationship between sociology as a new science and academic philosophy? Durkheim always remained a member of the philosophical community. A sociologist should take the importance of the social milieu of a thinker as primordial. Philosophers were his peers: he depended on them for basic evaluations but also for the construction of his reputation. He published in the two main philosophical journals of his time, the *Revue philosophique*, created in 1876 by the psychologist-philosopher Théodule Ribot, quite open to positive knowledge and new scientific thinking, and the *Revue de métaphysique et de morale*, launched in 1893 as a flagship of new philosophy: the founders, Xavier Léon and Elie Halévy, were less sympathetic to his views but he published decisive articles in it. This basic sociological fact seems too trivial for many historical sociologists of ideas, but it is a necessary condition to understand Durkheim's extremely complex relationship to philosophy.

Durkheim started his career with standard philosophical equipment, as his high-school lectures at the *Lycée* of Sens clearly show, but also with a growing disenchantment about the eclectic and metaphysical mainstream that had survived the establishment of the Third Republic. The sociologist was an ardent republican, and he was fully devoted to constructing a new rationalist philosophy, adapted to the progress of science as well as to the new democratic order. His lectures at the *Lycée* of Sens give us an idea of his philosophical positioning at an early stage of his career (Durkheim 2011). At that time, according to Giovanni Paoletti, his philosophical corpus was already stabilized (Paoletti 2012: 50–55). Of course, one should not give a decisive importance to his teaching in the development of his scientific endeavor. Like his colleagues, he recycled a lot of existing material, particularly the "spiritualist" philosopher Paul Janet's standard textbook. However, some elements deserve to be noted, as they will orient the following works. First, philosophy is no longer able to account for the synthesis or the unity of sciences, as in Comte or Spencer's architectonic constructions. This will be one of the key issues in *The Division of Labor in Society*. Philosophy is far too abstract and too general to deal with the recent growth of scientific invention. His critique of the French philosophical teaching is predicated on the obsolescence of its synthesizing properties. Fighting against abstractions or "generalities" is seen as a necessary task (Fabiani 2003). The main target here is Victor Cousin's eclecticism,[1] a kind of empty Hegelianism aiming at reconciling every theory in a noncontradictory world of ideas. The taste for "general views" is an epistemological obstacle to the development of sociology. In fact, particularly at an early stage of scientific development, sociology is unable to come up with easy generalizations. This is the reason why, according to Durkheim, one can consider that Antoine-Augustin Cournot, Gabriel Tarde, and Georg Simmel produce a form of impressionistic literature. However, in the Sens lectures, he does not condemn philosophy as such for its taste for uncontrolled or arbitrary metaphors. There is something to be saved, even in metaphysics, that can be serious and healthy: it keeps a regulatory function, indicating the limits of science and setting an agenda for the definition of problems. Here, he is close to Kant's critique, one of the main sources of his philosophical background. Metaphysics envisages the complexity of reality and is able to raise problems concerning it, but not to solve them. In the Sens lectures, some problems are listed: the soul, the body, God (Paoletti 2012: 33). Thus, one cannot consider Durkheim as an anti-metaphysician. Metaphysics set some limits, as the science of problems, but sociology must, in turn, set the limits of metaphysics in its fallible quest for substances. As a high-school teacher, Durkheim constantly warned his pupils against the temptation of substantialism.

As the founder of a new science based on the experimental method, Durkheim had to distinguish himself radically from philosophy, while remaining in the philosophical field on a full-time basis. The tension was extremely productive; it allows us to understand the sociologist's trajectory in the field, considered, in the Bourdieuan tradition, as a positional space (Bourdieu 1988; Fabiani 1988). Durkheim belonged to a group of new contenders, very often of provincial origins, provided with some amount of cultural capital. Their fathers were often primary school teachers or low-ranking civil servants. They were the most visible product of the new republican educational system, having entered the *Ecole normale supérieure* or having passed the *agrégation* at a high emotional and cognitive cost. Quite a few of them experienced bouts of depression after their success: it was the price to pay for scholarly achievement. Lacking economic and social capital, they relied only on the educational public institution to get recognition. They believed in its reconstruction and its reorientation toward more scientific thinking. Even the philosophers in charge of the new administration of education (then named *Instruction publique*) were convinced that philosophical teaching had to be reformed and modernized in order to account for the new cognitive and political environment. One can evoke at this point the cases of Louis Liard, Elie Rabier, and Ferdinand Buisson, renowned philosophers who planned successive reforms of the curriculum. All those newcomers had a very high sense of their legitimate ambitions, either as dedicated bureaucrats or as intellectual innovators. The aim was never to get rid of philosophy, but to reorient it in the direction of a new scientific development and a new form of rationalism, compatible with republican ideals. Durkheim's multiple remarks on the respective territory of philosophy and sociology must be analyzed as emerging within a specific *field* (see Bourdieu 1988 for an application of this concept to conflicts within academia): in order to gain a semiautonomous place, sociology had to shrink the space traditionally devoted to philosophy and to challenge the incumbent discipline. The new contenders fought against young bourgeois Parisians, provided with economic capital and social connections, such as Xavier Léon and Elie Halévy, cofounders of the *Revue de métaphysique et de morale*, who were skeptical, at best, about the promises of the new social sciences and devoted to restore metaphysics in an innovative way. Of course, field analysis has its shortcomings. One should not envisage a dichotomy between the two main groups of philosophers. In their inaugural address, the founders of the *Revue de métaphysique et de morale* claimed their commitment to the "vacillating little flame of reason" (*Revue de métaphysique et de morale* 1893: 3). Philosophers of the time were intensely connected: Durkheim presented his work at the *Société française de philosophie*, a professional association created in 1901 in order to strengthen links within the community. He attended many sessions of the *Société* (Baciocchi and Fabiani 2012), at least more than some dedicated metaphysicians.

Durkheim's early work, in spite of its incontestable inscription within the philosophical field, was not well received by his peers. The dissertation committee, composed of top-notch French philosophers of the time (Émile Boutroux, Paul Janet, Victor Brochard, Gabriel Séailles, Henri Marion, and Charles Waddington), mixing old "spiritualistes" and new leaders of the Sorbonne faculty, was quite reluctant to recognize its merits. "Your thesis is not sophisticated enough to have an effect on morality," Henri Marion said during a very tense defense. "It is a thesis on the physics of morals" (Fournier 2013: 154). The jury doubted the philosophical nature of Durkheim's endeavor, as did some reviewers. Tarde remarked that philosophy was drowned in the huge wasteland (*friche*) of the sociological field (Paoletti 2012: 60). This lack of recognition pushed Durkheim to adopt a more offensive position against the philosophical institution. In 1895, he replied twice to his philosophical opponents. The first was a quite elaborate critique of the traditional French philosophical teaching: it tended to ignore science, particularly in its recent developments. It expressed a love for vague generalities and substances (Durkheim 1895). It favored pupils' literary vision of the world and their quest for vain originality. It appeared as the consequence of a phenomenon of inertia in the educational system, Victor Cousin's inconclusive eclecticism having survived its own conditions of emergence. The article published in the *Revue philosophique* was a brilliant attempt to sketch a sociology of teaching contents, but it stirred a revolt among many French philosophers. They saw his critical comments as a fierce attack against the very existence of philosophy in the educational system, developing a sort of philosophical paranoia promised to a great success in the twentieth century. Devoid of any content and even ideological function, philosophy teaching became a mere formal exercise, Durkheim thought. This led philosophers to consider science as an "impediment" more than an object of study (Fabiani 1985). The sociologist blamed the game of distinction involved in philosophy teaching, which gave a privilege to brio, a quality less seen among the provincial newcomers than among their Parisian counterparts. Durkheim never advocated the suppression of philosophical teaching in secondary schools. On the contrary, he praised its capacity to prepare for social life. He just asked for a more science-oriented curriculum and for a less impressionistic and virtuoso mode of teaching. However, most philosophers did not like the sociologist's critical analysis. The editors of the *Revue de métaphysique et de morale* reacted promptly. They considered that the article was an example of the worst type of positivist reductionism. They saw in it a threat to the very existence of their discipline. They ended their answer by saying that "having M. Durkheim as an ally was dangerous" (*Revue de métaphysique et de morale* 1895: 232).

Durkheim's second reaction to his lack of recognition by philosophers occurred in 1895, too, at the core of his methodological manifesto, *The Rules of Sociological Method*. There, he claimed the total independence of sociology, although it might still contribute to provide philosophy with original material. The autonomy of the new science is predicated on the application of the principle of causality to social facts, which had been contested by Boutroux during the defense of *The Division of Labor*. The reception of the *Rules* was even harsher than the sharp criticisms that he had received for the dissertation. Philosophers blamed the "blind algebra" of the book or considered it as "dead letter," according to Lucien Herr, the socialist librarian at the *Ecole normale supérieure*, mentor of cohorts of young philosophers. It seemed that Durkheim was then estranged from his peers. He was put in a separate world. Philosophers turned the anti-substantialist argument against Durkheim himself: his social facts were the hypostasis of an ensemble of heterogeneous elements. At that stage, one could predict an unhappy divorce between Durkheim and philosophy. The autonomy of his endeavor was denied; his scientific ambition was ridiculed. The default of recognition undoubtedly humiliated him. At some point, he was tempted to apply his analysis of obsolete philosophical teaching to any type of philosophy, blaming the "abstract dissertations of philosophers who legislate every day on sociological method without having ever encountered social facts" (Durkheim [1900] 1970: 134).

In the years that followed 1895, Durkheim strove to consolidate his position as a scientist, moving away from philosophical controversy. He published *Suicide* in 1897. The book, however severely criticized, appeared instantly as the flagship of a new science based on a solid production of evidence. The author showed that the most private and psychological of human actions could be treated as a social fact, according to *The Rules of Sociological Method*. In the book, competitor sociologists were targeted more than philosophers. A sociological field was under construction. Durkheim had to fight with academic weapons to win over competitors such as René Worms, who launched the first sociology journal in 1893 (*Revue internationale de sociologie*) and the first French and international sociological association. "The sociological landscape suddenly looked quite different," Johan Heilbron writes (Heilbron 2015: 78). Durkheim did not want to compromise with dubious partners: he wanted to keep a monopoly over the new science. Sociology had to be distinguished from mundane endeavors. As it was much in fashion in the last decade of the nineteenth century (Mosbah-Natanson 2017), Durkheim decided to take an austere turn: "We believe, on the contrary, that the time has come for sociology to renounce worldly successes, so to speak, and take on the esoteric character which befits all science. Thus it will gain in dignity and authority what it will perhaps lose in popularity" (Durkheim [1895] 1982: 163). Tarde was the second target, as chapter I.4 in *Suicide* (Durkheim [1897] 2006), debunking imitation as an explanatory tool, has shown. By extending psychological observations to an allegedly nomothetic science of social relations, the author of *The Laws of Imitation* (1890) totally missed the point: he was unable to construct an autonomous science. Demarcating sharply sociology from psychology was thus a foremost endeavor: sometimes it led Durkheim to overlook individual dynamics in the construction of social facts.

Durkheim pursued simultaneously two goals: first, he established a firm demarcation line between philosophy and sociology, guaranteeing the full autonomy of the latter. Second, he benefited from his full membership in the philosophical institution to distinguish between the amateurs or even the "jokers" (a nickname he gave to Worms in his correspondence) and the professionals, that is, the Durkheimians, provided with full-fledged academic resources and, for most of them at an early stage of the existence of the group, with the prestige of philosophical training. Durkheim's necessary ambivalence permits us to avoid the oversimplification generated by strict disciplinary oppositions, particularly when disciplines have no institutional existence. He belonged to two partly interconnected worlds, academic philosophy and nascent sociology. Competition in the emerging field led him to use resources accumulated in the established one to sustain his own project. The creation of the *Année sociologique* in 1898 was another step toward the autonomization of sociology. Although he went on publishing in philosophy journals, he did not have to rely on them to develop his own endeavor any longer. He could compete with historians, in terms of erudition applied to social facts, and attract some of them. His lectures on the educational system, presented in 1904/1905 and unpublished before his death, increased his scientific legitimacy as he showed that he was able to take up philosophical and historical topics and treat them in a radically new way. *The Evolution of Educational Thought in France* (Durkheim [1938] 2009) was a brilliant lesson taught to historians. Durkheim identified different types and paces of temporality. Academic temporality was not analogous to the economic one: universities can be characterized by the intense activity of past elements in the present. A high level of inertia could characterize the educational system, as specific social features remained active long after their historical conditions of production had disappeared. This is not necessarily a mark of backwardness. The weight of the past is not always a handicap: specific levels of inertia may condition the relative autonomy of different spheres of activities. The relationship between spheres can be either synchronized or desynchronized, the second one being a potential source of social pathology. In *Moral Education* (Durkheim [1925] 1961), Durkheim distanced himself both from philosophy and from pedagogy, circumscribing the perimeter of a new form of sociological knowledge. Sociology constitutes its own disciplinary domain and its specific mode of knowledge production by debunking the illusions of philosophy. With respect to education, Kant and J. S. Mill fell into a trap, Durkheim wrote. They postulated that there was an ideal, perfect education that was relevant for all human beings in history. This abstraction is a fiction, since goals and modes of education have varied considerably throughout history. However, sociology is not a practical knowledge, such as pedagogy: it does not aim to offer a toolkit to improve schooling techniques. It is a theoretical endeavor of its own. Moral education is the object of its autonomous inquiry, although the study of morality traditionally belongs to philosophy. In this respect, sociology is a form of *Aufhebung* of philosophy.

If Durkheim never left the philosophical field, it is partly because he did not have the means, even at the acme of his career, to establish a sociological institution. He depended on philosophical resources to survive in academia and to increase his capital. However, the link to philosophy remained intense, since he shared with his fellow philosophers a common socialization, while he was not directly their competitor: his real enemies were would-be sociologists. The historians of academic disciplines have often neglected this complex imbrication.[2] In order to clarify the situation, one has to pay some attention to the philosophical sources of the republican idea, shared by all the members of the academic philosophical field. The idea appears as a paradoxical mix of two intellectual trends. The first one is the posthumous reconstruction of Auguste Comte's legacy. The second one is the neo-Kantian rationalism proposed by Charles Renouvier. Both thinkers remained outside the academic world, but they became foremost references in the reorientation of republican philosophy. One can be astonished to see Comte as a republican, since he developed some sort of counterrevolutionary theory. The reference to Comte was clearly reconstructed, particularly by Jules Ferry, according to the needs of republican ideology. His philosophical legacy appears in his epistemologically centered vision of the world. Although Durkheim dismissed his sociology as a prescientific attempt, he acknowledged his pedagogical usefulness (Fabiani 2002). Comte became the name for a republican pedagogy in which education and the development of knowledge institutions play a central role in the political project. Rational pedagogy is the main condition for the reconstitution of a cohesive society. More than his written work, Comte's figure became synonymous with the secularization of thought and of the sheer political efficiency of knowledge production and diffusion. When Foucault defined Comte as the point of departure of the French philosophy of concept, contrasting him to Maine de Biran and the philosophy of subject (Foucault 1985), he clearly defined a mix of scientific ambition and social commitment. At the beginning of the twentieth century,

Durkheimian sociologists and neo-metaphysicians editing the *Revue de métaphysique et de morale*, in spite of the conflicts described earlier, shared a common belief. Through the intensive use of the term "morality," they envisaged the social efficiency of intellectual work as the extension of rationality in society. Comte and Kant's legacy contributes to what the historian Stéphan Soulié called the "voluntarism of the idea" (Soulié 2009: 13). This point defines the conjunction of a rationalist optimism that leads scholars to think that they play an essential role in the progressive secularization of society and of a penetrating illusion about the social efficiency of academic speech. *The Evolution of Educational Thought in France* is a case in point in this respect: Durkheim thought that lecturing the would-be teachers (the *agrégatifs*) on the history of the educational system would be sufficient to inculcate a "scientific pedagogy."

The other philosophical reference with respect to the republican idea is less ambiguous. Charles Renouvier was a dedicated republican. The "criticist" philosopher was a companion to all the attempts to install a republic, as early as 1848, when he wrote a *Manuel républicain de l'homme et du citoyen*. From 1870 on, he coined the notion of moral education that was to be reused in a quite different way by Durkheim. He defined the republic as "the regime of principles." He criticized the most radical forms of republicanism and invited his fellow citizens to retrieve the republican spirit against revolutionary illusions. Criticist philosophy had Kantian roots: it invited honesty and candor into politics, a powerful tradition in France, often hidden by the loud voice of the tribune of the people. Humble character of the republic, Renouvier played a major role in the study of Kant and its connection to a political project. He was a central figure for the administrators of the new regime who were seeking solid theoretical references as well as for the new generation of philosophers who wanted to get rid of the old eclectic and "spiritualiste" philosophy. Renouvier grounded the concept of authority in the social world on critical competency, thus associating republic and philosophy in a theoretical-political construction that is undoubtedly a French singularity. Durkheim acknowledged his debt to Renouvier, without quoting him very often. The old philosopher was a tutelary figure. The sociologist kept a portrait of him on his desk.

Thus, Durkheim was never an alien in the philosophical field. Of course, most philosophers could not accept the objectivist epistemology that he defended, and they were extremely reluctant to acknowledge the idea of collective representations, as grounded in the postulation of a "'group mind,' distinct from that of its members taken together" (Lukes 1985: 11). In fact, the sociologist's position was more nuanced, but he always left some ambiguity when defining the relationship between the individual and the collective.

> He repeatedly denied reifying or hypostasizing society and wrote that "there is nothing in social life that is not in individual *consciences*"; on the other hand, he did use terms such as "*conscience collective*" and "*l'âme collective*" and wrote of "that conscious being which is society . . . a *sui generis* being with its own special nature,

distinct from that of its members, and a personality of its own different from individual personalities."

(Lukes 1985: 11)

In 1898, Durkheim published an article in the *Revue de métaphysique et de morale*, "Représentations individuelles et représentations collectives," three years after the controversy on philosophy teaching. This proves that he wanted to be understood by his colleagues on a philosophical basis. Although the editors of the *Revue* could not accept that sociology should now be the motor of philosophical investigation, they still considered the author of *The Elementary Forms of Religious Life* as a legitimate interlocutor. Other forms of sociology, either too far from minimal academic requirements or too close to social and political conservatism, never got this privilege.[3] When he published in the *Revue* or presented at the *Société française de philosophie*, he never chose issues that would make explicit a clear antagonism between philosophy and sociology. On the contrary, he focused on topics closer to moral issues. It seems that this cleavage is one of the keys to understand Durkheim's ambivalent reception by the philosophers of his time. On the one hand, the rationalist commitment to a reconstruction of morality is largely accepted. On the other hand, methodological prescriptions and epistemological collectivism are clearly rejected.

If one compares the list of contributors to the *Revue de métaphysique et de morale* and to the *Revue philosophique*, supposedly more welcoming to the new social sciences until 1914, one can see that most members of the Durkheimian circle published equally in both journals. This is the case for the master but also for Halbwachs, Hubert, Mauss, and Davy. Bouglé is an exception: he wrote mostly in the *Revue de métaphysique et de morale*. Neither Gustave Lebon, the founder of crowd psychology, nor Alfred Binet, who imagined the first IQ test, published in that journal. This gives some evidence to the fact that all social scientists were not equal in terms of philosophical legitimacy. The strongest element of divergence between Durkheim and the editors of the *Revue* is related to the deep meaning of philosophy teaching within the new republic. It became a bone of contention during the years of curriculum reform from 1880 to 1902. What was at stake? The philosophers-administrators, such as Louis Liard, who proposed reforms, were convinced that the system needed a vigorous modernization and that the curriculum should be more solidly grounded on experimental science. In contrast, conservative intellectuals, particularly Catholics, defended the status quo and supported the teaching of philosophy as it was, although it had been initially designed as a tool of secularization. In order to understand the paradox, one must turn to Durkheim's analytical grid presented in *The Evolution of Educational Thought in France*: the Church was led to defend classical humanities, based on a non-Christian legacy, since it saw in it a powerful tool to consolidate its position. In turn, the "liberals" were inclined to endorse the opposite cause (Durkheim [1938] 2009: 354). At the turn of the century, the situation was much more complex: both conservatives, such as Charles Maurras, the founder of monarchist *Action française*, and committed republicans, such as Alphonse Darlu, Proust's philosophy teacher, defended traditional philosophy teaching on opposite grounds (Fabiani 1988). The editors of the *Revue* considered that Durkheim was an enemy of philosophy teaching in high schools. This was not because he had designed a counterproposal, but because he had analyzed in-depth the functioning of virtuoso philosophy, a theme that would be taken up again by Claude Lévi-Strauss in *Tristes Tropiques* (1955) and by Pierre Bourdieu in *The Political Ontology of Martin Heidegger* (1988).

Durkheim was never entirely clear when he presented his view on the relationship between philosophy and sociology. Surprisingly enough, he gave the boldest form of his imperialist sociological vision in the first introduction to *The Elementary Forms* to the *Revue de metaphysique et de morale*, published in 1909. In the published version of the book, the last section, devoted to the relation between philosophy and sociology, was omitted (Durkheim 1909). In the first version, he tried to dismiss the accusation of being an anti-philosopher. He decided to confront it directly. He claimed that he was not the representative of a "narrow empiricism" and that we should not abandon metaphysical questions, since they had survived in a very long history. He just wanted to renew them in the light of the new experimental science of sociology. Far from being a weapon of destruction, sociology should be the best ally of philosophy. The eternity of metaphysics is an empirical fact. It is inscribed in collective representations that historical sociology brings to light. This point of view does not guarantee the rights of *philosophia perennis*, since the observation shows a radical change in knowledge production, brought about by the division of labor. "Philosophy is, so to speak, the collective consciousness of science and here, as elsewhere, the role of the collective consciousness diminishes as labour become more divided up" (Durkheim [1893] 1997: 301). As the queen of the disciplines is confronted with the growing specialization of knowledge, it has two possibilities: either it becomes a pure literary game, or it bears on a positive science that opens a window on totality. It does not come as a surprise that sociology is the adequate knowledge. It is restricted enough to be mastered by a single mind, but in the meantime, it is a discipline devoted to totality, as it covers all the civilizational facts in history. Durkheim did not say anything about the rather miraculous association of small and big items in a single knowledge, the only one apt to cancel the effects of the division of labor. This miracle was made possible by the complete historicization of philosophical concepts that became mere manifestations of collective consciousness. Philosophy is no longer what resists historical change as perennial, but what expresses it. This is an unbelievable sociological power grab. The new discipline now defines the tasks of philosophy. "Philosophy may hope to perceive unity of things only if it situates itself at the level of collective spirit" (Durkheim 1909: 757, my translation). Sociology thus represents the only chance of survival for philosophy. Durkheim removed that last section from the published book, probably because he did not want to offend philosophy in a moment when he wanted to be fully recognized by his fellow philosophers. His statement was undoubtedly one of the most ostensive manifestations of sociological imperialism in history. Although it was congruent with the central part of *The Elementary Forms* (Durkheim [1912] 2003), devoted to bring to light the social origins of mental categories, one can understand that

Durkheim preferred not to rattle his sociological saber in 1912. A time of reconciliation had come.

The philosophical reception of *The Elementary Forms* was clearly positive, in spite of the full historicization of mental categories. The *Société française de philosophie* held a full session on the book. The harsh comments by the venerable Catholic philosopher Jules Lachelier were the sole exception. He said: "The God I am thinking of is not the one that is adored at crossroads and the religion I am talking about ignores the cults you are alluding to" (*Bulletin de la Société française de philosophie* 1913: 90, my translation). Alphonse Darlu praised "the force and beauty in the book" and Henri Delacroix, who taught philosophy of religion at the Sorbonne, said to the author that his book "seemed masterly to him." Durkheim's appraisal was not purely circumstantial. In an earlier session of the Society devoted to the determination of the moral fact, which was less consensual, some agreement was reached. Léon Brunschvicg could address the sociologist in these terms: "It seems to me that I am able to follow most of the theses that you have presented, but you will forgive me if I succumb to the temptation to translate my approval in my own language" (*Bulletin de la Société française de philosophie* 1906: 169–212, my translation). Philosophers considered Durkheim, contrary to many social scientists of the time, as a peer. His book appeared in a specific context. It was part of an ongoing debate on science and religion that crossed diverse segments of French intellectual life. Contrary to the common picture of a fully secularized French philosophy, the issue of religion remained central in the mind of philosophers (Fabiani 2010). French rationalism had to fight what they called the "new mysticism" and the "crisis of reason" in the public. Durkheim contributed to the rational approach to religion that he shared with most of the French academic philosophers of the time, with the notable exception of Bergson. He tried to go beyond the antinomies of philosophical rationalism too. Traditional rationalism cannot properly answer this question: "Is it possible to submit to the procedures of science the very categories of thought that are the condition of possibility for science?" as Giovanni Paoletti writes (Paoletti 2012: 266, my translation). Durkheim considered that all collective representations have a double function: on the one hand, if they exist, this means that they are "socially true" as they express a social need. A member of society spontaneously acknowledges that form of truth. On the other hand, they can be analyzed as representations, mental states, or speculative forms by an external observer, either philosopher or scientist. The superiority of the sociologist over the philosopher lies in the fact that she is able to grasp both sides of the representation, the pragmatic and the speculative. As shown by Paoletti, Durkheim drew heavily on neo-Kantian philosophy to make his point, but added some new elements. In order to solve the contradiction between the personal (or subjective) basis for certainty and its impersonal dimension, a sociological approach is necessary: the logical validity of collective representations must be related to the authority exerted by society on individuals (Paoletti 2012: 268). Commenting on his move, the sociologist locates himself in the Kantian tradition: "Thus logical necessity would be simply another form of moral necessity, and theoretical certainty only another form of practical certainty. In this we remain firmly in the Kantian tradition" (Durkheim 1983: 102). This attachment to Kantianism appears in full force in *The Elementary Forms*. Sociology is in many ways a prolongation of Kant's questions with answers based on the collective status of concepts and beliefs.

After the positive reception of *The Elementary Forms*, the lectures on *Pragmatism and Sociology*, given in 1913 at the Sorbonne, consecrated Durkheim as *the* academic sociologist. For the first time in French history, a chair was devoted to sociology. There is some irony about the fact that the first theme was a philosophical one. It proved the sociologist's attachment to philosophical issues. Marcel Mauss remarked that the lectures were his uncle's "philosophical crowning," a note that shows the ambivalence of the situation. Although he considered that sociology and pragmatism was a question of either/or (the victory of the latter could destroy the former), Durkheim recognized, as he had already done in the *Forms*, the incontestable merits of the new Anglophone philosophy. In the first decade of the twentieth century, pragmatism became a hot issue, not only as a US import but also as an international philosophical revolution. As the founder of a new science, he had to position himself in the debate inaugurated by the rise of pragmatism, all the more since he had used as a strategic tool some insights of William James in his book on religion.[4] Being a foreign philosophy, pragmatism was easy to criticize and even to dismiss. Durkheim never did it, contrary to many French philosophers who were very hostile from the start. Pragmatism was a useful tool to secure Durkheim's theory, as it allowed conceptualizing the dimension of practice contained in collective representations (Baciocchi and Fabiani 2012: 27). On the one hand, pragmatism has a great capacity to identify changes in experiences and emotional diversity. On the other hand, it is very deficient when it comes to accounting for stability and regularity. Religion is an ideal object to study practice: every symbol must be put into practice if we want it to be efficient. In turn, the primacy of practice, as it exists in James's work, is a defeat of reason. Pure pragmatism is a death threat to rationalism, but some borrowings from its analysis of practice may extend rationalism and free it from the limitations of pure speculation. The term "effervescence" symbolizes the importance of performance in the display of symbols as well as in the constitution of belief: it remained largely undefined by Durkheim and led to the suspicion of irrationalism or, even worse, to a form of acquaintance with crowd psychology. The Jamesian approach to religious experience was a necessary step to understand the practical dimension of belief. This did not mean that the impressions of the faithful and the concept of religion were identical. There is no such thing as a pragmatic turn in Durkheim's later work. However, the theme of the nonillusory dimension of religion, attested by the dynamogenic aspect of religious performance, owes much to the active reading of Anglo-American pragmatism.

Quite a few readers saw, and still see, a new Durkheim appearing in *The Elementary Forms*, a thinker more interested in spiritual issues, undoubtedly more palatable to his contemporary philosophers. Reading together that book and the lectures on pragmatism leads to a different point of view. He never renounced to build an autonomous science, but he refined his tools along time. The *Forms* do not show any return to philosophy, but an improvement of the sociologist's toolkit. One can say largely that they radicalize the program of *The Rules of Sociological Method* (treating social facts as things) by "grasping facts as closely as possible," as Durkheim notes in his inaugural lecture on pragmatism in 1913 (see Baciocchi and Fabiani 2012: 33). This point is undoubtedly an opening toward a genuine sociological grasp of social reality that would be no longer dependent on philosophical concepts. One can see in the reemerging of the old conceptual pair mechanic/organic in the lectures on pragmatism a new way of distinguishing between philosophy and sociology. What he called mythological truth is definitely on the mechanical side. It is consensual, exegetic, and perennial, like academic philosophy. In contrast, scientific truth is on the organic side, not based on a social consensus, based on facts, and historical. Sociology is portrayed as the science in an age of complex division of labor. Durkheim did not elaborate much on the dichotomy, but it is not impossible to see in it the will to supersede traditional forms of philosophical problematizations, which he had to use in the course of his scientific program.

During his lifetime, Durkheim did not move from crude positivism to a form of spiritualist idealism. The illusion that such a change did happen is largely due to his many tactical moves. Properly speaking, he had to navigate between the philosophical field, from which he owned his credentials and his reputation, and an as-yet undefined zone of sociology, where he had to compete with amateurs, jokers, ideologists, and dubious specialists of curiosa. What is striking is his steadiness: he never abandoned a strong commitment to rationalism, although he had to adapt it in his later work to the analysis of practice and performance. Susan Stedman Jones is right when she pictures him as "a rationalist interested in the complex historical becoming of society" (Jones 2001: 218). He shared this orientation with many of his fellow philosophers, educated in an atmosphere of neo-Kantianism in part inspired by Renouvier. Nevertheless, he tried to go beyond the limits of pure philosophical rationalism. He tried particularly to integrate the issue of meaning in his theoretical framework and, contrary to Max Weber, was not much credited for it. He was certain from the start that his mission interlaced a scientific program and a moral imperative. He considered that historical processes were central in the configuration of society. Overall, he was much more complex than the caricature that depicts him as a rigid, narrow-minded, and positivist type of anti-philosopher. He wrote once to his disciple, Georges Davy, who owns a great responsibility in the success of the theme of his return to philosophy: "Having started from philosophy, I tend to come back to it, or, rather, I was naturally taken back to it by the nature of the questions that I encountered on my road" (Davy 1960: 10, my translation). We have seen that his partial return was not a regression. Studying religion as practice demanded a new type of philosophical investigation. Beside his constant tactical moves to ensure symbolic resources for his bold endeavor, he never changed direction. As Giovanni Paoletti (2012: 395–399) brilliantly shows, Durkheim never left aside his philosophical equipment, although he wanted to objectify and historicize it. In doing so, he moved from institutional tactics to conceptual strategy. At the beginning of his career he relied heavily on conceptual pairs inherited from philosophy. Steven Lukes's introduction to his unsurpassable biography draws a complete list of those pairs, starting with the social/individual and the sacred/profane oppositions (Lukes 1985: 16–30). Later in his life, he tried to get closer to a genuine grasp of social facts that would make smart use of pragmatism.

Durkheim was a great reader of ancient and modern philosophy. He participated in the main conceptual debates of his time with a great boldness and sometimes some peculiar ways of reasoning. Here again, it is not difficult for Lukes to list a set of questionable practices: *petitio principii*, argument by elimination, high-handed way with evidence (Lukes 1985: 31–34). His attitude can be analyzed in terms of "combat epistemology," a term used to define Bourdieu's conceptual fights (Fabiani 2015). When fighting, one does not have necessarily the choice of arms. Durkheim was a fighter who fought for a cause. He identified it very early, and never changed his mind about it: founding a new type of science equipped to deal with the complexity of the division of labor and the new social pathologies; reanimating philosophy by plugging its concepts in the analysis of social facts.

Notes

1. Victor Cousin (1792–1867) was one of the most famous French philosophers of the first half of the nineteenth century. He developed a theory based on eclecticism (taking the best of diverse authors in the canon) and became famous for his "spiritualisme" directed against Enlightenment materialism.
2. The best recent book on French sociology (Heilbron 2015) is a good example. Here, the claim of Durkheim's proximity to philosophy is seen as a posthumous reinscription that has been performed by non innovative disciples (Heilbron 2015: 103–104).
3. Frédéric Le Play's disciples are a good example. Le Play (1806–1882) was a pioneer in empirical research (*The European Workers*, 1855) and had many followers. However, his deep Catholicism and his incapacity to construct a theory made his work unpalatable for the republican philosophers.
4. In the conclusion of *The Elementary Forms of Religious Life*, Durkheim acknowledged the reality of the "religious experience" analyzed by William James in *The Varieties of Religious Experience*.

References

Baciocchi, Stéphane, and Jean-Louis Fabiani. 2012. "Durkheim's Lost Argument (1895–1955): Critical Moves on Method and Truth." *Durkheimian Studies* 18: 19–40.
Bourdieu, Pierre. (1984) 1988. *Homo Academicus*. Stanford, CA: Stanford University Press.
Callegaro, Francesco. 2015. *La science politique des modernes. Durkheim, la sociologie et le projet d'autonomie*. Paris: Economica.
Davy, Georges. 1960. "Emile Durkheim." *Revue française de sociologie* 1: 3–24.
Durkheim, Émile. 1895. "L'enseignement philosophique et l'agrégation de philosophie." *Revue philosophique de la France et de l'étranger* 39: 121–147.
Durkheim, Émile. 1898. "Représentations individuelles et représentations collectives." *Revue de métaphysique et de morale* 6: 273–302.
Durkheim, Émile. (1900) 1970. "La sociologie en France au XIXe siècle." In *La science sociale et l'action*, 118–141. Paris: PUF.

Durkheim, Émile. 1909. "Sociologie religieuse et théorie de la connaissance." *Revue de métaphysique et de morale* 17: 733–758.
Durkheim, Émile. (1925) 1961. *Moral Education: A Study in the Theory and Application of the Sociology of Education*. Translated by E. K. Wilson and H. Schnurer. New York: Free Press.
Durkheim, Émile. (1895) 1982. *The Rules of Sociological Method and Selected Texts on Sociology and Its Method*. Edited by Steven Lukes. London: Macmillan.
Durkheim, Émile. (1955) 1983. *Pragmatism and Sociology*. Edited by John B. Allcock. Cambridge: Cambridge University Press.
Durkheim, Émile. (1893) 1997. *The Division of Labor in Society*. Translated by W. D. Halls. New York: Free Press.
Durkheim, Émile. (1912) 2003. *The Elementary Forms of Religious Life*. Oxford: Oxford University Press.
Durkheim, Émile. (1897) 2006. *On Suicide*. Translated by Robin Buss. London: Penguin Books.
Durkheim, Émile. (1938) 2009. *The Evolution of Educational Thought: Lectures on the Formation and Development of Secondary Education in France* (Selected Writings on Education, vol. 2). London: Routledge.
Durkheim, Émile. 2011. *Durkheim's Philosophy Lectures: Notes from the Lycée de Sens Course, 1883–1884*. Edited by Neil Gross and Robert Alun Jones. Cambridge: Cambridge University Press.
Fabiani, Jean-Louis. 1985. "Enjeux et usages de la 'crise' dans la philosophie universitaire en France au tournant du siècle." *Annales. Economies, sociétés, civilisations* 40, no. 2: 377–409.
Fabiani, Jean-Louis. 1988. *Les philosophes de la République*. Paris: Editions de Minuit.
Fabiani, Jean-Louis. 2002. "Philosophie." In *Dictionnaire critique de la République*, edited by Vincent Duclert and Christophe Prochasson, 936–943. Paris: Flammarion.
Fabiani, Jean-Louis. 2003. "Clore enfin l'ère des généralités." In Émile Durkheim, *L'évaluation en comité: Textes et rapports de souscription au Comité des travaux historiques et scientifiques 1903–1917*, edited by Stéphane Baciocchi and Jennifer Mergy, 151–189. Oxford: Berghahn Books.
Fabiani, Jean-Louis. 2010. *Qu'est-ce qu'un philosophe français? La vie sociale des concepts (1880–1980)*. Paris: Editions de l'Ecole des hautes études en sciences sociales.
Fabiani, Jean-Louis. 2015. *La sociologie comme elle s'écrit: De Bourdieu à Latour*. Paris: Editions de l'Ecole des hautes études en sciences sociales.
Foucault, Michel. 1985. "La vie: L'expérience et la science." *Revue de métaphysique et de morale* 90, no. 1: 3–14.
Foucault, Michel. (1994) 2001. *Dits et écrits*. Vol. 1. Paris: Gallimard.
Fournier, Marcel. 2013. *Emile Durkheim: A Biography*. Cambridge: Polity Press.
Heilbron, Johan. 2015. *French Sociology*. Ithaca, NY: Cornell University Press.
Jones, Susan Stedman. 2001. *Durkheim Reconsidered*. London: Polity Press.
Karsenti, Bruno. 2006. *La société en personnes. Etudes durkheimiennes*. Paris: Economica.
Lukes, Steven. (1973) 1985. *Emile Durkheim: His Life and Work. A Historical and Critical Study*. Stanford, CA: Stanford University Press.
Mosbah-Natanson, Sébastien. 2017. *Une "mode" de la sociologie. Publications et vocations sociologiques en France en 1900*. Paris: Garnier.

Paoletti, Giovanni. 2012. *Durkheim et la philosophie. Représentation, réalité et lien social*. Paris: Garnier.

Rawls, Anne Warfield. 2005. *Epistemology and Practice: Durkheim's The Elementary Forms of Religious Life*. Cambridge: Cambridge University Press.

Sartre, Jean-Paul. 1947. *Situations 1: Critiques littéraires*. Paris: Gallimard.

Soulié, Stéphan. 2009. *Les philosophes en République. L'aventure intellectuelle de la* Revue de métaphysique et de morale *et de la Société française de philosophie (1891–1914)*. Rennes: Presses universitaires de Rennes.

CHAPTER 9

DURKHEIM'S TEAM
L'Année sociologique

MARCEL FOURNIER AND PAUL CARLS

DURKHEIM had a team of researchers who, strictly speaking, were his disciples. Many members of this team were collaborators on the journal *L'Année sociologique*, while others belonged to the network of this group of collaborators or had intellectual affinities with Durkheim. For example, Lucien Lévy-Bruhl, author of the book *La Morale et la sciences des moeurs* (1903), was a friend and colleague of Durkheim at the Sorbonne and close to Durkheim's disciples, but never collaborated with *L'Année sociologique*. Other scholars published articles in the journal but were not part of the group. For example, Henri Muffang (born in 1864), a colleague of Célestin Bouglé at the Lycée de Saint Brieuc, an *agrégé* in grammar, and a close follower of the German anthropologist Otto Ammon and the French anthropologist Georges Vacher de Lapouge, was excluded for being too close to anthroposociology, a form of racial anthropology that postulated a causal link between the physiology (i.e., the shape of the skull) and the psychosociology of racial groups. Gaston Richard ([1860] 1945) was a member of the first group of collaborators and responsible for the section on criminology, but he maintained a critical distance from Durkheim.

L'Année sociologique was founded in 1896, with the first volume published in 1898. This volume was the first in a series of twelve to be published under the direction of Durkheim. The second series of just two volumes (1925 and 1927) was published after World War I under the direction of Marcel Mauss (1872–1950).

The founder of the journal was Durkheim, but it would seem that Célestin Bouglé (1870–1940), a young *agrégé* in philosophy, was the one to have the idea. Upon his return from Germany in 1896, about which he (like Durkheim before him) wrote a report ("Les sciences sociales en Allemagne," 1896), he suggested launching an international journal to promote sociology. The publisher of the journal was Alcan, a major publishing house that published books and journals (*Revue historique*, *Revue philosophique*) in the social sciences and humanities. Durkheim debated the general orientation of the journal with Bouglé; the issue was the distinction between sociology and psychology. Durkheim agreed to define sociology as a form of psychology, but a specific one, that is, collective psychology (Besnard 1979). He succeeded in convincing Bouglé, who played an important role in bringing the team together and involving his friends Paul Lapie (1869–1927) and Dominique Parodi (1870–1955), both *agrégés* in philosophy, and colleague Henri Muffang in the project. Gaston Richard, an *agrégé* in philosophy who wrote his doctoral thesis on the origin of law (*Essai sur l'origine du droit*, 1892) and was one of Durkheim's colleagues at Bordeaux, also agreed to participate.

Émile Durkheim also succeeded in involving his nephew, Marcel Mauss, then a young *agrégé* in philosophy and a student in the history of religion at the École pratique des hautes études: "It's true that there don't need to be many of us [...] The fact that there are two of us is enough to make us stand out" (Durkheim [1897] 1998b: 81; trans. Macey 2013: 270). Mauss's job was to convince some of his friends, many of whom were also *agrégés*, to take part in the adventure and become sociologists: Henri Hubert (1872–1927), an *agrégé* in history with an interest in religion and archeology who was very close to Mauss and worked as his colleague at the École pratique des hautes études; Paul Fauconnet (1874–1938), an *agrégé* in philosophy with an interest in ethics who was part of the same class as Mauss and who published important introductory works to sociology with Mauss ("Sociologie," 1900) and Durkheim ("Sociologie et sciences sociales," 1903); Emmanuel Lévy (1871–1943), who had a doctorate in law and was interested in sociology; Albert Milhaud (1871–1955), an *agrégé* in history with an interest in economic sociology. The "top brass" of the team, and among the most active collaborators, included Bouglé, Fauconnet, Hubert, Mauss, and François Simiand (1873–1935). The latter was an *agrégé* in philosophy who wrote a yearly review of sociology publications in the *Revue de métaphysique et de la morale*, where he wrote a review of Durkheim's *Suicide* in 1897. Simiand was also, with Hubert and Mauss, close to the socialist librarian Lucien Herr at the École normale supérieure.

Simiand also had close connections to the Bourgin brothers, Hubert (1874–1955) and Gérard (1879–1958). Hubert was an *agrégé* in literature and held doctorates in literature and in law; his law thesis discussed the butcher industry in Paris and inspired one of his essays for *L'Année sociologique* ("Essai sur une forme d'industrie: la boucherie à Paris au XIXe siècle," 1903). Gérard had a double *licence* in law and literature, was an archivist, and was not a frequent contributor to *L'Année*. The Bourgin brothers were both active in the socialist and trade union movements.

The new journal had two parts: a first part consisting of two or three essays: the "Mémoires" in the first volume were a translation of Georg Simmel's paper, "The Persistence of Social Groups" ([1896] 1898), and an original paper by Durkheim, "Incest: The Nature and Origin of the Taboo" ([1898] 1963); and a second part with book reviews. According to Durkheim, it was the journal's "mission" to describe the "current state of literature" in the social sciences. He introduced a division of labor between his collaborators, giving each of them responsibility for sections of reviews. In the first issue of *L'Année*, these were as follows: General Sociology (Bouglé), Religious Sociology (Mauss and Hubert), Moral Sociology & Sociology of Law (Lapie, Lévy, Durkheim, Mauss), Criminal Sociology (Richard), Economic Sociology (Simiand),

Demography (Fauconnet), and miscellaneous (Muffang, Durkheim, Fauconnet, and Parodi).

The index to the journal contains a wide range of entries: crime and criminality, economy, education, sanctions and responsibilities, religion, women, suicide, the city, and so on. But it also includes entries on family, kinship, marriage, and sexuality (especially incest and prostitution). Over the following years, other themes related to religion took on more and more importance: belief, cult, God, dogma, church, ritual, fetishism, sacrifice, magic, myth, superstition, taboo, and totem. Such were the subjects that established Durkheim's program; at the Sorbonne, where Durkheim was elected professor in 1902, the nickname of his research group was "the totem-taboo clan."

Mauss and Hubert were the two pillars of the team. They were close friends, both born in 1872, both *agrégés*, both students of the India specialist Sylvain Lévi at the École pratique des hautes études and a few years later, both directors of studies at the same École pratique; they were "siamese brothers" and "working twins" (Mauss 1927). The story of *L'Année sociologique* was, from the beginning, to be the story of a family and a group of friends.

"Religious Sociology" and "Moral Sociology & Sociology of Law" were the two largest sections of *L'Année sociologique*. Hubert and Mauss were the coeditors of the Religious Sociology section; they published together in the second volume of the journal their first scientific paper, "Sacrifice: Its Nature and Function" ([1899] 1964). Durkheim published his article, "Concerning the Definition of Religious Phenomena" ([1899] 1975a), in the same volume, "because that is the only way to demonstrate in general terms that religion is something sociological [...] So it would not be a bad idea to show how, in general terms and in what sense, there is such a thing as a sociology of religion [...] My article will simply emphasize the social character of religious phenomena and show how private manifestations of religion are not central to it" (Durkheim [1898] 1998c: 108).[1]

Several years later, Hubert and Mauss penned another article, "A General Theory of Magic" ([1904] 1972), with a central reference to the notion of "mana." Hubert was at the time working with Isidore Lévy, an Orientalist and colleague at the École pratique des hautes études, on the major project of translating Pierre Daniel Chantepie de la Saussaye's handbook on the history of religions into French, for which he wrote a long introduction that was, according to Mauss, a "real manifesto [...] a persuasive defense of sociology's right to study all manifestations of religious life" (Mauss [1905] 1968: 177).[2] For Hubert, the notion of the sacred is the driving idea behind religion, which he defines as "the administration of the sacred" (Hubert 1904: xlvii).[3]

After the founding of *L'Année sociologique*, other prominent researchers would later join the team. Maurice Halbwachs (1877–1945), who received his *agrégation* in philosophy in 1901, joined in 1905 after meeting Durkheim and developing an interest in sociology. He was responsible for the sections on economic sociology and demography. Robert Hertz (1881–1915) received his *agrégation* in philosophy in 1904 and shortly thereafter began writing his doctoral thesis with Durkheim. He published especially on themes related to religion. Like Halbwachs and Hertz, Georges Davy (1883–1976) was an *agrégé* in philosophy, and he was also one of Durkheim's students; he took classes at the

École pratique des hautes études with Mauss as well. He published a number of works on the sociology of Durkheim, although he completed his doctoral thesis, *La Foi jurée*, only in 1922. Philologist, historian, and linguist Antoine Meillet (1866–1937) also contributed to *L'Année sociologique* beginning in 1902. He was a former student of Ferdinand de Saussure, an *agrégé* in grammar, and completed a doctorate in linguistics in 1897. In the 1890s he taught at the École pratique des hautes études, where he was one of Mauss's professors. The two would subsequently develop a close relationship.

L'Année's first series was the work of a real research laboratory, with not only collaborations between members—Durkheim and Mauss ("Primitive Classification"), Mauss and Hubert ("Sacrifice")—but also intense debates. The almost fifty collaborators published more than 2,800 book reviews.[4] Some of them contributed to all the volumes (Durkheim, Mauss, Hubert, Simiand), others to several volumes, and others to just one. Twenty-one essays (*Mémoires*) were published, mainly written by the "members" of the team, and only three were written by non-French scholars (Georg Simmel, Friedrich Ratzel, and Sebald Rudolf Steinmetz). According to Durkheim, "We will only be satisfied with articles that we write ourselves" (Durkheim [1900] 1976).[5] Durkheim, Mauss, and Hubert were the authors of a total of nine essays. The themes included totemism, magic, and religion but also economic sociology (François Simiand, Hubert Bourgin), language (Meillet), social crisis and criminality (Gaston Richard), the division of labor (Célestin Bouglé), and the caste system in India (Célestin Bouglé). *L'Année* also published Robert Hertz's essay, "A Contribution to the Study of the Collective Representation of Death" ([1907] 1960a).

The *Année*'s contributors came from different disciplines (philosophy, philology, archeology, and history, geography, linguistics, etc.). Durkheim held a central position, but there were different networks: Bouglé, Lapie, and Parodi; Simiand, Halbwachs, and the Bourgin brothers; Mauss, Hubert, and their students. It is possible to identify three generations: (1) the elders (born before 1860), including Durkheim, Richard, and colleagues (Meillet, Moret); (2) the generation born between 1870 and 1880, including the students of Durkheim at Bordeaux (Abel Aubin, Marcel Foucault, Jean-Paul Hourticq, Charles Lalo) and his nephew Marcel Mauss and his friends (Hubert, Fauconnet, Simiand); and (3) the generation of younger scholars, including students of Mauss and Hubert at the École pratique des hautes études (Henri Beuchat, Maxime David, Georges Davy, Louis Gernet, Robert Hertz, Henri Jeanmaire, Philippe de Felice, Jean-Paul Lafitte, Jean Marx, Jean-Pierre Reynier, Pierre Roussel).

Far from forming a homogeneous group, *L'Année sociologique*'s early contributors belonged to different circles or subgroups. On the one hand, there were the "teachers" (Bouglé, Lapie, Parodi, Richard, and Fauconnet), and on the other, the "researchers" (Mauss, Hubert, and Simiand). The first group largely began their careers at *Lycées* (high schools) before moving to universities once they had completed their doctorates, with some pursuing administrative positions as well. The second group also taught, but it did so in specialized institutions that were less prestigious, such as the École pratique des hautes études for Mauss or the Conservatoire des arts et des métiers for Simiand. Some from this group, such as Meillet, Mauss, and Simiand, moved on to take positions at the prestigious Collège de France. These different positions corresponded to different scientific habitus and fields of inquiry. The first group was interested in general sociology, morality, and law, while the second group was interested in religion, ethnography, archeology, economy, and linguistics.

The professional status of these two groups was to a large extent reflected in their mode of involvement in political life. On the one hand, the "researchers" were socialists and fought for equality. They were active in political parties, associations, and unions. On the other hand, the "teachers" were "liberals," writing philosophical essays and defending the values of justice, democracy, and freedom. Although the two groups related to politics in different ways and adopted different political positions, they were not entirely mutually exclusive. Both adopted a distant or critical stance with respect to political doctrines, with the socialists rejecting the dogmatism of the Marxists and the "liberals" distancing themselves from any form of ultra-liberalism. During the Dreyfus Affair, however, they all played the new role of "intellectual" and as Durkheim did, Bouglé, Lapie, Mauss, Hubert, Simiand, and H. Bourgin all signed the petition "*J'accuse*" in 1898, defending Dreyfus and calling for a retrial.

The rallying point of several of *L'Année* collaborators (Mauss, Hubert, Fauconnet, Simiand) was the *Société nouvelle de librairie et d'édition*, which had been founded by Lucien Herr and was close to the socialist movement. The *Société* wanted to base socialism on sociology and wanted socialist action to be rationalist. These *L'Année* collaborators also contributed in 1899 to political journals, such as the *Mouvement socialiste*, and to a bibliographical bulletin entitled *Notes critiques—Sciences sociales*, which like *L'Année sociologique* comprised several rubrics: general sociology, ethnography and folklore, religious sciences, science of law and mores, and economic sciences. Almost all the contributors to *L'Année sociologique*, including Durkheim, published reviews in *Notes critiques*, which continued publication until 1906. Of note is also that Mauss was friends with Jean Jaurès and during his life also wrote for the socialist newspaper *L'Humanité* and *Le Populaire*.

When the third volume of *L'Année* had been published, in 1900, Durkheim felt once more discouraged: the publication of the journal was too heavy a task; it absorbed him, and it burdened all his contributors with extra work. That was a first crisis at *L'Année sociologique*. Durkheim saw only one solution: *L'Année* and *Notes critiques* should merge. After nothing immediately came of the merger project, Durkheim began thinking of an alternative solution: shared editorial responsibility. He subsequently reorganized several aspects of the publications, which was required to deal with practical issues such as ordering books, preparing the manuscript, correcting proofs, translations, and the index. Hubert agreed to help Durkheim, who let him take more and more initiatives and responsibilities. Other crises emerged. For example, in 1907 Mauss thought of refusing to contribute to *L'Année*; at the time he was fully occupied by other responsibilities (teaching, political engagements, the writing of his doctoral thesis) and was annoyed with the behavior of his uncle who complained more than ever of the lateness with which his nephew would turn in reviews. Then, in 1910, in order to give themselves some respite and allow them to complete research projects which, in many cases, they had begun several years ago, Durkheim and his collaborators adopted a new formula, which introduced two major changes: *L'Année* would now appear every three years and could no longer publish original articles. What would have been articles would now appear in book form in the *Travaux de L'Année sociologique* collection published by Alcan.

The first series of *L'Année sociologique* was a challenging and difficult, but ultimately successful enterprise that gave visibility to the "French school of sociology," which was ultimately Durkheimian sociology. The institutionalization of this Durkheimian school was confirmed when its members gained positions in the educational system: in *lycées*, universities (Bordeaux, Toulouse, Paris), and other institutions (École pratique des hautes études, Conservatoire national des arts et métiers). Some of them also published papers and books discussing and defending the Durkheimian perspective in sociology. A former student of Durkheim, Georges Davy, published *La sociologie de Durkheim* (1911). The Durkheimian school was also acquiring visibility abroad through the publication of reviews of the first volume of *L'Année sociologique* in the British journal *Folk-Lore* and by A. W. Small in the *American Journal of Sociology*.

Durkheim's last and most ambitious book, *The Elementary Forms of Religious Life*, published in 1912, was a synthesis of the work that Durkheim and several of his collaborators had been doing for some years. Durkheim himself was aware of the collective nature of his research, and he often cited the work of Hubert and Mauss, as well as that of Robert Hertz. He also attached a great importance to the notion of *mana* (the totemic principle) because of the major role it plays in the development of religious ideas. When Henri Hubert received Durkheim's book, his first—and quite spontaneous—reaction was to write to Mauss: "I've received Durkheim's book. Perhaps you should have signed it, because there is a lot of you in it" (Hubert 1912).[6] Mauss had previously coauthored with his uncle the long and important essay "On Some Primitive Forms of Classification" (Durkheim and Mauss [1903] 1963, 1969a), and in his unfinished doctoral thesis, *On Prayer* (Mauss [1909] 2008), Mauss collected a great deal of data on indigenous Australian societies, which allowed him to describe in great detail their ritual ceremonies. In *L'Année sociologique* Mauss also published two summaries (one of which with Durkheim as a coauthor) of collections of observations on the Arunta and Loritja published by the German missionary Carl Strehlow (Durkheim and Mauss [1910] 1969b). This is the same data that Durkheim analyzed in *Elementary Forms*.

World War I brought tragedy to the Durkheimian school with the death of Émile Durkheim and his son André, as well as the loss of his young collaborators and students: Robert Hertz, Maxime David, Antoine Bianconi, and so on. "We lost a whole generation of our best and most vigorous collaborators. [...] We will see that, if it had not been for the war, sociology, science, and our country would have had a body of work that few studies have produced" (Mauss [1925] 1969a).[7]

One challenge was to keep alive the memory of Durkheim's work. Georges Davy published a long study, "Émile Durkheim: l'homme," in the *Revue de métaphysique et de morale* (1919). When he became a Professor at the Sorbonne, Paul Fauconnet devoted his inaugural lecture to Durkheim: "The Pedagogical Work of Emile Durkheim" ([1922] 1923). In August 1924, Célestin Bouglé, who had already published a *Guide de l'étudiant en sociologie* (1921), published an article, "Le spiritualisme d'Émile Durkheim" (1924) in the *Revue bleue*; he was also preparing to publish six of the master's articles under the title of *Sociologie et philosophie* (1924). Finally, Maurice Halbwachs published a long article entitled "La doctrine d'Emile Durkheim" (1918), and in a small book, *Sources of Religious Sentiment*, he produced what he called a "summary that is as accurate and literal as possible" of *The Elementary Forms of Religious Life* (Halbwachs [1925] 1962).[8] In the early 1930s, he reexamined Durkheim's study of suicide in light of a more sophisticated methodology: the result was *The Causes of Suicide* (Halbwachs [1930] 1978).

Across the English Channel, Alfred Radcliffe-Brown (1881–1955), an English anthropologist close to the Durkheimians and especially to Mauss, was active in disseminating the work of the Durkheim group in Great Britain. Beginning in the early 1910s he lectured on Durkheimian sociology at Cambridge and London University, discussing the topics of the sociological method, the evolution of social structure, religion, and morality. Although he recognized a "debt" to his French colleagues, Radcliffe-Brown was "disappointed" in Durkheim's great book on religion, which he saw as misinterpreting important ethnographic details of indigenous Australian societies (Radcliffe-Brown [1912] 1979).

Marcel Mauss, the "heir," "rekindled" *L'Année sociologique*, but only two volumes were published, in 1925 and 1927, with the participation of the "old" collaborators of the first series: Marcel Mauss, Henri Hubert, Célestin Bouglé, François Simiand, Paul Fauconnet, and Maurice Halbwachs. In the first of the two volumes, Mauss published "In Memoriam" ([1925] 1969a) and his famous essay *The Gift* ([1925] 1966). This initiative was well received abroad, especially in the United States. Charles Ellwood, at the time the president of the *American Sociological Association*, wrote to Mauss: "We look at France as the homeland of Sociology and we expect you still lead us in our endeavors to promote the development of science" (Ellwood 1924: 496).

In the 1930s, Durkheimians held three of the four chairs of sociology in French universities: Maurice Halbwachs at Strasbourg, and Paul Fauconnet and Célestin Bouglé at the Sorbonne. The fourth one, at Bordeaux, was held by Gaston Richard, a former collaborator. At the same time, Paul Lapie, then director of the Department of Primary Education in the Ministry of National Education, succeeded in introducing sociology into the curriculum of the *licence* (bachelor) in philosophy. In 1935 Célestin Bouglé became the director of the École normale supérieure, where he also led the Centre de documentation sociale, an institution that influenced a generation of young researchers, several of which became "Durkheimians." Durkheimian sociology saw a fresh start with many activities and initiatives: the creation of the Institut d'ethnologie de Paris (1925), Marcel Mauss's election to the prestigious Collège de France (1930), François Simiand's election to the Collège de France, and the recruitment of a new generation of collaborators (Françoise Henry, Michel Leiris, René Maunier, Robert Marjolin, Jacques Soustelle, etc.). Similarly, a continuation of *L'Année sociologique* began in 1934 in the form of the new journal *Annales sociologiques*.

Another "dark" period came with the deaths of François Simiand (1936), Paul Fauconnet (1938), Lucien Lévy-Bruhl (1939), and Célestin Bouglé (1940). By the beginning of the 1940s, the Durkheimian group had progressively faded and the Durkheimian project lost its coherence (Heilbron 1985). In 1942, *Annales sociologiques* ended publication. Maurice Halbwachs, elected to the Collège de France in 1943, died in 1945 in the Buchenwald concentration camp. Moreover, Marcel Mauss was ill; he died in 1950. This was, in a way, the end of the Durkheimian school, which had become the target of more frequent and very severe criticism in the 1930s and 1940s. Paul Nizan in *Les Chiens de garde* attacked Durkheim and his disciples, who he associated with the bourgeoisie and its conservative ideology (Nizan [1932] 1981). Jules Monnerot, a cofounder of the Collège de sociologie and a friend of Georges Bataille and Roger Caillois, published in 1946 a book entitled *Les Faits sociaux ne sont pas des choses*, which was an epistemological critique of Durkheim's methodology.[9] Finally, when Jean Stoetzel came back from the United States after World War II and gave his first lesson in sociology at Bordeaux, he concluded: "We should forget Durkheim" (Stoetzel 1946). In anthropology the dominant theme was the same. As Claude Lévi-Strauss, in a veiled reference to Durkheim, declared in his text on French sociology, which he dedicated to Marcel Mauss, "The time of dogmatic constructions appears to be definitively over" (Lévi-Strauss 1947).[10] Soon after Mauss's death, Lévi-Strauss edited a selection of Mauss's principal texts, entitled *Sociologie et anthropologie* (Mauss 1950). The time of structuralism had arrived.

But Durkheim has not been forgotten. A new generation of the students of *L'Année sociologique* collaborators renewed the publication of the journal in 1949 under the supervision of Henri Lévy-Bruhl, the son of Lucien. As they stated: "We consider ourselves the heirs (of Durkheim) and are proud to continue his work in the same spirit" (Les Rédacteurs 1949: ix).[11] The publication remains in print today, although in the postwar period the journal moved beyond its Durkheimian orientation to encompass a much broader sociological scope; the legacy of Durkheim and his original team of collaborators has nevertheless left an imprint (Mosbah-Natanson 2019). Despite the numerous obstacles and critics, Durkheim has also become a well-known classical sociologist in the academic world and is the subject of a number of commentaries and theoretical interpretations. For instance, 6.3 percent of the 8,353 articles published in the AJS and the ASR between 1895 and 1992 cite his texts. This is as many as Weber, the most influential sociologist of the era, who was cited in 6.5 percent of the articles over the same period. Thus "[t]he knowledge of Durkheim and of his books is a full part of the definition of what a sociologist is in America" (Vogt 1993: 227). Another analysis, which sampled thirty-four prominent American sociology journals, shows that between 1970 and 2012 Durkheim was the most cited of all the French sociologists with 2,018 citations. Pierre Bourdieu was second with 1,863 citations, while Bruno Latour was third with 662 (Ollion and Abbott 2016).

Part of Durkheim's resilience involved a kind of renaissance of Durkheimian thought that began in the 1970s. Steven Lukes (1973) published the first great intellectual biography of Durkheim. Many of Durkheim's texts were "reborn" when Victor Karady, also the editor of three volumes of Marcel Mauss's *Oeuvres* (1968–1969), edited and republished them in three volumes (Durkheim 1975b). In addition, new books gave a new perspective on Durkheim as a political thinker who is less conservative and more reformist—if not socialist (Filloux 1977; Lacroix 1981).

Continuing into the 1980s and beyond there has been a sustained interest in Durkheimian sociology. With the opening up of archives that have provided new information about Durkheim's life and work, there has been a proliferation of research on Durkheim's biography and intellectual development, as well as the reception of his ideas (Besnard 1979; Jones 1986, 1999; Besnard, Borlandi, and Vogt 1993; Leroux 1998; Mucchielli 1998; Borlandi and Cherkaoui 2000). In 1991, W. S. F. Pickering founded the British Centre for Durkheimian Studies at Oxford University; the decade also saw the publication of a new journal, *Études durkheimiennes*, which became *Durkheimian Studies / Études durkheimiennes*. In 2007, Marcel Fournier published a second great intellectual biography of Durkheim (Fournier 2007). In sociology, especially in the Anglo-Saxon world, but also in France, Germany, and Italy, there has been a renewal of Durkheimian Studies as well as the development of a neo-Durkheimian perspective (Goffman 1967; Bloor 1976; Joas 1984, 1993, 1996, 2000, 2008; Pickering 1984, 2009; Giddens 1971; Habermas 1987; Alexander 1988, 1996, 2002; Alexander et al. 2004; Meštrović 1988; Garland 1990; Gane 1992; Lehmann 1993; Turner 1993; Watts Miller 1996; Strenski 1997; Cotterrell 1999; Garfinkel 2001; Collins 2004, 2008; Rawls 1996, 2004; Alexander and Smith 2005; Bellah 2005; Grusky and Galescu 2005; Alexander, Giesen, and Mast 2006; Schmaus 2007; Smith 2008; Rosati 2009; Tiryakian 2009; Maryanski 2018; Müller 2019).[12]

There has also appeared a new interest in the work of some of Durkheim's close collaborators. The most attention has been given to Marcel Mauss. If Mauss was always widely discussed in anthropology due to his essay on *The Gift*, he was rediscovered by sociology in the 1980s and 1990s. Marcel Fournier (1994) wrote the first intellectual biography of Mauss, and the correspondence between Durkheim and Mauss was published (Durkheim 1998a). There was moreover the creation of the *Revue du M.A.U.S.S.* in 1981 and a proliferation of studies on gifting and philanthropy in modern societies, leading to the creation of a "new" paradigm of giving (Caillé 2004). Commentators recognized Mauss's originality as a thinker of the "total social fact" (Karsenti 1994) and as a pioneer in the study of both symbolism (Tarot 1999) and techniques of the body; in his studies of the latter, Mauss introduced the concept of habitus, which Bourdieu would later pick up. After the publication of his *Écrits politiques* (Mauss 1997) and the re-edition of his manuscript on the nation (Mauss 2013), a new interest in Mauss's political sociology developed, which saw him as a prophet of the solidarity economy (Dzimira 2007), a critic of chauvinistic nationalism who gave a definition of the nation not only as a cultural or ethnic community but also as a community of citizens (Schnapper 1994), and an ardent defender of internationalism (Mergy 2004). There is a strong relationship between his anthropological work on gifting (giving, receiving/debt, and giving back) and his political reflections, which touched on the best ways to restore order and solidarity in Europe after World War I, how to deal with the issue of German debt, and the issue of French colonial expansion (Mallard 2019).

Maurice Halbwachs's work has also generated great interest. He figures among the most prominent of Durkheim's collaborators due largely to his concept of "collective memory." Halbwachs rose to prominence beginning in the 1980s and early 1990s at a time when the humanities and social sciences were experiencing a "memory boom." In 1992 the University of Chicago Press published the first widely read English language version of Halbwachs's texts on memory, a collection edited by Lewis Coser, while in France there appeared re-editions of Halbwachs's most important texts on the subject, *Les cadres sociaux de la mémoire* (1994) and *La mémoire collective* (1997) (Hirsch 2016). Halbwachs is today generally seen as a "founding father" of the discipline of memory studies (Olick, Vinitzky-Seroussi, and Levy 2011; Gensburger 2016); his work is widely studied internationally across disciplines in the humanities and social sciences (Coser 1992; Marcel and Mucchielli 1999; Echterhoff and Saar 2002; Krapoth and Laborde 2005; Wetzel 2009). He is furthermore noted for his contribution to urban studies (Amiot 1986). On this topic scholarship draws attention to his relationship with the Chicago school of sociology (Grafmeyer and Joseph 1979).[13]

Other members of Durkheim's team have also attracted scholarly attention. There are studies of the life and work of Robert Hertz who, under the influence of Durkheim, outlined a research program that included work on collective representations of death and religious polarities. He is the author of a famous short essay on "The Right Hand" ([1909] 1960b) and his doctoral thesis deals with sin and expiation in primitive societies, although he died at the age of thirty-three in World War I before its completion (Parkin 1996). Alexander Riley (1999) sees in Hertz a combination of Durkheimian and Nietzschean thought that predates authors such as Georges Bataille, Roger Caillois, and Michel Leiris, all of whom, like Hertz, took courses with and read Mauss. François Simiand and his economic sociology has drawn interest (Steiner 2011), and he is well known in the humanities for his essay, "Historical Method and Social Science," in which he asserts that historians are too obsessed with three "idols": chronology, individuals, and events; he invites them instead to collect social facts and to strive for generality (Simiand 1903).

In the sociology of law and in legal studies, Paul Fauconnet's only book, *La responsabilité: Étude de sociologie* (1928), derived from his doctoral thesis, has drawn attention for its relevance to the study of law and the law's relationship with morality (Chateauraynaud 1991; Karsenti 2004; Combessie 2008). The work of Emmanuel Lévy and Paul Huvelin (1873–1924), both friends of Mauss, jurists, professors of law, and collaborators with the *Année*, is also noteworthy. Roger Cotterrell (2004a) argues that Lévy is an overlooked precursor to the critical legal studies movement in the United States. He also praises Huvelin's engagement with Durkheim's ideas and his attempt to go beyond Durkheim by thinking law in relation to power and politics (Cotterrell 2004b).

Along with the renewed interest and engagement with the work of Durkheim and his collaborators has also come a new set of critiques. For example, Durkheim and his collaborators have been met with postcolonial critiques. Critics point out problems with Durkheim's reliance on ethnographic fieldwork from English anthropologists, for example, or the fact that the mandate for the Institut d'ethnologie de Paris, which Mauss cofounded, was to help form future administrators for France's African colonies. Durkheim and his close collaborators did defend modern theories of progress, or the idea that Europe was continuously progressing toward a higher state of civilization. Nevertheless, they all maintained a variation of cultural relativism, according to which all cultures are different but equal in value and dignity (Kurasawa 2013).

Durkheim's work also continues to be the subject of neglect or even outright scorn. Charles Tilly (1981) published an essay called "Useless Durkheim," which criticizes Durkheim's account of the relation between societal growth, on one hand, and social differentiation, conflict, and disorder, on the other. Mustafa Emirbayer responded with "Useful Durkheim" (1996), which shows the usefulness of Durkheim's later works for historical comparative sociology. In his book *The Construction of Social Reality*, John Searle (1995) claimed to have discovered a groundbreaking new theory of social facts and social institutions, all while completely dismissing Durkheim's work. In a book review, Neil Gross (2006) pointed out that Searle's work is not all that different from Durkheim's. Searle (2006) responded to Gross and claimed that Durkheim's work was "impoverished," to which Steven Lukes (2007) responded by reaffirming Gross's points. While Durkheim's work continues to be maligned and misunderstood, it simultaneously proves its enduring usefulness and relevance.

There still might be some stigma attached to Durkheim's work and by extension those who would claim themselves to be "Durkheimian." Some observers wonder ironically if Durkheim's disciples, or even if Durkheim himself for that matter, were "Durkheimian" (Fournier and Leroux 1997; Boudon 2011). As evidence of this desire to limit direct contact with Durkheim, one can point to a text from Pierre Bourdieu and Jean-Claude Passeron, who at the end of the 1960s observed that Durkheim's influence on the social sciences in France at the time could only be indirect, that it was possible "to recognize the Durkheimian ancestry only through the most respectable relatives—the English cousin Radcliffe-Brown, or the testamentary executor, Marcel Mauss." Durkheim's imprint was nevertheless decisive, with dominant schools of thought such as structuralism or structural linguistics picking up on Durkheimian strands of thought. As Bourdieu and Passeron continued: "all the social sciences now live in the house of Durkheimism, unbeknownst to them, as it were, because they walked into it backwards" (Bourdieu and Passeron 1967: 166–168). Bourdieu himself, as seen in his book *Le métier de sociologue* (Bourdieu, Chamboredon, and Passeron 1968), kept both an admiration and a critical distance toward Durkheim while developing a strong affinity for the work of Durkheim's nephew, Mauss (Bourdieu 2004).

For those engaging with Durkheimian sociology, it remains perhaps easier to associate oneself with an intermediary, such as Mauss or Halbwachs, than with Durkheim directly. In the end, irrespective of whether researchers make reference to Durkheimian thought or actively seek to claim the Durkheimian mantel, the work of Durkheim and his colleagues has left an indelible imprint on the social sciences and humanities.

Notes

1. Translated by David Macey.
2. Translated by David Macey.
3. Translated by David Macey.
4. Only those who wrote reviews of at least six lines are considered here, as only these longer reviews were published with the author's name. The full list of the collaborators in the first series, ranked by how important their collaboration was (i.e., by the number of reviews they wrote), is E. Durkheim, M. Mauss, H. Hubert, F. Simiand, G. Richard, H. Bourgin, P. Fauconnet, C. Bouglé, M. Halbwachs, P. Lapie, P. Huvelin, D. Parodi, G. Bourgin, A. Meillet, R. Hertz, G. Davy, E. Lévy, A. Aubin, J.-P. Hourticq, A. Rey, H. Muffang, A. Bianconi, P. De Felice, I. Lévy, L. Gernet, A. Milhaud, E. Laskine, J. Marx, P. Reynier, H. Beuchat, M. David, R. Challié, G. Gelly, Ch. Poirot, J. Stickney, A. Vacher, E. Doutté, H. Jeanmaire, A. Demangeon, M. Foucault, F. Sigel, P. Roussel, Fossey, J.-P. Lafitte, Ch. Lalo, C. Maître, and A. Moret (Besnard 1979).
5. Translated by David Macey.
6. Translated by David Macey.
7. Translated by David Macey.
8. Translated by David Macey.
9. On the Collège de sociologie, see Moebius in this volume.
10. Our translation.
11. Our translation.
12. Outside of sociology, in related disciplines such as philosophy and psychology, one also sees Durkheim's influence. In political philosophy, Mark Cladis (1992) and Paul Carls (2019) see strong parallels between Durkheim's cult of the individual and John Rawls's notion of political liberalism, as well as Jürgen Habermas's concept of *Verfassungspatriotismus* (constitutional patriotism). In moral and evolutionary psychology, Durkheim's work on religion and morality has been the source of inspiration. Both Jonathan Haidt (2012) and David Sloan Wilson (2002) refer to Durkheim's insight that religion and morality serve to bind a group together. They do so to argue in favor of an evolutionary theory of group-level selection that would select positively for those individuals capable of forming the strong religious and moral bonds Durkheim describes.
13. However, as Topalov (2008) points out, while Halbwachs found the work of his Chicago colleagues stimulating, he did not see it as theoretically advanced or scientifically relevant.

References

Alexander, Jeffrey C., ed. 1988. *Durkheimian Sociology: Cultural Studies.* Cambridge: Cambridge University Press.

Alexander, Jeffrey C. 1996. "Cultural Sociology or Sociology of Culture?" *Culture* 10, no. 3–4: 1–5.

Alexander, Jeffrey C. 2002. "On the Social Construction of Moral Universals: The 'Holocaust' from War Crime to Trauma Drama." *European Journal of Social Theory* 5, no. 1: 5–85.

Alexander, Jeffrey C., and Philip Smith, eds. 2005. *Cambridge Companion to Durkheim.* Cambridge: Cambridge University Press.

Alexander, Jeffrey C., Bernhard Giesen, and Jason L. Mast, eds. 2006. *Social Performance: Symbolic Action, Cultural Pragmatics, and Ritual.* Cambridge: Cambridge University Press.

Alexander, Jeffrey C., Ron Eyerman, Bernhard Giesen, Neil J. Smelser, and Piotr Sztompka. 2004. *Cultural Trauma and Collective Identity*. Berkeley, CA: University of California Press.
Amiot, Michel. 1986. "Maurice Halbwachs: l'invention de la sociologie urbaine contre la primauté de l'économie, de l'histoire et de la politique." In Michel Amiot, *Contre l'état, les sociologues. Eléments pour une histoire de la sociologie urbaine en France, 1900–1980*, 13–33. Paris: Éditions de l'EHESS.
Bellah, Robert N. 2005. "Durkheim and Ritual." In *The Cambridge Companion to Durkheim*, edited by Jeffrey C. Alexander and Philip Smith, 183–210. Cambridge: Cambridge University Press.
Besnard, Philippe. 1979. "La formation de l'équipe de *l'Année sociologique*." *Revue française de sociologie* 20, no. 1: 7–31.
Besnard, Philippe, Massimo Borlandi, and Paul Vogt, eds. 1993. *Division du travail et lien social*. Paris: Presses universitaires de France.
Bloor, David. 1976. *Knowledge and Social Imagery*. London: Routledge & Kegan Paul.
Borlandi, Massimo, and Mohamed Cherkaoui, eds. 2000. *Le suicide. Un siècle après Durkheim*. Paris: Presses universitaires de France.
Boudon, Raymond, ed. 2011. *Durkheim fut-il durkheimien?* Paris: Armand Colin.
Bouglé, Célestin. 1924. "Le 'spiritualisme' d'Emile Durkheim." *Revue politique et littéraire. Revue bleue* 62, no. 16: 550–553.
Bouglé, Célestin, with Marcel Déat. 1921. *Le guide de l'étudiant en sociologie*. Paris: Garnier.
Bourgin, Hubert. 1903. "Essai sur une forme d'industrie. L'industrie de la boucherie à Paris au XIXe siècle." *L'Année sociologique* 8: 1–117.
Bourdieu, Pierre. 2004. "Marcel Mauss, aujourd'hui." *Sociologie et sociétés* 36, no. 2: 15–22.
Bourdieu, Pierre, and Jean-Claude Passeron. 1967. "Sociology and Philosophy in France since 1945: Death and Resurrection of a Philosophy without Subject." *Social Research* 34, no. 1: 162–212.
Bourdieu, Pierre, Jean-Claude Chamboredon, and Jean-Claude Passeron. 1968. *Le métier de sociologue, préalables épistémologiques*. Paris: Mouton–Bordas.
Caillé, Alain. 2004. "Marcel Mauss et le paradigme du don." *Sociologie et société* 36, no. 2: 141–176.
Carls, Paul. 2019. "Modern Democracy as the Cult of the Individual: Durkheim on Religious Coexistence and Conflict." *Critical Research on Religion* 7, no. 3: 292–311.
Chateauraynaud, Francis. 1991. *La faute professionnelle. Une sociologie des conflits de responsabilité*. Paris: Métailié.
Cladis, Mark. 1992. *A Communitarian Defense of Liberalism: Emile Durkheim and Contemporary Social Theory*. Stanford, CA: Stanford University Press.
Collins, Randall. 2004. *Interaction Ritual Chains*. Princeton, NJ: Princeton University Press.
Collins, Randall. 2008. *Violence: A Micro-Sociological Theory*. Princeton, NJ: Princeton University Press.
Combessie, Philippe. 2008. "Paul Fauconnet et l'imputation pénale de la responsabilité." In *Anamnèse, no 3, Trois figures de l'école durkheimienne: Célestin Bouglé, Georges Davy, Paul Fauconnet*, edited by Claude Ravelet, 221–246. Paris: L'Harmattan.
Coser, Lewis. 1992. "The Revival of the Sociology of Culture: The Case of Collective Memory." *Sociological Forum* 7, no. 2: 365–373.
Cotterrell, Roger. 1999. *Émile Durkheim: Law in a Moral Domain*. Edinburgh: Edinburgh University Press.
Cotterrell, Roger. 2004a. "Emmanuel Lévy and Legal Studies: A View from Abroad." *Droit et Société* 56/57: 131–141.

Cotterrell, Roger. 2004b. "Constructing the Juristic Durkheim? Paul Huvelin's Adaptation of Durkheimian Sociology." *Durkheimian Studies / Études Durkheimiennes*, New Series 10: 56–69.
Davy, Georges. 1911. "La sociologie de M. Durkheim." *Revue philosophique de la France et de l'étranger* 72: 42–71.
Davy, Georges. 1919. "Émile Durkheim: I—L'homme." *Revue de métaphysique et de morale* 26, no. 2: 181–198.
Davy, Georges. 1922. *La foi jurée*. Paris: Librairie Félix Alcan.
Durkheim, Émile. 1924. *Sociologie et philosophie*. Edited by Célestin Bouglé. Paris: Presses universitaires de France.
Durkheim, Émile. (1898) 1963. *Incest: The Nature and Origin of the Taboo*. Translated by Edward Sagarin. New York: Lyle Stuart. Originally published as "La prohibition de l'inceste et ses origines." *L'Année sociologique* 1: 1–70.
Durkheim, Émile. (1899) 1975a. "Concerning the Definition of Religious Phenomena." In *Durkheim on Religion: A Selection of Readings with Bibliographies*, edited by W. S. F. Pickering and translated by Jacqueline Redding and W. S. F. Pickering, 74–99. London: Routledge & Kegan Paul. Originally published as "De la définition des phénomènes religieux." *L'Année sociologique* 2: 1–28.
Durkheim, Émile. 1975b. *Textes*. 3 vols. Paris: Éditions de Minuit.
Durkheim, Émile. (1900) 1976. "Lettre de Durkheim à Bouglé, 13 June 1900." *Revue française de sociologie* 17, no. 2: 173–174.
Durkheim, Émile. 1998a. *Lettres à Marcel Mauss*. Edited by Philippe Besnard and Marcel Fournier. Paris: Presses universitaires de France.
Durkheim, Émile. (1897) 1998b. "Letter to Marcel Mauss, July 15, 1897." In Émile Durkheim, *Lettres à Marcel Mauss*, edited by Philippe Besnard and Marcel Fournier, 81–82. Paris: Presses universitaires de France.
Durkheim, Émile. (1898) 1998c. "Letter to Marcel Mauss," Bordeaux, Sunday (February 1898). In Émile Durkheim, *Lettres à Marcel Mauss*, edited by Philippe Besnard and Marcel Fournier, 110. Paris: Presses universitaires de France.
Durkheim, Émile, and Marcel Mauss. (1903) 1963. "On Some Primitive Forms of Classification." In *Primitive Classification*, translated by Rodney Needham. Chicago: University of Chicago Press. Originally published as "De quelques formes primitives de classification. Contribution à l'étude des représentations collectives." *L'Année sociologique* 6: 1–72.
Durkheim, Émile, and Marcel Mauss. (1903) 1969a. "De quelques formes primitives de classification. Contribution à l'étude des représentations primitives." *L'Année sociologique* 6. In Marcel Mauss, *Œuvres*, vol. 2, 3–53. Paris: Éditions de Minuit.
Durkheim, Émile, and Marcel Mauss. (1910) 1969b. "Compte rendu de C. Strehlow, *Die Aranda und Loritja-Staemme in Zentral-Australien*." *L'Année sociologique* 9. In Marcel Mauss, *Œuvres*, vol. 3, 434–439. Paris: Éditions de Minuit.
Dzimira, Sylvain. 2007. *Marcel Mauss, savant et politique*. Paris: La Découverte.
Echterhoff, Gerald, and Martin Saar, eds. 2002. *Kontexte und Kulturen des Erinnerns. Maurice Halbwachs und das Paradigma des kollektiven Gedächtnisses*. Konstanz: UVK.
Ellwood, Charles A. 1924. "Letter to Marcel Mauss. November 4" (Fonds Marcel Mauss, Archives du Collège de France). In Marcel Fournier, *Marcel Mauss*, 496. Paris: Fayard.
Emirbayer, Mustafa. 1996. "Useful Durkheim." *Sociological Theory* 14, no. 2: 109–130.

Fauconnet, Paul. (1922) 1923. "The Pedagogical Work of Emile Durkheim." *The American Journal of Sociology* XXVIII, no. 5: 529–553. Extracts of a lecture Fauconnet gave to the Sorbonne in 1922.
Fauconnet, Paul. 1928. *La responsabilité. Étude de sociologie*. Paris: Librairie Félix Alcan.
Filloux, Jean-Claude. 1977. *Durkheim et le socialisme*. Geneva: Droz.
Fournier, Marcel. 1994. *Marcel Mauss*. Paris: Fayard. English translation by Jane Marie Todd. Princeton, NJ: Princeton University Press, 1996.
Fournier, Marcel. 2007. *Émile Durkheim*. Paris: Fayard. English translation by David Macey. Cambridge: Polity, 2013.
Fournier, Marcel, and Robert Leroux. 1997. "Les collaborateurs de Durkheim étaientils en règle?" In *Durkheim d'un siècle à l'autre. Lectures actuelles des Règles de la méthode sociologique*, edited by Charles-Henry Cuin, 57–71. Paris: Presses universitaires de France.
Gane, Mike, ed. 1992. *The Radical Sociology of Durkheim and Mauss*. London: Routledge.
Garfinkel, Harold. 2001. *Ethnomethodology's Program: Working Out Durkheim's Aphorism*. Boulder, CO: Rowman & Littlefield.
Garland, David. 1990. *Punishment and Modern Society: A Study in Social Theory*. Chicago: University of Chicago Press.
Gensburger, Sarah. 2016. "Halbwachs' Studies in Collective Memory: A Founding Text for Contemporary 'Memory Studies'?" *Journal of Classical Sociology* 16, no. 4: 396–413.
Giddens, Anthony. 1971. "Durkheim's Early Works." In Anthony Giddens, *Capitalism and Modern Social Theory*, 65–81. Cambridge: Cambridge University Press.
Goffman, Erving. 1967. *Interaction Ritual: Essays on Face-to-Face Behavior*. Garden City, NJ: Anchor Books.
Grafmeyer, Yves, and Isaac Joseph, eds. 1979. "La ville-laboratoire et le milieu urbain." In Yves Grafmeyer and Isaac Joseph, *L'École de Chicago. Naissance de l'écologie urbaine*, 5–52. Paris: Éditions du Champ urbain.
Gross, Neil. 2006. "Comment on Searle." *Anthropological Theory* 6, no. 1: 45–56.
Grusky, David, and Gabriela Galescu. 2005. "Is Durkheim a Class Analyst?" In *The Cambridge Companion to Durkheim*, edited by J. C. Alexander and P. Smith, 322–359. Cambridge: Cambridge University Press.
Habermas, Jürgen. (1981) 1987. *The Theory of Communicative Action*, vol. 2: *Lifeworld and System: A Critique of Functionalist Reason*. Translated by Thomas McCarthy. Boston: Beacon Press.
Haidt, Jonathan. 2012. *The Righteous Mind: Why Good People Are Divided by Politics and Religion*. New York: Pantheon Books.
Halbwachs, Maurice. 1918. "La doctrine d'Émile Durkheim." *Revue philosophique de la France et de l'étranger* 85: 353–411.
Halbwachs, Maurice. (1925) 1962. *Sources of Religious Sentiment*. Translated by John Spaulding. New York: The Free Press of Glencoe. Originally published as *Les origines du sentiment religieux*. Paris: Librairie Stock.
Halbwachs, Maurice. (1930) 1978. *The Causes of Suicide*. Translated by Harold Goldblatt. London: Routledge & Kegan Paul.
Halbwachs, Maurice. 1994. *Les cadres sociaux de la mémoire*. Paris: Albin Michel.
Halbwachs, Maurice. 1997. *La mémoire collective*. Édition critique par G. Namer, avec la collaboration de M. Jaisson. Paris: Albin Michel.
Heilbron, Johan. 1985. "Les métamorphoses du durkheimisme, 1920–1940." *Revue française de sociologie* 26, no. 2: 203–237.

Hertz, Robert. (1907) 1960a. "A Contribution to the Study of the Collective Representation of Death." In *Death and the Right Hand*, translated by Rodney and Claudia Needham, 27–86. Glencoe, IL: The Free Press. Originally published as "Contribution à une étude sur la représentation collective de la mort." *L'Année sociologique* 10: 48–137.

Hertz, Robert. (1909) 1960b. "The Pre-eminence of the Right Hand: A Study in Religious Polarity." In *Death and the Right Hand*, translated by Rodney and Claudia Needham. 89–113 Glencoe, IL: The Free Press. Originally published as "La prééminence de la main droite. Étude sur la polarité religieuse." *Revue philosophique de la France et de l'étranger* 68: 553–580.

Hirsch, Thomas. 2016. "Une vie posthume. Maurice Halbwachs et la sociologie française (1945–2015)." *Revue française de sociologie* 57, no. 1: 71–96.

Hubert, Henri. 1904. "Introduction." In *Manuel d'histoire des religions*, edited by P. D. Chantepie de la Saussaye, V–XLVIII. Paris: Alcan.

Hubert, Henri. 1912. "Letter to Marcel Mauss, 4 July 1912." Fonds Hubert-Mauss, Archives du Collège de France.

Joas, Hans. 1984. "Durkheim et le pragmatisme. La psychologie de la conscience et la constitution sociale des catégories." *Revue française de sociologie* 25, no. 4: 560–581.

Joas, Hans. 1993. *Pragmatism and Social Theory*. Chicago: University of Chicago Press.

Joas, Hans. 1996. *The Creativity of Action*. Chicago: University of Chicago Press.

Joas, Hans. 2000. *The Genesis of Values*. Chicago: University of Chicago Press.

Joas, Hans. 2008. "Punishment and Respect: The Sacralization of the Person and Its Endangerment." *Journal of Classical Sociology* 8, no. 2: 159–177.

Jones, Robert Allen. 1986. *Emile Durkheim: An Introduction to Four Major Works*. Beverly Hills, CA: SAGE.

Jones, Robert Allen. 1999. *The Development of Durkheim's Social Realism*. Cambridge: Cambridge University Press.

Karsenti, Bruno. 1994. *Marcel Mauss. Le fait social total*. Paris: Presses universitaires de France.

Karsenti, Bruno. 2004. "Nul n'est censé ignorer la loi. Le droit pénal de Durkheim à Fauconnet." *Archives de philosophie* 67, no. 4: 557–581.

Krapoth, Hermann, and Denis Laborde, eds. 2005. *Erinnerung und Gesellschaft. Mémoire et Société: Hommage à Maurice Halbwachs (1877–1945)*. Wiesbaden: VS.

Kurasawa, Fuyuki. 2013. "The Durkheimian School and Colonialism: Exploring the Constitutive Paradox." In *Sociology and Empire: The Imperial Entanglements of a Discipline*, edited by George Steinmetz, 188–213. Durham, NC: Duke University Press.

Lacroix, Bernard. 1981. *Durkheim et le politique*. Paris and Montréal: Presses de la Fondation nationale des sciences politiques—Presses de l'Université de Montréal.

Lehmann, Jennifer. 1993. *Deconstructing Durkheim: A Post-Post-Structuralist Critique*. New York: Routledge.

Leroux, Robert. 1998. *Histoire et sociologie en France*. Paris: Presses universitaires de France.

Les Rédacteurs. 1949. "Avant-propos." *L'Année sociologique*, 3ᵉ série, tome 1 (1940–1948): ix–x.

Lévi-Strauss, Claude. 1947. "La sociologie française." In *La sociologie au XXe siècle*, tome 2, edited by Georges Gurvitch and Wilbert E. Moore, 513–545. Paris: Presses universitaires de France.

Lukes, Steven. 1973. *Émile Durkheim: His Life and Works*. Harmondsworth: Penguin Books.

Lukes, Steven. 2007. "Searle versus Durkheim." In *Intentional Acts and Institutional Facts: Essays on John Searle's Social Ontology*, edited by Savas L. Tsohatzidis, 191–202. Dordrecht: Springer.

Mallard, Grégoire. 2019. *Gift Exchange: The Transnational History of a Political Idea*. Cambridge: Cambridge University Press.
Marcel, Jean-Christophe, and Laurent Mucchielli. 1999. "Un fondement du lien social. La mémoire collective selon Maurice Halbwachs." *Technologies. Idéologies. Pratiques. Revue d'anthropologie des connaissances* 13, no. 2: 63–88.
Maryanski, Alexandra. 2018. *Émile Durkheim and the Birth of the Gods*. New York: Routledge.
Mauss, Marcel. 1927. "Henri Hubert." Fonds Hubert-Mauss, Archives du Collège de France.
Mauss, Marcel. 1950. *Sociologie et anthropologie*. Edited by Claude Lévi-Strauss. Paris: Presses universitaires de France.
Mauss, Marcel. (1925) 1966. *The Gift: Forms and Functions of Exchange in Archaic Societies*. Translated by Ian Cunnison. London: Cohen & West. Originally published as "Essai sur le don. Forme et raison de l'échange dans les sociétiés archaïques." *L'Année sociologique, nouvelle série* 1: 30–186.
Mauss, Marcel. 1968–1969. *Œuvres*, 3 vols. Edited by Victor Karady. Paris: Éditions de Minuit.
Mauss, Marcel. (1905) 1968. "Compte rendu de M. Chantepie de la Saussaye, *Manuel d'histoire des religions*." *L'Année sociologique* 8. In Marcel Mauss, *Œuvres*, vol. 1, 46. Paris: Éditions de Minuit.
Mauss, Marcel. (1925) 1969a. "In Memoriam. L'œuvre inédite de Durkheim et ses collaborateurs." *L'Année sociologique* n.s. 1. In Marcel Mauss, *Œuvres*, vol. 3, 473–499. Paris: Éditions de Minuit.
Mauss, Marcel. 1997. *Écrits politiques*. Edited by Marcel Fournier. Paris: Fayard.
Mauss, Marcel. (1909) 2008. *On Prayer*. Edited by W. S. F. Pickering and translated by Susan Leslie. New York: Berghahn Books. Originally distributed privately as *La prière*. New edition: *La prière*. Paris: Presses universitaires de France, 2019.
Mauss, Marcel. 2013. *La nation ou le sens du social*. Edited by Marcel Fournier and Jean Terrier. Paris: Presses universitaires de France.
Mauss, Marcel, and Henri Hubert. (1899) 1964. *Sacrifice: Its Nature and Functions*. Translated by W. D. Halls. Chicago: University of Chicago Press. Originally published as "Essai sur la nature et la fonction du sacrifice." *L'Année sociologique* 2: 29–138.
Mauss, Marcel, and Henri Hubert. (1904) 1972. *A General Theory of Magic*. Translated by Robert Brain. London: Routledge & Kegan Paul. Originally published as "Esquisse d'une théorie générale de la magie." *L'Année sociologique* 7: 1–146.
Mergy, Jennifer. 2004. "Teamwork across Disciplines: Durkheimian Sociology and the Study of Nations." *Revue européenne des sciences sociales / European Journal of Social Sciences* XLII, no. 129: 237–248.
Meštrović, Stjepan G. 1988. *Emile Durkheim and the Reformation of Sociology*. Lanham, MD: Rowman & Littlefield.
Mosbah-Natanson, Sébastien. 2019. "L'Année sociologique est-elle devenue 'boudonienne'? Les mutations d'une revue canonique (1964–2013)." *L'Année sociologique* 1, no. 69: 209–238.
Mucchielli, Laurent. 1998. *La Découverte du social. Naissance de la sociologie en France*. Paris: La Découverte.
Müller, Hans-Peter. 2019. "Emile Durkheims Moraltheorie." In Hans-Peter Müller, *Das soziologische Genie und sein solides Handwerk*, 127–155. Wiesbaden: Springer VS.
Nizan, Paul. (1932) 1981. *Les Chiens de garde*. Paris: François Maspero.
Olick, Jeffrey K., Vered Vinitzky-Seroussi, and Daniel Levy. 2011. *The Collective Memory Reader*. Oxford: Oxford University Press.

Ollion, Etienne, and Andrew Abbott. 2016. "French Connections: The Reception of French Sociologists in the USA (1970-2012)." *European Journal of Sociology* 57, no. 2: 331–372.

Parkin, Robert. 1996. *The Dark Side of Humanity: The Work of Robert Hertz and Its Legacy*. Amsterdam: Harwood Academic.

Pickering, W. S. F. 1984. *Durkheim's Sociology of Religion*. London: Routledge.

Pickering, W. S. F. 2009. *Durkheim's Sociology of Religion: Themes and Theories*. Cambridge: James Clarke & Co.

Radcliffe-Brown, A. R. (1912) 1979. "Lettre à Marcel Mauss, Birmingham, 6 août 1912." *Études durkheimiennes* 4: 2–7.

Rawls, Anne Warfield. 1996. "Durkheim's Epistemology: The Neglected Argument." *American Journal of Sociology* 102, no. 2: 430–482.

Rawls, Anne Warfield. 2004. *Epistemology and Practice: Durkheim's The Elementary Forms of Religious Life*. Cambridge: Cambridge University Press.

Riley, Alexander. 1999. "Whence Durkheim's Nietzschean Grandchildren? A Closer Look at Robert Hertz's Place in the Durkheimian Genealogy." *European Journal of Sociology* 40, no. 2: 304–330.

Rosati, Massimo. 2009. *Ritual and the Sacred: A Neo-Durkheimian Analysis of Politics, Religion and the Self*. London: Routledge.

Schmaus, Warren. 2007. *Rethinking Durkheim and His Tradition*. Cambridge: Cambridge University Press.

Schnapper, Dominique. 1994. *La communauté des citoyens. Sur l'idée moderne de nation*. Paris: Gallimard.

Searle, John. 1995. *The Construction of Social Reality*. New York: Free Press.

Searle, John. 2006. "Searle versus Durkheim and the Waves of Thought: Reply to Gross." *Anthropological Theory* 6, no. 1: 57–69.

Simiand, François. 1903. "Methode historique et science sociale." *Revue de synthèse historique*, tome 6, no. 1: 1–22, 122–157. Republished in: *Annales. Économies, sociétés, civilisations* 15, no. 1 (1960): 83–119.

Simmel, Georg. (1896) 1898. "The Persistence of Social Groups I-III." Translated by Albion Small. *American Journal of Sociology* 3, no. 5: 662–698; 3, no. 6: 829–836; 4, no. 1: 35–50. First published as "Comment les formes sociales se maintiennent." *L'Année sociologique* 1: 71–109.

Smith, Philip. 2008. *Punishment and Culture*. Chicago: University of Chicago Press.

Steiner, Philippe. 2011. *Durkheim and the Birth of Economic Sociology*. Princeton, NJ: Princeton University Press.

Stoetzel, Jean. 1946. "L'esprit de la sociologie contemporaine." *Bulletin de la Société de philosophie de Bordeaux*, no. 4: 2–20. Republished in *Revue française de sociologie* 32, no. 3 (1991): 443–456.

Strenski, Ivan. 1997. *Durkheim and the Jews of France*. Chicago: University of Chicago Press.

Tarot, Camille. 1999. *De Durkheim à Mauss. L'invention du symbolique*. Paris: La Découverte/ M.A.U.S.S.

Tilly, Charles. 1981. "Useless Durkheim." In Charles Tilly, *As Sociology Meets History*, 95–108. New York: Academic Press.

Tiryakian, Edward A. 2009. *For Durkheim: Essays in Historical and Cultural Sociology*. London: Routledge.

Topalov, Christian. 2008. "Maurice Halbwachs and Chicago Sociologists." *Revue française de sociologie* 49: 187–214.

Turner, Stephen, ed. 1993. *Emile Durkheim: Sociologist and Moralist*. London: Routledge.

Vogt, Paul W. 1993. "L'influence de la *Division du travail social* sur la sociologie américaine." In *Division du travail et lien social. Durkheim un an après*, edited by Ph. Besnard, M. Borlandi, and P. Vogt, 197–215. Paris: Presses universitaires de France.

Watts Miller, W. 1996. *Durkheim, Morals and Modernity*. Montreal: McGill-Queen's University Press.

Wetzel, Dietmar. 2009. *Maurice Halbwachs*. Konstanz: UVK.

Wilson, David Sloan. 2002. *Darwin's Cathedral: Evolution, Religion, and the Nature of Society*. Chicago: University of Chicago Press.

CHAPTER 10

DURKHEIM AND BERGSON, DURKHEIMIANS AND BERGSONIANS

HEIKE DELITZ

This chapter focuses on the tension between two contemporaneous "big" French systems of thought at the turn of the twentieth century, namely, between the philosophy of Henri Bergson, on the one hand, and Durkheimian sociology, on the other. Although this tension remained mostly implicit, it was very productive: the aversion of Durkheim and the Durkheim school to Bergson can be regarded as productive, to the extent that the cliché of Bergson's seemingly "irrational" and "metaphysical" thought enabled Durkheim to present his sociology as a thoroughly positivist, rationalist, and socio-centric discipline. And through his critical reading of Durkheimian sociology in *The Two Sources of Morality and Religion*, Bergson ([1932] 1935) elaborated a unique social theory, deeply inspired by Durkheim's religious sociology and, more generally, by the latter's functionalist perspective on social facts. At the same time, Bergson remained very critical of the Durkheimian way of posing the problem of social order, and of the dualism between society and individual posited by Durkheim. Since Bergson's death, a number of prominent French authors have, independently from each other, integrated these contrasting strands of thought. Here, one should mention not only all the theories of the "imaginary institution of society" that appear in the writings of authors such as Georges Canguilhem, Cornelius Castoriadis, Claude Lévi-Strauss, and Pierre Clastres but also the various theories of artifacts as social actors offered by André Leroi-Gourhan, Gilbert Simondon, and Gilles Deleuze. These social theories integrate a Bergsonian philosophy of becoming and a Bergsonian ontology. The result of this integration is nothing less than an alternative tradition in French sociology: a Bergsonian sociological theory. Hence, the historical relation between Durkheim and Bergson is of manifold interest for sociology: first, because of the productive rejection that led to the invention of the discipline of sociology; and second, because of the attraction of a new philosophy of social thought, or, in other words, because of both negative and positive "Bergson effects" (Delitz 2015).

In order to appreciate these effects, one must look beyond the boundaries of sociology—which were drawn by Durkheim in order to exclude other social theories and other academic projects. Also, it would be impossible to discuss the successive misreadings and rereadings of Bergson without providing the reader with at least a very brief general introduction to Bergson's work. More recent interpretations of this important twentieth-century French author have supplanted the two dominant pictures of Bergson's work—that is, as a metaphysics of life, and as a phenomenology of inner, or subjective, life (both of which regard Bergson as a theorist of a "stream of consciousness")—with a view of Bergson as the author of a philosophy of difference, of a non-Cartesian ontology, and of an ontology of process (see the introduction to Deleuze [1966] 1990): the name "Bergson" now connotes a philosophy of becoming, rather than a philosophy of being, or, an ontology of substance.[1] Moreover, he was always in touch with the empirical sciences. In each of his books, Bergson discussed one or more contemporary disciplines—psychology, biology, physics, and sociology-ethnology.

After briefly reporting the state of research, the chapter sketches the relation of Durkheim and his colleagues to Bergson. The first section focuses on the productive tension within the idea of sociology as a rationalistic, positivistic, and socio-centric discipline (opposed against irrationalism, metaphysics, and a philosophy of the subject). This first section also considers thematic similarities that are evident in the sociologizations of some of Bergson's core notions (as in the Durkheimian sociology of memory, and of time). The second section focuses on Bergson's own social theory. Indeed, *The Two Sources of Morality and Religion* was expressly conceived as a *livre de sociologie*. It is a productive result of the tension between these two authors and their works, as it reacts to the Durkheimian approach by integrating a social theory into a philosophy of becoming. To show this, the second part also provides a brief summary of Bergson's philosophical works and aims. The third section is dedicated to Bergsonian authors in French social thought beyond the boundaries of sociology, after 1945. If early Bergsonism celebrated the author for his seemingly anti-scientific and romantic philosophy, and for his critique of modernity, later "Bergsonians" highlight different productive intersections between Durkheim's and Bergson's strands of French thought.

The State of Research on Durkheim versus Bergson

Among the sociological classics, it was Claude Lévi-Strauss who brought Bergson and Durkheim together. For him, Bergson, not Durkheim, was fully aware of the *intellectual* character of totemism. Bergson "finds the solution to the problem of totemism in the field of oppositions and ideas," whereas Durkheim seeks the answer at the "level of indistinction" (Lévi-Strauss [1962] 1991: 95), and within "affective values" (Lévi-Strauss [1962] 1991: 97). More importantly, according to Lévi-Strauss, it was Bergson who rejected the idea that society is already given, and whose social theory tried to explain how societies constitute themselves. More recently, only a small number of authors have shown an interest in the relation between the two thinkers. This is true for both the French history of sociology (because of the sociological clichés surrounding Bergson) and the French historiography of philosophy (which shows little interest in questions of social theory). For example, Bergsonian scholars tend to read *The Two Sources* in a purely philosophical manner, seeing it exclusively as a philosophy of religion, or as metaphysics (Waterlot 2008; Sitbon-Peillon 2009). Durkheimian scholars, meanwhile, tend to oscillate between two assumptions when it comes to the pair's relationship, namely, Durkheim's hostility to Bergson, on the one hand, and Bergson's influence on Durkheim, on the other. According to Steven Lukes ([1973] 1985: 370–371), Durkheim regarded Bergson as "dangerous"; Marcel Fournier (2007: 652–653), like Grogin (1988), stresses Durkheim's rejection of Bergson.[2] By contrast, Lukes ([1973] 1985: 505–506), Pickering (1984: 404–405), and Namer (1994: 305) all assume a hidden Bergsonian influence on the concept of effervescence that Durkheim developed in *The Elementary Forms of Religious Life* ([1912] 1995). Stedman Jones (2001: 213–214, 80–81) also assumes a certain influence of Bergson on *The Elementary Forms*, but ultimately privileges the influence of Charles Renouvier. For Dominique LaCapra (2001 [1972]: 194, cf. 254–255), by contrast, the late Durkheim was heavily influenced by "Bergson's ideas of creative evolution and élan vital." Riley (2002), in turn, sees Bergson and Durkheim as sharing a common interest in the sacred. Within the history of French philosophy, Louis Pinto (2004: 42) understood the opposition between Bergson and Durkheim as the "main structuring line of the philosophical field" (for similar views, see Fabiani 2010; Paoletti 2012; Bianco 2015).[3]

Durkheim's "Becoming": Aversions to Bergson and Sociologizations of Bergson

In Durkheim's work, a twofold "Bergson effect" can be observed. First, the rejection of Bergson's philosophy—among other adversarial relations, like those to Gabriel de Tarde and René Worms—enabled Durkheim and his colleagues to invent the new discipline of sociology. Driven by manifold objections to Bergson, they could elaborate a firmly sociological position, even if—or perhaps, because—their references to Bergson mostly remained implicit. Despite their complete disavowal of Bergson's scientific methodology, the Durkheimians in fact adopted some of Bergson's themes, reformulating them sociologically. The following section will first survey the works of Durkheim and then those of some of his disciples and colleagues in the context of the *Année sociologique*.

Durkheim: A Meaningful Non-Relation to Bergson

In 1895, Durkheim wrote an article about the rise of anti-scientific tendencies in the teachings of his contemporary philosophers, where he talks about a new "mysticism" that promises "a world of pleasures" instead of scientific thought (Durkheim [1895] 1975a: 416). From *The Rules of Sociological Method* ([1894] 1964) to *Elementary Forms of Religious Life* ([1912] 1995), there is no explicit mention of Bergson. Apparently, Durkheim was not interested in reading Bergson's work in detail. Rather, his target was the contemporary *gloire* of Bergson (Azouvi 2007)—the fascination that Bergson provoked. In this context, one could argue that, in three important respects, *The Rules* were also written against Bergsonism: First, Durkheim introduces sociology as a rigid, positivist perspective on social facts—as an empirical science opposed to all philosophical speculation. Second, he stresses that the new discipline is a form of rationalism, as opposed to the "times of renascent mysticism" (Durkheim [1894] 1964: xi). And third, Durkheim defines the new science as socio-centric, asserting, against any philosophy of the subject, the nonpsychological character of the social. Of course, his immediate target is always Gabriel de Tarde, the personification of everything that the French school of sociology rejected, all the more so because Tarde (unlike Bergson at that time) claimed to be a sociologist. But the rejection of Bergson's philosophy can be seen as similarly constitutive for the new discipline. Given the omnipresent discussions of Bergson's work at the time, one could argue that Durkheim's elision of Bergson is a case of demonstrative ignorance. This argument becomes more compelling when one takes into account that the mainstream of French philosophy (except Lévy-Bruhl 1890) criticized the young Bergson in the same words that Durkheim used (i.e., dangerous "new mysticism" and "irrationalism"). Additionally, other accounts attest to a general hostility toward Bergson on the side of Durkheim's students (Agathon 1911, 1913); Romain Rolland spoke of Durkheim as the "Anti-Bergson" (Rolland 1971: 136), while the Durkheimian Célestin Bouglé (1935: 28–29) regarded both authors as being in a relation of "real opposition," and even in an "armed fight." It is interesting to note that Bergson and Durkheim knew each other from their time at the *École normale supérieure*. In the later stages of their careers, they remained rivals—Durkheim wanted to succeed Tarde as the chair of modern philosophy at the Collège de France, which Bergson eventually did.[4]

That Durkheim indeed had Bergson in mind becomes obvious in the lectures on *Pragmatism and Sociology* that he gave in 1913 (Durkheim [1955] 1983). Here, Durkheim explicitly paints Bergson as an anti-rationalist.[5] The final lecture, "Are Thought and Reality Heterogeneous?," is a critique of Bergson.[6] In these lectures, Durkheim consistently opposes the positions that he ascribes to Bergson. For instance, whereas Bergson (indeed) privileges continuous becoming and the "homogenous" as ontological features of reality, Durkheim writes: "reality [...] is far from resistant to any form of distinction" (Durkheim [1955] 1983: 94). While Bergson ([1907] 1944: 43) criticized Herbert Spencer's evolutionism as a theory which always negates the new, in these lectures Durkheim demonstratively accepts Spencer's view (Durkheim [1955] 1983: 95). And while Bergson elaborates a philosophy of process, Durkheim writes: States of reality express the "real elements of becoming" (Durkheim [1955] 1983: 96).

Durkheim's rejection of Bergson is also apparent in *The Elementary Forms of Religious Life*—although Bergson's name does not appear there. As the previously mentioned Durkheim scholars assume, there may be a Bergsonian influence in this work. This seems particularly true of the notion of *effervescence* (Durkheim [1912] 1995: 213, 429), as well as of related notions like *élan à croire* (translated as "leap"; cf. Durkheim [1912] 1995: 365; see Pickering 1984: 404–405, or Namer 1994: 305). Bergson's influence might also be apparent in Durkheim's discussions of social becoming and creativity (see Riley, Pickering, and Miller 2013). Nevertheless, *The Elementary Forms of Religious Life*, just like *Pragmatism and Sociology*, concludes with anti-Bergsonian arguments. In the conclusion of his final and perhaps most important book, Durkheim again argues for rationalism and against irrationalism, and declares the philosophy of identity to be the *only* rational one. Read in this light, the following sentences can be interpreted as a rejection of the core of Bergson's philosophy—at least if one regards Bergson as the philosopher of becoming, who seeks to rethink everything *sub specie durationis*: "To think logically, in fact, is [...] to think *sub specie aeternitatis*" (Durkheim [1912] 1995: 437). One can also point to Durkheim's discussion of the sociology of knowledge in the same book (and in Durkheim and Mauss [1903] 2009). Here, he develops the idea of a social genesis of the categories of thought and elaborates this idea also for the category of time, making reference to Henri Hubert's discussion of Bergson (Hubert [1905] 1999). Following Hubert, Durkheim says, against the notion of time as continuous change: One "can conceive of time only if we differentiate between moments"; moreover, "it is not *my time* that is organized in this way; it is time that is conceived of objectively by all men of the same civilization" (Durkheim [1912] 1995: 9–10). There was only one instance of positive cooperation between Durkheim and Bergson. In 1915, Durkheim invited him to contribute to his "war papers" (Durkheim and Denis 1915; Bergson 1915). This was, as Worms (2009: 185) states, a short-lived and "twice unexpected" cooperation—unexpected for both sides.

The Durkheimians (Hubert, Halbwachs, Mauss)

Similarly hostile attitudes toward Bergson appear in the works of Durkheim's disciples and colleagues—with the two exceptions of Robert Hertz and Gaston Richard, who were more impressed by, and more friendly to, Bergson (for Hertz, see Riley and Besnard 2002: 66; and see Richard 1994). Sometimes, these attitudes tended to be quite explicit. This is true, first, in the case of Henri Hubert. In his detailed discussion of Bergson's *Matter and Memory* (Bergson [1896] 1991) and *Time and Free Will* (Bergson [1889] 1910), Hubert ([1905] 1999) develops a sociology of time (cf. Isambert 1979, 1999). He emphasizes the social conditions of time consciousness, and the social structuration of duration, in the cases of magic and religious time. As Isambert (1999: 20) writes, unlike Bergson, Hubert doesn't "destructure time in order to make the duration the indefinitely varied and fluid course of the consciousness." Even today, Durkheimians see Bergson's philosophy as a plea for the idea of a "fluid stream of consciousness." In fact (as will become clear below), the ever-present starting point of Bergson's work was his differentiation between two notions of time, that is, between *durée*, or becoming, as the true character of time, on the one hand, and the disjoined time of physics (*temps* as a representation of time as divided), on the other. When speaking about calendars and time divisions as objects of a sociology of time, Hubert opposes Bergson, or he sociologizes Bergson's philosophy.

Maurice Halbwachs, a former disciple of Bergson, does the same thing with respect to the notion of memory. While inventing the notion of "collective memory" (Halbwachs [1950] 1980) and the related idea of "social conditions" of individual memory (Halbwachs 1992), he discusses Bergson's *Matter and Memory*, waging an "epistemological war" against Bergson (Namer 1997: 261). Here, Halbwachs always takes Bergson to be a philosopher of the subject whose interest lies in an "inner life" of emotions or thoughts. Contrary to this cliché, one of Bergson's core inventions in *Matter and Memory* is a non-Cartesian philosophy. In this philosophy, memory is not understood as a mere "inner" fact but as deeply related to affects and to activities of bodies. Nevertheless, Halbwachs ([1950] 1980: 90–92), while inventing a sociology of the social construction of memories, criticizes Bergson for the "hypothesis of purely individual and mutually inaccessible durations." Throughout his life, he regarded Bergson as a dangerous irrationalist.

Less important for his own work, but nonetheless of interest for us, are Marcel Mauss's critical discussions of Bergson. Mauss sociologizes Bergson's (less central) notion of homo faber, that is, his idea of the human being as the inventor of artifacts, feelings, and thoughts (Bergson [1907] 1944: 153–154). According to Mauss, Bergson has a false, solipsistic idea of technical inventions, which, in Mauss's view, are always social processes: instead of giving "techniques a place of honour in the history of humanity" but at the expense of reason, Bergson's ideas about an "individual and profound life of the spirit" should be replaced by a social theory (Mauss [1927] 2006: 50–51). Later, Mauss harshly criticized Bergson's *Two Sources* as a purely "literary point of view"; and for allotting to sociology only the "realm of the closed" (Mauss [1933] 1969: 436, my translation). Finally, Mauss saw Bergson as a forerunner of "Hitlerism" (Mauss [1938] 1990: 87).

BERGSON: A PHILOSOPHY OF BECOMING AND A SOCIOLOGY OF IMAGINED COLLECTIVE IDENTITY

In *The Two Sources of Morality and Religion* (1932 [1935]), Bergson wrote his own "livre de sociologie" (Bergson [1932] 2002: 1387). Here, he meticulously discusses Durkheim's approach, especially with regard to morals, religion, and more specifically, totemic societies. There, Bergson follows Durkheim far, but at the same time, he seeks a vitalist corrective for sociology. In Bergson's work, life is not only the object of society; it is, simultaneously, the subject of all social phenomena. In the words of Georges Canguilhem (1943 [2007]: 135–136; 1980 [2016]: 211), Bergson criticizes positivism as a self-description of social life, which transforms all phenomena into pure (unchangeable) "social facts," or which tends to discriminate against the new and the rare. Social inventions are of central relevance to Bergson's sociology: he is deeply interested in the emergence of new collectives. Therefore, the central notion of *The Two Sources* is positive imagination or *fabulation*, and not (negative, secondary) *constraint*. Social constraint might be necessary for any kind of collective life. The interesting phenomenon, however, is not constraint but rather the invention of new social ideals through which new societies institute themselves. Constraint explains nothing; there must first be an affective idea around which a collective is constituted—only then can this collective be stabilized by dogmas, taboos, and sanctions. A further point of contrast with respect to Durkheim is that, for Bergson, there is no such thing as a "closed" society. A collective identity is always imaginary; beyond such "fabulations," the reality of the social is a constant becoming another.

The Philosophy of Bergson: Becoming Instead of Being

A true "philosopher has only one idea," Bergson said ([1911] 1946: 131). His *idée directrice* is not so much the mysterious idea of an *élan vital*, but a more precise differentiation between time and space, or between "real" time—which is permanent, unforeseeable becoming—and divided, or "spatialized," time. The reality of all things—and, in particular, of living things—is heterogeneous and continuous becoming. In contrast to its ontological character, its epistemological representation—within the sciences as within daily life—is divided, homogenous, and discontinuous. Bergson's philosophy stresses that becoming another is real (which also means that it is not the becoming of some fixed thing). The real is a "change that is substance itself" (Deleuze [1966] 1990: 37). Because he sees reality not as a series of stages, but as permanent becoming another, Bergson rejects any philosophy of identity, or representation, in favor of a philosophy of temporal movement, or alteration.[7]

The first consequence of a philosophy of becoming is the rejection of Cartesianism: there is no matter which is formed by ideas; there is no clear distinction between mind and matter. Bergson sees all entities within the same ontological tableau. Mind and body, knowledge and world, thoughts and actions are only slightly different aspects of the same "attention to life" (Bergson [1896] 1991: 14), toward which all human actions are directed. From this perspective, thoughts are *bodily activities*. Or thoughts and emotions are "virtual actions" (Bergson [1896] 1991: 50), and matter, perceived by the attention to life, is "an aggregate of 'images' " (Bergson [1896] 1991: 9). In other words, matter and thought are different types of affects. They correspond to different "points of the universe which [our] movements could affect" (Bergson [1896] 1991:

41). In various affective states, the "inner" and "outer" worlds are only slightly different. Rather, Bergson speaks of various "tensions" of the attention to life or action. The second consequence of a philosophy of becoming, or a process ontology, can be called a philosophy of difference (Deleuze [1956] 2004). In *Creative Evolution*, Bergson elaborates such a philosophy for the realm of organic life (including human life). There, he also discusses the idea of an *élan vital*. According to Deleuze's interpretation, *élan vital* hereby means the whole of life, which is never actual, but virtual, as life is constant becoming. Life consists of permanent actualizations—that is, of the different living forms. In retrospect, these forms reveal themselves as "bifurcations" of life (Bergson [1907] 1944: 111)—between animals and plants, for instance. Therefore, Bergson regards life as "tendency," in the sense of a movement of differentiation ("creating, by its very growth, divergent directions" of life; Bergson [1907] 1944: 110). He also develops this idea of differentiation as bifurcation, or tending in opposite directions, for collective life, or types of society (cf. 2.2).

The third consequence of a philosophy of becoming is a critique of negative concepts and their underlying assumptions regarding opposed states of reality. He applies this critique to the central questions of classical philosophy. Of course, one could also apply this critique to the sociological question of social order (within Durkheimian sociology and beyond). For Bergson, both the epistemological question of "order" (i.e., Why is there order in our knowledge of reality?) and the ontological question of "being" (Why is there something rather than nothing?) are empty questions: First, both questions imply that there are two opposed states of reality (order vs. disorder, being vs. nothing), rather than actual becoming. Second, one of these states ("disorder") is defined in a purely negative way—as the simple opposite of a positive state ("order"), plus its absence (Bergson [1907] 1944: chap. IV, cf. Bergson [1930] 2012). The question, How is order possible instead of disorder?

> has meaning only if we suppose that disorder, understood as an absence of order, is possible, or imaginable, or conceivable. Now, it is only order that is real; but, as order can take two forms, and as the presence of the one may be said to consist in the absence of the other, we speak of disorder whenever we have before us that one of the two orders for which we are not looking. The idea of disorder [...] does not denote the absence of all order, but only the presence of that order which does not offer us actual interest.
>
> (Bergson [1907] 1944: 298)

The Social Theory of Bergson: The Imaginary Institution, or the Fabulation, of Society

Just as there was a Durkheimian critique of Bergson's philosophy, there was also a Bergsonian critique of Durkheim's sociology. Bergson always considered Durkheim to be an "enemy of freedom" (Benrubi 1942: 63). He spoke of Durkheim's sociology as a "false system," to the extent that it substitutes one reality (that of collective actions and representations) for another (that of individual actions and representations; cf. Chevalier 1959: 20 and 34). Both chronologically and systematically, Bergson's discussion of Durkheim's work has two stages.

An initial response to Durkheim can already be found in *Laughter*, Bergson's essays on the meaning of the comic, from 1900. Although Bergson takes a sociological perspective when stating that "laughter is always the laughter of a group" (Bergson [1900] 1911: 3), already here he explains this phenomenon by assuming that *life* is the subject of all social facts: in laughter, life corrects its own social constraints. Bergson's second, more elaborate, response to Durkheim can be found in *The Two Sources of Morality and Religion*. Here, Durkheim is explicitly mentioned, as are Mauss, Hubert, and Lévy-Bruhl. Working both with and against these authors, Bergson transforms his own philosophy into a theory of society. Seen from the vantage point of later French theories of society, especially that of Castoriadis, the core of Bergson's social theory lies in the pair of instituting and instituted society, that is, in the tension between social life as becoming and its imaginary fixation—or, in other words, in the tension between the becoming another of individuals and collectives, and their imagined identities. Collective identities and collective existence are counterfactual, but nonetheless necessary, imaginary institutions. Thus, one can see Bergsonian social theory as postfoundational: if the reality of the social is change, then collective identity is impossible; precisely for this reason, the fabulation of collective identities is necessary (cf. Marchart 2007: 104, 141).

The Two Sources is meant to be a work of sociology. It develops a social theory based on Bergson's philosophy, integrating Durkheim's notions and concepts along the way. This integration is obvious when Bergson speaks of "moral obligation," and of a "static religion"; likewise, when he discusses the social function of morality and religion, and the related idea of the necessity of social integration. Bergson also shares Durkheim's interest in totemism. He refers to Durkheim in at least three instances: First, he endorses the notion of collective representations, explicitly rejecting "only" the notion of a conflict between the social and the individual (Bergson [1932] 1935: 85). Second, he rejects the Durkheimian thesis that primitive thought is more "natural" than modern thought (Bergson [1932] 1935: 112 and 119–120). Third, Bergson reinterprets totemism: Totemic societies create collective identities by means of group differentiation. Neither their solidarity with animals nor their use of animals as symbols is of central importance, but rather the constitution of a group through the symbolic classification of nature (Bergson [1932] 1935: 156; cf. Durkheim and Mauss [1903] 2009). Of course, one already finds this thesis in *The Elementary Forms of Religious Life* (Bergson certainly was an unfair reader of Durkheim's final book). But a further argument is perhaps more important: Totemic societies may be extremely closed; they may stabilize themselves in an extreme manner—nonetheless, even here, social life remains perpetual change. By means of the same institution through which a society closes itself, and denies its own contingency, a new society can emerge that is made possible by "the myth-making function" of *fabulation* (Bergson [1932] 1935: 232). Fabulation, beyond being a mechanism of fixation, is also a capacity to invent new social forms. Here, too, Bergson is more interested in the opening aspects of societies and in the role of individuals in society—whereas he takes Durkheim to be accentuating the closing aspect. The "door will ever stand open to fresh creations," Bergson writes ([1932] 1935: 61), in spite of the fact that after "each occasion, the circle that has momentarily opened closes again," and that any new moral aspiration has to borrow its form of "obligation" "from the closed society" (Bergson [1932] 1935: 230). In short, fabulation is the mechanism by which a society fixes itself; and through fabulation, new collective lives emerge. Crucial for this interpretation of *The Two Sources* is a passage where Bergson reformulates Spinoza: social life and society are characterized as the relationship between *natura naturans* and *natura naturata*, or between "repose and movement" (Bergson [1932] 1935: 44–45). Thus, social life goes beyond any specific society; it is life which is real, whereas a fixation is always fabulated. The stopping point is always imaginary. The notions of closed society and open society do not denote two distinct types of societies, but the relation between social life, or social becoming, and its virtual stopping points (cf. Deleuze [1943] 2007: 84). Bergson's emphasis is on the instituting society, which is becoming, or "real and effective duration" (Deleuze [1943] 2007: 95). Therefore, Bergson speaks of a "vital impetus" (Bergson [1932] 1935: 91) beyond all given societies.

In sum, though Bergson affirms Durkheim's concept, he always emphasizes the moment of unforeseeable alteration and the imaginary character of social life. His concept of *élan vital* does not refer to some mystic life force but rather to the continuous becoming of another which exists only in the differentiation of collectives—as each society reveals, in a "latent" state, the "essential characteristics of most of the other manifestations" of social life (Bergson [1932] 1935: 98).

A Second "French School of Sociology": Bergsonian Social Theories

The relation between Durkheim and Bergson concerns not just the two authors but two styles of thought. Just as certain followers of Durkheim have been crucial for the development of a Durkheimian sociology, there are other authors from whom one can derive a Bergsonian social theory. Therefore, this chapter also examines Bergson's intellectual afterlife. A first attempt to criticize Durkheim on the basis of Bergson's philosophy can be seen in the work of Maurice Hauriou ([1925] 1970, [1928] 1986), whose "social vitalism" explicitly builds on Bergson. Later, more elaborate Bergsonian social theories appear. First and foremost, these are theories of the imaginary institution (fabulation) of society. Unlike Durkheimian vocabularies, such theories show a keen interest in the creativity of the social. Cornelius Castoriadis, in particular, regards "becoming" as primary. This kind of social theory does away with both the question of order and the related idea of the possibility of "disorder." A Bergsonian sociology takes unforeseeable change as the discipline's guiding problem. Social order must be imaginary, not because of disorder (which Bergsonians take to be nonexistent) but because of the reality of change. The focus here is wholly on the positivity of social phenomena. A second aspect of Bergson's legacy is the presence of Bergsonian arguments in the field of structural anthropology—especially when it comes to Bergson's critique of negative concepts. When Lévi-Strauss rejects the idea of a society "without" history, or when Pierre Clastres rejects the idea of a society "without" state, they do this because such negative concepts (and the inherent evolutionism or ethnocentrism of the corresponding social theories) have come to be seen as absurd. A third consequence of Bergson's philosophy relates to his theory of social interaction: a non-Cartesian ontology makes it possible to conceptualize interactions as involving bodies, be they human or not—and to include matter and artifacts in our analysis. Here one could mention the social theories of Gilles Deleuze, Gilbert Simondon, and André Leroi-Gourhan. A fourth Bergson effect amounts to a serious criticism of any (Durkheimian) positivism within the social sciences:

> As Bergson said, there is no disorder, but there are always two orders, of which the first is substituted by the second, which we want. [...] If there is life, there is a norm: life is a polarized activity [...] The normal is therefore a universal category of life, and the pathological must be regarded, without absurdity, as normal.
> (Canguilhem [1942/43] 2015: 104, my translation)

In his lecture *The Norms and the Normal* (Canguilhem [1942/43] 2015; cf. Le Blanc 2002: 130–140), Canguilhem criticizes sociological positivism from a Bergsonian point of view. At the same time, he reanimates vitalism as an attitude that expresses "the self-identity of life within the living human being" (Canguilhem [1952] 2008b: 62), and even as a kind of "rationalism" (Canguilhem [1952] 2008a: xx). Canguilhem's first critique of positivism refers to the vitality of norms. According to Canguilhem, norms are immanent in life (and do not simply act as external social constraints on life, as Durkheim thought). A second critique of Durkheim's positivism concerns the discourse of the normal and the pathological. According to Canguilhem, the truth of the social is the ability to disagree about norms; the pathological is never the "absence" of a norm, but is in itself a "norm" (Canguilhem [1943/1966] 1978: 82; cf. Canguilhem [1952] 2008c: 126, 131). It "is enough that one individual in any society question the needs and norms of that society"; a society is never a "harmonic whole," and a social invention is not a crisis (Canguilhem [1943/1966] 1978: 158; cf. Canguilhem [1955] 2012, referring to Bergson). Canguilhem criticizes Durkheim for methodologically presupposing a static concept of the social (which erroneously regards order and disorder as logical opposites) and for discriminating against individual inventions and social transformations.

On the question of who, or what, actively takes part in collective life (i.e., in their theories of social interaction), Bergsonian sociologies closely follow Bergson's non-Cartesian ontology. As mentioned, *Matter and Memory* offers a theory of the affective becoming of individuals, or of permanent individuation, that is, opposed to a philosophy of the self-identical subject. It also provided a new social ontology—in opposition to sociological anthropocentrism. André Leroi-Gourhan (1943, 1945), Gilbert Simondon, and Gilles Deleuze all share a social theory according to which artifacts and other non-organic matter are active participants in the social. Unlike Durkheimian theories, such social theories regard artifacts as being more than mere representations, or symbols, of a given social order. At the same time, all three of these authors share Bergson's interest in continuous becoming and social creativity. Simondon argues that, since becoming is the fundamental fact, an *énergétique sociale* is necessary. Sociology asks why societies change; Simondon's answer is: they do this because of their energetic potentials within moments of "high tension of information" during which a social idea is particularly affective (Simondon [1958] 2007: 63). Simondon's theory of society follows Bergson's philosophy. His analysis of modern societies is deeply concerned with the technical mode of collective existence (Simondon [1958] 2017). According to Simondon, it is technical activity that brings about a "veritable social reason," which in turn introduces the sense of "liberty" into the collective (Simondon [1958] 2007: 261, my translation), because only technical activity, defined as the intimate interaction between a human actor and matter, is free of normative constraints.

Deleuze also employs an ontology of immanence, as is made clear by his concept of assemblage. Deleuze understands the "assemblage" as "a constellation of singularities and traits deducted from the flow [of matter]—selected, organized, stratified—in such a way as to converge (consistency) artificially and naturally." An assemblage, in other words, "is a veritable invention" (Deleuze and Guattari [1980] 1987: 406). Recent social theories, particularly in the field of anthropology, exhibit such Deleuze-mediated Bergson effects.[8]

As mentioned earlier, while Bergson speaks of *natura naturata* and *natura naturans*, Castoriadis uses the terms *instituted society* and *instituting society*. For Castoriadis ([1975] 1998: 70), a society is based on nothing other than a vital, fluent ground which is the continuity of social becoming, or the "anonymous collective whole." Within this continuity, any given society is located on an imaginary line that includes all past and all future societies. This continuity of social life seems more than just conceptually similar to the continuity that Bergson's concept of *élan vital* claims with respect to living beings. Furthermore, Castoriadis shares Bergson's notion of the relationship between the vital and the social as a relation between underlying movements and imagined collective identities:

> The social-historical is the anonymous collective whole, the impersonal-human element that fills every given social formation but which also engulfs it, setting each society in the midst of others, inscribing them all within a continuity in which those who are no longer, those who are elsewhere and even those yet to be born are in a certain sense present. It is, on the one hand, given structures, "materialized" institutions [and] on the other hand, that which structures, institutes, materializes. In short, it is the union and the tension of instituting society and of instituted society, of history made and of history in the making.
>
> (Castoriadis [1975] 1998: 70)

Every society is based on a *societatis instituans*. Each societal life is an imaginary institution (fixation) of the social flux. Every society has to create such fixations, because social life is "perpetual [...] self-alteration," it is unpredictable and contingent. Society *as such* can only exist "by providing itself with 'stable' figures" (Castoriadis [1975] 1998: 126). It must deny its own alteration. At the same time, this mode of imaginary fixation constitutes the possibility of new societies. What "is given in and through history is not the determined sequence of the determined" society. Rather, it is the emergence of "radical otherness, immanent creation, non-trivial novelty." This character of social life is manifested by the "incessant transformation of each society," and also by the appearance of ever "new types of society" (Castoriadis [1975] 1998: 114). However, only when a new social form emerges does one recognize the vital becoming that is the foundation of the social.

If society is a fixation, if it is the imagination of an identity within time, every society *is*, first and foremost, the institution of a certain temporality. Capitalism *is* a "time of indefinite progress, unlimited growth, accumulation, rationalization, time of the conquest of nature, of the always closer approximation of a total, exact knowledge, of the realization of the phantasy of omnipotence" (Castoriadis [1975] 1998: 206–207). In this sense, Castoriadis implicitly develops a Bergsonian social theory, both in his concept of the instituting and instituted society, and in the central role he ascribes to imagination.[9] What he adds to Bergson from a Marxian perspective is the analytical difference between heteronomous and autonomous self-institutions of society. Moving beyond the apparent equivalence between self-institution and "self-alienation," an autonomous society would be a new mode of collective life. It would "make itself as explicitly self-instituting" (Castoriadis [1975] 1998: 372–373). Marcel Gauchet (1992) and Claude Lefort ([1980] 2006) may share such a theory of the instituted society.

And as mentioned earlier, another French Bergsonian sociology can be discerned in the methodology of structural anthropology (which is shared by the authors last mentioned, particularly by Gauchet). Criticizing negative concepts, structural anthropology compares societies as choices that are opposed to each other, not as different evolutionary stages. A society without history (Lévi-Strauss [1962] 1966: 233–234) can be better described as a society against history. Pierre Clastres ([1974] 1987) does not talk about stateless societies but about "societies against the state"—they do not lack a state; they actively refuse it. This view opposes the ethnocentric "conviction that history is a one-way progression" (Clastres [1974] 1987: 159), which permeates the entire Durkheim school.

Conclusion: Durkheim Versus Bergson—Durkheim Plus Bergson

Far from being of no interest (as the historiography of French sociology still suggests), Bergson's work gave rise to various "effects" within French social thought; if Bergson's new philosophy repelled some theorists, it attracted others. Although Durkheim and Bergson make almost no direct references to each other, the relationship between the two famous contemporaries was obviously hostile. In many ways, the relation between the two authors, and between their schools, is emblematic of a tension between opposing systems of thought. It is precisely because of this tension that the relationship between Durkheim and Bergson can be said to have been productive. The rejection of Bergson's work, or more precisely, the rejection of early Bergsonism, helped Durkheim and his colleagues to invent the discipline of sociology. In its rationalism, its positivism, and its socio-centrism, Durkheimian sociology was the opposite of the Bergsonian philosophy, which contemporaries interpreted as a kind of mysticism, speculative metaphysics, and subjectivism. At the same time, Henri Hubert, Maurice Halbwachs, and Marcel Mauss were able to transform central Bergsonian notions (concerning time, memory, and technique) into sociological concepts, thereby inventing a sociology of time, of collective memory, and of social techniques (for example, "techniques of the body"). For his part, Henri Bergson articulated his social theory as a critical response to Durkheim and his school, emphasizing the unforeseeable character of collective life and the fabulation of collective unity and identity; the role of individual inventions for new collectives; and the primacy of life, or of becoming, in general. Recourse to Bergsonian arguments enabled later authors to produce a critique of the identification of rare, or novel, social phenomena with pathological ones (Canguilhem); a critique of social theories that regard human beings as the only social actors (Simondon); a critique of ethnocentric theories of society (structural anthropology); and a critique of a sociology which denies the vital character of the social. Looking beyond the differences between the authors' respective social theories, one might consider the relation between these two prominent figures of twentieth-century French intellectual history from an even more abstract point of view; namely, from the point of view that regards French intellectual history as a history of polemics between two styles of thought. From this perspective, Bergson and Durkheim defined a "philosophical moment," in which they answered the same question—that of mentality—in opposite ways (Worms 2009: 12–14).

Notes

1. The rehabilitation of this author and his philosophical work is the merit of Maurice Merleau-Ponty, Jean Hyppolite, Jean Wahl, and, in particular, Gilles Deleuze.
2. Additionally, there are a few articles about the confrontational relation of both Maurice Halbwachs (Namer 1997) and Marcel Mauss (Schlanger 2006) to Bergson.
3. For an interpretation of Bergson's *livre de sociologie*, and of the ways in which it reacts to Durkheim's work, one should also mention the critical edition of *The Two Sources* (Bergson [1932] 2008), as well as Bouaniche et al. (2004), Lafrance (1974), Lefebvre and White (2010, 2012), Lefebvre (2013: 32–48), and Worms (2004, 2012). For a new interest in Bergson in sociology and social theory, see for instance Seyfert (2011).
4. For these and other institutional "affairs," see Clark (1973) and Besnard (1983).

5. Marcel Mauss (1923/24: 10) viewed these lectures as the "crown" of Durkheim's philosophical work, as Durkheim there showed himself "vis-à-vis James" and "vis-à-vis Bergson."
6. There is only one other recorded, albeit unpublished, mention of Bergson by Durkheim, a debate between him and Joseph Wilbois, an early Bergsonian (Durkheim [1914] 1975b).
7. Bergson discusses the consequences of this alternative view of the ontological realms for the different sciences, considering mental life in both *Time and Free Will* and *Matter and Memory*; organic life in *Creative Evolution*; and social, or collective, life in *The Two Sources of Morality and Religion*.
8. Cf. Viveiros de Castro ([2009] 2014), who shares a Bergsonian ontology of becoming and tries to decolonize our concepts of the social and the self.
9. For an explicit (and polemical) reference to Bergson, see Castoriadis (1985: 9–10).

References

Agathon. 1911. *L'esprit de la nouvelle Sorbonne*. Paris: Mercure de France.
Agathon. 1913. *Les jeunes gens d'aujourd'hui*. Paris: Mercure de France.
Azouvi, François. 2007. *La gloire de Bergson. Essai sur le magistère philosophique*. Paris: Gallimard.
Benrubi, Isaac. 1942. *Souvenirs sur Henri Bergson*. Neuchâtel, Paris: Delachaux & Niestlé.
Bergson, Henri. (1889) 1910. *Time and Free Will: An Essay on the Immediate Data of Consciousness*. London: George Allen & Unwin.
Bergson, Henri. (1900) 1911. *Laughter: An Essay on the Meaning of the Comic*. London: Macmillan.
Bergson, Henri. 1915. *The Meaning of the War: Life and Matter in Conflict*. London: Unwin.
Bergson, Henri. (1932) 1935. *The Two Sources of Morality and Religion*. London: Macmillan & Co.
Bergson, Henri. (1907) 1944. *Creative Evolution*. London: Macmillan & Co.
Bergson, Henri. (1911) 1946. "Philosophical Intuition." In *The Creative Mind*, 126–152. New York: Citadel.
Bergson, Henri. (1896) 1991. *Matter and Memory*. New York: Zone Books.
Bergson, Henri. (1932) 2002. "Bergson à [P. Masson-Oursel]." In *Correspondances*, 1386–1388. Paris: PUF.
Bergson, Henri. (1932) 2008. *Les deux sources de la morale et de la religion*. Paris: PUF.
Bergson Henri. (1930) 2012. "The Possible and the Real." In *The Creative Mind*, 73–86. New York: Dover.
Besnard, Philippe, ed. 1983. *The Sociological Domain: The Durkheimians and the Founding of French Sociology*. Cambridge: Cambridge University Press.
Bianco, Giuseppe. 2015. *Après Bergson. Portrait de groupe avec philosophe*. Paris: PUF.
Bouaniche, Arnaud, Frédéric Keck, and Frédéric Worms, eds. 2004. *Bergson: les deux sources de la morale et de la religion*. Paris: Ellipses.
Bouglé, Camille. 1935. *Bilan de la sociologie française contemporaine*. Paris: Alcan.
Canguilhem, Georges. (1943/1966) 1978. *On the Normal and the Pathological*. Dordrecht: Springer.
Canguilhem, Georges. (1943) 2007. "Commentaire au troisième chapitre de L'évolution créatrice." *Annales bergsoniennes* III, 113–160.
Canguilhem, Georges. (1952) 2008a. "Introduction: Thought and the Living." In *Knowledge of Life*, xvii–xx. New York: Fordham University Press.

Canguilhem, Georges. (1952) 2008b. "Aspects of Vitalism." In *Knowledge of Life*, 59–74. New York: Fordham University Press.
Canguilhem, Georges. (1952) 2008c. "The Normal and the Pathological." In *Knowledge of Life*, 121–133 New York: Fordham University Press.
Canguilhem, Georges. (1955) 2012. "The Problem of Regulation in the Organism and in Society." In *Writings on Medicine*, 67–78. New York: Fordham University Press.
Canguilhem, Georges. (1942/43) 2015. "Cours de philosophie générale et de logique." In *Œuvres complètes*, vol. 4: *Résistance, philosophie biologique et histoire des sciences, 1940–1965*, 81–110. Paris: Gallimard.
Canguilhem, Georges. (1980) 2016. "What Is Psychology?" *Foucault Studies* 21: 200–213.
Castoriadis, Cornelius. 1985. *Domaines de l'homme. Les carrefours du labyrinthe 2*. Paris: Seuil.
Castoriadis, Cornelius. (1975) 1998. *The Imaginary Institution of Society*. Cambridge, MA: MIT.
Chevalier, Jacques. 1959. *Entretiens avec Bergson*. Paris: Plon.
Clark, Terry Nichols. 1973. *Prophets and Patrons: The French University and the Emergence of the Social Sciences*. Cambridge, MA: Harvard University Press.
Clastres, Pierre. (1974) 1987. *Society against the State: Essays in Political Anthropology*. Cambridge, MA: MIT.
Deleuze, Gilles. (1966) 1990. *Bergsonism*. New York: Zone Books.
Deleuze, Gilles. (1956) 2004. "Bergson's Conception of Difference." In *Desert Island and Other Texts, 1953–1974*, 32–51. New York: Semiotext(e).
Deleuze, Gilles. (1943) 2007. "Lecture Course on Chapter Three of Bergson's 'Creative Evolution.'" *SubStance* 36 (3): 72–90.
Deleuze, Gilles, and Félix Guattari. (1980) 1987. *A Thousand Plateaus: Capitalism and Schizophrenia*. Minneapolis: University of Minnesota Press.
Delitz, Heike. 2015. *Bergson-Effekte. Aversionen und Attraktionen im französischen soziologischen Denken*. Weilerswist: Velbrück.
Durkheim, Émile. (1894) 1964. *The Rules of Sociological Method*. New York: Free Press.
Durkheim, Émile. (1895) 1975a. "L'enseignement philosophique et l'agrégation de philosophie." In *Textes 3: Fonctions sociales et institutions*, 403–434 Paris: Minuit.
Durkheim, Émile. (1914) 1975b. "Une confrontation entre bergsonisme et sociologisme. Le progrès moral et la dynamique sociale." In *Textes 1: Éléments d'une théorie sociale*, 64–70. Paris: Minuit.
Durkheim, Émile. (1955) 1983. *Pragmatism and Sociology*. Cambridge: Cambridge University Press.
Durkheim, Émile. (1912) 1995. *The Elementary Forms of Religious Life*. New York: Free Press.
Durkheim, Émile, and Ernest Denis. 1915. *Who Wanted War? The Origin of the War According to Diplomatic Documents*. Paris: Armand Colin.
Durkheim, Émile, and Marcel Mauss. (1903) 2009. *Primitive Classification*. Chicago: University of Chicago Press.
Fabiani, Jean-Louis. 2010. *Qu'est-ce qu'un philosophe français? La vie sociale des concepts (1880–1980)*. Paris: EHESS.
Fournier, Marcel. 2007. *Émile Durkheim (1858–1917)*. Paris: Fayard.
Gauchet, Marcel. (1977) 1992. "Primitive Religion and the Origins of the State." In *New French Thought: Political Philosophy*, edited by Mark Lilla, 116–122. Princeton, NJ: Princeton University Press.
Grogin, Robert C. 1988. *The Bergsonian Controversy in France, 1900–1914*. Calgary: University of Calgary Press.

Halbwachs, Maurice. (1950) 1980. *The Collective Memory*. New York: Harper & Row.
Halbwachs, Maurice. 1992. *On Collective Memory*. Edited by Lewis Coser. Chicago: University of Chicago Press.
Hauriou, Maurice. (1925) 1970. "The Theory of the Institution and the Foundation: A Study in Social Vitalism." In *The French Institutionalists*, edited by Albert Broderick, 93–124. Cambridge, MA: Harvard University Press.
Hauriou, Maurice. (1928) 1986. "Le pouvoir, l'ordre, la liberté et les erreurs des systèmes objectivistes." In *Aux sources du droit. Le pouvoir, l'ordre et la liberté*, 72–86. Caen: Centre de philosophie politique et juridique.
Hubert, Henri. (1905) 1999. *Essay on Time: A Brief Study of the Representation of Time in Religion and Magic*. London: Berghahn Books.
Isambert, François-André. 1979. "Henri Hubert et la sociologie du temps." *Revue française de sociologie* 20 (1): 183–204.
Isambert, François-André. 1999. "Introduction." In H. Hubert, *Essay on Time: A Brief Study of the Representation of Time in Religion and Magic*, 3–42. London: Berghahn Books.
LaCapra, Dominick. (1972) 2001. *Emile Durkheim: Sociologist and Philosopher*. Aurora: The Davies Group.
Lafrance, Guy. 1974. *La philosophie sociale de Bergson. Sources et interprétation*. Ottawa: Éditions de l'Université.
Le Blanc, Guillaume. 2002. *Canguilhem et la vie humaine*. Paris: PUF.
Lefebvre, Alexandre. 2013. *Human Rights as a Way of Life: On Bergson's Political Philosophy*. Stanford, CA: Stanford University Press.
Lefebvre, Alexandre, and Melanie White. 2010. "Bergson on Durkheim: Society sui generis." *Journal of Classical Sociology* 10 (4): 457–477.
Lefebvre, Alexandre, and Melanie White, eds. 2012. *Bergson, Politics, and Religion*. Durham, NC: Duke University Press.
Lefort, Claude. (1980) 2006. "The Permanence of the Theologico-Political?" In *Political Theologies: Public Religions in a Post-Secular World*, edited by Hent de Vries and Lawrence E. Sullivan, 148–187. New York: Fordham University Press.
Leroi-Gourhan, André. 1943. *Évolution et techniques 1: L'homme et la matière*. Paris: A. Michel.
Leroi-Gourhan, André. 1945. *Évolution et techniques 2: Milieu et techniques*. Paris: A. Michel.
Lévi-Strauss, Claude. (1962) 1966. *The Savage Mind*. London: Weidenfeld and Nicolson.
Lévi-Strauss, Claude. (1962) 1991. *Totemism*. London: Merlin Press.
Lévy-Bruhl, Lucien. 1890. Review: "Henri Bergson: Essai sur les données immédiates de la conscience. Étude critique." *Revue philosophique de la France et de l'étranger* 15, no. 29: 519–538.
Lukes, Steven. (1973) 1985. *Emile Durkheim: His Life and Work. A Historical and Critical Study*. Stanford, CA: Stanford University Press.
Marchart, Oliver. 2007. *Post-Foundational Political Thought: Political Difference in Nancy, Lefort, Badiou and Laclau*. Edinburgh: Edinburgh University Press.
Mauss, Marcel. 1923/24. "In memoriam. L'œuvre inédite de Durkheim et de ses collaborateurs." *L'Année sociologique* n.s. 1: 7–29.
Mauss, Marcel. (1933) 1969. "La sociologie en France depuis 1914." In *Œuvres 3: Cohésion sociale et division de la sociologie*, 436–450. Paris: Minuit.
Mauss, Marcel. (1938) 1990. "Lettre à Roger Caillois du 22 Juin 1938." *Actes de la recherche en sciences sociales* 84: 87.
Mauss, Marcel. (1927) 2006. "The Divisions of Sociology." In *Techniques, Technology and Civilisation*, 49–54. London: Berghahn Books.

Namer, Gérard. 1994. "Postface." In Maurice Halbwachs, *Les cadres sociaux de la mémoire*, 297–367. Paris: Albin Michel.
Namer, Gérard. 1997. "Postface." In Maurice Halbwachs, *La Mémoire collective*, 239–295. Paris: Albin Michel.
Paoletti, Giovanni. 2012. *Durkheim et la philosophie. Représentation, réalité et lien social.* Paris: Garnier.
Pickering, W. S. F. 1984. *Durkheim's Sociology of Religion: Themes and Theories.* London: Routledge & Kegan Paul.
Pinto, Louis. 2004. "Le débat sur les sources de la morale et de la religion." *Actes de la recherche en sciences sociales* 153: 41–47.
Richard, Gaston. (1923) 1994. "Dogmatic Atheism in the Sociology of Religion." In *Durkheim on Religion*, edited by W. S. F. Pickering, 228–276. London: Routledge.
Riley, Alexander T. 2002. "Durkheim contra Bergson? The Hidden Roots of Postmodern Theory and the Postmodern 'Return' of the Sacred." *Sociological Perspectives* 45 (3): 243–265.
Riley, Alexander T., and Philippe Besnard. 2002. "Présentation." In R. Hertz, *Un ethnologue dans les tranchées (août 1914–avril 1915). Lettres de Robert Hertz à sa femme Alice*, 5–20. Paris: CNRS.
Riley, Alexander T., W. S. F. Pickering, and William Watts Miller, eds. 2013. *Durkheim, the Durkheimians, and the Arts.* London: Berghahn Books.
Rolland, Romain. 1971. *Péguy.* Paris: Albin Michel.
Schlanger, Nathan. 2006. "Introduction: Technological Commitments. Marcel Mauss and the Study of Techniques in the French Social Sciences." In Marcel Mauss, *Techniques, Technology and Civilisation*, 1–29. New York: Berghahn Books.
Seyfert, Robert. 2011. *Das Leben der Institutionen. Zu einer allgemeinen Theorie der Institutionalisierung.* Weilerswist: Velbrück.
Simondon, Gilbert. (1958) 2007. *L'individuation psychique et collective: à la lumière des notions de forme, information, potentiel et métastabilité.* Paris: Aubier.
Simondon, Gilbert. (1958) 2017. *On the Mode of Existence of Technical Objects.* Minneapolis: Univocal.
Sitbon-Peillon, Brigitte. 2009. *Religion, métaphysique et sociologie chez Bergson. Une expérience intégrale.* Paris: PUF.
Stedman Jones, Susan. 2001. *Durkheim Reconsidered.* Cambridge: Cambridge University Press.
Viveiros de Castro, Eduardo. (2009) 2014. *Cannibal Metaphysics.* Minneapolis: Univocal.
Waterlot, Ghislain, ed. 2008. *Bergson et la religion. Nouvelles perspectives sur Les Deux Sources de la morale et de la religion.* Paris: PUF.
Worms, Frédéric. 2004. *Bergson ou les deux sens de la vie.* Paris: PUF.
Worms, Frédéric. 2009. *La philosophie en France au XXe siècle. Moments.* Paris: Gallimard.
Worms, Frédéric. 2012. "The Closed and the Open in *The Two Sources of Morality and Religion*: A Distinction That Changes Everything." In *Bergson, Politics, and Religion*, edited by Alexandre Lefebvre and Melanie White, 25–39. Durham, NC: Duke University Press.

CHAPTER 11

DURKHEIM, PRAGMATISM, AND SOCIOLOGY

ROMAIN PUDAL

Introduction

ALTHOUGH writings on Durkheim rarely attach much importance to the course on pragmatism that he delivered in 1913–1914, it was a milestone in his theoretical development, sometimes considered to be a sort of intellectual manifesto but at the very least a high point in the synthesis of his conceptions of truth, rationalism, and the role he reserved for sociology.[1] Marcel Mauss went so far as to consider the course the "philosophical crowning of Durkheim's work," writing in *In Memoriam*:

> In the same way, we must deplore the loss of the entirely new course that Durkheim gave, in 1913–14, just before the war. The purpose that he proposed was to make known to the students this still novel form of philosophical thought: Pragmatism. [...] He seized the opportunity, not only to help [*young students*] to know of this philosophy, but also to define the correspondences, the concordance and the discordance, that he was establishing between this system and philosophical evidence that seemed to him to be emerging from Sociology, in its early stages. He situated himself and his philosophy vis-à-vis Bergson, vis-à-vis William James, vis-à-vis Dewey and the other American pragmatists. Not only was he summarizing their doctrine with power and perceptivity, but he was filtering what should be retained from it, from his own point of view. He took account, above all, of Dewey, for whom he had an ardent admiration."
>
> (Mauss [1925] 2016: 32)[2]

This course included the bulk of Durkheim's thinking on pragmatism, both positive and critical, which had already been introduced less systematically in *The Elementary Forms of Religious Life* (Durkheim [1912] 2001).

We will start, like Durkheim, with his extremely positive initial assessment of pragmatism: "it has, in common with sociology, a sense of *life* and *action*. Both are children of the same era" (Durkheim [1913] 1983: 1). Over the course of his lectures, Durkheim proceeded to develop the fundamental points of convergence between sociology and pragmatism (Deledalle 2002). Briefly put, both were in opposition to two great forms of dogmatism; the first, empiricism, considered truth as a given in the sensory world; and the second, rationalism, believed that truth could be found in thought or absolute Reason. Durkheim deplored the inability of either to comprehend the historical and human dimensions of truth, and this inability to understand the very historicity of reason—its principles, categories, realizations—is precisely what Durkheimian sociology (in many regards, like pragmatism) was trying to counteract. Indeed, they share this antidogmatic intellectual posture, both of them challenging the idea that "the true" is already present in things and is only waiting to be discovered or, to the contrary, that it belongs to a world of ideas existing in and of itself and is waiting for the mind to find the means to reproduce it (in a Platonic conception). A. Cuvillier (1961: 77), who wrote the preface to the published version of Durkheim's lectures, indicated that this shared attitude explained Durkheim's great sympathy for pragmatism because, like sociology, it tries to understand the connections linking thought to existence and life.

However, this glowing introduction was quickly counterbalanced by a series of three precautions, which Durkheim resumes as follows:

> I do part company totally, however, with the conclusions of pragmatism. [...] The problem raised by pragmatism is indeed of a very serious nature [...] Consequently, the problem is of threefold importance.
> 1. In the first place, it is of *general* importance. Pragmatism is in a better position than any other doctrine to make us see the need for a reform of traditional rationalism, for it shows us what is lacking in it.
> 2. Next, it is of *national* importance. Our whole French culture is basically an essentially rationalistic one. The eighteenth century is a prolongation of Cartesianism. A total negation of rationalism would thus constitute a danger, for it would overthrow our whole national culture. If we had to accept the form of irrationalism represented by pragmatism, the whole French mind would have to be radically changed.
> 3. Lastly, it is of specifically *philosophical* importance. Not only our culture, but the entire philosophical tradition, right from the very beginnings of philosophical speculation (with one exception, which we shall discuss shortly) is inspired by rationalism. If pragmatism were valid, we should have to embark upon a complete reversal of this whole tradition. (Durkheim [1913] 1983: 1)

The task at hand is to rapidly review the issues at stake in this encounter between Durkheim's thinking and pragmatism in order to explore the fundamental ambivalence characterizing his position. Joas's description of the reception of pragmatism among German thinkers can be applied to the French case, too:

> [W]e can exclude there being any validity to the simplistic explanation that the misunderstanding of pragmatism resulted from some major implicit difference between German and American thought. [...] [M]isunderstandings arose not only among positions which were irreconcilable with pragmatism, but also among positions which were similar to it.
>
> (Joas 1993: 95)

To dig deeper into these positions and their consequences, we will first summarize the main theoretical stumbling blocks in a Durkheimian reading of pragmatism, then proceed to a more general analytical frame for examining Durkheim's ambiguous reaction to pragmatism in relation to the ideological, political, and historical contexts of the time.

THEORETICAL CRITIQUES

The genuine affinities between sociology and pragmatism that Durkheim so often emphasized (see especially Durkheim [1913] 1983: 67–68) cannot hide the deep theoretical divide between the two intellectual endeavors. While pragmatism, and especially the pragmatism of William James so copiously commented upon by Durkheim,[3] claims to explain truth psychologically and subjectively, and thus, in his attempt to understand how reason spreads across time and space, sticks to a strictly individual level, Durkheim says that sociology shows how "truth, reason, and morality are the results of a becoming that includes the entire unfolding of human history" (Durkheim [1913] 1983: 67). This is the first essential rift: Durkheim saw pragmatism as still being trapped in a strictly individual, and thus subjective, conception of the historical spread of human reason, and as failing to touch upon the distinctly social dimension of this process. According to Durkheim, however, taking the social into account makes it possible to explain how reason and truth are connected to the concrete existence of humans, how they are effectively rooted in their lived reality, and how they extend beyond each distinct individual. From this difference of conception follows another no less important one: since pragmatism considers truth to be a purely individual creation, ever-changing and shifting, it always seems ready to adopt a purely relativist conception of what is true, and does not comprehend the impersonal and imperative dimension of truth. "This pressure that truth is seen as exercising on minds is itself a symbol that must be interpreted," Durkheim ([1913] 1983: 68) wrote, "even if we refuse to make of truth something absolute and extra-human."

These two rifts between sociology and pragmatism are at the heart of Durkheim's theoretical critique. For Durkheim, pragmatism ultimately represents a form of modern irrationalism and sophism: the idea that "the mind remains free with regard to truth" ([1913] 1983: 2), which Durkheim saw as common to all pragmatists, obviously found no favor in his eyes. It is this erroneous conception of truth, he said, that imperceptibly leads pragmatists to associate what is true with what is useful, and he assembled many quotes from James and Schiller to prove his point. If, as they would have it, the true is not imposed on us and has no logical value of its own, then "the 'true,' to put it very briefly, is only the expedient in the way of thinking" (Durkheim [1913] 1983: 44, quoting James [1907] 1978: 106), nothing more, and the ever-changing true is what is useful to each of us, taken individually. Here again, this logical utilitarianism flies in the face of Durkheim's rationalist conception, which holds that truth does not change as such, but is enriched instead by the multiplicity of human experiences over time and across space, and thus appears to be something "living. [...] [I]t is a product of that higher form of life, social life" (Durkheim [1913] 1983: 196). The subjectivism of pragmatism that denies the social leads to its utilitarianism that levels everything. As a consequence of all that, in wanting to "'soften' truth" (Durkheim [1913] 1983: 67), pragmatism is ultimately incapable of explaining the historical and social development of the truth.

Durkheim's critique of pragmatism is not, however, limited to the theoretical and conceptual discussion in his course, and it can also be found in connection with his analysis of ethnographic studies of Australian rituals published in *The Elementary Forms of Religious Life*. As A. W. Rawls (2004) explains, it is in this book that Durkheim's theory of knowledge can be found. Not only does he contest pragmatist conceptions on principle, as it were; in this book, he also tries to concretely demonstrate why he still sees pragmatism as a failure, despite its praiseworthy effort to overcome the dualism between thought and reality by turning to action. Action is always conceived in a strictly individualist way, especially in James: the true is only valid as long as the action lasts and only for the person doing it. Against this, Durkheim set out to demonstrate that actions must be approached as shared practices in order to comprehend what might be rational about the categories of understanding and the concept of truth, and what they might have in common; his goal was to do this without falling back on the dualism to which he also objected, since "society has provided the canvas on which logical thought has operated" (Durkheim [1912] 2001: 115). According to Durkheim, this is precisely the point that pragmatism cannot elucidate, because only a concrete study of the collective accomplishment of ritual practices makes it possible to observe how categories of understanding are created. As A. W. Rawls put it, "Durkheim argued that the categories of the understanding enter the minds of individual persons during enacted practice in such a way as to be empirically valid" (1996: 435). This is how Durkheim developed his analysis of "scientific truth and collective conscience," the title of the nineteenth lesson of his course on pragmatism. "The fact is," he wrote, "that truth, the 'copy' of reality, is not merely redundant or pleonastic. It certainly 'adds' a new world to reality, a world which is more complex than any other: That world is the human and social one. Truth is the means by which a new order of things becomes possible, and that new order is nothing less than *civilisation*" (Durkheim [1913] 1983: 92).

So for Durkheim, one should consider truth as something social and human, without falling into relativism or individualism: while it is superior to the individual conscience, it is nevertheless only achieved by individuals; while, as a human thing, it is close to us, it still maintains authority over us, precisely because of its social character. Where James remains focused on individuals and on the constant flow of action in which they are caught up, Durkheim uses the analysis of ritual practices to show how "the 'givens' were always socially constructed phenomena resting on a foundation of socioempirically valid categories of thought" (Rawls 1996: 476).

Durkheim's arguments concerning pragmatism were thus focused on certain essential aspects of this wide-ranging philosophical current of thought; this is a vitally important point, as Durkheim took care to distinguish between James, Dewey, and Peirce. Radical empiricism, pluralism, continuism, phenomenalism, instrumentalism, subjectivism, and utilitarianism are the words he used most often in his effort to characterize pragmatism. Durkheim insisted on pragmatism's embodied, realistic, and anti-intellectualist dimensions, those with which nascent sociology had undeniable affinities, but he ultimately summed up his position in decisive terms:

> We can therefore conclude that pragmatism is much less of an undertaking to encourage action than an attack on *pure speculation and theoretical thought*. What is really characteristic of it is an impatience with any rigorous intellectual discipline. It aspires to "liberate" thought much more than it does action. Its ambition, as James says, is to "make the truth more supple." We shall see later what reasons it adduces to support its view that truth must not remain "rigid."
>
> (Durkheim [1913] 1983: 64)

As H. Joas (1993: 56) put it, "Durkheim made it clear from the very beginning that his analysis was not intended as a discussion which weighed one approach against another, but rather as a 'political' act in defence of a certain theory." This is the path we must follow in order to understand why Durkheim took the trouble to devote an entire year's worth of lectures to pragmatism and indicate his deep interest for this heterogeneous current while launching lively critique its way. And why indeed would he have notified his audience from the outset that pragmatism might incarnate a sort of threat to both philosophical and national orders? The reason is that, as Durkheim wrote with a certain gravity, "we are currently witnessing an attack on reason which is truly militant and determined" ([1913] 1983: 1). Nonetheless, Durkheim's desire to defend a "typically" French rationalism is not merely linked to a specific situation, as Jean-Louis Fabiani (2001) has indicated and Bernard Lacroix (1976: 218) emphasized in his commentary on Davy: "Sociology should be the philosophy that would contribute to permanently establishing the Republic and inspiring its rational reforms while at the same time giving the Nation a principle of order and a moral doctrine." To better comprehend Durkheim's position in detail, we will now put this debate in context.

Contextualizing the French Debate: Rationalism = the Republic?

For Durkheim and other French intellectuals, the early twentieth century was marked by a struggle in favor of rationalism, which was also considered to be the philosophy most suited to spreading the ideals of the French Republic. There was an intense critical activity around pragmatism in France, especially in the best-known philosophy journals renowned for publishing the great names of the discipline that have been the subject of several historical and sociological texts to this day.[4] Hence, in the *Revue philosophique de France et de l'étranger*, founded in 1876 by Théodule Ribot, twenty-one articles were devoted to pragmatism between 1876 and 1887, and no less than ninety-two between 1896 and 1912. The journal averaged forty-some articles per year overall, adding up to about six hundred over the period in question; this means that a little less than one in six published articles made at least passing reference to pragmatism. Another important fact is that articles by the three great American pragmatists themselves were among them. Overall, there was a strong rise in the number of articles devoted to pragmatism (and William James in particular) in 1906–1912: the critical tone suggests that these articles are not all laudatory—far from it.

In the journal *Revue de métaphysique et de morale*, founded in 1895 by Xavier Léon, Elie Halévy, and Léon Brunschvicg and counting Couturat, Lalande, Bergson, Durkheim, Boutroux, and Ravaisson among its early contributors, the number of articles on pragmatism tripled between the 1893–1909 period (three articles) and the next, 1910–1929 (nine articles)—although this is still relatively few.

But an enhanced count based on J. Shook's bibliography (of the period 1898–1940) in its January 2001 version[5] corroborates and enriches our survey and reveals that interest in pragmatism was a massive and Europe-wide phenomenon. In addition to articles and books, Shook included book reviews and summaries of conference and seminar papers on pragmatism in his bibliography. There were three references to pragmatism per year from 1898 through 1904, then nine in 1905, eight in 1906, twenty in 1907 and again in 1908, no less than twenty-two in 1909, twenty-six in 1910, twenty-eight in 1911, nineteen in 1912 and again in 1913. World War I (1914–1918) led to a sharp drop in intellectual activity on this issue (and many others), and figures for 1920–1950, never higher than ten and often fewer than five, demonstrate that the fervor for pragmatism had waned.

A list of French books devoted to pragmatism over the entire period demonstrates the extent of this engagement: M. Hébert, *Le pragmatisme*, 1908; J. Bourdeau, *Pragmatisme et modernisme*, 1909; A. Schinz, *Anti-pragmatisme*, 1909; E. Boutroux, *William James*, 1911; R. Berthelot, *Un romantisme utilitaire*, volume 1 in 1911, volume 2 in 1913, volume 3 in 1922; A. Fouillée, *La pensée et les écoles anti-intellectualistes*, 1911; J. Wahl, *Les philosophies pluralistes d'Angleterre et d'Amérique*, 1920; G. Sorel, *De l'utilité du pragmatisme*, 1921. Abel Rey, in a summary of the International Conference of Philosophy (held in Bologna,

April 6–11, 1911) published in the *Revue philosophique* in July 1911, offers the following observations on the situation of pragmatism in Europe:

> In Heidelberg [*i.e. at the 1908 International Conference of Philosophy*], it was certainly pragmatism that had been the focus of attention for the junior faculty. "It's the Pragmatism Conference," one of them had said, and it was true. And according to the opinion of many, this Pragmatism conference demonstrated pragmatism's very felicitous efforts to rejuvenate the questions by putting them in touch with current experience, but at the same time, it demonstrated its inadequacy and its failures to offer a coherent and consistent theory, a philosophy that was truly and fully a philosophy. The Bologna Conference in a way justified this impression, by its very existence. As a general philosophy, pragmatism went almost unnoticed [...]. So it seems to me that I have been present during a collapse of that philosophy, as a general system, that W. James believed to be the philosophy of the future. But on the other hand, it seemed to me that the influence of this attitude was making itself felt on the main philosophical concerns that I thought I saw taking shape among the masters of contemporary thought and among their disciples. Pragmatism may thus retain tremendous historical significance.
>
> (Rey 1911: 4–5)

Some commentators of the period preferred to see the success of pragmatism as nothing but a "state of mind," a "fashion," or even a simple "mood of the times."[6] As we shall see, the majority of philosophers shared the elitist view that pragmatism's very popularity cast suspicion on its purely philosophical and intellectual quality. Speaking of it in terms of "fashion" and "trend of the day," expressions commonly found in writings on the subject, unquestionably conveys a value judgment that denies pragmatism genuine philosophical dignity. The purely philosophical value of pragmatism was decidedly a major issue of the day. But more generally speaking, pragmatism was a bone of contention insofar as both its adversaries and its zealots in France sought to make it an intellectual resource to fuel all sorts of conflicts along the fault lines of the national intellectual space. Robert Nye (1975: 98) has provided what is probably the best summary of this general context: "On French terrain pragmatism was quickly absorbed by those who in one way or another were opposed to the 'official' rationalism and scepticism of the dominant political and philosophical elements in the Third Republic."[7] This is, for instance, the setting in which Bergsonism, which bonded with James's pragmatism due to their great affinity, could be a philosophy for fighting the dominant scientism and rationalism (at least until Pope Pius X placed Bergson's *Creative Evolution* on the Index of Forbidden Works).[8] The religious issues around a pragmatism adapted to the Bergsonian style were also what led Durkheim ([1913] 1983: 41) to bitterly declare that "in France pragmatism appears above all in the neo-religious movement." An ideological division running through the entire period was an important aspect of the context in which pragmatism was received and discussed. Nevertheless, although Durkheim saw connections between the reception of pragmatism and the neo-religious movement in France, other writers classified pragmatism as supporting social democracy.[9] Defended among others by Bergson (friend and ally of William James), Edouard Le Roy (a disciple of Bergson), and George Sorel, pragmatism was supposed to be able to represent the anti-rationalist, post-Kantian philosophical renewal that was ostensibly needed by fossilized French philosophy.

Two figures who sparred over the subject of pragmatism embody these ideal types: Léon Brunschvicg, the university-based representative of rationalist philosophy; and Henri Bergson, who practiced a "philosophical magisterium" (Azouvi 2007) at the Collège de France. Their affiliations show how this divided representation of pragmatism was also embodied in institutions. Despite his undeniable fame, and despite and having applied there twice, Bergson never worked at the Sorbonne, and instead taught with great success at its competitor, the Collège de France, from 1904 until he entered the Académie Française (Azouvi 2007: 59).[10] Here we offer just one example of this kind of confrontation (of which there were many): Edouard Le Roy, at that time a well-known disciple of Bergson, published two articles in the *Revue de métaphysique et de morale* (1901a, 1901b), where he defended what he called "the new philosophy," which was actually largely inspired by pragmatism:

> That is the second part adopted by the new philosophy: it is not intellectualist. It sees rationalism as the negation of the mind. It sees it as abandonment to content oneself with representations when one can get at the truth through actions. It seeks the path, truth, and life, but truth as a path through life. It agrees with Ravaisson who says that intelligence is still in certain regards only the physique of the mind. Let us go more deeply into ourselves and penetrate to the mysterious point where our integration into the universal reality occurs through the effectiveness of deep action. There, and only there, does verification take place.
>
> (Le Roy 1901b: 298)

Léon Brunschvicg lost no time condemning the vitalist and anti-rationalist tone of Le Roy's "new philosophy":

> What Mr. Le Roy thus challenges with each of his theses is the right to a spiritual life of clear thought and of pure thought, engaged neither in the compromises of action nor in the reminiscence of dogma. We believe that it is necessary to defend this right in this very *Revue* [*de métaphysique et de morale*], not because we have ever pursued or even desired some sort of doctrinal unity, which would be sufficient for abruptly stopping the progress of philosophical speculation, but because this progress is only possible under certain conditions of intellectual discipline; it supposes certain principles of method.
>
> (Brunschvicg 1901: 434)

Hence, over the entire period there was a struggle over the definition of legitimate philosophical practice, in which pragmatism played a significant role. James's pragmatism, as it was acclimatized in France by Bergson and somewhat popularized by Le Roy, was one of the critics' weapons against university philosophy, and Durkheim was a full participant in this struggle that was as much ideological as it was philosophical. As a result, his critique not only challenged the pragmatism of James but also all the uses made of it in France, from Le Roy to Bergson, from Sorel to Le Bon. Durkheim consequently found himself in a difficult position: he manifested a clear theoretical interest in pragmatism (especially that of Dewey, according to Mauss[11]) and as we saw earlier, he even detected some real intellectual affinities between it and the project of founding a new positive science like sociology. But when confronted with the dominant ways in which pragmatism was appropriated in France, in the service of what he considered an armed assault on Reason and a turn against the Nation, he had no choice but to be reticent and critical. His rationalist ideal found embodiment in the institutions of the French Republic, or at any rate such was his deepest conviction. But it is clear that pragmatism serves above all to fuel his critics and enemies. Thus, Durkheim wrote:

> To a very great extent, James' whole argument [against conceptual thought] closely follows developments in Bergson.[12] The positive conclusions at which the two men arrive are not identical, but their attitude toward classic rationalism is the same. Both have the same hypersensitivity to everything that is mobile in things, the same tendency to present reality in its obscure and fugitive aspect, the same inclination to subordinate clear and distinct thought to the troubled aspect of things. But the main thing that James has borrowed from Bergson is the form of argumentation that directly challenges conceptual thought. ([1913] 1983: 32)

Durkheim's defiance of James's version of pragmatism in particular can be better understood if we heed the fact that James had shown himself critical of the sociological school of Durkheim and much more enthusiastic about the conceptions of Tarde. Several of James's texts emphasized their affinities, as David Lapoujade (2007: 130–145) has pointed out. Their attention to individual differences and to the indefinite potential of each individual places Tarde and James in the same hostile posture relative to the collective social fact. In this spirit, James wrote in his essay "The Importance of Individuals" (first published in 1890, and reprinted in 1896 in *The Will to Believe*):

> And for my part I cannot but consider the talk of the contemporary sociological school about averages and general laws and predetermined tendencies, with its obligatory undervaluing of the importance of individual differences, as the most pernicious and immoral of fatalisms. Suppose there is a social equilibrium fated to be, whose is it to be,—that of your preference, or mine? There lies the question of questions, and it is one which no study of averages can decide. ([1896] 1979: 194–195)

Once again, in order to better understand Durkheim's position, it is advisable to remember who the French allies of pragmatism were (in this case, followers of James).

Conclusion

The fact that pragmatism was never a homogeneous current of thought is, of course, one explanation for the varieties of ways in which it was received. The ambivalence of Durkheim's reaction to pragmatism should be understood in light of the deep theoretical divergences between them—especially vis-à-vis James and his radical forms of anti-intellectualism and anti-rationalism—but also in the light of this specific context of reception. This is a fine example of a classic phenomenon in the history of ideas that "consists of adopting foreign cultural elements by making them subject to autochthonous objectives" (Bayart 1996: 80): pragmatism was used, mobilized, and discussed as it related to the intellectual, institutional, political, and ideological issues that were current in the French national space at the time. Durkheim was thus obliged to take a position on the original pragmatism, whose theses he discussed in minute detail and which he took great care to present as completely and impartially as possible. As a major player on the intellectual scene, however, he was led to take a position on the uses made of pragmatism within France.

Having quickly summarized how rifts between various conceptions of the social sciences and philosophy were traced and redrawn, we will turn to Cuvillier's assessment of the situation, which is nearly as relevant today as it was at the time. It respects the classic Durkheimian tradition by associating both of the major inclinations of the social sciences, fluctuating between objective analysis of the social world and social critique:

> Indeed pragmatism accepts one and only one framework for being and experience, and in this way it "levels everything out": it reduces values in relation to the useful and subjective experience, it disregards this fundamental dualism that exists between the individual and the social, like that between the empirical and the rational, which according to Durkheim provides a foundation for our action on the world: in the name of what can we expect to transform something, if we accept that everything should be put on the same level, that there is no difference between values and raw existence?
>
> (Cuvillier 1961: 86)

In the end, one might wonder if Durkheim's ambivalence to pragmatism might not ultimately accord with Vincent Descombes's assessment that "[i]n France, the development of a political position remains the decisive test, disclosing as it does the definitive meaning of a mode of thought" (1980: 7).[13] Here Descombes draws attention to the French penchant for evaluating thoughts in function of, and *even above all by*, their political and ideological implications.[14] In his assessment of pragmatism, Durkheim thus adopted a split posture, part theoretical discussion and part "ideological" critique, while presenting himself as a defender of rationalism and of the French Republic.

Notes

1. This course was reconstructed from students' notes and published in French in 1955, with an introduction by A. Cuvillier (Durkheim [1913] 1955), and then translated into English (Durkheim [1913] 1983).
2. Johan Heilbron (1985: 216), too, stresses the importance of this philosophical current for Durkheim.
3. Durkheim was rather selective in his initial remarks on pragmatism, devoting little discussion to Peirce and considering James to have been the first to use the term clearly; he also considered Dewey and Schiller as protagonists of the movement. It is nonetheless clear that the radicalism of James's theses and their success in France led Durkheim to see him as a key figure.
4. For instance, Fabiani (1993). See also Worms (2009: chapter 1); Vogt (1982); Soulié (2009); Karady (1983); Karsenti (2005); Gross (1997); and Heilbron (1985).
5. Available online at the Pragmatism Cybrary (http://www.pragmatism.org/research/prag_in_france.htm).
6. For an overview, see Azouvi (2007); for contemporary statements, see Sorel (1921); Parodi (1908, 1920); Paulhan (1912); and Benda ([1927] 1975).
7. So what are the main elements? Generally speaking, the entire period is dominated by the consolidation of the "radical Republic," to use Madeleine Rebérioux's term (1975). Its main milestones were the Dreyfus Affair, the education reform of 1902, the anticlerical policies enacted while Émile Combes was prime minister, and the December 9, 1905, law separating church and state.
8. The existence of correspondence between Bergson and Le Bon should be emphasized: "The idea that societies and individuals are not governed by purely rational sense—even if they think that they are—is an idea to which I arrive myself, although by other paths than you" (letter from Bergson, June 1912). In March 1914: "Although you are not registered under the banner of pragmatism, the pragmatists will certainly be those who will be the most welcoming to your ideas. [...] You probably do not reduce the true to the useful, but you see in the truth some kind of social force, variable and relative like all forces of this sort. William James would have been delighted" (Bergson 1972: 120 and 99).
9. Albert Schinz's book (1909) exemplifies this political reading of pragmatism. Schinz was a university professor of philosophy and a regular contributor to *Revue philosophique*, as Paul Vogt (1982) indicates in his article on the intellectual communities of France from 1900 to 1939. His thoroughly hostile argument against pragmatism owed more to political considerations than to theoretical ones. It was evident to Schinz that pragmatism was contributing to a general movement degrading the traditional values and hierarchies, which he firmly condemned because he feared a down-classing of the "legitimate heirs" of the "intellectual aristocracy."
10. For more on the split between Bergson and Brunschvicg, see Worms (2009: chapter 1).
11. Mauss ([1925] 2016); the subject was also discussed by Pierre Bourdieu (2004).
12. Obviously, this assertion is debatable from a theoretical perspective, but it seems that Durkheim was mainly intent on identifying the French academic thinkers that were the closest to pragmatism, Jamesian in particular. James and Bergson's correspondence, from their first letters in 1902 until James's death in 1910, attests to this affinity: Bergson's esteem and admiration never flagged, since he republished the preface that he had written for the French translation of James's *Pragmatism* in 1911 in his 1934 book *La pensée et le mouvant*. See Bergson (1972).

13. For Paul de Gaudemar (1969: 81), there can be no doubt about the connection between Durkheim's positions on pragmatism and socialism: "Although there was no question of it in *Pragmatism and Sociology*, we must not forget G. Sorel's attacks on Durkheim going back to the time of *The Division of Labour*. Although the question of pragmatism is indirectly tied to that of socialism, and although the ambiguity of Durkheim's position toward socialism is, in a way and under a different light, found in his critique of pragmatism, an important difference remains: Durkheim was practically always a 'sympathizer' of socialism, he was never an ally of pragmatism."
14. For example, Bruno Latour (2003: 70) writes that, if Dewey deserves praise, it is because he made it possible to break out of French "national-rationalism": "minds remain stuck on what I call national-rationalism, to which Durkheim gave brilliant expression in his course on the pragmatists in 1914, and which has not budged an inch for nearly 100 years: If, he said, France one day had to change its rationalist conception of science, it would disappear! What country has ever built its national idea on such a conception?"

References

Azouvi, François. 2007. *La gloire de Bergson. Essai sur le magistère philosophique*. Paris: Gallimard.
Bayart, Jean-François. 1996. *L'illusion identitaire*. Paris: Fayard.
Benda, Julien. (1927) 1975. *La trahison des clercs*. Paris: Grasset.
Bergson, Henri. 1972. *Mélanges: L'idée de lieu chez Aristote. Durée et simultanéité, correspondance, pièces diverses, documents*. Paris: Presses universitaires de France.
Bourdieu, Pierre. 2004. "Présences de Marcel Mauss." *Sociologie et sociétés* 36, no. 2: 15–22.
Brunschvicg, Léon. 1901. "La philosophie nouvelle et l'intellectualisme." *Revue de métaphysique et de morale* 9: 433–478.
Cuvillier, Armand. 1961. *Sociologie et problèmes actuels*. Paris: Vrin.
Deledalle, Gérard. 2002. "French Sociology and American Pragmatism: The Sociology of Durkheim and the Pragmatism of John Dewey." *Transactions of the Charles S. Peirce Society* 38: 7–11.
Descombes, Vincent. 1980. *Modern French Philosophy*. Translated by L. Scott-Fox and J. M. Harding. Cambridge: Cambridge University Press.
Durkheim, Émile. (1913) 1955. *Pragmatisme et sociologie*. Paris: Vrin.
Durkheim Émile. (1913) 1983. *Pragmatism and Sociology*. Translated by J. C. Whitehouse. Cambridge: Cambridge University Press.
Durkheim, Émile. (1912) 2001. *The Elementary Forms of Religious Life*. Translated by Carol Cosman. New York: Oxford University Press.
Fabiani, Jean-Louis. 1993. "Métaphysique, morale, sociologie. Durkheim et le retour à la philosophie." *Revue de métaphysique et de morale* 98, no. 1–2: 175–191.
Fabiani, Jean-Louis. 2001. "La tradition latente: à propos des usages de la philosophie comtienne de la science dans l'histoire de la sociologie française." In *Le goût de l'enquête. Pour Jean-Claude Passeron*, edited by J.-L. Fabiani, 389–416. Paris: L'Harmattan.
Gaudemar, Paul de. 1969. "Les ambiguïtés de la critique durkheimienne du pragmatisme." *La Pensée* 145: 81–88.
Gross, Neil. 1997. "Durkheim's Pragmatism Lectures: A Contextual Interpretation." *Sociological Theory* 15, no. 2: 126–149.
Heilbron, Johan. 1985. "Les métamorphoses du durkheimisme, 1920–1940." *Revue française de sociologie* 26: 203–237.

James, William. (1907) 1978. "Pragmatism: A New Name for Some Old Ways of Thinking." In *Pragmatism and the Meaning of Truth*. Cambridge, MA: Harvard University Press.

James, William. (1896) 1979. "The Importance of Individuals." In *The Will to Believe and Other Essays in Popular Philosophy*, 190–195. Cambridge, MA: Harvard University Press.

Joas, Hans. 1993. *Pragmatism and Social Theory*. Chicago: University of Chicago Press.

Karady, Victor. 1983. "Les professeurs de la République. Le marché scolaire, les réformes universitaires et les transformations de la fonction professorale à la fin du XIXe siècle." *Actes de la recherche en sciences sociales* 47–48: 90–112.

Karsenti, Bruno. 2005. "La sociologie à l'épreuve du pragmatisme. Réaction durkheimienne." In *La croyance et l'enquête*, edited by B. Karsenti and L. Quéré, 317–349. Paris: Editions de l'EHESS.

Lacroix, Bernard. 1976. "La vocation originelle d'Émile Durkheim." *Revue française de sociologie* 17: 213–245.

Lapoujade, David. 2007. *William James. Empirisme et pragmatisme*. Paris: Seuil.

Latour, Bruno. 2003. "Il ne faut plus qu'une science soit ouverte ou fermée." *Rue Descartes* 41: 66–81.

Le Roy, Edouard. 1901a. "Un positivisme nouveau." *Revue de métaphysique et de morale* 9, no. 2: 138–153.

Le Roy, Edouard. 1901b. "Sur quelques objections adressées à la nouvelle philosophie (I et II)." *Revue de métaphysique et de morale* 9, no. 3: 292–327.

Mauss, Marcel. (1925) 2016. "In Memoriam." In *The Gift. Expanded Edition*. Selected, annotated, and translated by Jane I. Guyer, 29–51. Chicago: HAU Press.

Nye, Robert. 1975. *The Origins of Crowd Psychology: Gustave Le Bon and the Crisis of Mass Democracy in the Third Republic*. Thousand Oaks, CA: SAGE.

Parodi, Dominique. 1908. "La signification du pragmatisme." *Bulletin de la Société française de philosophie* 8: 249–296.

Parodi, Dominique. 1920. *La philosophie contemporaine en France*. Paris: Alcan.

Paulhan, Frédéric. 1912. "Review of *Un romantisme utilitaire* by René Berthelot." *Revue philosophique de la France et de l'étranger* 73: 211–217.

Rawls, Anne Warfield. 1996. "Durkheim's Epistemology: The Neglected Argument." *The American Journal of Sociology* 102: 430–482.

Rawls, Anne Warfield. 2004. *Epistemology and Practice: Durkheim's The Elementary Forms of Religious Life*. Cambridge: Cambridge University Press.

Rebérioux, Madeleine. 1975. *La République radicale? 1899–1914*. Paris: Seuil.

Rey, Abel. 1911. "Le Congrès International de Philosophie: Bologne, 6–11 Avril 1911." *Revue philosophique de la France et de l'étranger* 72: 1–22.

Schinz, Albert. 1909. *Anti-pragmatisme. Examen des droits respectifs de l'aristocratie intellectuelle et de la démocratie sociale*. Paris: Alcan.

Sorel, Georges. 1921. *De l'utilité du pragmatisme*. Paris: Rivière.

Soulié, Stéphan. 2009. *Les philosophes en République. L'aventure intellectuelle de la Revue de métaphysique et de morale et de la Société française de Philosophie (1891–1914)*. Rennes: Presses universitaires de Rennes.

Vogt, Paul. 1982. "Identifying Scholarly and Intellectual Communities: A Note on French Philosophy, 1900–1939." *History and Theory* 21, no. 2: 267–278.

Worms, Frédéric. 2009. *La philosophie en France au XXe siècle*. Paris: Gallimard.

CHAPTER 12

ÉMILE DURKHEIM'S GERMANY

WOLF FEUERHAHN

In the context of the French academic landscape at the end of the nineteenth century, one country stands apart on the globe: Germany. It was considered the most "advanced" scientific nation in the world. The Prussian victory at Sadowa and the French defeat at Sedan were interpreted as victories of the German academic system. For example, Ernest Renan asserted: "what has conquered at Sadowa is Germanic science, it is Germanic virtue, it is Protestantism, it is philosophy, it is Luther, it is Kant, it is Fichte, it is Hegel" (Renan 1868: VII; see also Renan 1871; on this crisis: Digeon 1959; Charle 1994; Barbey-Say 1994).[1] This led to two transformations in France. First, a political decision to prepare for an intellectual revenge by promoting, more than ever since 1842,[2] "missions" for young members of the French academic elite (mainly former students of the *Ecole normale supérieure*) who are sent to Germany to study the strength of German science and to make up for lost time. Second, the development of an academic practice which was seen as typical of German science, namely, creating journals mostly dedicated to international book reviews.

Émile Durkheim participated in both of these reforms. In 1885, as a twenty-seven-year-old "normalien" and "agrégé de philosophie," he was given a sabbatical ("congé d'inactivité"[3]) to travel to Germany from January to August 1886.[4] There is no evidence that he had the official status of a "missionnaire," but, like most of the *missionnaires* from the Third Republic, after coming back, he published two articles. In his case one on the teaching of philosophy at German universities, in the *Revue internationale de l'enseignement* (Durkheim 1887a), and one on the "Positive Science of Morality in Germany" in the *Revue philosophique de la France et de l'étranger* (Durkheim 1887b).[5] Ten years later, he launched a new journal mainly dedicated to reviews of international social sciences: *L'Année sociologique*.

Along all his career, his reviewing activity testifies to the importance that academic work written in German had for him. In order to present a general overview of the ratio of Durkheim's reviews of books written in German,[6] we may distinguish two periods between his first review and his death (1885–1917) with the year 1898 as a turning point—turning point not because the weight of German reviews would strongly decrease after 1898, but because, from then onward, Durkheim published his own journal *L'Année sociologique*, and the number of his reviews increased dramatically. In 1913, he stopped reviewing books.

Between 1885 and 1897, the ratio between reviewed books written in German and those in other languages is 35 to 65 percent. Between 1885 and 1889, the percentage of works written in German rises to 50 percent. In total, Durkheim reviewed 557 books and 540 after 1898 (97 percent). The ratio of works written in German remains high (40 percent) between 1898 and 1907, when Durkheim gives all his effort in order to develop his yearbook.

The importance of German science for Durkheim seems indubitable.[7] But writing about his relationship with Germany is not easy because first this very relationship became the main reason for attacks against Durkheim. Indeed, in 1905, the Belgian Simon Deploige, professor at Louvain University, wrote articles accusing him of having imported German science into France without saying that it was "German" science.[8] In the tense political international context of the time, the accusation had potentially important consequences because he, as a Jew, and shortly after the Dreyfus Affair, was eventually accused to be a German spy.

How should historians deal with this topic? If we are talking about a German "influence" on Durkheim, we may be adopting the point of view of an actor of the time (namely, Deploige). In order to avoid this mistake, I will not use the term "influence," which suggests that it is received passively (Espagne and Werner 1987: 970). In order to emphasize Durkheim's role and the importance of the context in which he worked, one should rather speak of "appropriation" and "resemantization." Also, what do we mean by "Émile Durkheim's Germany": the country, the new Empire, German-language science, German colleagues? As a historian, if I consider all these aspects, I have to be careful in using this national adjective ("German") and to differentiate from Durkheim's usage of both: adjective ("German") and locative ("in Germany"). Because of the limited length of the chapter, I will focus on Durkheim's presentation of Germany; I will not analyze the reception of his work in the German-speaking countries. In addition, I will not postulate that an author who writes in German is considered by Durkheim as "German"; Durkheim did not consider Kant at all as "German," as we shall see. I will therefore focus on the way Durkheim uses the adjective "German" and its semantics. Furthermore, one has to be careful of the chronological evolution of his usage of the German "reference." The impact of the political context has to be taken into account if one wants to understand the shift from his rather positive reviews of some academic books written in German in the 1880s to his harsh propagandistic booklet *"Germany above all"* in 1915.

THE GERMAN SCIENCE OF MORALITY: A WEAPON IN DURKHEIM'S SCIENTIFIC STRUGGLE IN FRANCE (1885–1894)

The reports written by the young French academics constituted a genre of its own. Published in the *Revue internationale de l'enseignement*, a journal widely read by French academics, they were never fully apologetic; in fact, they always stressed the "esoteric character" or even "heaviness" of the "German spirit" (Charle 1994: 30–32), with the goal of overcoming what was seen as the French delay, and of surpassing German science. In the case of Durkheim, he has a more specific genre in mind: in 1887, he was the third "normalien agrégé" to write the same type of article: before him, Henri Lachelier (1881) and Gabriel Séailles (1883) had done the same.[9] His report is twice as long as those of his predecessors, as if there had been a competition between them. Knowledge about German science was symbolic capital in the French academic world. Durkheim's report is mostly critical, particularly where the organization of the teaching is concerned: "the general organization is far from perfect; the plethora of lectures is only an apparent wealth; for philosophy at least, teaching is too general; students are too worried about their exams" (Durkheim 1887a: 436 / 1975b: 481). This allows him to praise the French system and the central role of the "classe de philosophie" at secondary schools. Nevertheless, there is something Durkheim wants to import into France: the "morality" or what he calls the "Positive Science of Morality" (*science positive de la morale*): "While in our country, morality remains an autonomous science, which hardly maintains more than a few quite distant relations with psychology, in Germany, it tends to get closer and closer to its neighbouring sciences like political economy, law, and history, in order to look for the concrete material it needs" (335–336/463).

In France, the "old morality" still prevails: from its point of view, "the individual is a self-contained whole that belongs entirely to himself, by virtue of his absolute freedom. He is the only agent and the sole purpose of social evolution" (337/465). This

> mechanical conception of the society is being replaced, in the new school, by an organic conception. It demonstrates that this alleged autonomy is only apparent; that there is no abyss between each of us and other human beings, that heredity reduces us to being nothing but a continuation of our predecessors, that the existence of common sentiments erases at every moment the purported line of demarcation that is said to separate our consciences […]. The individual is an integral part of the society into which he was born; it penetrates him from all sides. To isolate oneself from it and to withdraw from it is to diminish oneself. (337/465)

For Durkheim, it is urgent to import those studies into France, for political reasons: "what we need most right now is to awaken in us the taste of collective life" (437/482);

"the German conceives the state as a power that is superior to individuals" (337/465). The French people have to break with a critique that sees the state as "a vast machine, destined to constrain that multitude of unsociable beings which Rousseau imagined and in which, to our misfortune, we continue to believe" (337n35/465n35). Against this, he praises the "German" conception of the state as a "spontaneous product of social life" (337n35/465n35). In order to treat our "national evil," we have to promote these "studies of morality" (440/486).

In this presentation of the studies of morality, Durkheim uses many national characterizations ("our national character," "the German morality," "the German spirit") (334–335/461–462). These qualifications can be found everywhere in the text, mostly in a pejorative sense. Here, this is not the case. As Mosbah-Natanson (2008) has rightly shown, in the first period of Durkheim's work (until 1895), international and especially German scientific references play the role of resources that enable him to assert his centrality in the emerging landscape of French sociology. But not all German academics are praised. In his reviews written during that period, Durkheim builds an ideal library of the "positive science of morality": the *Lehrbuch der politischen Oekonomie* by Adolph Wagner (1872), *Ueber einige Grundfragen des Rechts und der Volkswirthschaft* by Gustav Schmoller (1875), *Bau und Leben des socialen Körpers* by Albert Schäffle (2nd ed. 1881), *Der Zweck im Recht* by Rudolph von Ihering (1884), *Ethik: Eine Untersuchung der Thatsachen und Gesetze des sittlichen Lebens* by Wilhelm Wundt (1886), the *System der Staatswissenschaft* (1852–1857) and *Gegenwart und Zukunft der Rechts- und Staatswissenschaft Deutschlands* by Lorenz von Stein (1876), and *Die Grundlagen des Rechts und die Grundzüge seiner Entwickelungsgeschichte* by Albert Hermann Post (1884).

A historian of German academic life in the second half of the nineteenth century would be very surprised to see all these authors being put together as belonging to the same "school."[10] Durkheim is aware of the possibility of this objection but pretends that the publication of Wundt's *Ethik* "has given a framework to these endeavors which until then had remained rather vague and poorly conceived both in themselves and in the goal toward which they were directed. To fully appreciate this important work, it is necessary to know the movement of which it is, one might say, the philosophical expression" (Durkheim 1993: 57 / 1887b: 33). He portrays himself as capable of making explicit an "ethical movement [...] [which] remained unknown and in part latent for a long time" (58/34). For Durkheim its starting point has to be found in political economy (58/34) where he delineates a "German school" (60/35) for which, in contrast to the "British" school of "utilitarianism," "ethics and political economy" do not merge. Morality and political economy are "distinct entities, but they carry on a constant dialogue with one another" (60/35). Adolph Wagner and Gustav Schmoller are presented as its representatives. Against the "Manchester School" (63/37), Durkheim emphasizes that they stress that it is wrong to say "that the whole is equal to the sum of its parts" (64/37). Nevertheless, they still defend an artificialist conception of the social laws (72/45). Even if he emphasizes that Albert Schäffle, author of the magnum opus *Bau und Leben des socialen Körpers* (Construction and Life of the Social Body, 1875–1878), "is not a member of any school" (73/45), in order to insert him into his history of the "positive science of morality," Durkheim describes him as having been influenced by the German economic school. Within this teleological history, Schäffle's work is presented as a next step because, unlike Wagner and Schmoller, he considers that "the legislator does not invent its [i.e., society's] laws; he or she can only ascertain them and formulate them clearly" (75/47). Results of this movement is a "dismemberment of the old philosophy" (77/48–49). Just as psychology, which autonomized itself from philosophy thanks to its contact to physiology, "the study of morality [...] more and more [...] ceases to revolve around metaphysics [...], drawn as it is into the sphere of influence of the social sciences" (77/49).

After the "Economists and Sociologists," the second group—the "Jurists"—are represented by Rudolph von Ihering, who increased the "contact" between the "philosophy of law" and the "science of law" (78/50). Emphasizing that "to live is not to think, it is to act" (80/51), Ihering enabled Durkheim to conclude that "the image of a goal [...] [t]he final cause" is "the chief motive of our behavior" (80/51). That is why "to explain a rule of law is not to prove that it is there, but to show that it is of use for something, that it is well adapted to the purpose it ought to fulfill" (80/51). But the historical movement described by Durkheim reaches its culmination with the "Moral Philosophers," especially with Wundt's *Ethik* (89–122/113–142). This book, which Durkheim describes as a "synthesis of all the isolated perspectives and special studies," appears to him as a "natural" consequence of this movement of thought.[11] For Durkheim, Wundt's *Ethik* "marks progress in two ways" (116/136): first, he breaks "completely" (116/137) with the tendency to attribute an important role to "calculation" and "will" in the "evolution of moral ideas" (116/136); second, after Schäffle, Wundt stresses that morality is not simply an art but a science; he "shows that if moral ideas evolve, their evolution follows laws that science can determine" (117/138). But this does not put into question the existence of a "German school." What links all these works is first that they introduce a "genuinely inductive method" (127/278). In contrast, even the British utilitarians are described as deductivists (123–125/275–276). That is also the reason why the "Kantians" do not belong to this "German school": "The Kantians make morality into a specific but transcendent fact which escapes scientific observation; the Utilitarians make it into a fact of experience, but one which is not specific. They reduce it to this confused notion of utility and see nothing in it but an applied psychology or sociology" (127/278).[12] These symmetrical errors enable Durkheim to insist on the originality of the "positive science of morality": "Only the German theorists understand moral phenomena as facts which are at once empirical and *sui generis*" (127/278).[13] The expression "facts which are *sui generis*"— which serves to emphasize that social facts cannot be reduced to psychological or physiological phenomena—would stay the trademark of Durkheim's sociology. Already in this early article, Durkheim repeats what will be his holistic mantra: the whole is not the sum of the parts (63, 64, 110 / 37, 131). This autonomy of "morality" is the second most important feature of this "German school" (129/280).

In his review of Gumplowicz (1885b), Durkheim's diagnosis is clear: in the international competition, France has lost its leadership on sociology: "So it is that sociology, French in origin, increasingly becomes a German science" (Durkheim 1989: 7 / 1885b:

627). French academics have to go back to the classroom and read this German school; about Schäffle, Durkheim asserts:

> It is by the practice of such patient and laborious studies that we shall fortify our spirit, now too slender, too thin, too fond of simplicity. It is by learning to face the infinite complexity of facts that we free ourselves of those too narrow frameworks in which we tend to compartmentalize things. It is perhaps no exaggeration to say that the future worth of French sociology depends on this.
>
> (Durkheim 1978: 110 / 1885a: 97)

This critique of "French sociology" is harsh, but its aim is clear: Durkheim wants to impose a new definition of sociology in France and to appear as the French leader of this newly defined science. Indeed, his reviews of German authors are intimately linked to characteristics of the French academic landscape. He did not discover Schäffle during his travel to Germany. He published his review of the second edition of *Bau und Leben des socialen Körpers* before leaving. Indeed, Durkheim does not belong to the first generation of philosophers who wanted to legitimate sociology in France, and he has learned a lot from one of his predecessors: Alfred Espinas, a *normalien agrégé* like him. His doctoral dissertation, *Des sociétés animales*, had provoked a scandal in France. The spiritualists accused him of negating the boundary between man and animal (Feuerhahn 2011). In the second edition (1878), Espinas praised Schäffle's work and stressed that "whoever had the courage to execute the translation of this volume would render a service to sociology in France" (Espinas 1878: 139). Espinas's work was immediately remarked in Germany: Wundt positively reviewed his book, which was translated into German in 1879 (Wundt 1878; Espinas 1879). And Schäffle augmented his introduction to the second edition of *Bau und Leben* (1881) with "a short overview on the very interesting results of Espinas's research" (Schäffle 1881: X). But this overview by Schäffle included objections which Durkheim sums up in order to distinguish himself from Espinas: "sociology is not [...] the final chapter of biology. Between these two sciences, just as between their respective subject matters, there exists a break in continuity. [...] sociology [*la science sociale*], since it studies a new world, must have a new method" (Durkheim 1978: 95 / 1885a: 86). By emphasizing the autonomy of sociology in relation to biology, Durkheim could appear as a better interpreter of German science, and as defending a sociology that was compatible with the credo of the spiritualists who were still dominating French philosophy at that time, and who, in the context of the reception of Darwin, emphasized the difference between human and animals. In 1893, Durkheim would dedicate his doctoral dissertation to Émile Boutroux, one of the most important representatives of the spiritualists at the Sorbonne, who had had a conflict with Espinas in the 1880s (see Cabestan et al. 2023).[14]

In 1887, Durkheim had been appointed *Chargé de cours de Science sociale et de Pédagogie à la Faculté des Lettres de Bordeaux*. His inaugural lecture sketches a history of social science. It is structured as a history of ideas punctuated by great thinkers responsible for advances. Plato's *Politeia* is described as responsible for the assertion that social science was impossible. Taking society as "the work of man, the result of skill and reflection" (Durkheim 2008: 189 / 1888: 24), the numerous authors who followed Plato's view were unable to perceive that it was a "natural product." The first turning point took place with Montesquieu, Condorcet, and what Durkheim calls "the economists." They were "the first to state that social laws are as necessary as physical laws" (189/25), but they suggested "that there is nothing real in society but the individual" (191/28); therefore, economics remained "an abstract and deductive science." Auguste Comte was the first to consider that the object of sociology was not the "individual," but "society" and that a "whole is not identical to the sum of its parts" (192/29–30). But Comte assumed that there is only one single "human evolution which is one and the same everywhere and that societies are only different varieties of a single type" (194/31). Spencer, however, does not speak anymore of "society in a general and abstract way" but "distinguishes between social types" (196/35). Still, for Durkheim, he remains a "philosopher" (196/35); and because of his "English prejudices" (197/37), Spencer attributes value to liberty in itself and not because of its "fruits." Alfred Espinas, Durkheim's new colleague at Bordeaux, is praised: "His book constitutes the first chapter of Sociology" (197/38). But in this history of progress, Durkheim points out that Espinas's objects of study remained animal and not human societies. Thanks to "a German scholar" (Schäffle), who "has too deep a feeling for the complexity of things to be so easily satisfied with such a simplistic solution [i.e., Kantian individualism]," "the German school" (Wagner, Schmoller) as well as the jurists Ihering and Post, "sociology now no longer seems like a kind of science of the whole, general and confused [...]. We see it rather as splitting off into a number of specific sciences concerned with increasingly defined problems" (197–199/38–40).[15]

Between 1885 and 1894, Schäffle remains the German author whom Durkheim quotes most often. By contrast, in 1889, he describes Ferdinand Tönnies as a "systematician," a "dialectician" and therefore classifies him as belonging not to the group of "German moralists," but to that of "German logicists" (Durkheim 1889: 422 / 1975a: 390), which for Durkheim is an insult.

But his defense of Schäffle caused difficulties for Durkheim. He was accused of defending state socialism: "Since such a conception of collective life does not lead to one of those systems of clear ideas which our French temperament loves, we feel we have dealt with it justly when we disdainfully accuse it of being a German import. It cannot be demonstrated that the sphere of social action extends itself to the degree that societies develop without being accused of state socialism and treated as an enemy of liberty" (Durkheim 1973a: 40–41 / 1890: 454). Perhaps as a reaction to these accusations, Durkheim stopped reviewing German books from 1890 until 1898.

Nationalizing Sociology (1895–1915)

From 1895 on, Durkheim regularly wrote presentations on the history of sociology. We will focus on this corpus and on the way in which it treats the topic of nationality, especially of German nationality. As Mosbah-Natanson (2008) has noted, in this second period, Durkheim insists on the predominance of a French national tradition in sociology. In 1895, he wrote an article on "The Current State of Sociological Studies in France" for an Italian journal (Durkheim 1895 / 1975a: 73–108). He attributes the most important role to himself (Durkheim 1975a: 93–104); the German science of morality is no longer seen as the best incarnation of social science. Durkheim seems to have completely changed his criteria of scientificity: "If the German mind is more sensitive than ours to the complex nature of social things, on the other hand, as it is poorly analytical, it seemed to him very difficult if not impossible to submit entirely to scientific analysis a reality so complex [...]. The French spirit, on the contrary, although it embraced the new ideas of which we spoke, remained what it has always been, profoundly rationalist" (106). Rationalism is no longer a sign of scientific weakness, but of strength. Durkheim concludes: "France is in the most favourable conditions to contribute to the progress of sociology" (107).

This change can already be observed in Durkheim's two dissertations. German-language authors are very little quoted in the *Division of Labour in Society* (1893); there is no mention of a "German school" of the science of morality. In his *Thèse secondaire* on Montesquieu (1892), Durkheim states that, by forgetting the French past, he had overestimated the German precedence, and that French scholars should rehabilitate Montesquieu, who was the real founder of sociology:

> Unmindful of our history, we have fallen into the habit of regarding social science as foreign to our ways and to the French mind. The prestige of recent works on the subject by eminent English and German philosophers has made us forget that this science came into being in our country. Not only was it a Frenchman, Auguste Comte, who laid its actual foundations, distinguished its essential parts and named it sociology—a rather barbarous name to tell the truth—but the very impetus of our present concern with social problems came from our eighteenth-century philosophers. In that brilliant group of writers, Montesquieu occupies a place apart. It was he, who, in *The Spirit of Laws*, laid down the principles of the new science.
> (Durkheim 1960b: 1 / 1966: 25)

Reading these works as well as *The Rules of Sociological Method* (1894–95) and *Suicide* (1897) leads to the following conclusion: Durkheim retains the idea that he previously said to owe to the German moralists—in particular, the idea that social facts are *sui generis* facts, irreducible to psychological or biological facts—but ceases to refer to the German moralists and even insists that it was the French who first became aware of this specificity of social facts.

In 1895, Célestin Bouglé, *normalien* and *agrégé de philosophie* like Durkheim, followed his steps and travelled to Germany in order to follow the teachings of Georg Simmel, von Ihering, and Wagner. During his travel, he published articles on these authors in the *Revue de métaphysique et de morale*, which were collected in a book: *Les sciences sociales en Allemagne: Les méthodes actuelles* (1896). The book presents a challenge to Durkheim: Bouglé stresses that his knowledge of German science is more up to date than Durkheim's, and he highlights that there has been an important change in German academia since 1886—psychology has replaced biology as a model for sociology.[16] Furthermore, he mobilizes the works of three opponents of Durkheim—Gustave Le Bon, Paul Lacombe, and Gabriel Tarde—in order to emphasize that in France, too, the role of psychology had been reevaluated. And unlike Durkheim who, in *The Rules of Sociological Method*, insisted on the autonomy of sociology toward psychology and, in his article in *La riforma sociale*, on the domination of French sociology over German sociology, Bouglé asserts that there are "many concordances between French thinkers and German thinkers" (Bouglé 1896: 147). The book ends with a long critique of Durkheim. Surprisingly, Durkheim did not answer with anger. On the contrary, he tried to enrol Bouglé in his team,[17] accepted his assertion that sociology is "a psychology, *but distinct from individual psychology*," and inscribes Bouglé's book into his Franco-German competition over sociology:

> It is a study which cannot fail to bring great honour to us on the other side of the Rhine; and by showing the Germans with what care and kind feeling we are studying them, it will perhaps bring them to display more interest in what we are doing. For—and I do not know whether I am mistaken—it seems to me that Germany is committing the same error as we did before 1870 by shutting itself off from the outside world.
>
> (Letter from Durkheim to Bouglé, December 14, 1895; Durkheim 1982: 249 / 1976: 166)

In 1900, Durkheim publishes two articles that present the discipline of sociology— one for the French general public, "Sociology in France in the Nineteenth Century" (Durkheim 1900a), one for the Italian readership, "Sociology and Its Scientific Field" (Durkheim 1900b). In the first article, sociology is described as a French science: "To determine France's part in the progress made by sociology during the nineteenth century is to review, in large part, the history of that science. For it is in our country and in the course of this century that it was born, and it has remained an essentially French science" (Durkheim 1973b: 3 / 1900a: 609). As in his inaugural lecture, each author that is mentioned in the article represents a step in the progressive history of the science. But in this article, Durkheim's pantheon is French: Durkheim quotes Montesquieu, Condorcet, Saint-Simon, Comte, Cournot, Espinas, and himself. Spencer is the only foreigner, and he gets only a short paragraph. No Germans are quoted and, as in the article of 1895, a large part is devoted to Durkheim's own work. Durkheim had criticized Tarde already in 1895, but now the criticism is even harsher: Tarde's sociology is presented as standing apart from what is common to all the other approaches that "In effect, they all originate from the same thought—that social phenomena are natural, that is to say, rational, like the other phenomena of the universe" (Durkheim 1973b: 18 / 1900a: 649). Finally, the capacity to incarnate sociology is presented as a French destiny:

> Moreover, everything predestines our country to play an important role in the development of this science. Two causes have determined its appearance and,

consequently, are likely to favor its progress. The first is a sufficiently marked weakening of traditionalism. [...] The second factor is what could be called the rationalist state of mind. One must have faith in the power of reason in order to dare submit to its laws this sphere of social facts where the events, by their complexity, seem to escape the formulations of science. Now, France fulfills these two conditions to the highest degree. (21–22/651)

Germany and the German school of moral science have completely disappeared from the historiographical landscape of sociology. Professor at Bordeaux University since 1895, leader of a "scientific team" of young *agrégé normaliens*, director of a journal—*L'Année sociologique* (1898)—Durkheim now has a central position in France. One thing is missing: he is still professor at a provincial university and has failed to be elected at the *Collège de France* (Benthien 2015) where Tarde has taught since 1900. Maybe that is one reason why he felt it necessary to criticize Tarde. In the second article (1900b), the readership is Italian. Here, Durkheim tries to enlarge his international visibility. Maybe because of this, the article is structured differently. Durkheim does not propose a history of sociology but organizes his text as a critique of Georg Simmel's definition of sociology. Since the beginning of the 1890s, Simmel tries to compensate for his difficulties to get tenure in Germany by increasing his international fame. He could arrange that his programmatic article "Das Problem der Sociologie" (1894) was translated into English, French, and Italian.[18] His main ambassador in France was Célestin Bouglé. Structured as an answer to Simmel, Durkheim's article was probably a way to limit the international success of his German colleague. His objections are severe: Simmel's formal sociology is presented as a practice which maintains sociology in the "metaphysical ideology" (Durkheim 1975a: 16).

In 1902, Durkheim was one of the numerous French scientists and artists whom Jacques Morland, a young translator of Nietzsche, asked about the "German influence" in France (on the survey, see Schockenhoff 1986: 212–258). This survey was directed by a critical historical diagnosis. After a period of "childish imitation" (Morland 1902: 292) of Germany, French intellectuals had to be conscious that "numerous symptoms testify to the decline of the authority we had given to Germanic culture" (293); he looks for "expert testimonies" in order to enlighten the French and even the German public opinion on the German intellectual influence (294). Durkheim's answer does not represent the most conflictual version of this geopolitics; nevertheless, he opposes German and French science as whole entities and asserts that the hierarchy between both has changed:

> Personally, I owe a lot to the Germans. It was partly thanks to them that I acquired a sense of social reality, its complexity and its organic development. Through the contact with them, I have better understood the meagreness of the conceptions of the French school [...]. So much for the past. For the present, I have the very clear impression that, for some time now, Germany has not been able to renew its formulas. Production remains abundant, more abundant than in our country. But I do not see any new impetus in the social sciences. Sociological studies, which are now enjoying

an almost excessive popularity among us, have almost no representatives. The fact seems all the more remarkable to me because, when I began eighteen or twenty years ago, in the studies I am pursuing, it was from Germany that I expected enlightenment. Germany has ceased to be a vibrant country with novelties from abroad. I know she is saturated with her own production. I wonder, however, whether this is not also the sign of a certain incuriosity, of a sort of self-centeredness [...] which is opposed to new advances.

(Durkheim 1902: 647 / 1975a: 400)

Durkheim certainly recognizes his debts toward Germany, but he considers that this country is not anymore a cradle of curiosity toward foreign science. Its German-centered outlook seems to him as narrow as that of French science in 1870.

Durkheim's critical discourse about contemporary Germany and his French genealogy of sociology met harsh criticism a few years later. In a series of articles published between 1905 and 1907 in the *Revue néo-scolastique*, Simon Deploige, a professor of law at the University of Louvain, scrutinizes the references of Durkheim's works and concludes: "if it is still not demonstrated that sociology was not 'born in France,' it is established that it did not 'remain an essentially French science.' The work of Mr Durkheim, currently its most eminent representative, is *made in Germany*" (Deploige 1911: 151).[19] Deploying quotations from German academics (Wagner, Schmoller, Schäffle), Deploige attempts in particular to establish the German origin of Durkheim's social realism, which asserts that the social whole is irreducible to the sum of the individuals.[20]

In the years following the Dreyfus Affair, this claim was far from being politically innocent,[21] but it could appear plausible because Deploige was very precise and Durkheim had indeed been one of the mediators of German science in France. Durkheim answered by asserting the French origin of his scientific practice.[22] He systematically replaced the German names quoted by Deploige by French names (Deploige 1911: 401). In his answer, Deploige does the contrary and stresses the inauthenticity of Durkheim's national genealogy (404–413).

Deploige transformed his series of articles in a book first published in 1911; two other editions followed in 1912 and 1923. Durkheim wrote a review in which he denunciated the work as an "apologetical pamphlet" (405). For him, Deploige's goal was clear: "to discredit our ideas [...] for the greater glory of the doctrine of Saint Thomas" and to "present our designs as the product of a Germanic import" (405). Here again, he systematically contests Deploige's German genealogy of his works and stresses a French[23] and English one.[24]

At the same time, under the pseudonym of Agathon, Henri Massis and Alfred de Tarde (the son of Gabriel) published a denunciation of what they called "the spirit of the new Sorbonne" (Agathon 1911). For these authors, the newly refunded university was obsessed by the "imitation of Germany" (11–12); people like Durkheim are presented as the promoters of the triumph of the spirit of specialization: Durkheim "is the regent of the Sorbonne, the all-powerful master, and we know that the professors of the section of philosophy, reduced to the role of simple officials, follow his orders" (98).[25]

The German Enemy (1915–1917)

During World War I, Durkheim took an active role in the French propaganda against Germany. In 1915, for the international exhibition in San Francisco, he wrote an article for a book presenting "French science" in which he strengthened his national genealogy of sociology: "To set forth the role which belongs to France in the establishment and development of sociology is almost tantamount to writing the history of this science; for it was born among us, and, although there is no country today where it is not being cultivated, it nevertheless remains an essentially French science" (Durkheim 1960a: 376 / 1915a: 5). This article is almost the same as "Sociology in France in the Nineteenth Century" (Durkheim 1900a). Just like in the first version, Spencer is the only foreign sociologist who is quoted, and France is described as destined to exert the leadership on sociology at an international scale.

An active intellectual propagandist during the war (Prochasson and Rasmussen 1996: 189), Durkheim, together with eleven other prominent French professors, founded the book collection "Etudes et documents sur la guerre" (published by Armand Colin) and collaborated on three books of this collection.[26]

Let us focus our attention on the last one, which is entirely dedicated to Germany. The nation is personified and all its "behaviour" is presented as deriving from a "mental attitude" which has a "morbid character" (Durkheim 1915b: 2). In order to characterize this "mentality," Durkheim makes no statistical survey but chooses one historian, the strongly nationalist Heinrich von Treitschke (1834–1896), and presents him as "a personality pre-eminently representative" who "expresses the mental attitude of his surroundings" (5). Durkheim who, in 1898, had emphasized, against the psychologists, the qualitative gap between individual and collective representations (Durkheim 1898) now defends the possibility to erect an individual into a representative of the whole.[27] Doesn't Durkheim, by denouncing a homogeneous "German mentality," take the risk of weakening the epistemological model that he borrowed from the German "positive science of morality"? Is it still possible for him to reason in terms of "mentality" if he considers the German mentality and all its intellectual productions as dangerous? How to separate the intellectual tool—the notion of "mentality"—from the Pan-Germanic discourse? A passage from his booklet shows how he tries to solve the problem. He first acknowledges, and praises, a German scientific peculiarity: "Many Schools of German scientists (Niebuhr, Savigny, Latzarus [sic!] and Steinthal) have, it is true, attributed to the nation, as distinguished from the State, a kind of soul (*die Volksseele*) and consequently, a personality. [...] It was indeed one of the services rendered to the world by German science of the past to have called attention to these impersonal, anonymous and obscure forces which are not the least important factors in history" (Durkheim 1915b: 28–29). In order to avoid being accused of contradicting himself, he stresses that Treitschke was specifically opposed to this type of distinction between state and people or civil society. But this remark does not stop him from keeping his presentation of

German "mentality" on the level of generality chosen by Treitschke—that of the state—and from ending his book by saying that Germany's will to be "above all" is a "morbid hypertrophy of the will, a kind of will-mania," compared to the wills of other nations who, "normal, healthy," accept "the necessary relations of dependence inherent in the nature of things" (44).[28]

Conclusion

To speak, as Deploige, about a "German influence" on Durkheim, as if he were passive, would be incorrect. On the contrary, even during the period when he reviewed a lot of German authors, Durkheim was always selective about the works that he praised and emphasized his disagreements. For him, Germany was more of a resource for presenting himself as a real scientist, in contrast to what he considered as the dominance of *lettres* and humanities in France.

Between 1895 and 1915, there is indeed an evolution: there is no praise of German science as such left in his works. This is probably linked to the impact of the Dreyfus Affair on French political life. After his engagement for Dreyfus, hard-line nationalists saw Durkheim as a Jew and even, during the war, as a German spy.[29] His nationalization of the history of sociology and, more generally, his nationalist views were probably also an answer to these accusations. In any case, compared to colleagues like Émile Boutroux, Charles Richet, and Xavier Léon, who were much more engaged in the internationalist arena, Durkheim had been much less of an internationalist before the war and was much more engaged in the French war propaganda against Germany (Prochasson and Rasmussen 1996: 213).

Notes

1. "In the struggle which has just ended, the inferiority of France has been above all intellectual; what we missed was not the heart, it is the head. Public education is a subject of capital importance; the French intelligence has weakened; it must be strengthened. [...] The lack of faith in science is the profound defect of France; our military and political inferiority has no other cause" (Renan 1871: 95).
2. The "Service des missions" had been created in 1842 (Bourquin 1993, 2004).
3. His career file (dossier de carrière: AN F17/25768 [Archives nationales / French National Archives]) says: "On leave of absence with pay for one year from October 1, 1885." The decree of August 28, 1885, says that it is for "health reasons" and not, as the rector of the Douai academy (August 4, 1885) writes, "in order to prepare his doctoral thesis."
4. AN F17/25768: In a letter to Louis Liard (August 10, 1886), Durkheim states that he is back. He reminds the Director for Higher Education that he had made Durkheim "hope that it [...] might be possible to entrust me to the next academic year a position as lecturer in philosophy [*maîtrise de conférences*]."

5. On the importance of this article for the *Division of Labour in Society*, see Jones (1999: chapter 4).
6. My statistics are based on the bibliography in Lukes (1973: 561–588).
7. Gephardt (1982) remains fundamental here even if he focuses on Durkheim's relations to Schäffle, Tönnies, and Simmel. As will be seen, our perspective here focuses more on Durkheim's use of the label "German" when talking about science.
8. Simon Deploige, "Le conflit de la morale et de la sociologie." *Revue néo-scolastique* 12 (1905): 405–417; 13 (1906): 49–79, 281–313; 14 (1907): 329–392; Émile Durkheim, "Lettre au directeur de la *Revue néo-scolastique* du 20 octobre 1907." *Revue néo-scolastique* 14 (1907): 606–607; Deploige, "Réponse, 24 octobre 1907." *Revue néo-scolastique* 14 (1907): 607–611; Durkheim, "Lettre au directeur de la *Revue néo-scolastique* du 8 novembre 1907." *Revue néo-scolastique* 14 (1907): 612–614; Deploige, "Réponse, 12 novembre 1907." *Revue néo-scolastique* 14 (1907): 614–621; Deploige, *Le conflit de la morale et de la sociologie* (Louvain, 1911); Durkheim, "Review of Simon Deploige, *Le conflit de la morale et de la sociologie*." *Année sociologique* 12 (1913): 326–328.
9. Durkheim also quotes Hollenberg (1881).
10. On "schools" in the history of science and human sciences, see Orain (2018).
11. "It was natural, however, that this movement would produce a study of the whole of the moral life" (Durkheim 1993: 89 / 1887b: 113).
12. See also his text on the teaching of philosophy, where Kant is described as a representative of individualism in morality (Durkheim 1887a: 337 / 1975b: 465).
13. See also Durkheim (1993: 77 / 1887b: 49): "All the moral theorists mentioned here see in moral phenomena *sui generis* facts which must be studied in themselves, for themselves, by a special method."
14. At the same time, Durkheim criticized the interpretation of Schäffle as a socialist by French political economists (Feuerhahn 2014: 87–90).
15. At the end of the academic year 1888, the *Recteur* of the Académie of Bordeaux wrote the following observation: "Distinguished spirit, whose originality is emerging, well acquainted with a domain of study little cultivated here" (AN F17/25768).
16. "[…] biological metaphors are out of fashion and psychology is universally regarded as the soul of the social sciences" (Bouglé 1896: 144).
17. Bouglé became in fact a "Durkheimian" and could not impose Simmel as an international partner of *L'Année sociologique* (Papilloud 2002; Rol 2006).
18. English: "The Problem of Sociology." *The Annals of the American Academy of Political and Social Science* 6, no. 3 (1895): 52–63; French: "Le problème de la sociologie." *Revue de métaphysique et de morale* 2, no. 5 (1894): 497–504; Italian: "Il problema della sociologia," trad. A. Bartolomei. *Riforma sociale* 6 (1899): 629–637.
19. On the Deploige–Durkheim debate, see Firsching (1995).
20. A defender of neo-Thomism, Deploige wrote his articles as a reaction against the publication of Lucien Lévy-Bruhl's *La morale et la science des mœurs* (1903). He criticizes the postulates and conclusions of Lévy-Bruhl's "science des mœurs" via an analysis of Durkheim's "system" which, to him, is Lévy-Bruhl's main theoretical reference. Deploige asserts that Lévy-Bruhl and Durkheim miss their target: Saint Thomas's moral philosophy cannot be criticized by sociologists because, like sociology, it is opposed to natural rights theory. Therefore neo-Thomism and sociology have the same enemy, namely, rationalism: "the sociological movement that developed in the nineteenth century, as a whole, is a return to the Thomistic conception of moral science" (Deploige 1911: 424).

21. See the reaction of Georges Sorel, who at that time is close to the Catholic Right, and who praises the book (Serry 2004: 70).
22. He also stresses the importance of English social science: "I certainly owe a debt to Germany, but I owe much more to her historians than to her economists, and Mr Deploige does not seem to be aware that I owe at least as much to England" (Deploige 1911: 403).
23. "[…] it is from Renouvier that we got the axiom: a whole is not equal to the sum of its parts" (Deploige 1911: 405).
24. At the same time, Durkheim stresses the differences between his and Wundt's conceptions of totemism (Rol 2012).
25. See Fournier (2013: 570–573). On Durkheim's answers, see Bompaire-Evesque (1988: 159–160). Agathon does not quote Deploige, but Jean Bourdeau, one of the critics of the "new Sorbonne," refers to Deploige's book (Bompaire-Evesque 1988: 173n7).
26. Émile Durkheim and Ernest Denis, *Qui a voulu la guerre? Les origines de la guerre d'après les documents diplomatiques* (Paris: Colin, 1915); Émile Durkheim, *"L'Allemagne au-dessus de tout": La mentalité allemande et la guerre* (Paris: Colin, 1915); Émile Durkheim et al., *Lettres à tous les Français* (Paris: Comité de publication, 1916). On the "French science" involvement in the manifesto warfare, 1914–1918, see Rasmussen (2004).
27. Strangely, Bruno Karsenti proposed an interpretation of this text as a methodological manifesto for sociology (Durkheim 2015).
28. Hartmann Tyrell notes that in this text, Durkheim interprets German militarism as a remnant of ancient paganism and as the clue to oblivion of Christian inheritance, and concludes: "It is rare to see Durkheim identify with this point from the Christian point of view" (Tyrell 2011: 91).
29. In 1916, a senator attacked him as a "Frenchman of foreign descent, probably representative of the German 'Kriegsministerium.' Louis Liard required the senator to apologize" (AN F17/25768).

References

Agathon. 1911. *L'esprit de la nouvelle Sorbonne. La crise de la culture classique, la crise du français*. Paris: Mercure de France.
Barbey-Say, Hélène. 1994. *Le voyage de France en Allemagne, de 1871 à 1914*. Nancy: Presses universitaires de Nancy.
Benthien, Rafael. 2015. "Les durkheimiens et le Collège de France (1897–1918)." *Revue européenne des sciences sociales* 53, no. 2: 191–218.
Bompaire-Evesque, Claire-Françoise. 1988. *Un débat sur l'université au temps de la troisième république. La lutte contre la nouvelle Sorbonne*. Paris: Aux amateurs de livres.
Bouglé, Célestin. 1896. *Les sciences sociales en Allemagne. Les méthodes actuelles*. Paris: Alcan.
Bourquin, Jean-Christophe. 1993. "L'état et les voyageurs savants: Légitimités individuelles et volontés politiques. Les missions du ministère de l'instruction publique, 1842–1914." Doctoral thesis, Université Paris 1.
Bourquin, Jean-Christophe. 2004. "National Influences on International Scientific Activity: The Case of the French *Missions Littéraires* in Europe, 1842–1914." In *Transnational Intellectual Networks: Forms of Academic Knowledge and the Search for Cultural Identities*, edited by Christophe Charle, Jürgen Schriewer, and Peter Wagner, 451–472. Frankfurt am Main: Campus.

Cabestan, Bérenger, Wolf Feuerhahn, and Thibaud Trochu, eds. 2023. *La philosophie made in France*. Paris: La Découverte.

Charle, Christophe. 1994. *La république des universitaires, 1870–1940*. Paris: Seuil.

Deploige, Simon. 1911. *Le conflit de la morale et de la sociologie*. Louvain: Institut supérieur de philosophie.

Digeon, Claude. 1959. *La crise allemande de la pensée française (1870–1914)*. Paris: Presses universitaires de France.

Durkheim, Émile. 1885a. "Review of 'Albert Schaeffle, Bau und Leben des socialen Körpers (Organisation et vie du corps social), Erster Band, 2e édition.'" *Revue philosophique de la France et de l'étranger* 19: 84–101.

Durkheim, Émile. 1885b. "Review of 'Dr Ludwig Gumplowicz, Grundriss der Sociologie (Esquisse d'une sociologie).'" *Revue philosophique de la France et de l'étranger* 20: 627–634.

Durkheim, Émile. 1887a. "La philosophie dans les universités allemandes." *Revue internationale de l'enseignement* 13: 313–338, 423–440.

Durkheim, Émile. 1887b. "La science positive de la morale en Allemagne." *Revue philosophique de la France et de l'étranger* 24: 33–58, 113–142, 275–284.

Durkheim, Émile. 1888. "Cours de science sociale: Leçon d'ouverture." *Revue internationale de l'enseignement* 15: 23–48.

Durkheim, Émile. 1889. "Review of 'Ferdinand Tönnies, Gemeinschaft und Gesellschaft. Abhandlung des Communismus und des Socialismus als empirischer Culturformen.'" *Revue philosophique de la France et de l'étranger* 27: 416–422.

Durkheim, Émile. 1890. "Les principes de 1789 et la sociology" (Review of *Les principes de 1789 et la science sociale* by Thomas Ferneuil). *Revue internationale de l'enseignement* 19: 450–456.

Durkheim, Émile. 1895. "Lo stato attuale degli studi sociologici in Francia." *La riforma sociale* 3: 607–622, 691–707. French version: "L'état actuel des études sociologiques en France" In Durkheim 1975a, 73–108.

Durkheim, Émile. 1898. "Représentations individuelles et représentations collectives." *Revue de métaphysique et de morale* 6: 273–302.

Durkheim, Émile. 1900a. "La sociologie en France au XIXe siècle." *Revue bleue* 13, no. 20: 609–613, no. 21: 647–652.

Durkheim, Émile. 1900b. "La sociologia ed il suo dominio scientifico." *Rivista italiana di sociologia* 4: 127–148. French version: "La sociologie et son domaine scientifique," In Durkheim 1975a, 13–36.

Durkheim, Émile. 1902. "Contribution to 'Enquête sur l'influence allemande.'" *Mercure de France* 44 (156): 647–648.

Durkheim, Émile. 1915a. "La sociologie." In *La science française* (Exposition universelle et internationale de San Francisco), vol. 1, 39–49. Paris: Larousse.

Durkheim, Émile. 1915b. *"Germany above all": German Mentality and War*. Translated by J. S. Paris: Colin.

Durkheim, Émile. (1915a) 1960a. "Sociology." In *Emile Durkheim, 1858–1917*, edited by Kurt H. Wolff, 376–385. Columbus: Ohio State University Press.

Durkheim, Émile. (1892) 1960b. "Montesquieu's Contribution to the Rise of Social Science." In *Montesquieu and Rousseau: Forerunners of Sociology*, translated by Ralph Manheim, 1–64. Ann Arbor: University of Michigan Press.

Durkheim, Émile. (1892) 1966. "La contribution de Montesquieu à la constitution de la science sociale." In *Montesquieu et Rousseau, précurseurs de la sociologie*, 25–113. Paris: Marcel Rivière.

Durkheim, Émile. (1890) 1973a. "The Principles of 1789 and Sociology." In *Emile Durkheim: On Morality and Society*, edited by Robert N. Bellah, 34–42. Chicago: University of Chicago Press.

Durkheim, Émile. (1900a) 1973b. "Sociology in France in the Nineteenth Century." In *Emile Durkheim: On Morality and Society*, edited by Robert N. Bellah, 3–22. Chicago: University of Chicago Press.

Durkheim, Émile. 1975a. *Textes*, vol. 1: *Eléments d'une théorie sociale*. Paris: Minuit.

Durkheim, Émile. 1975b. *Textes*, vol. 3: *Fonctions sociales et institutions*. Paris: Minuit.

Durkheim, Émile. 1976. "Lettres à Célestin Bouglé." *Revue française de sociologie* 17, no. 2: 165–180.

Durkheim, Émile. (1885a) 1978. "Review of Albert Schaeffle, *Bau und Leben des sozialen Körpers: Erster Band*." In *Emile Durkheim on Institutional Analysis*, edited and translated by Mark Traugott, 93–114. Chicago: University of Chicago Press.

Durkheim, Émile. (1895) 1982. *The Rules of Sociological Method and Selected Texts on Sociology and Its Method*. Translated by W. D. Halls. New York: Free Press.

Durkheim, Émile. (1885b) 1989. "Durkheim's Review of Gumplowicz's *Grundriss der Soziologie* (1885)." *Etudes Durkheimiennes / Durkheim Studies* 1, no. 1: 7–11.

Durkheim, Émile. (1887b) 1993. *Ethics and the Sociology of Morals*. Edited and translated by Robert T. Hall. Buffalo, NY: Prometheus Books.

Durkheim, Émile. (1888) 2008. "Course in Social Science—Inaugural Lecture." *Organization & Environment* 21, no. 2: 188–204.

Durkheim, Émile. 2015. *L'Allemagne au-dessus de tout. Commentaire à vive voix*. Edited by Bruno Karsenti. Paris: Editions de l'EHESS.

Espagne, Michel, and Michaël Werner. 1987. "La construction d'une référence culturelle allemande en France. Genèse et histoire (1750–1914)." *Annales. Economies, sociétés, civilisations* 42, no. 4: 969–992.

Espinas, Alfred. 1878. *Des sociétés animales*. Paris: Germer-Baillière.

Espinas, Alfred. 1879. *Die thierischen Gesellschaften. Eine vergleichend-psychologische Untersuchung*. Braunschweig: Vieweg.

Feuerhahn, Wolf. 2011. "Les 'sociétés animales': Un défi à l'ordre savant." *Romantisme* 154: 35–51.

Feuerhahn, Wolf. 2014. "Zwischen Individualismus und Sozialismus. Durkheims Soziologie und ihr deutsches Pantheon." In *Europäische Wissenschaftskulturen und politische Ordnungen in der Moderne (1890–1970)*, edited by Gangolf Hübinger, 79–98. Munich: Oldenbourg.

Firsching, Horst. 1995. "Emile Durkheims Religionssoziologie—Made in Germany? Zu einer These von Simon Deploige." In *Religionssoziologie um 1900*, edited by Volkhard Krech and Hartmann Tyrell, 351–363. Würzburg: Ergon.

Fournier, Marcel. 2013. *Émile Durkheim: A Biography*. Cambridge: Polity Press.

Gephart, Werner. 1982. "Soziologie im Aufbruch. Zur Wechselwirkung von Durkheim, Schäffle, Tönnies und Simmel." *Kölner Zeitschrift für Soziologie und Sozialpsychologie* 34, no. 1: 1–25.

Hollenberg, Wilhelm A. 1881. "La philosophie dans les gymnases allemands." *Revue internationale de l'enseignement* 1: 257–266.

Jones, Robert Alun. 1999. *The Development of Durkheim's Social Realism*. Cambridge: Cambridge University Press.

Lachelier, Henri. 1881. "L'enseignement de la philosophie dans les universités allemandes." *Revue philosophique de la France et de l'étranger* 11: 152–174.

Lévy-Bruhl, Lucien. 1903. *La morale et la science des mœurs*. Paris: Alcan.

Lukes, Steven. 1973. *Emile Durkheim: His Life and Work*. London: Allen Lane.
Morland, Jacques. 1902. "Enquête sur l'influence allemande." *Mercure de France* 44, no. 155: 289–294.
Mosbah-Natanson, Sébastien. 2008. "Internationalisme et tradition nationale. Le cas de la constitution de la sociologie française autour de 1900." *Revue d'histoire des sciences humaines* 18, no. 1: 35–62.
Orain, Olivier. 2018. "Les Écoles en sciences de l'homme. Usages indigènes et catégories analytiques." *Revue d'histoire des sciences humaines* 32: 7–38.
Papilloud, Christian. 2002. "Simmel, Durkheim et Mauss. Naissance ratée de la sociologie européenne." *Revue du MAUSS* 20, no. 2: 300–327.
Prochasson, Christophe, and Anne Rasmussen. 1996. *Au nom de la patrie. Les intellectuels et la Première Guerre mondiale (1910–1919)*. Paris: La Découverte.
Rasmussen, Anne. 2004. "La 'science française' dans la guerre des manifestes, 1914–1918." *Mots. Les langages du politique* 76: 9–23.
Renan, Ernest. 1868. *Questions contemporaines*. Paris: Michel Lévy.
Renan, Ernest. 1871. *La réforme intellectuelle et morale de la France*. Paris: Michel Lévy.
Rol, Cécile. 2006. "'Sur la psychologie sociale de l'hostilité.' Ou la dernière apparition de Georg Simmel sur la scène sociologique française." *L'Année sociologique* 56, no. 1: 137–168.
Rol, Cécile. 2012. "Animisme et totémisme: Durkheim *vs* Wundt." *L'Année sociologique* 62, no. 2: 351–366.
Schäffle, Albert. 1881. *Bau und Leben des socialen Körpers*. Erster Band. Neue zum Theil umgearbeitete Ausgabe. Tübingen: Laupp.
Schockenhoff, Andreas. 1986. *Henri Albert und das Deutschlandbild des Mercure de France 1890–1905*. Frankfurt am Main: Peter Lang.
Séailles, Gabriel. 1883. "L'enseignement de la philosophie en Allemagne." *Revue internationale de l'enseignement* 6: 956–976.
Serry, Hervé. 2004. "Saint Thomas sociologue? Les enjeux cléricaux d'une sociologie catholique dans les années 1880–1920." In *Pour une histoire des sciences sociales. Hommage à Pierre Bourdieu*, edited by Johan Heilbron, Rémi Lenoir, Gisèle Sapiro, and Pascale Pargamin, 59–82. Paris: Fayard.
Simmel, Georg. 1894. "Das Problem der Sociologie." *Schmollers Jahrbuch für Gesetzgebung, Verwaltung und Volkswirtschaft im Deutschen Reich* 18: 1301–1307. English translation: "The Problem of Sociology." *The Annals of the American Academy of Political and Social Science* 6, no. 3 (1895): 52–63.
Tyrell, Hartmann. 2011. "Religion und Politik: Max Weber und Émile Durkheim." In *Religionen verstehen. Zur Aktualität von Max Webers Religionssoziologie*, edited by Agathe Bienfait, 41–91. Wiesbaden: Verlag für Sozialwissenschaften.
Wundt, Wilhelm. 1878. "Ueber den gegenwärtigen Zustand der Thierpsychologie." *Vierteljahrsschrift für wissenschaftliche Philosophie* 2: 137–149.

CHAPTER 13

THE MODERN INDIVIDUAL

W. WATTS MILLER

An account of the modern individual is a central feature of the sociological landscape of Durkheim's first great work, his doctoral thesis on the division of labor, which took many years to write and was eventually published as a book in 1893. But the account changed in significant ways in writings of the late 1890s and early 1900s. In turn, further developments came with the emerging sociological landscape of his last great work, *Les formes élémentaires de la vie religieuse*, which again took many years to write and eventually appeared in 1912.

Even so, Durkheim's approach to the modern individual also involves basic continuities. One of these is his interest, shared with so many contemporaries, in an understanding of modern life that is rooted in a story of human evolution and early origins. Another is his more distinctive, much disputed insistence on a sui generis realm of human social life, irreducible to either biology or psychology. At the same time it is essential to notice how, throughout his career, he combined a theoretical commitment to sociology as science with practical commitments to social critique and social reform. This is especially linked with how, again throughout his career, he was concerned with far-reaching modern pathologies and a state of crisis. Indeed, in my chapter's concluding exploration of ways in which Durkheim's sociology of the modern individual is still relevant, a key question is how it might illuminate an ongoing crisis nowadays.[1]

THE INDIVIDUAL IN DURKHEIM'S THESIS ON THE DIVISION OF LABOR

The French Revolution, conventionally dated as beginning in 1789, sparked off a period of turmoil in which it is possible to count, over the hundred years that followed, four forms of monarchy, two empires, and three republics. Durkheim was born during the regime of the Second Empire, which collapsed in defeat to the Germans in 1870, and, after a time of often bitter struggle, the arrival of a Third Republic was confirmed by elections of 1878. Durkheim, who very much welcomed the new republic, was by now a student in Paris, preparing for the entrance examinations to do philosophy at the prestigious *Ecole normale supérieure* (ENS). The son of the rabbi of the little town of Epinal in eastern France, he came from a relatively modest background. But, like many bright young men of his class and generation, he made his way with the help of the public educational system (like the emancipation of the Jews, one of the many legacies of the Revolution). He graduated from the ENS in 1882 and then taught philosophy at various provincial *lycées*, but he was already turning toward sociology in turning his mind to what to do for a doctorate. Indeed, in recently discovered student notes of a course given by Durkheim at the *Lycée de Sens* in 1883/84 (Durkheim 2004), there is a revealing discussion of individualistic versus socialist ideologies. Individualism treats society as an artificial construction and fails to see it as a complex living reality. Yet socialism so exalts society and the state that it denies individual rights and crushes the individual personality. However, "The solution to this problem is the division of labor" (Durkheim 2004: 259). In any case, and partly thanks to his interest in sociology, Durkheim was picked out as a rising star and in 1887 took up an appointment at Bordeaux to the first post in social science at a French university.

A Modern Dynamic

Durkheim's inaugural lecture was a high-profile public occasion that ended with a vision of how sociology could contribute to social renewal and reform, especially through an understanding of solidarity, which then helped to introduce a course on solidarity itself. There is now no known detailed record of this course. However, a summary was given at the start of the following session and reveals a distinction between two basic types of social organization.

> The analysis of these two social types then led us to discover two very different forms of social solidarity, one that is due to the similarity of consciousnesses, to the community of ideas and sentiments, the other that is on the contrary a product of the differentiation of functions and of the division of labor.
>
> (Durkheim 1888: 258; 1975, vol. 3: 10)

As the summary continues, these two forms of solidarity—the "mechanical" and the "organic"—usually coexist in some way with one another, but modern societies especially depend on a solidarity based on the division of labor, "which allows individuals independence while reinforcing the unity of the whole" (Durkheim 1888: 258; 1975, vol. 3: 10).

Clearly, Durkheim was teaching his very first students at Bordeaux the basic ideas of his thesis. But although, by this time, he must already have made good progress with it, he took until 1892 to write up a final manuscript, which was then printed for his examining jury early in 1893 and published as a commercial book later the same year. Even so, and perhaps surprisingly, he managed to complete his thesis without offering any definition of *solidarité*. However, it is apparent from textual analysis that, in line with established French usage of the time, it is not a mere matter of sentiment—as in the English *fellow feeling*—but is about a sense of social attachment in webs of definite links, relations, and responsibilities. Thus, Durkheim's story of an evolution from "mechanical" to "organic" solidarity especially involves a move away from his paradigmatic case of early traditional worlds—societies made up of a system of clans. This is not just a move away from likeness based on the traditional collective consciousness of a group's detailed, far-reaching set of shared sentiments and beliefs. It is also a move away from likeness based on the traditional social structure of interlinked yet essentially similar, internally homogeneous groups exemplified by clans and discussed, more abstractly, as "segments." Looked at another way, it is a story of a move toward a solidarity in difference and diversity, driven by the modern dynamic of a division of labor that, among other things, helps to transform the collective consciousness into an affair of generalities, open to many interpretations. But also and not least, it increasingly converts a "segmental" into an "organic" structure, made up of a diversity of groups and individuals attached to one another through a web of different interlocking roles and functions. So a fundamental message of the thesis is not simply about the modern individual. Rather, it involves a modern social dynamic that makes possible an increasing development of individuality itself.

However, one of many problems with Durkheim's thesis is that he might appear to contradict himself on this issue. Picturing an early social world in which the power of the collective consciousness is at a maximum, he writes that "at that moment our individuality is zero" (Durkheim 1893: 139 / 1984: 84). Indeed, several chapters later in his work's increasingly complex argument, he again remarks on and even emphasizes a time when the individual personality "*did not exist*" (212/142). Yet perhaps this is an instance of his stylistic fondness for overstatement, rather than something to take literally. Only a few pages further on he makes clear that the individual personality always exists. The reason is that one of the sources of psychic life's realm of representations is the human being's physical embodiedness. "This first basis of all individuality is inalienable and does not depend on the social world" (216/cf. 145). The discussion then also makes clear his concern with the social world itself as the other and more significant source of individuality. The message driven home by his earlier rhetoric is that every human being's character as an individual personality is not just a matter of biology but is above all "the fruit of historical development" (217/146)—a message with the added significance that it is the earliest identifiable expression of Durkheim's interest in a universal duality of human nature.

Another challenging yet seldom noticed or examined feature of the thesis is its use of two discourses, which could be called the "functionalist" and the "republican." Both of these discourses are concerned with the individual as a distinct, particular character, and both of them are concerned with how individuality and solidarity can combine through a common basis in difference. However, the functionalist discourse centers round a harmony of roles in an overall integrated system, to cast the individuals filling these roles as mere "parts of a whole," indeed, as "organs of an organism." Yet even Durkheim stops short of talking about an organic individual and instead invokes the "individual personality." This is more in line with the republican discourse, with its attention to individuals not only as persons but also as citizens, with its appeal to a whole set of ideals encapsulated in the motto of the Revolution, readopted in the Third Republic, *Liberté, Égalité, Fraternité*, or, not least, with its insistence on moral diversity and autonomy. Thus, as eventually explained in Book III of the thesis: "Functional diversity entails a moral diversity that nothing can prevent, and it is inevitable that one grows at the same time as the other" (405/cf. 298). Or, as explained early on in the work, it arose from an interest in the division of labor as a way of resolving an "apparent antinomy," in which the individual personality increasingly combines autonomy with solidarity (ix/xxx).

Autonomy, Solidarity, and a Commonwealth of Persons

Durkheim's simultaneous reference both to an antinomy and to autonomy is unmistakably Kantian in inspiration, and even or especially in criticizing as well as sympathizing with Kant, he had a long involvement with his work. Kant was by far and away the author most frequently cited by Durkheim in his course at the *Lycée de Sens* in 1883/84, a point evident from the detailed research on Durkheim's philosophical interests and concerns undertaken by Giovanni Paoletti (2012: 47–48). But as his research also shows, Kant was the philosopher most often cited by Durkheim throughout the whole of his sociological career (41–42).

The picture can be further filled out thanks to the even more recent discoveries, by Nicolas Sembel and Matthieu Béra, of Durkheim's library loans both at Bordeaux and Paris (Sembel and Béra 2013; Béra 2016). This new research helps to reveal a "hidden Durkheim," who consulted works and authors never explicitly cited in his surviving publications, and often difficult or even impossible to infer from these. In the case of interest here, the discoveries show that he borrowed a wide range of works by Kant, both in the original German and in French translations, together with various commentaries on Kant, again both in German and French. Notably, his loans included German editions and French translations of Kant's *Groundwork of the Metaphysics of Morals*, as well as of all three of his critiques, *The Critique of Pure Reason*, *The Critique of Practical Reason*, and *The Critique of Judgement*.[2]

Yet how, in what survives of Durkheim's writings, did he attack but also support and try to go on from Kant? His enduring and most fundamental criticism is already evident in his 1883/84 *Lycée de Sens* lectures. These reject a Kantian dualism of two radically different worlds, which attempts to overcome the apparent antinomy between causation and freedom by locating one in the accessible outer world of phenomena, the other in a mysterious inner realm of the noumenal. It is necessary to look for an alternative solution to the problem, since "the freedom that Kant offers us is metaphysical, virtual, sterile" (Durkheim 2004: 163–164). There is then an attempt to build in a more realistic and practical way on Kant's work, as "one of the greatest efforts ever made to push humanity toward the ideal" (242).

A similar pattern of criticism and sympathy can be found in Durkheim's thesis. It starts with a ringing declaration—"This book is above all an effort to treat the facts of moral life according to the method of the positive sciences"—and adds for good measure that any possible transcendental realm can be left to the metaphysician, since "what is above all certain" is that morality "develops in history and under the influence of historical causes" (Durkheim 1893: i–ii / cf. 1984: xxv–xxvi). But, as already noted, it is then in an interest in the historically evolving dynamic of the division of labor as a key to overcoming an apparent antinomy between autonomy and solidarity. Or again, in posthumously published lectures of the late 1890s, an aim is to replace the timelessness of a merely metaphysical, Kantian autonomy with something more practically meaningful, a "progressive autonomy" that evolves and develops in history (Durkheim 1925: 126, 130 / 1961: 110, 114).

Even so, and given all this, a drawback would be if any effort to combine autonomy with solidarity is hopelessly un-Kantian. On the contrary, however, it can seem very much in line with an argument that must have been known to Durkheim and that was first made in *The Groundwork*, originally published in 1785. But if we cite the editions that Durkheim himself consulted, the argument links autonomy with the ideal of a "kingdom of ends," an ideal clearly open to interpretation as an affair of solidarity, since it is defined as a "systematic union of different rational beings through common laws" (Kant 1854: 81, 1867: 281).

In the overall conclusion to his thesis, Durkheim highlights his work's key arguments for seeing the division of labor as a route to a modern interlinkage of autonomy and solidarity. In doing so, he also brings out his view of autonomy itself and how it is especially an affair of individual personalities who are free and distinct. "In effect, to be a person is to be an autonomous source of action," a developing, historically situated power of agency that human beings owe, not to a shadowy, metaphysically fixed free will, but to processes of a growing individualization in which "the very materials of their consciousness have a personal character" (Durkheim 1893: 453–454 / cf. 1984: 335). Moreover, it is this essentially republican concern with each different individual's same moral status as a person that underlies the account, in Book III, of ideals of equality and justice in which society frees everyone to develop, flourish, and live up to their potential (422–423/313).

A great mistake of many commentators has been to pay little or no attention to Book III, and to concentrate instead on Books I and II, with their basic message that the division of labor is the place to look for a solidarity of modern times. But Book III is about a failure to generate this in modern everyday scenes of alienation, anomie, injustice, and class war, and in an ongoing crisis especially bound up with a "constrained" as against a "spontaneous" division of labor. Indeed, as the work now reveals, "the division of labour produces solidarity only if it is spontaneous and to the extent that it is spontaneous" (422/cf. 312).

Moreover, although Durkheim continues to use a functionalist discourse in Book III, it is also here that, in the end, his republican discourse wins out. In particular, although he continues to invoke a "harmony of functions," a key reason why this can get nowhere on its own is that any modern harmony of functions depends on a modern "need for justice" (434/cf. 321–322). More generally, modern solidarity depends on movement toward the ideal of a spontaneous division of labor, which is above all discussed as an ideal of a society of freedom, justice, everyone's flourishing, and an interlinkage of autonomous persons, and so in ways connected with the Revolution's *Liberté, Égalité, Fraternité* but also with Kant's "kingdom of ends."

Although Kant's "kingdom" is never explicitly mentioned in Durkheim's thesis, it must have been familiar to him, though not just because he had read *The Groundwork*. It was part of his intellectual milieu and had been reworked as a "society of persons" in a text well known to him and indeed by his philosophical hero, Charles Renouvier (1869, vol. 1: 168). In turn, it was reinterpreted as a "republic of persons" in lectures given in the 1890s by the man to whom the thesis was dedicated, Émile Boutroux (1926: 373). Or, in picking out a Durkheimian version, we could discuss it as an ideal of a "commonwealth of persons."

A Time of Crisis and Transition

In worrying about an ongoing modern crisis, Durkheim was also hopeful enough to see it as a passing, transient crisis that would one day be overcome. In the meantime, it stimulated a developing analysis in his work of forms of individualism he condemned or even saw as pathological. Some of these clustered round the anomie of a radical deregulation, whether in an unchaining of desires or of a coldly calculated self-interest. But perhaps a more fundamental malaise was the alienation of a radical separateness from others and lack of solidarity itself, whether an individual becomes isolated in a private world of thought and the imagination, or, again, by absorption in his or her own desires and interests. Indeed, the individualism that Durkheim most ferociously opposed throughout his career was the alienation of the atomized, economistic individual, absorbed in the calculation and pursuit of self-interest.

However, in Book III of his thesis, the worries about an ongoing crisis are above all about social rather than merely individual pathologies, since they especially center round a critique of the division of labor's constrained as well as anomic forms. A concern running through his critique is not only with an underlying "antagonism between labour and capital" but also open "class wars," and in any case involving an alienating social gulf between whole groups, rather than simply individuals, in which vast numbers are forced into "degrading" work but also into "exploitative" contracts, bound up with gross inequalities and the scandal of "rich and poor at birth" (Durkheim 1893: 397–430 / cf. 1984: 292–320). In sum, a basic theme is a breakdown of solidarity in the underlying tensions and overt conflicts of a class-divided society.

If we ask what helped to bring about this situation as well as what might help to overcome it, the beginnings of answer can be found in Durkheim's first sociological publication, around the time of getting started in earnest on his thesis. The French Revolution suppressed the guilds of the old regime without replacing them, and in the process it helped to unleash two extreme tendencies, a conflict of "unfettered egoisms," arising from individualism but generating class war, and a "despotic socialism," centralizing power in the state. The only solution to this crisis is to re-establish intermediate groups like the guilds, but in "a new organization, less narrow and fixed, and better adapted to today's mobile life and to a far-reaching division of labour" (Durkheim 1885: 96 / cf. 1978: 108).

Or, as argued in his thesis itself, it is necessary to rebuild solidarity through new occupational groups to replace the old guilds, swept away in times of social change "that required, not so much this organization's radical destruction, as its transformation" (Durkheim 1893: 238–239 / cf. 1984: 165). However, the work has only a few references to such groups, since he was planning a whole follow-up volume on them, as he explained in the preface to a revised edition of his thesis (Durkheim 1902: i–ii / 1984: xxxi). This volume never materialized, and instead the preface became a substitute for it, but as part of a landscape in which his picture of the individual was no longer quite the same.

New Developments: 1897–1902

The notion of a religious or religious-like cult of the person, lying at the core of a modern collective consciousness, was originally floated by Durkheim in his thesis, in two quite brief but also contrasting passages, one relatively early on in the work, the other in the conclusion's final overview of things. The first of these passages attacks a modern collective cult of the individual, since "it is not to society that it attaches us; it is to ourselves" (Durkheim 1893: 187 / cf. 1984: 122). This might make sense as an attack on a Durkheimian *bête noire*, the individual as a radically alienated, interest-calculating atom. It makes little or no sense as an attack on the individual either as a functionalist organ of an organism or as a republican socially attached personality. It is this republican character that is clearly at stake in the passage in the work's overall conclusion, which recognizes that belief in everyone's same status and dignity as a person is nowadays a moral "rallying-point" (450/333). Yet despite the evident sympathy with a cult of the person, it is in insisting that it can only be a minor source of solidarity nowadays and that by far the major source—even or especially in Durkheim's hopes for reform—is to be found in a division of labor's webs of interlinking groups and relations. The issue of the relative importance of a cult of the person compared with a whole wider vision of a moral commonwealth can then be seen as underlying key developments in subsequent work. This involves *Suicide*, completed in 1897, an essay on individualism and the intellectuals written in 1898, and the preface on occupational groups for *The Division of Labour*'s revised edition of 1902.

If we start with *Suicide*, it is worth noticing that the author devotes roughly equal space both to what constitutes his first significant sustained account of a modern cult of the person (Durkheim 1897: 377–384 / 1951: 332–338) and to what constitutes his first significant sustained account of the need for reform through new occupational groups (434–451/378–392). But it is also worth noticing that he keeps these accounts more or less separate and places them some distance away from one another, so that it requires an effort—not always made by commentators—to link them together and ask about their combined overall message.

In line with his thesis, the cult is still seen as arising from a division of labor's social dynamics of increasing individualization (382/336–337). In contrast with his thesis, it now centers round the person as "a sacred thing and even the sacred thing *par excellence*" (378/cf. 333). Not least, it has also become a source of solidarity that, "far from detaching individuals from society," unites them in an essentially collective ideal—an ideal of "humanity in general" in one formulation and of "the human person" in another, yet which in any case is not just very different from a focus on the embodied, "sensate" individual but also transcends everyone as "individual personalities" (382–383/336–337). Yet although this represents a significant new development, he continues to look for a modern solidarity's strongest roots in a division of labor's webs of relations, above all in his campaign for a web of new occupational groups—a campaign especially concerned with these as social practices that can develop an effective moral code based on ideals and demands of modern times, not least a demand for "distributive justice" (440/383).

In sum, a combined overall message is that a cult of the person, even if centered round a new sacred thing par excellence, has only a secondary importance compared with reforms for a moral commonwealth. This is not just because it originates anyway in a division of labor, nor is it just because it is a subsidiary source of solidarity, but it is also because a concept of humanity in general, far from offering a solution to the problem of translating ideals of justice and so on into an effective, detailed moral code, is part of the problem itself.

A similar overall message can be gleaned from reading together the two quite separate texts already mentioned, the essay on "Individualism and the Intellectuals" and the preface on occupational groups. Certainly, the essay is where Durkheim is at his most eloquent in defending a humanist cult of the person, and the preface is where he is at his most cogent in arguing for new intermediate occupational groups. Even so, the essay is careful to say how the cult can unite modernity's increasingly dissimilar individuals as a "system of beliefs"—rather than as a web of relations—and this is in continuing to view it as arising from a division of labor's dynamics of increasing difference and diversity (Durkheim 1898a: 10–11 / 1973: 50). Or again, the essay helps to illuminate what a sacralization of the person is actually about, in seeing it as an uncompromising attachment to a core moral principle, in contrast with a "sordid," interest-driven, economistic individualism, in which nothing is sacred since everything is negotiable (7/cf. 44). It remains the case that the cult revolves around a concept of humanity in general, and that whatever the impassioned, uncompromising attachment to such a concept, there is still a need for social practices that can work out and translate its ramifications into a detailed, developing moral code—precisely one of the main roles of the preface's web of intermediate occupational groups, in an empowerment of individuals both as autonomous persons and active citizens, drawn into "the general torrent of social life" (Durkheim 1902: xxxiii / cf. 1984: liv). Indeed, an overlap between the two texts is how the essay warns against forms of individualism that combine with an "authoritarian conception of society" (Durkheim 1898a: 9 / 1973: 47), which links with the preface's warning against an elimination of intermediate groups that leaves only a mass of atomized individuals plus an authoritarian overblown state, a combination described as a "sociological monstrosity" (Durkheim 1902: xxxii / 1984: liv). In another key area of common ground, the essay looks to ways of "completing, extending and organizing individualism" that help to introduce "more justice" in socioeconomic relations (Durkheim 1898a: 13 / cf. 1973: 56)—again, one of the main roles of the preface's new occupational groups (Durkheim 1902: xxxiv–xxxvi / 1984: lv–lvii).

It is essential, however, to bear in mind the circumstances in which Durkheim felt impelled to write the essay. He finished *Suicide* early in 1897, while also getting on with preparing the first issue of his new journal, the *Année sociologique*, for publication the following year, and in 1898 itself was busy preparing the journal's next issue. Yet this was at the very height of the Dreyfus Affair, and the furor over whether or not a Jewish army captain, convicted of selling secrets to the Germans, was the victim not only of a miscarriage of justice but also of an establishment cover-up, protecting the real traitor, a down-at-heel aristocrat. Durkheim was at first reluctant to get too closely involved in the Affair, not least thanks to the heavy burden of producing the *Année*. However, the members of the team he had gathered around the journal were all becoming keen pro-Dreyfusards, he himself was deeply shocked by the wave of vitriolic antisemitism that swept through France, and in the end he not only helped to found a League for the Defense of Human Rights but was also provoked into responding to an article by a prominent right-wing Catholic, Ferdinand Brunetière. This sneered at intellectuals as jumped-up nobodies who dared to challenge established authority, and it condemned their attachment to individualism, "the great sickness of the present time" (Brunetière 1898: 445).

But it is not just that Durkheim's essay marshals a whole set of arguments against such views, including, not least, his stress on two very different forms of individualism. It also expresses, in its conclusion, his worries over a strategic dilemma in which, even in urging the need to go beyond and enlarge an earlier, limited individualism of basic rights, he insists that in the current situation such reform is a work of the future. For now, "the urgent task that must come before everything else is to save our moral patrimony" (Durkheim 1898a: 13 / cf. 1973: 56). However, even if this is not a reference to the Revolution's legacy of aspirations toward a moral commonwealth, an improbable interpretation of the "moral patrimony" that requires defense is that it is simply a collection of a few basic rights won for individuals in the past. On the contrary, the target of reactionary forces is the very idea of everyone's equal moral status as a person—an idea at stake in struggles *both* for its enlargement through long-term reform *and* for its defense in an immediate crisis.

The Individual, Creative Effervescence, and *The Forms*

In asking about the individual in the landscape of Durkheim's last great work, my main concern will be with how, through its picture of an early elementary Australia, it offers an account of continuing elemental features of all social life and so also of bases of reform nowadays. But a place to begin is with a fundamental tenet of his whole sociology and with new approaches to it.

A Sui Generis Realm of the Social

An opening announcement in *The Forms* is that "society is a *sui generis* reality" (Durkheim 1912: 22 / cf. 1995: 15). However, Durkheim is unconvincing in making this claim in his early writings. This is because he is unclear about the need to identify and address two key problems, or at least two aspects of the same problem. One is how a realm of the social does not just magically emerge out of nothing, yet is nonetheless irreducible to human biology or psychology. The other is how there can be such a realm without a break in chains of causation, that is, without some sort of indeterminacy and freedom.

But there were significant moves on this front in his essay on "Individual and Collective Representations," especially in its final section (Durkheim 1898b: 293–302 / 1974: 23–34). Its key terms are "synthesis" and "fusion" in an argument explaining how one order of reality can have roots in the elements of another, yet is irreducible to these—in effect, it does not just emerge out of nothing, yet is nonetheless distinct. In one case, individual representations have roots in a "synthesis" of physiological elements that are transformed by the very fact of their "fusion"; in another, collective representations have roots in a "synthesis" and "fusion" of individualistic elements that are transformed in the very process itself (295–296/26–27).

Or again, in arguing for sui generis orders of reality, he still insists that they can have only a relative autonomy. More mysteriously, he denies any "break of continuity" between his interlinked orders of reality, even in invoking "suppleness, flexibility, and contingence" as characteristics of a higher realm compared with its substratum, and in asserting that it becomes relatively "free" from its roots in this (298–299/cf. 29–30). I would suggest, then, that what is in fact at stake is a relative break in chains of causation. Indeed, this is perhaps the only way to make sense of his argument, in the same overall passage, that collective representations can cut loose from close initial links with a substratum, to combine with one another in all kinds of new syntheses and to take on "a life of their own," as in the case of the "luxuriant growth" of myths and legends that are constructions of religious thought itself rather than simply epiphenomena of social morphology (299/cf. 31).

Even so, the essay has only a single reference to creativity and makes no mention of effervescence. Accordingly, let us now move on to *The Forms* and an idea at the core of the work.

Creative Effervescence

Just as god is described, in *The Forms*, as a "creative power," so is society; indeed, it is a creative power with no equal in the world of actual, observable life, and it is added for good measure that creation, far from being a merely mystical process, is the product of a "synthesis" (Durkheim 1912: 637 / 1995: 447). Accordingly, what we have now is an explicit idea of a creative synthesis, systematically interlinked with a similarly explicit idea of creative effervescence. It is this idea that underlies the wholly general claim that a "society can neither create nor recreate itself without, in the very act, creating an ideal" (603/cf. 425), but that is also overtly at stake in hope for social reform and a renewal of idealism through another moment of "creative effervescence" (611/429).

Moreover, if we examine the work's accounts of its two star cases of effervescence— a ceremony among the Warramunga people in Australia, and the French Revolution in the modern west—it is evident from how it concretely describes these that the extraordinary creative energies of effervescence combine the power of assembly, the power of symbolism, and the power of art. Or, turning to the work's more abstract theorizations of things and starting with assembly, complete with its close proximity and interaction of embodied individuals, this helps to generate "a state of effervescence that alters the conditions of psychic activity" (602–603/424). In the case of symbolism and how it creates and constitutes collective concepts through fixing them on material objects, "social life makes this fusion possible through the great mental effervescence it brings about" (339/cf. 238). Or, in the case of art, its "free creations of the mind" and "free combinations of thought and action" are characterized in terms of a "surplus" and energies that sweep far beyond the practically appropriate or necessary (544–546/385–386). The importance of this case is not just because of the explicit reference to "free creations," but because art is integrally part of the work's concretely described paradigmatic examples of effervescence, just as it is also bound up with the luxuriant growth and "great independence" of "a whole world of feelings, ideas, and images" (605/426).

In sum so far, the essay on individual and collective representations helps to prepare the way for *The Forms*, which, in continuing concerns with a freedom, independence, and sui generis distinctiveness of an order of reality that nonetheless still has roots in another, continues to repeat talk of a "relative autonomy" (388/274). But it clarifies and crystallizes these concerns in linking them, through a new web of argumentation, with a new, key, explicitly formulated idea of creative effervescence.

At the same time it is possible to identify, in *The Forms*, two other relevant, highly significant developments in Durkheim's approach to things. In one of these, he now insists that collective beliefs are always individualized. In his account of Australia, the totemic principle, like god, is simultaneously transcendent and immanent, at once a vast external power going over and beyond individual members of the clan and an inner energy active in each of them, and in penetrating inside them, "it is inevitable that it is itself individualized" (356/cf. 251). Or, in a far-reaching generalization, the "impersonal forces that arise from collectivity" can only become established through their incorporation within individual consciousness, "where they are themselves individualized" (382/cf. 269)—a point repeated in the work's conclusion (605/425).

One of its many implications is how, as a process of internalization and individualization necessarily going on even or especially in Durkheim's key collective times of effervescence, it applies to both the main forms of these he had come to distinguish, involving the rites and festivals of an established social calendar as against the great upheavals of historically transformative times. Here, by way of conclusion, I want to focus on his concern with these great historic times, exemplified by all his interest in the French Revolution and hope for another transformative moment of creative effervescence.

The Individual, an Ongoing Crisis, and Possibilities of Reform

It is in no way the case that a pathology of the modern individual is the core of Durkheim's account of a modern crisis in Book III of his thesis. On the contrary, the overwhelming majority of individuals are at the receiving end of the hurts and injustices of a system in serious disrepair. The account might have lost force for a time, in the welfare reforms and general mood of progress in Western societies around the 1950s. Yet there has been an increasing return to a world of exploitative contracts, distributive injustice, the scandal of rich and poor at birth, and an extreme concentration of wealth and power reminiscent of a prerevolutionary old regime. *The Division of Labour*'s analysis of a crisis, first published in 1893, cannot nowadays just be consigned to the museum of the history of ideas. Moreover, the analysis was republished in full in the work's revised edition of 1902 and developed even further in Durkheim's new preface to this. Its concerns resurface in his conclusion not only to *The Forms* itself but also to a talk of 1914 explaining what his new work was all about (Durkheim 1919/1975). These concerns are again evident in his final writings and are very clearly expressed in a recently discovered article of 1917, rearticulating *The Division of Labour*'s view of an ongoing modern crisis and entitled "The Politics of the Future" (Durkheim 1999). It is historically inaccurate and simplistic to construct a "new" Durkheim around a narrative of a "cultural turn" (Smith and Alexander 2005), in which he is pictured as abandoning the concerns of *The Division of Labour* for those of *The Forms*. But it is sociologically misguided to construct an account of the modern world that emphasizes the cultural and ritual-symbolic while paying little or no attention to underlying structures and dynamics at work in a time of socioeconomic crisis and moral malaise. Indeed, it can seem an exercise in fiddling while Rome burns.

In rethinking the crisis, however, it could be considered a built-in, permanent feature of the modern world, thanks to a built-in, ever-expanding agenda around its concept of the person, sparking off conflicts around issues of women's equality, gay rights, educational opportunities, ethnic pluralism, everyone's developing and flourishing, and so on in the never-ending work of actualizing ideals of a commonwealth. This is nonetheless quite different from a situation, reminiscent of the Dreyfus Affair, in which "culture wars" are used by right-wing forces to mask an agenda that does not just involve an increasing concentration of private wealth and power, but that targets the very concept of the person itself. A paradox in Durkheim's work is that he saw this concept as deeply rooted in the modern world yet also as quite fragile, one of the things at stake in a critical analysis of his "new religion" by W. S. F. Pickering (1984), and more recently explored, in an enquiry on how the person became sacred, by Hans Joas (2013). But there is also the related Durkheimian worry about a tension between rallying round a core idea of the person in an immediate crisis and working for a commonwealth, which helps to lead on to some concluding remarks about creative effervescence.

It is evident from Durkheim's article on the politics of the future—perhaps the last to be published in his lifetime—that he never abandoned *The Division of Labour*'s concerns with identifying modern ideals but also with the structural organization required to articulate and actualize them. However, in reapproaching his campaign for a new web of intermediate occupational groups, there is a strong case for retheorizing them as "constitutive practices," as in the work of Anne Rawls (2012). Yet, on the one hand, a crucial part of Durkheim's account of a modern crisis is about a hollowing out of such groups, so that a way of understanding the importance of what is at stake is that it is a hollowing out of the constitutive practices of modern society itself. On the other hand, it also means that an effervescent renewal of idealism depends for any long-term success on a renewal of on-the-ground organization and a whole web of these socially constitutive practices. Indeed, something else that is evident from Durkheim's writings, including *Suicide*, the essay on the Dreyfus Affair, and *The Forms* itself, is that he was well aware of various dangers built into effervescence—high hopes soon followed by bitter disenchantment and despair, or, separately or together, a bloodbath, a renewal of fogs of mystification, a return of authoritarian regimes, a collapse of the idea of the person itself. But an altogether basic point, following from new developments in his view of a sui generis social realm, is that its effervescent creation comes with serious risks, even with only a relative indeterminacy and freedom.

Notes

1. See also Watts Miller (2012, 2017). Except for recently discovered student notes, all translations of Durkheim are my own and are based on original editions of his work. These are essential for scholarly historical purposes and are cited first. Available English editions vary in character and are cited afterward in two ways—as in the reference (Durkheim 1912: 611 / 1995: 429) when a translation is the same as mine, but as in the citation (Durkheim 1912: 382 / cf. 1995: 269) when it is different.

2. A suggestion some years ago by Warren Schmaus (2004) was that Durkheim did not consult Kant's work itself, but just relied on how it was interpreted by certain other French writers. This suggestion had only a flimsy basis at the time, and it is no longer plausible in light of the new evidence.

REFERENCES

Béra, Matthieu. 2016. "Les emprunts de Durkheim dans les bibliothèques de l'École normale supérieure et de la Sorbonne / Durkheim's Loans from the Libraries of the ENS and the Sorbonne, 1902–1917." *Durkheimian Studies / Etudes Durkheimiennes* 22: 3–46.

Boutroux, Émile. 1926. *La philosophie de Kant. Cours professé à la Sorbonne en 1896–1897.* Paris: Vrin.

Brunetière, Ferdinand. 1898. "Après le procès." *Revue des Deux Mondes* 146 (March): 428–446.

Durkheim, Émile. 1885. "Review of Albert Schaeffle, *Bau und Leben des sozialen Körpers: Erster Band*." *Revue philosophique* 19: 84–101. Reprinted in Durkheim 1975, vol. 1, 355–371. Translation Durkheim 1978.

Durkheim, Émile. 1888. "Introduction à la sociologie de la famille." *Annales de la Faculté des lettres de Bordeaux* 10: 257–281. Reprinted in Durkheim 1975, vol. 3, 9–34.

Durkheim, Émile. 1893. *De la division du travail social. Etude sur l'organisation des sociétés supérieures.* Paris: Alcan 1893. Revised edition Durkheim 1902.

Durkheim, Émile. 1897. *Le suicide. Etude de sociologie.* Paris: Alcan. Translation Durkheim 1951.

Durkheim, Émile. 1898a. "L'individualisme et les intellectuels." *Revue bleue*, 4e série 10: 7–13. Reprinted in Émile Durkheim, *La science sociale et l'action*, edited by Jean-Claude Filloux, 261–278. Paris: Presses universitaires de France, 1970. Translation Durkheim 1973.

Durkheim, Émile. 1898b. "Représentations individuelles et représentations collectives." *Revue de métaphysique et de morale* 6: 273–302. Reprinted in Émile Durkheim, *Sociologie et philosophie*, 273–302. Paris: Alcan, 1924. Translation Durkheim 1974.

Durkheim, Émile. 1902. *De la division du travail social.* 2nd ed. Paris: Alcan. Translation Durkheim 1984.

Durkheim, Émile. 1912. *Les formes élémentaires de la vie religieuse. Le système totémique en Australie.* Paris: Alcan. Translation Durkheim 1995.

Durkheim, Émile. (1914) 1919. "La conception sociale de la religion." In *Le sentiment religieux à l'heure actuelle*, edited by F. Abauzit, 97–105. Paris: Vrin. Reprinted in Durkheim 1970, 305–313. Translation Durkheim 1975.

Durkheim, Émile. 1925. *L'éducation morale.* Edited by Paul Fauconnet. Paris: Alcan. Translation Durkheim 1961.

Durkheim, Émile. (1897) 1951. *Suicide: A Study in Sociology.* Translated by John A. Spaulding and George Simpson. New York: Free Press.

Durkheim, Émile. (1925) 1961. *Moral Education: A Study in the Theory and Application of the Sociology of Education.* Translated by E. K. Wilson and H. Schnurer. New York: Free Press.

Durkheim, Émile. (1898) 1973. "Individualism and the Intellectuals." In *Emile Durkheim: On Morality and Society*, edited by Robert N. Bellah, 43–57. Chicago: University of Chicago Press.

Durkheim, Émile. (1898) 1974. "Individual and Collective Representations." In Émile Durkheim, *Sociology and Philosophy*, edited and translated by D. F. Pocock, 1–34. New York: Free Press.

Durkheim, Émile. (1919) 1975. "Contribution to Discussion 'Religious Sentiment at the Present Time.'" In *Durkheim on Religion: A Selection of Readings with Biographies and Introductory Remarks*, edited by W. S. F. Pickering, 181–189. London: Routledge & Kegan Paul.

Durkheim, Émile. 1975. *Textes*. Edited by Victor Karady. 3 vols. Paris: Editions de Minuit.
Durkheim, Émile. (1885) 1978. "Review of Albert Schaeffle, *Bau und Leben des sozialen Körpers: Erster Band*." In *Emile Durkheim on Institutional Analysis*, edited and translated by Mark Traugott, 93–114. Chicago: University of Chicago Press.
Durkheim, Émile. (1902) 1984. *The Division of Labour in Society*. Translated by W. D. Halls. London: Macmillan.
Durkheim, Émile. (1912) 1995. *The Elementary Forms of Religious Life*. Translated by Karen E. Fields. New York: Free Press.
Durkheim, Émile. (1917) 1999. "La politique de demain." *Durkheimian Studies / Etudes Durkheimiennes* 5: 8–12.
Durkheim, Émile. 2004. *Durkheim's Philosophy Lectures: Notes from the Lycée de Sens Course, 1883–1884*. Edited and translated by Neil Gross and Robert Alun Jones. Cambridge: Cambridge University Press.
Joas, Hans. 2013. *The Sacredness of the Person: A New Genealogy of Human Rights*. Washington, DC: Georgetown University Press.
Kant, Immanuel. 1854. *Fondement de la métaphysique des mœurs*. In *Principes métaphysiques de la morale*, 3rd ed., edited and translated by Joseph Tissot. Paris: Ladrange.
Kant, Immanuel. 1867. *Grundlegung zur Metaphysik der Sitten*. In *Immanuel Kant's sämmtliche Werke*, vol. 4, edited by Gustav Hartenstein. Leipzig: Voss.
Paoletti, Giovanni. 2012. *Durkheim et la philosophie. Représentation, réalité et lien social*. Paris: Garnier.
Pickering, W. S. F. 1984. "The New Religion: The Cult of Man or Society?" In W. S. F. Pickering, *Durkheim's Sociology of Religion: Themes and Theories*, 476–499. London: Routledge & Kegan Paul.
Rawls, Ann Warfield. 2012. "Durkheim's Epistemology: Continuities between *The Elementary Forms* and *The Division*." *Etnografia e ricerca qualitativa* 5 (3): 335–364.
Renouvier, Charles. 1869. *Science de la morale*. 2 vols. Paris: Ladrange.
Schmaus, Warren. 2004. *Rethinking Durkheim and His Tradition*. Cambridge: Cambridge University Press.
Sembel, Nicolas, and Matthieu Béra. 2013. "Emprunts de Durkheim à la bibliothèque universitaire de Bordeaux / Durkheim's Loans from Bordeaux University Library, 1889–1902." *Durkheimian Studies / Etudes Durkheimiennes* 19: 49–71.
Smith, Philip, and Jeffrey C. Alexander. 2005. "Introduction: The New Durkheim." In *The Cambridge Companion to Durkheim*, edited by Jeffrey C. Alexander and Philip Smith, 1–37. Cambridge: Cambridge University Press.
Watts Miller, William. 2012. *A Durkheimian Quest: Solidarity and the Sacred*. New York and Oxford: Berghahn Books.
Watts Miller, William. 2017. "Creativity: A Key Durkheimian Concern and Problematic." *Revue européenne des sciences sociales* 55 (2): 17–40.

CHAPTER 14

DURKHEIM AND ECONOMIC SOCIOLOGY

PHILIPPE STEINER

BEYOND its philosophical dimension, the theme chosen by Durkheim for his doctoral dissertation had an economic dimension. After Adam Smith's considerations about its profound impact on the economy, the division of labor became a central theme in nineteenth-century political economy; when Auguste Comte gave it a significant place in his lectures on positive philosophy, it entered sociological thinking as well. But this is not the only economic theme that Durkheim considered in his work, as the last part of his study on suicide rates in France and European countries makes it clear with its strong emphasis on the professional group as the key socioeconomic basis of the social reform that he had in mind.

Durkheim had a limited but significant knowledge of the political economy of his time. He had read the famous *Traité d'économie politique* (*Treatise on political economy*) by Jean-Baptiste Say, still considered the founding father of that science in France, and the books of the leading French liberal economists of his time such as Paul Leroy-Beaulieu. In addition to that, his economic background came from his reading of German political economists belonging to the historical school, notably Albert Schäffle, Gustav Schmoller, and Karl Bücher, who were most influential in that period of time, in Europe and the United States (Steiner 2011: 8–17). Beyond some theoretical and methodological issues, Durkheim never entered into the technicalities of economic theory proper and limited himself to issues related to economic policy and economic reform as many economists did at that time. Then, in the middle of the 1890s, Durkheim left out economic issues because he had the feeling that religious issues were much more important for understanding modern societies than he thought at the beginning of his sociological career. Thus we may understand why he did not write a single review for the "economic sociology" section of *L'Année sociologique*. Nevertheless, even in the last period of his life, economic issues were still lurking behind the curtains, and some important insights of his economic sociology are to be found in his last great book, *The Elementary Forms of Religious Life*.

This is not the whole story. It is well known that Durkheim produced not only a personal work but also a collective one through the building of a sociological group around *L'Année sociologique*. So, beyond Durkheim's own achievement, a proper understanding of the strength of the Durkheimian economic sociology must also consider the work of some members of that group, notably François Simiand (1873–1935) and Maurice Halbwachs (1877–1945), who were at the head of the "economic sociology" section of *L'Année sociologique*. The third author to be considered is no other than Marcel Mauss (1872–1950) for his work on nonmarket forms of economic transactions such as gift-giving. Finally, the strength of the Durkheimian approach to economic sociology is illustrated through some contemporary inquiries.

Economic Themes in Durkheim's Works

Durkheim was strongly influenced by neo-Kantian philosophy, notably by the version developed by the French philosopher Charles Renouvier. This means that all through his intellectual life, Durkheim endorsed a nonutilitarian view of human beings and society. This is explicit when he claimed that "Never do we admit that a moral value can be expressed in terms of economic values" (Durkheim [1906] 1974: 57–58).

Beyond this general consideration, Durkheim's contributions to the birth of economic sociology can be organized along two lines: first, his critique of political economy because of its unsatisfactory theoretical and methodological basis; second, his social reform grounded on some specific institutions necessary to trigger a social transformation on the basis of a sound understanding of the functioning of modern societies.

Methodological Issues

Following Comte's critique of political economy that was hammered out in the *Course of Positive Philosophy* (lecture 47), Durkheim explained how dissatisfied he was with the theoretical underpinnings of this social science. This is particularly developed in the articles he wrote before the completion of his PhD.

As many sociologists after him, Durkheim had a negative appreciation of the "economic man" that fills the world of most economists. Durkheim did not condemn the use of abstraction, but the use of inappropriate abstractions, as he explained in the following passage in his opening lecture at the University of Bordeaux: "To simplify things economists have artificially impoverished matters. Not only do they abstract from all circumstances of time, place, and country in imagining the abstract type of man in general, but in this ideal type itself they have neglected everything that does not relate to a life that is strictly individual, so that this abstraction from an abstraction leaves them nothing more than the cheerless image of a purely selfish self" (Durkheim [1888] 1970: 85). Abstractions are a necessary component of scientific inquiry, but for this purpose abstractions must offer the possibility to isolate one part of reality so that it may be studied according to the principles of the experimental sciences. Instead, said Durkheim, economists were substituting for reality ideas that they tried to render coherent through the use of a rationality principle. In the process, the very nature of society disappeared: "Whether one likes it or not, whether it is a good thing or a bad one, societies exist. Economic activity takes place within constituted societies. Logic is powerless if confronted with the fact that complicates a problem, but which cannot be excluded by abstraction" (Durkheim [1886] 1970: 208). In modern parlance, Durkheim here is pointing out the necessity to embed economic activity within the social world.

The methodological critique is developed in chapter 2 of *The Rules of Sociological Method* when Durkheim explained that the law of supply and demand has never received a scientific demonstration, grounded on empirical data: "All that could be done, and has been done, has been to demonstrate by dialectical argument that individuals should act in this way if they perceive what is in their best interest; any other course of action would be harmful to them [. . .] But this entirely logical necessity in no way resembles the one that the true laws of nature reveal. These express the relationships whereby facts are linked together in reality, and not the way in which it would be good for them to be linked" (Durkheim [1895] 1982: 68–69).

Having said that, how did Durkheim proceed to link economic activity and society? Obviously, as the examples he offered in chapter 1 of *The Rules of Sociological Method* make clear, economic events are social events; they are "ways of acting, thinking and feeling" (Durkheim [1895] 1982: 51) that impose themselves on economic actors, as is the case with the currency system, credit arrangements, and the organization of the factory that an entrepreneur builds for running his business. A departure from the expected behavior would find its sanction in bankruptcy. Then, after having adopted the terms of institution, the new vocabulary proposed by Marcel Mauss and Paul Fauconnet in their paper on sociology published in the *Grande Encyclopédie*, Durkheim defined economic sociology in the following way:

> Finally, there are the economic institutions: institutions relating to the production of wealth (serfdom, tenant farming, corporate organization, production in factories, in mills, at home, and so on), institutions relating to exchange (commercial organization, markets, stock exchanges, and so on), institutions relating to distribution (rent, interest, salaries, and so on). They form the subject matter of *economic sociology*.
> (Durkheim and Fauconnet [1909] 2004: 150)

We have to follow him in his dissertation on the division of labor and in his study of suicide to understand the meaning and consequences of this view of economic sociology.

Division of Labor, Contract, and Exchange

Still in line with Comte's views, according to which the greatest, but incomplete, scientific achievement of political economists was the study of the division of labor,

Durkheim built his work as an endeavor to consider the social dimension of the division of labor since economists were focusing only on its efficiency side, hence his approach of the subject in terms of the form of social cohesion—the so-called organic solidarity—based on the differences and complementary between the individuals involved in any complex task.

All along his inquiry, Durkheim addressed some important economic issues through the division of labor and its ineluctable consequence, the development of market transactions.

Generally speaking, Durkheim is reluctant to consider exchange as a binding force able to produce some kind of durable solidarity among market participants. Exchange entails an opposition of interest between the two parties since one would like to buy at a cheaper price, whereas the other would sell at a higher one and, in this process, their objective solidarity (the division of labor) is lost: "For if mutual interest draws men closer, it is never more than for a few moments. It can only create between them an external bond [...] For where interest alone reigns, as nothing arises to check the egoisms confronting one another, each self finds itself in relation to the other on a war footing, and any truce in this perpetual antagonism cannot be of long duration. Self-interest is, in fact, the least constant thing in the world. Today it is useful for me to unite with you; tomorrow the same reason will make me your enemy" (Durkheim [1893] 1984: 152).

This conceptualization of market exchange is in line with the negative or external solidarity similar to the one provided by the property laws that link material objects to individuals. This is not enough to build such a solidarity, for: "Negative solidarity is only possible where another kind is present, positive in nature, of which it is both the result and the condition" (Durkheim [1893] 1984: 75). Where does this positive solidarity come from? From the division of labor that provides a profound and long-standing feeling of mutual dependence instead of the superficial one that results from the exchange itself:

> It presumes that two beings are mutually dependent upon each other because they are both incomplete, and it does no more than interpret externally this mutual dependence. Thus it is only the superficial expression of an internal and deeper condition. Precisely because this condition remains constant, it gives rise to a whole system of images which function with a continuity that is lacking in exchange. The image of the one who complements us becomes inseparable within us from our own, not only because of the frequency with which it is associated with it, but above all because it is its natural complement.
>
> (Durkheim [1893] 1984: 22)

Nevertheless, Durkheim is not an opponent of the market economy: his main objective is to understand its institutional foundation and then to suggest a reform in order to add social justice to the market economy.

The first institutional underpinning of the market economy is the contract that legally binds together the buyer and the seller. Contrary to the view upheld by Herbert Spencer, according to whom it is possible and desirable to build a society on the basis of contracts agreed upon by the members of a society, Durkheim explained that the contract and the wishes of the parties are not enough for such a task. Any contract entails many obligations that are not the result of the wishes of the parties, and this is necessarily so since in the opposite case they would have to bargain on so numerous legal clauses that it would take too much of their time, they would be blocked. This argument is similar to the now well-known theory of transaction costs (i.e., market exchanges entail cost of transaction that should be compared to the cost of a similar task in a hierarchical organization), but Durkheim did not go further in that direction; instead, he stressed the noncontractual basis of the contract, that is, the social basis without which contractual behavior would be socially meaningless. Accordingly, "We co-operate because we have wished to do so, but our voluntary co-operation creates for us duties that we have not desired" (Durkheim [1893] 1984: 161). This view led to the well-known statement: "Summing up, therefore, the contract is not sufficient by itself, but is only possible because of the regulation of contracts, which is of social origin" (Durkheim [1893] 1984: 162). Beyond this general statement, Durkheim is adamant in claiming that modern contracts should be just to be considered legally binding, a claim that stresses notably the importance of an equal position of the two parties when they bargain the various clauses of their contract: "In short, for the obligatory force of the contract to be entire, it is not sufficient for it to have been an object of express assent. It must also be fair, and it is not fair by the mere fact that it has been agreed verbally" (Durkheim [1893] 1984: 318).

Hence, we may understand why Durkheim had a negative view of the law of bequest—a position that was uncommon at that time, since there was a large majority of economists and social thinkers who fully endorsed the equalitarian (i.e., the same amount for each child) stance of the current law of bequest formulated in the *Code civil* promulgated in 1804. The reason is plain: the wealth received through bequests gives to the happy heirs a marked advantage in the economic life; their economic condition is improved without any effort or contribution to social life, and the disequilibrium thus created is conceived as an impediment to the socializing effects of the division of labor.

His study of these two economic institutions—the contract and the laws of bequest—with the strong emphasis on justice are significant contributions to an economic sociology of exchange in the sense that they offer a way to link economic activity and society. They show how the process of exchange is directly grounded on social representations and formal institutions without which they cannot operate. However, Durkheim's approach left out the market itself as an institution. In other words, one should bear in mind that Durkheim restricted his study to interindividual transactions, on the one hand, and the legal apparatus that makes these transactions possible, on the other. But the market as a social gathering and a structured entity in which exchanges are performed according to a set of rules is never the center of his attention. Prices are not conceived as the result of the collective forces at work in a market limiting the expectations of individuals; in other words, competition as a set of behaviors mutually constraining the actors of the market is not taken into account. Nevertheless, his approach to the exchange process and its defects led him to elaborate two key points of his economic sociology.

Social Evaluation and the Professional Groups

These important contributions are to be found notably in the last part of Durkheim's book on suicide. Unexpectedly, the study of the evolution of suicide rates in Europe led Durkheim to offer some innovative ideas in terms of economic sociology. The issue of justice appeared then as the central value thanks to which a sociological assessment of the present industrial society could be delivered. The problem to solve required the finding of an institution able to give a social underpinning to this idea, beyond the personal view of the sociologist. Durkheim pointed out two such institutions: the first one is the public opinion, the second was to be created under the name of the professional groups.

As explained earlier, Durkheim did not provide a sociological theory of price formation, de facto leaving this "technicality" to the economists. However, Durkheim considered the normative assessment that public opinion may express when prices and revenues were escaping the domain of moral validity, so to speak, that they should not trespass. This is what can be called the social evaluation of market prices:

> Economists protest in vain: it will always scandalize public sentiment that any individual can devote too great a quantity of wealth to completely superfluous consumption, and indeed it seems that this intolerance relents only in times of moral disturbance. So there is a veritable regulation which, though it does not always have a juridical form, none the less unceasingly sets with relative precision the maximum of comfort that each class of society can legitimately seek to obtain. But a scale set up this way is in no way immutable. It changes as collective income rises or falls, and with changes occurring in the moral ideas of society.
>
> (Durkheim [1897] 2006: 276, translation modified)

This evaluative process is certainly at work when the public opinion gets the feeling that something wrong is happening—the moral and political reactions to the last major financial crisis with the Spanish *Indignados* and the American movement *Occupy Wall Street* are examples of the surge of this evaluative function of public opinion. But the process of social evaluation has no social structure dedicated to its existence and is left to the vagaries of the public opinion and the merging of social movements. This lack in structure leaves open the possibility to end up in what Durkheim called a constrained social solidarity, in which revenues and prices do not match with the different contributions to the production process. Something more was needed, and this is the reason why Durkheim elaborated his views on the professional group (Plouviez 2013).

The rapid changes that had provoked the growth of the division of labor rendered the older process of socialization inadequate; religious, political, and family processes of socialization were ineffective in the thriving domain of economic activity. Accordingly, a new institution was needed to fill this gap. Based on the gathering of workers and bosses, Durkheim's professional groups were first providing interactions between economic actors of the industrial society; these interactions would help finding agreements and regulation about working conditions, level of wages, forms of competition, and the like (Durkheim [1890/1900] 2001: lecture 3). This stronger and encompassing network of relations would moderate the passions of each category through the mutual knowledge they would get from these interactions, and finally, this new collective entity would be able to create the ideals that were lacking in the present organization of the industrial society. Furthermore, Durkheim boldly suggested that these professional groups could become the basis of the political organization, with a pooling system grounded on professional categories instead of geographical ones (Durkheim [1890/1900] 2001: lecture 9).

In the period in which Durkheim wrote his book on suicide, he went through the so-called revelation according to which the importance of religion for understanding the functioning of the social realm appeared to him of the utmost importance. Does economic sociology survive this revelation? Apparently no, since in the introduction of the second edition (1902) of his *Division of Labor*, Durkheim made clear that he was abandoning his work on the professional groups and the social reform that was attached to it. Nevertheless, economic sociology did not disappear altogether, even if Durkheim's contributions were less salient.

Religion, Knowledge, and the Economy

Was the economy still a significant dimension of *The Elementary Forms of Religious Life*? The answer could have been negative, following what Durkheim wrote to Mauss when he was trying to convince his nephew to take the leadership in the "religious sociology" section of the *L'Année sociologique*: how erroneous are those theories that derive all social life from material foundations, either territorial (Friedrich Ratzel) or economic (Karl Marx), since they forget that collective representations are realities and forces. Paradoxically, economic life still plays a role in Durkheim's book on religion for two reasons: first, there is an opposition between economics and religion; second, there exist links between both realms, some of them still to be discovered.

The Elementary Forms are built around the idea of *homo duplex*, according to which "man is double." This duality entails the irreducibility of moral ideas to utilitarian motives and, more generally, the distinction of two different forms of social life among primitive tribes with dispersion in order to get the resource for its subsistence, and gathering for social life and religious activities: "Sometimes the population is broken up into little groups who wander about independently of one another, in their various occupations; each family lives by itself, hunting and fishing, and in a word, trying to procure its indispensable food by all the means in its power. Sometimes, on the contrary, the population concentrates and gathers at determined points for a length of time varying from several days to several months" (Durkheim [1912] 1915: 214–215). The theme of alternating between work and the economy, on the one hand, and festivals and religious practices, on the other, runs through the entire book and plays a key role since it is the basis for the phenomenon of collective effervescence in which religious ideas emerge.

Economy as it appears in that book thus lies in the shadow of the light projected by religion and the fabric of symbolism and ideals.

Nevertheless, Durkheim does not forget to mention the existence of connections between economic life and religious beliefs. In many of their daily activities, primitive peoples consider religious rites as factors of production. Rites performed for the fertility of the soil or the fecundity of the animal species on which they nourish themselves were in their eyes as rational as technical processes used by modern farmers. Similarly, Durkheim links *totem* and a form of ownership because before consuming the totemic animal or plant on whose territory one is located, one must obtain the authorization of the head of the clan. So the opposition between the religious and the economic realms is far from being absolute.

Second, due to his interest in the process through which symbolism and the sacred are created in a society, Durkheim proposed to link the sacred and the notion of value. There is an indirect but potentially strong link between both domains when Durkheim briefly alludes to what we now call exchange of symbolic goods; when a man loans to another one his *churinga*, as a form of acknowledgment, the recipient makes a present of some of his hairs, and thus the two symbolic objects belong to the same order of things and are of the same symbolic value. Durkheim perceived that such exchange supposes a social process of valorization and commensuration, albeit different from the one implemented for economic goods (utility or work), that entails social representations that are, as the religious representations, "well-founded delirium." Finally, there is a striking passage relegated in a note of the concluding part of the book, pointing to an important relation between religion and economic life through the notion of value:

> Only one form of social activity has not yet been expressly attached to religion: that is economic activity. Sometimes processes that are derived from magic have, by that fact alone, an origin that is indirectly religious. Also, economic value is a sort of power or efficacy, and we know the religious origins of the idea of power. Also, wealth can confer *mana*; therefore it has it. Hence it is seen that the idea of economic value and of religious value are not without connection. But the question of the nature of these connections has not yet been studied.
>
> (Durkheim [1912] 1915: 418n1)

A final consideration is necessary in order to take into account the theory of knowledge that is developed in the concluding part of the *Elementary Forms*. Durkheim's sociology of knowledge is relevant in the sense that he showed that the process of creating categories and classification is a social process. And since economic activity and economic theories are based on a large series of such categories (things that can become commodities versus those that cannot, fair versus unfair exchange, etc.), this issue is one that could be studied for a better understanding of the functioning of the economy (see Radin 1996; Steiner and Trespeuch 2015). Even if Durkheim himself did not illustrate this idea with economic examples, the following statement is relevant to the economic world as a whole: society "is possible only when the individuals and things which compose it are divided into certain groups, that is to say, classified, and when these groups are classified in relation to each other. Society supposes self-conscious organization which is nothing other than a classification" (Durkheim [1912] 1915: 443).

Economic Sociology in the Durkheimian Group

Durkheim left out economic sociology after the publication of his study on suicide, since he had now a quite negative view of the scientific achievements of political economists as he wrote to his colleague Célestin Bouglé: "I hope that the reading of economists serves you better than it has me. When I began, fifteen years ago, I too thought that I would find here answers to the questions that concerned me. I spent many years with such reading and have learned nothing more than that which a disheartening experience teaches. All the same, it is true that this domain is wide open for exploration. No doubt one could make some interesting discoveries here with the help of statistics and history" (Durkheim to Bouglé, May 16, 1896; Durkheim 1975, II: 392). Does it mean that the impetus for a Durkheimian economic sociology was exhausted? No, because Durkheim was not an isolated scholar. His sociology was strongly associated with a collective entity and the collective work done by the group of scholars who worked around the *Année sociologique*. *L'Année sociologique* had many different sections, from "general sociology" to the "sociology of esthetics," but the most important one in terms of place and efforts were the section on "religious sociology" under the direction of Mauss and "economic sociology" under the direction of Simiand—Halbwachs joined him in 1908. Accordingly, the development of the Durkheimian approach to economic sociology is to be found in the pages of the thirteen volumes of the *Année sociologique* and, then, in Simiand's and Halbwachs's works, the two men in charge of the "economic sociology" section of the journal. Finally, Mauss's work on the gift must be mentioned as a path-breaking masterpiece.

François Simiand and Maurice Halbwachs

The critical tone is certainly what is the most salient in the numerous reviews that Simiand wrote for *L'Année sociologique* (Steiner 2011: 69–76). He was a bold and a harsh critic of political economy, whether the liberal version of it, so common among French political economists, or the historical approach, which was of the greatest importance in Germany of course, but as well in England and the United States. Simiand was the one who adopted Durkheim's views on this issue in the sense that economic sociology should be grounded on a careful and demanding historical and statistical approach, similar to the structure of the experimental procedure set forth in *The Rules of Sociological Method* (definition, observation, classification, explanation, and administration of the proof). Simiand was adamant in linking both elements; thus, he published many reviews in which he slashed important economists (e.g., Irving Fisher) because their statistical data were too limited (about thirteen years) for the theory (the quantitative theory of money) they were supposed to give a scientific support. Simiand was also bold in the sense that he did not hesitate to publish a harsh critique of the mathematical approach in that domain even if, as a philosopher, his knowledge of mathematics was limited. The main review essays were later published in a volume in which the critical dimension of his economic sociology, or positive political economy (*l'économie positive*), was the main characteristic of the book (Simiand 1912). Nevertheless, this did not put him in the cold, since North American institutional economists, such as Thorstein Veblen and Wesley C. Mitchell, were on the same line (Gislain and Steiner 1999); furthermore, Simiand, and then Halbwachs, became members of the *Revue d'économie politique*, the main French academic journal at that time.[1]

Beyond these methodological skirmishes, Simiand's research was focused on wages and money issues. The formation of wages was a long-standing research interest since it was the topic of his PhD in economics (Simiand 1907) and one of the topics of his great book *Le salaire, l'évolution sociale et la monnaie* (*On Wages, Social Change and Money*) (Simiand 1932). His theory of wage formation is built on a conflict theory of action in order to give an account of the variations in nominal wages according to the phase of the business cycle. According to the phase of the cycle, workers will opt for one strategy based on their perception of the trade-off between effort and monetary gain, while in the opposite camp, the bosses would do the same. This was highly innovative within the Durkheimian school since, first, the sociology of conflict was not a dimension of the French sociological cluster; second, the theory had a "methodological individualism" flavor that is generally and rightly considered foreign to Durkheim's sociology. Later on, in his last great book, Simiand would acknowledge this point and explain that, nonetheless, his individualistic approach was empirically grounded and experimentally proved. His trade cycle theory—the most important topic of interwar political economy—was built on the idea that the basic engine of these fluctuations was provided by the fluctuation in the monetary creation, since a raise in the quantity of money produced a raise in monetary prices and thus an euphoric feeling favorable to the growth of activity—the reverse in the case of a contraction in the quantity of money. It is interesting to note that this approach differs from Durkheim's approach in *Suicide*, where this euphoria generates an economic anomie with negative consequences, due to the loss of landmarks and the suffering it causes. Simiand rather takes up the idea of a positive effervescence as described by Durkheim in *The Elementary Forms of Religious Life*.

After a PhD in political economy dedicated to the study of housing market speculation (Halbwachs 1909), Halbwachs studied with great scrutiny the consumption patterns of the working classes in order to go beyond the statistical results known as Engel's laws (Halbwachs 1912). Accordingly, in order to reach the social representations at the root of these behaviors, Halbwachs sorted out the three classical categories of expenditures (food, clothing, housing) according to their amount and frequency. As food is bought on a daily basis, its prices are considered as given and buyers do not haggle, considering that they get value for money. When expenditures are less frequent, economic representations change and suspicion prevails, buyers haggle because they are no longer able to link a price to the good. Uncertainty on the quality of the clothes leads them toward the cheap clothes so that the buyer will not be much of a dupe; the highest uncertainty comes with the price of their apartment, which appears always too high for the service received and thus, according to Halbwachs, escaping the payment of the rent was not considered as specially blameworthy.

Finally, the connection between religion and economic life was also emerging in one of the most innovative works done by Simiand. In a paper written for the new Durkheimian journal—*Annales sociologiques*—he claimed that money was a social reality (i.e., a social fact). The reason behind this view comes from the fact that the value of money, which has no specific usefulness, was a kind of mystery for the main economists of that time—and this is still the same today. Accordingly, in contradistinction to economists who try to explain the emergence of money through a utilitarian process leading to the selection of the most convenient good for simplifying their transactions, Simiand suggested to define money as collective belief, securing the continuity between the present conditions of monetary exchanges and its future:

> Gold is made up of appreciation, of estimation, of belief, of confidence, product of sentiment as much as of reason, which cannot be distinctly separated one from the other […] This representation, at once intellectual and affective, which is a money of this kind [fiat money], is not made from competent and informed individuals, but rather by groups, by collectivities, by a nation; it is social. It has a character and a role manifestly objective, because it is *a belief and a social faith*, and, as such, a *social reality*.
>
> (Simiand 1934: 38–39)

Thus, the functioning of this key economic institution is based on collective beliefs, on faith that can be studied scientifically as religious beliefs were studied by religious sociologists. In this sense, he was joining Mauss in providing an answer to the question left open by Durkheim in the footnote of the *Elementary Forms* about the connection between religious and economic life.

Marcel Mauss

Mauss was focused on the sociology of religion, and he spent most of his time reviewing the books for the "religious sociology" section of *L'Année sociologique*. However, from time to time he touched economic issues, notably in the interwar period when he wrote a series of articles on money when the French Franc was under fire. However, his encounter with economic sociology was strong in the mid-1920s when he wrote two papers about the Soviets in the USSR and his famous essay on the gift.

In the essay on the Soviets, Mauss ([1924] 1997) explained that the Russian communists were misled with their policy aiming at suppressing market exchanges.

Markets, he said, were present throughout human history, and it makes no sense to try suppressing them. That does not mean that Mauss was a market monger since the essay on the gift (Mauss [1925] 1966) stressed the existence of this form of exchange from archaic tribes to the modern world. Mauss's interest in gift-giving derives from his previous work on sacrifice, in which the last sentences are, as are the opening sentences of his essay on the gift, stressing the intricate connection between interested and disinterested behavior.[2] So this study is to be understood as a contribution of the Durkheimian program in religious sociology to economic sociology. As a result, Mauss's theory is similar to Karl Polanyi's views on the economic role of reciprocity: for both of them, there exist two different realms within the economy (I leave out here redistribution, the third one in Polanyi's conceptualization): market economy on the one side, the most salient form in our modern societies, and gift-giving or exchange-gift, on the other, a less visible behavior but still important.

Gift-giving is a form of transaction that is difficult to understand from the point of view of the economist since it means that you give something against nothing, creating on a micro-scale a form of "free lunch." This asymmetry is crucial in the sense that for the lawyer, a gift means precisely such unusual behavior to be sorted out as a gift; in any other circumstances, the transaction would be considered as a covert form of interested behavior. This is a position that economists are keen to adopt since at least the donor gets a positive view of himself as a reward attached to her gift. Mauss does not pay attention to these views and admits straightforwardly that from a sociological point of view, gift-giving is both altruistic and self-interested, both free and compulsory. This last idea is the key point in Mauss's definition of gift-giving behavior organized around the obligation to give, the obligation to receive, and the obligation to give back. Adam Smith had endeavored to explain the rules that men follow in exchanging goods on the market, so one can read Mauss's definition as the equivalent for the gift: there, instead of the monetary equality in market exchange and the end of the social relation once the transaction is over, gift-giving involves inequality in value but the obligation to keep in touch for the potentially endless process of giving. The gift is therefore a specific transaction, distinct from exchange, thanks to which things can change hands. The circulation of things is a necessity to societies, but the manner in which this circulation occurs is a mode of being that characterizes one society relative to others; and this applies to our present societies since many transactions are achieved through gift-giving, for example in the biomedical domain either for blood (Titmuss 1970) or human organs (Healy 2006; Steiner 2010).

Contemporary Economic Sociology and the Durkheimian Approach

Contemporary economic sociology may be conceived along three different approaches: in the Paretian approach, economic sociology, as the final layer of economic theory, deals with the nonrational forms of behavior, whereas economics is busy with rational ones; in the Weberian approach, economic sociology aims at producing an encounter between history and theory, notably through a specific attention given to economic actions and institutions. The Durkheimian approach has a different flavor with a strong bent toward the critique of economic theory and an emphasis on the institutional approach to the functioning of the economy.

From a methodological point of view, the Durkheimian critical approach is still relevant since there exists a great number of sociologists who consider that economic theory is not very well done, notably because the interplay between social phenomena and economic ones is generally left out of their research in order to get a "tractable" mathematical form. For example, there exists a large body of sociological critiques of economic thinking based on the (infamous) *homo oeconomicus* (Steiner 2016: ch. 1): Pierre Bourdieu's book on the social structures of the economy is a perfect illustration of this critical approach in contemporary sociology (Bourdieu 2000). In this respect, the Durkheimian approach is close to the North American institutional school of political economy, notably those who claim to follow the Veblenian tradition. But other currents in institutional economics are also in line with the Durkheimian approach, as it is the case with the French economists of the *Economie des conventions* (Economy of Convention) and *L'Ecole de la régulation* (The Regulation School). Notably, the last group of economists sticks to some key elements of Simiand's approach with a strong methodological critique of economic theory and an emphasis on the role of institutions, their complementarity (Amable 2003), and the use of statistical data beyond the usual theory-cum-econometrics of mainstream economics. However, these economists give much more attention to political issues than the Durkheimians were ready to do. To illustrate more specifically the Durkheimian legacy, André Orléan's book on value and money is a case in point. The book is first a vigorous critique of the theory of value, whether under its Marxian or its Walrasian form, since both of them leave out the relational dimension of the market and congeal social relations into the issue of value, whether based on labor or on utility. How then to account for money and value if they are no longer based on utility or work? Orléan (2014: ch. 5) proposes to consider value as a collective representation and money as a social institution, assuming that at their starting point there is an effervescent group whose affects will converge toward an object (gold) from which common evaluations will be produced and received as socially relevant. This process, he said, is similar to that of the formation of the ideal in effervescent groups as described by Durkheim in the *Elementary Forms*. In a nutshell, Orléan considers that the process coming from the Durkheimian theory of religion offers a better explanation of the creation of money than savvy mathematical models grounded on utility maximization.

Such a connection between the Durkheimian approach and the work of contemporary economists remains rather uncommon, and economic sociologists are more involved in the maintenance of the Durkheimian legacy.

The first example comes with Jens Beckert's work. Beyond his general assessment of Durkheim's contribution to economic sociology, stressing the role of moral order

(Beckert 2002: ch. 2), he has studied the law of bequest (Beckert 2008), a major economic institution since, with the rise of inequalities in incomes and wealth (the latter being much more important than the former), a huge amount of wealth is transferred from one generation to the following each year. Contrary to Durkheim's wishes, inheritance has not been abolished, but the taxes paid by wealthy people are decreasing sharply since the 1970s in the United States and in the European countries. Following Durkheim's sociological interpretation of law as an indicator of social solidarity (for example, considering the issue of equality among the children or the status of the surviving spouse), and following a comparative approach, Beckert examines how modern laws of bequest were created and how they were transformed during the last two centuries. Empirically, he conceptualizes political discourses as a combination of an institution and its related social representations. The main result comes with a definition of this intergenerational solidarity that balances the legal claims of the individual, of the family, and of the State, in a different way according to the values that a society cherishes most: the individual in the United States, the family in Germany, and the State in France. It is worth stressing the fact that Beckert's approach has a strong sociology of economic knowledge dimension, since the discourses that he studies are grounded on social and economic arguments. The importance of this sociological dimension can be as well seen in his recent research on the role of social representations, and more precisely what he calls "fictional expectations" or "capacity to imagine futures," which then can be institutionalized through planning and forecasting departments, statistical apparatus (Beckert 2016). Here again, collective representations play a key role for understanding the modern capitalist society.

The second example is related to the development given to Mauss's approach to gift-giving. This approach is important for two reasons. First, it fits rather well with the great importance that contemporary economic sociology gives to the seminal work of Polanyi ([1944] 2001), notably his threefold division of economic activity with market exchange, redistribution when a hierarchical entity grasps a part of the resources in order to proceed to its redistribution, and reciprocity between members of the society. Gift-giving is, of course, a perfect example of this reciprocity principle. Second, some sociologists have gathered behind Alain Caillé's claim that the Maussian gift is a powerful tool for modifying the functioning of the capitalist economy (Caillé and Godbout 1998). There is thus a significant number of scholars, notably in France and Europe, who endorse that view; they are then close to the sociologists who pay attention to nonprofit organizations and the so-called third sector as an alternative way to organize the economy or, at least, as a key element to add to our understanding of the functioning of a society able to provide more social justice.

A more specific development was recently proposed in the domain of gift-giving with what I have suggested calling "organizational gift-giving" (Steiner 2015), a form of gift-giving in which an organization or a series of organizations step in between the donor and the recipient, so that a solidarity at a distance emerges (Naulin and Steiner 2016).

Maussian gift-giving is strongly associated with a direct connection between the donor and the recipient, and this connection is the rational basis of the formation of a strong social bond between them. In this sense, using the classical distinction introduced by Durkheim in *The Division of Labor in Society*, we may say that the Maussian gift is a mechanical one: the people involved are directly and strongly connected; they have common practices and common social representations and expectations. This is no longer the case when organizations stand in between the initial donor and the final receiver. In that case, and in contradistinction to the *mechanical gift* set up by Mauss, we observe the growing importance of the *organic gift*, that is, a gift subjected to a form of division of labor thanks to which the gift at a (social and geographical) distance may occur. This form of gift-giving is grounded on a different set of principles than the three moral obligations that structure the Maussian gift: the organizational gift does not involve direct contact; organizations are supposed to do a huge logistic work in order to transform the initial gift (most often money) into the relevant resources needed by the recipient, and they have to secure a steady flow of donations in order to provide the continuity necessary for helping the recipients; market transactions and gifts usually are intertwined, and, due to the lack of direct connection between the donor and the recipient, reciprocity is difficult to achieve beyond the "local" reciprocity in which the recipient may give back or reciprocate to the person who actually gives her a resource and not to the initial donors who remain unknown. Organizations are thus producing a solidarity at a distance, permitting the people who have the feeling that something must be done to help their fellow human being suffering from natural disasters, famines, difficulties in providing basic education and health services, to act according to their beliefs and values. But this solidarity is weak in the sense that it does not entail any sense of continuity from the donors who are not committed to any continuity in their altruistic behavior.

All these examples prove that the Durkheimian approach in economic sociology is still alive; it maintains the sociologists' scrutiny in the methodological feuds about the theoretical underpinnings of economic thinking, and it is at the root of many empirical studies about the institutional dimensions of the economic basis of modern societies, notably in the areas where market exchanges are ruled out.

Notes

1. These two appointments resulted from a peer-to-peer co-option procedure; they can be explained as follows: in addition to the social recognition provided by their training at the *Ecole normale supérieure*, Simiand and Halbwachs had a PhD in law, as had all the professors of economics in France at that time, and they were *agrégés*; their work as statisticians and socioeconomists was known to economists. Finally, like the Durkheimians, the *Revue d'économie politique* opposed the liberalism of the *Journal des économistes*.
2. In the conclusion of their *Essay on Sacrifice*, Hubert and Mauss explain: "In any sacrifice there is an act of abnegation since the sacrifier deprives himself and gives. Often this abnegation is even imposed upon him as a duty. For sacrifice is not always optional; the gods demand it. [...] But this abnegation and submission are not without their selfish aspect. The sacrifier gives up something of himself but he does not give himself. Prudently, he sets

himself aside. This is because if he gives, it is partly in order to receive. Thus sacrifice shows itself in a dual light; it is a useful act and it is an obligation. Disinterestedness is mingled with self-interest" (Huber and Mauss [1899] 1964: 100). Twenty-five years later, presenting the research program of his *Essay on the Gift*, Mauss states that he studies gifts as being "in theory voluntary, disinterested and spontaneous, but [...] in fact obligatory and interested. The form usually taken is that of the gift generously offered; but the accompanying behaviour is formal pretence and social deception, while the transaction itself is based on obligation and economic self-interest" (Mauss [1925] 1966: 1).

REFERENCES

Amable, Bruno. 2003. *The Diversity of Modern Capitalism*. Oxford: Oxford University Press.
Beckert, Jens. 2002. *Beyond the Market: The Social Foundations of Economic Efficiency*. Princeton, NJ: Princeton University Press.
Beckert, Jens. 2008. *Inherited Wealth*. Princeton, NJ: Princeton University Press.
Beckert, Jens. 2016. *Imagined Futures: Fictional Expectations and Capitalist Dynamics*. Cambridge, MA: Harvard University Press.
Bourdieu, Pierre. 2000. *Les structures sociales de l'économie*. Paris: Seuil.
Caillé, Alain, and Jacques T. Godbout. 1998. *The World of the Gift*. Montreal: McGill-Queen's University Press.
Durkheim, Émile. (1912) 1915. *The Elementary Forms of the Religious Life*. Translated by Joseph Ward Swain. London: Allen & Unwin.
Durkheim, Émile. (1886) 1970. "Les études de science sociale." In *La science sociale et l'action*, edited by Jean-Claude Filloux, 184–214. Paris: Presses universitaires de France.
Durkheim, Émile. (1888) 1970. "Cours de science sociale: Leçon d'ouverture." In *La science sociale et l'action*, edited by Jean-Claude Filloux, 77–110. Paris: Presses universitaires de France.
Durkheim, Émile. (1906) 1974. "The Determination of Moral Facts." In Émile Durkheim, *Sociology and Philosophy*, 35–62. New York: Free Press.
Durkheim, Émile. 1975. *Textes*, vol. 2: *Religion, morale, anomie*. Edited by Victor Karady. Paris: Les Editions de Minuit.
Durkheim, Émile. (1895) 1982. *The Rules of Sociological Method and Selected Texts on Sociology and Its Method*. Translated by W. D. Halls. New York: Free Press.
Durkheim, Émile. (1893) 1984. *The Division of Labor in Society*. Translated by W. D. Halls. New York: Free Press.
Durkheim, Émile. (1890/1900) 2001. *Professional Ethics and Civic Morals*. Translated by Cornelia Brookfield. London: Routledge.
Durkheim, Émile. (1897) 2006. *On Suicide*. Translated by Robin Buss. London: Penguin Books.
Durkheim, Émile, and Paul Fauconnet. (1909) 2004. "Sociology and the Social Sciences." In *Readings from Emile Durkheim*, edited by Kenneth Thompson, 9–14. London: Routledge.
Gislain, Jean-Jacques, and Phillippe Steiner. 1999. "American Institutionalism and Durkheimian Positive Economics: Some Connections." *History of Political Economy* 31, no. 2: 273–296.
Halbwachs, Maurice. 1909. *Les expropriations et le prix des terrains à Paris (1860–1900)*. Paris: Cornély.
Halbwachs, Maurice. 1912. *La classe ouvrière et les niveaux de vie. Recherches sur la hiérarchie des besoins dans les sociétés industrielles contemporaines*. Paris: Alcan.

Healy, Kieran. 2006. *Last Best Gifts: Altruism and the Market for Human Blood and Organs.* Chicago: University of Chicago Press.
Hubert, Henri, and Marcel Mauss. (1899) 1964. *Sacrifice: Its Nature and Function.* Chicago: University of Chicago Press.
Mauss, Marcel. (1925) 1966. *The Gift: Forms and Functions of Exchange in Archaic Societies.* London: Cohen & West.
Mauss, Marcel. (1924) 1997. "Appréciation sociologique du bolchévisme." In Marcel Mauss, *Écrits politiques,* edited by Marcel Fournier, 537–566. Paris: Fayard.
Naulin, Sidonie, and Philippe Steiner, eds. 2016. *La solidarité à distance. Quand le don passe par les organisations.* Toulouse: Presses universitaires du Midi.
Orléan, André. 2014. *The Empire of Value: A New Foundation for Economics.* Cambridge, MA: MIT Press.
Plouviez, Mélanie. 2013. "Le projet durkheimien de réforme corporative. Droit professionnel et protection des travailleurs." *Les études sociales* 157/158: 57–103.
Polanyi, Karl. (1944) 2001. *The Great Transformation: The Political and Economic Origins of Our Time.* Boston: Beacon Press.
Radin, Margaret Jane. 1996. *Contested Commodities.* Cambridge, MA: Harvard University Press.
Simiand, François. 1907. *Le salaire des ouvriers des mines de charbon en France. Contribution à la théorie économique du salaire.* Paris: Cornély.
Simiand, François. 1912. *La méthode positive en science économique.* Paris: Alcan.
Simiand, François. 1932. *Le salaire, l'évolution sociale et la monnaie. Essai de théorie expérimentale du salaire.* Paris: Alcan.
Simiand, François. 1934. "La monnaie réalité sociale." *Annales sociologiques,* Series D, Vol. 1: 1–58.
Steiner, Philippe. 2010. *La transplantation d'organes. Un commerce nouveau entre les êtres humains.* Paris: Gallimard.
Steiner, Philippe. 2011. *Durkheim and the Birth of Economic Sociology.* Princeton, NJ: Princeton University Press.
Steiner, Philippe. 2015. "The Organizational Gift and Sociological Approaches to Exchange." In *Re-Imagining Economic Sociology,* edited by Patrik Aspers and Nigel Dodd, 275–298. Oxford: Oxford University Press.
Steiner, Philippe. 2016. *Donner . . . Une histoire de l'altruisme.* Paris: Presses universitaires de France.
Steiner, Philippe, and Marie Trespeuch, eds. 2015. *Marchés contestés. Quand le marché rencontre la morale.* Toulouse: Presses universitaires du Midi.
Titmuss, Richard M. 1970. *The Gift Relationship: From Human Blood to Social Policy.* London: Allen & Unwin.

CHAPTER 15

REFLECTING ON DURKHEIM AND HIS STUDIES ON LAW THROUGH CANCELLATION OF BRITISH CITIZENSHIP

DEVYANI PRABHAT

Introduction

> However future society is organized [...]. There will be a place for all.
> —Durkheim 1899: 438, quoted in Lukes 1973: 324

> The consul banged the table and said: "If you've got no passport you're officially dead": But we are still alive, my dear, but we are still alive.
> —W. H. Auden in his poem *Refugee Blues*

Émile Durkheim is called the father of sociology because of his life's work in consolidating the disciplinary features of sociology. However, it is not just sociology that he has established, Durkheim has also steered the purposes and effects of criminology and deviance by connecting observable macro-processes with the large questions in the field (such as who commits crime and why, and why punish). Law is an important theme in Durkheim's research; his scholarship is widely cited in law and society literature. He used law and legal data as observable facts in empirical studies and developed a conceptual understanding of legal evolution connected to modernity, social solidarity, and moral individualism. His work on law is spread out in the breadth of his writings ranging from his first monograph *The Division of Labour* ([1902] 1984), to his lectures on civic morals in *Professional Ethics and Civic Morals* ([1950] 1957), and in later works such as *The Rules of Sociological Method* ([1895] 1982), *The Elementary Forms of Religious Life* ([1912] 1995), and *Suicide* ([1897] 1951). Thus, Cotterrell (1995: 179) observes,

"Durkheim's writings on law are voluminous, if largely fragmentary." Yet, apart from being dispersed in his writings, Durkheim's work on law is also complex in orientation as it is well integrated with his general ideas about sociology and morality. Durkheim's aim was to formulate an accessible methodology for the study of morality using law.[1]

Law and morality are not distinct domains. Legal rules constitute a subset of moral rules: law and morality are too intimately related to be radically separated. Legal rules are distinguished from moral rules not by their character—for example, by their content or form or by the nature of the behavior they regulate—but rather by the way that the sanctions are administered. Moral sanctions are diffuse—"administered by everybody without distinction." Legal sanctions are, by contrast, organized—"applied only through the medium of a definite body," "specially authorized representatives" charged with the task of enforcement (Cotterrell 1999: 60). Law involves some institutionalized means for publicly declaring and enforcing norms. Durkheim seeks ways to operationalize "social solidarity." He says that "we must therefore substitute for this internal datum, which escapes us, an external one which symbolizes it, and then study the former through the latter. That visible symbol is the law" (Durkheim [1902] 1984: 24).

Applying Durkheim

Despite Durkheim's popularity in the law and social sciences, critics often find a simplistic assumption of cause and effect in Durkheim's work, which has led to criticisms of positivism and functionalism (Black 1972: 1091, 1094–1095, 1098; Griffiths 1984: 39). Positivism in Durkheim's work refers to the manner in which he linked the study of sociology with a similar rationale as studying science through observable phenomena (e.g., in his book *The Rules of Sociological Method*, in French in 1895). Functionalism refers to the social value of observable social facts in Durkheim's work, which again he puts forward as a central idea in his book *The Rules of Sociological Method*. Both of these approaches appear rather superficial but are situated in complex contexts in his writings. In his defense, scholars also propose an earlier Durkheim and a later Durkheim (the "two Durkheim" thesis) (Lukes 1973; Cotterrell 1977). According to this "two Durkheim" thesis, the later Durkheim is the complex and more mature scholar while his earlier works were less mature and more committed to functionalism and positivism. For law, this rings especially true: Durkheim has an initial positivist approach linked to rules he formulates in relation to law, which later develops into a more nuanced study in which law is important, but not always critical, for morality.

To demonstrate both the potential of Durkheim's sociology of law and its limitations, this chapter focuses on cancellation of British citizenship. Stripping people of citizenship for counterterrorism purposes involves an increased use of law such as legislations which authorize such acts, the executive power to implement these, and judicial power in reviewing the limits of the law. Most people who have been stripped of British citizenship are from ethnic and religious minority communities, and they have been stripped for being national security threats. Such situations raise questions about breakdown of social solidarity because minority ethnicity individuals are expelled from national citizenry. While cancellation can appear to be punitive in nature, it also has expressive elements such as a deeply symbolic gesture of expulsion. Human rights principles (such as statelessness) have been raised to challenge citizenship stripping. Thus, on one hand, there are solidarity issues of allegiance and patriotism and, on the other, issues of rights such as equality and nondiscrimination. As such, the conditions appear fertile for a Durkheimian analysis of law and morality.

CANCELLATION, COUNTERTERRORISM, AND MINORITY COMMUNITIES

Cancellation laws are applied at present to largely prevent the re-entry into the United Kingdom of terrorism suspects who travel to conflict-ridden areas (such as Syria), as well as to stop future travels which create national security concerns (Anderson 2016). The UK government has increasingly used its powers to strip people of their British citizenship status and also refused to issue British passports for travel in recent times.[2] Such measures have applied mostly to British Muslims and have created a sense of second-class citizenship where some people are more prone to experiencing cancellation than others.

Cancellation laws are an index of societal solidarity as these laws target those who are considered as disloyal to the country and therefore are denied protection. This "loyalty and protection" framework has been recently reiterated in the Pham case (Pham v. SSHD [2018] EWCA Civ 2064). Mr Pham was born in Vietnam in 1983 but later became British. The government deprived him of his British citizenship for terrorism-related activities in Yemen. Eventually, while in an US prison, he appealed on the ground that he was not a current risk to UK public safety. The Court of Appeal rejected Mr Pham's appeal and said, "In the present case, the appellant has over a significant period of time fundamentally and seriously broken the obligations which apply to him as a citizen and put at risk the lives of others whom the Crown is bound to protect. I do not consider that it would be sensibly argued that this is not a situation in which the state is justified in seeking to be relieved of any further obligation to protect the appellant" (para. 51).

The current legislation (British Nationality Act 1981) permits some citizens to be left stateless through citizenship stripping, while others cannot be rendered stateless. Table 15.1 shows how people become British citizens, what other nationalities they hold, and whether their citizenship can be cancelled.

In the instance of citizens born in the United Kingdom, if they do not hold another nationality, they cannot be left stateless through cancellation. Those who hold another nationality are categorized as at no risk of statelessness and therefore their citizenship can

Table 15.1 Cancellation of British Citizenship for Reasons of Conduct

British Citizen Born in the United Kingdom?	Any Other Nationality?	Can British Citizenship Be Cancelled for Conduct?	Can Be Rendered Stateless?
Yes	No	No	No, cancellation prohibited because of risk of statelessness.
Yes	Yes	Yes	There is no risk of statelessness.
No	Yes	Yes	There is no risk of statelessness.
No	No	Yes	Yes, can be cancelled even if rendered stateless.

(arguably) be cancelled without violating any convention obligations. The last column illustrates when a person could potentially be rendered stateless by a cancellation order. For those who naturalize, there is a risk of statelessness as they can be stripped even without another nationality in place. This can happen if they have no other nationality, but whether or not there is any alternative existing nationality is often disputed in court. The Home Office raises claims they have national connections with other countries through their ethnicity or parental links.

The most high-profile of these instances is the situation of Shamima Begum, which has been reported at length in international media. Shamima Begum was born in Britain to British parents of Bangladeshi heritage. As a teenage schoolgirl she joined IS fighters in Syria. At age nineteen she found herself in a refugee camp in Syria with no British citizenship. The claim of the Home Office is that Shamima Begum has an eligibility for Bangladeshi nationality through her parents and is therefore not stateless. Yet, on February 20, 2019, Bangladesh issued a statement saying Begum did not have Bangladeshi nationality and would not be allowed into Bangladesh. In May 2019, Bangladesh stated it would seek the death penalty for Begum if she ever visited Bangladesh because of her connection with terrorism. Ironically, this means that whether a cancellation measure survives a court challenge by affected people largely depends on the text and interpretation of Bangladeshi nationality provisions and case law.[3] But the fact that Bangladesh says she has no claim to Bangladeshi citizenship now means that she is effectively stateless in Syria and elsewhere.[4] An immediate implication of this case is that anyone with any other national connection is now at greater risk of losing their British citizenship and becoming effectively stateless (Prabhat 2020). The situation raises concerns among migrants who naturalized to citizenship and other second-generation migrants born as British in terms of their legal status in the country.

The effects on minority communities of contemporary counterterrorism in many ways mirror the effects on French Jews of the war-time measures and trials which Durkheim experienced during his own lifetime. These also resonate with other episodes of suspicion of minorities such as the Irish during the heyday of the Northern Irish conflict (1980s/1990s). Many researchers point out that the experiences of British Muslims in particular, after the events of 9/11 and 7/7, resonate with the experiences of the Irish in the United Kingdom (Ramraj 2006; Hickman et al. 2011). Marie Breen-Smyth (2014: 223) explains how "a community created in and by the securitised imagination and enacted in a process of 'othering' through a range of security practices of counter-terrorism" can become a "suspect community."[5] These experiences also resonate with those of Jews in Durkheim's lifetime. He was most certainly aware of anti-Semitism and its emergence in the context of political developments of his days. He wrote an essay on anti-Semitism (Durkheim [1899] 2008). An awareness of it also permeated his other writings such as his response to the French Revolution and its legacy (Goldberg 2011: 248).

Given such close parallels in circumstances, to what extent do Durkheim's general concepts such as anomie and collective conscience, as well as specific ideas on the relationship between law and sociology, have any explanatory value for cancellation of citizenship? While addressing this question, this chapter has two main arguments to present: first, that Durkheim's work was complex and multicausal and did not merely have a simplistic or positivist orientation and, second, that there are strong thematic connections between Durkheim's earlier writings and his later works especially on basic theoretical premises and on methodology.

Durkheim consistently and incrementally develops his ideas on the sociology of law and refines how to study these. Most gaps that are identified in his work relate to contemporary rethinking of legal and social methodology. A post-Durkheimian reading that critiques his methodology is likely to ascribe meanings to Durkheim anachronistically, based on a legal sociology that had not yet been established. Thus, William Watts Miller (1988: 653) writes that, ironically, Durkheim has been accused of being "insufficiently durkheimian" in his sociological methods. Indeed, recent ideas on sociology of law and criminology owe much in their origins to Durkheim's efforts at unpacking the links between law and morality (e.g., Garland 1990).

THE INSIDER-OUTSIDER VIEW ON THE BREAKDOWN OF BONDS

An analysis of the life stories of scholars may not always be necessary to understand their ideas but Durkheim has a unique insider-outsider perspective which he brings to his social science because of his own biography. Before analyzing each of the aforementioned strands in Durkheim's work, therefore, we should trace Durkheim's journey of ideas and examine how his own life experience influenced his sociological imagination. His background as son of a poorly paid Rabbi father and an embroiderer mother in rural France meant he was a class outsider in the elite echelons of French academia. Indeed, it took him three attempts to enter the elite *Ecole normale supérieure* because he had to undertake family responsibilities when his father became ill. He reported feelings of emptiness and isolation in Paris (Lukes 1973: 42). Similarly, being from Jewish heritage but holding an atheist/agnostic approach to religion meant he was an outsider to most Jewish circles. This is not surprising as his view about religion was in part functional: religion serves a purpose in society (Mars 2016). The early influence of a much-admired Catholic teacher reinforced his religious outsiderness and heightened awareness of pluralism in religious beliefs (Lukes 1973: 41).

Being an outsider-insider, or insider-outsider, Durkheim often asked the question about what keeps society together despite differences rather than focusing on conflict which brings about breakdown. It seemed more natural to him that differences would lead to breakdowns in social order but why that would not happen all the time was more puzzling. Similarly, other key life events have influenced his research. He had experienced personal upheaval which led him along different research avenues. A close friend's suicide while in school made him think deeply about how suicides can be prevented (Lukes 1973: 191). This prompted his study of suicide in which he looked at its social causes through empirical data (Durkheim [1897] 1951). The trial of Captain Alfred Dreyfus, a Jewish French officer who was wrongly convicted of treason (popularly known as the Dreyfus Affair), politically galvanized Durkheim.

These life experiences provide Durkheim's work a unique moral perspective: since law exists within a moral domain it has moral meaning (Durkheim 1925: 37, in Cotterrell 1999: 21). Even when there is a differentiated society there is a moral core which is identifiable and universal, and this core is respect for basic humanity (moral individualism). As Davy states, morality was "the center and end of his work" (Davy 1920: 71). Law is an important part of the empirical project for studying morality. With time Durkheim looks more closely at the basis of belief, moral attachment, and independence, but there always remains a tendency to conflate law and morality as one and the same because morality was for Durkheim the most important subject of study.

The impact of this perception is profound. Cotterrell (1999) explains how the centrality of the moral in Durkheim's work rescues him from lapsing into mere positivism. For instance, Durkheim gives some telling examples to illustrate the effects for individuals of the social causes of suicide. Despite his attempts to separate out sociology from psychology, he had to account for the impact of anomie, egoism, and so on on individuals. When it comes to law, Durkheim virtually equated it with morality so that law is "treated as an undistorted reflection of society's collective morality" and ignored other factors which may have also influenced law and/or morality (Lukes and Scull 1983: 6; Lukes and Prabhat 2012: 367).

According to Durkheim, there are three major rules about law (Lukes and Scull 1983: 1, 33, 38, 69). First, law is conceived of as an "external" index, symbolizing the nature of social solidarity in any society in which it exists. Second, legal development has a relatively consistent evolutionary pattern from the predominance of penal law with repressive sanctions (aimed at the punishment of wrongdoing such as in criminal law) to a predominance of "civil law, commercial law, procedural law, administrative and constitutional law" (where the primary aim is restitution or restoration of the status quo in social relationships). Durkheim connects to the development of law and legal systems the evolution of societies "from less to more advanced forms, from an all-encompassing religiosity to modern secularism, and from collectivism to individualism" in an anthropological manner. Third, crime is a violation of collective sentiments, and punishment an expression of them, so that punishment's "real function is to maintain inviolate the cohesion of society by sustaining the common consciousness in all its vigour."

In his later work each of these rules is connected to Durkheim's work on moral individualism. Thus, when society progresses from mechanical to organic solidarity, the predominant form of social solidarity becomes one of common humanity so that other aspects of functional differentiation (such as different kinds of labor or different ethnicities) do not subvert solidarity. The law in this understanding is one that supports common humanity through a protective framework (such as human rights laws) rather than through punishment or contractual regulation.

Viewed through the lens of these three hypotheses about law and subsequent connections with moral individualism, cancellation of citizenship laws reveals a great deal of information about underlying morality and society in contemporary Britain. As an external index, cancellation laws expose the weakness of social solidarity. Increasingly minority ethnicity groups are targets of such national security measures, making them the "other" in British society and indicating there is a lack of multicultural space, whether demonstrated in lack of inclusion or lack of loyalty. Yet the direction of modernity predicted by Durkheim toward moral individualism does not appear to ring wholly true in the case of cancellation of citizenship where the law has serious repressive and retributive consequence: the individuals are expelled from national territorial and legal jurisdiction without any judicial determination of their conduct.

The Index View of Law and Mechanical to Organic Solidarity

The first rule, the index view of law, is the one arguably the most positivist in nature. Durkheim writes that law is conceived of as an "external" index, which symbolizes the nature of social solidarity in any society in which it exists. Studying this external index, Durkheim develops a thesis of evolution of social solidarity in society. He writes in the *Division of Labour* that solidarity based on sameness (mechanical solidarity) proceeds to a deeper solidarity between people over time irrespective of their different positions in society (organic solidarity). He argues that traditional societies were made up of homogenous people that were more or less the same in terms of values, religious beliefs, and backgrounds. Mechanical solidarity occurs when individuals within structural units are alike and self-sufficient. For example, in traditional societies, people grew their own food, made their own clothes, and had little need for extensive social contact with others because they did not have to rely on others for daily needs. They develop solidarity based on sameness such as between farmers in remotely located villages.

Organic solidarity is based on deeper connections made between people who are different but who find they need each other because of, or despite, their differences. An example would be a community with differentiated labor where people can exchange or sell different skills and goods. Modern societies, in contrast, are made up of a complex division of labor, beliefs, and backgrounds. Organic solidarity occurs when a large population is stratified into smaller structural units. There is a high level of interdependence among individuals and structures, but there is still a division of people along the lines of labor. Organic solidarity has the capacity to include diverse identities, while mechanical solidarity excludes those who are different.

Thus, in modern societies, mechanical solidarity based on the authority of custom and tradition must be replaced by a new and different sort of solidarity in which greater scope is allowed for individuality and "authority is rationally grounded" (Durkheim [1898] 1973: 49).

In this new form of solidarity, which Durkheim termed organic, "reflection" and "criticism" would "exist next to faith, pierce that very faith without destroying it, and occupy an always larger place in it" (Durkheim [1928] 1958: 215).

According to Durkheim, organic solidarity would be propelled and enhanced by heterogeneity as people search for deeper connections with one another. However, deeper connections may not always be forged and there may be a lack of mutual obligations and respect. An example of such failure of solidarity could be the reason for why citizens act against their own countries.

Contrary to Durkheim's predictions, cancellation laws indicate a move away from organic solidarity to mechanical solidarity as these seem to operate on the basis of difference rather than sameness. How law changes in character as morality evolves is obviously not always in the same direction as Durkheim sets out in his work. One explanation for this is suggested by Lukes and Scull (1983: 5) as the narrow focus of Durkheim's "index" view of law. In reality there are many more complex factors to be considered. In the case of cancellation of citizenship laws, other potential moral conflicts are underplayed. For example, national security concerns are heightened whenever there are acts of terrorism so it is important to see evidence of the participation of citizens in acts of terrorism and whether those citizens are indeed the ones who are stripped of citizenship through the new laws. Scholars view cancellation laws as continued means to control mass migration—in many ways a project of "crimmigration" (criminalization of immigration) (e.g., Stumpf 2006; Aas and Bosworth 2013).

Moreover, as Cotterrell (1999: 33) writes, "Legal provisions may be more or less detailed depending on the intentions or skill of the law creator, the extent to which common understandings governing circumstances in which the law is to apply can be assumed, and prevailing attitudes to interpretation of law. [Durkheim] fails to note that repressive and restitutive sanctions may often be mixed and that their relation to particular rules may be indirect and complex." In short, the index thesis, as he explains it, seems to show the worst aspects of the positivist orientations of his sociology. However, this is mitigated later when he looks at minority rights and the presence of ethnic minorities in society. Perhaps these writings, penned at a time of heightened persecution of the Jewish minority in France, are relevant for analyzing whether cancellation rules have disproportionate effects on ethnic minorities.

Durkheim's essays on individualism and the intellectuals and on anti-Semitism contain practical suggestions on how to combat racial prejudice. Chad Goldberg (2011: 249) writes that Durkheim maintained strong relations with his Jewish family and never discarded his Jewish roots. He also collaborated in his scholarly work with other Jewish intellectuals, especially during the Dreyfus Affair. Goldberg concludes that Durkheim's sense of Jewish identity was not traditionalist, but neither was it absent or nonexistent. Durkheim viewed anti-Semitism as a thermometer for measuring the pathology of society. He recognized that punishment for incitement was not going to change people's minds by itself, but he argued that it would strengthen and reinvigorate public revulsion at such behavior. Opponents of racism must condemn it in both theory and practice, and the government had to take responsibility for enlightening the masses. Durkheim viewed this moral education as a means of repairing social disorder. These are complex solutions penned for his day but also relevant for modern society.

Repression to Restitution

The second rule Durkheim developed about law and society was to predict that legal rules were evolving in character from the predominance of penal law with repressive sanctions (aimed at the punishment of wrongdoing such as in criminal law) to a predominance of "civil law, commercial law, procedural law, administrative and constitutional law" (where primary aim is restitution or restoration of the status quo in social relationships). In his search for the most visible external indicators of morality, Durkheim focused on the law's effects evoked when laws are violated, namely sanctions. Distinguishing two broad types of sanction, he connected these to successive types of solidarity—mechanical and organic—sustained and revealed by distinctive types of law, namely repressive law, focusing on punishing the offender, and restitutory law, focusing not on the infliction of suffering but rather on restoring the status quo ante, making the victim "whole" again, as in contract law, administrative law, and civil law generally. This was presented in *The Division of Labour* as the thesis that law is an index of the two kinds of solidarity, repressive law indicating the extent of mechanical solidarity and restitutory law the extent of organic solidarity.

Contrary to this position, it may be argued that cancellation laws are not criminal laws and these aim to simply remove the threat to national security. When cancellation is for fraud (such as a fraudulent application), indeed, it has a contractual element. However, cancellation laws seem to contradict the predictions of the second hypothesis, which indicate a move from the predominance of penal law with repressive sanctions (aimed at the punishment of wrongdoing such as in criminal law) to a predominance of restitutory laws because in many ways cancellation laws are even more punitive than penal laws.

There are now many studies that challenge Durkheim's proposed general pattern of evolution from a preponderance of penal or repressive law to one of cooperative or restitutive law (e.g., Barnes 1966; Gatrell, Lenman, and Parker 1980). Further, political centralization, rather than being a contingent and subordinate factor as Durkheim suggested, appears to be directly and consistently associated with greater reliance on repressive controls and with greater punitive intensity (Spitzer 1975; see Lukes and Scull 1983: ch. 4). Cancellation is a further example of how repressive measures resurface and state power plays a central role. However, there is evidence for Durkheim's ideas of moral individualism. Although the distinct possibility of statelessness has returned in the context of cancellation, such measures still operate within the limitations of international law. Most governments have tailored national laws to fit commitments to human rights conventions. The United Kingdom has commitments to two UN conventions in 1954 and 1961 designed to prevent statelessness.

Function of Punishment

Durkheim's third hypothesis about law is about the function of punishment. Lukes and Scull note three separate claims in this hypothesis. The first claim is that crime and punishment promote social integration. When a crime is punished, there is a clear indication of what collective beliefs have been violated by the crime. Therefore, when such violation is punished, it reaffirms collective beliefs and sentiments, thereby enhancing social solidarity. The second claim is that crime is normal in society because any society will define certain kinds of conduct as crime. Durkheim gave an example of a society of saints and asserted that even in that society there would be some conduct that would be deemed unacceptable and would be proscribed (Lukes and Scull 1983: 100). The third point Durkheim highlighted was that crime would sometimes change the moral framework of society. Civil disobedience is an example of when this could happen.

If we think of crime as a violation of collective sentiments, and punishment an expression of them, so that punishment's "real function is to maintain inviolate the cohesion of society by sustaining the common consciousness in all its vigour" (Lukes and Scull 1983: 1, 69), perhaps cancellation laws fit the third hypothesis as these seem to punish terrorism and reflect collective sentiments against disloyalty and lack of patriotism. Garland points out that for Durkheim the motivations to punish are about revenge rather than any rehabilitation or restitution. "Crimes are thus a violation of society's morality *and* a personally felt outrage against every 'healthy' individual. The result is a passionate, hostile reaction from the public" (Garland 1990: 31). Cancellation is similarly a punishment driven by a sense of outrage. It is banishment from society or ostracization and is in that sense a primal reaction. But it could have a utilitarian function as well, as for the state cancellation is a form of crimmigration as it extends state oversight over migrants entering the country illegally to the domain of migrants who stayed legally and naturalized or others who have connections with foreign countries. Punishment can also follow the rebranding of certain acts as crime. For example, travel to Syria has become a crime connected to national security only after the heightened threat to terrorism when British fighters travelled to join rebel groups fighting there.

With respect to the idea that crime and punishment are functional to social integration, Lukes and Scull argue that the primary difficulty of the thesis is its vagueness. It is not possible to identify how the thesis operates empirically in society as the boundaries and constituents of society are unclear as are the effects of what it would look like if it did disintegrate (Lukes and Scull 1983: 18). It is easy to draw on the thesis to argue for preserving any dominant practice or institution and quelling any kind of dissent or disagreement. In democracies, protests can lead to new reform movements, but if punishment is used to maintain the status quo all the time, there is unlikely to be any health progress or innovation through reimagination.

Some critics argue that "the law," through professionalization, formal institutionalization, and other aspects of functional differentiation, has loosened its ties to common everyday morality; hence, it no longer "mirrors" social morality, as Durkheim assumes (Garland 1991: 153). Others, such as Prosser (2006), have shown how diverse laws, such as regulatory rules, which appear functionally differentiated from criminal and contract laws, are still connected to underlying issues of social solidarity in a Durkheimian sense.

Garland, while looking at the social character of punishment, reflects on Durkheim's work and criticisms of his approach. He concludes that criticisms of Durkheim do not take away from the strength of his complex reflections on punishment and society (Garland 1990: 49). Durkheim does not just assert that crime is the only factor that supports social integration but, in its regulation, there are a range of factors contributing to social integration of which legal regulation (through punishment) is but one of the means of rendering that regulation effective. Removal of legal regulation will not automatically lead to disintegration if other factors continue to exist. Indeed, the framework of Durkheim's *Suicide* rests on the multiple layers of integration and regulation of a person within society (religious, occupational, familial, and political) which extend beyond the legal. Indeed, *Suicide* can be viewed as a work that demonstrates empirically that in many circumstances disorder does not accompany the weakening of regulative norms and integrative institutions. After all, because of the multiple layers of integration, even when several changes take place in the law, suicide still remains a deviant act. What this demonstrates is that law is an important factor in Durkheim's exploration of social solidarity and moral regulation, but it is not the only relevant factor.

Sanctity of the Human

In his work, Durkheim does not distinguish between sources of law (whether judicial, executive, or legislative) but has an interest in treating all of law as data (observable facts). He has "a strong interest in how the role of punitive justice had changed on the way to modernity" (Joas 2008a: 141) and thus in his "Two Laws of Penal Evolution" ([1901] 1983), he goes beyond the general evolutionary thesis of *The Division of Labour*. The Individual emerges as important in modern penology but in premodern societies, sacrilege, blasphemy, and regicide were the worst crimes as these were directed against the sovereign. Crimes against the person mattered less. Moreover, not only the evaluation of the gravity of crimes but also of what counts as acceptable punishment has shifted. The greater emphasis on the person makes society more egalitarian, since "the only ways of acting that are moral are those which are fitting for all men equally, that is to say, which are implied in the notion of man in general"; it was "the glorification not of the self, but of the individual in general" (Lukes 1969: 21, 24).

Durkheim's evolutionary approach is not just about time or quantity of rules but also about the quality of the values that transform with modernity. Durkheim through his anthropological approach connects Kantian enlightenment values with the evolution of societies "from less to more advanced forms, from an all-encompassing religiosity to modern secularism, and from collectivism to individualism" (Lukes and Scull 2013: 5). Thus, the penal aspect of law becomes more humane over time and becomes a means of strengthening the conscience collective by protecting the sanctity of the Individual. More generally, Durkheim's idea is that, in modern differentiated and plural societies, there are a range of increasingly humane core moral norms which progressively instantiate the "cult of the individual" or sacralization of the person (see Joas 2008b). These are evident in various spheres of social life, both private and public. When violated, as they often are, they need to be reaffirmed by being enforced. Failing to do so can, under certain conditions, have the consequence that social practices and relationships become less humane.

As modernity led to the progressive emancipation of the individual from traditional sources of influence, there was greater scope for the "cult of the individual" or "religion of humanity" to emerge. For this cult, as in other concepts developed by Durkheim, the state was not so significant. This is a weakness in Durkheim's approach since the state is necessary for protecting the rights that are implied by the "cult of the individual." Indeed, modern international human rights systems require states to be defenders of rights. As Hannah Arendt (1973: 287) has pointed out, without nation-state interventions, people cannot put into effect rights and are excluded from the dignity of human sacredness.

Durkheim writes,

> the human person (*personne humaine*) [...] is considered sacred in the ritual sense of the word. It partakes of the transcendent majesty that churches of all time lend to their gods; it is conceived of as being invested with that mysterious property which creates a void about sacred things, which removes them from vulgar contacts and withdraws them from common circulation. And the respect which is given it comes precisely from this source. Whoever makes an attempt on a man's life, on a man's liberty, on a man's honor, inspires in us a feeling of horror analogous in every way to

that which the believer experiences when he sees his idol profaned. Such an ethic is therefore not simply a hygienic discipline or a prudent economy of existence; it is a religion in which man is at once the worshipper and the god.

(Durkheim [1898] 1973: 46)

Individualism thus understood has as its motive force "not egoism but sympathy for all that is human, a wider pity for all sufferings, for all human miseries, a more ardent desire to combat and alleviate them, a greater thirst for justice." It is a "cult of man" that has "for its primary dogma the autonomy of reason" and for its "primary rite the doctrine of free inquiry" (Durkheim [1898] 1973: 49). It is, moreover, henceforth the only system of beliefs which can ensure the moral unity of the country. For with ever greater social complexity and diversity, traditions and practices adapt to social change by becoming ever more plastic and unstable: social and cultural differentiation has developed almost to a point at which the members of a single society retain only their humanity in common. Society was evolving, Durkheim wrote, toward a state in which "the members of a single social group will have nothing in common among themselves except their humanity, except the constitutive attributes of the human person in general." Thus the "idea of the human person," given different emphases in accordance with the diversity of national temperaments, is "the only idea which would be retained, unalterable and impersonal, above the changing torrent of individual opinions" (Durkheim [1898] 1973: 51–52). Yet such an exalted view of the human as a basis of rights is not borne out always in reality. In any society there are stigmatized and marginalized groups of people who just appear to count less or do not matter at all (Garland 1990).

In his short article about anti-Semitism, Durkheim called for repression of "all incitement of hatred of citizens against one another." Such punishment, he recognized, would not by itself "change people's minds," but it could strengthen and reinvigorate public revulsion against such incitement (Durkheim [1899] 2008: 322). In *Suicide* (first published in 1897), Durkheim offers a similar reason for why legal and other kinds of intervention are required in order to prevent suicides: the human person—the individual in general—is sacred and has to be preserved. Durkheim connects suicide to the conceptual structure of morality. He observes that by "calling the evil of which the abnormal increase in suicides is symptomatic of a moral evil, we are far from thinking to reduce it to some superficial ill which may be conjured away by soft words" (Durkheim [1897] 1951: 387). He distinguishes a greater harm to society from the smaller harm to the individual. Thus, a

> man who kills himself, the saying goes, does wrong only to himself and there is no occasion for the intervention of society; for so goes the ancient maxim *Volenti non fit injuria*. This is an error. Society is injured because the sentiment is offended on which its most respected moral maxims today rest, a sentiment [that is] almost the only bond between its members, and which would be weakened if this offense could be committed with impunity. How could this sentiment maintain the least authority if the moral conscience did not protest its violation? From the moment that the

human person is and must be considered something sacred, over which neither the individual nor the group has free disposal, any attack upon it must be forbidden.

(Durkheim [1897] 1951: 337)

From these statements it is clear that Durkheim believes in legal and other kinds of regulation of suicide because of harm to "the individual," because of the need to protect the sacredness of the Individual as it permeates the collective conscience, rather than because of a particular harm to particular, actual empirical individuals.

When discussing the legal prohibition of suicide, Durkheim writes that the harm consists in suicide's subversion of human individuality. It is the "cult of the individual" which is a feature of modern morality and which Durkheim considers needs protection. In the case of suicide, such protection is afforded not just by laws but also by religious traditions and popular sentiment (Durkheim [1897] 1951: 334). But Durkheim sees such protection taking multiple forms in various contexts. In the economic and industrial sphere, he so regarded policies favoring social justice and reducing exploitation. In essence, he lays out a Kantian universal human rights perspective in which a progressively reinterpreted conception of the Individual lies at the core of what constitutes the "conscience collective." In the subject matter of cancellation of citizenship, we can see how this retraction from the sanctity of the Individual takes place. The retraction of the sacred individual and the creation of relations which do not respect human rights and dignity are apparent in contemporary legal developments in this area in the United Kingdom.

Begum's case highlights that somebody who has lost their citizenship has no right to re-enter the United Kingdom or to seek diplomatic protection from the British government. As a consequence of citizenship stripping, former British citizens have been left in war zones and died in drone attacks (Woods and Ross 2013; Gjevori 2019). Some have been sent to foreign countries for trial. Thus, in cancellation cases we can see the complete degeneration of the individual into "the other" who can be killed or violated with impunity. Honig (2003) writes that the link between deprivation and deportation is that "we almost always make foreign those whom we persecute." Clearly, this drive to render foreign is not consistent with Durkheim's account of the structure of modern industrial societies and the "religion of individualism" as the sole surviving common link between human beings.

Critics tend to agree that a general theory of power or a theory of the state is missing in Durkheim's work. Cotterrell (2011: 17) writes, "Durkheim's sociology of law has been criticized for its focus on law's links to morality, rather than to power." Perhaps the explanation for the mismatch in law and morality in the instance of cancellation of citizenship lies in Durkheim's failure to consider the limits of national citizenship and state power. Without the guarantees of national citizenship, general rights principles become abstract and metaphorical. As Joas (2008a: 144) has pointed out, Durkheim's work on religion of individualism lacks a cult in the sense of special rituals of a genuine church, a community of the faithful. In *Suicide* and in *Elementary Forms* as well as in

Moral Education, Durkheim often discusses the role of non-state actors, such as schools and trade unions in civic engagement. Such institutions are potential spaces for greater solidarity in modern British society, but the creation of plural spaces of belonging is not at the forefront of counterterrorism today when citizenship has become conditional and fragmented in nature. The drive to cancel matches a different kind of solidarity, one which Garland (1990) refers to as the emotional solidarity of aggression which engenders a simplistic mechanical solidarity.

Conclusion: The Overoptimism of Durkheim?

In this chapter, emulating Durkheim's own approach of using law as an observable social fact in sociological analysis, I have used the specific example of cancellation of British citizenship to demonstrate the links Durkheim sets out in his work among the individual, morality, and social solidarity. Studying the cancellation of citizenship has provided a good opportunity to reveal the strengths and expose the limits of Durkheim's hypotheses because cancellation is directly about social solidarity but also draws on issues of power which may have been overlooked by Durkheim.

The Home Secretary's power to strip people of their citizenship creates different kinds of effects for different citizens. While those British by birth and descent are unaffected, naturalized citizens are at greater risk of statelessness. Specific groups who are mostly ethnic and religious minority groups in Britain can become abandoned outside the United Kingdom and/or rendered stateless. Such developments undermine the concept of equal citizenship in a diverse and democratic society. The measures subvert multiculturalism as multicultural practices require space for different cultural identities and practices to coexist and flourish.

What does the case study of cancellation reveal about Durkheim's framework on law, morality, and social solidarity? Do Durkheim's ideas on law and sociolegal research have any traction in explaining the links between law and society in contemporary times? The main challenge posed to Durkheim's ideas comes from his tendency to wax lyrical about individualism as a religion and the progressive inclusion of rights. As mentioned in the epigraph to this chapter, he foresaw a role for everyone in society in the future, yet cancellation of citizenship presents the picture of Auden's poem *Refugee Blues*, where the passportless become the living dead in modern society. Instead of outsiders seeking refuge, it is the insider who is expelled and made foreign through cancellation powers. The surge in number of cancellations indicates that denationalizing of minorities is the preferred solution of the executive. Such a trend would have been disturbing to Durkheim in his pursuit of moral individualism as a source for social solidarity. Nevertheless, the example of cancellation of citizenship developed in this chapter demonstrates how social solidarity, and a Durkheimian inquiry into morality through law, is still a valid enquiry for sociologists of law. Cancellation laws have the power to make people nonexistent in a country, and this is a social fact which is not just dependent on individual conduct. Such laws are about social solidarity and fractures in social solidarity. However, the developments in this area indicate that the evolutionary approach of Durkheim's work does not bear out in reality because of its overoptimistic reliance on a progression toward greater rights and safeguards for all.

Decades back, Durkheim wrote about the presence of minorities and xenophobia as a means of studying the strength of social integration in his piece "Anti-Semitism and Social Crisis" ([1899] 2008), thereby opening up many avenues of exploration when looking at cancellation or other emerging issues of discrimination. Even though Durkheim does not develop his own empirical project on the issue of minority rights and xenophobia, he inspires other scholars to engage with these issues. His legacy is the scholarship that his work galvanized—the criminologists who examine punishment and the sociolegal scholars who deepen ideas of moral individualism.

Acknowledgement

The chapter draws liberally on my prior work in Lukes and Prabhat (2012) for the framework on moral individualism as a basis for rights while extending it to cancellation of citizenship.

Notes

1. There is a distinction in Durkheim's work between the use of the word "individual" as referring to any single person and a capitalized word the "Individual" which is more of a collective concept of humanity so this chapter uses these words in the different ways as employed by Durkheim.
2. See, for example, Melanie Gower and Terry McGuinness, Parliamentary Briefing, June 9, 2017, on Deprivation of British Citizenship and Withdrawal of Passport Facilities, https://commonslibrary.parliament.uk/research-briefings/sn06820/—81 deprivation of citizenship orders had been made in the years 2006 to 2015.
3. The Begum case is still ongoing in UK courts at the time of writing and submission of this chapter for publication. Begum's appeal is currently before the Special Immigration Appeals Commission, and the UK Court of Appeal in July 2020 had permitted her to return to the United Kingdom to instruct her lawyers and participate in her appeal. However, the UK Supreme Court reversed this decision to prevent Begum's return to the United Kingdom (February 26, 2021, *Begum v Home Secretary* [2021] UKSC 7).
4. https://www.trtworld.com/magazine/what-shamima-begum-s-case-says-about-the-future-of-muslims-in-the-uk-24381.
5. See also Hickman et al. (2011: 5): "Despite anti-discrimination legislation, Muslim communities today are subjected to a similar process of construction as 'suspect' as Irish communities in the previous era."

References

Aas, Katja F., and Mary Bosworth, eds. 2013. *The Borders of Punishment: Migration, Citizenship, and Social Exclusion.* New York: Oxford University Press.

Anderson, David. 2016. "Citizenship Removal Resulting in Statelessness: First Report of the Independent Reviewer on the Operation of the Power to Remove Citizenship Obtained by Naturalisation from Persons Who Have No Other Citizenship." UK Government Publication for presentation in Parliament, April.

Arendt, Hannah. 1973. *The Origins of Totalitarianism.* New York: Harvest.

Barnes, J. A. 1966. "Durkheim's *Division of Labour in Society*." *Man* 1, no. 2: 158–175.

Black, Donald J. 1972. "The Boundaries of Legal Sociology." *The Yale Law Journal* 81, no. 6: 1086–1100.

Breen-Smyth, Marie. 2014. "Theorising the 'Suspect Community': Counterterrorism, Security Practices and the Public Imagination." *Critical Studies on Terrorism* 7, no. 2: 223–240.

Cotterrell, Roger. 1977. "Durkheim on Legal Development and Social Solidarity." *British Journal of Law and Society* 4, no. 2: 241–252.

Cotterrell, Roger. 1995. *Law's Community: Legal Theory in Sociological Perspective.* Oxford: Clarendon Press.

Cotterrell, Roger. 1999. *Émile Durkheim: Law in a Moral Domain.* Edinburgh: Edinburgh University Press.

Cotterrell, Roger. 2011. "Justice, Dignity, Torture, Headscarves: Can Durkheim's Sociology Clarify Legal Values?" *Social & Legal Studies* 20, no. 1: 3–20.

Davy, Georges. 1920. "Durkheim: II—L'œuvre." *Revue de métaphysique et de morale* 27, no. 1: 71–112.

Durkheim, Émile. 1899. "Merlino, Saverio, *Formes et essence du socialisme*, avec une préface de G. Sorel." *Revue philosophique* 48: 433–439.

Durkheim, Émile. (1897) 1951. *Suicide: A Study in Sociology.* Translated by John A. Spaulding and George Simpson. New York: Free Press. Originally published as *Le suicide. Etude de sociologie.* Paris: Alcan.

Durkheim, Émile. (1950) 1957. *Professional Ethics and Civic Morals.* Translated by Cornelia Brookfield. London: Routledge & Kegan Paul. Originally published as *Leçons de sociologie. Physique des mœurs et du droit.* Paris: Presses universitaires de France.

Durkheim, Émile. (1928) 1958. *Socialism and Saint-Simon.* Translated by Charlotte Sattler. London: Routledge & Kegan Paul. Originally published as *Le Socialisme*, edited by Marcel Mauss. Paris: Alcan.

Durkheim, Émile. (1925) 1961. *Moral Education: A Study in the Theory and Application of the Sociology of Education.* Translated by E. K. Wilson and H. Schnurer. New York: Free Press. Originally published as *L'éducation morale*, edited by Paul Fauconnet. Paris: Alcan.

Durkheim, Émile. (1898) 1973. "Individualism and the Intellectuals." In *Emile Durkheim: On Morality and Society*, edited by Robert N. Bellah, 43–57. Chicago: University of Chicago Press. Originally published as "L'individualisme et les intellectuels" in *Revue bleue*, 4e série 10: 7–13.

Durkheim, Émile. (1895) 1982. *The Rules of Sociological Method and Selected Texts on Sociology and Its Method.* Translated by W. D. Halls. New York: Free Press. Originally published as *Les règles de la méthode sociologique.* Paris: Alcan.

Durkheim, Émile. (1901) 1983. "Two Laws of Penal Evolution." In *Durkheim and the Law*, edited by Steven Lukes and Andrew Scull, 102–132. Oxford: Martin Robertson. Originally published as "Deux lois de l'évolution pénale" in *L'Année sociologique* 4: 65–95.

Durkheim, Émile. (1902) 1984. *The Division of Labor in Society*. Translated by W. D. Halls. New York: Free Press. Originally published as *De la division du travail social. Etude sur l'organisation des sociétés supérieures*. Paris: Alcan, 1893; 2nd ed. Paris: Alcan, 1902.

Durkheim, Émile. (1912) 1995. *The Elementary Forms of Religious Life*. Translated by Karen E. Fields. New York: Free Press. Originally published as *Les formes élémentaires de la vie religieuse. Le système totémique en Australie*. Paris: Alcan.

Durkheim, Émile. (1899) 2008. "Anti-Semitism and Social Crisis." *Sociological Theory* 26, no. 4: 321–323. Originally published as a contribution to *Enquête sur l'antisémitisme*, edited by Henri Dagan, 59–63. Paris: Stock. Republished as "Antisémitisme et crise sociale" in Émile Durkheim, *Textes*, vol. 2: *Religion, morale, anomie*, edited by Victor Karady, 252–254. Paris: Les Editions de Minuit, 1975.

Garland, David. 1990. *Punishment and Modern Society: A Study in Social Theory*. Chicago: University of Chicago Press.

Garland, David. 1991. "Sociological Perspectives on Punishment." *Crime and Justice* 14: 115–165.

Gatrell, V. A. C., Bruce Lenman, and Geoffrey Parker. 1980. *Crime and the Law: The Social History of Crime in Western Europe since 1500*. London: Europa Publications.

Gjevori, Elis. 2019. "What Shamima Begum's Case Says about the Future of Muslims in the UK." https://www.trtworld.com/magazine/what-shamima-begum-s-case-says-about-the-future-of-muslims-in-the-uk-24381, March 11, 2019.

Goldberg, Chad Alan. 2011. "The Jews, the Revolution, and the Old Regime in French Anti-Semitism and Durkheim's Sociology." *Sociological Theory* 29, no. 4: 248–271.

Gower, Melanie, and Terry McGuinness. 2017. "Parliamentary Briefing, June 9, 2017, on Deprivation of British Citizenship and Withdrawal of Passport Facilities." https://commonslibrary.parliament.uk/research-briefings/sn06820/.

Griffiths, John. 1984. "The Division of Labor in Social Control." In *Toward a General Theory of Social Control*, vol. 1: *Fundamentals*, edited by Donald Black, 37–70. New York: Academic Press.

Hickman, Mary J., Lyn Thomas, Sara Silvestri, and Henri Nickels. 2011. "*Suspect Communities?" Counter-Terrorism Policy, the Press, and the Impact on Irish and Muslim Communities in Britain*. London: London Metropolitan University.

Honig, Bonnie. 2003. "A Legacy of Xenophobia: A Response to David Cole's 'Their Liberties, Our Security.'" *Boston Review*, http://bostonreview.net/archives/BR27.6/honig.html.

Joas, Hans. 2008a. "Human Dignity: The Religion of Modernity?" In *Do We Need Religion? On the Experience of Self-Transcendence*, 133–147. Boulder, CO: Paradigm.

Joas, Hans. 2008b. "Punishment and Respect: The Sacralization of the Person and Its Endangerment." *Journal of Classical Sociology* 8: 159–177.

Lukes, Steven. 1969. "Durkheim's 'Individualism and the Intellectuals.'" *Political Studies* 17, no. 1: 14–30.

Lukes, Steven. 1973. *Emile Durkheim: His Life and Work*. London: Allen Lane.

Lukes, Steven, and Devyani Prabhat. 2012. "Durkheim on Law and Morality: The Disintegration Thesis." *Journal of Classical Sociology* 12, no. 3–4: 363–383.

Lukes, Steven, and Andrew Scull, eds. 1983. *Durkheim and the Law*. Oxford: Martin Robertson.

Lukes, Steven, and Andrew Scull, eds. 2013. *Durkheim and the Law*. New York: Macmillan.

Mars, Leonard. 2016. "Reflections of an Atheist Jew." *Sociology and Anthropology* 4, no. 1: 37–42.

Prabhat, Devyani. 2020. "Political Context and Meaning of British Citizenship: Cancellation as a National Security Measure." *Law, Culture and the Humanities* 16, no. 2: 294–312.

Prosser, Tony. 2006. "Regulation and Social Solidarity." *Journal of Law and Society* 33, no. 3: 364–387.
Ramraj, Victor V. 2006. "Counter-Terrorism Policy and Minority Alienation: Some Lessons from Northern Ireland." *Singapore Journal of Legal Studies* (Dec.): 385–404.
Spitzer, Steven. 1975. "Punishment and Social Organization: A Study of Durkheim's Theory of Penal Evolution." *Law & Society Review* 9, no. 4: 613–638.
Stumpf, Juliet. 2006. "The Crimmigration Crisis: Immigrants, Crime, and Sovereign Power." *American University Law Review* 56, no. 2: 367–419.
Watts Miller, William. 1988. "Durkheim and Individualism." *The Sociological Review* 36, no. 4: 647–673.
Woods, Chris, and Alice Ross. 2013. "Former British Citizens Killed by Drone Strikes after Passports Revoked." *The Bureau of Investigative Journalism*, February 27, 2013. https://www.thebureauinvestigates.com/stories/2013-02-27/former-british-citizens-killed-by-drone-strikes-after-passports-revoked.

CHAPTER 16

ÉMILE DURKHEIM AND THE SOCIOLOGY OF RELIGION

MATTHIAS KOENIG

AFTER years of relative neglect, religion has moved back to the center of theoretical debates in sociology. The emergence of new religious movements, the rise of fundamentalism and religious nationalism, and contentious politics of religious diversity across the globe have called into question grand narratives of secular modernity. Long enjoying paradigmatic status in the discipline, orthodox secularization theory assumed that modernity would entail a decline of religious beliefs, a privatization of religious practices, and increased functional differentiation of religion from politics and other social systems (see Casanova 1994). Refuting the inevitability of these processes, revisionist sociologists of religion have shifted attention to the historically contingent, culturally variegated, and globally entangled interplay of religious traditions with modern nation-states, civil societies, capitalist markets, and international law (for reviews, see Ebaugh 2002; Gorski and Altınordu 2008; Smith 2008; Edgell 2012). In doing so, they have contributed to sociology's critical revision of modernization theory.

Revising secularization theory has implied revisiting the sociology of religion as formulated during the discipline's foundational period. One of its most prominent classics, next to Max Weber, is Émile Durkheim (1858–1917). In his late book *Les formes élémentaires de la vie religieuse* (1912), the only one translated into English during his lifetime (1915), he formulated a highly influential theory of the sacred, its relation to society, and its impact on morality and knowledge. Devoting substantial space of his school's flagship journal, *L'Année sociologique* (AS [1896–1912]), to the sociology of religion (*sociologie religieuse*), he carved out an intellectual space for that subfield in French academia, and his repeated interventions in French public debates over secularism (*laïcité*) attest to early sociology's acute interest in the fate of religion in modern society.

How does Durkheim's *sociologie religieuse*, which has had such enduring influence in anthropology and religious studies (for review, see Pickering 2007; Paden 2011), relate to the revisionist sociology of religion? Is it just another version of obsolete narratives of secular modernity or does it offer analytical tools to grasp the reconfigurations of religion in the twenty-first century? To address these questions, the present chapter proceeds in two steps. First, it reviews how the "New Durkheim" as recovered by the recent historiography of classical sociology defined, explained, and assessed religion. Second, after acknowledging Durkheim's ambivalent legacy in the sociology of religion and cultural sociology more broadly, it discusses its potential and limitations for analyzing the persistence and the production of collective religious forms in a global age.

Theorizing the Sacred in a Secular Age: Durkheim's Sociology of Religion

Long dismissed as a positivist, as a hopelessly holistic social theorist, and as a staunch proponent of moral conservatism, Durkheim has attracted renewed attention among sociologists since the 1970s. Contextual readings of early sociology have generated nuanced interpretations of his positional moves in the academic field (Clark 1973; Lukes 1973; Besnard 1983; Leroux 1998; Jones 1999). At the same time, archival material including his letters, lecture notes, and unpublished manuscripts (e.g., Karady 1975) has led to better appreciation of the collaborative nature of *L'Année sociologique* and has cast his entire oeuvre in novel light. Decades of historiographical research have uncovered a "New Durkheim" whose situated writings helped shape the contours of early French sociology (Strenski 2006; Fournier 2007).

Spearheaded by Pickering's editorial and exegetical work (Pickering 1975, 1984), scholars have also reappreciated Durkheim's sociology of religion. Biographically, they have explored his Jewishness, relating his religious sensitivity to his ambivalent identity as son of a rabbi (e.g., Fields 1995: xxx) and situating his academic ambitions in Reform Judaism's debates over assimilation and rising anti-Semitism (Strenski 1997; Goldberg 2011). Intellectually, they have not only tracked his dialogue with British anthropologists of religion but also scrutinized less familiar sources such as his teacher Numa Denis Fustel de Coulanges's religious history of ancient Rome (Jones 1993) or Albert Mathiez's study of French revolutionary cults (Tiryakian 1988). Institutionally, they have explored how Durkheim's promotion of sociology intersected with French university reforms, such as disciplinary reconfigurations of the *Nouvelle Sorbonne* and transformations within the fifth section for religious studies (*sciences religieuses*) at the *Ecole pratique des hautes études* (Strenski 2006: 181–228; Fournier 2007: 259).

Yet the pivotal context for Durkheim's sociology of religion is political (Müller 1993; Jones 1999: 9–44; Riley 2010: 37–55). From its inception in 1870, the Third French Republic was afflicted by intense conflict that pitted republican secularists against Catholic reactionaries. Aiming to break Catholicism's hegemony over public life, republicans pursued a policy of secularism (*laïcité*), implemented in Jules Ferry's reform of public school curricula (1882), in the overhaul of the teaching body (1886), the fight against religious orders (1900–1904), and eventually in the law separating church and state (1905). What has been called the "war of the two Frances" (Poulat 1987), featuring both Catholic assaults on Jews, Protestants, and Free Thinkers and repressive anticlericalism under the government of Émile Combes (1902–1906), only ended with the *union sacrée* at the onset of World War I. The French culture wars provided the background for Durkheim's recruitment as professor for pedagogics and social sciences in Bordeaux (1887), where he founded a secularist student union (*La jeunesse laïque*), as well as for his appointment to the chair vacated by Ferdinand Buisson, one of the major architects of French *laïcité*, at the Sorbonne (1902). Durkheim repeatedly defended the republican cause, notably at the height of the famous Dreyfus Affair, and he lectured continuously on secular morality (*morale laïque*) in Bordeaux and Paris. Arguably, his lifelong project of restituting the social bond (*lien social*) not by postulating moral principles—as in the neo-Kantian rationalism of Charles Renouvier—but by grounding them in the empirical study of social facts (*faits sociaux*), including "religious facts" (*faits religieux*), was an attempt to resolve the Third Republic's deep moral and political crisis.

Different emphases on these biographical, intellectual, institutional, and political contexts have led scholars to different interpretations of Durkheim's sociology of religion. Some emphasize discontinuity between an early, positivist and a later, idealist stage in his thinking, citing the "revelation" he self-confessedly had about religion's essential role, when reading William Robertson Smith's *The Religion of the Semites* and preparing his first lecture course on the sociology of religion in 1894/95 (Parsons [1937] 1968: 409n; Lukes 1973: 237–244; Alexander 1982: 235). Others stress his continued interest in, and consistent approach to, religion as eminently social fact—from his earliest reviews of Herbert Spencer and Jean-Marie Guyau to his last unfinished manuscript on morality (Pickering 1984: 51–52; Wallwork 1985; Rawls 2004: 322; Tarot 2008: 263). Without settling that controversy, it seems safe to say that his sociology of religion developed into a full-fledged theory of the sacred through various transitional periods (Pickering 1984: 51–52; Fournier 2007: 282), while continuously displaying internal tensions and paradoxes (see Willaime in Durkheim [1912] 2008). The following sections, organized in systematic rather than chronological fashion, highlight some of these tensions as articulated in Durkheim's definition, explanation, and assessment of religious facts.

Defining Religion by the Sacred

According to the *Règles de la méthode sociologique* (Durkheim [1895] 2013), the initial task for a sociologist of religion is to define his or her object of research. In one of his first essays published in *L'Année sociologique* (AS 2 [1898]: 1–18 / Durkheim [1898] 1975), Durkheim takes up just that task to define religious facts by delineating a comprehensive set of externally observable phenomena. Bracketing previous preconceptions, he rejects definitions that refer to the supernatural (Edward Tylor) for presupposing a modern notion of nature, and he criticizes those that refer to the idea of gods or spiritual beings (Max Müller) for ignoring religions such as Buddhism, Jainism, or totemism. Instead, he starts from ritual or cult (*culte*) understood as practice concerned with sacred objects, specifying that objects derive their sacredness from beliefs (*croyances*), such as myths and dogmas, that were collectively held due to a sense of obligation. He thus arrives at an initial definition of religious facts as "obligatory beliefs, connected with clearly defined practices which are related to given objects of those beliefs," religions being unified systems of such facts (Durkheim [1898] 1975: 93).

With its emphasis on obligatory beliefs that distinguish religion from both morality (obligatory practices) and science (voluntary beliefs), Durkheim's initial definition prefigures his mature theory of the sacred but partially. He successively developed that theory by systematizing arguments advanced by Henri Hubert and Marcel Mauss in their essays on sacrifice (AS 2 [1897/98]: 29–138) and magic (AS 12 [1902/03]: 1–146) (see Isambert 1976; Jones 2005; Watts Miller 2012). In his opus magnum, *Les formes élémentaires de la vie religieuse*, an elaboration of his 1906/07 Sorbonne lecture on the origins of religion, he modifies his initial definition in three respects. First, he affirms that what truly characterized religion was the radical separation between the sacred and the profane. Second, he refines the concept of the sacred by highlighting its ambiguity of both demanding obligation and eliciting attraction. Third, he distinguishes religious from magical beliefs and practices by relating them to a solidary group. As his well-known definition reads: "A religion is a unified system of beliefs and practices relative to sacred things, that is to say, things set apart and forbidden—beliefs and practices which unite into one single moral community called a Church, all those who adhere to them" (Durkheim [1912] 1995: 44).

Within the classical sociology of religion, Durkheim's theory of the sacred stands out by combining substantial and functional definitions. The former define religion by its content (the supernatural, gods, transcendence, etc.), the latter by the needs it addresses (e.g., ultimate meaning, legitimacy, etc.). Durkheim combines both by identifying the sacred/profane binary as content of religion and social integration as its pivotal function; and he adds a formal component defining religion as a system of beliefs and practices (see Tarot 2008: 208, 684). This composite definition, however, sets his sociology of religion on quite a distinctive track. Treating the sacred/profane binary as universal content of religious beliefs, he downplays the cross-cultural variability of religious worldviews so forcefully analyzed, for instance, in Weber's comparative sociology of religion. Presuming that religious practices always integrate society, he also sidetracks typological distinctions of religious organizations (churches, sects, etc.) and roles (priests, prophets, laity, etc.) as well as different relationships between religious and political authority as explored by Weber and Ernst Troeltsch.[1] In short, unlike the Weberian tradition that situated traditional religions in their historical contexts while emphasizing their distinctiveness from other value spheres, notably politics, Durkheim's theory of the sacred focuses on religion per se and its constitutive function for society (see Tyrell 2008). This focus, deeply rooted in his larger project of resolving the Third Republic's moral and political crisis, also undergirds his sociological explanation of the sacred.

Explaining the Sacred by Society

In explaining the social origins and functions of religion per se, Durkheim follows the evolutionist paradigm of his time. From his essays on incest prohibition (AS 1 [1898]:

1–70), totemism (*AS* 5 [1902]: 82–121), and collective representations (*AS* 6 [1903]: 1–72) onward, he turns to "primitive," morphologically simple societies to dissect the most elementary religious beliefs and practices. As he argues in *Formes*, the most archaic religious system was neither animism (Tylor) nor naturism (Müller) but totemism as described in Baldwin Spencer's and Francis J. Gillen's famed ethnographies of Central Australian Aboriginal tribes (1899 and 1904). In his detailed analysis of Australian totemism, Durkheim advances the theoretical claim that religious beliefs and practices symbolically represented and ritually revitalized society.

Durkheim starts his analysis of totemistic *beliefs* from the observation that the Aboriginals attributed sacred character to clan names, emblems, and ritual instruments, to animals and plants, and to parts of the human body, thus constituting an entire cosmological system. Instead of deducing these beliefs from previous religions (Tylor) or reducing them to magical thought (Frazer), he insists on treating them as elementary forms of religion. For the multiplicity of sacred things found their unity in the quasi-divine principle of the totem, which symbolically represented an impersonal force similar to the Melanesians' *mana*. Durkheim's key sociological claim is that "the god of the clan, the totemic principle, can be none other than the clan itself, but the clan transfigured and imagined in the physical form of the plant or animal that serves as totem" (Durkheim [1912] 1995: 208). A force constraining and empowering the individual, the sacred was thus homologous to society. In fact, it also emerged from society, more precisely from experiences of "collective effervescence" that characterized Aboriginals' gatherings (*corroboree*) periodically interrupting their everyday economic life.

Whereas totemistic beliefs symbolically represented society, totemistic *practices* ensured its ritual revitalization. This holds particularly for the positive cult, which—unlike the negative cult—did not just separate the sacred from the profane but also made it accessible. The Aboriginals' *intichiuma*, a quasi-sacrificial rite combining offerings with alimentary communion, facilitated contact among the clan members and regenerated their shared collective consciousness. Without such positive cults, be they sacrificial, mimetic, or commemorative, the clan would cease to exist—in the minds of its members that is. Explaining the sacred sociologically, Durkheim thus advances both a genetic and a functionalist explanation of religion.

> However complex the outward manifestations of religious life may be, its inner essence is simple, and one and the same. Everywhere it fulfills the same need and derives from the same state of mind. In all its forms, its object is to lift man above himself and to make him live a higher life than he would if he obeyed only his individual impulses. The beliefs express this life in terms of representations; the rites organize and regulate its functioning.
>
> (Durkheim [1912] 1995: 417)

Durkheim's sociology of religion amounts to a full-scale theory of society that derives all social institutions—to some limited extent even economic ones (see Steiner

2012)—from an initially religious form. He particularly highlights religion's "practical" and "speculative" functions. In *practical* terms, religion provided the binding force of normativity. Moral facts (*faits moraux*), defined as rules of conduct that were not only obeyed out of obligation but also performed out of desirability, partook in the ambiguity of the sacred (Durkheim [1906] 1953: 36, 45, 70). Legal norms, enforceable through organized sanctions, similarly had a sacred core; penal law emerged from ritual taboo norms, contract law from religious oath formulas, and property law from negative religious rites (Durkheim [1950] 1957: 150–158). In *cognitive* terms, religion delivered the generic quality of conceptual thought. That the categories of understanding, which Kant's transcendental philosophy treated as a priori (time, space, classification, force, causality, and totality), emerged from the sacred/profane binary—hence from society—is indeed a central theme in *Formes*. Some interpreters regard Durkheim's socially based epistemology, according to which shared knowledge is formed through enacted practices, even as key to his entire oeuvre (Rawls 2004).

From its publication to its centenary, Durkheim's *Formes* has elicited celebratory comments but also sharp criticism, whether for its misinterpretation of ethnographic sources or for its dogmatic atheism (see notably Arnold van Gennep [1913] and Gaston Richard [1923] in Pickering 1975: 205–208, 228–276; see also Hausner 2013; *Archives de sciences sociales des religions* 159 [2012]). Indeed, Durkheim had to defend his *Formes* on several occasions. To his fellow philosophers, he anchored his genetic explanation of religion in the duality of human nature that consisted of individual as well as collective consciousness, the latter a fruit of the communion of minds (Durkheim [1914] 1975). Addressing fellow republicans, associated by Buisson in the *Union de libres penseurs et de libres croyants pour la culture morale* (Union of Free Thinkers and Free Believers for Moral Culture), he clarified the primary function of religion as consisting in the "dynamogenic influence it exercises on the conscience" (Durkheim [1914/1919] 1975: 184). Religion per se was not only inherent in the human condition but, due to its "dynamogenic" character, met a key functional requirement of any society.

Yet despite these self-explications, two major conceptual tensions within his theory of the sacred remain largely unresolved. First, Durkheim's very notion of the sacred oscillates between "hot" and "cold" moments, between the emotionally intense experiences of sociality, on the one hand, and the institutionalization of shared beliefs and practices, on the other (Desroche 1969: 85). As a result, Durkheimian *sociologie religieuse* could inspire radically different strands of thought—the phenomenology of the sacred associated with the *Collège de sociologie* but also the structuralist analysis of symbolic systems (see second section). Second, Durkheim's explanation of the sacred oscillates between nonreductionist and reductionist arguments. Thus, he argues against reductionist explanations of religion as a psychologically or materialistically based illusion, by stressing that religion was anchored in real forces, for once even agreeing with American pragmatist William James, whose subjectivist account of those forces he otherwise rejects (Durkheim [1912] 1995: 420). Yet at the same time, he argues that religion misrepresented these forces, transfiguring them in symbols without acknowledging their real social origins as unveiled by modern science. These unresolved tensions intimately relate to Durkheim's paradoxical pursuit of the sacred in secular society.

Searching the Sacred in Secular Society

Preoccupied with the Third Republic's culture wars, Durkheim explicitly motivates his *sociologie religieuse* with a desire to understand "present-day humanity" and its "religious nature" (Durkheim [1912] 1995: 1). Given this motivation, it may seem striking how little empirical research he actually conducted on religious facts of his contemporary society. In *Suicide*, he certainly does discuss confessional suicide statistics in Europe, explaining higher rates among Protestants (compared to Catholics and Jews) with their lack of social cohesion (Durkheim [1897] 1951: 105–125). Occasionally, he also commented upon religious statistics that documented declining rates of baptisms and marriages in France (*AS* 6 [1903]: 550–551). Yet, as Mauss would later regretfully acknowledge, primitive and folk religions remained the Durkheimians' primary empirical research objects.[2]

However, even Durkheim's primitivist project (see Crapanzano 1995) ultimately served to understand the future of religion in modern society. At first glance, his sociology encapsulates key features of orthodox secularization theory. That theory is typically based on the distinction of evolutionary stages and tells what Charles Taylor (2007: 26, 428) calls a "subtraction story," whereby science tears apart the veils of enchantment and releases social institutions from religious tutelage. Such a stage consciousness most pronouncedly underlies Durkheim's *Division of Labor*. "Mechanical" solidarity as expressed in penal laws, which were rooted in a religious collective consciousness (e.g., sacrilege prohibitions), characterized primitive, segmentary societies (Durkheim [1893/1902] 1984: 94). Modern, differentiated societies, by contrast, developed an "organic" solidarity where restitutive laws facilitated individuals' cooperation without requiring shared religious beliefs any longer. As Durkheim unambiguously states, "if there is one truth that history has incontrovertibly settled, it is that religion extends over an ever diminishing area of social life" (119). That revealed religions were irreversibly losing their practical as well as speculative functions remained Durkheim's conviction—even long after his own "revelation." Prepared by Christianity's inward faith, and accelerated by the Protestant Reformation, behavioral obligations toward God were giving way to secular morality, and dogmatic beliefs were being superseded by science as the more accurate representation of natural and social reality (Durkheim [1912] 1995: 432).

Politically, Durkheim's secularization theory translates into a committed defense of republican *laïcité*. Speaking as public sociologist, he welcomed the Combes government's anticlericalism (Durkheim [1904] 1973: 60). When discussing the draft law separating church and state, he supported abolishing the Concordat by creating decentralized cult associations (*associations cultuelles*). Bemoaning that "the church was, in sociological perspective, a monster" ("L'Église, au point de vue sociologique, est un monstre") (Durkheim [1905] 1975: 166), he expected the law to unleash natural processes of internal differentiation hitherto repressed by the church hierarchy. His position was actually more rigorously secularist than the eventually adopted law that, in its liberally amended Article 4, would leave the organizational unity of the Catholic Church intact (Baubérot 2008). An assertive secularism also permeates Durkheim's Sorbonne lecture course on moral education (1902/03). While justifying the introduction of secular morality (*morale laïque*) in French public schools with arguments of historical necessity, he criticizes its half-hearted implementation and lack of inspiration. Educators should not just strip religious allegories away from morality, but they should replace them with "rational substitutes" (Durkheim [1925] 1961: 9). Moreover, they should complement the two traditional elements of morality—discipline and group attachment—with a third, purely secular element, namely human autonomy (121).

Yet Durkheim's assertive secularism paradoxically translates into a search for new forms of the sacred and its "dynamogenic" force. In his short response to an international survey on the future of religion, Durkheim thus claims that while traditional religious forms were dissolving ("Il paraît de toute évidence que nous assistons à la dissolution d'une forme religieuse"; Durkheim [1907] 1975: 169), modern secular society would generate novel religious forms. He speculates that these forms would fully embrace rationalism and hence articulate the real forces experienced in religion more directly ("Tout ce que l'on peut présumer, c'est que [les formes religieuses de l'avenir] seront encore plus pénétrées de rationalité que les religions même les plus rationnelles d'aujourd'hui, et que le sens social, qui a toujours été l'âme des religions, s'y affirmera plus directement et plus expressément que par le passé, sans se voiler de mythes et de symboles"; 170). Against utilitarian thinkers (e.g., Spencer) and liberal Protestants (e.g., Sabatier), he stresses that these forms did not amount to a privatization of religion but were thoroughly collective and public (Durkheim [1912] 1995: 43). Crucially, unlike Comte, whose positivist religion he regards as artificial, he expects these new religious forms to emerge spontaneously from within society, notably among the working classes (Durkheim [1914/1919] 1975: 187).

What for Durkheim comes closest to a modern form of religion is the sacredness of the human person (*personne humaine*) emerging in the French Revolution and being reaffirmed in the Third Republic. Already in his early writings, Durkheim interprets the revolutionary principles of 1789, albeit false as scientific propositions, as "a religion which has had its martyrs and apostles, which has profoundly moved the masses, and which, after all, has given birth to great things" (Durkheim [1890] 1973: 35). At the height of the Dreyfus Affair, he justifies the intellectuals' principled defense of individual rights against those misinterpreting the latter as egoistic utilitarianism. The moral individualism, philosophically conceived in the eighteenth century (Kant, Rousseau) and politically realized in republican constitutions and rights declarations, attributed sacred quality not to the individual self, but to the human person and thus to humanity. In modern differentiated societies, "this religion of humanity, of which the individualist ethic is the rational expression, is the only one possible" (Durkheim [1898] 1973: 51; see also Durkheim [1893/1902] 1984: 122). The sacredness of the human person underlay the third element of secular morality (Durkheim [1925] 1961: 107), and it was legally enshrined in rights to life, liberty, and equality (Durkheim [1950] 1957).

Interpreters disagree whether Durkheim's religion of humanity strictly qualifies as religion under Durkheim's own theory of the sacred (for review, see Isambert 1992; Karsenti 2006: 78–82). Some regard his attempt to explicate the universalistic ideals of human dignity and rights in religious terms as a rhetorical move to deflect the criticism of anti-intellectual conservatives during the French culture wars. Others regard him as a true believer in these sacred ideals, and yet others stress that, compared to the revolutionary cults studied by Mathiez, the cult of the individual seemed to Durkheim as lacking the emotional heat necessary to revitalize society. Aware of living through times of crisis and transition, Durkheim articulated ambivalent stances vis-à-vis the religion of humanity at best. In *Formes*, he tellingly ends his pursuit of the sacred in a secular age on a prophetic note:

> In short, the former gods are growing old or dying, and others have not been born. [...] But that state of uncertainty and confused anxiety cannot last forever. A day will come when our societies once again will know hours of creative effervescence during which new ideals will again spring forth and new formulas emerge to guide humanity for a time.
>
> (Durkheim [1912] 1995: 429)

Durkheimian Legacies in the Sociology of Religion

Durkheim's sociology of religion left a massive imprint on French social sciences, not least thanks to Mauss, Hubert, and Hertz, who in their writings on magic, prayer, sin, time, and death continuously refined and revised the sociological theory of the sacred. After Durkheim's death, Mauss launched a new *Année* series (*AS* n.s. [1923–1925]) and, subsequently, established the *Annales sociologiques* (notably series B [1934–1939]), featuring exhaustive review sections on *sociologie religieuse* as well as major essays on rituals among Kabyle Berbers, Chinese kinship relations, and changing religiosity in rural France (see Le Bras 1966). Durkheimian anthropology of religion, firmly anchored in the Institute of Ethnology in Paris, cofounded by Mauss in 1926, informed French colonial sociology of North Africa, the Arab World, and Indochina (see, e.g., Bayly 2000). The *Collège de Sociologie*, initiated by Georges Bataille and Roger Caillois in 1937, radicalized Durkheim's concept of the "dynamogenic" sacred in its order-maintaining and transgressive versions to explore the affective power of modern mass movements such as fascism (see Richardson 1992: 34–36; Riley 2010: 212–219). Claude Lévi-Strauss, in turn, supplemented Durkheimian and Maussian concepts of collective representation with Saussurian linguistic methods to dissect the symbolic structures of human culture (see Tarot 2008: 378–384).

However, Durkheim's theory of the sacred has become startlingly marginal to the contemporary sociology of religion. As elsewhere, the sociology of religion in France became a specialized subfield ever since Gabriel Le Bras founded the *Groupe de sociologie des religions* (GSR 1954, today GSRL) and launched the *Archives de sociologie des religions* (ASR 1956, today ASSR). Empirically, it has left Durkheim's elementary forms of religion largely to anthropologists and historians, instead using sophisticated statistical data and in-depth field studies to compare changes in church membership, worship attendance, beliefs in God, and individual religiosity across Western societies (see Lassave 2012). Theoretically, it has conceptualized religious change by departing considerably from Durkheim's definition of religion whose pretension of universal applicability was seen as masking the historical genealogy of the *sacré* (Isambert 1982). Danièle Hervieu-Léger has criticized the concept of the sacred for bringing "more confusion than clarity into the debate on religious modernity" (Hervieu-Léger 2000: 50), instead proposing a formal definition of religion as a distinctive mode of believing (*croire*) legitimized by an authoritative tradition. In the Anglo-Saxon literature, sociologists of religion have articulated similar skepticism toward Durkheim's notion of the sacred, advocating a substantial definition of religion as a set of practices oriented toward superhuman powers (Riesebrodt 2010: 78; Smith 2017: 24). Focusing on new cults, religious markets, or ethno-religious identification, the subfield seems to have moved quite far away from Durkheim's theory of the sacred.

At the same time, Durkheimian cultural sociologists, often implicitly subscribing to conventional secularization theory, largely remained disinterested in historical religious traditions. In its micro-sociological version, Erving Goffman, Harold Garfinkel, and Randall Collins mobilized Durkheim's theory of the sacred to explain how interaction rituals, characterized by bodily co-presence, shared attention focus, and common mood, generate the collective effervescence that sustains sacred symbols, moral norms, group solidarity, and emotional energy (Collins 2004: 48). In its macro-sociological version, Jeffrey Alexander and others read Durkheim's late sociology of religion as "structural hermeneutics" uncovering societies' meaning systems as built around binaries of sacred/profane, pure/polluted, or good/evil (e.g., Alexander 1988; Alexander and Smith 2005); the legal system, in particular, appears in Durkheimian fashion to rest on sacred foundation (Sarat et al. 2007). However, absent sustained empirical or theoretical scrutiny of traditional religions and their contemporary reconfigurations, this cultural sociology of the sacred (Lynch 2012) has remained relatively detached from the aforementioned developments in the sociology of religion.

Given this ambivalent legacy, how does Durkheim's theory of the sacred relate to the contemporary revisionist sociology of religion? On the one hand, its inherent tensions and paradoxes, notably its inbuilt "subtraction story" of secularization (see first section), seem to stand at odds with the current vitality, public visibility, and political contestation of religious traditions. On the other hand, it offers analytical tools that sensitize to the persistence and production of collective religious forms, thus contributing to the revision of orthodox secularization theory. Durkheim's project of restituting the social bond (*lien social*) particularly resonates with the search for shared values in religiously diverse societies, arguably one of the most pressing political challenges across the globe. The following sections highlight some Durkheimian perspectives in the revisionist sociology of religion, arguing that they require closer integration with Weberian legacies in the field to grasp religious reconfigurations in the twenty-first century.

Persistence of the Sacred in Multiple Modernities

A major strand in the revisionist sociology of religion focuses on the persistence of elementary and other forms of religious belief and practice in "multiple modernities" (Smith 2008: 1569). Orthodox secularization theorists typically assumed modernization processes to converge in the decline of religious belief. In an ingenious adaptation of Durkheim, for instance, Jürgen Habermas interpreted cultural rationalization as a "linguistification of the sacred," whereby communicative action took the burden of social integration previously guaranteed by religious myths and rituals (Habermas 1987: 77–111; for a critique, see Casanova 1994: 231). By contrast, revisionist sociologists of religion emphasize the persistence of historically contingent and culturally divergent religious traditions, thus sensitizing to the inherent cultural diversity of today's global age.

Most important in the search for persisting religious layers is the debate over what German philosopher Karl Jaspers dubbed the "Axial Age," the period around the mid-first millennium BCE when historic religions emerged across Afro-Eurasia. Unlike preaxial religion of tribal societies and archaic kingdoms, historic religions such as Confucianism, Hinduism, Buddhism, Greek philosophy, Judaism, Christianity, and Islam featured greater reflexivity, a radical distinction of transcendent and immanent orders, and distinctive visions of "world rejection." A rich comparative literature pioneered by Shmuel N. Eisenstadt has studied sociological preconditions for the axial breakthrough and has explored how, carried by a new stratum of intellectual elites, it generated novel modes of political accountability, created conflicts between orthodoxy and heterodoxy, and accelerated dynamics of civilizational change. As this literature suggests, different axial religions have persistently shaped political centers, collective identities, and protest movements, thus sustaining multiple varieties of modernity's cultural and political program (Eisenstadt 2003, vol. 2).

Evidently, the debate on axial religions and multiple modernities draws most heavily on Weber's comparative sociology of world religions. However, scholars have also started mobilizing Durkheimian analytical tools to identify persisting religious beliefs and practices across modern societies. The most prominent proponent is Robert Bellah, who, in his mature theory of religious evolution, draws on Durkheim's definition of religion to specify the sacred as "realm of non-ordinary reality" with which humans engage through various forms of religious representation (Bellah 2011: 1, 11). He bolsters Durkheim's sociological explanation of religion with insights from neuroscience and evolutionary biology about the phylogenetic primacy of ritual. What cognitive scientist Merlin Donald called "episodic," "mimetic," and "mythical culture" corresponded to elementary forms of religious representation found in tribal societies such as the

Australian Walbiri (Bellah 2011: 146). Despite the emergence of a "theoretic culture" during the Axial Age (Bellah 2011: 273), these deep-seated layers of human culture, where religious and political community are coextensive, continued to permeate modernity, for instance, in what Taylor (2007: 455) calls "paleo-Durkheimian" social forms.

The Durkheimian tradition not only sensitizes to the persistence of preaxial forms of religious representation, however, but also contributes more than generally acknowledged to capturing the diversity of (axial) civilizational trajectories. After all, early studies on the *literati*'s official religion in ancient China (Marcel Granet), on the Indian caste system (Célestin Bouglé), and on the historical anthropology of ancient Greece (Louis Gernet) took strong inspiration from Durkheim's sociology of religion. Together with Mauss, Durkheim himself actually ventured the possibility of a comparative civilizational sociology (AS 12 [1913]: 46–50; see Arjomand 2010: 365). The *Année* group's proto-structuralist approach to preaxial as well as axial societies, while tacitly presuming European colonialism and benefiting from its supply of raw data, can therefore help reorient comparative sociology away from narratives of civilizational progress (Kurasawa 2013) and, by implication, revise grand narratives of secular modernity.

Productions of the Sacred and Civil Religions in a Global Age

Other important strands in the revisionist sociology of religion focus on the production of novel religious forms. For a long time, functional differentiation of religion from other social systems, notably politics, was held to entail its privatization; if anything, modern societies generated highly individualized forms of religiosity variably called "invisible religion" (Thomas Luckmann), "spirituality" (Paul Heelas), "believing without belonging" (Grace Davie), or "post-Durkheimian" belief (Taylor 2007: 487). Without denying the prevalence of these forms in parts of the world, revisionist sociologists of religion have added novel insights into thoroughly collective religious practices, ranging from quotidian lived religion to public theologies and fundamentalist movements (for review, see Edgell 2012: 253). Responding to the challenge of religious diversity, two lines of empirical inquiry have taken inspiration from Durkheim's pursuit of the sacred, while incorporating Weberian insights into the variable relationship between religious and political authority, church and state.

The *first* line rectifies modernist and secularist biases in the nationalism literature, which long tended to regard the imagined community of the nation as superseding or replacing traditional religions. The (sometimes violent) rise of religious nationalisms in countries such as India or Sri Lanka, Israel or Turkey has prompted scholars to analyze *exclusionary* forms of sacralizing the nation (for reviews, see Friedland 2001; Brubaker 2012; Gorski and Türkmen-Dervişoğlu 2013). They draw on Durkheim in regarding the nation as "sacred communion of the people" with its own symbols and rituals (Smith 2003: 19–43). Yet at the same time, they acknowledge that historical religious traditions, by virtue of narrative prototypes (e.g., "chosen people"), ritual templates (e.g., "sacrifice"), and codes of collective identity, provide cultural repertoires for modern nationalism (Gorski 2000). Its *inclusionary* forms, by contrast, are explored in reinvigorated debates on "civil religion." Originating in Rousseau's political philosophy, that concept was famously forged by Bellah in his analysis of American founding myths which, while drawing on various denominational traditions, provided a nondenominational and hence integrative sacred center for a pluralistic political community (Bellah 1975; for a similar analysis of the British monarchy, see Shils and Young 1953). Recent scholarship has explored how American civil religion with its characteristic fusion of biblical prophecy and civic republicanism differs from polarizing currents of religious nationalism and radical secularism (Gorski 2017). It has likewise detected civil religions in countries such as China (Zhe 2013), Turkey (Kucukcan 2010), and, last but not least, France where collective imaginations have long merged both republican and Catholic traditions (Willaime 1993).[3] While all these analyses take up Durkheim's theory of the sacred, however, they eschew its reductionist and secularist tendencies, treating sacralizations of the nation as intricately intertwined with hardwired power struggles among religious and nonreligious actors over symbolic boundaries of the polity and over control over the state apparatus.

The *second* line of empirical inquiry focuses on productions of the sacred under conditions of globalization. Revisions of orthodox secularization theory owe indeed heavily to globalization studies and their insights on intercivilizational encounters, the invention of "world religions," and the formation of transnational religious communities facilitated by mission, mass media, and migration (see notably Robertson 1992; Juergensmeyer 2005; Beyer 2006). Within this broader literature, Durkheim's vision of a "religion of humanity" has inspired neo-institutionalist sociologists to scrutinize the global rise of beliefs and practices that invest the human individual with legitimate actorhood (Meyer 2010). They have amply documented how ideals of human dignity and human rights are promoted by inter- and nongovernmental organizations and institutionalized in international conventions, national constitutions, public policies, school curricula, and textbooks, thus amounting to a "civil religion for world society" (Elliot 2007; Cole 2012). Moving beyond Durkheim, however, scholars treat such global processes of sacralizing the human person as interacting with axial religious traditions that provided cultural repertoires of universalistic values (e.g., Stamatov 2013) and affected their local adaption (Swidler 2010).

Theorizing Religious Sacralization Processes

Capturing the persistent influence of preaxial and axial religions upon, and the production of novel religious forms within, global modernity ultimately calls for closer conceptual integration of Durkheim's *sociologie religieuse* with Weber's comparative sociology of religion. The systematic challenge lies in theorizing how the binaries of sacred/profane and transcendence/immanence relate to each other, and how both relate to the modern distinction of religion and the secular (see Casanova 2008).

To meet this challenge, recent scholarship has pursued different analytical strategies. One starts with elementary processes of sacralization. For instance, tempting objects acquire sacred status when being invested with absolute moral qualities in situations where temptation collides with tradition (Marshall 2010: 68). On such an account, religions appear as broader sets of elementary practices of singularization (Taves 2009). Another strategy is to cross-tabulate Durkheimian and Weberian distinctions to detect typological "modalities of the sacred," whether religious or secular (Mellor and Shilling 2014: 21). The most ambitious strategy is to canvas an analytical framework that mobilizes Durkheimian as well as Weberian tools to explain theoretically distinctive cultural processes of sacralization. This strategy is prominently pursued in Hans Joas's (2017) pragmatist theory of religion. Joas starts from the premise that humans spontaneously attributed qualities of the sacred to situational elements in which they made emotionally intensive "experiences of self-transcendence," Durkheim's collective effervescence being just one item in a phenomenologically variegated repertoire (Joas 2017: 434). Attributions of sacredness varied by the form of their semiotic articulation, ranging from prereflexive, situation-specific symbols (as in Durkheim's *Formes*) to reflexive, situation-independent ideals including transcendent visions (as in universal religions). The former typically entailed a "self-sacralization of the collectivity" (453), but it was undermined by the latter that emerged in historically contingent moments of creative ideal-formation during the Axial Age and characterized as "reflexive sacralization." Joas's analytical framework sensitizes to cultural processes of sacralization, including notably the genesis of values of human dignity and rights captured in Durkheim's "religion of humanity" (Joas 2013), while perceptively relating them to religio-political power configurations so central to the legacy of Weber (and Troeltsch).

Disentangling various processes of sacralization, all these analytical strategies ultimately contribute to revising grand narratives of secular modernity and attest to the analytical payoff of conceptually integrating classical legacies of the sociology of religion. They illustrate that even under vastly different political circumstances than those of the French Third Republic, the Durkheim tradition offers relevant insights into the complex interplay of emotion and embodiment, cognition and normativity in forging societies' sacred bonds. Despite its internal tensions and despite its undeniable limitations, it seems that the "new" Durkheim theory of the sacred continues to offer powerful tools for the revisionist of sociology.

Notes

1. Mauss, as should be noted, did briefly acknowledge the transformative power of "sects" within both national and universalistic religions (*AS* 8 [1903/04]: 293–295).
2. "[N]ous étudions peut-être trop, les 'primitifs' et pas assez les grandes religions, les nôtres, les mouvements de sentiments et d'idées qui les agitent" (Mauss in *AS* n.s. 2 [1924/25]: 123).
3. Ironically, French civil religion actually turns out to differ starkly from Durkheim's anticlerical position, thus betraying his portrayal as "high priest and theologian of the civil religion of the Third Republic" (Bellah in Durkheim 1973: x).

REFERENCES

Alexander, Jeffrey C. 1982. *Theoretical Logic in Sociology*, vol. 2: *The Antinomies of Classical Thought: Marx and Durkheim*. Berkeley: University of California Press.

Alexander, Jeffrey C., ed. 1988. *Durkheimian Sociology: Cultural Studies*. Cambridge: Cambridge University Press.

Alexander, Jeffrey C., and Phillip Smith, eds. 2005. *The Cambridge Companion to Durkheim*. Cambridge: Cambridge University Press.

Arjomand, Saïd Amir. 2010. "Three Generations of Comparative Sociologies." *European Journal of Sociology* 51 (3): 363–399.

Baubérot, Jean. 2008. "Durkheim und die Debatte um die Laizität." In *Religionskontroversen in Frankreich und Deutschland*, edited by Matthias Koenig and Jean-Paul Willaime, 182–203. Hamburg: Hamburger Edition.

Bayly, Susan. 2000. "French Anthropology and the Durkheimians in Colonial Indochina." *Modern Asian Studies* 34 (3): 581–622.

Bellah, Robert N. 1975. *The Broken Covenant: American Civil Religion in Time of Trial*. New York: Seabury Press.

Bellah, Robert N. 2011. *Religion in Human Evolution: From the Paleolithic to the Axial Age*. Cambridge, MA: Harvard University Press.

Besnard, Philippe, ed. 1983. *The Sociological Domain: The Durkheimians and the Founding of French Sociology*. Cambridge: Cambridge University Press.

Beyer, Peter. 2006. *Religions in Global Society*. London: Routledge.

Brubaker, Rogers. 2012. "Religion and Nationalism: Four Approaches." *Nations and Nationalism* 18 (1): 2–20.

Casanova, José. 1994. *Public Religions in the Modern World*. Chicago: University of Chicago Press.

Casanova, José. 2008. "Public Religions Revisited." In *Religion: Beyond a Concept*, edited by Hent de Vries, 101–119. Fordham, NY: Fordham University Press.

Clark, Terry Nichols. 1973. *Prophets and Patrons: The French University and the Emergence of the Social Sciences*. Cambridge, MA: Harvard University Press.

Cole, Wade M. 2012. "A Civil Religion for World Society: The Direct and Diffuse Effects of Human Rights Treaties, 1981–2007." *Sociological Forum* 27 (4): 937–960.

Collins, Randall. 2004. *Interaction Ritual Chains*. Princeton, NJ: Princeton University Press.

Crapanzano, Vincent. 1995. "The Moment of Prestidigitation: Magic, Illusion, and Mana in the Thought of Emile Durkheim and Marcel Mauss." In *Prehistories of the Future: The Primitivist Project and the Culture of Modernism*, edited by Elazar Barkan and Ronald Bush, 95–113. Stanford, CA: Stanford University Press.

Desroche, Henri. 1969. "Retour à Durkheim? D'un texte peu connu à quelques thèses méconnues." *Archives de sociologie des religions* 27: 79–88.

Durkheim, Émile. (1897) 1951. *Suicide: A Study in Sociology*. Translated by John A. Spaulding and George Simpson. New York: Free Press.

Durkheim, Émile. (1906) 1953. "The Determination of Moral Facts." In Émile Durkheim, *Sociology and Philosophy*, translated by D. F. Pocock, 35–62. New York: Free Press.

Durkheim, Émile. (1950) 1957. *Professional Ethics and Civic Morals*. Translated by Cornelia Brookfield. London: Routledge & Kegan Paul.

Durkheim, Émile. (1925) 1961. *Moral Education: A Study in the Theory and Application of the Sociology of Education*. Translated by E. K. Wilson and H. Schnurer. New York: Free Press.

Durkheim, Émile. 1973. *On Morality and Society.* Edited by Robert N. Bellah. Chicago: University of Chicago Press.
Durkheim, Émile. (1890) 1973. "The Principles of 1789 and Sociology." In *Emile Durkheim: On Morality and Society*, edited by Robert N. Bellah, 34–42. Chicago: University of Chicago Press.
Durkheim, Émile. (1898) 1973. "Individualism and the Intellectuals." In *Emile Durkheim: On Morality and Society*, edited by Robert N. Bellah, 43–57. Chicago: University of Chicago Press.
Durkheim, Émile. (1904) 1973. "The Intellectual Elite and Democracy." In *Emile Durkheim: On Morality and Society*, edited by Robert N. Bellah, 58–60. Chicago: University of Chicago Press.
Durkheim, Émile. (1898) 1975. "Concerning the Definition of Religious Phenomena." In *Durkheim on Religion*, edited by W. S. F. Pickering, 74–99. London: Routledge & Kegan Paul.
Durkheim, Émile. (1905) 1975. "Débat sur les conséquences religieuses de la séparation des Églises et de l'État." In Émile Durkheim, *Textes*, vol. 2: *Religion, morale, anomie*, edited by Victor Karady, 165–168. Paris: Editions de Minuit.
Durkheim, Émile. (1907) 1975. "Remarque sur l'avenir de la religion." In Émile Durkheim, *Textes*, vol. 2: *Religion, morale, anomie*, edited by Victor Karady, 169–170. Paris: Editions de Minuit.
Durkheim, Émile. (1914) 1975. "Le dualisme de la nature humaine et ses conditions sociales." In Émile Durkheim, *Textes*, vol. 2: *Religion, morale, anomie*, edited by Victor Karady, 314–332. Paris: Editions de Minuit.
Durkheim, Émile. (1914/1919) 1975. "Contribution to Discussion 'Religious Sentiment at the Present Time.'" In *Durkheim on Religion*, edited by W. S. F. Pickering, 181–189. London: Routledge & Kegan Paul.
Durkheim, Émile. (1893/1902) 1984. *The Division of Labour in Society.* Translated by W. D. Halls. London: Macmillan.
Durkheim, Émile. (1912) 1995. *The Elementary Forms of Religious Life.* Translated by Karen E. Fields. New York: Free Press.
Durkheim, Émile. (1912) 2008. *Les formes élémentaires de la vie religieuse. Le système totémique en Australie.* Paris: Presses universitaires de France.
Durkheim, Émile. (1895) 2013. *The Rules of Sociological Method and Selected Texts on Sociology and Its Method.* Edited by Steven Lukes and translated by W. D. Halls. New York: Free Press.
Ebaugh, Helen Rose. 2002. "Return of the Sacred: Reintegrating Religion in the Social Sciences." *Journal for the Scientific Study of Religion* 41 (3): 385–395.
Edgell, Penny. 2012. "A Cultural Sociology of Religion: New Directions." *Annual Review of Sociology* 38: 247–265.
Eisenstadt, Shmuel N. 2003. *Comparative Civilizations and Multiple Modernities.* 2 vols. Leiden and Boston: Brill.
Elliot, Michael A. 2007. "Human Rights and the Triumph of the Individual in World Culture." *Cultural Sociology* 1 (3): 343–363.
Fields, Karen E. 1995. "Religion as an Eminently Social Thing: Translator's Introduction." In Émile Durkheim, *The Elementary Forms of Religious Life*, translated by Karen E. Fields, xvii–lxxiii. New York: Free Press.
Fournier, Marcel. 2007. *Emile Durkheim (1858–1917).* Paris: Fayard.
Friedland, Roger. 2001. "Religious Nationalism and the Problem of Collective Representation." *Annual Review of Sociology* 27: 125–152.

Goldberg, Chad Alan. 2011. "The Jews, the Revolution, and the Old Regime in French Anti-Semitism and Durkheim's Sociology." *Sociological Theory* 29 (4): 248–271.
Gorski, Philip S. 2000. "The Mosaic Moment: An Early Modernist Critique of Modernist Theories of Nationalism." *American Journal of Sociology* 105 (5): 1428–1468.
Gorski, Philip S. 2017. *American Covenant: A History of Civil Religion from the Puritans to the Present*. Princeton, NJ: Princeton University Press.
Gorski, Philip S., and Ateş Altınordu. 2008. "After Secularization?" *Annual Review of Sociology* 34: 55–85.
Gorski, Philip S., and Gülay Türkmen-Dervişoğlu. 2013. "Religion, Nationalism, and Violence: An Integrated Approach." *Annual Review of Sociology* 39: 193–210.
Habermas, Jürgen. 1987. *The Theory of Communicative Action*, vol. 2: *Lifeworld and System: A Critique of Functionalist Reason*. Boston: Beacon Press.
Hausner, Sondra L., ed. 2013. *Durkheim in Dialogue: A Centenary Celebration of* The Elementary Forms of Religious Life. New York: Berghahn Books.
Hervieu-Léger, Danièle. 2000. *Religion as a Chain of Memory*. Cambridge: Polity Press.
Isambert, François-André. 1976. "L'élaboration de la notion de sacré dans l' 'école' durkheimienne." *Archives de sciences sociales des religions* 42: 33–56.
Isambert, François-André. 1982. *Le sens du sacré. Fête et religion populaire*. Paris: Editions de Minuit.
Isambert, François-André. 1992. "Une religion de l'homme? Sur trois interprétations de la religion dans la pensée de Durkheim." *Revue française de sociologie* 33: 443–462.
Joas, Hans. 2013. *The Sacredness of the Person: A New Genealogy of Human Rights*. Washington, DC: Georgetown University Press.
Joas, Hans. 2017. *Die Macht des Heiligen. Eine Alternative zur Geschichte von der Entzauberung*. Berlin: Suhrkamp.
Jones, Robert Alun. 1993. "Durkheim and *La Cité Antique*: An Essay on the Origins of Durkheim's Sociology of Religion." In *Emile Durkheim: Sociologist and Moralist*, edited by Stephen P. Turner, 23–50. London: Routledge.
Jones, Robert Alun. 1999. *The Development of Durkheim's Social Realism*. Cambridge: Cambridge University Press.
Jones, Robert Alun. 2005. "Practices and Presuppositions: Some Questions about Durkheim and *Les Formes élémentaires de la vie religieuse*." In *The Cambridge Companion to Durkheim*, edited by Jeffrey C. Alexander and Philip Smith, 80–100. Cambridge: Cambridge University Press.
Juergensmeyer, Mark, ed. 2005. *Religion in Global Civil Society*. Oxford: Oxford University Press.
Karady, Victor, ed. 1975. *Émile Durkheim: Textes*, vol. 2: *Religion, morale, anomie*. Paris: Editions de Minuit.
Karsenti, Bruno. 2006. *La société en personnes. Etudes durkheimiennes*. Paris: Economica.
Kucukcan, Talip. 2010. "Sacralization of the State and Secular Nationalism: Foundations of Civil Religion in Turkey." *George Washington International Law Review* 41 (4): 963–983.
Kurasawa, Fuyuki. 2013. "The Durkheimian School and Colonialism: Exploring the Constitutive Paradox." In *Sociology and Empire: The Imperial Entanglements of a Discipline*, edited by George Steinmetz, 188–209. Durham, NC: Duke University Press.
Lassave, Pierre. 2012. "Les *Formes* dans les *Archives*. Filiation, refondation, référence." *Archives de sciences sociales des religions* 159: 89–111.

Le Bras, Gabriel. 1966. "Note sur la sociologie religieuse dans *l'Année Sociologique*." *Archives de sociologie des religions* 21: 47–53.

Leroux, Robert. 1998. *Histoire et sociologie en France. De l'histoire-science à la sociologie durkheimienne*. Paris: Presses universitaires de France.

Lukes, Steven. 1973. *Emile Durkheim: His Life and Work*. London: Allen Lane.

Lynch, Gordon. 2012. *The Sacred in the Modern World: A Cultural Sociological Approach*. Oxford: Oxford University Press.

Marshall, Douglas A. 2010. "Temptation, Tradition, and Taboo: A Theory of Sacralization." *Sociological Theory* 28 (1): 64–90.

Mellor, Philip A., and Chris Shilling. 2014. *Sociology of the Sacred: Religion, Embodiment and Social Change*. London: SAGE.

Meyer, John W. 2010. "World Society, Institutional Theories, and the Actor." *Annual Review of Sociology* 36: 1–20.

Müller, Hans-Peter. 1993. "Durkheim's Political Sociology." In *Emile Durkheim: Sociologist and Moralist*, edited by Stephen P. Turner, 95–110. London: Routledge.

Paden, William E. 2011. "Reappraising Durkheim for the Study and Teaching of Religion." In *The Oxford Handbook of the Sociology of Religion*, edited by Peter B. Clarke, 31–47. Oxford: Oxford University Press.

Parsons, Talcott. (1937) 1968. *The Structure of Social Action: A Study in Social Theory with Special Reference to a Group of Recent European Writers*. New York: Free Press.

Pickering, W. S. F., ed. 1975. *Durkheim on Religion*. London: Routledge & Kegan Paul.

Pickering, W. S. F. 1984. *Durkheim's Sociology of Religion: Themes and Theories*. London: Routledge & Kegan Paul.

Pickering, W. S. F. 2007. "Emile Durkheim." In *The Oxford Handbook of Religion and Emotion*, edited by John Corrigan, 438–456. Oxford: Oxford University Press.

Poulat, Émile. 1987. *Liberté, laïcité. La guerre des deux France et le principe de la modernité*. Paris: Cerf & Cujas.

Rawls, Anne Warfield. 2004. *Epistemology and Practice: Durkheim's* The Elementary Forms of Religious Life. Cambridge: Cambridge University Press.

Richardson, Michael. 1992. "Sociology on a Razor's Edge: Configurations of the Sacred at the College of Sociology." *Theory, Culture & Society* 9 (3): 27–44.

Riesebrodt, Martin. 2010. *The Promise of Salvation: A Theory of Religion*. Chicago: University of Chicago Press.

Riley, Alexander Tristan. 2010. *Godless Intellectuals? The Intellectual Pursuit of the Sacred Reinvented*. New York: Berghahn Books.

Robertson, Roland. 1992. *Globalization: Social Theory and Global Culture*. London: SAGE.

Sarat, Austin, Lawrence Douglas, and Martha Merrill Umphrey, eds. 2007. *Law and the Sacred*. Stanford, CA: Stanford University Press.

Shils, Edward A., and Michael Young. 1953. "The Meaning of the Coronation." *Sociological Review* 1 (2): 63–81.

Smith, Anthony D. 2003. *Chosen Peoples: Sacred Sources of National Identity*. Oxford: Oxford University Press.

Smith, Christian. 2008. "Future Directions in the Sociology of Religion." *Social Forces* 86 (4): 1561–1589.

Smith, Christian. 2017. *Religion: What It Is, How It Works, and Why It Matters*. Princeton, NJ: Princeton University Press.

Stamatov, Peter. 2013. *The Origins of Global Humanitarianism: Religion, Empires, Advocacy.* Cambridge: Cambridge University Press.

Steiner, Philippe. 2012. "Religion et économie chez Durkheim. Deux formes de cohésion sociale?" *Archives de sciences sociales des religions* 159: 247–263.

Strenski, Ivan. 1997. *Durkheim and the Jews of France.* Chicago: University of Chicago Press.

Strenski, Ivan. 2006. *The New Durkheim.* New Brunswick, NJ: Rutgers University Press.

Swidler, Ann. 2010. "The Return of the Sacred: What African Chiefs Teach Us about Secularization." *Sociology of Religion* 71 (2): 157–171.

Tarot, Camille. 2008. *Le symbolique et le sacré. Théories de la religion.* Paris: La Découverte.

Taves, Ann. 2009. *Religious Experience Reconsidered: A Building-Block Approach to the Study of Religion and Other Special Things.* Princeton, NJ: Princeton University Press.

Taylor, Charles. 2007. *A Secular Age.* Cambridge, MA: Harvard University Press.

Tiryakian, Edward A. 1988. "Durkheim, Mathiez, and the French Revolution: The Political Context of a Sociological Classic." *European Journal of Sociology* 29 (2): 373–396.

Tyrell, Hartmann. 2008. "Kulturkämpfe in Frankreich und Deutschland und die Anfänge der Religionssoziologie." In *Religionskontroversen in Frankreich und Deutschland*, edited by Matthias Koenig and Jean-Paul Willaime, 97–181. Hamburg: Hamburger Edition.

Wallwork, Ernest. 1985. "Durkheim's Early Sociology of Religion." *Sociological Analysis* 46 (3): 201–217.

Watts Miller, William. 2012. *A Durkheimian Quest: Solidarity and the Sacred.* New York: Berghahn Books.

Willaime, Jean-Paul. 1993. "La religion civile à la française et ses métamorphoses." *Social Compass* 40 (4): 571–580.

Zhe, Ji. 2013. "Return to Durkheim: Civil Religion and the Moral Reconstruction of China." In *Durkheim in Dialogue: A Centenary Celebration of* The Elementary Forms of Religious Life, edited by Sondra L. Hausner, 47–66. New York: Berghahn Books.

CHAPTER 17

DURKHEIM'S AMBIVALENCE TOWARD ART

EDWARD A. TIRYAKIAN AND JOSEFINA CINTRON TIRYAKIAN

INTRODUCTION

PIERRE Bourdieu's *boutade* that "sociology and art do not make good bedfellows" ([1984] 1993: 139) has struck social scientists and humanists as deplorable, but it is a telling point of departure for inquiry, despite efforts by "humanist sociologists" like Robert Nisbet (2002) and Vera Zolberg (1990) to bring the two together. Among the many trails in Europe and in America which in the past have marked exclusion rather than collaboration between the arts and sociology, special attention is due to Émile Durkheim because of his dominant role in the formation and development of sociology as the science of society. In these pages we trace as a primary theme what may be interpreted as Durkheim's ambivalence toward art.

For Émile Durkheim, recently installed at the University of Bordeaux (1887–1888) and who had demonstrated his talents with new courses on sociology and a spate of well-received articles on intellectual currents in the social sciences in Germany, the future held much promise. This, not only for himself but also for sociology becoming a science complementary to history, as he announced in the first volume of his major project, *L'Année sociologique* (Durkheim 1898: II–IV).[1]

Durkheim came alive as a sociologist in the 1890s, one of the great creative periods of the French Third Republic (later known as the Republic of the Professors), which was recovering from the demoralizing double crisis of 1870 (at the hands of Germany and the civil war of the *Communes*). A rising new generation made great advances in the natural sciences: Pierre and Marie Curie and Henri Becquerel in radioactivity, magnetism, and uranium, while Louis Pasteur established his world-famous Pasteur Institute, a center for microbiological research and combating infectious diseases. Positivism, formulated by a "modern" French philosopher, Auguste Comte, became accepted as a key collective evolutionary platform for the nascent social sciences, anchoring Durkheim's sociology. But this was not all to the creative outburst; the last decade of the nineteenth century, extending from 1890 to its seismic crash in 1914, was also the scene of much artistic ferment: Van Gogh, Chagall, Matisse, Cézanne, and Picasso in painting; Maillol and Rodin in sculpture; and Debussy, Schoenberg, Fauré, Saint-Saëns, Stravinsky, Mahler, and Berg in music.

In her introduction to Durkheim's classic *The Elementary Forms of Religious Life*, Karen Fields (1995: xxii) pinpoints turn-of-century Paris as "a place that fizzed with experiments in artistic representation." This is just a short step away from the pregnant "collective effervescence" of the Australian Arunta described in *The Forms*. But before getting there, we need to consider the concept *scandale* introduced by Fields as it applied to both the Parisian artistic scene and Durkheim's theory of the *totem*. Scandale was used to denote artworks or ideas that undermined middle-class values and traditions and consequently led to widespread criticism or, as in the case of works of art, emotional outbursts and even violent reactions from the public. This was so with the tumult that shook the Parisian art scene at century's end as a reaction to avant-garde artistic expressions such as Alfred Jarry's 1896 play *Ubu roi*, a precursor of the theater of the absurd and modernism, Picasso's Cubism (*Les Demoiselles d'Avignon*, 1907), capped in 1913 by the tumultuous world premiere of Diaghilev's Ballets Russes's *Le Sacre du printemps* (The Rite of Spring). In such instances of *scandale*, a riot in the theater was seen as a success for the performance, despite the critics' negative reviews. These violations of societal values and provocation of fractures in social solidarity might have contributed to Durkheim's critical comments of art. However, Durkheim's unorthodox perspective of the *totem* as the ground of religion was also a *scandale* among some in his intellectual peer group, and it was forcefully criticized and rejected (Fields 1995: xx).

As the driving spirit of the *Année sociologique*, how did Durkheim, its undisputed head, organize the materials for the nonscientific creative field, of what may be called "the arts"? He had shown awareness of the need to add a residual category, "Divers," to the five major classificatory types in the first volume (1898). In volume 6 (1903) the residual "Divers" became the seventh section with subsections for Aesthetics, Technology, Linguistics, and Socialism. It is in the following volume 7, published in 1904, that a new head for the subsection "Aesthetics" appears: Charles Lalo. Sandwiched between reviews of Durkheim, Mauss, and Hubert, Lalo (1904) headed Aesthetics with a one hundred–line review of Richard Wallaschek's *Anfänge der Tonkunst*, an enlarged translation of a work published in London as *Primitive Music* (Wallaschek 1893). While praising Wallaschek for his contribution to aesthetics, including the history of instruments, Lalo ends with a gentle criticism: Why has the author, who has so well defended the specific character of music in relation to language, not done the same in relation to *la mesure*? Lalo concluded that not taking into account the latter, which—according to him—should be considered the sociological element par excellence in music, could lead readers to believe that the development of music in itself is not a sociological datum.

Agrégé of philosophy, and Durkheim's student at Bordeaux, where he prepared his doctoral research on scientific musical aesthetics, Charles Lalo seemed well qualified to join Henri Hubert and Marcel Mauss as permanent reviewers of aesthetics. This field of studies was to be his special domain the length of his productive academic career culminating at the Sorbonne as Professor of Aesthetics at the end of World War I.[2] But after this one review, Lalo disappears as reviewer from all subsequent volumes of the journal during Durkheim's lifetime. Hubert returns in volume 8 as the head of the Aesthetics section of the Divers category, and Lalo, in volume 11 (1910), is only listed for his book, *Esquisse d'une esthétique musicale scientifique*. Could it be that Lalo's emphasis on aesthetics jarred Durkheim's primary focus on art's contribution to solidarity? Or was it a reflection of Durkheim's temperament, that he was not "a man to sing the beauty of primitive art" (Hennion [1993] 2015: 22)?[3] Lalo made a comeback when the *Année* resumed publication in the postwar years. A new series appeared briefly for two issues under the faltering leadership of Mauss (volume 1 for 1923/1924 published in 1925) with Lalo listed as a collaborator, contributing extensive reviews of German works. With volume 2 (1924/1925, appearing in 1927) and never completed, an important phase of the sociology of art as a stepchild of the *Année* ended.

It is now time to turn to Durkheim directly to seek a response to a central theme of this chapter: How did Durkheim's ambivalence toward the world of the arts manifest itself? To encapsulate Durkheim's perspective on art, we first consider the place of art in his writings in two major periods: what he said initially while at Bordeaux in his more direct "positivistic" sociological writings (*The Division of Labor*, *Suicide*, and *Moral Education*), and what he said after his professional move to the Sorbonne. There took place his great "cultural turn," manifest in *The Elementary Forms*, exploring the cultural life of the *expérience vécue* of the Australian "primitives" recorded by Spencer and Gillen (1899) in their ethnographic studies, with a focus on belief systems and rituals.

Moral Education and the Arts: The Early Years

In his doctoral dissertation, *The Division of Labor in Society* (1893/1902), Durkheim had little positive to say about the function of art in the moral progress of society: "it is a luxury, [...] outside of the realm of obligation, in the domain of liberty [...] even if it becomes involved in moral phenomena, it is not in itself moral." He added emphatically that in individuals as well as in societies, an intemperate development of aesthetic faculties is "a serious symptom from a moral point of view" (Durkheim 1902: 14).[4] A more balanced view is found after Durkheim's mid-career move to Paris and the Sorbonne.

Recall that at the start of the twentieth century, Durkheim had become a well-known French intellectual in pedagogical and center-left political circles, a reputation enhanced by his activism in the Dreyfus Affair that rocked France in a sustained political crisis (1894–1906). After Ferdinand Buisson, professor of education at the Sorbonne (1896–1902), resigned to enter politics and continue as a Radical Socialist deputy in the National Assembly (eventually receiving the Nobel Peace Prize), he threw his support to Durkheim as his successor. Durkheim was then drafted from Bordeaux to the coveted vacancy in Paris and became professor of education and sociology. Establishing intellectual continuity with his predecessor, Durkheim began his new position with lectures on a subject close to his heart: these were reassembled after his death by a trusted colleague and published in 1925, and reissued in English in 1973 as *Moral Education*.

It should be borne in mind that in this set of lectures Durkheim was addressing an audience of teachers who, in keeping with the reforms of primary education in the Third Republic, would have an important task "for creating not merely a literate electorate, but an electorate steeped in republican"—read "secular"—"principles" (Bergen 1986: 274).[5] Moral education, integral to this task, was a fundamental secularist endeavor, for both republican principles and for Durkheim's stress on social consciousness. Imparting morality to youth was an important foundation of citizenship, necessary for the maintenance of social solidarity and the moral community. How did this impact aesthetics?

Having earlier discussed the important role of the teaching of science in moral education, Durkheim ([1925] 1973: 267) notes the secondary importance of the teaching of art and literature. Being essentially idealistic, art—both beaux arts and literature—qualifies as an instrument of moral education. On the positive side, adds Durkheim, there is a healing power of art that removes us from our ordinary cares yet leads us away from self-centeredness; aesthetic education can hence prepare youth for their moral education. Still, Durkheim cautions, aesthetic education diverges radically from moral education because the domain of the former is not that of reality. Art is not conveyed to us by precepts or concepts, he states, but by our imagination. "The artist's world is the world of images, and the world of images is the world of dreams, of untrammeled mental play" (271). When all is said and done, both art and morality draw out the person from herself, the one links us only to ideals or "mental creations," the other to the real world of the living. Without laboring the point, Durkheim downgrades the artistic for shielding the viewer from seeing people in "their ugliness and wretchedness"—which, he adds, would be necessary "if we want to help them" (271–272). Moral education has practical ends, including the patriotic one of "energetically participating in the common life" (272). Morality is life in earnest (*la vie sérieuse*), the very distance that separates play from work.[6] Moreover, Durkheim further distances himself from playing the game of art: it is not from art that "we learn to do our duty," he admonishes (273). Doing one's duty was indeed a cardinal virtue of secular moral education, and, it might be said, of Durkheim's austere personal code of conduct—a legacy of Kantian ethics that permeated Third Republic intellectuals and was embodied by Durkheim the length of his career.

Near the end of his transitional *Moral Education*, Durkheim voices a softer approach to art by viewing it as having a positive albeit "only a secondary and accessory role in moral education" (267). Art is a game, and games are very much part of life, for we cannot work all the time; we must have leisure, and art is a refined form of play which may otherwise appeal to "gross and selfish and sometimes even brutal instincts, like certain sports" (273). Art implies a certain detachment from the coarsest material interests, adding even a spiritual tinge to our feelings and our will. Still, art retains limited sociological appeal, insufficient to qualify for treatment as a component of *la vie sérieuse*. This might serve as a rationale for the delayed start of reviewing aesthetics in the *Année*.

Newer Approaches to Durkheim and the Arts

Discussions of Durkheim have become greatly enriched in the past generation from new findings in libraries, archives, and letters to and from Durkheim, examination of texts, and new research published in journals like the *Journal of Classical Sociology* and especially *Durkheimian Studies*. Among the many topics which have provided a frame for a specialized treatment of Durkheim is his ambivalence toward the sociology of aesthetics. The question of this reticence in a recognized founder of modern sociology is one that has present relevance as a condition in marginalizing the broad field of aesthetics from attracting young sociologists to study it empirically and theoretically as a bona fide area of specialization in an academic career. To probe more deeply into the etiology of the ambivalence, we need to consider some of the recent studies of Durkheim's ambivalence, as prefatory to an important change in his outlook.

Jean-Paul Callède (2008), a French specialist in the sociology of sports, has explored Durkheim's concern toward the "ludic" in *Moral Education* that also reflects Durkheim's ambivalence toward the aesthetic life. Citing the preface of the second edition of Durkheim's *Division of Labor in Society*, which refers to art as "refractory to everything which resembles obligation because it is the realm of liberty" (Durkheim 1902: 14),[7] Callède infers that Durkheim views the game as breaking humans out from constraints, though moderation is necessary: "The need to play, without any goals for action, only for the pleasure of playing, can only be developed beyond a certain point without losing interest in *la vie sérieuse*" (Durkheim 1902: 219).[8] The latter, Callède notes, is, for Durkheim, basic for the health of the individual and for that of society. The source of Durkheim's ambivalence toward the ludic seems to be that it is superfluous but necessary; this applies equally to art.

Fournier (1987) emphasizes Durkheim's negative views of art: "Durkheim himself was not interested in art at all. For this ascetic intellectual art belongs to the superfluous [...]." And quoting Durkheim, he adds "too large an artistic sensibility is a sickly phenomenon which cannot be generalized without danger to society." Fournier notes that "Durkheim takes art seriously only within the frame of religious sociology which he elaborates in the 1890s and in which he gives primacy to collective representations more extensively treated in the *Elementary Forms*" (5).

A recent collective volume on *Durkheim, the Durkheimians, and the Arts* (Riley et al. 2013) makes readily available some of the most trenchant writings regarding the Durkheimian school, particularly in the neglected area of art. One of the editors, Alexander Riley, provides salient clues to Durkheim's reticence:

> Perhaps if in modernity one could hope to find an art that recaptured the ethos of the whole people and was morally centered in the life of the community, Durkheim might have treated it with more explicit attention, and earlier, than he did. It is precisely insofar as art leads not to integration and social solidarity, which were guiding principles in his life and thought, but to alienation and individualism that Durkheim was something less than an obvious partisan of this variety of human action.
>
> (Riley 2013: 6)

W. S. F. Pickering (2013: 44) addresses Durkheim's ambivalence, if not hostility, to the plethora of artistic activity in the Paris around him. Pickering points out that Durkheim's lectures on *Moral Education* warned about the dangers of the aesthetic culture in the educational process. Art, Durkheim held, does not bring people face to face with reality: the artist's imagination, which has no constraints—mental, moral, or social—stands in stark opposition to science, which aims to find truth as rationally ascertained. Art, like games, makes people forget the reality of life and does not seek to contribute to knowledge. Worse, when removed from the control of religion, the secular art of the modern age, freed from the restraints of the sacred, which for Durkheim is the basis of society, becomes a drawing card for *la vie légère* (45). Seeking to go deeper in Durkheim's background to find factors operative in his downgrading of art, Pickering notes that Durkheim, as a child growing up in a middle-class Jewish family, was cognizant of the iconoclastic tradition that frowned at impressionist representations of the body and the joyous gaiety of the outdoors. To live simply, with austerity even, was a way of life he could comply with, at home and throughout his career, evoking "a stern, puritanical figure"—like distant Puritans known for their "strict moral code" and "opposition to many of the arts" (48–49). When Durkheim married his lifelong devoted wife Louise, he forbade her playing the piano, much as she enjoyed doing it, and she returned to doing so only after his death (49).[9]

Pierre-Michel Menger (2013), professor of the sociology of creative work at the Collège de France, posits that the question of the value of art has been an ongoing challenge for sociology: How can we account for the production of artworks by individual artists, for the uniqueness of these works, and for the universal aesthetic pleasure they give? Drawing on *The Division of Labor*, Menger emphasizes a dilemma that a Durkheimian sociology of art comes up with: artwork—artistic innovation—is made possible by creative energy which adds desire to basic human needs; this promotes the civilizing process and an individualization of behavior and thereby leads to changes that enhance social solidarity. However, when the artistic imagination crosses society's moral boundaries, its aesthetic activity cannot be developed without depriving oneself of serious life-acting (*la vie sérieuse*) and hence, without weakening of the social order and its code of morality: "all aesthetic activity [...] is healthy only if moderated. [...] Too great an artistic sensibility is a sickly phenomenon which cannot become general without danger to society" (80).

Here, then, is a source of ambivalence: when art is contained by the social organization of society, it adds to the well-being of individuals by complementing the serious hard work of quotidian activity. Yet, because it draws on imagination and desire, it seeks to go out of the boundaries of organization; it promotes deregulation and immorality. That is the dark shadow cast by art that may well be present in Durkheim's reticence to credit art's social function.

Thus, there is a functional need for a regulatory norm apparatus—moral rules, religious beliefs, and behavioral models of conduct—to check what those who have read the second edition of *The Division of Labor* ([1902] 2013) and *Suicide* ([1897] 1951) can readily identify as the social pathology of anomie.[10] It has become part of professional lore that Durkheim obtained the now classic term *anomie* from Jean-Marie Guyau who had discussed it, in positive terms, as a creative evolutionary force of freedom. Menger (2013: 78) emphasizes that Guyau, in his original account saw anomie not as a hamper but as an emancipatory force in the civilizational process: "The consummate form of *anomie* thus defined was aesthetic activity, an activity in which individualism might express itself unfettered, thereby manifesting the immense power of creative freedom." (We will return shortly to Guyau as an alternative theorist of anomie.) Menger posits that for Durkheim, the bonding interaction of individual consciousnesses is the source of creative power—of collective effervescence—liberated through play or violence in moments of crisis. This collective effervescence is so intense that it leaves a surplus of energy for works of luxury, that is, works of art (88). When, over time, social bonds between group members become slack in "cool" historical periods, with individuals sensing "a separation between the ideal and the real," "art is one means of keeping up and 'revivifying' memory of group ideals" (87). Menger thus draws from the *Elementary Forms* Durkheim's later discussion on the function of art in the bonding interaction of individual consciousnesses. Ultimately, Menger adds, art works "for the unique purpose of projecting and symbolizing group unity and ideals. This is art's one positive accomplishment, since it is usually imbued with individualist intemperance and is therefore a threat to group cohesion. [...] When art revivifies those ideals [i.e., group unity and collective ideals (E. T./J. T.)] through its function of recollection, then and only then, for Durkheim, is it doing what art should do" (88).

Before closing this section there is need for additional remarks on the notions of anomie held by Durkheim and Guyau. Jean-Marie Guyau had a strong interest in Greek Epicurean moral philosophy before seeking an original synthesis of modern morality. His *Sketch of a Morality without Obligation or Sanction* (1885) and the follow-up, *The Unreligion of the Future: A Sociological Study* (1887), caught the immediate attention of a new generation, including Durkheim at Bordeaux, who published a favorable book review of *The Unreligion of the Future* in the scholarly *Revue philosophique* (Durkheim 1887).[11]

Durkheim found much in *The Unreligion of the Future* that agreed with his assessment of the waning of traditional religious authority. But whereas Guyau welcomed the trend favoring increased diversity of beliefs, which he felt should be furthered in artistic creativity,[12] Durkheim saw anomie as a pathogen for human association. Both Guyau and Durkheim saw the absence of fixed traditions and moral rules as a growing fixture of modern (industrial) life. Whereas for Guyau ([1889] 1891: xix) this increased individualization favored "a profound harmony underlying the antinomies between individual existence and collective existence," for Durkheim, anomie as disorder, and lack of social cohesion, equaled evil (Orru 1983: 514–515).

A later positive perspective on anomie and its function in the historical process of modernity is found in a French sociologist who approached Durkheim's ambivalence toward art by reversing the image of anomie in the shadow of Guyau. This is the late Jean Duvignaud (1921–2007), a specialist in Durkheim, in sociological aesthetics based on field studies in Northern Tunisia, and in theories of the theater. Duvignaud (1972) seeks to situate a sociology of art in terms of the creative imagination (*l'imaginaire*) which crystallizes in his work as an invisible community of artists that holds the secret of our future existence (20). The task for a sociology of art is to understand the artist not as a mere part of collective life but to understand him "in his unique, irreducible individuality" (21). This implies, he adds, finding the extent to which the imaginary is rooted in a collective life that is always a dynamic, changing reality in which man finds his freedom. Duvignaud traces Durkheim's concept of anomie to the "overall state of disorder caused by the continuous process of change in the social structure. […] the important factor is that people, separated from the norms which until then controlled and ordered their desires, suddenly find themselves confronted with unrestricted aspirations" (59). What follows is worth noting:

> At this point […] we disagree with Durkheim whose obdurate moralism leads him to prefer a "social harmony" which is another way of saying "moral order." This "erethism," which he regards as a cause of suffering and distress, appears to us, on the contrary, to be an important factor in the creation of new human possibilities. During these periods of disorder or anomy, both collective and individual freedom find expression in small or nation-wide "dramas," and can even produce hitherto unknown opportunities, capable of creating stable relationships and real development. (59)

Before examining Durkheim's major change in his outlook of the relation between art and society in *The Elementary Forms*, consider a summary statement he gave at a conference in 1910, "The Teaching of Morality in Primary School."[13] He stresses that teaching morality in secular terms to young children, without reference to "revealed religion" or "rational theology," had been a major concern of his all his life (3). Morality is a system of rules, maxims, and actions which tell us how to behave in different circumstances. When we act morally, there is an effort, a sacrifice; a moral act too easy to do is not a moral act (6). And Durkheim continues: "the role of morality is to allow human beings to live together, rather than to let them die. Morality is not a bookish thing; it springs from the sources of life. It is only in society and from society."

Durkheim then mentions all the goods from society which we internalize, and which are external to us: language, ways of thinking, science, moral norms, and family sentiments. There is nothing new here, but what is missing is a reference to art—yet, the reader may ask, what society does not have a form of music, of art, of acting? Still, this statement may be taken as a representative summation of Durkheim's major ambivalence in his first creative period.

Moral Education and the Arts: Transition

We turn now to Durkheim's cultural shift in *The Elementary Forms* and his focus on arts and aesthetics in his interpretation of the religious life of the Australian Arunta, as depicted in the great ethnographies of Spencer and Gillen (1899). In noting "primitive" rites which cannot possibly have physical efficacy, the ethnographic recording pointed to rites "whose sole purpose is to arouse certain ideas and feelings, to join the present to the past and the individual to the collectivity" (Durkheim [1912] 1995: 382). There are also rites whose sole purpose is "to amuse, to provoke laughter by laughter—that is, to cultivate gaiety and good humor within the group." These ceremonies "bring out an important element of religion: its recreational and aesthetic element." They are "akin to dramatic performances" (383). They "make men forget the real world so as to transport them into another where their imagination is more at home; they entertain" (384); "the world of religious things is partly an imaginary world [...] and, for this reason, one that lends itself more readily to the free creations of the mind" (385).

Ritual performances entertain, transporting the audience away from the quotidian into another world. "[G]ames and the principal forms of art," Durkheim reflects, "seem to have been born in religion and that they long maintained their religious character." The religious cult has among other functions that of recreation. It is especially involved in the symbolization of sacred things—the impressions really felt by human beings—which become interpreted, elaborated, and transformed "to the point of becoming unrecognizable." Yet the emotional forces generated in the situation of collective effervescence that the assembly experiences are so intense that a surplus of energy is engendered, for "supplementary and superfluous works of luxury—that is, [...] works of art" (385).

> [R]eligion would not be religion if there was no place in it for free combinations of thought and action, for games, for art, for all that refreshes a spirit worn down by all that is overburdening in day-to-day labor. That which made art exist makes it a necessity. It is not merely an outward adornment that the cult can be thought of as dressing up in, in order to hide what may be too austere and harsh about it; the cult in itself is aesthetic in some way. (385–386)

"The truth is that there is a poetry inherent in all religion"—but this is not the only or the most important aspect of religion. The cult "exerts its influence in a different direction than does a pure work of art": through moral forces, real forces, not through "empty images that correspond to nothing in reality." These moral forces "are necessary to the good order of our moral life [...]. It is through them that the group affirms and maintains itself, and we know how indispensable the group is to the individual." However, the unreal and imaginary element of the aesthetic still plays a role, for "Recreation is one form of the moral remaking that is the primary object of the positive cult." Placing us in contact with a higher source of energy and replenishing our capacities, fulfillment of our ritual duties helps us return to profane life "with more energy and enthusiasm," "less tense, more at ease, and freer," thus providing to religion an appeal "that is not the least of its attractions" (386).

Furthermore, as William Watts Miller (2012: 148) points out, Durkheim considered the sacred as a "vast elemental force" that generated not only art but science. Given Durkheim's firm belief in and promotion of science, his attributing to both fields a common lineage represents a profound shift in his conception of the relation of art and society. His ambivalence morphs into a more comprehensive and appreciative perspective of art—art in the service of religion and of society, which he had previously described as fundamentally linked—"religion is first and foremost a system of ideas by means of which individuals imagine the society of which they are members and the obscure yet intimate relations they have with it" (Durkheim [1912] 1995: 227). This statement marks the culmination of Durkheim's questioning of the role of art in society and the stages of his progressive understanding of art's contributions to society: art as a facilitator of the teaching of morality, art as leisure and recreation, and art as instrumental in enhancing solidarity and group identity.

It is near the end of his sustained interpretation of religion that Durkheim mentions another set of sacred rituals generated by death or natural calamities: piacular rites.[14] Piacular rites have two functions: they express the tribal anger, sadness, and resentment brought forth by calamities, and they are restorative and healing. The violence of the tribal display expresses the shared sorrow and evidences that "even at this moment, society is more alive and active than ever." The "excess of energy" that the rites produce "erases the effects of the crippling that occurred to begin with"; it dissipates "the sensation of cold that death everywhere brings"; people come out of the rites feeling "confidence and security" having recovered their "original feelings of tenderness and solidarity" (405).

Related to piacular rites is the concept of the ambiguity of the sacred for which Durkheim acknowledged Robertson Smith. Durkheim points out that the sacred has two faces: the "pure" (beneficent, life-sustaining, and divine) and the "impure" (maleficent, death-inducing, and demonic).[15] Further, the divine can become demonic, and the demonic can become divine. Durkheim underlines, however, that "the pure and impure are not two separate genera but two varieties of the same genus that includes all sacred things" (415).

While Durkheim—as well as Mauss, Hubert, and especially Hertz—took notice of the dichotomy of the sacred "pure" and "impure," the Great War soon after publication of *The Elementary Forms* plunged France and the world into a nonfictive set of piacular rites. Of the small group that had contributed during Durkheim's life to the slender Aesthetics section of the *Année*, only Hubert and Mauss survived (as did Lalo).[16] However, as we have seen, that does not terminate the influence of Durkheim's analysis of the arts and his aesthetic theories.

ART AND MEDIATION

We terminate with a brief discussion of a volume relevant to the subject, although it does not mention Durkheim's ambivalence toward art: *The Passion for Music: A Sociology of Mediation* ([1993] 2015) by the French sociologist Antoine Hennion. Hennion explores Durkheim's methodological legacy to the sociology of art, as well as to the discipline, and its restrictive inflection on both. This he does in the context of the book's subject, which seeks "to redefine the sociology of music, taking as its theme and material the complex relationships between the social sciences and the arts" (ix). To this end he proposes a sociology of mediation that would vastly enrich present sociological thinking; an approach which he states is inspired by that of the sociology of science and technology practiced by the Center of Science and Innovation at the *Ecole des mines* (10). In short, Hennion revisits the relations between art and society through the lens of the notion of mediation. He begins with an exposition of Durkheim's account of cultural mediation. The question revolves around the source of the power of the *totem*—the emblem of the group. Does it, as "primitives" believed, reside within the *totem*—the cultural object (linear causality)—or behind the object, in society—in the group that selected it as a sacred object (circular causality)? Durkheim interpreted the power of the *totem* to be firmly anchored in society. His account of cultural mediation, "the least mediating of mediation theories" (24), set the path of sociology: since then "sociology [has] highlighted with increasing complexity the theoretical mechanism linking objects to the social. To what, to whom, and how should the cause which animates objects be attributed?" (32).

Mediation points to the filter that lies between the subject and the object, facilitating their seeing each other. However, adds Hennion, Durkheim's theory of emblems overlooks the mediators.[17] It overlooks that the "'subject' of artistic production and its product is not the artist but the whole set of agents who are involved in art" ("social, institutional, human, material") that define the relationship between art and society: "patrons, merchants, salons or academies, pigments, formats, programmes or commissions, etc." (17, 159). Observing them moves us "towards a reinstatement of the resources which compose it [i.e., art] and ensure its duration" (10). Durkheim laid the foundations for today's sociological discourses that apply his ethnological hypotheses to the modern world: he made the "separation between social and natural objects the very principle of the sacred" (18). Hennion proposes contemporary history of art as a discipline which has successfully and fruitfully added mediation to its methodological toolbox, and as a template for sociology of art and sociology, incorporating what he calls "unruly mediators." Contrasting the perspectives of sociology and art history, he points out that sociology seeks a reductive explanation while art history seeks a diversity of explanations.

> Although sociology initially needs mediators in order to counter the causes which others have established, in the end it seeks to eliminate these others behind the new social cause [...]. By contrast, art history lavishly multiplies the mediations that exist between art and the most varied aspects of the reality surrounding it, usually without bothering to theorise this constant work of restoration, which it treats as an end in itself. (42)

In the rest of his book, Hennion explores how mediation has enriched our understanding of the complex relation between music (and art in general) and society. He also successfully explores the ability of music to help us understand how the art history model of mediation is able to replace the traditional sociological explanation, which is "unable to overcome its need to assert its authority over the ethnic objects that it studies" (10).

Conclusion

The evaluation of Durkheim's imprint on the sociology of art is a recent development which we have sought to trace in this chapter. Much of Durkheim's perspective on art and aesthetics reflects his personality—a highly intellectual scientist not prone to music or the visual arts. A major theme noted by Durkheimian scholars is his seeming ambivalence toward art, despite the plethora of artistic flourishing and creativity in Paris during his lifetime. In this essay we note his aversion to *la vie légère*—the life of pleasure and entertainment as a mode of conduct detracting from his own basic code of *la vie sérieuse*—work and the life of the mind in the service of society.

During the early period of his career, art was for Durkheim a zone of human activity which provided temporary pleasure and relaxation from the world of work. It was also a vehicle that prepared youth for moral education. However, while it fostered creativity, art, he felt, could weaken social bonds by increasing human desire and leading to disorder. This was the specter of anomie, prominent in Durkheim's Bordeaux period.

After his promotion to the Sorbonne, his reading of Robertson Smith and of the ethnographies of Spencer and Gillen on the Australian Aborigines' rites and collective effervescence led Durkheim to reconsider the religious base of the social order, and of the place of art and aesthetics in society. The aesthetic dimension of the belief system of the cult and its rites was recast as enhancing group solidarity, always a primary value for Durkheim, in the forefront of his intellectual, political, and personal journey.

To conclude, in reviewing Durkheim's perspective on art, we have sought to present a fuller perspective of his writings on art and society. Ultimately, what needs to be considered is how what he has to say about art and aesthetics relates to his primary emphasis on social solidarity, given that his overarching lifetime goal was the reconstruction of a moral community for the industrial age—a secular equitable moral code appropriate for modern industrial society. We should also keep in mind that as a parting message, he included art as one of the essential contributions of humans to society: "Let language, sciences, arts, and moral beliefs be taken from man, and he falls to the rank of animality; therefore the distinctive attributes of human nature come to us from society. On the other hand, however, society exists and lives only in and through individuals" (Durkheim [1912] 1995: 351).

Notes

1. On the emergence of the *Année* amid the bourgeoning French *academe*, see Besnard (1983) and Karady (1983). Both Hubert and Mauss were contributors to the first volume and remained to the end, an intellectual sacrifice of time that could have been spent on their own writings.
2. For a list of Lalo's considerable publications, see Nandan (1977). In Harry Alpert's doctoral dissertation on Durkheim, published as *Durkheim and His Sociology*, Lalo's *L'art et la vie sociale* (1921) (*Art and Social Life*) is cited in the discussion of social factors in the sociology of values (Alpert 1939: 207).
3. Hennion ([1993] 2015: 45) points out that Lalo "invented 'sociological aesthetics.'"
4. Translation by E. Tiryakian.
5. For a detailed review of works pertinent to Third Republic school reforms, see Bergen (1986).
6. For a discussion of *la vie sérieuse*, a term coined by Durkheim, its opposite *la vie légère*, and their ties with rituals and the arts, see Pickering (1984: 352–361).
7. Translation by E. Tiryakian.
8. Translation by E. Tiryakian.
9. In contrast to his uncle, Marcel Mauss "considered himself 'broad-minded,' regularly listened to jazz and marveled at both contemporary and 'native' art" (Fournier 2006: 285). Mauss's openness to modern art was shown in his contribution to Georges Bataille's "Hommage to Picasso" (Mauss 1930: 177): "shall I tell you that I was in the first years of the century one of the young persons who found your paintings and drawings so appealing [...] or shall I say how your painting and your drawings bring us near the purest sources of impression and expression?"
10. On Durkheim's definitions of the concept of anomie, see Besnard (1987).
11. Durkheim declined to review Guyau's *L'art au point de vue sociologique* (1889).
12. "If two men think in a different way, all the better; they are closer to the truth than if they would both think the same way" (Guyau 1885: 232, quoted in Orru 1983: 511).

13. This is a fifteen-page typed manuscript, part of a series of undated conferences, probably written between 1908 and 1910, that came into the collection of the *Ecole normale d'instituteurs de Paris* (now the *Institut universitaire des maîtres*) in 1910.
14. It is likely that Durkheim got the important concept of piacular from Hubert's and Mauss's *Année sociologique* essay on sacrifice (1899: 31). A contemporary public display of piacular rites was shown in Grand Central Station, New York, following the 9/11, 2001, attack on the United States.
15. On Robertson Smith's influence on Durkheim, see Pickering (1984: 62–70).
16. Maurice Halbwachs was another notable "second generation" Durkheimian who survived World War I and continued to be creative in the sociology of aesthetics; see Daynes (2013) on Halbwachs's study of collective memory of musicians.
17. Hennion ([1993] 2015: 19) gives an example of the modernization of the Durkheimian causal model: "Faced with the power of the totem—that is, nowadays, the media, consumer goods or works of art—'the native'—i.e. the televiewer [...], the consumer, the art lover—attributes to the object (and to himself, as subject) what he feels to be its effects on him (whether to submit to or reject them): the model he adopts is linear, indeed natural, physical."

References

Alpert, Harry. 1939. *Emile Durkheim and His Sociology*. New York: Columbia University Press.
Bergen, Barry H. 1986. "Primary Education in Third Republic France: Recent French Works." *History of Education Quarterly* 26 (2): 271–285.
Besnard, Philippe. 1983. "The *Année sociologique* Team." In *The Sociological Domain: The Durkheimians and the Founding of French Sociology*, edited by Philippe Besnard, 11–70. Cambridge: Cambridge University Press.
Besnard, Philippe. 1987. *L'anomie: Ses usages et ses fonctions dans la discipline sociologique depuis Durkheim*. Paris: Presses universitaires de France.
Bourdieu, Pierre. (1984) 1993. *Sociology in Question*. London: SAGE. Originally published as *Questions de Sociologie*. Paris: Minuit.
Callède, Jean-Paul. 2008. "Jeu et sport chez Durkheim et le groupe de L'Année sociologique." *Durkheimian Studies* 14: 23–34.
Daynes, Sarah. 2013. "Too Marvelous for Words...: Maurice Halbwachs, Kansas City Jazz, and the Language of Music." In *Durkheim, the Durkheimians, and the Arts*, edited by Alexander Riley, W. S. F. Pickering, and William Watts Miller, 154–177. New York: Berghahn Books.
Durkheim, Émile. 1887. Review of "Guyau. L'irréligion de l'avenir, étude de sociologie." *Revue philosophique de la France et de l'étranger* 23: 299–311.
Durkheim, Émile. 1898. "Préface." *L'Année sociologique* 1: I–VII.
Durkheim, Émile. (1897) 1951. *Suicide: A Study in Sociology*. Translated by John A. Spaulding and George Simpson. New York: Free Press. Originally published as *Le suicide*. Paris: Alcan.
Durkheim, Émile. (1925) 1973. *Moral Education: A Study in the Theory and Application of the Sociology of Education*. Translated by Everett K. Wilson and Herman Schnurer. New York: Free Press. Originally published as *L'education morale*, edited by Paul Fauconnet. Paris: Alcan.

Durkheim, Émile. (1912) 1995. *The Elementary Forms of Religious Life*. Translated by Karen E. Fields. New York: Free Press. Originally published as *Les formes élémentaires de la vie religieuse. Le système totémique en Australie*. Paris: Alcan.
Durkheim, Émile. (1893/1902) 2013. *The Division of Labour in Society*. Edited by Steven Lukes and translated by W. D. Halls. Houndmills: Palgrave Macmillan. Originally published as *De la division du travail social. Etude sur l'organisation des sociétés supérieures*. Paris: Alcan, 1893; 2nd ed. Paris: Alcan, 1902.
Duvignaud, Jean. 1972. *The Sociology of Art*. New York: Harper & Row.
Fields, Karen E. 1995. "Translator's Introduction: Religion as an Eminently Social Thing." In Émile Durkheim, *The Elementary Forms of Religious Life*, translated by Karen E. Fields, xvii–lxxiii. New York: Free Press.
Fournier, Marcel. 1987. "Durkheim, *L'Année sociologique* et l'art." *Etudes Durkheimiennes* 12: 1–10.
Fournier, Marcel. 2006. *Marcel Mauss: A Biography*. Princeton, NJ: Princeton University Press.
Guyau, Jean-Marie. 1885. *Esquisse d'une morale sans obligation ni sanction*. Paris: Alcan. English translation: *A Sketch of Morality Independent of Obligation or Sanction*. London: Watts, 1898.
Guyau, Jean-Marie. 1887. *L'irréligion de l'avenir. Etude sociologique*. Paris: Alcan. English translation: *The Non-Religion of the Future: A Sociological Study*. New York: H. Holt, 1897.
Guyau, Jean-Marie. 1889. *L'art au point de vue sociologique*. Paris: Alcan.
Guyau, Jean-Marie. (1889) 1891. *Education and Heredity: A Study in Sociology*. Translated by William John Greenstreet. London: Walter Scott. Originally published as *Éducation et hérédité. Étude sociologique*. Paris: Alcan.
Hennion, Antoine. (1993) 2015. *The Passion for Music: A Sociology of Mediation*. Farnham: Ashgate.
Karady, Victor. 1983. "The Durkheimians in Academe: A Reconsideration." In *The Sociological Domain: The Durkheimians and the Founding of French Sociology*, edited by Philippe Besnard, 71–89. Cambridge: Cambridge University Press.
Lalo, Charles. 1904. Review of "Richard Wallaschek, Anfaenge der Tonkunst." *L'Année sociologique* 7: 667–670.
Lalo, Charles. 1921. *L'art et la vie sociale*. Paris: Doin.
Mauss, Marcel. 1930. [Hommage à Picasso]. *Documents* 2 (3): 177.
Menger, Pierre-Michel. 2013. "The Power of Imagination and the Economy of Desire: Durkheim and Art." In *Durkheim, the Durkheimians, and the Arts*, edited by Alexander Riley, W. S. F. Pickering, and William Watts Miller, 77–94. New York: Berghahn Books.
Nandan, Yash (compiler). 1977. *The Durkheimian School: A Systematic and Comprehensive Bibliography*. Westport, CT: Greenwood Press.
Nisbet, Robert. 2002. *Sociology as an Art Form*. New Brunswick, NJ: Transaction.
Orru, Marco. 1983. "The Ethics of Anomie: Jean Marie Guyau and Émile Durkheim." *British Journal of Sociology* 34 (4): 499–518.
Pickering, W. S. F. 1984. *Durkheim's Sociology of Religion: Themes and Theories*. London: Routledge & Kegan Paul.
Pickering, W. S. F. 2013. "Durkheim, the Arts, and the Moral Sword." In *Durkheim, the Durkheimians, and the Arts*, edited by Alexander Riley, W. S. F. Pickering, and William Watts Miller, 43–58. New York: Berghahn Books.

Riley, Alexander. 2013. "Introduction." In *Durkheim, the Durkheimians, and the Arts*, edited by Alexander Riley, W. S. F. Pickering, and William Watts Miller, 1–15. New York: Berghahn Books.

Riley, Alexander, W. S. F. Pickering, and William Watts Miller, eds. 2013. *Durkheim, the Durkheimians, and the Arts*. New York: Berghahn Books.

Spencer, Baldwin, and F. J. Gillen. 1899. *The Native Tribes of Central Australia*. London: Macmillan.

Wallaschek, Richard. 1893. *Primitive Music: An Inquiry into the Origin and Development of Music, Songs, Instruments, Dances, and Pantomimes of Savage Races*. London: Longmans, Green, and Co.

Watts Miller, William. 2012. *A Durkheimian Quest: Solidarity and the Sacred*. New York: Berghahn Books.

Zolberg, Vera L. 1990. *Constructing a Sociology of the Arts*. Cambridge: Cambridge University Press.

CHAPTER 18

DURKHEIM AND SOCIAL MOVEMENTS

KERSTIN JACOBSSON

DURKHEIM's influence on social movement theorizing often has been more implicit than explicit. It seems symptomatic, for instance, that a great article on "Ideology, Symbolic Action and Rituality in Social Movements" (Sassoon 1984) could be published without even mentioning Durkheim. The fact that social movement scholars have readily focused on collective identity and solidarity without any association to Durkheim led Crossley to remark that many "avoid uttering the 'D-word' except in contempt" (Crossley 2002: 15).

One reason for the uneasy relationship between Durkheim and social movement scholars is the fact that he came to be placed among the strain and breakdown theorists of collective action—as noted by Traugott (1984), Crossley (2002), and Buechler (2004), among others, and as discussed later in this chapter. Here, social movements were seen as responses to social disintegration and were classified as one type of collective behavior along with crowds, panics, or riots. The frequent association of Durkheim to Parsons's structural functionalism, especially in the US context (following, e.g., Smelser 1962), was not helpful either. When the pendulum swung back in the 1970s, and structural and functionalist approaches were replaced by notably agent-centered and rationalist social movement theories, Durkheimian approaches for a time seemed even more out of place.

Since then, there has been a renewed interest in Durkheimian approaches in social theory in general, focusing inter alia on the symbolic dimensions of social life (e.g., Alexander 1988; Smith and Alexander 2005; Alexander and Mast 2006), on microsociological analysis of emotions (e.g., Collins 2001, 2004), and on social network and relational analyses (e.g., Emirbayer 1996; Segre 2004). All these approaches have in various ways also fertilized social movement theorizing (e.g., Alexander 1996; Emirbayer 1996; Emirbayer and Goodwin 1996; Jasper 1997, 1998; Crossley 2002; Olesen 2015; Jacobsson and Lindblom 2016). Especially Durkheim's late work, *The Elementary Forms of Religious Life*, has greatly inspired social movement scholars, stressing in particular the role of collective effervescence, generated in ritual action, for empowerment and collective agency (e.g., Tiryakian 1995; Emirbayer 1996; Jasper 1997; Peterson 2001; Pettenkofer 2010; Jacobsson 2014).

Nevertheless, I argue in this chapter that Durkheim's potential contribution to social movement theorizing goes beyond both the social disintegration and the collective effervescence and the ritual life-inspired analyses. Thus, I suggest that there are other openings in Durkheim's works that can be made productive for social movement theorizing. While most social movement theorists have drawn their inspiration from either Durkheim's early more structural works or his late more ideational work, I will stress the relevance of less frequently used parts of his production, such as his sociology of morality as developed in *Moral Education* (Durkheim [1925] 1961), and his, admittedly rather fragmentary and posthumously published, political sociology, in *Professional Ethics and Civic Morals* (Durkheim [1950] 1992; see also Giddens 1978). Whatever changes Durkheim's thinking underwent during the course of his career, a continuity was the stress on the moral dimension of social life. I argue that a distinctly Durkheimian understanding of social movements will entail a moral understanding of social movements as essentially moral phenomena.

In the remaining parts of this chapter, I will first account for the major ways in which Durkheim's work has been used in social movement theorizing. Second, I will outline my own neo-Durkheimian approach to social movements, as developed jointly with Jonas Lindblom (e.g., Jacobsson and Lindblom 2016). Finally, I will briefly conclude and suggest some venues for future research.

Durkheim and Social Movements

Durkheim obviously did not provide a full theory of social movements. Rather, he provided insights, sometimes in the form of hints and glimpses, that can be made productive for social movement theorizing but require a fair amount of sociological imagination on behalf of the researcher to fill in the gaps or even rethink some assumptions.

While Durkheim himself did not use the term "social movements," he spoke of "social currents," which he considered a social fact alongside other types of social facts such as legal or financial systems or religious belief systems (e.g., Durkheim [1895] 1982: 52–53, 70). In his political sociology he wrote: "There exist too at all times social currents wholly unconnected with the State, that draw the collectivity in this or that direction. Frequently it is a case of the State coming under their pressure, rather than itself giving the impulse to them" (Durkheim [1950] 1992: 49). This remark is interesting as Durkheim here explicitly acknowledges the dimension of societal groups and forces exerting political pressure.

It is reasonable to conceive of social movements as part of "political society," which Durkheim saw as "formed by the coming together of a rather large number of secondary social groups" subject to the same authority, which for Durkheim was the national state (Durkheim [1950] 1992: 45). While Durkheim came to see the state as the liberator of the individual, he also stressed secondary groupings as a counterbalance to the state; the state "must be restrained by other collective forces [...]. And it is out of this conflict of social forces that individual liberties are born" (Durkheim [1950] 1992: 63). Even if Durkheim frequently singled out professional associations as a key type of secondary grouping, in other parts of his work he spoke of other groupings as well as forming part of political society.

Additionally, there are numerous other references in Durkheim's production of obvious relevance for the analysis of what we would conceptualize as social movements. For instance, he spoke of "lasting movements of opinion which relate to religious, political, literary and artistic matters" (Durkheim [1895] 1982: 53), waves of enthusiasms or indignation (52–53), outbursts of collective emotions in assemblies (56), collective action (Durkheim [1925] 1961: 150), collective aspirations (Durkheim [1950] 1992: 56), "the spirit of association" and "grass-roots sentiment" (Durkheim [1925] 1961: 238) as well as revolutions. Durkheim considered the French Revolution as "a social fact of the greatest importance" and a prime example of a "creative era" (Durkheim 1973: 34, 41). The aspirations of the French Revolution, in his view, have amounted to "a religion which has had its martyrs and apostles, which has profoundly moved the masses, and which, after all, has given birth to great things" (Durkheim 1973: 35; see also [1925] 1961: 259). "It is [...] at such moments of collective ferment that are born the great ideals upon which civilizations rest" (Durkheim [1924] 1974: 91).

In *Moral Education*, Durkheim ([1925] 1961: 238) lamented, "it is true that the radical disappearance of intermediate groups has impaired public morality." He concluded that:

> What we must do is to try to bring to life new groupings, which are in harmony with the present-day social order and with the principles on which it reposes. But the only way of succeeding in this is to breathe life into the spirit of association. These groups cannot be created by force. If they are to have any real life they must be created by public opinion. Men must feel the need for them and be inclined to form groups of their own accord. (235)

I find it close at hand to conceive of a social movement as such a "force of moral opinion" (195), or public opinion (196), but requiring some level of social organization in order for "the spirit of association" to be maintained over time (see also Durkheim [1893] 1984: 25) and in order to be able to effectively exert some pressure on the state. Indeed, as Durkheim ([1925] 1961: 150) noted, "Collective action, according to the way its influence is used, may enhance the good or increase the evil." A mob or a crowd "move quickly to excesses" as they lack rules or regulatory organs ([1925] 1961: 150), which was why Durkheim saw moral regulation and moderation as key also to the secondary groups and their internal functioning. I will later in this chapter return to the opening for social movement theorizing that I see in Durkheim's sociology of morality (as developed in *Moral Education*).

However, first I will briefly account for the major ways in which Durkheim has been treated and used in social movement theorizing. These can be largely summarized as social disintegration approaches in the study of social movements, analyses of the mobilizing power of collective effervescence and ritual processes, and—albeit less developed—relational approaches to social movements.

Social Disintegration Approaches

As already mentioned, one reason for the uneasy relationship between Durkheim and many contemporary social movement scholars is the fact that his work served as a theoretical basis for the strain and breakdown theorists of collective action—as noted by among others Traugott (1984), Crossley (2002), and Buechler (2004, 2016). According to these theories, collective protest results from a breakdown of social control and normative order connected with social change, which led activists to become associated with unruly crowds and deviant behavior. This was maybe most clearly articulated in the "collective behavior" tradition, represented by authors such as Le Bon ([1895] 1960) and Smelser (1962). Social disintegration approaches in relation to social protest came in different versions, variously stressing anomie (e.g., Gurr 1970), structural strain (e.g., Smelser 1962; Turner and Killian 1987), or relative deprivation (e.g., Gurr 1970). Mass society theorists (e.g., Kornhauser 1959) also claimed a Durkheimian heritage.

As social disintegration approaches in relation to social protest came to be increasingly criticized on both empirical and theoretical grounds, Durkheim also came under fierce attack. The most forceful critique came from Charles Tilly, whose interest was the link between large-scale social change and collective action. Tilly (1978: 18) claimed that Durkheim's theory of anomie "leads us to anticipate finding the populations newly created or displaced by differentiation at the center of collective action. It predicts a close association among suicide, crime, violence, and nonroutine collective action." In an article tellingly entitled "Useless Durkheim," Tilly (1981) derived three hypotheses for which he found no historical validity: (1) weakened social control (as a consequence of anomie) leads to heightened levels of social conflict; (2) periods of rapid social change increase levels of social conflict and protest; and (3) different forms of social disorder, such as suicide, crime and protest, tend to coincide since they stem from the same cause (lack of moral regulation due to social change). He concluded: "Breakdown theories of collective action [...] suffer from irreparable logical and empirical difficulties. Some sort of solidarity theory should work better everywhere. No matter where we look, we should rarely find uprooted, marginal, disorganized people heavily involved in collective violence. All over the world we should expect collective violence to flow out of routine collective action and continuing struggles for power" (Tilly et al. 1975: 290). It should be mentioned that Tilly (1978: 17) also briefly acknowledged the solidarity-producing consequences of ritualized collective action, but he clearly did not turn to Durkheim for theorization of solidarity.

The association of Durkheim to breakdown theories has been rightly criticized. In his work on anomie (Durkheim [1897] 1951), Durkheim did not focus explicitly on protest. As Traugott (1984: 322, 326) remarked: "It is Smelser, not Durkheim, who explicitly links such individual responses as "anxiety, hostility, and fantasy" to collective responses including various forms of social movements [...]. Far from advocating a disintegration theory, Durkheim might more reasonably be expected to stress the role of social solidarity and the need to adopt a group unit of analysis." Social movements should, in Traugott's view, be seen primarily as "the collective response to shared discontents which binds participants together in social action and which constitutes a prototypical emergent phenomenon" (326). Also, Crossley (2002: 101–102) argued that Durkheim's prime interest was in moral regulation and solidarity rather than disintegration, and that it is from there that his contribution to social movement theorizing would come.

Ritual and Emotional Approaches

Thus, while the early usage of Durkheim by social movement scholars built on his early and more structuralist works (*The Division of Labor in Society* and *Suicide*), more recently it has been his later (admittedly partly functionalist) *Elementary Forms of Religious Life* (Durkheim [1912] 2001), which stressed the symbolic and cognitive dimensions of social life, that has been the main source of inspiration, stressing the importance of symbols and rituals in movement life as well as the collective feelings they generate. Durkheim's sociology of religion provides crucial insights into the mechanisms of internal solidarity in activist communities as well as into the sources of individual and collective agency. Rituals create a heightened sense of awareness and aliveness, what Durkheim called collective effervescence, without which activists would not be able to transcend their individual self-interest and to produce symbols, norms, heroes, and villains, and achieve history-making change. Activists' participation in rituals such as demonstrations, acts of civil disobedience, or meetings, strengthens their moral ties, creating and reinforcing bonds of solidarity and a we-feeling and sense of common purpose in social movements. Mobilizing symbols (e.g., Alexander 1996) such as injustice symbols (Olesen 2015), songs (Eyerman 2006), dancing and moving together (Jasper 1997), and thus experiences of corporality and co-presence, are key for the "fusion" of activist groups (Peterson 2001: 59). Indeed, rituals have been shown to have a positive effect on the level of engagement in collective action (e.g., Tiryakian 1995; Jasper 1997; Barker 1999; Peterson 2001; Casquete 2006; Gould 2009; Gasparre et al. 2010; Jansen 2017). In ritual, an emotional transference occurs, which produces a collective emotional energy, and a sense of belonging to some force greater than oneself. As Eyerman (2006: 195) notes (but without citing Durkheim), this is key to understanding what *moves* social movements: "most of all movement refers to an experience of moving and of being moved by forces greater than one's self." Rituals, moreover, constitute and construct the fundamental boundary between inside and outside without which no community can exist (e.g., Giesen 2006; Jacobsson and Lindblom 2016).

Drawing on Durkheim's sociology of religion and based on a study of animal rights activists, I identified a number of elementary forms and experiences of religious life in animal rights activism, including overwhelming conversion experiences as eye-opening events moving individuals into activism; a division of the world into sacred and profane; concern about protecting the sacred ideal (of animal rights) fueling taking action and entailing a strong commitment to spreading the message and living out one's faith; the feeling that one's own suffering and guilt have meaning, explaining activists' willingness to self-sacrifice; and finally the constitutive role of common symbols and rituals in activist community-building, reinforcing bonds of solidarity and renewal of commitment (Jacobsson 2014; Jacobsson and Lindblom 2016). A Durkheimian lens helps us see that it is in the light of the sacred ideal (of animal rights) that activists' fervor, zeal, and sometimes uncompromising attitudes can be understood.

Nevertheless, for Durkheim ritual life is not just reinforcing, and thus conserving, the group ideals; collective effervescence is both creative and transformative. He wrote: "Man does not recognize himself; he feels he is transformed, and so he transforms his surroundings" (Durkheim [1912] 2001: 317). Durkheim saw the French Revolution, the Reformation, and the birth of socialism as such creative moments in which currents of social change emerged (e.g., Hunt 1988; Tiryakian 1995), with the power to transform the social order. Social movement scholars have pointed to the creative dynamics in situations of intense social interaction giving rise to new definitions of the situation (Crossley 2002: 102), enabling the challenging of institutionalized authority. As put by Tiryakian (1995: 274): "this sentiment of empowerment, which occurs only in certain moments, transforms the group into a charismatic community, transforms, ultimately, social structure into agency." At the same time Durkheim's perspective calls attention to unintended consequences of such moments (Tiryakian 1995). And Emirbayer, in a reply to Tilly entitled "Useful Durkheim," pointed to the relevance of Durkheim's sociology of religion for historical-comparative analyses of collective action precisely because it takes into account both the structural contexts for action and the "dynamic moment of *human agency*" (Emirbayer 1996: 111; see also Alexander 1996).

At an individual level, collective effervescence, generated in rituals, invigorates and empowers the activist, giving her a momentary feeling of everything being possible, and thus a feeling of being able to transcend her own self-limitations and egoistic desires, surrendering to forces greater than herself. Durkheim pointed to the dualism of human nature, conceptualized as *homo duplex* (Durkheim [1925] 1961: 152; see also Shilling and Mellor 2011); as human beings, we are internally divided between egoistic dispositions and moral dispositions, the latter of which follow from our attachment to a social group. Participation in group rituals pushes the individual toward the moral side of her person, tying her more closely to the group and its moral ideal.

The sacredness of the ideals and the group dynamics of collective effervescence has also been used to analyze collective violence (Hunt 1988; Mukherjee 2010; Wahnich 2012), such as the explosive sociality of militancy in high-risk activist groups (e.g., Peterson 2001). As Alexander (1996: 208) has argued, the "secularized" versions of social movement theory, stressing the individual and collective rational choice of action repertoire, tend to see even violence as merely an efficient instrument that is used if "it works." However, the sacrality of ideals helps us understand why activists may resort to violence even in contexts or situations where it does not actually "work" or is counterproductive to their cause (Jacobsson and Lindblom 2016). Rather than being the outcome of instrumental calculation, it is the burning passion for the sacred that occasionally leads to violent action.

Durkheim's sociology of religion has also inspired emotional approaches in the study of social movements (e.g., Collins 2001; Jacobsson and Lindblom 2013) but less so than one would expect, given the centrality of emotions in Durkheim's sociology. According to Durkheim ([1925] 1961: 94), emotions "are the moving forces of conduct" and thus central for agency. Moreover, what constitutes a group is that they feel together. For Durkheim, collective conscience consists of beliefs and sentiments, and in particular moral ideas and moral feelings (Durkheim [1925] 1961: 9). Thus, in a Durkheimian perspective, shared moral emotions are primarily what constitute collective identity in social movements (Jacobsson and Lindblom 2016). Moral emotions, such as righteous anger and indignation (e.g., Jasper 1997; Jansen 2017), evoked by violations of moral ideals, frequently mobilize individuals into collective action, as can emotionally disruptive experiences, which Jasper and Poulsen (1995) conceptualize as "moral shocks." Drawing on Durkheim's analysis of ritual effects, Collins (2001) elaborated the role of interaction ritual and emotional energy as motivational force in social movements. Collins's approach in turn inspired a number of contributions on the role of emotions in social movements (see, e.g., contributions in Flam and King 2005, many of which without mentioning Durkheim).

Emotional refill by participation in group rituals and support by fellow activists are necessary to sustain commitment over time (e.g., Jacobsson and Lindblom 2013), as well as being key for the development of communities able of critical consciousness and resistance (e.g., Taylor and Whittier 1995; Summers-Effler 2002; Gould 2009). Rather than being merely driven by emotions, as the crowd theorists would have it, activists have been found to pursue reflexive emotion work in a variety of ways (Ruiz-Junco 2013; Jacobsson and Lindblom 2013), for instance converting shame into pride (Gould 2001).

Relational Approaches

Finally, while Durkheim has not been a key figure in the recently emerging network and relational approaches to collective action (e.g., Diani and McAdam 2003), there are some relational approaches that explicitly draw on Durkheimian thinking. Emirbayer (1996) argued that Durkheim's ontological commitment to a "relational social realism" opened a theoretical perspective able to account for, and integrate, the cultural, the social-structural, and the social-psychological environments of action as well as bridging structure and agency (see Alexander 1988). Similarly, Emirbayer and Goodwin (1996) stressed the usefulness of a relational focus in the study of revolutions and collective action, underlining that social action is simultaneously embedded in, and shaped by, a plurality of relational contexts. They argued: "Revolutionary movements, for example, will potentially reconfigure not only networks of social relationships [...] but also patterns of relationships among symbols within cultural structures [...] *as well as* more emotional, psychical bonds of identification and idealization among individuals, groups, and leaders" (Emirbayer and Goodwin 1996: 374).

Segre (2004) stressed Durkheim's contribution to network theory, conceiving structure as a network of networks, where the whole pattern of direct and indirect relations between social actors constrain actors' behavior; he argued that such relations (rather than actors and their attributes) should be the unit of analysis (Segre 2004: 226). Nevertheless, the distinctly Durkheimian contribution, according to Segre, consists of emphasizing not only on ties and networks but actors' *awareness* of their various social roles, their "sense of community" (230), and how cooperation flows from, and upholds, a common social, and therefore moral, attitude (226). Segre's reading of Durkheim as network theorist stresses the moral dimension of bridging (and not only bonding) ties. Relevant research questions in a Durkheimian network perspective would be the conditions that make bridges possible, the relevance of cultural and moral contexts of interaction, and the moral effects of bridges and networks (231), identifying the multiplex ties and ties bridging different clusters as well as the consequences for cooperation. Segre suggested this research agenda could be pursued in future social movement research, among others.

A Neo-Durkheimian Approach to Social Movements

Few social theorists have been subject to so many misunderstandings as Durkheim; conventional wisdom holds that he has ignored power, conflict, and change (e.g., Taylor and Whittier 1995), was conservative (Nisbet 1965), and has opened "the door to irrationality" and thus paved the way for crowd theorists (Buechler 2016: 52). Despite excellent critiques of such readings, such as Stedman Jones's *Durkheim Reconsidered* (2001; see also Emirbayer 1996, 2003), this mainstream view has remained remarkably "sticky." This may explain the overall limited interest that social movement scholars have paid to Durkheim, especially in the last decades.

Nevertheless, the social disintegration and the collective effervescence approaches that have dominated Durkheimian analyses of social movements so far do not exhaust what Durkheim has to offer social movement analysis. In the following, I will briefly outline a neo-Durkheimian approach to social movements (developed jointly with Jonas Lindblom), which draws primarily on Durkheim's sociology of morality (Durkheim [1925] 1961). We argue that a distinctly Durkheimian understanding of social movements will entail an understanding of social movements as essentially moral phenomena operating in a moral context (Jacobsson and Lindblom 2016). While the moral aspects of contemporary forms of collective action were frequently acknowledged in previous research (e.g., Smelser 1962; Jasper and Nelkin 1992; Jasper 1997; Crossley 2002), this is to go one step further and say that it is the moral dimension that is constitutive of social movements. Who social movements are (collective identity), and what they do (action and strategy), is fundamentally based on a moral grammar.

We suggest that Durkheim's reflections on morality in *Moral Education* allow for a theoretical perspective which is able to reconcile structure and agency, encompass a parallel focus on conflict and consensus, and allow for the theorization of emotional intensity as well as reflexivity in the analysis of social movements' struggle for social change. Durkheim's analysis here is located mainly at the meso-level, focusing on the social group as the main unit of analysis. Here, it is useful to recall Durkheim's view of society, which refers to all kinds of social groups. Durkheim pointed to our simultaneous membership in many different groups, such as family, occupational organization, company, political party, nation, even humanity (Durkheim [1893] 1984: 298; [1887] 1993: 100; [1925] 1961: 73ff.), and, we can add, the activist group. Thus, as Collins (1988: 109) argued, we should "take 'society' in its generic sense, as any instance of prolonged sociation, whatever its boundaries in space or in time." As in modern societies, the individual belongs to many different social groups that all exert pressure on her, we even have several collective consciences operating within us (Durkheim [1893] 1984: 67). Thus, as Collins (2004: 15) noted: "'Collective conscience' can exist in little pockets rather than as one huge sky covering everybody." Being "at once complex and a single whole," Durkheim acknowledged the tensions and contradictions of moral reality (Durkheim [1925] 1961: 111). As morality is group-specific, and groups exist at different levels, there will be competing ideals and norms in a pluralist world. Durkheim's sociology of morality is compatible with moral consensus as well as conflict (see Collins 1988).

A social movement can be conceptualized as a society in Durkheim's sense. According to Durkheim, societies are formed around moral ideals, denoting a conception of what the world should be like; indeed, for Durkheim, the moral ideal is the group's principle raison d'être (Durkheim [1887] 1993: 20). While moral ideals are perceived as desirable (Durkheim [1925] 1961: 96), Durkheim in addition identified a second component of morality that we usually speak of as norms: an element of obligation that prescribes or proscribes certain behaviors or types of behaviors and that are backed up by sanction. Thus, morality is both external and internal to the individual; it is both imposed through social pressure and internalized as embraced ideals (Durkheim [1925] 1961: 96ff.). The distinction between ideals and norms is important for our neo-Durkheimian understanding of social movements. Ideals tend to be unrealized and as yet untranslated into social obligations. We suggest that what social movement activists do is to *interpret and pursue these ideals in order to achieve social change*. Drawing on Durkheim's ideas, we conceptualize social movement activists as *pursuers of moral ideals* as they interpret, formulate, and bring forward new societal visions on matters of concern, such as peace, democracy, and animal rights. As pursuers of ideals, however, activists readily come into *conflict with established social norms*. Thus, activists are constrained by norms as well as being a prominent force in changing norms.

Drawing on the distinction between ideals and norms, our approach stresses social movement activists' inherently ambiguous standing in relation to the moral order of society at large, as pursuers of sacred moral ideals *as well as* norm transgressors. On the one hand, social movement activists may be seen as defending important ideals. Being in conflict with established social norms, on the other hand, activists may *also* be perceived as outsiders, threats, or even criminals by the general public. Being dependent on public reactions for the advancement and success of their cause, social movements must make an effort to downplay the prominence and importance of their norm-breaking while underlining the ideal-conforming aspects of the actions they perform. As Eyerman (2006: 204) argued,

> To be recognized as a movement, rather than a "terrorist" organization, for example, can confer a degree of legitimacy on a group and its actions in that they impute political and in that sense popular, rather than merely criminal, motivations. Part of a group's representational struggle may indeed be to achieve recognition as a movement [...].

It is important in a Durkheimian analysis that moral order, as a social fact, in various ways imposes constraints on activists. This has several implications for social movement theorizing. First, activists have to take existing norms (moral, legal, and ceremonial ones) into account when carrying out their actions. Second, as activists are committed to their sacred ideals, and have to stay true to them when carrying out their actions, morality is not something that can simply be "used" and "traded" instrumentally as more actor-oriented and voluntaristic models on protest would have it (such as the highly influential framing approaches; see Benford and Snow 2000). After the critique of structural-functionalism, actor-oriented approaches came to dominate the study of social movements, stressing social movements as institutionalized and strategic actors. These approaches frequently see even morality as a cultural resource that actors interpret and use (e.g., Swidler 1995; Williams 1995; for a critique, see Alexander 1996; Crossley 2002), rather than focusing on the structural dimensions of morality. As Alexander has argued in a critique of the strategic action paradigm in social movement theory, such approaches make social movements "resemble complex maximizing machines" (Alexander 1996: 208). Indeed, the most important contribution that a Durkheimian lens would bring to social movement theorizing is to rectify the strategic action framework by complementing the actor-oriented models of morality with a conception of morality as social fact. Opportunity structures are, in this perspective, first and foremost moral, whether they manifest in a political, legal, cultural, or discursive context. Or in Durkheim's terms, "social life is nothing other than the moral milieu or better, the collection of different moral milieux which surround the individual" (Durkheim cited in Stedman Jones 2001: 15).

Durkheim's moral-sociological perspective is able to reconcile structure and agency. Moral ideals are central to action and transformation in Durkheim's understanding (see also Stedman Jones 2001). Belonging to the sphere of "the sacred," collective ideals are vested with prestige (Durkheim [1912] 2001), giving ideals an action-motivating force; the sacred ideals and the emotions that these ideals evoke are the driving force that propels social movement activists to pursue a social change agenda. Rather than seeing the sacred as being abolished in modern societies, we can, as Emirbayer argued, speak of a "developmental history of the sacred," and of the rise "of conflicts over the very meaning and legitimate definition of sacred ideals" (Emirbayer 1996: 115; see also Alexander and Mast 2006: 7ff.). It is precisely in such conflicts that social movement activists engage.

Moreover, Durkheim's sociology of morality allows not only for agency but also for reflexive action. Durkheim stressed the "active and creative energy that is developed through the most continuous and intimate communication with the very source of moral energy—that is to say, society" (Durkheim [1925] 1961: 100) *as well as* "the active and imaginative forces of the conscience" which must be stimulated, in order for morality to develop (102). Few authors have acknowledged that Durkheim identified, alongside ideals and norms, a third element of morality, which he called *autonomy* (see, however, Stedman Jones 2001; Dawson 2017). The modernization process—secularization, the development of modern science, and, especially, individualism—entails an increased autonomy of the individual in relation to collective imperatives (e.g., Durkheim [1925] 1961: 1–14):

> Society is continually evolving; morality itself must be sufficiently flexible to change gradually as proves necessary. But this requires that morality not be internalized in such a way as to be beyond criticism or reflection, the agents par excellence of all change.
>
> (Durkheim [1925] 1961: 52)

Moral autonomy gives reflection a key role in social change. "Reflection alone makes possible the discovery of new and effectual practices, for it is only by reflection that the future can be anticipated" (Durkheim [1950] 1992: 90). That was why Durkheim saw deliberative assemblies as key to achieve the "changes that present-day conditions of collective existence demand" (90). Reflection and deliberation were thus key to Durkheim's conception of agency (e.g., Emirbayer 2003; Stedman Jones 2001).

Even so, Durkheim-inspired analyses of rituals have tended to stress the empowering but nonreflexive nature of such processes (see, however, Giesen 2006). Nevertheless, even in *The Elementary Forms of Religious Life*, Durkheim opened for some level of reflexivity: "The emotions provoked by these periodic crises of external things make the men who witness them determined to reunite and consult one another on an appropriate course of action. But they find mutual comfort in the very fact of assembling; they find the remedy because they seek it together" (Durkheim [1912] 2001: 256). For Durkheim, group effort is key to achieve change and to handle social evils: "One can act effectively upon society only by grouping individual efforts in such a way as to counter social forces with social forces [...]. Individual energies must be grouped, concentrated, organized to produce any effect" (Durkheim [1925] 1961: 84). Moreover, ideals must be actively willed: "Our wills alone can make it a living reality" (Durkheim [1924] 1974: 89). Thus Durkheim clearly identified both reflection and collective effort as sources of change, along with deliberation.

Our neo-Durkheimian perspective stresses the role of moral reflexivity in social movements, and especially social actors' potential awareness of discrepancies between ideals and norms (Jacobsson and Lindblom 2016). Activists seek to change dominant social practices and moral codes to bring them more in tune with their ideals. In doing so, they must both stay true to their ideals and handle their partial clash with existing norms, indeed the success of which requires moral reflexivity. Reflexivity is both a resource of the individual (the individual's agency and ability to think and reflect) and a property of the social structure (reflexivity is linked to the social norms and moral ideals of society). For social movement theorizing, this means that activists have the competence to alter a given condition known to them, yet are constrained by a moral-social order that exists as a social fact.

While social movement activists must take their moral environments into account in their struggle for social change, here they can draw on achievements from previous struggles. For instance, the now commonly shared ideal of democracy makes it easier to win battles in new areas in society where this ideal has not yet been implemented. And in the course of history, the sacralization of the individual (Durkheim [1925] 1961; see Joas 2013) has been extended to new groups, such as women or people of color. "For the necessary progress is possible only thanks to progress already achieved. It is a matter of completing, extending, and organizing individualism, not of restraining and combating it. It is a matter of using reflection, not of imposing silence upon it" (Durkheim 1973: 56). For Durkheim, the development of individualism has the effect of opening moral consciousness to new ideas and rendering it more demanding: "Since every advance that it makes results in a higher conception, a more delicate sense of the dignity of man, individualism cannot be developed without making apparent to us as contrary to human dignity, as unjust, social relations that at one time did not seem unjust at all" (Durkheim [1925] 1961: 12). In our analysis of animal rights activism, we have suggested that these activists extend the sacralization of the human person to the sacralization of the animal-individual, thus expanding individualism to encompass animal individuals as well. In doing so, they also challenge established boundaries between sacred and profane, when dismantling the symbolic boundary between humans and animals (Cherry 2010), which may seem provoking to mainstream norms.

Durkheim ([1925] 1961: 107) spoke of the evolution of morality and said that great moral transformations take time. I find it close at hand to see social movements as such forces of moral evolution, as well as the collective force that Durkheim argued, were necessary as a counterbalance to the state (Durkheim [1950] 1992: 63).

Conclusion

A major benefit of Durkheim's sociology lies in the avoidance of both oversocialized and undersocialized versions of society (e.g., Alexander 1988; Meštrović 1988;

Emirbayer 2003), which is also the main benefit of a Durkheimian perspective on social movements. Social movements emerge as the collective response to shared discontents (Traugott 1984: 326), on the basis of shared moral ideals that are actively willed and form the basis for social and political action. A conception of morality as desired ideal as well as existing social fact, enabling and constraining actions, helps to rectify overly actor- and strategic-action-oriented models, while allowing us also to theorize collective agency and, indeed, to theorize what moves, "fuses," and energizes social movements. As argued earlier in this chapter, these emotional processes are not mindless. Emotional refill and renewal of moral commitment are fully compatible with the exertion of moral reflexivity in collective action (Jacobsson and Lindblom 2013, 2016; see Durkheim [1925] 1961). Indeed, a Durkheimian approach allows us to integrate the cognitive, emotive, and moral dimensions of social action. Moreover, it allows us to see social movements as emergent phenomena with intended as well as unintended consequences.

Moreover, a Durkheimian lens allows for a parallel focus on conflict and consensus, the combination of which is characteristic of the moral order in modern societies. Many of the great conflicts of our time appear around clashing norms, or divergent interpretation of sacred ideals (most importantly, the role and status of the individual), conflicts in which social movements frequently engage. Less explored in research so far is the fact that Durkheim is also useful for theorizing the consequences of engaging in such conflicts, such as the challenges that social movement activists encounter in their pursuit of social change, as well as experiences of estrangement and deviance that activists may have when they go against the stream (Lindblom and Jacobsson 2014). Durkheim teaches us that it is at such occasions that the social forces are most apparent (Durkheim [1895] 1982: 51ff.). Contrary to structuralist readings of Durkheim, a Durkheimian lens allows us to integrate the macro-meso-micro-levels of analysis: analytically integrating the social-moral milieu in all its complexity, the social movement as a collective (including social relationships, shared symbols, practices, emotions), as well as the implications for the lifeworlds of the individual activists.

A potential for future research lies in the reading of Durkheim as a relational theorist (as argued by, e.g., Emirbayer 1996; Emirbayer and Goodwin 1996; Stedman Jones 2001; Segre 2004) and in the implications of Durkheim's relational ontology for the bridging of agency and structure in social movement theory.

To conclude, rather than a developed theory of social movements, what Durkheim provides is a general theoretical, and deeply sociological, outlook on social life; he offers a starting point for theorization on social movements rather than the end product. In this project, the researcher is well advised to incorporate dimensions on which Durkheim was less articulate, such as power relationships. Developing middle-range theory based on a Durkheimian ontology is also a way in which social movement analysis, rather than remaining a confined field of study, could again be fruitfully integrated within general social theory, without the limitations set by structural functionalism and the disintegration paradigm.

REFERENCES

Alexander, Jeffrey C. 1988. *Action and Its Environments: Toward a New Synthesis.* New York: Columbia University Press.

Alexander, Jeffrey C. 1996. "Collective Action, Culture and Civil Society: Secularizing, Updating, Inverting, Revising and Displacing the Classical Model of Social Movements." In *Alain Touraine*, edited by Jon Clark and Marco Diani, 205–234. London: Falmer Press.

Alexander, Jeffrey C., and Jason L. Mast. 2006. "Introduction. Symbolic Action in Theory and Practice: The Cultural Pragmatics of Symbolic Action." In *Social Performance: Symbolic Action, Cultural Pragmatics, and Ritual*, edited by Jeffrey C. Alexander, Bernhard Giesen, and Jason L. Mast, 1–28. Cambridge: Cambridge University Press.

Barker, Colin. 1999. "Empowerment and Resistance: 'Collective Effervescence' and Other Accounts." In *Transforming Politics: Power and Resistance*, edited by Paul Bagguley and Jeff Hearn, 11–31. Basingstoke: Macmillan.

Benford, Robert D., and David A. Snow. 2000. "Framing Processes and Social Movements: An Overview and Assessment." *Annual Review of Sociology* 26: 611–639.

Buechler, Steven M. 2004. "The Strange Career of Strain and Breakdown Theories of Collective Action." In *The Blackwell Companion to Social Movements*, edited by David A. Snow, Sarah A. Soule, and Hanspeter Kriesi, 47–66. Oxford: Blackwell.

Buechler, Steven M. (2011) 2016. *Understanding Social Movements: Theories from the Classical Era to the Present.* London: Routledge.

Casquete, Jesus. 2006. "The Power of Demonstrations." *Social Movement Studies* 5, no. 1: 45–60.

Cherry, Elizabeth. 2010. "Shifting Symbolic Boundaries: Cultural Strategies of the Animal Rights Movement." *Sociological Forum* 25, no. 3: 450–475.

Collins, Randall. 1988. "The Durkheimian Tradition in Conflict Sociology." In *Durkheimian Sociology: Cultural Studies*, edited by Jeffrey C. Alexander, 107–128. New York: Cambridge University Press.

Collins, Randall. 2001. "Social Movements and the Focus of Emotional Attention." In *Passionate Politics: Emotions and Social Movements*, edited by Jeff Goodwin, James M. Jasper, and Francesca Polletta, 27–44. Chicago: University of Chicago Press.

Collins, Randall. 2004. *Interaction Ritual Chains.* Princeton, NJ: Princeton University Press.

Crossley, Nick. 2002. *Making Sense of Social Movements.* Buckingham: Open University Press.

Dawson, Matt. 2017. "Morality as Rebellion: Towards a Partial Reconciliation of Bauman and Durkheim." *Distinktion: Journal of Social Theory* 18, no. 3: 255–273.

Diani, Mario, and Doug McAdam. 2003. *Social Movements and Networks: Relational Approaches to Collective Action.* Oxford: Oxford University Press.

Durkheim, Émile. (1897) 1951. *Suicide: A Study in Sociology.* Translated by John A. Spaulding and George Simpson. New York: Free Press.

Durkheim, Émile. (1925) 1961. *Moral Education: A Study in the Theory and Application of the Sociology of Education.* Translated by E. K. Wilson and H. Schnurer. New York: Free Press.

Durkheim, Émile. 1973. *On Morality and Society.* Edited by Robert N. Bellah. Chicago: University of Chicago Press.

Durkheim, Émile. (1924) 1974. *Sociology and Philosophy.* Edited and translated by D. F. Pocock. New York: Free Press.

Durkheim, Émile. (1895) 1982. *The Rules of Sociological Method and Selected Texts on Sociology and Its Method.* London: Macmillan.

Durkheim, Émile. (1893) 1984. *The Division of Labor in Society*. Translated by W. D. Halls. New York: Free Press.
Durkheim, Émile. (1950) 1992. *Professional Ethics and Civic Morals*. Translated by Cornelia Brookfield. London: Routledge.
Durkheim, Émile. (1887) 1993. *Ethics and the Sociology of Morals*. Buffalo, NY: Prometheus Books.
Durkheim, Émile. (1912) 2001. *The Elementary Forms of Religious Life*. Translated by Carol Cosman. Oxford: Oxford University Press.
Emirbayer, Mustafa. 1996. "Useful Durkheim." *Sociological Theory* 14, no. 2: 109–130.
Emirbayer, Mustafa. 2003. "Introduction. Emile Durkheim: Sociologist of Modernity." In *Emile Durkheim: Sociologist of Modernity*, edited by Mustafa Emirbayer, 1–28. Malden, MA: Blackwell.
Emirbayer, Mustafa, and Jeff Goodwin. 1996. "Symbols, Positions, Objects: Toward a New Theory of Revolutions and Collective Action" (Review of *Debating Revolutions* by Nikki R. Keddie). *History and Theory* 35, no. 3: 358–374.
Eyerman, Ron. 2006. "Performing Opposition or, How Social Movements Move." In *Social Performance: Symbolic Action, Cultural Pragmatics, and Ritual*, edited by Jeffrey C. Alexander, Bernhard Giesen, and Jason L. Mast, 193–217. Cambridge: Cambridge University Press.
Flam, Helena, and Debra King, eds. 2005. *Emotions and Social Movements*. London: Routledge.
Gasparre, Anna, Serena Bosco, and Guglielmo Bellelli. 2010. "Cognitive and Social Consequences of Participation in Social Rites: Collective Coping, Social Support, and Post-Traumatic Growth in the Victims of Guatemala Genocide." *Revista de Psicología Social* 25, no. 1: 35–46.
Giddens, Anthony. 1978. *Durkheim*. London: Fontana.
Giesen, Bernhard. 2006. "Performing the Sacred: A Durkheimian Perspective on the Performative Turn in the Social Sciences." In *Social Performance: Symbolic Action, Cultural Pragmatics, and Ritual*, edited by Jeffrey C. Alexander, Bernhard Giesen, and Jason L. Mast, 325–367. Cambridge: Cambridge University Press.
Gould, Deborah B. 2001 "Rock the Boat, Don't Rock the Boat, Baby: Ambivalence and the Emergence of Militant AIDS Activism." In *Passionate Politics: Emotions and Social Movements*, edited by Jeff Goodwin, James M. Jasper and Francesca Polletta, 135–157. Chicago: University of Chicago Press.
Gould, Deborah B. 2009. *Moving Politics: Emotion and ACT UP's Fight against AIDS*. Chicago: University of Chicago Press.
Gurr, Ted Robert. 1970. *Why Men Rebel*. Princeton, NJ: Princeton University Press.
Hunt, Lynn. 1988. "The Sacred and the French Revolution." In *Durkheimian Sociology: Cultural Studies*, edited by Jeffrey C. Alexander, 25–43. New York: Cambridge University Press.
Jacobsson, Kerstin. 2014. "Elementary Forms of Religious Life in Animal Rights Activism." *Culture Unbound* 6, no. 2: 305–326.
Jacobsson, Kerstin, and Jonas Lindblom. 2013. "Emotion Work in Animal Rights Activism: A Moral-Sociological Perspective." *Acta Sociologica* 56, no. 1: 55–68.
Jacobsson, Kerstin, and Lindblom, Jonas. 2016. *Animal Rights Activism: A Moral-Sociological Perspective on Social Movements*. Amsterdam: Amsterdam University Press.
Jansen, Annette. 2017. *Anti-Genocide Activists and the Responsibility to Protect*. London: Routledge.

Jasper, James M. 1997. *The Art of Moral Protest: Culture, Biography, and Creativity in Social Movements.* Chicago: University of Chicago Press.
Jasper, James M. 1998. "The Emotions of Protest: Affective and Reactive Emotions In and Around Social Movements." *Sociological Forum* 13, no. 3: 397–424.
Jasper, James M., and Dorothy Nelkin. 1992. *The Animal Rights Crusade: The Growth of a Moral Protest.* New York: Free Press.
Jasper, James M., and Jane D. Poulsen. 1995. "Recruiting Strangers and Friends: Moral Shocks and Social Networks in Animal Rights and Anti-Nuclear Protests." *Social Problems* 42, no. 4: 493–512.
Joas, Hans. 2013. *The Sacredness of the Person: A New Genealogy of Human Rights.* Washington, DC: Georgetown University Press.
Kornhauser, William. 1959. *The Politics of Mass Society.* New York: Free Press.
Le Bon, Gustave. (1895) 1960. *The Crowd: A Study of the Popular Mind.* New York: Viking Press.
Lindblom, Jonas, and Kerstin Jacobsson. 2014. "A Deviance Perspective on Social Movements: The Case of Animal Rights Activism." *Deviant Behavior* 35, no. 2: 133–151.
Meštrović, Stjepan G. 1988. *Émile Durkheim and the Reformation of Sociology.* Lanham, MD: Rowman & Littlefield.
Mukherjee, S. Romi, ed. 2010. *Durkheim and Violence.* Chichester: Wiley-Blackwell.
Nisbet, Robert A. 1965. *Émile Durkheim.* Englewood Cliffs, NJ: Prentice Hall.
Olesen, Thomas. 2015. *Global Injustice Symbols and Social Movements.* New York: Palgrave Macmillan.
Peterson, Abby. 2001. *Contemporary Political Protest: Essays on Political Militancy.* Aldershot: Ashgate.
Pettenkofer, Andreas. 2010. *Radikaler Protest: Zur soziologischen Theorie politischer Bewegungen.* Frankfurt am Main: Campus.
Ruiz-Junco, Natalia. 2013. "Feeling Social Movements: Theoretical Contributions to Social Movement Research on Emotions." *Sociology Compass* 7, no. 1: 45–54.
Sassoon, Joseph. 1984. "Ideology, Symbolic Action and Rituality in Social Movements: The Effects on Organizational Forms." *Social Science Information* 23, no. 4–5: 861–873.
Segre, Sandro. 2004. "A Durkheimian Network Theory." *Journal of Classical Sociology* 4, no. 2: 215–235.
Shilling, Chris, and Philip A. Mellor. 2011. "Retheorising Emile Durkheim on Society and Religion: Embodiment, Intoxication and Collective Life." *The Sociological Review* 59, no. 1: 17–41.
Smelser, Neil J. 1962. *Theory of Collective Behaviour.* London: Routledge & Kegan Paul.
Smith, Philip, and Jeffrey C. Alexander. 2005. "Introduction: The New Durkheim." In *The Cambridge Companion to Durkheim*, edited by Jeffrey C. Alexander and Philip Smith, 1–37. Cambridge: Cambridge University Press.
Stedman Jones, Susan. 2001. *Durkheim Reconsidered.* Malden, MA: Polity.
Summers-Effler, Erika. 2002. "The Micro Potential for Social Change: Emotion, Consciousness, and Social Movement Formation." *Sociological Theory* 20, no. 1: 41–60.
Swidler, Ann. 1995. "Cultural Power and Social Movements." In *Social Movements and Culture*, edited by Hank Johnston and Bert Klandermans, 25–40. Minneapolis: University of Minnesota Press.
Taylor, Verta, and Nancy Whittier. 1995. "Analytical Approaches to Social Movement Culture: The Culture of the Women's Movement." In *Social Movements and Culture*, edited by Hank Johnston and Bert Klandermans, 163–187. Minneapolis: University of Minnesota Press.

Tilly, Charles. 1978. *From Mobilization to Revolution*. New York: Random House.
Tilly, Charles. 1981. "Useless Durkheim." In *As Sociology Meets History*, 95–108. New York: Academic Press.
Tilly, Charles, Louise Tilly, and Richard Tilly. 1975. *The Rebellious Century 1830–1930*. Cambridge, MA: Harvard University Press.
Tiryakian, Edward A. 1995. "Collective Effervescence, Social Change and Charisma: Durkheim, Weber and 1989." *International Sociology* 10, no. 3: 269–281.
Traugott, Mark. 1984. "Durkheim and Social Movements." *Archives Européennes de Sociologie* 25, no. 2: 319–326.
Turner, Ralph H., and Lewis M. Killian.1987. *Collective Behavior*. 3rd ed. Englewood Cliffs, NJ: Prentice Hall.
Wahnich, Sophie. 2012. *In Defence of the Terror: Liberty or Death in the French Revolution*. London: Verso.
Williams, Rhys H. 1995. "Constructing the Public Good: Social Movements and Cultural Resources." *Social Problems* 42, no. 1: 124–144.

CHAPTER 19

DURKHEIM AND THE SOCIOLOGY OF HUMAN–ANIMAL RELATIONS

ROBERT SEYFERT

Introduction

STANDARD introductions define sociology as "the scientific study of *human* social life, groups and societies" (Giddens 2006: 4; italics mine). Ever since its founding, the discipline has tended to consider the *socius* whose life it studies as an exclusively human phenomenon. In recent years, sociology has been accused of being an anthropocentric discipline, and even of "reactionary humanism" (McFarlane 2013: 46). Émile Durkheim's work, too, has not escaped this charge of anthropocentrism (e.g., Nimmo 2011: 74; Ross 2017: 21). In turn, approaches such as actor network theory (ANT) (e.g., Law and Hassard 1999; Latour 2005) and the sociology of nonhuman animals (e.g., Arluke and Sanders 1996; Sanders 2007) have convincingly argued that nonhumans in general (ANT) and animals in particular (sociology of nonhuman animals) are simply too widespread and too relevant as actors within everyday social life to be ignored in sociological investigations.

Durkheim's work appears doubly distant from these newly expanded circles of sociological concern. At first glance, relations between humans and nonhuman animals do not seem to be of primary importance in Durkheim's writing, since accounts of them are subsumed under the study of totemism. These accounts of totemism are, on the one hand, often classed under the rubric of sociology of religion and, on the other hand, seen as specialist studies of practices peculiar to totemism, and of limited applicability to contemporary globalized, industrialized, and postindustrial societies. Finally, Durkheim's typology of societies has been accused of casting cultural distinctions as evolutionary differences, of introducing a false teleology to cultural forms.

The idea that Durkheim relegates totemism to some kind of "primitive"—that is, less differentiated—"mentality" is an unfortunate consequence of the functionalist and structuralist reception of his work.[1] Claude Lévi-Strauss's influential interpretation of Durkheim posits that nonhuman totemic figures are all-too-human mental representations that aid in the structuring of human societies. However, such a reading fails to take seriously the self-understanding of totemic societies, a failure that stems in part from the very unfamiliar ways in which totemic societies organize relations between humans and other nonhuman animals. The inability to truly come to terms with a "totemic otherwise" (Povinelli 2016) has meant that subsequent scholarship has glossed over Durkheim's careful analysis of those features of totemic societies that prove especially challenging to our own anthropocentrism.

Through a careful reading of Durkheim's work on totemism, this chapter shows how Durkheim, by taking seriously the self-understanding of totemic societies, generated a historically dynamic theory of totemic societies and their relations to their nonhuman "others." In doing so, he has shown how the preoccupations and practices of totemic societies, often deemed so distant, have the capacity to speak to us about our own present struggles with how to make ethical and social sense of new challenges: genetic codes, artificial intelligence, how to treat nonhuman others, and so forth. I will briefly touch on some of these issues in the final section of this chapter.

In the following discussion, I focus mainly on three Durkheim texts: *Concerning the Definition of Religious Phenomena* ([1898] 1975), *On Totemism* ([1900/1901] 1985), and *The Elementary Forms of Religious Life* ([1912] 1995; hereafter, *Elementary Forms*).

Ritual or Myth?

To understand the impact of Lévi-Strauss's interpretation on the reception of Durkheim's work, we have to turn to a classical debate in the sociology of religion and religious studies, one that predates Durkheim's work. This is the question of whether rituals enact myths or, conversely, whether myths are the result of ritual performances: Do rituals enact pre-existing symbolic beliefs (in the form of myths, narratives, etc.) or, vice versa, do symbols emerge from the practices of rituals, which are then "translated" into language and semantic meaning, taking the form of myths, narratives, and stories? Do collective beliefs drive and motivate common action, or are the former the product of the latter?

Claude Lévi-Strauss came down on the side of the symbol, and his structuralist reading strongly influenced later work, such as Mary Douglas's theory of social processes of symbolization (Douglas 2001: 22) and the "cultural turn" of the 1980s (Alexander and Smith 2008: 12). Lévi-Strauss's structural symbolism emerged from a criticism of previous studies of totemism. Most importantly, Lévi-Strauss wanted to show that the so-called primitive thinking of totemic societies is by no means irrational but in fact analytical, and as such, similar to the scientific thinking of "modern" societies. Symbolic structuralism characterizes totemic societies as consisting of a vast universe of (human) cognitive operations: the totemic identification of human beings with animals, plants, or objects is a mental projection of, and symbolization by, humans (see, e.g., Knoblauch 1999: 64). In Lévi-Strauss's famous phrase: "The animal world and that of plant life are not utilized merely because they are there, but because they suggest a mode of thought" (Lévi-Strauss 1963: 13). I call this the *symbolic hypothesis*: a systematic reduction of all social constructions to the mental projections, social imagination, and collective representations of human members. Before demonstrating the problems involved in the application of this symbolic hypothesis to both Durkheim's work and the study of totemic societies, it is important to note what Lévi-Strauss tried to achieve with this research tool. The symbolic hypothesis tried to achieve what recent scholars would call a decolonization of anthropology; it was an attempt to erase the difference between "rational modernity" and "irrational primitivism." What Lévi-Strauss did achieve, however, is an intellectualization of non-Western societies, including totemic societies (as well as modern societies). Recent critiques of such intellectualizations not only help us (Western scholars) to re-evaluate modern societies, which have never been so modern after all (Latour 1993), they also help us to approach non-Western societies on their own terms (e.g., Kwek and Seyfert 2018). They help us to understand that non-Western thought cannot easily be identified as either analytical or irrational, for both descriptions are different sides of the same (binary) classificatory system. Thus, such a re-evaluation and demodernization is not an attempt to reirrationalize non-Western societies, but rather an effort to overcome the reductionism of scientific approaches, such as the reduction of social life to cognitive operations that symbolic structuralism performs.

I am arguing that a re-evaluation of Durkheim's work can be particularly useful here, since he avoided the reductionisms of symbolic structuralism. Even though many scholars identify his work with some form of symbolic theory, it is important to note that Durkheim develops a far more complex approach. On a first glance, Durkheim himself seems to adopt ambiguous stances toward the ritual-or-symbol question in different parts of his work. In *Elementary Forms*, he famously says that, "in all its aspects and at every moment of its history, social life is only possible thanks to a vast symbolism" (Durkheim [1912] 1995: 233); and that "the rite serves and can only serve to maintain the vitality of [...] beliefs and to prevent their memory from being obliterated—in other words, to revitalize the most essential elements of the collective consciousness and conscience" (379). However, he also states at the very end of the same book that it

> is through common action that society becomes conscious of and affirms itself; society is above all an active cooperation. [...] even collective ideas and feelings are possible only through the overt movements that symbolize them. Thus it is action that dominates religious life, for the very reason that society is its source. (421)

Durkheim's seeming ambiguity is neither a sign of indecision or unclear conceptual framing, nor a matter of changing positions in his earlier and later work. Nor does the solution lie in the "parity" of rituals and myths (Pickering 1984: 373–379). Instead of a universally applicable theory privileging either symbol or ritual, Durkheim develops a dynamic and processual model. Durkheim's account of totemic societies does not present static societies, frozen in time, but includes a dynamic account of the compositional changes to totemic societies over time—changes in which nonhuman animals and human–animal relations play a key role. Whether rituals or symbols are primary depends on historical changes in the composition of the social group. The following sections examine the role of ritual in Durkheim's understanding of totemic societies, which has been neglected by interpretations that emphasize the symbolic.

Consubstantiality and Sacrifice

In a letter from 1907, Durkheim calls the anthropological work of William Robertson Smith a "revelation" (Durkheim 1907: 613). While scholars disagree over the nature of this revelation (Pickering 1984: 65; see also Goldenweiser 1915: 722; Evans-Pritchard 1965: 56; Kippenberg 1997: 106–108), Durkheim himself clearly states in his *Elementary Forms* what he derived from Robertson Smith. The revelation has to do with Robertson Smith's definition of totemism (see Robertson Smith 1894). One of the most important totemic rituals is the ritual of the sacrificial meal, which is commonly defined as a symbolic closure of the social group (Lévi-Strauss 1966: 226; Turner and Rojek 2001: 28). However, Durkheim adopted Robertson Smith's analysis of totemism and emphasizes two features of the totem ritual that render the symbolic hypothesis highly unlikely: "First, it is a meal; the substance of sacrifice is food. Second, it is a meal of which the faithful who offer it partake at the same time as the god to whom it is offered" (Durkheim [1912] 1995: 341). The fact that the ritual is related to a meal in which the faithful are as much involved as the gods makes it highly unlikely that the meaning of this ritual is only symbolic. For where, according to the symbolic hypothesis, images and symbols should reign, vital matter moves—the revitalizing substance of food. The totem ritual is a vitalist and social operation: the recreation of bodily strengths in a shared meal. The sacrificial meal is a ritual that distributes a common substance among all members of the group: "totemism presupposes a consubstantiality of man and animal (or plant), whether natural or acquired" (Durkheim [1912] 1995: 87). Those who adhere to some version of the symbolic hypothesis might find the very idea of "consubstantiality" challenging, if not incomprehensible. Durkheim explains clearly what he means:

> [S]ince food constantly remakes the substance of the body, shared food can create the same effects as shared origin. According to Smith, the object of sacrificial banquets is to have the faithful and the god commune in one and the same flesh, to tie a knot of kinship between them. From this perspective, sacrifice came into view in an altogether novel way. Its essence was no longer the act of renunciation that the word

"sacrifice" usually expresses, as was so long believed; it was first and foremost an act of alimentary communion. (341)

Totem societies perform "alimentary communion" for the production of a common substance, a consubstantiality of all group members.

Very often, interpretations of totemism skip over the precise nature of this consubstantiality and concentrate on kinship relations, on symbolizations, or on the production of a group identity that sustains a distinction from other groups (Lévi-Strauss 1966: 105). Thus, the symbolic hypothesis neglects the most important aspect of consubstantiality, namely, what Durkheim, pace Robertson Smith, calls the *substantial identity* of animals, plants, humans, and other objects within one group:

> Indeed, the essential principle of this religious system is that the man and the animal which serves him as totem are united by a close bond of kinship. But this is an understatement; for in reality, there is virtually a *substantive identity* between them. The animal is a member of the clan just as the man who bears his name is of the animal species.
>
> (Durkheim [1900/1901] 1985: 112, italics mine)

What decisively rules out symbolic representation and subjective projections (of humans, always humans) at this stage of ritual imitation is the utter absence of any (idea of) human exceptionalism. Durkheim drew extensively on Karl von den Steinen's empirical research on totemism in *Unter den Naturvölkern Zentral-Brasiliens* (*Among the Indigenous Peoples of Central Brazil*), where von den Steinen cautions against assuming that these societies are based on phantasies and symbolizations: "To suggest that previous times, where the legends originated, *only symbolized* and mixed up descendants, name, and object is a convenient insinuation but an inadmissible one because if this was the case the entire tradition would only consist of confusion" (von den Steinen 1894: 353, italics mine).[2] Thus, von den Steinen insists, "we have to imagine the boundary between human and animal as non-existing" (von den Steinen 1894: 351). Durkheim follows von den Steinen in *insisting on taking totemic societies at their word* and in attempting to fully depict their ways of sense-making:

> In general, the clan has been viewed as merely a group of human beings, merely a subdivision of the tribe. As such, it seems, the clan could only be made up of men. But when we reason this way, we substitute our European ideas for those the primitive has about the world and society. For the Australian, things themselves—all of the things that make up the universe—are part of the tribe. Since they are constituents of it and, in a sense, full-fledged members, they have a definite place in the scheme of society, just as men do.
>
> (Durkheim [1912] 1995: 141)

As Durkheim insists, "all of the things that make up the universe [...] are part of the tribe" (141). To suggest otherwise is to introduce differences that do not exist in these societies. Thus, if we carefully follow Durkheim's own reasoning, and drop the interpretive frame of the symbolic hypothesis, we will see a conception of consubstantiality that demonstrates a radical inclusion of nonhuman things that the contemporary discourse of nonhuman rights is just beginning to catch up with.[3]

It is imperative for Durkheim to analyze the precise relation of the "likeness in nature" of all social members. First, Durkheim repudiates the false parallelism that sees the relation of humans to their totem figure as equivalent to that of a worshipper to his or her god(s):

> we must be careful not to see totemism as a kind of zoolatry. Since man belongs to the sacred world, his attitude toward the animals or plants whose name he bears is by no means the attitude a believer has toward his god. Rather, their relations are those of two beings who are basically at the same level and of equal value. (139)

In other words, these beings identify with one another. These processes of identification are not simply symbolic; instead, they are solidary relations: A totemic group is solidary insofar as humans, animals, plants, objects, spirits, and so on all are on an equal footing. They are "alter egos" for each other (160). They form solidary systems in which both humans as well as nonhumans can become equal members of the group. The relation is substantial and vital. In other words, this relation is not simply one where passive objects (symbols, signs, images) are manipulated by active humans, but a relation of social reciprocity, and thus, a vital relation: "By their joining, then, the people of the clan and the things classified in it form a unified system, with all its parts allied and vibrating sympathetically" (150). This is a substantial or ontological identity, not an imaginary one.

Here, Durkheim describes alter-ego relationships that far exceed what, in classical sociology, is commonly understood as intersubjective relations. This sphere of alter-ego relations is not limited to human relations; it includes all relevant members of a specific culture, including nonhuman ones: "They are all persons with varying appearances and varying qualities" (von den Steinen 1894: 351). In other words, totemic societies are heterological societies, where logic of the social structure (*logos*) allows for the inclusion of radical other (*hetero*) *socii* or members of the group (Kwek and Seyfert 2018).

Totemic societies and our modern society share the focus on a single figure. While totemism most commonly centers on a totem figure that is nonhuman, our modern societies have the human being as its guiding figure. However, both types of societies differ in their degrees of integrability and expandability of this figure, that is, in the ways in which they keep this figure open for outsiders.

For instance, in her anthropological studies of the Malaysian Chewong, Signe Howell has shown that members of this group clearly "differentiate between 'us' and 'them.'" They do not extend their membership indiscriminately to everybody; they clearly exclude others. However, it is important to note that these groups have a mechanism to include almost anybody and anything. While totemic societies tie membership to a particular figure (an animal, a plant, an object), almost everybody can become this figure—thus, everybody can *become* part of this group. In order to become a group member, one has to perform certain ritual practices. For the Chewong, one has to reveal oneself to the group: "Until something has revealed itself as a personage, the Chewong have an agnostic attitude to every plant, stone, or moving creature in the forest" (Howell 1996: 135–136). Relatively uncommon for heterological societies, the Chewong have a preference for the human figure. Like in our societies, the central figure is the human. However, what makes Chewong society heterological, and thus differentiates it from our "modern" societies, is that they accept the possibility that nonhuman members within the group may become human persons; they allow for the extension of humanity to nonhuman beings:

> The continuity, or extension, of humanity is, as it were, moving in and out and around the numerous named and enumerated beings and objects in their environment—in the many worlds that they maintain exist in the forest. What is of interest, however, is that such boundaries are far from absolute, and "us" is a fluid category. (141–142)

As I said, membership depends on rituals and processes rather than biological characteristics and inheritance. Thus, while "modern" human societies define the figure of the human biologically, the totemic classification is cultural. Consequently, it is crucial to understand the rituals and processes that drive this process of *inclusion*: a ritual process of *becoming other*. Karl von den Steinen has shown that changing one's own persona, transforming from one figure into another, is unproblematic and rather common within totemic groups: "You only need to be a shaman who can do everything, to transform from one person into another, to understand all languages that are spoken in the forest or in the sky or in the water" (von den Steinen 1894: 351). The process of transforming one being into another is at its core a ritual, and so is social inclusion.

In contrast, modern human (anthropistic) societies are characterized by the impossibility of such fluidity. It is the most restrictive type of society, in which the most urgent task is always to maintain an anthropological differences vis-à-vis the other, to keep those others out, to remain a homological society.

The Chewong is a heterological society with the human figure at its center. I have mentioned that this is rather uncommon for totemic societies. Durkheim emphasizes that totemic societal forms do not necessarily involve a "favoritism toward the humans" (Durkheim [1900/1901] 1985: 112), nor do they presume a hierarchy in which the human stands at the apex. In fact, Durkheim saw "*the animal form* [as] *the fundamental form*" of totemism (Durkheim [1912] 1995: 64), and he describes complex relations between humans and their nonhuman totem figure:

> For its part, the animal protects the man and is a kind of patron. It alerts him to possible dangers and to means of escaping them; it is said to be the man's friend. [...] Nevertheless, the man's ties with his patron are not ones of dependency, pure and simple. The man, for his part, can act upon the animal. He gives it orders and has power over it.
>
> (Durkheim [1912] 1995: 160–161)

The relation between humans and nonhumans is reciprocal and thus far from being a form of domination or hegemony, animals do not constitute a ruling class in this type of societies; rather, the totem figure is an orientation, a guiding figure that all members of a group strive to become. It defines the nature of a group member (see also Seyfert 2007, 2008). Thus, in totem societies humans strive to become animals (or plants, etc.) in the pursuit of *substantial identity*, through ritual practices of sacrifice.

RITUAL IDENTIFICATION IN TOTEMIC SYSTEMS: ON IMITATION

Like sacrificial rites, imitative rites, which include imitative ritual practices (such as putting on fur, feathers, and masks) and speech and bodily movements that mimic the guiding totem, are ways of identifying with a nonhuman group member that are primarily somatic, corporeal, and praxeological (rather than mental, cognitive, or symbolic). Such rituals affectively distribute the substance of the group among all its members (Seyfert 2012). Durkheim explicitly states that, in order for humans to reach their nonhuman companions:

> there will be only one way for them to affirm their collective existence: to affirm themselves as animals of that same species—and this not only in the silence of consciousness but by physical doing. It is this doing that will form the cult, and obviously it can only be movements by which the man imitates the animal with which he identifies himself.
>
> (Durkheim [1912] 1995: 391)[4]

In other words, these rites are not based on "subjective belief" but on concrete, somatic, corporeal, praxeological—that is, ritual—contact. Again, we can see how reducing Durkheim's work to the symbolic hypothesis fails to account for his analysis of totemic rituals. This particular societal stage is clearly described by the ritual hypothesis, which is at the same time a precognitive and preintellectual hypothesis. It argues that ideas and cognitive processes are secondary phenomena. Ideas and thoughts emerge from the bodily movements and ritual practices. As we will see, from such practices also emerges the idea of the absence of something (e.g., of bodily faculties, skills, elements) that in turn leads to cognitive classifications: I am different from you, because I cannot fly, dance, move like you, and so on.

Anne Rawls argues that imitative rites in fact *create* social relations: "imitative rites invoke and produce a direct relation between action and effects, actually creating and recreating the group that enacts them" (Rawls 1996: 441). By imitating the guiding totem creature, individuals identify with the group, and, at the same time, are able to identify those who belong to the group and those who do not. Imitative rites are thus not merely imaginary productions of lineage, or acts of symbolic representation, but practices that produce a "group substance." There is an obvious reason why symbolic identification is not sufficient for the production of group solidarity in heterological societies: symbolism is not a universal medium of communication.

SOCIETAL TRANSFORMATIONS: STAGES OF TOTEMIC SOCIETIES

Durkheim shows that totemic societies already contain the seed of a transition toward human-centered societies, and that this transition is a gradual evolution,[5] rather than a rupture. In fact, totemism itself, as Durkheim notes, goes through different stages, moving from a ritual to a mythical or symbolic phase. This dynamic or transformative theory of totemic societies is developed in his text *On Totemism* (Durkheim [1900/1901] 1985), which is not regularly cited in debates on Durkheim's work. Far from simply describing the structures and functions of totemic societies, it describes in detail different phases of totemism, which, according to Durkheim's theory, result in social transformations that reach beyond totemic societies. The first phase consists of totemic society in which ritual is primary (T-*r*); in the second phase, *symbol* and *myth* become primary in the totemic society in question (T-*s*); finally, the third phase is a human-centered or anthropistic society (A-*s*). In this third phase, symbol, rather than ritual, is the primary medium of social cohesion.

We have examined in detail the first phase of totemism, with its substantial identity of human and nonhuman members. Indeed, in *Concerning the Definition of Religious Phenomena*, Durkheim explicitly states, "one must recognize that in less advanced religions, rites are already developed and definite when myths are still very rudimentary" (Durkheim [1898] 1975: 99n25). Here, the symbolic hypothesis fails again. Rather, Durkheim is referring to a societal transformation from a ritual to a symbolic stage. What happens to or in totemic societies that makes rituals lose their importance and give way to the symbol as the main medium of social cohesion?

Lillian Lawler's classical analysis of the corporeal-affective dimensions of ritual dances provides a clue about the subtle mechanisms that trigger this transformation. She notes:

> Frequently animal dances of the serious type are characterized by the phenomenon known as "possession." In other words, as the dancer performs he suddenly becomes slightly crazed, [...] [h]is eyes roll wildly, he utters animal cries, he breaks away from the circle of dancers, and sometimes he even crawls on all fours. His companions look upon him with reverence; for the sacred animal, or the god to whom the animal is sacred, is believed to be "within him."
>
> (Lawler 1952: 318–319)

The moment of substantial identification can always, at the same time, create a moment of cognitive disjunction, when his "companions look upon him with reverence." It is precisely the ritual identification with appearances, sounds, and bodily images that draws attention to a primary lack of such features (language, feathers, etc.). Paradoxically, therefore, a difference between human and nonhuman beings emerges precisely in the midst of these rituals, in the very process of identification with other (nonhuman) beings. Ritual identification, which serves to create and protect the consubstantiality of all group members, contains the very undercurrent that has the potential to de-differentiate this identity. Thus, paradoxically, it is in the very rituals of imitation—rituals that are meant to produce a substantial identification—that the differences between humans and their guiding totem are made visible. It is this rendering visible of—for want of a better word—"species" difference within the very ritual that is supposed to generate *identity*, that leads to the transformation of totemic society, and to the second phase where *symbols* become primary.

The transition from the first (T-r) to the second phase (T-s) of totemism is the process of symbolizing the totem figure. Durkheim shows that the totemic symbol, which represents the group and is borrowed from the image of a particular group member, does not originate from the totem figure itself, but from the introduction of a transcendent aspect within the society, when "the representations of the totem are more efficacious than the totem itself" (Durkheim [1912] 1995: 133). From this historical moment on, it is no longer the group members who are sacred, but the represented gods and images. Gilles Deleuze and Félix Guattari (1983: 33) call this process "overcoding" (*surcodage*); the heterogeneous elements within this society become unified by a "transcendent unity" (Deleuze and Guattari 1983: 196).

Thus, the symbolic phase of totemism implies the gradual exclusion of nonhuman (animal and plant) members of the group. It is a twofold process: on the one hand, a process of stripping nonhuman beings of their status as group members, and on the other, a subsequent codification and symbolization that turns the former nonhuman companions into totem images and symbols, which involves a "transformation of totemism" (Durkheim [1900/1901] 1985: 115). Thus, Durkheim's On Totemism is not simply a universal or abstract definition of totemism, but rather an examination of transformations within totemic societies.[6]

What Lévi-Strauss has criticized as a "totemic illusion" (Lévi-Strauss 1963: 15–32)[7]—the indiscriminate subsuming of unrelated and heterogeneous phenomena under a single concept of "totemism"—is in fact a dynamic theory of transformations within totemic societies that also shows how those transformations lead to anthropistic forms.

The symbolism that has been deemed so central to totemism is therefore a late stage; it only appears after the solidary relationship between humans, animals, plants, and objects has been lost. It is an "autochthonous evolution" of totemic societies, one which explains why totemic societies are "losing certain features and acquiring others, so that their present state recalls their original nature only imperfectly" (Durkheim [1900/1901] 1985: 96). The second, symbolic phase of totemism might even be seen as a liminal moment, a threshold that marks the transition from the totemic to the anthropistic type of society. While the first step in the transition from totemic to anthropistic societies consists in a shift from an identification with the totem figure (by eating or imitating it) to its symbolic representation, the next step consists of transformation of the totem into a human figure. So, "[a]t the beginning, sacred beings are conceived of in the form of animals or plants, from which human form has slowly emerged" (Durkheim [1912] 1995: 64). The fact that, from now on, totem figures do not serve as guiding figures for imitative identifications but as sacred symbols for transcendent gods indicates a gradual shift toward another societal form. It implies that the move to the anthropistic stage has been finalized.

The emergence of a symbolic system introduces an anthropistic hierarchy. In anthropistic societies, nonhuman beings, such as animals, plants, rivers, etc. are removed from the realm of the social. While participation in the social requires a human nature, it is decoupled from the realm of the sacred. From now on, the sacred is a transcendent and entirely symbolic space, populated with an abstract image of the human itself. The sacred being emerges in the image of man, a symbol in the shape of a transcendent god: "To find a god constructed entirely out of human elements, one must come almost to Christianity. In Christianity, the God is a man, not only in the physical aspect in which he temporarily manifested himself but also in the ideas and feelings he expresses" (64). In most of today's societies, the totem figure is the human, and all members strive or are forced to become human (see Kwek and Seyfert 2018).

An anthropistic society is a human-centered one, but it is not necessarily anthropocentric. ("Anthropism" is my own term, not Durkheim's.) While *anthropocentrism* is the belief in the superiority of human beings, drawn from the human exceptionalism of the Christian tradition, *anthropism* simply designates social forms that limit inclusion, participation, and membership to humans. (Durkheim's theory is purely analytical and normatively agnostic as far as anthropocentrism is concerned; his interest in anthropological difference, too, is entirely analytical.) In contrast, totemic societies, in which human individuals consider their nonhuman companions as equals, are *heterological societies* (Kwek and Seyfert 2018).[8]

In a way, the transition from totemic to anthropistic societies is also a process of simplifying complexity. Critics have often accused Durkheim of an evolutionary approach that presents history as a process of increasingly complex differentiation (see, e.g., Knoblauch 1999: 60) and thus introduces a teleological bias into his study of cultural forms. What has less often been noted is that, in the transition from totemic to anthropistic societies, Durkheim also shows how this "evolution" can sometimes be a process of de-differentiation. This transformation will end in human exclusivity, the result of a *reduction* in social complexity. It also leads to less differentiated social structures, for example, in family relations. While totemic societies are genuinely heterogeneous with highly diverse and complex social relations, anthropistic societies are characterized by simple homogenous relationships. Totemic societies are defined by a heterogeneity in the membership of a group, with human and nonhuman members, with highly complex family relations and plural forms of subjectivity. Such group members do not only have human family members but also various relations to a variety of nonhuman beings, each of which is defined by family ties of varying strength. For instance, every group member has different levels of kinship relations and thus always a vast variety of totem references, with private totems, group totems, family totems, and so on. A member of a totemic society truly is part of what we might today call a postmodern patchwork family. The transition from totemism to anthropism is a process of de-differentiation that leaves only human members and limited family relations.

However, this reduction in complexity, and the exclusive focus on interhuman relations, extensively draw on relations to nonhuman others, relations that remain mostly hidden and implicit. Arnold Gehlen, building on Durkheim's work, has described the constitution of human beings as a *parasitism* upon nonhumans. Aside from the "exploitation of animal procreation" that serves as an "infinite supply" for human nutrition and biological constitution (Gehlen 2004: 102), human social identity, too, is derived from nonhumans. Gehlen argues that "the human being cannot make any directly applicable propositions about itself; it only grasps itself by proxy of nonhumans, by identifying with them and differentiating itself from them at the same time." He calls this process a *"differentiating identification* with an animal" (Gehlen 2004: 119; italics mine). Thus, a specifically human social identity relies on the exclusion of nonhuman others, with humans denying that their very nature is constitutively dependent on nonhuman others whom they refuse to accept as group members. Thus, in that transition from the ritual to the symbolic phase of totemism, the experience of the otherness of the animal within the very ritual that is meant to create a human identity with his or her totem guide, the seed of a *differentiating identification* is planted.

Contemporary and Future Societal Forms

In this final section, I would like to show how a Durkheim-inspired analysis of society, and his understanding of rituals as practices of identification that produce group membership, can help us understand the potential transformations and future differentiations of our anthropistic societies. Contemporary societies self-identify as essentially human societies. The human "person" is its sacred center, ideologically manifested in humanist philosophy and human rights (Joas 2013). Thus, in anthropistic societies, the guiding totem is the human. The human "nature" of anthropistic societies is produced in various identification rituals that can be epistemological, juridical, political, corporeal, and experimental.

Anthropistic identification rituals include juridical definitions of "personhood." Obviously, only humans are allowed to be persons. However, even humans are subjected to processes of becoming human, for example, through humanist education efforts and through constant reminders of the fragility of human rights. Conversely, in order to facilitate the extension of certain social protections to nonhuman companions, juridical rituals are necessary. Thus, the notion of "personal dignity" or juridical "personhood" is increasingly extended beyond humans: this can be seen in a variety of recent legal revisions. Examples of these transformations abound, including the changes to Article 120 of the Swiss constitution in 1992 (which refers to the dignity of sentient creatures in general and explicitly accounts for plants), the New Constitution of Ecuador (2008), which recognizes nature as a legal subject, the law on Mother Earth (Pacha Mama) adopted by the Bolivian government in 2011, which recognizes the right of nature independent of its value for human beings, the granting of legal personhood to the Whanganui River in New Zealand in 2017, and the declaration of the Ganges and the Yamuna Rivers in India as living and legal entities in 2017. However, with the exception of Pacha Mama, this extension of the status of personhood to nonhumans imposes on them human characteristics; the arguments for the acknowledgment of personhood are often made by noting the extent to which these nonhumans resemble humans, for example, by pointing to the sentience of plants or animals, to the nurturing relation of a river to a people, and so on.

From a ritualistic point of view, the scientific study of human nature is an epistemological ritual identification of humans. This is nowhere more clearly demonstrated than in those cases where the right to participate in some or all aspects of human social life has been denied to certain groups. Likewise scientific studies of nonhumans, for example, animal ethology, can also be understood as forms of ritual identification, as early studies of animal behavior by Oskar Heinroth and Konrad Lorenz have shown (Lorenz 1965; Heinroth 1990). If brought up under human guardianship (e.g., in a laboratory), a freshly hatched gray goose will immediately start to adopt and imitate a human as its "mother." It will be strongly convinced that it is of the same kind as its companions. All later attempts to have the young goose befriend other gray geese will fail. It will refuse to become a companion of other gray geese. This identification goes beyond a particular individual—the young gray goose does not only identify with its particular human "mother"; it will consider every human being it meets a potential companion (Heinroth 1990: 633–634). The animal is identifying itself with its human companion—it is becoming human. It is not the biological marking that determines this identification. Rather, companionship triggers social membership. It is safe to say that most studies of animal behavior are somehow related to making nonhumans imitate and identify with humans. For instance, to "test" whether or not an animal can count numbers is nothing but an imitation and identification ritual. Only in anthropistic societies do animals have to count numbers. In other words, rather than a study of the nature of an animal, the study of animal behavior is a performative process of making this animal human.

However, just as the rituals of identification with animals in totemic society led to *differentiating identification* that generated differences within the very act of producing substantial identification, in anthropistic societies, too, the attempts to make both nonhumans and humans more human also always have the unintended side effect of making them—making us—a little more nonhuman. The auto-identification of humans as humans leads to further differentiations (perhaps of a different kind) on the human plane.

The paradox of anthropological exclusivity has the unintended side effect of making us more nonhuman. Thus, while all scientific thought is performed in the name of humans, it makes us ever more nonhuman. A classical epistemological example of humans becoming nonhumans can be found in Darwin's theory of biological evolution. The quest for the origins of (hu)man famously dissolves anthropological exclusivity and recreates the human–animal bond from the inside. Like totemism, the theory of evolution creates lineages of descent from a kind of ur-totem-creature. Humans also always share relations to nonhuman relatives. This ranges from the differentiating identification of the human relation to primates, to the discovery of our "inner fish" Tiktaalik, an ancient predator fish to which humans and all mammals owe their five fingers (Shubin 2008). Once such epistemological and conceptual differentiations (or differentiating identifications) have taken off, anthropistic societies seem to be unable to stop the retroactive incursion of nonhumans, as can be seen in the discovery that an overwhelming percentage of genes is common to humans and other animals, even mushrooms, or in the fact that 90 percent of the human body consist of bacteria cells. Furthermore, attempts to improve human nature also tend to nudge humans toward more nonhuman-ness. Examples can be found in today's medicine (e.g., the use of pig heart valves) or technology (e.g., cyborgs, AI, etc.).

In anthropistic societies, lines of human ancestry and descent are being recoded, and it is worthwhile studying the rituals and other practices that accompany such recodings, or indeed, to question the absence of rites and practices that would help us make practical social sense of these recodings.

It remains to be seen whether these recodings will lead to the decline of anthropistic society, to a radical change of the guiding figure, just as it happened to totemic societies. Perhaps the signs of becoming nonhuman I have just described are early signs of an emerging new societal type, or perhaps we are in a liminal phase, where neither the animal nor the human or the plant is the dominant form. It might be too early to give a name to this societal type, but as our various examples show, it might be a type in which various kinds of *socii* will equally participate in the membership of the group. Perhaps we are on the way to a heterological society (Kwek and Seyfert 2018).

Notes

1. For an overview of this debate, see Pickering (1984: 362–379).
2. The following quotations from Karl von den Steinen are my translations.
3. Durkheim appears to have prefigured the recent "ontological turn" in anthropology and the other human sciences, with its emphasis on the importance of nonhuman members in social groups (Descola 1992; Viveiros de Castro 2012; Kohn 2013; Holbraad, Pedersen, and Viveiros de Castro 2014), though perhaps the full import of his ideas could only be understood once the "turn" had been made.
4. For instance, Edward Sapir has shown that the Takelma, an indigenous tribe in North America, imitates the phonetics of their totem figure. "*l* is freely prefixed to any word spoken by the bear. Its uneuphonious character is evidently intended to match the coarseness of the

bear [...] The prefixed sibilant *s·* serves in a similar way as a sort of sneezing adjunct to indicate the speech of the coyote. *Gwi'di* where? says the ordinary mortal; *Igwi'di*, the bear; *s·gwi'di*, the coyote" (Sapir 1922: 8n2).
5. Durkheim adopted Darwin's theory of evolution, but his interpretation is quite idiosyncratic. It is also radically different from Spencer's social Darwinism. For Durkheim evolution is a process to circumvent conflict and competition rather than a struggle for survival and so on (see Seyfert 2015).
6. His main argument is that the functional mechanism of economic reciprocity is not the core of totemism (as Frazer has argued), but rather a phenomenon of a later stage.
7. As often in such cases, Lévi-Strauss was not the first who formulated this criticism (e.g., Goldenweiser 1910: 266; Boas 1910: 321).
8. It is true that Durkheim's theory operates with a difference between humans and animals. He defines humans by a duality—they are at the same time individuals and units of a collective entity. The "homo duplex," as he calls the human being, is made of two parts, "one purely individual, which has its roots in our organism, the other social, which is nothing except an extension of society" (Durkheim [1914] 2005: 37, 44).

References

Alexander, Jeffrey C., and Philip Smith. 2008. "Introduction: The New Durkheim." In *The Cambridge Companion to Durkheim*, edited by Jeffrey C. Alexander and Philip Smith, 1–37. Cambridge: Cambridge University Press.

Arluke, Arnold, and Clinton R. Sanders. 1996. *Regarding Animals*. Philadelphia: Temple University Press.

Boas, Franz. 1910. "The Origin of Totemism." *The Journal of American Folklore* 23: 392–393.

Deleuze, Gilles, and Félix Guattari. 1983. *Anti-Oedipus: Capitalism and Schizophrenia*. Minneapolis: University of Minnesota Press.

Descola, Philippe. 1992. "Societies of Nature and the Nature of Society." In *Conceptualizing Society*, edited by A. Kuper, 107–126. London: Routledge.

Douglas, Mary. 2001. *Purity and Danger: An Analysis of Concepts of Pollution and Taboo*. London: Routledge.

Durkheim, Émile (1898) 1975. "Concerning the Definition of Religious Phenomena." In *Durkheim on Religion: A Selection of Readings with Bibliographies and Introductory Remarks*, edited by W. S. F. Pickering, 74–99. London: Routledge.

Durkheim, Émile. (1900/1901) 1985. "On Totemism." *History of Sociology* 5, no. 2: 91–121.

Durkheim, Émile. 1907. "Lettres au Directeur de la *Revue néo-scolastique*." *Revue néo-scolastique* 14: 606–607, 612–614.

Durkheim, Émile. 1912 (1995). *The Elementary Forms of Religious Life*. New York: Free Press.

Durkheim, Émile. (1914) 2005. "The Dualism of Human Nature and Its Social Conditions." *Durkheimian Studies* 11: 35–45.

Evans-Pritchard, Evans E. 1965. *Theories of Primitive Religion*. Oxford: Oxford University Press.

Gehlen, Arnold. 2004. *Urmensch und Spätkultur. Philosophische Ergebnisse und Aussagen*. Frankfurt am Main: Klostermann.

Giddens, Anthony. 2006. *Sociology*. 5th ed. Cambridge: Polity Press.

Goldenweiser, Alexander A. 1910. "Totemism, an Analytical Study." *The Journal of American Folklore* 23: 179–293.

Goldenweiser, Alexander A. 1915. "Review of 'Les Formes élémentaires de la vie religieuse.'" *American Anthropologist* 17: 719–735.
Heinroth, Oskar. 1990. *Beiträge zur Biologie, namentlich Ethologie und Psychologie der Anatiden*. Vienna: Verein für Ökologie und Umweltforschung.
Holbraad, Martin, Morten Axel Pedersen, and Eduardo Viveiros de Castro. 2014. "The Politics of Ontology: Anthropological Positions." *Cultural Anthropology Online*, Jan. 13, 2014. https://culanth.org/fieldsights/462-the-politics-of-ontology-anthropological-positions (2017-10-26).
Howell, Signe. 1996. "Nature in Culture or Culture in Nature? Chewong Ideas of 'Humans' and Other Species." In *Nature and Society: Anthropological Perspectives*, edited by Philippe Descola and Gísli Pálsson, 127–144. London: Routledge.
Joas, Hans. 2013. *The Sacredness of the Person: A New Genealogy of Human Rights*, Washington, DC: Georgetown University Press.
Kippenberg, Hans G. 1997. "Émile Durkheim (1858–1917)." In *Klassiker der Religionswissenschaft: von Friedrich Schleiermacher bis Mircea Eliade*, edited by Axel Michaels, 90–119. Munich: Beck.
Knoblauch, Hubert. 1999. *Religionssoziologie*. Berlin: de Gruyter.
Kohn, Eduardo. 2013. *How Forests Think: Toward an Anthropology Beyond the Human*. Berkeley: University of California Press.
Kwek, Dorothy H. B., and Robert Seyfert. 2018. "Affect Matters: Strolling through Heterological Ecologies." *Public Culture* 30, no. 1: 35–59.
Latour, Bruno. 1993. *We Have Never Been Modern*. Cambridge, MA: Harvard University Press.
Latour, Bruno. 2005. *Reassembling the Social: An Introduction to Actor-Network-Theory*. New York: Oxford University Press.
Law, John, and John Hassard, eds. 1999. *Actor Network Theory and After*. Oxford: Wiley-Blackwell.
Lawler, Lillian B. 1952. "Dancing Herds of Animals." *The Classical Journal* 47, no. 8: 317–324.
Lévi-Strauss, Claude. 1963. *Totemism*. Boston: Beacon Press.
Lévi-Strauss, Claude. 1966. *The Savage Mind*. London: Weidenfeld and Nicolson.
Lorenz, Konrad. 1965. *Über tierisches und menschliches Verhalten. Aus dem Werdegang der Verhaltenslehre*, Gesammelte Abhandlungen, vol. 1. Munich: Piper.
McFarlane, Craig. 2013. "Relational Sociology, Theoretical Inhumanism, and the Problem of the Nonhuman." In *Conceptualizing Relational Sociology*, edited by Christopher Powell and François Dépelteau, 45–66. New York: Palgrave Macmillan.
Nimmo, Richie. 2011. "The Making of the Human: Anthropocentrism in Modern Social Thought." In *Anthropocentrism: Humans, Animals, Environments*, edited by Rob Boddice, 59–80. Leiden: Brill.
Pickering, William S. F. 1984. *Durkheim's Sociology of Religion: Themes and Theories*. London: Routledge.
Povinelli, Elizabeth A. 2016. *Geontologies: A Requiem to Late Liberalism*. Durham, NC: Duke University Press.
Rawls, Anne Warfield. 1996. "Durkheim's Epistemology: The Neglected Argument." *The American Journal of Sociology* 102, no. 2: 430–482.
Robertson Smith, William. 1894. *Lectures on the Religion of the Semites*. London: Adam and Charles Black.
Ross, Jeremy A. 2017. "Durkheim and the Homo Duplex: Anthropocentrism in Sociology." *Sociological Spectrum* 37, no. 1: 18–26.

Sanders, Clinton R. 2007. "The Sociology of Nonhuman Animals and Society." In *21st Century Sociology*, vol. 2, edited by Clifton D. Bryant and Dennis L. Peck, 2–7. Thousand Oaks, CA: SAGE.

Sapir, Edward. 1922. "The Takelma Language of Southwestern Oregon." In *Handbook of American Indian Languages*, Part 2, edited by Franz Boas, 1–296. Washington, DC: Bulletin/Bureau of American Ethnology.

Seyfert, Robert. 2007. "Wissen des Lebens. Lebenssoziologische Beiträge zur Wissenssoziologie." *Sociologia Internationalis* 44, no. 2: 193–215.

Seyfert, Robert. 2008. "Zum historischen Verhältnis von Lebensphilosophie und Soziologie und das Programm einer Lebenssoziologie." In *Die Natur der Gesellschaft. Verhandlungen des 33. Kongresses der DGS in Kassel*, edited by Karl-Siegbert Rehberg, 4684–4694. Frankfurt am Main: Campus.

Seyfert, Robert. 2012. "Beyond Personal Feelings and Collective Emotions: A Theory of Social Affect." *Theory, Culture & Society* 29, no. 6: 27–46.

Seyfert, Robert. 2015. "'I Am Inclined Not To': Circumventing Contestation and Competition." In *Rethinking Order: Idioms of Stability and De-stabilization*, edited by Nicole Falkenhayner, Andreas Langenohl, Johannes Scheu, Doris Schweitzer, and Kacper Szulecki, 139–158. Bielefeld: transcript.

Shubin, Neil. 2008. *Your Inner Fish: A Journey into the 3.5 Billion-Year History of the Human Body*. New York: Pantheon.

Turner, Bryan S., and Chris Rojek. 2001. *Society and Culture: Principles of Scarcity and Solidarity*. London: SAGE.

Viveiros de Castro, Eduardo. 2012. "Cosmological Perspectivism in Amazonia and Elsewhere." *HAU Masterclass Series*, vol. 1. https://haubooks.org/cosmological-perspectivism-in-amazonia.

von den Steinen, Karl. 1894. *Unter den Naturvölkern Zentral-Brasiliens. Reiseschilderung und Ergebnisse der zweiten Schingú-Expedition, 1887–1888*. Berlin: Reimer.

CHAPTER 20

DURKHEIM AND THE SOCIALITY OF SPACE

MARKUS SCHROER

ÉMILE Durkheim is generally considered to be a theoretician of social order, morality, and anomie. Less consideration has been given to the fact that he also identified the material aspects of society as a major sociological concern. Within the new discipline of sociology—a discipline yet to be established as a science—the materiality of society becomes the object of a branch of science in its own right: a field of inquiry called "social morphology" (Mauss [1904] 1979: 19). Though social morphology was mainly developed and elaborated by Durkheim's pupils Marcel Mauss (1872–1950) and Maurice Halbwachs (1877–1945), it nonetheless plays a central role in Durkheim's thinking. His engagement with the writings of philosopher Montesquieu (1689–1755), sociologist Herbert Spencer (1820–1903), historian Numa Denis Fustel de Coulanges (1830–1889), economist and social scientist Gustav Schmoller (1839–1917), and geographer Friedrich Ratzel (1844–1904), as well as his ethnological research, all lead to the insight that society has material groundings which should not be theorized away when thinking about social development. The spatial organization of society is claimed to be of paramount importance.

The following chapter highlights the significance of space within Durkheim's notion of sociology in three steps. First, the research program of social morphology is outlined. Subsequently, his theory of modern society will be examined with regard to its propositions on spatial order. In a third and final step, it will be argued that, in addition to his treatment of space within the context of a theory of society, Durkheim also proposes an epistemological perspective which allows one to think of space as social. In conclusion, it will be shown that Durkheim's sociology of space proves to be of a surprisingly contemporary value, especially if read against the background of current developments in the social and cultural sciences.

Social Morphology—The Examination of the Society's Material Substratum

Émile Durkheim divided sociology into two fields of study: social physiology, on the one hand, and social morphology, on the other (Durkheim [1934] 1961, [1900] 1964; Jonas 1980: 83; Schroer 2017a). While physiology deals with functional aspects of society, morphology studies the "material forms of society" (Durkheim [1900] 1964: 362). His interest in the material manifestations of society and its physical nature propel him to thoroughly engage in sociology's neighboring disciplines. Social morphology was given space within *L'Année sociologique*, a journal founded by Durkheim and inaugurated with an article of programmatic nature—written by Durkheim himself (Durkheim 1897–1898). The journal serves as a platform for taking up and discussing research findings within the neighboring fields of economy, ethnology, anthropology, demographics, social geography, and anthropogeography. A thorough treatment is given to zoologist and geographer Friedrich Ratzel, who worked toward laying the foundations for a science called "anthropogeography." As an "application of geography to history" (Ratzel [1882] 2005) and a "school of space" (Ratzel 1923: 262, transl. M.S.), anthropogeography is supposed to inform politics, thus, in effect, turning it into "political geography" (Ratzel 1923: 262, transl. M.S.). Although it is Durkheim's contention that Ratzel is taking the dependence of social processes on geographical conditions too far, his appraisal of Ratzel's writings is nevertheless remarkably affirmative (Gephart 2004). Partial findings of Ratzel's research time and again find their way into Durkheim's own writings.

However, up until today, and despite its obvious significance, social morphology has received a rather stepmotherly treatment by scholars of Durkheim's work—without good reason and wrongly so! For if René König's claim holds true that the importance of religion in Durkheim's work is evidenced by "the fact alone that, as early as 1898, in the first issue of 'Année sociologique,' Émile Durkheim awarded religion its own rubric" (König 1978: 239, transl. M.S.), then the same argument can be made for social morphology: it likewise was given its own rubric following the second of altogether twelve issues of the journal. Far from being an insignificant add-on to his sociology, Durkheim introduced social morphology as a "fundamental branch of sociology" ([1900] 1964: 360). Accordingly, exemplifications of social morphology's tasks and aims can be found in several of his other writings as well as in the aforementioned journal article (Durkheim [1893] 1933, [1950] 1958, [1934] 1961, [1900] 1964, [1912] 1976). Even in cases where the label is not explicitly used, the subject matter of his writings frequently falls into social morphology's domain, which includes those phenomena which render society perceivable and tangible in a material sense—notably its volume (extension and number of population); the density and territorial distribution of its population; its internal division into villages, cities, and provinces; its forms of land use and cultivation; and its specific kind of architecture. Social morphology is thus tasked with attending to the "composition of society" (Durkheim [1900] 1964: 360), its material forms, whereas social physiology deals with functional requirements of collective life (Durkheim [1900] 1964: 362). Durkheim leaves no doubt about the fact that a sufficiently comprehensive understanding of society's formation, organizational structure, and functions is achieved only if the interplay between morphology and physiology is taken into account (Durkheim [1900] 1964: 374). The sociologist's task is not only to describe the material-social substratum of society but also to explain it by determining its causes as well as its functions. Specifically, a sociologist operating within this field of study will ask questions such as these: Why would societies prefer to be located on the periphery? What is the significance of territory for nation-states? Why do borders take so variedly different shapes, as Ratzel has shown? What circumstances lead to the formation of villages and cities? What factors contribute to the development of urban centers (Durkheim [1900] 1964: 361)? Durkheim considers the external or material form of the social substratum to be defined by three factors: "(1) the size of the territory; (2) the space which the society occupies [...]; and (3) the form of its frontiers" (Durkheim [1900] 1964: 360).[1]

Durkheim explicitly repudiates the notion that social morphology's investigation of the material forms of society is "a science of statics" (Durkheim [1900] 1964: 362):

> It is not a question of looking at society arrested at a given moment by abstraction (as has sometimes been said), but of analyzing its formation and accounting for it. Undoubtedly, the phenomena that have to do with structure have something more stable about them than have functional phenomena, but there are only differences of degree between these two orders of fact. Structure itself is encountered in *becoming*, and one cannot illustrate it except by pursuing this process of becoming. It forms and dissolves continually; it is life arrived at a certain measure of consolidation; to disconnect it from the life from which it derives or from that which it determinates is equivalent to dissociating things that are inseparable.
>
> (Durkheim [1900] 1964: 362)[2]

Spatial structures, therefore, are not an impediment to a dynamic social process. On the contrary, they are part and parcel of social change. While they do provide a certain degree of stability, they also do not stand in the way of "movements" (Durkheim [1900] 1964: 361), which Durkheim considers to be both the "causes" and the "effects" of social development.[3] Durkheim thus, quite early on, goes against a common view which equates time with mobility, the dynamic and progressive, change, development, and history, while space stands for immobility, stagnation, the reactionary, and solidity (Foucault 1980: 70).

What is noteworthy about this formulation of sociology's objectives by one of its founding fathers is that things and material relations are decidedly considered to be part of its subject matter—contrary to the otherwise predominant "excommunication of things and material relations from sociology" (Linde 1972: 78, transl. M.S.): "The composition of society consist in certain combinations of things which by necessity are connected in space" (Durkheim [1900] 1964: 360). Housing, tools, routes of transportation, and clothing are to be regarded as social things just as institutionalized rules of conduct or behavioral constraints (codified in either statute law or prevailing moral norms) are. What both "worlds of things" have in common is that they have an existence of their own—independent of the individual's volition. They force themselves upon individuals and determine their actions. It is this quality which, according to Durkheim, makes them a "social fact." As his study on suicide programmatically says: "First, it is not true that society is made up only of individuals; it also includes material things, which play an essential role in the common life. The social fact is sometimes so far materialized as to become an element of the external world. For instance, a definite type of architecture is a social phenomenon; but it is partially embodied in houses and buildings of all sorts which, once constructed, become autonomous realities, independent of individuals" (Durkheim [1897] 1951: 313–314).

It is central to Durkheim's understanding of society that the formed material environment conveys that the collective always precedes the individual. From traffic routes to the built monument: the living are faced with the mark left on the present by what was "bequeathed by previous generations" (Durkheim [1897] 1951: 314).[4] Through spatial conditions, cities, squares, and buildings, as well as through the world of things, artifacts, apparatuses, and objects, we are presented with a past that surrounds us like a "silent and immobile society" (Halbwachs [1950] 1980: 128)—albeit with inventors, creators, and builders long gone.[5] Durkheim's predominant focus on social physiology and functional analysis notwithstanding, it would be inaccurate to pose social morphology as a negligible, marginal concept or as an idea of no further bearing on his work. On the contrary, Durkheim will consistently return to stressing the importance of studying the morphological structure of a society.

The inception of social morphology is but the natural consequence of Durkheim's conviction that sociology's autonomy should not come at the expense of narrowing its field of study. It should be achieved by dividing the domain of sociology into subfields rather than restricting it (Durkheim [1900] 1964: 369). Durkheim's project of establishing sociology as an autonomous scientific discipline is not built upon excluding neighboring disciplines, but upon their inclusion. Social morphology allows sociology to tackle certain topics which otherwise would have to be relinquished to the expertise of geographers. Durkheim does not want to cede accounting for the geographical and material factors which were, in any case, already taken up by Montesquieu and Herbert Spencer, and thus declares them a field of sociology study in its own right. Last but not least, he contends that the formation of a society is the result of particular circumstances of life on earth:

> Let us suppose that the earth were an infinite plain, and that human beings were dispersed over it in such a way that they did not form any community amongst themselves: in these conditions it would not be possible for them to have any possession in common. But the earth is spherical and hence of limited surface area. Men are thus compelled by the unity of habitat to be in relation—thus they form

a whole and this whole is the natural owner of the total habitat which it occupies, that is, of the earth.

(Durkheim [1950] 1958: 129)

It is thus not the will to cooperate or the fear of one's fellow human beings which initiates the formation of social relations, but the fact that available physical space is finite and a scarce resource.

Theory of Modernity: The Organization of Space in Simple and Complex Societies

In his 1893 study on *The Division of Labor in Society* (1933), Durkheim formulates a theory of modernization which delineates the evolution of simple, archaic societies to complex, modern societies. Following a "historical law" (174), the primitive, simple *type* of society is successively being supplanted by a complex *type* of society. In terms of terminology, Durkheim's argument largely follows the theoretician of state Montesquieu, to whom he attests having discovered "the two fundamental ideas necessary for the establishment of social science, namely the ideas of *type* and of *law*" ([1892] 1965: 62). Both terms play to his ideal of modeling sociology after the natural sciences.

It is characteristic of Durkheim's study on the social division of labor that it does not concede to the voices speaking of the transition to modern society as a process of decline. Contrary to the overall pessimistic diagnosis of his time, he poses that societal solidarity is being fundamentally transformed rather than destroyed, thereby making it a top priority for sociology to give an adequate account of this transformation. His comparison of the two types of societies uncovers, as a result, two different forms of differentiation, solidarity and law: premodern or simple societies are shaped by segmental differentiation; modern societies by functional differentiation. In simple societies mechanical solidarity (cohesion based on similarities) is predominant, whereas in modern societies social cohesion is achieved through organic solidarity (cohesion based on differences and diversity). Restitutive law (restitution of balance) replaces repressive law (punishment of physical harm or loss of life). A further characteristic of simple societies is a strong collective consciousness (a shared reservoir of common beliefs, values, norms, and feelings) and a poorly developed individuality of its members. In modern society, the relationship between individuality and collective consciousness is reversed. The same applies to the division of labor: hardly existent in simple societies, it becomes dominant in modern society.

However, this list of differences between simple and complex societies might give the impression that these two types of societies are being schematically contrasted, as if there were no overlap or interference. Despite his theory of differentiation having drawn criticism (and not without reason) for failing to provide a concrete and detailed description of the processes leading to this social change (Alexander 1988: 60), Durkheim is yet at pains to delineate step by step the emergence of modern society—including the transitional phases. He also takes care to point out that modern society does not completely supplant the prior social formation. It is rather the case that the modern type becomes dominant, its traits gradually assuming a "preponderance" (Durkheim [1893] 1933: 174), without, however, entirely suppressing the traits of its predecessor. Segmentary differentiation and mechanical solidarity do not vanish entirely, but persist to a certain degree.

In addition to these various traits of simple as opposed to complex societies, both types of society differ in terms of their relationship to territory and in their spatial divisions—differences which will be discussed in the next section. It will be shown that, in this case as well, the old is not entirely superseded by the new. On the contrary, according to Durkheim ([1893] 1933: 261), it can be regarded as a sort of underlying principle of social evolution that "traces of the most primitive social organization [are found] among the most advanced peoples."

From Clan to Nation-State Society

Simple societies are of rather a small dimension. They are made up of similar and homogeneous segments, like hordes, clans, tribes, or families, which coexist side by side and without crossover. Each segment constitutes a world of its own, in strict separation from others: "We give the name *clan* to the horde which has ceased to be independent by becoming an element in a more extensive group, and that of *segmental societies with a clan-base* to peoples who are constituted through an association of clans" (Durkheim [1893] 1933: 175). It is characteristic of the clans' spatial organization that their territories never lie next to each other. Even within clans, one field never directly touches the other. Every field is fenced in by an enclosure which spatially separates it from the other allotments. This piece of in-between-land was to remain undeveloped and uncultivated (Durkheim [1950] 1958: 150) and therefore considered a no man's land ([1893] 1933: 258). Whoever did not bend to this rule and desecrated this hallowed ground was ostracized and could even be killed with impunity. The border between one's own and the hallowed ground was regularly reinforced through religious practices and a procession down the path. The border "thus assumed a character that was decidedly sacred" (Durkheim [1950] 1958: 151).

It was nearly impossible for clan members to switch from one clan to the other. This, however, changes in the course of a development which Durkheim ([1893] 1933: 186–187) describes as the successive transition from closed circles to a more open organization of social space: "When a person is born into a clan, he can in no way ever change the fact of his parentage. The same does not hold true of changing from a city or a province. No doubt, the geographical distribution generally coincides, in the large, with a certain moral distribution of population. Each province, each territorial division, has its peculiar customs and manners, a life peculiar unto itself. It therefore exercises over the individuals who are affected by it an attraction which tends to keep itself alive, and to repel all opposing forces. But, in the case of the same country, these differences would be neither very numerous, nor very firmly marked out. The segments are each more exposed to the others." With the spread of cities, "segmental organization lost its distinction" ([1893] 1933: 187). It was common for the newly founded cities in the Middle Ages to open their gates to strangers, making their populations more heterogeneous. For Durkheim, the village—"which is originally only a fixed clan" ([1893] 1933: 282, note 13)—is a kind of hold-over from or remnant of simple society. City and village thus turn out to be two coexisting forms of social organization, each with a distinctive prevailing pattern of social relations. Whereas "the village is a much more hermetically closed system to the outside and more sufficient unto itself" ([1893] 1933: 184) and of "domestic nature" ([1893] 1933: 183), the city is marked by the increasing permeability of its social milieus and the resulting openness and diversity of modern society. The city stands for a state of permanent change and innovation, for volatility and a fast-changing tempo of life. The village, however, exudes a statically dormant uniformity. It stands for the power of tradition, which makes the villagers cling to their habits. The rural population in civilized society has in common with "primitive people" ([1893] 1933: 252) that they "aspire to nothing new" ([1893] 1933: 252) and have no "desire for changes" ([1893] 1933: 252).[6] Durkheim is by no means blind to the negative sides of modern life in the big cities. To him, they are not only the site of heterogeneity, diversity, education, civilization, art, and progress but also of neuroses, bustling industriousness, and anomie (Schroer and Wilde 2012). But here, as in other cases, he thinks it crucial to adequately describe the transformations and search for innovative solutions to problematic developments rather than to seek refuge in a nostalgic romanticization of the past. Furthermore, Durkheim holds that this transformation will not stop at the boundary between village and city; it will go on to affect the way of thinking and living of the inhabitants of small towns:

> Separated from the rest of society by barriers more or less difficult to clear, nothing turns us from local life, and, therefore, all our action is concentrated there. But as the fusion of segments becomes more complete, the vistas enlarge, and the more so as society itself becomes more generally extended at the same time. From then on, even the inhabitant of a small city lives the life of the little group immediately surrounding him less exclusively. He joins in relations with distant localities which are more numerous as the movement of concentration is more advanced. His more frequent journeys, the more active correspondence he exchanges, the affairs occupying him outside, etc., turn his attention from what is passing around him. He no longer finds the center of his life and preoccupations so completely in the place where he lives. He is then less interested in his neighbors, since they take a smaller place in his life.
>
> (Durkheim ([1893] 1933: 300)

In "Professional Ethics and Civil Morals" (Durkheim [1950] 1958), a treatise devoted to tracing society's developmental path into modernity, the formation of nation-states is identified as another important milestone on this path. Man's relation to land and ground changes fundamentally in this process. However, contrary to the commonly held conviction, formulated in legal scholar Kaspar Bluntschli's (1808–1881) theory of state, that a state's population is indissolubly connected with a state's territory, Durkheim ([1950] 1958: 43) maintains that a population's close ties to a territory historically precedes the formation of the nation-state: "The family, too, has its domain from which it is inseparable, since that domain is inalienable. We have seen that the patrimony of landed estate was sometimes the very kernel of the family; it is this patrimony that made its unity and continuity and it was about this focus that domestic life revolved. Nowhere, in any political society, has political territory had a status to compare with this in importance." Durkheim furthermore challenges Bluntschli's alleged connection between state population and state territory by arguing that it was the number of citizens, rather than territory, which initially laid the foundation of the nation-state: "To annex a State was not to annex the country but its inhabitants and to incorporate them within the annexing State" ([1950] 1958: 43). Instead of being a prerequisite of state formation, a state population's identification with a state territory is of relatively recent date: "It is not a great while since the peoples became so identified with the territories they inhabit, that is, with what we should call the geographical expression of those peoples" ([1950] 1958: 43). In Durkheim's life time, this connection was once again intensified: "The society of which we are members is in our minds all the more a well-defined territory, since it is no longer in its essence a religion, a corpus of traditions peculiar to it or the cult of a particular dynasty" ([1950] 1958: 44).

What Durkheim ([1893] 1933: 186) seeks to highlight is that the close bond between a society and its territory is not solely a modern-day phenomenon, but occurs wherever nomadism is replaced by a settled populace and sedentary families: "Thus it is that all peoples who have passed beyond the clan-stage are organized in territorial districts (counties, communes, etc.) which [...] connected themselves with other districts of similar nature, but vaster, sometimes called the Hundred, sometimes the assembly, sometimes the ward, which, in their turn, are often enveloped by others, still more extensive (shire, province, department), whose union formed the society." According to Durkheim, the survival of this kind of spatial differentiation of society is the reason "why mechanical solidarity persists even in the most elevated societies" ([1893] 1933: 186). Organic solidarity, however, which becomes dominant with the progression of the division of labor, finds its spatial expression in the formation of nation-state societies.

With the formation of nation-states, the development toward an increasing significance of territory has, for the time being, come to its conclusion. Durkheim conceives of societies as nation-state societies, which may be composed of heterogeneous elements, but present themselves as homogeneous entities to the outside world. Each societal formation, though, contains its historic precursor from which it has emerged: "Thus, the tribe is formed of an aggregate of hordes or clans. The nation [...] and the city are formed of an aggregate of tribes; the city, in turn, with the villages subordinate to it, enters as an element of the most complex societies, etc. Thus, the social volume cannot fail to increase, since each species is constituted by a repetition of societies of the immediately anterior species" ([1893] 1933: 261).[7]

From the National to the Global?

The close interrelation with a spatial formation is no longer a characteristic trait of modern societies in their present stage of development. The ties to territory are loosening. Territorial divisions—which unavoidably "have something artificial about them" (Durkheim [1893] 1933: 186), because the ties "arising from consanguinity" ([1893] 1933: 186) knit together more profoundly than the ties resulting from mere "cohabitation" ([1893] 1933: 186)—become less and less significant in the course of social evolution. Villages, provinces, and cities, as territorial units, "no longer awaken in us profound sentiments" ([1893] 1933: 28). The individual's activities have long transgressed beyond the narrow bounds of the neighborhood, to an extent which inevitably must make local concerns seem provincial: "Territorial divisions are thus less and less grounded in the nature of things, and, consequently, lose their significance. We can almost say that a people is as much more advanced as territorial divisions are more superficial" ([1893] 1933: 187). That segments lose their individuality through the dissolution of boundaries does not mean, however, that the "diversity of environments" ([1893] 1933: 187) must disappear completely. It only means that they are divested of their foothold in a territory, so that, going forward, they have to uphold their difference by other means. With the dissolution of boundaries, segments collide and are forced into competition. This leads to an increase in specialization and division of labor. As the division of labor unfolds, social relations are severed from their territorial groundings, so that social and spatial proximity no longer coincide: "Indeed, although very often the most highly solidary organs tend to come closer to each other, nevertheless, in general, their material proximity very inexactly reflects the more or less great intimacy of their relations. Certain of them are very distant, although they are directly dependent upon each other. Others are near, yet their relations are only mediate and distant. The manner of human grouping which results from the division of labor is thus very different from that which expresses the partition of the population in space" ([1893] 1933: 189).

On the one hand, Durkheim sees the increasing permeability of boundaries as leveling all differences, as it is manifested by the disappearance of local religions, and by dialects being absorbed into a national language. Yet on the other hand, he stresses that these demolitions of boundaries also create opportunities for forming new social ties and relationships. One is no longer bound, without alternative, to one's place. With the spread of means of communication and transportation, "the gaps separating social segments" ([1893] 1933: 259–260) are being overcome. They thereby increase the density of society.

The unhampered growth of society, however, makes it difficult for the individual to find his orientation. Because the individual's wants and talents need reigning in in order for a labor-divided society to function, the environment in which the individual moves also needs to be delimited: "And the more the dimensions of societies increase and the more the markets expand, the greater the urgency of some regulation to put an end to this instability. Because, as discussed earlier, the more the whole exceeds the part, the more the society extends beyond the individual, the less can the individual sense within himself the social needs and the social interests he is bound to take into account" (Durkheim [1950] 1958: 16).

However much Durkheim may be in favor of society's expansion on account of the ensuing emancipation of the individual from the "yoke" of the common conscience ([1893] 1933: 167), he also stresses certain functional requirements that come with it: the increase in volume and density of society can only be maintained if individuals are allowed to differentiate themselves, being given their own tasks, and choosing their own ways of life (Durkheim [1888] 1978: 207). In an undifferentiated society, the individual is being drowned out. Without clearly established boundaries, the required cooperation between social groups operating alongside each other is lacking. Only limitation creates the pressure to implement specialization and division of labor. Without boundaries, people would drift apart. Durkheim considers professions ([1893] 1933: 1–31; Schroer 2000: 175–184) to be capable of establishing a new social bond between individuals. It is through professional groups that social integration can be achieved in modern societies. Professions establish an intermediate level between society and the individual. With family, religion, and the state losing significance, it falls to professional groups to both reign in the individual's egotisms and protect them from the brutal laws of the market. Only within the limited social context of a professional organization do individuals recognize the necessity of containing their egotistical passions, which is indispensable to society's continued existence.

Durkheim thus conceives of modernization as a process of the continued liberation from narrow local circumstances, a process promoting a more global orientation while at the same time giving rise to a growing indifference toward one's immediate environment. And even though Durkheim does not condemn this process, he is skeptical of the cohesive powers of a spatially expanding society which has stripped itself of its local shackles. He unequivocally demands: "If each State had as its chief aim, not to expand, or to lengthen its borders, but to set its own house in order and to make the widest appeal to its members for a moral life on an ever higher level, then all discrepancy between national and human morals would be excluded. If the state had no other purpose than making men of its citizens, in the widest sense of the term, then civic duties would be only a particular form of the general obligations of humanity" (Durkheim [1950] 1958: 74).

It has not yet come to this, however. His age is marked by "a clash between cosmopolitanism [...] and patriotism" (Durkheim [1950] 1958: 74), a conflict which is the result of citizens' obligation toward the state, on the one hand, and their obligations toward an ideal of humankind, on the other. Moral individualism, which Durkheim categorically distinguishes from a merely egotistical individualism, is the "only system of beliefs which can ensure the moral unity of the country" ([1898] 1973: 50), for in modern society, "man has become a god for man" ([1898] 1973: 52; Schroer 2000: 166–167). The overall tendency seems to be that patriotism is being overcome by cosmopolitism:

> No matter how devoted men may be to their native land, they all to-day are aware that beyond the forces of national life there are others, in a higher region and not so transitory, for they are unrelated to conditions peculiar to any given political group and are not bound up with its fortunes. There is something more universal and more enduring. It is true to say that those aims that are the most general and the most unchanging are also the most sublime. As we advance in evolution, we see the ideals men pursue breaking free of the local or ethnic conditions obtaining in a certain region of the world or a certain human group, and rising above all that is particular and so approaching the universal.
>
> (Durkheim [1950] 1958: 72)

Although he considers an overcoming of national particularities to be favorable, Durkheim is not willing to chime in with those who consider patriotism an atavism soon to disappear from history. Completely dispensing of the individual's ties to the nation-state in favor of a kind of global or world society is not a solution to the problem, for "man is a moral being only because he lives within established societies" (Durkheim [1950] 1958: 73). Humankind, however, is not a society, but merely an abstract regulatory idea (Durkheim [1934] 1961: 67). What is lacking is the material basis for the realization of the idea of general human rights. However, social development need not stop at nation-states in their current form. They do not signify the end of history. For Durkheim, there is no reason to suppose that the development toward ever larger and ever more general associations, spanning from tribes to cities and on to nations, should have found its conclusion (Durkheim [1934] 1961: 76) in a "confederation of European States" (Durkheim [1950] 1958: 74). Even if the emergence of "a state embracing the whole of humanity" (Durkheim [1934] 1961: 76) is unlikely, the vision of a developmental stage in which the current spatial order of nation-state societies existing alongside each other is transcended is yet presented as the only solution to the problem of reconciling patriotism and cosmopolitism: "The more societies concentrate their energies inwards, on the interior life, the more they will be diverted from the disputes that bring a clash between cosmopolitism—or world patriotism, and patriotism; as they grow in size and get greater complexity, so will they concentrate more and more on themselves. Here we see how the advent of societies on an even bigger scale than those we know will constitute an advance in the future. So that what breaks down the paradox is the tendency of patriotism to become, as it were, a fragment of world patriotism" (Durkheim [1950] 1958: 74–75).

Durkheim thus neither advocates retreating to the local nor moving on to the global plane. As long as no alternative is in sight that would be able to guarantee the realization of the ideal of humankind, one should refrain from prematurely abandoning existing forms of moral order. In light of our current experiences with globalization, Durkheim's judicious reflections seem very current and worth consideration.

Space as a Social Category

With his agenda for a social morphology, Durkheim has given the material substratum of societies a significance in its own right. Accordingly, thoughts on the spatial organization of different types of society have found their way into his theory of society which has at its core the transition from archaic to modern nation-state societies. In his late work on *The Elementary Forms of Religious Life* (Durkheim [1912] 1976), Durkheim again approaches the topic of space, this time primarily from an epistemological perspective.

His argument differs from that of Friedrich Ratzel,[8] who, in his anthropogeographical studies of the effects of space on social structures, endows space with an inordinate potency and thereby, in effect, turns space into a hypostacized subject. By contrast, Durkheim ([1912] 1976: 9) argues that not only a society's material substratum, or the content of its knowledge, is socially constructed but also its elementary categories of thought, such as time and space (see also Joas 1993: 62). Like Kant, Durkheim is not interested in space *per se*, but in how the categories which shape our perception came to be. Yet he decidedly argues against Kant's notion of a priori modes of perception. "Space is not the vague and indetermined medium which Kant imagined; if purely and absolutely homogeneous, it would be of no use, and could not be grasped by the mind" (Durkheim [1912] 1976: 11). Space and time are not a priori, but socially constructed and socially preconfigured categories of perception. They are "the product of collective thought" (Durkheim [1912] 1976: 10) and thus of social origin. Social organization precedes these categories, the latter essentially being its mirror-image. The order of thought follows the social-spatial order with its distinctions of above/below, left/right, north/south, west/east, and so on. These kinds of directional vectors are neither rooted in subjective perception, nor are they qualities pertaining to space itself. Rather, these categorizations are collectively shared attributions. Just as notions of space are the same for all members of a society, so are the "sympathetic values [which] have been attributed to various regions" (Durkheim [1912] 1976: 11). This alone is sufficient proof to Durkheim (Durkheim [1912] 1976: 11) that the spatial distinctions and divisions are of social origin. "[S]ocial space" (Durkheim [1912] 1976: 444), Durkheim argues, "could not be what it is if it were not, like time, divided and differentiated" (Durkheim [1912] 1976: 11). It follows that "[t]o dispose things spatially there must be a possibility of placing them differently, of putting some at the right, others at the left, these above, those below, at the north of or at the south of, east or west of, etc., etc." (Durkheim [1912] 1976: 11). Behind this argument lies Durkheim's fundamental belief that society can only function if "the individuals and things which compose it are divided into certain groups, that is to say, classified" (Durkheim [1912] 1976: 443). He further elaborates: "Society supposes a self-conscious organization which is nothing other than a classification. This organization of society naturally extends itself to the place which this occupies. To avoid all collisions, it is necessary that each particular group have a determined portion of space assigned to it: in other terms, it is necessary that space in general be divided, differentiated, arranged, and that these divisions and arrangements be known to everybody" (Durkheim [1912] 1976: 443). The same applies to time. Time also would be inconceivable without its division into specific amounts of time, that is, into minutes, hours, days, weeks, months, and years. Time ultimately consists of the intervals into which we divide it, just as space consists of the parts we partition it into. Without these divisions, space and time would remain abstract and without bearing on social life. In the case of time, also, divisions are not the product of an arbitrarily erected system of classification, artificially imposing itself upon reality. The divisions of time spring from life, making it a "social time" (Durkheim [1912] 1976: 444). Calendars, for instance, ensure the regularity of reoccurring social activities (Durkheim [1912] 1976: 10). And just as spatial distributions, and the respective places taken up by various social groups, work to prevent "collisions" (Durkheim [1912] 1976: 443), so does a collectively shared understanding of time allow events like a feast, hunt, or a war to take place. Without these spatial and temporal regulations, the protagonists of these and other activities simply could not get together, and thus these activities could not take place. Individuals have to share basic notions of elementary categories such as time and space: "If men did not agree upon these essential ideas at every moment, if they did not have the same conception of time, space, cause, number, etc., all contact between their minds would be impossible, and with that, all life together" (Durkheim [1912] 1976: 17, 443–444).[9]

Space and time serve as guarantees of reliability and stability. This applies to higher as well as simple forms of society. Durkheim looks for further corroboration of his thesis about the spatial manifestation of any given social organization in accounts of North American and Australian tribal societies. It is in these societies that Durkheim finds evidence for his argument that social organization inscribes itself in space. For instance, "space is conceived in the form of an immense circle, because the camp has a circular form; and this spatial circle is divided up exactly like the tribal circle, and is in its image. There are as many regions distinguished as there are clans inside the encampment which has determined the orientation of these regions. Each region is defined by the totem of the clan to which it is assigned" (Durkheim [1912] 1976: 11–12). From the fact that the number of clans changes in line with the number of differentiated regions, Durkheim infers that "the social organization has been the model for the spatial organization and a reproduction of it. It is thus even up to the distinction between right and left which, far from being inherent in the nature of man in general, is very probably the product of representations which are religious and therefore collective" (Durkheim [1912] 1976: 12).

What is crucial for Durkheim is the insight that these distinctions are not prompted by an individual's *will* to classify. Nor are they inherent in things. Physical space or territory is above all a manifestation of social relations. His theory of space can therefore be summed up as follows: physical space has always already been social space.

Successors and Current Relevance

As the previous sections should have made clear, Émile Durkheim is an author to whom the allegation generally that sociology has not dealt with space does not apply (Schroer 2006: 17–28, 48–60). Across the range of topics covered in his writings, a treatment of the problem of space in all its facets can be found. As we have seen, social morphology is of particular importance in this respect. His fundamental tenet that spatial order represents the social was taken up and further pursued by Maurice Halbwachs and Marcel Mauss. The case can also be made that it has left its mark on Pierre Bourdieu's social theory (Schroer 2006: 82–106). It is through social morphology, in particular, that Durkheim's sociology can be linked to current debates in the social and cultural sciences. His remarks on the material substratum of society make him a point of reference for the proponents of both the "spatial turn" (Schroer 2012) as well as the "material turn" (Hicks 2010). What is particularly current about Durkheim is that he did not shy away from discussing aspects of the earth environment or from embracing territory as a categorical means for grasping social phenomena. He is therefore an important candidate for furnishing a geosociology, a field of study which aims for the intensified study of environmental earth, particularly in light of the challenges posed by the Anthropocene (Schroer 2017b). His contention that "even if society is a specific reality it is not an empire within an empire; [that] it is a part of nature" (Durkheim [1912] 1976: 18) and that the social world is not "separated by some abyss from the rest of nature" ([1934] 1961: 265), has most certainly an up-to-date ring to it. It is also true, however, that his theory of modernization is largely based on the assumption that modern society is progressively being disembedded from its territorial groundings. But this has never led him so far as to propose the end of space or geography, as some of the fervid contemporary proponents of globalization have done. His thorough treatment of the material substratum of society is precisely what keeps him from making such an audacious proposition. By contrast, what was to follow was a "notion of the social [...] which [...] wafts through the air without touching the earthly ground" (König 1972: VII, transl. M.S.). Durkheim's theory can make an important contribution to the reintegration of social phenomena into the "ecosphere" or "biosphere," an endeavor which was advocated by René König and rightly so. This holds even more true in our current age of the Anthropocene, in which the "ecosphere" and "biosphere" have become an even more contentious and pertinent topic of discussion.

Notes

1. Durkheim ([1900] 1964: 360) continues: "As Friedrich Ratzel has demonstrated, the nature and aspects of frontiers chance according to the countries involved: in one instance, they may be represented by more or less extensive surfaces; in another, by geometrical lines; in a

third, they enter like wedges into contiguous countries or fold and thrust themselves back into the interior."
2. Durkheim's reference to "life" shows that he was not immune to the influence of the vitalist philosophy and sociology of his time (Durkheim [1955] 1983: 95–97; see also Delitz 2015: 51).
3. In this respect, he is in accordance with Ratzel ([1882] 2005: 157, transl. M.S.): "Ceaseless movement is part of the nature of the human spirit; it is measured and bound by time and space, even if it progressively makes them smaller. Ceaseless movement is likewise in the nature of nations and their populaces, which, as a history, unfolds in space and finds its limitations in it."
4. Maurice Halbwachs directly follows up on this notion by writing: "In routes of communication we vaguely sense the presence of those who determined their direction. Trails marked in the brush or mountain paths cut into rock more than a thousand years ago, Roman roads, highways of the Middle Ages paved with cobblestones, modern roads whose gradients have been calculated by engineers—these routes seem to reveal the footprints of those who first pushed ahead and carved them out, and we recognize the marks of the tools used to construct them" (Halbwachs 1960: 36).
5. In light of this delineation of social morphology's scope of investigation, it can only be deemed astounding that Bruno Latour made Durkheim the antipode of his theory. The similarities between the two approaches are obvious (Schroer 2009).
6. Claude Lévi-Strauss will turn this difference into the distinction between "hot" and "cold" societies: hot societies strive toward change and innovation, whereas cold societies try to thwart change. They are at peace with themselves and immune to social process (Lévi-Strauss 1966: 233–234).
7. This notion seems to have also served as an inspiration for Durkheim's vision of the progression of the sciences: sociology will not become fully fledged science by categorially excluding, in the name of autonomy, other scientific disciplines. It is rather about incorporating them. From this perspective, sociology would be a synthesis of other sciences: "In fact, in nature everything is so connected that there can be neither a complete break in continuity nor any too exact boundaries, which are necessarily indeterminate anyway" (Durkheim [1900] 1964: 354).
8. Friedrich Ratzel (1844–1904) is considered the founder of anthropogeography and political geography. Durkheim deals extensively with his writings (Köster 2002: 90–94).
9. Spatial divisions are also of the utmost significance to religion: "In the first place, the religious life and the profane life cannot coexist in the same place. If the former is to develop, a spatial spot must be placed at its disposition, from which the second is excluded. Hence comes the founding of temples and sanctuaries: these are the spots awarded to sacred beings and things and serve them as residences [...]. Likewise, the religious life and the profane life cannot coexist in the same time. It is necessary to assign determined days or periods to the first, from which all profane occupations are excluded" (Durkheim [1912] 1976: 308).

REFERENCES

Alexander, J. 1988. "Durkheim's Problem and Differentiation Theory Today." In J. Alexander, *Action and Its Environments: Toward a New Synthesis*, 49–77. New York: Columbia University Press.

Delitz, H. 2015. *Bergson-Effekte. Aversionen und Attraktionen im französischen soziologischen Denken*. Weilerswist: Velbrück.
Durkheim, É. 1897–1898. "Note sur la morphologie social." *L'Année sociologique* 2: 520–521.
Durkheim, É. (1893) 1933. *The Division of Labor in Society*. Glencoe, IL: Free Press.
Durkheim, É. (1897) 1951. *Suicide: A Study in Sociology*. New York: Free Press.
Durkheim, É. (1950) 1958. *Professional Ethics and Civic Morals*. Glencoe, IL: Free Press.
Durkheim, É. (1934) 1961. *Moral Education*. New York: Free Press.
Durkheim, É. (1900) 1964. "Sociology and Its Scientific Field." In *Émile Durkheim: Essays on Sociology and Philosophy*, edited by K. Wolff, 354–375. New York: Harper & Row.
Durkheim, É. (1892) 1965. "Montesquieu's Contribution to the Rise of Social Science." In É. Durkheim, *Montesquieu and Rousseau: Forerunners of Sociology*, 1–64. Ann Arbor: University of Michigan Press.
Durkheim, É. (1898) 1973. "Individualism and the Intellectuals." In *On Morality and Society: Selected Writings*, edited by R. N. Bellah, 43–57. Chicago: University of Chicago Press.
Durkheim, É. (1912) 1976. *The Elementary Forms of Religious Life*. London: Allen & Unwin.
Durkheim, É. (1888) 1978. "Introduction to the Sociology of the Family." In *Emile Durkheim on Institutional Analysis*, edited by M. Traugott, 205–228. Chicago: University of Chicago Press.
Durkheim, É. (1955) 1983. *Pragmatism and Sociology*. New York: Cambridge University Press.
Foucault, M. 1980. *Power, Knowledge: Selected Interviews and Other Writings 1972–1977*. New York: Pantheon Books.
Gephart, W. 2004. "Der Raum, das Meer und die Gesellschaft. Der deutsch-französische Diskurs zwischen Geographie und Soziologie um die Wende vom 19. zum 20. Jahrhundert." *Sociologia Internationalis* 42, no. 1: 143–166.
Halbwachs, M. (1938) 1960. *Population and Society: Introduction to Social Morphology*. Glencoe, IL: Free Press.
Halbwachs, M. (1950) 1980. *The Collective Memory*. New York: Harper & Row.
Hicks, D. 2010. "The Material-Cultural Turn: Event and Effect." In *The Oxford Handbook of Material Culture Studies*, edited by D. Hicks and M. C. Beaudry, 25–99. Oxford: Oxford University Press.
Joas, H. 1993. "Durkheim and Pragmatism: The Psychology of Consciousness and the Social Constitution of Categories." In *Pragmatism and Social Theory*, 55–78. Chicago: University of Chicago Press.
Jonas, F. 1980. *Geschichte der Soziologie*, vol. 2: *Von der Jahrhundertwende bis zur Gegenwart*. Opladen: Westdeutscher Verlag.
König, R. 1972. "Vorwort." In *Soziologie der geographischen Mobilität. Zugleich ein Beitrag zur Soziologie des sozialen Wandels*, edited by G. Albrecht, V–VIII. Stuttgart: Enke.
König, R. 1978. "Die Religionssoziologie bei Émile Durkheim." In R. König, *Émile Durkheim zur Diskussion. Jenseits von Dogmatismus und Skepsis*, 239–256. Munich: Hanser.
Köster, W. 2002. *Die Rede über den "Raum." Zur semantischen Karriere eines deutschen Konzepts*. Heidelberg: Synchron.
Lévi-Strauss, C. 1966. *The Savage Mind*. Chicago: University of Chicago Press.
Linde, H. 1972. *Sachdominanz in Sozialstrukturen*. Tübingen: Mohr Siebeck.
Mauss, M. (1904) 1979. *Seasonal Variations of the Eskimo: A Study in Social Morphology*. London: Routledge & Kegan Paul.
Ratzel, F. 1923. *Politische Geographie*. Munich: R. Oldenbourg.
Ratzel, F. (1882) 2005. *Anthropo-Geographie oder Grundzüge der Anwendung der Erdkunde auf die Geschichte*. Leipzig: Elibron Classics.

Schroer, M. 2000. *Das Individuum der Gesellschaft. Synchrone und diachrone Theorieperspektiven*. Frankfurt am Main: Suhrkamp.

Schroer, M. 2006. *Räume, Orte, Grenzen. Auf dem Weg zu einer Soziologie des Raums*. Frankfurt am Main: Suhrkamp.

Schroer, M. 2009. "Materielle Formen des Sozialen. Die 'Architektur der Gesellschaft' aus Sicht der sozialen Morphologie." In *Die Architektur der Gesellschaft. Theorien für die Architektursoziologie*, edited by J. Fischer and H. Delitz, 19–48. Bielefeld: transcript.

Schroer, M. 2012. "Spatial Turn." In *Lexikon Raumphilosophie*, edited by S. Günzel, 380–381. Darmstadt: WBG.

Schroer, M. 2017a. *Soziologische Theorien. Von den Klassikern bis zur Gegenwart*. Paderborn: W. Fink (UTB).

Schroer, M. 2017b. "Geosoziologie im Zeitalter des Anthropozäns." In *Raum und Zeit. Soziologische Beobachtungen zur gesellschaftlichen Raumzeit 4. Sonderband der Zeitschrift für theoretische Soziologie*, edited by A. Henkel, H. Laux, and F. Anicker, 126–152. Weinheim: Juventa.

Schroer, M., and J. Wilde. 2012. "Emile Durkheim." In *Handbuch Stadtsoziologie*, edited by F. Eckart, 59–82. Wiesbaden: VS Verlag.

CHAPTER 21

ÉMILE DURKHEIM AND THE MODERN FAMILY

FRANÇOIS DE SINGLY

BORDEAUX, a Friday in early December 1888. Émile Durkheim leaves the family home in Talence to take the tramway (Béra 2014). He is going to the university to give his first public sociology lecture on the family to an audience of ten or so students (Béra 2017) and a few professors (Fournier 2007: 131). The previous year, his first year teaching at the university, he gave a "Course in Social Science" on solidarity (Durkheim [1888] 2008). This year, 1888, he drafts a research agenda in his first lecture, entitled "Introduction to the Sociology of the Family" (Durkheim [1888] 1978). Durkheim will reuse part of his course on the family in the 1891/92 academic year, still in Bordeaux. Marcel Mauss (son of Durkheim's oldest sister, who joined his uncle in the autumn of 1890) takes this new version of the course. In 1921, Mauss will publish his notes from the seventeenth (and last) lecture, given on Saturday, April 2, 1892, entitled "The Conjugal Family" (Durkheim [1921] 1978).

Back to 1888. When Durkheim gives this first lecture, he has been a father since early September, a year after his marriage to Louise Julie Dreyfus. He begins his married and paternal life while reading in preparation for his course on the sociology of the family.[1] Is there a connection between personal experience and academic work? Durkheim's answer is an explicit no—he justifies his choice of the family as the subject of his course differently. In 1887/88, he had identified two kinds of social solidarity: "The first of these results from the similarity of consciousnesses and the community of ideas and feelings. The other, on the contrary, is a product of the differentiation of functions and the division of labor" (Durkheim [1888] 1978: 206). Durkheim wants to devote the following year to studying "the simplest group of all, the one whose history is the most ancient: the family" (207), although he has a "profound sense of the complexity of the subject" (218).

Durkheim had read widely, citing thirty-odd writers in his first lecture. He takes particular care to set himself apart from Frédéric Le Play, a writer of monographs on the family.[2] For the conservative Le Play, the history of the family reflects a decline of society, and he "look[s] upon the families of previous ages as models" which he offers up "for our imitation." Durkheim adopts the opposite attitude, which he saw as scientific and "impartial" (220). "Today's family is neither more nor less perfect than that of yesterday; it is different because circumstances are different" (219). He will forget this posture a few years hence, during the debate over the reinstatement of divorce by mutual consent, when he will assert the moral superiority of marriage without the possibility of separation.

The fact that Durkheim's written lectures were lost when the Paris home of his daughter-in-law Marie Halphen was requisitioned by the Gestapo, combined with the lack of a book on the family, has led many to think that the theme was of secondary importance. Mary Ann Lamanna (2002) asserted as much, even while trying to prove the contrary. Regardless, it was not secondary to Durkheim. He proves this, for example, by providing numerous reviews of books on marriage and the family in *L'Année sociologique*. Marcel Mauss stresses Durkheim's commitment, stating that Durkheim "wanted to devote the end of his life to this natural and comparative history of the family and marriage up to our own day. [...] But he knew that this work surpassed the capacity of one man, and he had wondered whether to ask me to devote myself to it with him. We planned to spend several years of our lives on this" (Mauss [1925] 2016: 35–36).[3] Durkheim had a great many projects before he slipped into depression after the death of his son André. Mauss insisted, however, that he "held above all else only to publish his 'Morality' and his 'Family'" (41). While the birth of his first child coincides with his first course on the family, the premature death of his son brings an end to the father's work on this institution.

Although personal experience of the family is an obstacle to analysis because it makes it difficult to study the institution as undiscovered country, it does make it more enticing. Whatever reasons lay behind Durkheim's choice of this theme, reading his work on the family today is useful in two regards. First, it helps us to comprehend the "conjugal family," which corresponds to what Ulrich Beck (1992) identified as the first modernity, and second, it allows us to see the tensions and contradictions within Durkheim's social theory.[4]

Personal Ties

This course still deserves to be studied because Durkheim had an intuition of what would make the modern family distinctive. He wrote that "Domestic solidarity becomes entirely a matter of persons. We are attached to our family only because we are *attached to the person* of our father, our mother, our wife, or our children" (Durkheim [1921] 1978: 234, my emphasis). More precisely, we are attached to our father because of his status and because of his person. This amounts to thinking that the personal dimension supplants that of status. Durkheim understood that the nature of the connection was changing, even if he did not anticipate all the consequences this would have. Based on his own argument, not to mention his personal experience (his grief over the death of his mother,

Mélanie, in 1902 and his son, André, in 1915), he ought to have argued that the modern family is "relational," not merely "conjugal" (see Singly 2016).

This powerful idea was frequently obscured by other, contested, declarations. Indeed, for Durkheim, this focusing on specific persons was associated with a contraction of the family; he believed that the "central zone" of the modern family was composed of the husband, the wife, and young children, surrounded by "secondary zones" of ascendants and descendants. According to historical demography and ethnology, this is not so: the nuclear family is not a form original to Western societies in the modern era. There is no question that Durkheim was a victim of the evolutionism that was in fashion at the end of the nineteenth century. To better understand Durkheim, it is probably best to reformulate his claim in the following way: the conjugal family is *one* form of the nuclear family whose specificity lies in the number of people concerned and the kind of ties between them. Historian Philippe Ariès (1960) demonstrates the gradual change in how parents relate to their children, also becoming personal (coming close to Durkheim's thesis on this point). Personal attachment was not limited to the spouse, although love marriage was taking hold and arranged marriage was gradually disappearing at the end of the nineteenth century. Research on World War I correspondence has revealingly documented this rising sentimentality between spouses (Vidal-Naquet 2014a, 2014b).

While Durkheim's thesis on the contraction of the conjugal family (relative to previous family types) is debatable because the nuclear family had existed at other times and places, this thesis can be understood in a way that makes it relevant (see, for example, Laslett 1988). According to this interpretation, the contraction refers to the limitation of the number of births. For Philippe Ariès (1948), this limitation derives from causes beyond the merely objective (the decline in infant mortality) and includes the central position occupied by the child.[5] In this regard, the focusing on personal relations went hand in hand with a reduced family. Doesn't the end of large families reveal the need to concentrate efforts on a few children and to personalize relations?

The "personalities of the family members" increasingly break free of the modern family. These individual differences were "accentuated, consolidated, and, as they were the property of the individual personality, they necessarily tended to develop. Each individual increasingly assumed his own character, his personal manner of thinking and feeling" (Durkheim 1978 [1921]: 233–234). Durkheim repeated his diagnosis in a review of a book on the falling of the birth rate, stating that "the abstract personality of the familial society is no longer the object of the same feelings; it is no longer the family that we love, but the individual persons that comprise it, and most of all our children" (Durkheim 1898/99: 560–561).

The fact that individuals have more personal rationales results in a limitation of family communism, since the latter "presupposed the identity and fusion of all consciousness within a single common consciousness which embraced them" (Durkheim [1921] 1978: 234). Hence, this increase in individual autonomy had significant consequences for how the domestic sphere functioned. In families where the transmission of economic patrimony was the priority, patrimony held the central position. Karl Marx also expressed this idea: "The beneficiary of the entail, the eldest son, belongs to the land. The land inherits him" (Marx quoted in Bourdieu 1976: 117). In the modern family, to the contrary, family ties were less dependent on property and the possessions of the family as a group; "things cease, to an ever greater extent, to act as cement for domestic society" (Durkheim [1921] 1978: 234). Instead, the relationships between husband and wife and between parents and children would animate the family spirit.

Mutual Dependence and Conjugal Differences

Durkheim expanded on his course of 1888 in his dissertation, which he defended at the Sorbonne in 1893.[6] Here, he better articulated the value of applying the concept of the division of labor to the conjugal group than he had in his two published lectures on the family. Durkheim held that in societies where labor is only to a small degree divided by gender, "the two sexes are only slightly differentiated," which "bears witness to the fact that conjugal solidarity is itself very weak" (Durkheim [1893] 2014: 48). In more modern societies, the division of labor increases and leads to a greater solidarity in the couple. Husband and wife are in "mutual dependence" (50). The most compelling idea today is that the feeling of friendship between spouses is rooted in their differences, which "can be a cause of mutual attraction." To justify this distinction, Durkheim built on Aristotle's two types of friendship, one based on the principle that "like goes with like" and the other on its opposite: "the finest harmony is born from differences" (45), and asserted that they are both equally important.

Yet sociological work on the choice of life partners, especially since Alain Girard (1964) and Pierre Bourdieu (1976), has forgotten Durkheim's words. It mainly focuses on the interests of each family line and emphasizes that these interests tend to lead to "matched" marriages, that is, marriages between a man and a woman possessing equivalent capitals. This is how most textbooks state "the rule of homogamy," based solely on the primacy of the principle that similar interests are in play. This rule was less obvious to Durkheim, who "married well" (in the words of Christophe Charle 1984) in wedding Louise Julie Dreyfus, who brought him a significant dowry.

This social reproduction approach neglects something that men and women are nonetheless quite aware of: they are also complementary and complete each other.[7] According to Durkheim, such differences between spouses—associated with the division of labor between the sexes[8] and reinforced by the presence of children—connect them to each other. They saturate their whole existence, Durkheim stated, unlike their sexual life, which is too limited. It would be interesting to test Durkheim's ideas—for example, are egalitarian couples more fragile than those with a pronounced division of labor?[9]—to see if the observed resistance to the slightest reduction in gender differentiation has functions other than maintaining masculine domination in married life.

This division of labor is also the source of the mutual dependence that today is usually criticized in the name of gender equality and individual independence. This should not put an end to the Durkheimian line of thought. From the opening lecture of his first social science course in December 1887, he asserted that "It is sociology which will [...] teach [the individual] that he is not an empire enclosed within another empire [...]. Sociology will make the individual feel that solidarity and dependence on someone else does not diminish him" (Durkheim [1888] 2008: 204). Durkheim can be read alongside contemporary work on individuals and their vulnerability, such as that of Peter Berger and Hansfried Kellner (1964; see also Singly 1996a), who greatly believed in the necessity of conjugal conversation: according to them, the personal world would be strengthened by the spouse's validation as "significant other." Mutual dependence has a positive side, ensuring "ontological security."

THE DANGERS OF PERSONAL TIES

In 1902, his very first year as professor at the Sorbonne, Durkheim gave a course, entitled "On Moral Education" (Durkheim [1925] 1961). He particularly emphasized "the spirit of discipline" (129). The family setting allows the child to "acquire regular habits with respect to everything bearing on the chief circumstances of his life" (138), especially times for nursing and bottles. But this is only "a first feeling for moral authority" because the child also has to explicitly learn to obey the rules. Durkheim considered "education within the family inadequate" (144) and preferred school discipline. The educating family's childrearing limitations arise from the nature of family ties: "The family, especially today, is a very small group of persons who know each other intimately [...]. As a result, their relationships are not subject to any general, impersonal, immutable regulation [...]. Familial duties [...] [can] accommodate themselves to differences in personality and circumstance." For Durkheim, "the morality practiced in this [family] setting is above all a matter of emotion and sentiment." Thus, family members are too close to each other for the child to learn abstract rules.[10] Durkheim restated something he had said in his "Conjugal Family" course: in the current day and age, "family relationships have lost their earlier impersonality and have a personal and quite volitional character" (147). This personalization of family ties makes the school the leading institution for moral education, not only because it includes a larger number of individuals, but even more so because the rules must be obeyed "for altogether general and abstract reasons" (149). A child obeys her mother because it is her mother who is asking, but she obeys the teacher because she must follow the rules.

The (relative) decline of the family's role in moral education and the rise of the school's would be picked up, in other terms, in the work of George Herbert Mead (1934), Jean Piaget ([1932] 1997), and Lawrence Kohlberg (1981). They considered abstract obedience to be a higher stage of moral development than a conditional obedience that takes account of the circumstances and people present. Reference to a "generalized other" is morally superior to reference to a "concrete other," to use Mead's terms.

This ranking would not be criticized until the 1980s, when Carol Gilligan (1982) condemned it for hiding the imposition of an abstract posture that defends men as being responsible for the common good, without taking the role of emotions into account. Gilligan proposed the term "care" in order to raise the social value and recognition of "taking care of people" (for a discussion, see, for example, Larrabee 1993). By implication, the family would have to be seen as being equally important as the school for the moral development of the child, since the child must learn to be attentive to others as well as to respect the rules. If, according to Durkheim, European modernity is typified by a rise in the importance of personal relationships, then apprenticeship in caring and paying attention to others becomes necessary, and the school is not the best setting for providing this education. The question remains which balance can be struck between the two levels of morality—abstract and concrete, impersonal and personal—when they are no longer ranked.[11]

The Virtues of the Institution of Matrimony

Durkheim's entire oeuvre on the family is rife with tensions between his observations of social changes and his conception of what is normal within the domestic circle. The issue of divorce, which was already a hotly debated topic in France early in the Third Republic, is another case in point. On the one hand, Durkheim became aware of the specificity of "the conjugal family," that is, a greater attachment to the personal dimension than to status.[12] On the other hand, consistent with his research on suicide (Durkheim [1897] 2007), Durkheim believed that men and women need strong institutions to contain their urges. He also thought that divorce by mutual consent was unfavorable to individual happiness because a weakened marital institution would not be strong enough to "hold" individuals.

No reference was made to divorce in his course on "The Conjugal Family," despite the ratification, after much passionate debate, of the so-called Naquet law on July 27, 1884. Divorce by mutual consent had been voted into being on September 20, 1792, the same day that the Assembly voted to establish civil marriage. This form of divorce was repealed by the Bonald law of May 8, 1816, during the reign of Louis XVIII, after a campaign to this end led largely by Louis de Bonald (1801). Some groups sought to reinstate it after the founding of the Third Republic in 1870, but conservatives successfully barred that eventuality with the Naquet law.

The Naquet law only reinstated divorce for a few serious situations. It did little to calm the debates that would resume, particularly with the publication of the novel *Les deux vies* by Paul and Victor Margueritte (1902), which Durkheim cites ([1906] 1978: 240).

The novelists were favorable to divorce by mutual consent, and they demonstrated the hypocrisy of maintaining a marriage when the conjugal relationship no longer means anything. They revived the sense of the preamble of the law of 1792 establishing divorce by mutual consent: "The ability to divorce results from individual freedom, for which an indissoluble engagement would be a loss." Durkheim took a public position against the restoration of divorce by mutual consent in the *Revue bleue* (1906), going against the progressive camp to which he belonged (he was a friend of leading socialist Jean Jaurès, who founded the newspaper *L'Humanité* in 1904 and would be assassinated in 1914; Durkheim's nephew Marcel Mauss was involved in *L'Humanité* from the beginning).

Durkheim also agreed to present his position at a debate on marriage and divorce held by the *Union pour la vérité* (Union for Truth) (Durkheim 1909). He refused to place spousal consent at the heart of the institution of marriage. For Durkheim, marriage is characterized by the presence of a "third party": "It is he who pronounces the words that bind, it is he who creates the conjugal tie. This tie thus depends, from its very creation, on a will and a moral power other than the individuals who are uniting. In other words, so that they cannot get rid of it as they wish, they cannot break it as they please" (258). "Marriage is a discipline" (276), and as such it is necessary. It is a "restraint" that moderates desires (Durkheim [1906] 1978: 248). Durkheim claimed to have proved this by showing that married men are less likely to commit suicide than either single or divorced men. He conceded that women have less need of marriage because, he thought, they have less of a "sexual instinct." Durkheim was thus opposed to marriage conceived as a contract: "the obligations that marriage brings into the world, although willingly contracted, are, once they are formed, subject to the arbitrary power of the individuals" (Durkheim 1906: 441).

Durkheim evoked his famous rule of the method, "social facts must be treated as things" (Durkheim [1895] 1982: 35)—meaning observing their external traits without going through the consciousness of individuals—to justify his condemnation of divorce by mutual consent: "The matter at hand is an objective fact, that is to say the manner in which their union functions; and this fact requires an objective appreciation of itself alone. Why would the manner in which the concerned parties represent this functioning be decisive?" (Durkheim 1906: 442). Continuing, he explained that "they only see things from their perspective, all individual and subjective; they feel the clashes and strains of everyday life. But as to knowing if these strains are of such a nature as to invalidate the conjugal union, to prevent it from fulfilling its social role, this is a problem that is beyond them." Durkheim concludes that "The conception they have of their relationship is thus a very bad criteria for judging the true state of relations" (442).

In making such a judgment, Durkheim does not take account of the thesis of his "Conjugal Family" course, according to which attachments to people are stronger than those to status. So what made him decide to favor objectivation, risking the disappearance of the affective dimension so characteristic of ties in the modern family? Durkheim seems to have been caught in the tension between his observations—the new nature of family ties—and his ideological concerns—preserving marriage as an institution. Everyone close to Durkheim agreed that he never recovered from the death of his son,

André, in December 1915. In a manner of speaking, he let himself die from that day until November 15, 1917, not writing another word. Durkheim began to worry the moment his son left for the front, a fact he confessed to Marcel Mauss and asked him to keep to himself so as not to further trouble Louise: "The situation up there is becoming quite tenuous. I am thus living in anxiety. Of course, not a word of this in your letter" (December 1, 1915). In a later letter, having no news of his son, Durkheim wrote again to Mauss: "Pointless to analyse our state for you. You imagine it easily for yourself. We suffer and we live" (February 5, 1916).

We find this tension (or even contradiction) once again in Durkheim's writing on cohabitation. He condemns free unions because "any sexual union which is not contracted in the matrimonial form disturbs the familial duty and the familial bond. [...] There is no moral society in which the members do not have obligations toward one another. [...] Free union is a conjugal society in which these obligations do not exist. It is, therefore, an immoral society" (Durkheim [1921] 1978: 238–239). Referring both to his attachment to the rules constraining individuals and to his observation of the concentration on the conjugal family, Durkheim concluded that "While the family loses ground, marriage, on the contrary, becomes stronger" (239).

There seems to be a confusion of two levels here. Durkheim rightly insisted on the couple's greater autonomy from its kinship networks and earlier generations. But after making this observation, he lets the meaning of the concept of marriage oscillate between "marriage as conjugal life" and "marriage as institution." Durkheim would have liked the force of the institution of marriage to compensate for the lost social force of kinship and the extended family. This is why he wanted the institution of marriage to become mandatory (by rejecting "free unions") and indissoluble (by rejecting divorce by mutual consent). Once again, this position (which is a legitimate ideological option) rejects his own theoretical propositions on the importance of personalization. If "relations continue to assume an exclusively personal character" (239), it is difficult to see why marriage would become stronger as an institution. The century following Durkheim's lecture on "The Conjugal Family" proved him wrong, with gradual increases in divorce, conjugal separations, and cohabitation, the destabilization of marriage as an institution, and a rising percentage of births outside of marriage. Durkheim's statement should be rephrased: while personalization gains ground, marriage, on the contrary, is eroded.

The Contemporary Family Has No Intergenerational Perspective

Durkheim thought that inheritance should be put to an end, since such transmissions of economic capital were contrary to the principle that individuals should earn their social positions for themselves, through merit, instead of inheriting resources from the family. The primacy of personal identity tends to sap the value from status-based identities such as "child of." At the very least, Durkheim thought, one could imagine having the freedom to decide how to make a will—the right to be able to decide the sums allotted to each person, or even which people will inherit—since children are defined more as individuals than as "son of" or "daughter of." Durkheim, moreover, emphasized that the chain of inheritance is disrupted by another factor—professions that are defined not by the quantity of economic capital, but by other (cultural or educational) resources: "there is a whole category of workers who can no longer transmit to their children the fruits of their labor, namely, those whose work brings only honor and respect rather than wealth" (Durkheim [1921] 1978: 235). Durkheim may have had himself and his intellectual renown in mind, along with his son, André, who was a student at the *Ecole normale supérieure* when the war broke out. He is indirectly demanding better recognition for intellectual work.

These pages on the transmission of inheritance reveal the ambivalence in Durkheim's attitude to the modern family. Consistent with his value system, he approved of the devaluation of inheritance, which he saw as the means by which "the external inequalities with which individuals are faced are leveled" so that "no social inequalities other than those which derive from the personal worth of each individual" would remain (236). He believed that personalization implied holding merit in high esteem. Each according to his abilities, and not according to his inheritance. This is why he approvingly thought that "the right of inheritance, even in the form of a will" was "destined progressively to disappear." For him, the emphasis on interpersonal relations is a corollary of building oneself through one's own work and merit. But at the same time, Durkheim feared that the individual would then become the end in and of itself. As seductive as personalization may be, it could lead to a form of laziness: "what binds us to our work is the fact that it is our means of enriching the domestic patrimony, of increasing the well-being of our children" (236). How, Durkheim wondered, can it be arranged that we will "be stimulated to work by something other than personal or domestic interest"? What group will take over from the family?

Although Durkheim believed that the conjugal society is "almost completely indissoluble" and he observed that communism and community are both strong within the couple, he did not see that as the future, because the conjugal group's lifespan is "too ephemeral for that" (237). Spouses "cannot be for one another an object sufficient to tear them from the search for fleeting sensations" (238), regardless of conjugal communism, because of death and the couple's certain dissolution resulting from it.

In comparison with other forms of the family, the conjugal family as Durkheim described it is the only one that does not offer familial prospects, in the strict (that is, intergenerational) sense of the term. It is significant that Durkheim suggested in his course on the family that the solution might be a greater attachment of individuals to their professional lives, outside the domestic circle. This indicates how pessimistic Durkheim was when he designated the modern family with the term "conjugal family."

But just because children leave their parents at majority and start out in life without recourse to inheritance does not mean that relations between parents and their children move into the background. Durkheim's mistake came from the fact that he overlooked new and more complex forms of exchange between generations. Despite being a sociologist of education, Durkheim forgot the effects the school had on the modern family. It would not be until Pierre Bourdieu and Jean-Claude Passeron ([1964] 1979) that the knowledge and legitimate forms of language which are explicitly or implicitly passed from generation to generation in the family would be called "inheritance" (see also Bernstein 1971). As his own life shows, Durkheim knew this form of inheritance without theorizing it. Although he was an ardent supporter of public "Republican" schools, his son, André, stayed home rather than attending primary school, his father playing schoolmaster until André was ten: "For a long time," Durkheim said, "I was his sole master," which led to "an intellectual intimacy that was as complete as possible" (Durkheim [1917] 1975). In their relationship, the transmission of cultural and educational capital (to put it in Bourdieu's terms) was spun into the thread of strong affective ties.

The Corollary of Personalization: State Intervention

What Durkheim found novel and distinctive in this new family type was "the ever increasing intervention of the state into the internal life of the family" (Durkheim [1921] 1978: 231). He gave the example of the control the state exercises over the father's "paternal power of chastisement." Indeed, it was during this period that public child protection policy was established in France, defending the youngest from excesses in "paternal authority" with a law in 1889 on the decline of "paternal authority" to the benefit of Public Assistance and an 1898 law against the mistreatment of children (Cabantous 1990; Rollet-Echalier 1990). In 1935 "paternal power of chastisement" was abolished, and in 1970 the notion of "paternal authority" was replaced with "parental authority."

The movement toward a greater concentration on individuals and personal identity, associated with the family's greater autonomy from the broader kin group, neighbors, and the rest of society, was accentuated by a rationale of greater dependence on the state: "the state has become a factor in domestic life" (Durkheim [1921] 1978: 231). The decline of domestic communism, and thus of a mutual dependence between family members, turns into an increasing dependence on the state. Closing the domestic circle with its charms of intimacy has a flip side: the control of this private life by the state. And so, at the same time that Durkheim was giving his course, a Public Assistance inspector trying to use social hygiene laws to establish a system of protection for all children expressed his approval that "breaches have been opened in the walls of the household enclosure, through which society is trying to see and penetrate, to defend the child, should there be need" (quoted in Rollet 1993). Hygienic and childrearing concerns serve to legitimate this surveillance of parental conduct. Hence, calling the undisputable gains in personal intimacy[13] a "privatization" of the modern family might be a fallacy, given that these gains come with such an increase in interventions by the state and its institutions.

This trend became stronger in the late twentieth century, with the establishment of family mediation to teach parents how to be parents (and to successfully manage their possible separation),[14] and, in France, with the creation of an independent High Authority in 2000, "The Defender of Children": any child can directly denounce what he or she believes to be parental mistreatment to a representative of the state.[15] The state has supported (and still supports) the actions of hygienists, doctors, psychologists, social workers, social assistants, marriage counsellors, family mediators, and many others to observe and regulate private relations (Donzelot 1977).

The state also intervenes in family affairs through the long-term and large-scale schooling of the children. This schooling has gradually led to the predominance of educational capital in the family patrimony (Bourdieu 1998). Because the power to grant degrees comes from the school and not directly from the family, the mother and father are partly dispossessed of the power to validate their child's social worth. They still have the power to act so that their child can do as best as possible in his or her studies, although this power is unequally distributed. Identifying this permanent intervention of the state and the concentration on the personal dimension of family members are Durkheim's core contributions to the sociology of the family.

Translated from the French by Juliette Rogers.

Notes

1. In 1892, the year his son, André, was born, Durkheim also chose to devote his course to the family (Fournier 2007: 158).
2. His ideas are summarized in Le Play (1982).
3. However, the content of Durkheim's "family" manuscript is not known.
4. This article studies the analyses that Durkheim made of the family of late nineteenth-century Europe. Hence, there are few references to lectures and publications on research concerning the elementary forms of marriage and family, which are too dependent on the dominant evolutionary perspective of the late nineteenth century. In order to show relative continuity between family types, Durkheim tended to forget what he observed in the conjugal family. A reader of "La prohibition de l'inceste" (Durkheim 1897) can only be astonished to read that "The family has nonetheless remained saturated by religiosity; it is still the holy ark, forbidden to touch precisely because it is the school of respect, and respect is the religious sentiment par excellence" (60). In his course on the conjugal family, as we will see, Durkheim especially emphasizes weakening feelings for the family as a communal unit and the development of personal ties.
5. To such an extent that Philippe Ariès dubbed the modern family "the educative family." Durkheim and Ariès each emphasized one of the relationships, forgetting that the other is also moving in the same direction.
6. It was published as *De la division du travail social* (Durkheim [1893/1902] 2014).
7. If one is to believe certain descriptions of the couple by friends and family, Louise was distinctly more likely to smile than Émile.

8. This idea has been forgotten because it might seem to justify the unequal distribution of domestic work.
9. The man, centered on his salaried work, better succeeds at his career than a woman who must take over more domestic work; see, for example, Singly (1996b).
10. Durkheim would have liked to conform to the rules and be strict, but he was unable to hide his affection and sensitivity. After his death, his friend Maurice Holleaux wrote: "Few knew that his severity concealed an almost feminine sensitivity, or what treasures of goodwill were contained in this heart, enemy of ready outpourings" (quoted in Davy 1960: 8).
11. Some of Gilligan's writings seem to indicate that she was reversing the hierarchy; the proposal to not rank them is this author's suggestion.
12. On the literary and philosophical history of this inversion, see Singly (2017).
13. This translates into the attachment to a domestic space, both enclosed and well maintained; see Murard and Zylberman (1976: 25); Perrot (1990).
14. Divorce by mutual consent was reinstated in France in 1975. But the state requires that parents continue to exercise their authority together. This is the concept of "joint parental authority." Durkheim thought that the state would defend the indissolubility of marriage (Durkheim [1921] 1978: 231), and he did not anticipate the compromise found in the 1980s: the couple of spouses may separate, but not the couple of parents.
15. Since 2011, this "defender" has been part of the *Défenseur des droits*, a state-sanctioned independent authority for the protection of rights.

References

Ariès, Philippe. 1948. *Histoire des populations françaises et de leurs attitudes devant la vie depuis le XVIIIe siècle*. Paris: Editions Self.
Ariès, Philippe. 1960. *L'enfant et la vie familiale sous l'Ancien Régime*. Paris: Plon.
Beck, Ulrich. 1992. *Risk Society: Towards a New Modernity*. London: SAGE.
Béra, Matthieu. 2014. *Emile Durkheim à Bordeaux (1887–1902)*. Bordeaux: Editions Confluences.
Béra, Matthieu. 2017. "Sociologie des premiers étudiants de Durkheim (Bordeaux, 1887–1902)." HDR thesis, Ecole normale supérieure de Cachan.
Berger, Peter, and Hansfried Kellner. 1964. "Marriage and the Construction of Reality: An Exercise in the Microsociology of Knowledge." *Diogenes* 12 (46): 1–24.
Bernstein, Basil. 1971. *Class, Codes and Control*, vol. 1: *Theoretical Studies towards a Sociology of Language*. London: Routledge & Kegan Paul.
Bonald, Louis de. 1801. *Du divorce, considéré au XIXe siècle relativement à l'état domestique et à l'état public de société*. Paris: Leclere.
Bourdieu, Pierre. 1976. "Marriage Strategies as Strategies of Social Reproduction." In Pierre Bourdieu, *Family and Society: Selections from the* Annales. Economies, Sociétés, Civilisations, edited by Robert Forster and Orest Ranum, 117–144. Baltimore: Johns Hopkins University Press.
Bourdieu, Pierre. 1998. *The State Nobility: Elite Schools in the Field of Power*. Stanford, CA: Stanford University Press.
Bourdieu, Pierre, and Jean-Claude Passeron. (1964) 1979. *The Inheritors: French Students and Their Relation to Culture*. Chicago: University of Chicago Press.
Cabantous, Alain. 1990. "La fin des patriarches." In *Histoire des pères et de la paternité*, edited by Jean Delumeau and Daniel Roche, 323–348. Paris: Larousse.

Charle, Christophe. 1984. "Le beau mariage d'Emile Durkheim." *Actes de la recherche en sciences sociales* 55: 45–49.

Davy, Georges. 1960. "Emile Durkheim." *Revue française de sociologie* 1 (1): 3–24.

Donzelot, Jacques. 1977. *La police des familles*. Paris: Minuit.

Durkheim, Émile. 1897. "La prohibition de l'inceste et ses origines." *L'Année sociologique* 1: 1–70. Republished in Émile Durkheim, *Journal sociologique*, 37–101. Paris: Presses universitaires de France, 1969.

Durkheim, Émile. 1898/99. Review "Dumont (Arsène), Natalité et démocratie." *L'Année sociologique* 3: 558–561. Republished in Émile Durkheim, *Journal sociologique*, 237–240. Paris: Presses universitaires de France, 1969.

Durkheim, Émile. 1906. Review "Valensi (Alfred), *L'application de la loi du divorce en France*." *L'Année sociologique* 9: 438–443.

Durkheim, Émile. 1909. Contribution "Débat sur le mariage et le divorce." In *Libres Entretiens. Sur la condition économique et juridique des femmes*, 258–293. Paris: Union pour la vérité, fifth series. Partially republished in Émile Durkheim, *Textes*, vol. 2, edited by Victor Karady, 206–215. Paris: Minuit, 1975.

Durkheim, Émile. (1925) 1961. *Moral Education: A Study in the Theory and Application of the Sociology of Education*. Translated by E. K. Wilson and H. Schnurer. New York: Free Press. Originally published as *L'éducation morale*, edited by Paul Fauconnet. Paris: Alcan.

Durkheim, Émile. (1917) 1975. Obituary "Durkheim (André-Armand)." In Émile Durkheim, *Textes*, vol. 1, edited by Victor Karady, 446–452. Paris: Minuit. Originally published in *Annuaire de l'association amicale des anciens élèves de l'Ecole normale supérieure*, 201–205.

Durkheim, Émile. (1888) 1978. "Introduction to the Sociology of the Family." In *Emile Durkheim on Institutional Analysis*, edited and translated by Mark Traugott, 205–228. Chicago: University of Chicago Press. Originally published as "Introduction à la sociologie de la famille" in *Annales de la Faculté des lettres de Bordeaux* 10: 257–281.

Durkheim, Émile. (1906) 1978. "Divorce by Mutual Consent." In *Emile Durkheim on Institutional Analysis*, edited and translated by Mark Traugott, 240–252. Chicago: University of Chicago Press. Originally published as "Le divorce par consentement mutuel" in *Revue bleue* 44 (5): 549–554.

Durkheim, Émile. (1921) 1978. "The Conjugal Family." In *Emile Durkheim on Institutional Analysis*, edited and translated by Mark Traugott, 229–239. Chicago: University of Chicago Press. Originally published as "La famille conjugale" in *Revue philosophique* 91: 1–14.

Durkheim, Émile. (1895) 1982. *The Rules of Sociological Method and Selected Texts on Sociology and Its Method*. Translated by W. D. Halls. New York: Free Press. Originally published as *Les règles de la méthode sociologique*. Paris: Alcan.

Durkheim, Émile. (1897) 2007. *On Suicide*. Translated by Robin Buss. London: Penguin Classics. Originally published as *Le suicide: Etude de sociologie*. Paris: Alcan.

Durkheim, Émile. (1888) 2008. "Course in Social Science—Inaugural Lecture." *Organization & Environment* 21 (2): 188–204. Originally published as "Cours de science sociale: Leçon d'ouverture" in *Revue internationale de l'enseignement* 15: 23–48.

Durkheim, Émile. (1893/1902) 2014. *The Division of Labor in Society*. Edited by Steven Lukes and translated by W. D. Halls. New York: Free Press. Originally published as *De la division du travail social. Etude sur l'organisation des sociétés supérieures*. Paris: Alcan, 1893; 2nd ed. Paris: Alcan, 1902.

Fournier, Marcel. 2007. *Emile Durkheim (1858–1917)*. Paris: Fayard.

Gilligan, Carol. 1982. *In a Different Voice*. Cambridge, MA: Harvard University Press.

Girard, Alain. 1964. *Le choix du conjoint. Une enquête psycho-sociologique en France.* Paris: Presses universitaires de France.

Kohlberg, Lawrence. 1981. *Essays on Moral Development*, vol. 1: *The Philosophy of Moral Development: Moral Stages and the Idea of Justice.* San Francisco: Harper & Row.

Lamanna, Mary Ann. 2002. *Emile Durkheim on the Family.* Thousand Oaks, CA: SAGE.

Larrabee, Mary Jeanne, ed. 1993. *An Ethic of Care: Feminist and Interdisciplinary Perspectives.* London: Routledge.

Laslett, Peter. 1988. "Family, Kinship and Collectivity as Systems of Support in Pre-Industrial Europe: A Consideration of the 'Nuclear-Hardship' Hypothesis." *Continuity and Change* 3 (2): 153–175.

Le Play, Frédéric. 1982. *Frédéric Le Play on Family, Work, and Social Change.* Edited and translated by Catherine Bodard Silver. Chicago: University of Chicago Press.

Mauss, Marcel. (1925) 2016. "In Memoriam: The Unpublished Work of Durkheim and His Collaborators." In Marcel Mauss, *The Gift.* Expanded Edition, translated by Jane I. Guyer. Chicago: HAU Books.

Mead, George Herbert. 1934. *Mind, Self, and Society.* Chicago: University of Chicago Press.

Murard, Lion, and Patrick Zylberman. 1976. *Le petit travailleur infatigable.* Paris: Recherches.

Perrot, Michelle. 1990. "At Home." In *A History of Private Life*, vol. 4: *From the Fires of Revolution to the Great War*, edited by Michelle Perrot, 341–357. Cambridge, MA: Harvard University Press.

Piaget, Jean. (1932) 1997. *The Moral Judgement of the Child.* Translated by Marjorie Gabain. New York: Free Press.

Rollet, Catherine. 1993. "De l'intérêt de l'état aux droits de l'enfant." *Le groupe familial* 138 (1): 4–11.

Rollet-Echalier, Catherine. 1990. *La politique à l'égard de la petite enfance sous la IIIe République.* Paris: Presses universitaires de France.

Singly, François de. 1996a. *Le soi, le couple et la famille.* Paris: Nathan.

Singly, François de. 1996b. *Modern Marriage and Its Cost to Women: A Sociological Look at Marriage in France.* Newark: University of Delaware Press.

Singly, François de. 2016. *Sociologie de la famille contemporaine.* 6th ed. Paris: Armand Colin.

Singly, François de. 2017. *Double Je: Identité personnelle et identité statutaire.* Paris: Armand Colin.

Vidal-Naquet, Clémentine. 2014a. *Correspondances conjugales 1914–1918. Dans l'intimité de la Grande Guerre.* Paris: Laffont.

Vidal-Naquet, Clémentine. 2014b. *Couples dans la Grande Guerre. Le tragique et l'ordinaire du lien conjugal.* Paris: Les Belles Lettres.

CHAPTER 22

DURKHEIM, TARDE, LATOUR

BJØRN SCHIERMER

THIS chapter discusses the current critique of Durkheim's work and of Durkheimian sociology initiated by French sociologist, anthropologist of science, and actor-network theorist Bruno Latour. Latour aims for nothing less than a reevaluation of the sociological canon and wishes, at the expense of Durkheim, to repatriate his historical adversary Gabriel Tarde as the "*real* founder of French Sociology" (Latour 2004: 245, original emphasis). Thus, reviving the debate between Durkheim and Tarde that echoed through French academic life from 1894 to Tarde's death in 1904, Latour constructs a decisive "academic battle" between Durkheim and Tarde. Recently, he has even played a catalyst role in the theatrical "re-enactment"—at a Cambridge conference on the relationship between Durkheim and Tarde held in 2008 (Candea 2010)—of the "legendary" face-to-face confrontation between the two adversaries that originally took place in Paris in 1903.[1] In Latour's view, the fact that Durkheim came out on top of the dispute with Tarde has had fatal consequences for the discipline.

This chapter investigates the central issues to the historical discussion between Durkheim and Tarde, and it discusses Latour's recent appropriation of it, his interpretation of Tarde, and his critique of Durkheim. First, I delve into the young Durkheim's programmatic ideas for his new science of sociology and seek to make Tarde's objections intelligible. I also investigate Durkheim's critique of the concept of imitation, Tarde's key concept, and demonstrate that while it is true that the young Durkheim was critical toward the concept, it stands, rather surprisingly, at the very center of his late sociology of religion. In the third part of the chapter, I shortly engage Tarde's sociology, highlighting the ambivalences that makes it objectionable to Durkheim and attractive to Latour. In the fourth part, I introduce Latour's critique of Durkheim; I seek to assess the merits of this critique, and, based on my own work, I intimate a possible compromise between Latour and Durkheim. While sharing the anti-holistic impetus of Tarde's and Latour's critique of Durkheim, I demonstrate that this critique misses crucial and fruitful reorientations in Durkheim's late thought. Notably, the recent interest in the Durkheim-Tarde constellation seems to ignore that imitation plays a central role in Durkheim's late conception of ritual and thus in his very construction of the sacred object.

The Durkheim-Tarde Debate

When writing about Durkheim and Tarde, it is imperative to avoid the simplifying reduction of ten years of debate to one spectacular event taking place in 1903.[2] Such a focus on an isolated event not only obscures the developments within a debate which lasted more than ten years; it also leaves aside transformations in Durkheim's late sociology which, as we will see, turn directly on central issues to the debate.[3] Even if lack of space forces me to refrain from tracing the course of their continuous and prolonged "dialogue," I shall shortly list the relevant texts and dates.

The first critical remarks on the concept of imitation are found in Durkheim's first major work, *The Division of Labour in Society* ([1893] 2013a: 295). This book is reviewed respectfully although critically by Tarde (1893). Durkheim extends and deepens his critique in the first chapters of *The Rules of Sociological Method* ([1895] 2103b: 20–28, esp. 27). There is no doubt that Durkheim, at this point seeking to contour his version of the new discipline, thinks he must prove Tarde's basic ideas wrong. This time, however, Tarde reacts: one finds no less than six texts from his hand, all written within a year after the publication of *Rules* (the first chapters of which were published in advance as journal articles), and all strongly critical of Durkheim (the most important one being Tarde [1894] 1969: see esp. 114–125; cf. Besnard 1995: 228–229). Durkheim retorts within the same year—1895—criticizing Tarde's work in an extended review of French sociology written for an Italian journal ([1895] 1975a: esp. 81–89).

Suicide ([1897] 2002a) is meant as a final refutation of Tarde—a fact duly noted by Tarde himself (Tarde [1897] 2000: 233). While large parts of the third part's first chapter (Durkheim [1897] 2002a: 269–290) deal extensively with Tarde's objections to the *Rules*, an entire chapter in the first part (74–94) is meant to dismiss the concept of imitation as sociologically irrelevant. Tarde announces a response to this tour de force but never completes it (see his notes in Tarde [1897] 2000). Another critical (and shorter) review of Tarde's work from Durkheim's hand surfaces in 1900 (1973: 18–20). The ultimate "physical confrontation" follows in 1903 (Tarde and Durkheim 1969). After Tarde's death in 1904, Durkheim publishes a negative review of Tarde's book on "inter-psychology" in 1905 (Durkheim 1905). Durkheim's last—and decidedly more positive—assessment of Tarde's sociological merits is from 1915 (Durkheim 1975b: 115–116).

Except for this very last text, a deep sense of disagreement—and a note of personal contempt—is tangible in these exchanges. Basically, in Durkheim's eyes, Tarde is a dilettante.[4] Tarde, Durkheim feels, takes his point of departure in an abstract "philosophical" concept of imitation, which explains everything and nothing; he recurs to literary sources or mere "anecdotes" and knows little about "scientific" methodology; he remains "individualistic" and "psychological" and too close to the "biological"—impulses which run counter to the young Durkheim's scientific ideals and to his attempt to demarcate a sui generis concept of the social. Tarde was no less hostile. In Tarde's eyes, Durkheim is a metaphysician or even a mystic. Again and again, Tarde challenges

Durkheim's strong holism or "emergentism" as an "ontological scholasticism" which is "illusionary" or even "mystic" or "fantastic" ([1894] 1969: 115), insisting that the social can only take place among real human beings; he criticizes Durkheim's emphasis on coercion and constraint as reductionist and one-sided ([1894] 1969: 118–119), highlighting instead "spontaneous" imitation ([1894] 1969: 118–119) or "instincts of sociability" (Tarde [1893] 2012: 30). He even seeks to demonstrate, against Durkheim, the presence of imitation in Durkheim's own work (Tarde [1894] 1969, [1897] 2000). To these theoretical and scientific differences, major political and personal ones should be added: Tarde was conservative while Durkheim was republican (and *Dreyfusard*); Tarde, the flamboyant Parisian, was as much at home in the literary salons as in the academic world, while Durkheim was known for his austere personality, had little regard for culture (in the narrow sense), and only gained an academic position in Paris in 1902.

The next section analyzes the main issues of this debate, focusing on Durkheim's work: it critically investigates Durkheim's holism, his coercive account of the social, his sociology of the crowd, and his critique—and final incorporation—of the concept of imitation. By making intelligible the Durkheim that Tarde and Latour revolt against, I also seek to assess the merits of their critique.

Durkheim

A Sociology of Constraint

There is a tight relationship between the programmatic and foundational gesture of *Rules* and the understanding of the social that the book promotes and that underlies much of Durkheim's sociology. Durkheim's wish to secure a proper object for the new science of sociology leads him to the idea of the social sui generis, demarcated from the "psychological" and "individual," and this leads him in turn to focus on a certain genre of social phenomena:

> [L]egal and moral rules, aphorisms and popular sayings, articles of faith in which religious or political sects epitomize their beliefs and standards of taste drawn up by literary scholars etc. ([1895] 2013b: 24)

For Durkheim, such phenomena count as paradigmatic expressions of the social. Why? Because they show the characteristics that he needs in order to separate the social from the individual. By focusing on such sedimented expressions of the social—manifested in our written laws and in our traditions, of course, but also in an abundance of ways in our material culture—Durkheim means to show that the social has its own life independent of us—the living and breathing individuals. These "signs" point to an underlying reality of social norms and duties which survive us and into which we are socialized as we grow up.

These inveterate norms and rules are then, Durkheim repeatedly emphasizes, "external" to the individuals in several ways (cf. Lukes 1973: 8–23; Borlandi 1995). They are persistent not only in the sense that they outlast the single individual but also in the sense that she *must* adapt to them. They are "obligatory" to the individual who cannot (singlehandedly) change them; they are opposed to her and "impose" themselves upon her. This is why Durkheim insists that "constraint is *the* characteristic trait of *every* social fact" ([1895] 2013b: 97, my emphasis). The social *is*—essentially—normative "constraint" (cf. Lukes 1973: 13).

Despite Durkheim's reservations against the "psychological," this definition has clear psychological or experiential implications: the paradigmatic experience of the social is shaped by fear of collective sanctions and by sentiments of opposition to other human beings. Durkheim's insistence that the sociologist should "treat the social as a thing" ([1895] 2013b: 29–49) only reinforces this repressive phenomenology. True, on the one hand, by insisting on "external observation," and forbidding "mere" introspection, "psychology," or "understanding" (from the perspective of the individual, as in Weber), Durkheim tells us to focus on the objectified manifestations or "signs" of the social—think, for instance, of his investigation of historical changes in penal law as indications of different forms of solidarity in *Division* ([1893] 2013a) or of his use of statistics in *Suicide* ([1897] 2002a). Yet on the other hand, the very insistence on the social as external is inseparable from the "psychology" of the social as an external source of discipline:

> A thing is principally recognisable by virtue of not being capable of modification through a mere act of the will. [...] We have seen that social facts possess this property of resistance. Far from being a product of our will, they determine it from without. They are like moulds into which we are forced to cast our actions. This necessity is often ineluctable. [...] Thus in considering facts as things, we shall be merely conforming to their nature.
>
> (Durkheim [1895] 2013b: 37)

The social is, by "nature," hard and solid as a physical "thing." It does not yield if you bump into it and is thus capable of forcing you back onto the beaten path. This is the psychological side to Durkheim's infamous social "realism." However, the reader should recognize this schema. We are dealing with a crude version of the dichotomy of actor versus structure and its concomitant dualities: internal versus external, freedom versus determinism, and active versus passive. Thus, even though, in Durkheim's account, "free" action—free will—is the prerogative of the human individual, the social assumes an explanatory role simply because it limits this freedom decisively. This template goes hand in hand with Durkheim's methodological "holism": the social is *more* than its parts (the individuals); it is not reducible to the actions of the individuals, but rather *explains* (large parts) of their behavior.

To sum up: Durkheim's attempt to demarcate an object for sociology leads him to insist on the "externality" of the social, which then goes hand in hand with a reduction of the social to repressive "external" norms. This, in turn, forces Durkheim into the traditional dichotomy of actor versus structure, with an exclusive interest in the structural aspects.

Moreover, the reader should remark the *individualist tenor* of this understanding of the social. This may come as a surprise, yet there can be no doubt that the reduction of the social to a rather decontextualized grid of norms essentially *decollectivizes* it. Not only does it "naturalize" the social in its normative and repressive guise, it also turns it into a rather abstract entity (a structure of norms and rules), and thus cleanses it of experiences of concrete others. The internalization of this structure through education and socialization ([1895] 2013b: 25) does not make the individual less lonely. It installs society inside the individual instead of installing the individuals in the collective.

… and Integration

The reader should notice the unmistakable anti-Tardean thrust of this sociology. Literally, in early Durkheim the social is held together through the *fear of being different*, not through the *desire—*conscious or not*—to be similar*. It is a sociology of conformist individuals, but not of collectivist ones; a sociology of isolated individuals facing a normative structure, not of porous individuals always-already connected with other individuals, let alone imitating these other individuals. It is highly understandable that Tarde misses, in Durkheim's sociology, a notion of "natural attraction" among humans, an inherent "tendency toward association" ([1894] 1969: 123) or what he elsewhere calls "the lively instinct of sociability which makes men want to agglomerate themselves" ([1893] 2012: 30).

Yet matters are more complex. First of all, as readers familiar with Durkheim's *Suicide* ([1897] 2002a) will know, Durkheim was soon to complement his normative concept of the social with a more positive and affirmative one. In *Suicide*, the "regulative" side of the social is complemented with an "integrative" side (105–174); in the lectures on *Moral Education*, the "disciplinary" side is complemented with a dimension of "attachment to society" ([1903] 2002b: 71ff.); in the text on "The Moral Fact" ([1906] 1965), the aspect of "duty" is complemented with the aspect of "love" and even "desire" (for the sacred).[5]

Unfortunately, Durkheim cannot really give substance to this move. Even though, for instance, *Suicide* contains a number of passages on concrete collective sentiments, intensities and energies related to family life or to participation in political effervescent events (cf. esp. [1897] 2002a: 159–168), these concrete observations and experiences disappear at the end of the section. Again, the abstract concept of "society" imposes itself:

> The influence of society is what has aroused in us the sentiments of sympathy and solidarity drawing us toward others; it is society which, fashioning us in its image, fills us with religious, political and moral beliefs that control our actions. […] We can cling to these forms of human activity only to the degree that we cling to society itself. ([1897] 2002a: 170)

It is not the sentiments of sympathy or solidarity which draw us toward others, but "society" which first teaches us to feel this way. Despite his emphasis on these positive sentiments, Durkheim ultimately isolates the individuals. This time around, however, it is not about constraint or discipline, but rather about making them understand their positive moral and cultural dependence on society. This is the project of *Moral Education* ([1903] 2002b). Concrete collective attachment is "sublimated" into "attachment to society." Indeed, it is in the high-flown register of the descriptions of this need "to cling" to "society" as a vast moral and cultural power that Durkheim's own sacralization of "society" becomes salient (Adorno [1967] 1979; Latour 2014; cf. also Riley 2012; Pickering 1984: 244).

Thus, unsurprisingly, Durkheim's opening toward an "integrative" dimension to the social does not bring him any closer to Tarde. Nevertheless, the reader feels how Durkheim balances on a knife's edge here: How to make sense of the concept of "integration" without falling back into an individualistic "psychology" of concrete collective experiences (with concrete others)? At this point, Durkheim's answer is the sacralization of society. More than ever, "society" is indeed "infinitely" more than its parts—which it constitutes, comforts, and transcends like a divine being. Ultimately, the dimension of integration ends up just as decollectivized as the dimension of constraint or regulation. In both cases we are dealing with a sole individual facing a "society" bereft of concrete collectivity, the only difference being whether this society is pictured as a treasure of cultural riches or as a system of norms and rules.

What to think of this abstract collective? Probably, to the Durkheimian, bent on avoiding "psychology" and having no quarrels with the abstract idea of "society," this maneuver may seem straightforward; to the Tardean, bent on concrete (imitational) interchanges between "real" people (mediated or not), it is metaphysical and speculative. It rubs salt in Tarde's wounds: Durkheim reacts to his critique of the one-sidedness of the picture of the social as coercive not by giving admissions to the collective or the social-psychological, but by even further consecrating the very holism that Tarde so despised.

However, there remains a difficult subject that Durkheim has yet to deal with; a subject that will really test his anti-psychologism. This subject is the *crowd*.

The Crowd

The crowd was a hot topic in *fin de siècle* France. It was also dear to Tarde, and it was normally theorized in terms of imitation and suggestion. Gustave Le Bon's famous *Psychologie des foules* (1905) came out in 1895, the same year as Durkheim's *Rules* (2013b). Durkheim had to show that his new sociology was capable of accommodating the crowd without "falling back" into crowd psychology.

This time, however, Durkheim cannot abstract from concrete experience of others and of a sense of participation. Then, this is really what crowd experience *is*. But is it possible to give voice to this *feeling* of excitement and collective presence while at the same time insisting upon the social as something "external"? It is difficult. Take the following quote from *Rules*:

> But even when the social fact is partly due to our direct corporation, it is no different in nature. An outburst of collective emotion in a gathering does not merely express the sum total of what individual feelings share in common, but is something of a very different order [...]. If all hearts beat in unison, this is not as a consequence of a spontaneous pre-established harmony, it is because one and the same force is propelling them in the same direction. ([1895] 2013b: 25)

But is it really possible to talk about "direct corporation" or "spontaneity" ([1895] 2013b: 23) or about actively "*sharing* a common feeling" (instead of merely having it *in common*) ([1897] 2002a: 80) *and* at the same time insist that the individuals are "propelled" (by forces coming) from without. Durkheim's holism simply forbids resorting to the individual level in explaining the social—and this produces ambivalences:

> [I]n a public gathering the great waves of enthusiasm, indignation and pity that are produced have their seat in no one individual consciousness. They come to each one of us from outside and can sweep us along in spite of ourselves. If perhaps I abandon myself to them, I may not be conscious of the pressure that they are exerting upon me, but that pressure makes itself felt immediately if I attempt to resist them. [...] Now, if this external coercive power asserts itself so acutely in cases of resistance, it must be because it exists in the other instances cited above without our being conscious of it. Hence we are the victims of an illusion which leads us to believe we have ourselves produced what has been imposed upon us externally. [...] It is then we perceive that we have undergone the emotions much more than generated them. ([1895] 2013b: 22)

It is a mere "illusion" on the part of the members of the crowd to think that they have actually "generated" or "produced" the collective emotions they "undergo." The active and the passive cannot overlap, nor can the internal or the external or the individual and the social. Durkheim thus reinforces these dichotomies even when analyzing situations where they are absent from experience. The consequences are obvious: the active *and* passive, the spontaneous production of determination, the internal *and* external, the activity of letting oneself "be swept away" finds no place in Durkheim's account.[6] But, arguably, when we do not notice that we are transported into a "completely other state of mind" when participating in the crowd, isn't it exactly because there is *no clean break* between the individual (or the psychological) and the social? Between the internal and the external? Durkheim, however, *must* enforce this dichotomy.

Nevertheless, as we will see, it is exactly this rupture between the individual and the social that Durkheim mends in his late, ethnography-inspired work. To understand this, however, we need a careful introduction of the concept of imitation.

Imitation—Before and After

Imitation is Tarde's key notion, and it is important for Durkheim to show that it cannot serve as a foundational sociological concept. His argument takes up a whole chapter of *Suicide* ([1897] 2002a: 74–94) and cannot be done justice here (but see Besnard 1995; Karsenti 2010; Schiermer 2019). Yet his main strategy consists in constructing the phenomenon of imitation in an extremely impoverished version and then showing that it cannot produce sociality in any substantial sense:

> That imitation is a purely psychological phenomenon appears clearly from its occurrence between individuals connected by no social bond. A man may imitate another with no link of either one with the other or with a common group on which both depend, and the imitative function when exercised has in itself no power to form a bond between them.
> (Durkheim [1897] 2002a: 74)

Not only are imitational dynamics instinctive, automatic, and blind—and thus independent of any prior social structure—but they are also unidirectional. Thus thinned out, imitation remains "purely psychological." It leaves no social "bond." Having reduced imitation to a mere one-way transport, Durkheim ([1895] 1975a: 84) can claim that its cultural and social significance is "very secondary." There may be imitational rays or waves, but no imitational crowds.

Now, this total rejection of the concept of imitation on Durkheim's part is where all the contemporary interpreters—the Durkheimians as well as the Tardeans—usually halt their investigations. I think this is a mistake. Then, the concept of imitation emerges in Durkheim's own work in 1912, eight years after Tarde's death, in a central, implicit yet entirely *positive* role. I am thinking about Durkheim's account of (informal) ritual:

> It is by shouting the same cry, saying the same words, and performing the same action in regard to the same object that [the Australians] arrive at and experience agreement [...].
> The individual minds can meet and commune only if they come outside themselves, but they can do this only by the means of movement. It is the homogeneity of these movements that makes the group aware of itself, and that, in consequence, makes it be. ([1912] 1995: 232)

Imitation is at the very heart of ritual in the late work. Here, in strict opposition to Durkheim's earlier critique of Tarde, the very creation of collectivity is imitational. What has happened?

First, the reader should note that this new concept of imitation bears little resemblance to the impoverished version found earlier. This time imitation *is* capable of engendering collective energies. We are not dealing with automatic one-way copying, but with reciprocal self-reinforcing entrainment. This means, second, that the individuals, in contrast to the scenarios found in *Rules* and *Suicide*, *actively co-produce* the collective sentiments that will overtake them. There is a sense of acuity and presence to these paragraphs which is absent from the accounts in *Rules* and *Suicide*. Forced by his encounter with ethnographic accounts of ritual, Durkheim must mitigate the dualism of his early descriptions—even though the notions of "exteriority" and "imposition" are still amply present in the late text. Nevertheless, here collective sentiments—"experience of agreement"—are actively sought for and enjoyed, and animated through dynamics of mutual tuning in, mutual engagement, and self-abandonment—that is through active co-production of collective determination. Such intricate mixtures of activity and passivity found no room, as we saw, in the early work.

This should not be misunderstood. Imitation is but one aspect—albeit a crucial one—of ritual. It is the motor of effervescence. But the collective energies are then projected upon an *object* which thereby become sacred. Imitation *and* projection are what account for the sacred in the late Durkheim's work. There is a potentially self-enforcing circle here: projections of collective energies explain the importance and salience of the object, and the salience and importance of the object engender imitation and entrainment taking place around it.

Tarde

Tarde as Methodological Individualist?

In this section, I shall concentrate on two ambiguous aspects of Tarde's relation to Durkheim: first, his alleged "individualism" (and psychologism) and, second, his idea of a sociological "monadology." These two themes must be analyzed if we want to understand Durkheim's quarrels with Tarde, and Latour's recent attempt to enlist the latter as a "respectable forefather" of actor-network theory (2002: 117; 2005: 13).

Is Tarde an individualist? This was the point behind Durkheim's critique of the concept of imitation in *Suicide* ([1897] 2002a: 74–94): Imitation, we saw, creates no "social bond"; it remains on the individual or psychological "level." The categorization of Tarde as a methodological individualist is not without a certain textual base in Tarde himself. He repeatedly insists on the individual—the "genius," the "great scientist," the "leader"—as the locus of invention and thus as the point of departure for imitational "rays." But the imitators, too, should be seen as actually existing individuals:

> The truth is that any social thing, a word in a language, a religious rite, a trade secret, an artistic process, a legal provision, a moral maxim, is transmitted and passed not from *the social group taken collectively* to the individual, but from one individual—parent, teacher, friend, neighbour, comrade—to another individual [...]. ([1894] 1969: 115)

Many of Tarde's anti-holistic arguments—not only his polemic against Durkheim's "fantastic" or "mystic" notion of a "new" and "superior" societal "being" with a life of its own ([1894] 1969: 122)—have an individualist ring to them. However, again, matters are more complex. Often, critics seem to assume that the individualist position is the only possibility left once holism is denounced (see Lukes 1973: 302–313; Besnard 1995; Jones 1999; and for an exception, Karsenti 2010). But Tarde is not that easy to place. He is not an individualist in the Weberian sense. He is not interested in the inventors—but in the imitators. And *these* "individuals" are often strangely porous and plastic. Ultimately, he denies the very distinction between the social and the individual. To Durkheim's allegation that "psychological explanation cannon help but overlook [...] the social" (cf. Durkheim [1895] 2013b: 86), he answers:

> I reply yes, if one wishes to account for a collective fact only through the logic of individuals and of real individuals, but not if one also considers the psychology and the logic of the masses and the dead. ([1894] 1969: 123)

Despite the metaphors, the message is clear: we cannot explain the social by taking our point of departure in self-conscious and "intentional" individuals; such individuals are from the outset (at least partly) dissolved in the imitational content they share with others—living or "dead." In short, *the individuals cannot be considered apart from their relations*. Tarde is *not* a methodological individualist.

Monadolgy

This brings us to the other ambivalent trait in Tarde's work: his "monadological" ideas contoured in *Monadology and Sociology* ([1893] 2012). Even though the book was written before the debate with Durkheim took off—it is published in the same year as Durkheim's *Division of Labour*—one hardly finds a less Durkheimian understanding of what sociology ought to be.

In contrast to Durkheim's idea that the elements (the behavior of the individuals) should be explained by the sui generis laws, forces, or rules of the whole (through the "external" limits they place on these elements), the impetus of Tarde's monadology is that the relations among the elements should, as it were, "explain themselves," that is, that only "immanent" explanations should be allowed (cf. Tarde [1894] 1969: 112–125).

To really understand what is meant here it is necessary to appreciate how this immanentism goes hand in hand with an *extension of the concept of the social* to the "nonhuman" ([1893] 2012: 28ff.). On the one hand, Tarde is inspired by contemporary scientific insights into the complexities on the level of cells, bacteria, and molecules and by the constant discoveries of ever more minuscule elements of nature. On the other hand, the book presents one long rejection of different attempts to "master" the concrete and individual level of relations through (explanations resorting to) natural laws, functional or organicist principles, essences, or "divine guarantees." Order, organization, or stability is, Tarde insists, created from the ground up or, rather, inside out, through reciprocal relations between the elements: they are not held from without; not to be explained from without. Societies are not organisms; instead organisms are societies—and they unfold and function due to internal relations and connections (Tarde [1893] 2012: 28). The deeper into the infinitesimal we move, the more complex and connected everything becomes. Social phenomena do not need the support of "external forces" to keep them stable; again, we do not need, Tarde notes polemically, Durkheim's "explanatory talisman" of the (social) "environment" to explain them ([1894] 1969: 124). The human level is but one instance of this dynamic—yet at all levels we should explain by delving into the complex and "microscopic"; it is here we find the myriad of relations which hold things together. In other words: the whole is always *less* than its parts. Or even: the part is *more* than the whole, even in human societies ([1893] 2012: 33).

In order to create a conceptual framing around these thoughts, Tarde uses the concept of the "monad" (articulated by the seventeenth-century German philosopher Gottfried Wilhelm Leibniz) which contains the principle of its *immanent* unfolding or self-realization. "A monad has no windows," as Leibniz famously says. Yet in contrast to Leibniz's monads, those of Tarde are "open" ([1893] 2012: 26). They "penetrate each other reciprocally, rather than being mutually external" ([1893] 2012: 26), or, as he creatively expresses it, they "have" each other—are part of each other, constitute or presuppose each other—rather than merely "being" identical with themselves ([1893] 2012: 87–98). Nothing acts alone. An example:

> From our point of view, what is signified by the great truth that every activity of the soul is linked to the functioning of some bodily apparatus? It comes down to the fact that in a society no individual can act socially, or show himself in any respect, without the collaboration of a great number of other individuals, most of them unknown to him. [...] Thus, left to its own devices, a monad can achieve nothing. ([1893] 2012: 34)

The "individuals" on which "the soul" leans here are the millions of other human individuals; but it is also the cells of his "bodily apparatus." And the latter are "individuals" too—yet, to be sure, in a sense, "unknown" to me, even while I "collaborate" with them. The reader should notice the profoundly anti-Cartesian, anti-dualist thrust of the formulations here ([1893] 2012: 15ff.). Ultimately, Tarde turns the human individual into a network—and not just a network with other humans, but rather a network of a multitude of interrelated, mutually constitutive and empowering "individuals" or "elements," the composite nature of which bridges traditional ontological distinctions between soul and body and mind and matter (and thus also action and behavior).

We now see how Tarde's "relationalist" position transcends not only Durkheimian "structural" accounts but also "Weberian" individualistic ones. What explains action is not placed behind the individual's back, "forcing" her to comply, being "external" to her whether internalized or not (as in Durkheim); but neither is it placed inside the conscious subject (as in Weber). Instead, Tarde embeds the individuals in their concrete mutual and co-constitutive relations at the same time as he generalizes to "individuals" and relations *of all kinds*. One understands why Latour sees a prefiguration of actor-network theory here.

Latour on Durkheim and Tarde

This is not the place for an introduction to actor-network theory, nor to Latour's reading of Tarde (cf. Latour 2002, 2005: 13–16, 2010; Latour and Lépinay 2008), yet a few remarks are in order.

First, like Tarde, Latour (2005: 43–62) wants to promote a "relational" concept of agency: no one or nothing acts alone. This goes hand in hand with the network metaphor that is meant to convey a sense of ontological "hybridity" and of mutually enabling forms of agency. Agency is a network of interlaced actors that call forth certain actions and capacities in each other. These actors cannot be conceptualized without taking into account their relations. Second, actor-network theory wants to draw in "nonhuman" artifacts—technology, instruments, tools, and other "nonhuman" entities—as potential actors into this network. Evidently, such "beings" *do* play a major role in "our" lives or in important practices, and one understands why Latour insists on integrating them in any explanation of agency.

How far does Tarde go into this direction? On the one hand, as we saw earlier, Tarde makes a similar metaphysical move in his *Monadology*. Tarde *does* see "society" as a form of network, his understanding of action *is* relationalist, he *does* criticize metaphysical dualism and draw into his account "nonhuman" forms of agency. Yet, on the other hand, there is no question that Tarde ([1893] 2012: 28), despite his "universalization" of the concept of society, often separates the realms of the physical, the biological, and the psychological. The networks or societies described by Tarde are only rarely as "hybrid" as those described by Latour. Nevertheless, Durkheim saw in this not only a runaway metaphysics but also a direct threat to his own attempt to demarcate the social and to contour his new sociology *in contrast* to the biological and physical sciences.

So is there really enough ontological mixing and mingling in Tarde to categorize him as an actor-network theory sociologist *avant la lettre*? I am less sure. There may be many sorts of "societies" in Tarde—from "ant societies" to "solar systems" to "atom societies"—yet they rarely blend into one another. Tarde does not collapse the distinction between culture and nature, the human and the nonhuman, at least not to the same degree as Latour.

Latour's reading of Tarde is also selective in another respect: Latour's Tarde is no Durkheimian, nor a Weberian individualist, but he is *not a social psychologist* either. As we saw, the porosity of the individuals in the network perspective is not about being carried away by the crowd; it is not about group imitation or mass psychology. Rather, it is what makes it possible for the human individuals to delegate agency and to invest themselves in large hybrid networks. Tarde's notion of imitation, Latour insists, could not be "further from psychology" (2002: 126–127). According to Latour, imitation in Tarde merely amounts to an empty "principle of connections" (2005: 13) or even to an "odd metaphor" which—this is no surprise!—may simply be replaced with the concept of "actor network" (2002: 126–127). However, while this move may work for Tarde's

Monadology, it obscures the social-psychological aspects of the concept of imitation found in much of Tarde's other work, not least in his work on *crowds*.[7]

What about Latour's relation to Durkheim then? There is no doubt that much of Latour's critique is already to be found in Tarde. As we have seen, from a "relationalist" perspective on action, Durkheim's holism is both reductionist and "sociologistic." As soon as the social is understood as a substance or a form of "stuff" (Latour 2005)—the social sui generis, which is drawn upon as an *explanation* of this or that phenomenon—the immanent and relationalist perspective becomes inaccessible. Durkheim's very separation and externalization of the social—the social understood as a prior, "external" structure—"explains away" what interests a Latourian or Tardean "sociology of relations." In their view, the social is what must *be explained*, not what explains.

Hence, it is no surprise that Latour's only extended engagement with Durkheim (cf. Latour 2014) is profoundly critical. Latour sees in Durkheim's late sociology of religion an attempt to consecrate the holist attitude. We saw earlier how Durkheim's more "integrative" texts—the ones highlighting the individual's "attachments" to "society"—often express a quasi-religious attitude toward society. This exaltation of the social, Latour notes, goes together with an ambivalence toward the individual:

> [...] Durkheim's diagnostic of the individual's weaknesses is without mercy. Not only is it separated from its fellow human beings [...] [but] [i]t is small, incapable, mean, closed off, a prisoner inside the narrow confines of its body. However, first of all it is debased, constantly made flat; made flat just to make sure that it needs to be elevated by the immense sadomasochist machinery of society which will make it love the violence it is subjected to as the only means to avoid the animal existence.
>
> (Latour 2014: 164)

The idea of an all-powerful and oppressive society goes hand in hand with the construction of decollectivized and isolated individuals who need the social to set limits to their desires and to discipline their vile bodily natures. Latour's critique is surprisingly similar to the critique of Durkheim voiced in early critical theory (cf. Adorno [1967] 1979). Yet Latour (2014: 269) is more interested in the emancipation of the nonhumans than in that of the humans:

> Nevertheless, as always among great minds, other forms of existence escape the moulds imposed upon them by this curious mixture of epistemology and spirituality which in France passes for the paradigmatic expression of social "science." Even though he seeks to occult them, Durkheim ends up revealing, in the experience of the social and through his readings of the Australian cults, other divinities than the monotheistic one he thinks he professes to.

In fact a close reading of Durkheim will show, Latour insists, that "monotheist" society is not the only "divinity," "entity," or "being" who asserts itself, gains agency and takes hold of the individuals in *The Elementary Forms* ([1912] 1995). Attachments to other "nonhuman" beings or forms of existence are being cultivated and empowered, too. I cannot here go into details regarding the "revelation" of these nonhuman beings allegedly asserting themselves in Durkheim's late text despite of him. What is interesting, however, is the "relationalist" character of Latour's emancipative engagement: we humans can only be free if our most important "nonhuman" relations are freed, too; then they must be allowed to help us and act on us inside the relations we cultivate and animate together with them. This requires that we allow them their crucial and active role in our practices, and this, in turn, entails a rupture with explanatory templates—holist or individualist—which place agency elsewhere and thus separate us from these beings, silence them, rationalize them, or explain them away.

Inspired by Tarde, Latour thus focuses on the coercive Durkheim and on Durkheim's consecration of a transcendent yet all-pervading "society." Yet, in contrast to Tarde (who died before Durkheim's ethnographical turn), Latour must take into account Durkheim's account of ritual, imitation and entrainment, and the essential role in these accounts played by (material) objects upon which collective sentiments are projected. In *Reassembling the Social* (2005) Latour is critical to the idea of projection since it tends to pacify the object—and thus neglects the contributions coming from the object-side in gathering the crowd and keeping it together. Still, he relates positively to these "constructivist" passages and points to the (few) instances where Durkheim describes how the very *material* nature of the sacred object contributes to provide permanence to the social (Latour 2005: 38; cf. Durkheim [1912] 1995: 231–233). In the more recent paper on *The Elementary Forms* (Latour 2014), from which I cited above, the tone is less positive:

> To the degree that Durkheim must respond to the objection constantly made by Tarde that external coercion does not suffice to explain the conformism pertaining to the social, a periodic resuscitation of the argument to make sure that the gulf between the individual and society remains provisionally closed [...] is needed. *Exterior* coercion is reversed into *interior* respect and celebration. This is the role played by effervescence and materiality; a provisional and limited role solidly encased but essential to the argument. (2014: 266–267)

Seeing the late Durkheim's participatory collectivism as a concession to a rival who had been dead almost ten years at this point is, however, rather far fetched. More importantly, Latour here neglects exactly what demarcates the late Durkheim from the younger one: the move from an individual consecration of a sacred "society" to a collective and relational construction of the sacred object taking place in concrete ritual.

Conclusion

Is it possible to circumscribe a compromise between the two doctrines? I do think so, and I think such compromise must pass through the role of the sacred *object*. In short, I think Latour is wrong: it *is* possible to sacralize an object without pacifying it. In other words: to make its proper contributions tangible, we do not need to cleanse a sacred object of *all* the social substance projected upon it. Why would we have to insist, as Latour does, that *all* their sensuous attraction, *all* their powers of fascination, all their love and comfort, in short, *all* the agency that we help to bring forth in our sacred objects, derives *solely* from our *mutual* relation with them in our mundane practices. Projection does not exclude relation. It is the other way around: our relations are *further* animated by the very fact that we treasure these "nonhuman" beings or objects together *with other humans*, that is, that they stand at the center of collective attention, that they circulate everywhere. Isn't the allure of the fashionable object, the force of God, the songs we sing, the enigma of the scientific object, the hobby we cultivate, the enemy we detest, the charisma of the great politician—aren't the actions of all these objects *further* animated by the fact that we entrain, collectivize, and imitate around them?

We constantly reinforce our relations to important "nonhumans" by reinforcing our relations to other humans—and vice versa (Schiermer 2016). The subjective, the objective, and the collective constantly bleed into one another, resonate together, and reinforce each other. In order to understand what takes place inside this complex triangular matrix, we need to combine concepts from all three authors. This way, the combination of Durkheim's, Tarde's, and Latour's templates presents an extremely powerful matrix apt to make the empirical resonate in new and exciting ways.

Notes

1. Latour, together with Bruno Karsenti, sought to reenact the face-to-face debate between the two adversaries at the conference *Tarde/Durkheim: Trajectories of the Social* held in Cambridge in 2008 (cf. Candea 2010). It should be emphasized that we do not know much of what was actually said at the historical event, since the transcripts have been lost. For an English version of the script read by Latour and Karsenti, see Durkheim and Tarde (2010). This script just is a shortened version of a longer French compilation of paradigmatic textual excerpts from the two historical sociologists' work (Durkheim and Tarde 2008). A very rudimentary resumé of the real Paris encounter, probably written by Rene Worms (and published in 1904), can be found in Tarde and Durkheim (1969).
2. I am again thinking about the set-up of the Cambridge conference, the contributions to which can be found in Candea (2010). There is a certain anachronistic feel to the very idea of a "re-enactment" of an allegedly "decisive" historical event of 1903, notably because it obscures all subsequent (successful) attempts at canonical formation and reformation. At the time of his death in 1904, Tarde was an international celebrity, in possession of far more power and prestige in French academia than Durkheim. Neither should it be forgotten that the rather "local" debate with Durkheim made little difference to the reception of Tarde in the United States, where Tarde's name and the concept of imitation continued to resonate long after it was silenced in Europe—at least until Talcott Parsons's ([1937] 1968) authoritative construction of the history of the discipline (pitting Weber against Durkheim) gained hegemony. And even at that point, Tardean impulses overwinter in the "social behavior"

tradition still vital in Herbert Blumer's work. For a historical account of the early years of American sociology with a special focus on Tarde and imitational "crowd semantics," see Borch (2012: 131–140). Another account, less positive toward the persistence of Tardean themes among the Chicago scholars, can be found in Snow and Davis (1995).
3. On the historical unfolding of the debate, see Lukes (1973: 302–313); Jones (1999: 257–268); Besnard (1995); Besnard and Borlandi (2010); and Borlandi (2001). The most thorough and most balanced text on Durkheim, Tarde, and the concept of imitation is Karsenti (2010).
4. Durkheim goes as far as to allude to Tarde as a "bluffer" or "charlatan" ("faiseur") in his correspondence—though it must be noted that he uses the same expression in his correspondence with Tarde about yet other (shared) enemies (cf. Borlandi 2001: 107–108, 110; Besnard 1995: 230)
5. Also, the later Durkheim repeatedly denies that his focus on coercion in *Rules* is anything but methodological or didactical. See, for instance, the "Second Introduction" to *Rules* ([1901] 2013b: 16) or the notes in *The Elementary Forms* ([1912] 1995: 211, 214).
6. In Durkheim's depictions of the crowd, effervescence often seems to fall upon the individuals as by surprise. And even where other individuals are present—see for example the scenarios in *Suicide* ([1897] 2002a: 76–77)—these individuals seem strangely immobilized and disembodied. In the later work, action often is literally taken over by mental "representations" and mental "states" which "combine" on their own accord and thus create powerful "collective representations."
7. For a critique of Latour's construction of Tarde, see (among others) King (2016) and Mucchielli (2000). One of the (all too) rare moments where Latour admits a distance between him and the historical Tarde is to be found in Latour (2005: 216).

References

Adorno, Theodor W. (1967) 1979. "Einleitung zu Emile Durkheim, 'Soziologie und Philosophie.'" In *Soziologische Schriften I* (Gesammelte Schriften, vol. 8.1), 245–279. Frankfurt am Main: Suhrkamp.
Besnard, Philippe. 1995. "Durkheim critique de Tarde: des *Règles* au *Suicide*." In *La sociologie et sa méthode. Les Règles de Durkheim un siècle après*, edited by Massimo Borlandi and Laurent Mucchielli, 221–243. Paris: Editions L'Harmattan.
Besnard, Philippe, and Massimo Borlandi. 2010. "Gabriel Tarde: Contre Durkheim à propos de son Suicide." In *Le Suicide: Un siècle après Durkheim*, edited by Massimo Borlandi and Mohamed Cherkaoui, 219–222. Paris: Presses universitaires de France.
Borch, Christian. 2012. *The Politics of Crowds*. Cambridge: Cambridge University Press.
Borlandi, Massimo. 1995. "Les faits sociaux comme produits de l'association entre les individus. Le fil conducteur des *Règles*." In *La sociologie et sa méthode. Les Règles de Durkheim un siècle après*, edited by Massimo Borlandi and Laurent Mucchielli, 139–164. Paris: Editions de L'Harmattan.
Borlandi, Massimo. 2001. "Informations sur la rédaction de *Suicide* et sur l'état du conflit entre Durkheim et Tarde de 1895 à 1897." In *Emile Durkheim: Critical Assessments of Leading Sociologists*, vol. 4, edited by W. S. F. Pickering, 99–115. London: Routledge.
Candea, Matei, ed. 2010. *The Social after Gabriel Tarde: Debates and Assessments*. London: Routledge.
Durkheim, Émile. 1905. "Tarde G, L'interpsychologie." *Année sociologique* 9: 133–135.

Durkheim, Émile. (1906) 1965. "The Determination of the Moral Facts." In *Sociology and Philosophy*, 35–79. London: Cohen & West.
Durkheim, Émile. (1900) 1973. "Sociology in France in the Nineteenth Century." In *Emile Durkheim: On Morality and Society*, edited by Robert N. Bellah, 3–22. Chicago: University of Chicago Press.
Durkheim, Émile. (1895) 1975a. "L'état actual des études de sociologie en France." In *Textes I: Éléments d'une théorie sociale*, 73–108. Paris: Les Editions de Minuit.
Durkheim, Émile. (1915) 1975b. "La Sociologie." In *Textes I: Éléments d'une théorie sociale*, 109–118. Paris: Les Editions de Minuit.
Durkheim, Émile. (1912) 1995. *The Elementary Forms of Religious Life*. New York: The Free Press.
Durkheim, Émile. (1897) 2002a. *Suicide*. London: Routledge.
Durkheim, Émile. (1902–1903) 2002b. *Moral Education*. Mineola, NY: Dover.
Durkheim, Émile. (1893) 2013a. *The Division of Labour in Society*. Basingstoke, UK: Palgrave Macmillan.
Durkheim, Émile. (1895) 2013b. *The Rules of Sociological Method*. Basingstoke, UK: Palgrave Macmillan.
Durkheim, Émile, and Gabriel Tarde. 2008. "The Debate between Tarde and Durkheim." Edited by Eduardo Viane Vargas, Bruno Latour, Bruno Karsenti, Frédérique Aït-Touati and Louise Salmon. *Environment and Planning D: Society and Space* 26: 761–777.
Durkheim, Émile, and Gabriel Tarde. 2010. "The Debate." In *The Social after Gabriel Tarde*, edited by Matei Candea, 27–43. London: Routledge.
Jones, Robert Alun. 1999. *The Development of Durkheim's Social Realism*. Cambridge: Cambridge University Press.
Karsenti, Bruno. 2010. "Imitation: Returning to the Tarde–Durkheim Debate." In *The Social after Gabriel Tarde*, edited by Matei Candea, 44–61. London: Routledge.
King, Anthony. 2016. "Gabriel Tarde and Contemporary Social Theory." *Sociological Theory* 34, no. 1: 45–61.
Latour, Bruno. 2002. "Gabriel Tarde and the End of the Social." In *The Social in Question: New Bearings in History and the Social Sciences*, edited by Patrick Joyce, 117–132. London: Routledge.
Latour, Bruno. 2004. "Why Has Critique Run out of Steam? From Matters of Fact to Matters of Concern." *Critical Inquiry* 30, no. 2: 225–248.
Latour, Bruno. 2005. *Reassembling the Social: An Introduction to Actor-Network-Theory*. Oxford: Oxford University Press.
Latour, Bruno. 2010. "Tarde's Idea of Quantification." In *The Social after Gabriel Tarde*, edited by Matei Candea, 145–176. London: Routledge.
Latour, Bruno. 2014. "Formes élémentaires de la sociologie. Formes avancées de la théologie." *Archives des sciences sociales des religions* 167: 255–275.
Latour, Bruno, and Vincent Lépinay. 2008. *L'économie, science des intérêts passionnés*. Paris: La Découverte.
Le Bon, Gustave. (1895) 1905. *Psychologie des foules*. Paris: Felix Alcan.
Lukes, Steven. 1973. *Emile Durkheim: His Life and Work*. London: Penguin Books.
Mucchielli, Laurent. 2000. "Tardomania?" *Réflexions sur les usages contemporains de Tarde* 2, no. 3: 161–184.
Parsons, Talcott. 1968. *The Structure of Social Action*. London: The Free Press.
Pickering, W. S. F. 1984. *Durkheim's Sociology of Religion: Themes and Theories*. Cambridge: James Clarke & Co.

Riley, Alexander. 2012. *Godless Intellectuals? The Intellectual Pursuit of the Sacred Reinvented.* New York and Oxford: Berghahn Books.

Snow, David A., and Phillip W. Davis. 1995. "The Chicago Approach to Collective Behavior." In *A Second Chicago School: The Development of a Postwar American Sociology*, edited by Gary Alan Fine, 188–220. Chicago: University of Chicago Press.

Schiermer, Bjørn. 2016. "Fetishes and Factishes: Durkheim and Latour." *British Journal of Sociology* 67, no. 3: 497–515.

Schiermer, Bjørn. 2019. "Durkheim on Imitation." In *Imitation, Contagion, Suggestion: On Mimesis and Society*, edited by Christian Borch, 54–72. Abingdon: Routledge.

Tarde, Gabriel. 1893. "Questions sociales." *Revue philosophique* 35: 618–638.

Tarde, Gabriel. (1894) 1969. "Sociology, Social Psychology, and Sociologism." In *Gabriel Tarde: On Communication and Social Influence*, edited by Terry N. Clark, 112–135. Chicago: University of Chicago Press.

Tarde, Gabriel. (1897) 2000. "Contre Durkheim à propos de son Suicide." In *Le Suicide: Un siècle après Durkheim*, edited by Massimo Borlandi and Mohamed Cherkaoui, 222–255. Paris: Presses universitaires de France.

Tarde, Gabriel. (1893) 2012. *Monadology and Sociology*. Melbourne: Re.press.

Tarde, Gabriel, and Émile Durkheim. (1903) 1969. "A Debate with Emile Durkheim." In *Gabriel Tarde: On Communication and Social Influence*, edited by Terry N. Clark, 136–140. Chicago: University of Chicago Press.

CHAPTER 23

SOCIOLOGY OF THE SACRED

The Revitalization of the Durkheim School at the Collège de Sociologie and the Renewal of a Sociology of Sacralization by Hans Joas

STEPHAN MOEBIUS

In 1937, George Bataille, Roger Caillois, and Michel Leiris launched the Collège de Sociologie. The Collège was devoted to studying the sacred in the tradition of the Durkheim school. Some years prior, these thinkers had already begun to take interest in the Durkheim school and the sociology of the sacred. Bataille wrote in a 1933 study on the psychological structure of fascism that "Durkheim faced the impossibility of providing it [the sacred] with a positive scientific definition: he settled for characterizing the sacred world negatively as being absolutely heterogeneous compared to the profane" (Bataille [1933/34] 1979: 69). Via their contact with Durkheim's nephew Marcel Mauss, Caillois and Leiris were also thoroughly familiar with the Durkheimians' sociology of religion. The Collège de Sociologie was a group of intellectuals that addressed the sacred from very different angles, including sociology, ethnology, philosophy, and literary and religious studies (see Moebius 2006a). The Collège conducted its analyses of the sacred under the common notion of "sacred sociology." Bataille used the following words to describe the objective of the overall venture that had both a theoretical and political thrust: "Indeed, for us sacred sociology is not just a part of sociology as is, for example, religious sociology, with which it risks confusion. Sacred sociology may be considered the study not only of religious institutions but of the entire communifying movement of society" (Bataille [1937] 1988a: 74). The study of the sacred was to detect or spark new types of community in a society experienced as extremely individualized. Their sociology of the sacred was thus not limited to religion in the narrow sense; rather it delved into all those sacredly charged areas in society that spawn sociality and induce a communifying movement of the kind that Durkheim described in his later sociology of religion by referring to collective ecstasy, for instance. In this view, the sacred is not only the normative elevation of things, people, experiences, places, and times but also a kind of communication, a fusion and an experience of loss of self.[1]

Although neither the analytical concepts nor the academic careers of the Collège's main protagonists clearly followed a completely straight path, they were still inextricably bound to the tradition of the Durkheim school.[2] In the following, I will take a closer look at these links. What we will see is that the Collège initially adopted a notion of the sacred that is virtually identical to the one found in the Durkheimians' ethnological studies of religion but gave it its own twist. In contrast to the Durkheim school, the Collège put a much greater focus on the sacred in the culture and everyday life of its own society. Its mission was to carry on the sociology and ethnology of religion of the Durkheim school during the interwar period and provide insights, by means of the Collège's interdisciplinarity, that benefit other areas of society as well (e.g., politics, art, literature). Hans Joas is currently developing a sociology of the sacred, which also builds centrally on Durkheim, but in contrast to the Durkheim school and the Collège, he primarily emphasizes the historical and action-theoretical dimensions of sacralization.

In the following, I will begin by briefly characterizing the Collège de Sociologie and its goals. Each of the subsequent three sections is then devoted to key works of the sociology of religion of the Durkheim school: Émile Durkheim's *The Elementary Forms of Religious Life* ([1912] 1995), Robert Hertz's studies on the left sacred, and Marcel Mauss's analyses of the sacrifice, the gift, and seasonal effervescence. I will briefly recall these works by the Durkheimians and demonstrate in exemplary fashion how the Collège de Sociologie picked up on them in a specific way. The article concludes with a discussion of current analyses of sacralization processes by Hans Joas, which also build on Durkheim's sociology of religion. Referring to Joas's work, I will briefly draw out the implications that research on the sacred—most of which is in the tradition of the Durkheim school—has for contemporary sociology and social theory.

The Collège de Sociologie

The Collège de Sociologie was among the first recipients of the Durkheim school's ethnology and sociology of religion (cf. Richman 1990; Mürmel 1997: 220). It was an intellectual circle that gathered for discussions every two weeks from 1937 to 1939. Apart from the three founders, some of the other participants were Alexandre Kojève, Pierre Klossowski, Jean Paulhan, Denis de Rougemont, the Mauss student Anatole Lewitzky, and André Masson, as well as three German scholars in exile: Walter Benjamin, the literary studies scholar Hans Mayer, and the Max Scheler student Paul Ludwig Landsberg. Both the outbreak of World War II and internal disagreements about the appropriate adoption of the Durkheim school, particularly over methodological issues, triggered the Collège's disbandment in 1939.

Despite its short existence, the Collège and its sacred sociology have continued to influence theory and debates to the present day (cf. Albers and Moebius 2012; Moebius 2018a). Many of the members of the Collège had known each other since attending Alexandre Kojève's Hegel seminars in 1934, which he held at the *Ecole pratique des hautes études* from 1933 to 1939.³ But there were also other networks in which the members of the Collège had previously organized and become acquainted with one another, such as the surrealist movement, the surrealist-ethnological journal *Documents*, the political group *Contre-Attaque*, and the secret society *Acéphale* (cf. Bataille 1999; Moebius 2003, 2009a). Apart from these networks and seen from the perspective of the history of ideas, the theoretical and thematic continuity of the positions of Émile Durkheim and his students Marcel Mauss, Henri Hubert, and Robert Hertz in the fields religious sociology and ethnology played a key role for the *collégiens* (cf. Fournier 1994: 707–711; Richman 2002; Moebius 2006a, 2006b; Moebius and Papilloud 2007; Moebius 2012). The Collège continued down the path, which the Durkheim school had already embarked on, of bringing sociology and ethnology closer together; this resulted in its further institutionalization in France. Caillois, Lewitzky, and Leiris were students of Mauss. With regard to the influence of the Durkheim school and the attention that the Collège received among the academic community at the time, Claude Lévi-Strauss wrote that the Collège de Sociologie "was a success. This close connection between sociology and every tendency or current having Man, and the study of Man, as its center, is one of the more significant traits of the French school" (Lévi-Strauss 1945: 508).⁴

The Collège saw its mission as establishing "sacred sociology." This sociology was geared toward investigating and breathing new life into the vital and sacred elements of communal bonds in modern society, such as collective emotional experiences of self-loss, affective intensity and ecstasy sparked by rituals, myths, festivals, or games. For the Collège, symbolizations of death or of dreams, practices of engaging in unproductive lavishness, collective expenditure in festivals, or immersion in experiences of crossing boundaries as well as sexuality, ecstasy, dance, madness, violence, or myths were all areas, experiences, and phenomena associated with the sacred. What all these phenomena had in common is, in their view, that they involve experiences of being in the grip of emotion, of affective intensity, and of self-transcendence.⁵

With its analytical focus on *modern* societies, the Collège sought to extend the Durkheimians' previous sociological and ethnological work on nonmodern societies to its own society and reinvigorate sociology and ethnology altogether in the process (cf. Richman 2002: 114). However, this did not lead to it adopting the Durkheim school's brand of sociology of religion in its entirety. In spite of the pivotal significance that the Durkheim school had for the *collégiens*, we can identify three pronounced differences:

(1) The Collège de Sociologie criticized the Durkheimians for having primarily focused on the sacralization practices in other (nonmodern) societies. In accordance with their own peculiar interpretation of the Durkheim school, the protagonists of the Collège perceived this focus to reflect a cowardly, bourgeois, and positivist understanding of sociological and ethnological research because of its detached stance (cf. Moebius 2006a: 491–495). For them, attention was instead to be directed to the sacred in their own culture.⁶ I will later show that this criticism of Durkheim was not fully justified. What anyone familiar with the Durkheim school knows, however, is that the latter's goal was precisely to analyze modern societies by identifying the "elementary"—yet still

effectual in modern society as well—forms of religion along with the origins of our present categories of thought by way of the indirect route via ethnology.

(2) The Collège accused Durkheim in particular of scientism, which it countered by proposing a subjectivistic approach to science, that is, an approach that is closely guided by subjective experience. This is exemplified in Leiris's autoethnographic texts ([1938] 1995, 1939). This understanding of science was due not least to the fact that surrealism had a strong influence on most of the Collège's protagonists (cf. Moebius 2003, 2009a).

(3) Finally, we see significant differences in their political ideas. Whereas Durkheim and Mauss pursued political rationalism and reform socialism (cf. Moebius 2006d), the Collège aimed to establish new sacred communities and myths for the purpose of fundamentally transforming society as a whole. It considered experiences that had already underpinned the conception of the sacred in Durkheim's sociology of religion—for instance, the experience of being in the grip of emotion—as modes of human experience that have deeper worth beyond rational agreement and that create opportunities for "community" and social cohesion. This insight was to be politically utilized (cf. Richman 1990: 207, 2002: 110–154; Falasca-Zamponi 2011). Accordingly, the Collège did not simply want to be a debating society but associated its *sociologie sacrée* with goals reflecting a critical view of society. The reason for advocating community-building and myths originated in the assumption that modern societies were characterized by pervasive fragmentation, rationalization, and anomie, which makes them especially susceptible to fascist propaganda and mass arousal. The Collège saw the most effective safeguard against fascism in creating "acephalous" communities based on voluntary membership and sacred experiences, so that people's desire for affective bonds was not left to right-wing groups and fascists to exploit. What we see here is that the *collégiens* subscribed to a conception of sociality that revolves around emotional and experiential dimensions in particular and interprets these along anthropological/life-philosophical lines as vital collective energies. Durkheim did not share such an anthropological/life-philosophical assumption that all human beings had a need for sacred experiences. This becomes apparent in Durkheim's interpretation of his own time as one of "moral mediocrity" (Durkheim [1912] 1995: 429) and an absence of the sacred (cf. Pettenkofer 2010: 228–229).[7]

We can hold that the Collège was interested in only *one* strand (although a central one) of the Durkheim school's endeavor to explain the social: its sociology of the sacred. Hardly any mention was made, by contrast, of the social processes involved in the division of labor or organic solidarity. Whereas, in Durkheim's work, these processes are linked to questions about the sacred, the formation of ideals, and the genesis and binding force of values, the Collège adopted from the Durkheim school only insights into the binding power of the social/sacred at the level of emotions, experiences, and values that a society perceives to be sacred. The *collégiens*' interest in the Durkheim school thus focused particularly on the latter's works in the sociology of religion and ethnology since it was there where they believed that the key insights into the genesis and forms of sacralization processes were to be found. In addition to Durkheim's late sociology of religion, their reception centered on Marcel Mauss's *Essai sur le don* (1925) and Robert Hertz's sociology of religion.

Émile Durkheim's Late Sociology of Religion

Regardless of differences in their scientific approach and their assessment of scientific rationalism, the Collège shared with Durkheim his criticism of utilitarian, atomistic individualism, which, with an eye to social cohesion, he attested to have a destructive impact on social bonds. Like Durkheim, the Collège was also interested in whether a new morality could be detected in society, while both were convinced that this morality would have to be of a sacred nature that deeply pervaded the subjects (Durkheim 1974: 68–72). As early as 1898, in the course of the Dreyfus Affair, Durkheim directed attention to a specifically modern kind of morality that is diametrically opposed to a destructive utilitarian individualism (Durkheim [1898] 1973): the sacralization of the individual. Durkheim believed that, against the backdrop of a functional division of labor and the territorial expansion of humanity and Christian morality, modern societies had developed a new morality, a kind of "religion of humanity" (48), which had become manifest, for instance, in the belief in universal human dignity and human rights.[8]

The Collège de Sociologie took up these ideas but devoted its attention to the sacralization of the community, without losing sight of the individual. In this context, the Collège considered two of Durkheim's theorems to be of key significance: first, the Collège maintained that society is not equal to the sum of its parts (Durkheim [1895] 1982: 128; Bataille 1988a: 74–75, [1946] 1994: 110); second, Bataille and his friends agreed with Durkheim that the sacred is a constitutive element of a society's power to create social bonds. This assumption that society is more than the sum of its parts led the Collège (as it did Durkheim) to reject individualism on methodological grounds and to subject its manifestation in the form of radical individualism to sociological critique. And again in line with Durkheim, this criticism of utilitarian, anomic individualism was inextricably bound to those analyses concerned with the role of religious and moral forces in the emergence of collective processes and social institutions and seeking answers to the question of how a "moral community" or society could emerge in the first place (as stated in the second point of the Collège's founding document; cf. Hollier 1988: 10; Moebius 2006a: 127).

In this context, Durkheim's *The Elementary Forms of Religious Life*, published in 1912, gained particular significance for studying the sacred as well as the social integration and collective ecstasy associated therewith, which the Collège perceived to be an integrative force (Caillois [1939] 1988: 282–283, 298; Bataille [1946] 1994: 104–105). Durkheim's late sociology of religion was significantly influenced by the previous work of his disciples in this area and their ethnological interests (cf. Condominas 1972a, 1972b; Tarot 2008; Moebius 2012). In *The Elementary Forms*, Durkheim started from the assumption that the object of religious reverence is society *itself*. He saw collective life—the intense experience of self-transcending community in particular—as the origin of religious beliefs.[9]

In this context, Durkheim defined "religion" as a "unified system of beliefs and practices relative to sacred things, that is to say, things set apart and forbidden—beliefs and practices which unite into one single moral community called a Church, all those who adhere to them" (Durkheim [1912] 1995: 44, italics deleted). Religion in this sense does not necessarily imply the idea of gods or spirits. For Durkheim, the crucial aspect for a religious pattern of interpretation and perception was the binary division of the world into the world of the sacred and that of the profane (214, 220).[10]

This dichotomy at the heart of the "religious idea" is the product of extremely emotional and intense interaction and community experiences, which Durkheim called *effervescence* (220) and which suggest to the participants that they draw a distinction between profane everyday life and extraordinary sacred situations. As Andreas Pettenkofer specified in his instructive analysis of Durkheim's sociology of religion, the extraordinary experiences of *collective effervescence* (mediated by and repeatedly experienced in rituals) are the result of a situational, mutual, symbolically mediated, and meaningful (cognitive as well as emotional) perception of commonality (Pettenkofer 2010: 222–224). Such experiences lead to situations in which the participants are overwhelmed and temporarily lose their sense of self (cf. Joas 2000: 58–68). "It is not difficult to imagine that a man in such a state of exaltation should no longer know himself. [...] It seems to him that he has become a new being" (Durkheim [1912] 1995: 220).

It is these experiences of collective effervescence that are then interpreted as reflecting the influence of external powers instead of recognizing them as what they actually are: effects of sociality itself (in the context of which rituals serve as means of producing and regularly stabilizing social cohesion). The idea of the sacred—or, in Durkheim's words, "the sacred principle"—"is nothing other than society hypostasized and transfigured" (351). Whether or not a thing or action is associated with these experiences of collective ecstasy is essential to whether it is perceived as profane or sacred. "Sacred is that which corresponds to this experience—in however mediated a form" (Joas 2000: 59).

The analysis of collective experiences and the processes of sacralization and idealization that they give rise to are of crucial importance for both Durkheim and the Collège. This led Bataille to acknowledge that Durkheim's research on religion and the sacred had captured the "*constitutive* element of everything that is society" (Bataille [1946] 1994: 110, emphasis added) and provides another reason to suggest that the Collège was totally unjustified in criticizing Durkheim as well as Mauss and Hertz for restricting their focus to so-called "primitive" societies. The whole purpose of Durkheim's investigation of the elementary forms of religious life and the rituals of collective effervescence was to protect for the future the social cohesion endangered in modern society (cf. also Durkheim [1912] 1995: 1).[11] "For him, such events are not primitive or irrational marginal phenomena of sociality, but the constitutive precondition for all emotionally charged social ties to collectives and values" (Joas 2000: 67). In Durkheim's view, his religious-sociological analysis of religion was not to reinvigorate traditional religions but to understand how a new secular morality might assume the role of religion. In this sense, Durkheim viewed sacralization as a social necessity (Durkheim 1974: 69).

Bataille insisted that it was impossible to comprehend the sacred purely rationally or scientifically, but that, strictly speaking, it could be understood only through lived experience. Overall, the Collège de Sociologie favored a notion of science that is reminiscent of surrealism with its drive toward overcoming the division between art and everyday practice (cf. Bürger 1984; Clifford 1988). Even though the Collège continued down the path of the Durkheim school by adopting the sacred as its object of research, it distanced itself from the latter's sociological methodology. As Bataille put it in a letter to Michel Leiris (Hollier 1995: 827), by invoking the imperative to think of social phenomena objectively as "things," Durkheim methodologically excluded the possibility of basing the analysis on lived experience. Leiris had criticized his colleagues at the Collège for neglecting the strict methodological standards of the Durkheim school (cf. Hollier 1988: 354–355; Fournier 1994: 707–711; Marcel 2003: 147–149; Tarot 2009: 21).[12] In the preceding years, they had still agreed that not only the scientific mind but also practical, lived experience—*life*, that is—could yield insight and reflection (cf. Clifford 1988; Hollier 1988: 98–102, 1995: 119; Leiris [1938] 1995). This perspective reflects the Collège's general understanding of science: the members of the Collège perceived the detachment from the object of research, which institutionally established sociology had made the imperative of its methodology, along with the neutralization and negation of subjective experience that this entails, as being a genuine trait of the despised "bourgeois" science and "bourgeois" discourse on the social world. The alternative that they proposed instead was the sublation of science in everyday life (cf. Jamin 1980: 16).

All in all, the Collège regarded Durkheim with ambivalence: its main protagonists shared Durkheim's key assumptions—namely, his statements on the power of collective effervescence in which the sacred can be experienced as hands-on reality, his theorem of the duality of the sacred, his idea of the necessity of a morality that can be experienced as sacred, and the dictum that society represents a reality sui generis. Yet there were several areas of disagreement. These differences were not limited to disregarding the Durkheim school's scientific methodology (cf. Clifford 1988; Hollier 1988: 98–102, 1995: 119; Leiris [1938] 1995). Another difference to Durkheim was that they did not believe that a rational understanding of the sacred binding forces of the social would give rise to a new morality in society but that this would require a mythological foundation that could be experienced emotionally (cf. Wiechens 1999: 242). Durkheim and the *collégiens* also differed in that Durkheim saw the sacred as emerging primarily in extraordinary spheres of action, whereas the members of the Collège perceived the sacred as originating in everyday life. In summary, my impression is that the motivation behind the *collégiens'* attempts to draw these distinctions had less to do with the Durkheimians as such and was more about defining the group's own identity and giving it a nonconformist profile.[13]

Despite their criticism of Durkheim's methodology, his special significance to and influence on the *collégiens'* work is evident in the formulation of their key concepts and theoretical assumptions (Bataille [1937] 1988a: 74, 1989: 123–124; Bataille and Caillois [1938] 1988: 158; Caillois [1939] 1988: 282–283; cf. Richman 2002). In particular, the Durkheim school's analyses of the *bipolarity* of the sacred found a strong echo among the *collégiens*. Durkheim assumed the sacred to be ambiguous in that it has a pure and impure side. He gained this insight into the ambiguity of the sacred—and the Collège along with him—from Robertson Smith and especially from Robert Hertz's studies in religious sociology (Durkheim [1912] 1995: 12, n12; cf. Jamin 1980: 22; Riley 1999; Marroquín 2005: 76–79), even though Durkheim never explicitly mentioned this (cf. Needham 1973: xiii; Mürmel 1997: 214).

Robert Hertz and the Two Sides of the Sacred

Of particular significance to the *collégiens* were Hertz's studies on "The Pre-Eminence of the Right Hand" ([1909] 1960b) and "A Contribution to the Study of the Collective Representation of Death" ([1907] 1960a). His concept of the ambiguity of the sacred was at the heart of the Collège's reception of his work. This concept not only separates the sacred from the profane but also divides it into a pure and impure sacred, a right and left sacred. Today, we are familiar with this in our conception of St. Nicholas and his helper Krampus.[14]

The right and left side are significant for the Collège's definition of the sacred (cf., e.g., Bataille [1938] 1988b; Parkin 1996: 77). Michel Leiris's lecture "Le sacré dans la vie quotidienne," held in 1938, for instance, attests to this. In this lecture, he gave an autoethnographic account of the sacred in his childhood (Leiris [1938] 1995: 102).[15] Apart from the many "sacred" everyday objects (specific things that belonged to his father or a heating stove that resembled a guardian spirit), there were also "sacred" places in Leiris's childhood—among them, for instance, his parents' bedroom or the bathroom—that marked the right and left pole of the sacred (105–106).

At the Collège, Roger Caillois ([1938] 1995: 371–380) also addressed the ambiguity of the sacred in more detail.[16] The pure is attractive, he argued, the impure repulsive; the one is noble, the other vicious; the one side is met with respect, love, and gratitude, the other with fear, aversion, and horror (379–380). Caillois, too, made reference to Hertz.

In a conversation with Michèle Richman in 1983, Leiris reported that the Collège was not interested in the sacred per se but in its "left" side specifically, that is, in all that bourgeois society regards as the impure, lowly, outcast, and heterogeneous (Richman 1990: 213–214; cf. Jamin 1980: 20–24; Riley 2005). At times, the *collégiens* even considered the "left" side as the more genuine and primordial side of the sacred, which can transform into an element of the right sacred (Bataille [1938] 1988b: 122). To some degree, this coincides with Hertz: according to Marcel Mauss ([1925] 1969: 493), Hertz was especially interested in the dark and sinister sides of human mentality.

Bataille mentioned the ambiguity of the sacred early on in his 1933 contribution "The Psychological Structure of Fascism" (Bataille [1933/34] 1979) to the journal *La Critique sociale*. This ambiguity plays a key role in his elaboration of the concept of "heterology," which is particularly concerned with the excluded and the ostracized (cf. Moebius 2006a: 123–128). The contribution is a sociopsychological analysis of German and Italian fascism. At the same time, the study revolves around the attractive and repulsive forces that emanate from the sacred and heterological and affect the unconscious layers of personality. *Heterology* refers to an analysis and activation of those segments of society that are usually outcast and relegated to the margins of society. Fascist leaders, Bataille holds, exploit fascination for "heterological" and unconscious "realities," such as death or violence, to control the masses and tie them to the leadership. Bataille studied the fascination that emanates from charismatic leaders—also drawing on Freud's *Group Psychology and the Analysis of the Ego*—to shed light on the collective glorification and legitimation of fascism.

He applied the concept of the duality of the sacred in his studies of fascism, differentiating more precisely but analogously to Durkheim ([1912] 1995: 412–417; cf. Pickering 1984: 126–129) between the pure and impure sacred and the profane and relating this distinction to Hertz's concepts of right and left. In his reasoning, there is a pure, useful, productive right side of the sacred and an impure, subversive, unproductive left side. The form of the sacred that serves to sacralize the leaders is directed against the other people; in Bataille's view, it belongs to the right, orderly side of the sacred and can be distinguished from the heterogeneous or left side of the sacred, which extends to groupings, such as the "lumpenproletariat" for example, that are usually regarded as a "lower" form in "bourgeois" society and even by the proletarians (Bataille [1933/34] 1979: 65; cf. Stallybrass 1990). Accordingly, Bataille does not understand the terms "lower" or "higher form" according to the usual standards of valuation that prefer the higher to the lower but reverses the binary hierarchy of valuation to give precedence to the lower form.

Against the backdrop of these considerations, Bataille sees two questions that need to be addressed to assess a social order. First, how does a society and the individual deal with the ambiguity of the sacred, especially with the heterogeneous elements? Second, how can the elements of the "left" sacred be put to subversive use in favor of achieving a more humane community?

Marcel Mauss and Theories of the Gift, the Sacrifice, and Seasonal Effervescence

"No one other than Marcel Mauss should have been designated to write a book on the sacred. Everyone is convinced that this book would have been for a long time *the* book on the sacred" (Caillois [1939] 2001: 14). Roger Caillois wrote these sentences in the preface to his book *Man and the Sacred*, which originated directly from his lectures at the Collège.[17] Caillois was not the only member of the Collège directly influenced by Mauss. Mauss was one of the most important teachers for Leiris as well (Leiris 1948: xxiv).

Among the Durkheim school, Marcel Mauss was the first to emphasize and investigate the central significance of the sacred for religious ideas and practices (even before Durkheim himself; cf. Moebius 2012). Thus, compared to his early sociology of religion, we can see that Durkheim's key concepts of the sacred and effervescence as well as his interest in ethnological research on religion were already inherent and had been developed in the work of his students Mauss, Hubert, and Hertz at a much earlier point in time. We can trace the disciples' pioneering role in Durkheim's later sociology of religion particularly in Mauss's early work on the origins of criminal law (Mauss [1896] 1968: 651–698), in which Mauss, before Durkheim, anticipates the relevance of the distinction between the sacred and the profane and introduces the equation of "religion = society," which was later attributed to Durkheim (cf. Tarot 2008: 295–297; Moebius 2012).[18] We can also already find some of Durkheim's key ideas in Mauss and Henri Beuchat's study on "Eskimos" ([1906] 2004) as well as in Mauss and Hubert's analyses of the sacrifice ([1899] 1964) and of magic ([1903] 2001).

In *Man and the Sacred*, Caillois draws on Mauss and Hubert's essay collection *Mélanges d'histoire des religions* (1906/09). In particular, Caillois and other *collégiens* were enthusiastic about Mauss and Hubert's theory of sacrifice as it was presented in the "Essai sur la nature et la fonction du sacrifice," an article published in *Année sociologique* in 1899 and reprinted in the *Mélanges* (see also Bataille 1989: 43–61; Caillois [1938] 1995: 376).[19] They perceived it to provide an analysis of how something is rendered sacred. The act of sacrificing involves not only giving something but also *making* something sacred, to "sacralize" it; the term "sacrifice" (Latin: *sacrum facere*) very clearly reflects this. The sacrifice is important for the functioning of society as the act of destruction involved in the sacrifice gives rise to the sacred in society and society periodically renews and creates itself anew in the sacrifice. In their analysis, Mauss and Hubert describe an *interdependent alternation between sacralization and desacralization* (Hubert and Mauss [1899] 1964: 95).

The *collégiens*' reception of Mauss also centered on two other works: Mauss and Henri Beuchat's *Seasonal Variations of the Eskimo: A Study in Social Morphology* (Mauss and Beuchat [1906] 2004) and Mauss's *The Gift* ([1925] 1966). In a lecture on the festival, given on May 2, 1939, Roger Caillois again underlined the significance of Durkheim's distinction between the sacred and profane; the effervescent festival (*l'effervescence de la fête*) stands in contrast to everyday life, he argued, like the sacred to the profane. In his analysis of the festival as a sacred time of social purification and renewal, he also mentions the central significance of Mauss and Beuchat's study: "Mauss's study of Eskimo societies furnishes the best example of violent contrast between the two sorts of life, which can always be perceived among peoples condemned by climate or economic organization to prolonged inactivity for part of the year" (Caillois [1939] 1988: 283). As the seasons change, so does the social morphology of society: in wintertime, when society pulls closer together, everything is done together, whereas in summertime each family makes a living on its own. Winter appears to society as a time of religious exaltation, Caillois argued, like a festival, like a sacred time (282–283). Today, in modern societies, he claimed, the sacred time is individualized, the annual vacation has now replaced the time of the once sacred festival. Here, too, there is a demarcation from everyday life, but unlike the festival, vacation time is "a phase of relaxation and not of paroxysm. [...] Rather than communication with the group in its moment of exuberance and jubilation, it is further isolation. [...] Is a society with no festivals not a society condemned to death?" (302).[20]

Mauss's *The Gift / Essai sur le don* ([1925] 1966), first published in the founding year of the *Institut d'ethnologie*, also played a central role for the *collégiens*. Georges Bataille in particular picked up on *The Gift*. He developed Mauss's study into a full-fledged theory of expenditure (Bataille [1933] 1985), which he related to sacred sociology in his work at the Collège (Bataille [1938] 1988b: 123; cf. Moebius 2009b). In Mauss's *The Gift*, we re-encounter both the sacred expenditure at festivals and the sacralizing sacrifices and acts of destruction. What the members of the Collège were particularly interested in was Mauss's description of the practices of giving associated with the *potlatch*. Instead of pure exchange, the potlatch is marked by rivalry and antagonism (Mauss [1925] 1966: 4–5, 33), even to the point of open fights and the killing of chiefs and noblemen. In addition, it features the "purely sumptuous destruction of accumulated wealth" (4), an aspect that particularly Bataille's theory of expenditure draws attention to.[21]

To the Collège, the unproductive, anti-utilitarian element of the gift is especially important to show that sociality and social action are not sufficiently accounted for in terms of (re-)production and the strategic-instrumental pursuit of predefined goals. "But without free loss, without expense of energy, no collective existence, or even individual existence is possible," said Bataille (1988b: 123) in his lecture at the Collège on February 5, 1938. Like the sacrifice, expenditure, too, serves the making of sacred things (cf. Marroquín and Seiwert 1996: 147). In contrast to the *collégiens* and to Bataille specifically, who viewed expenditure as an activity largely devoid of interests, Mauss saw the lavish, risk-embracing, and luxurious gift exchange associated with the potlatch as bound to an interest in forging social bonds, enhancing prestige, and wielding symbolic power. Inherent in Mauss's study of the gift, however, is a conceptual ambiguity that alternates between gift as exchange and as expenditure, which was subsequently differentiated in the reception of the study by, for example, Claude Lévi-Strauss or Jacques Derrida. Yet it was clear to both Mauss and the Collège that the practice of giving creates and renews social bounds in a nonutilitarian, sacred manner, as it were, thus making a crucial contribution to the creation of communities and social cohesion.

Mauss could not but view Bataille's thinking as an attack on his rationalism, his understanding of science, and his belief in reason and progress (cf. Marcel 2003: 142). There was a deep gulf between the values of his generation and those of these nonconformist intellectuals. Bataille's admiration for Mauss's thought on the gift met with no equivalent interest on Mauss's part. Rather, Mauss sought to save Caillois and Leiris from the pitfalls of irrationalism (Mauss [1938] 1990). The special emphasis given to the left sacred and the Collège's irrationality contradicted Mauss's insistence, inherited from Durkheim, on keeping with rational verifiable standards of analysis; perhaps he also feared that the Collège's approach might discredit the new discipline of ethnology.

Mauss's political thinking was also very distant from that of the Collège. He was not concerned with the formation of new communities but rather, under the influence of Jean Jaurès's reform-socialist thought, with measures to protect social and economic standards to promote and maintain corporative solidarity (cf. Mauss 1997; Moebius 2006c; Dzimira 2007). This is especially apparent in his criticism of the Collège's thematic foci and its irrationalism in a letter to his student Caillois on the occasion of the publication of the latter's book *Le mythe et l'homme* (1938). In Mauss's view, Caillois was a victim of Heidegger's and Bergson's irrationalism,[22] and Heidegger's philosophy in turn legitimated an irrationalism-besotted Hitlerism (Mauss [1938] 1990; cf. Fournier 1994: 709–710; Marcel 2003: 150).

Both the Collège and Mauss expected their analyses of the sacred and of archaic practices of gift exchange to yield insights that could be translated into specific policies for modern society. Their strategies, however, differed radically. Mauss wanted nothing to do with either reviving myths or with strategies of collective effervescence (cf. Moebius 2006d). Rather, he pursued a rational *conception of politics as educational practice* (cf. Chiozzi 1983: 658).

As the previous discussion has demonstrated, however, the Collège represented a serious attempt to continue and advance the Durkheim school's research in the ethnology and sociology of religion as well as to apply it to the social problems of its time and, pursuing an interdisciplinary approach, put it to productive scientific, aesthetic, and political use. Theoretically, we can identify the following commonalities: the experiences of self-loss and collective ecstasy and of the realm of the sacred in its entirety at the center of the Durkheimians' and *collégiens'* analyses contradict simple theories of modernization because they show that certain, variable conceptions of the sacred exist in modern societies as well and that, in this respect, there has been no comprehensive process of secularization and that such a process is perhaps not even desirable.[23] Both the Durkheimians and the *collégiens* therefore not only emphasized the relevance of ethnological research for sociology but generally stressed the significance of these phenomena of the sacred for a sociological theory of action and the explanation of social cohesion. Just as interesting as the question of which ideas made an imprint on the Durkheimians and the Collège is hence the question of what present-day sociology can learn from their research.

On the Renewal of Sociology of Sacralization: The Sociology of Hans Joas

The dimensions of experience and action associated with the sacred provide a path toward an explanation of the binding, corporal-affective, and other-pervaded nature of the social that the productive relationship between the sociology and ethnology of the Durkheimians and the Collège de Sociologie was able to capture. However, this was later largely ignored by the primarily utilitarian or normativistic social theories that followed, and today it has not yet been articulated with sufficient clarity in contemporary social-theoretical discourses. A significant exception in this respect is the social theory of Hans Joas. Following Joas, we might say that Mauss, Hertz, and Durkheim, as well as the sacred sociology of the Collège de Sociologie, were all concerned with the phenomenon of "primary sociality" (Joas 1996: 184–195). What Joas means by this is those social processes that are of constitutive importance in the formation of identity, agency, and a moral stance toward the world, processes—not limited to early childhood socialization—in which the experience of self-transcendence and being in the grip of emotion play a constitutive role. As opposed to making the assumption of an autonomous, self-interested individual the starting point of social theory, primary sociality also comprises the sacred experience of liminality and self-transcendence that is not a

> primitive or irrational marginal phenomenon of sociality; in fact it is the constitutive precondition for all affectively charged social bonds to other individuals, collectives or values. Durkheim consequently regards the emergence of the "sacred" as the core of social bonds. It is not accessible to reflective thought and is by no means limited to primitive cultures or times of revolutionary upheaval, but is an ongoing process. [...] In the occasional dissolution of its symbolic and social structures, the collective does not dissolve into nothingness, but rather experiences that it always extends beyond what is contained in its own structures.
>
> (Joas 1996: 194)

As Joas has shown in *The Genesis of Values* (2000), it is not so much cognitive beliefs or rational arguments that bind us to values but (apart from processes of "self-formation") experiences of self-transcendence. We already find this insight in Durkheim's work (Joas 2000: 54–68) as in that of Mauss and Hertz (cf. Moebius 2009b, 2012). The members of the Collège de Sociologie attempted to apply this insight practically to the everyday world around them.[24] In Joas's perspective, Durkheim's originality for sociology is especially apparent in his late sociology of religion (Joas 1996: 49–65). For the Durkheimians and the Collège, primary sociality involves those dimensions of experience associated with the sacred that refer to contexts of experience and action, beyond instrumental rationality, in which meaning is created and social cohesion is forged and that can be described by terms such as effervescence, being in the grip of emotion, devotion, sacrifice, expenditure, self-surrender, or self-loss. Sacredness thus originates from human experiences of being gripped by emotion and self-transcendence. These experiences of self-transcendence comprise not only enthusiastic experiences but also experiences of fear, in which we become aware of the boundaries of the self, or of experiences of violence (Joas 2017: 433).

Though already inherent in Joas's earlier work (1996, 2000, 2008), it is only in recent publications (2013, 2014, 2016, 2017) that he has expressly devoted attention to the dynamic processes of sacralization and desacralization, thus lending sacred sociology new relevance.[25] Apart from Ernst Troeltsch, William James, John Dewey, Josiah Royce, and Charles Taylor, the key point of reference for Joas's analysis of sacralization processes is specifically Émile Durkheim. In Durkheim's work, Joas sees the "clearest expression" of an analysis of sacralization and the notion that "a society can neither create itself nor recreate itself without at the same time creating the ideal" (Joas 2016: 29–30). Taking up the thread of *The Genesis of Values* (2000) and *Do We Need Religion? On the Experience of Self-Transcendence* (2008), he describes the "genesis of sacredness" not as an intentional process but as a

> fundamentally anthropological phenomenon. People sometimes have experiences in which they feel drawn beyond the boundaries of the self—in other words, experiences of "self-transcendence." [...] It is vital to understand that the formation of ideals is not an intentional process. We cannot decide to regard something as an ideal. We must instead be seized by it, which is why in all such cases we experience ourselves as passive, as recipients of a gift, as hearers of a message, as receptacles of inspiration.
>
> (Joas 2016: 28)

As in the case of Durkheim, we must also not confuse sacredness and religion in Joas's work. They are not identical, for religions are "attempts to interpret the experience of the sacred, to facilitate this experience through practices and narratives and give it enduring form through institutions" (27).[26] Other, secular content can also "take on the qualities characteristic of sacrality; namely, subjective self-evidence and affective intensity. Sacredness may be ascribed to new content. It may migrate or be transferred" (Joas 2013: 5).

Taking Durkheim's analyses of the sacred and his interpretation of human rights as the result of a sacralization of the individual (cf. Durkheim [1898] 1973) as a starting point, Joas shows in detail in his major study *The Sacredness of the Person* (2013), by tracing the genealogy of human rights, that sacralization and desacralization are the product of historically contingent, collective processes. They involve "certain states of a collectivity that have been experienced as particularly intense, states that have given rise to the ideal. *The sacralization of particular meanings is, originally, also the sacralization of the collectivity*" (Joas 2016: 31). To a much greater extent than Durkheim and to some degree similar to Bataille in his analysis of fascism, Joas understands the dangers of processes of self-sacralization, like those that could be observed, for instance, in the context of the totalitarianisms of the twentieth century (38–39).

This critical view of tendencies toward the self-sacralization of collectives is, however, not the only difference between Joas's social theory of the sacred and the sacred sociology of the Durkheimians and the *collégiens*. Despite all commonalities between these perspectives in terms of attributing the sacred a central role in sociology and the analysis of sociality, Joas goes beyond the sacred sociology of the Durkheim school and the Collège de Sociologie in three points. These three points can be described as (1) an account of the articulation of experience, (2) the grounding of sacralization processes in a theory of action, and (3) the contextualization of sacralization processes in terms of a sociology of institutions and power.

(1) Neither Durkheim nor the *collégiens* took into account that sacralization cannot be understood as an endogenous process that derives from collective effervescence alone (cf. Joas 2000: 67; Pettenkofer 2010: 220–230). In Durkheim's account, "even the collective interpretation of collective experience evolves from the latter without the individuals who participate in the collective experience having developed differing interpretations of this experience" (Joas 2000: 67–68). Durkheim and the *collégiens* "neglect the role played by the interpretation of experience" (68; cf. Pettenkofer 2010: 222–224). That is to say, it is not only experiences of self-transcendence that are crucial for sacralization processes but also the interpretation and articulation of these experiences. These experiences cannot be separated from their interpretation. They can be interpreted and articulated in very different ways in light of specific, pre-existing patterns of interpretation and depending on the situation, which in turn can entail changes in these patterns of interpretation (cf. Pettenkofer 2010: 240–241). Sacralization thus does not simply emerge automatically from experiences of self-transcendence but, as Joas emphasizes in several places, from a complex "interplay between the situation experienced, our prereflective experience, our individual articulation, and the cultural repertoire of interpretative patterns. We may constantly strive for an attunement between these levels, but we will only rarely and never permanently attain it. But in this very process—in the attempts to achieve this attunement—new values are produced" (Joas 2002: 514; cf. Joas 2000: 134–136, 2008: 46; for an example of such an analysis of this interplay, see Joas 2013; see also the example of the storming of the Bastille in Pettenkofer 2010: 239–242). Drawing on Charles Taylor, Joas (2017: 436–437) distinguishes four levels in the process of articulation that are intertwined and between which fissures and contradictions can emerge: the level of lived experience, of prereflective experience, of individual interpretation of experience, and of the cultural repertoire of interpretive patterns. The key aspect is that the process of articulation, which largely occurs in interaction with others, can indeed bear something new. Moreover, the articulation of an experience does not leave that experience unchanged (Joas 2017: 437). That articulation must not necessarily be verbal; images or performative practices can express experiences as well (438).

(2) Closely related to this is another point. According to Joas, the analyses of sacralization processes by Durkheim, the Collège de Sociologie, and others who have attended to the phenomenon of sacralization not only fail to consider the interaction between experience, articulation, and cultural patterns of interpretation but also lack an action-theoretical grounding. Only an action-theoretical perspective, as spelled out in *The Creativity of Action* (Joas 1996), can account for the dynamics of sacralization processes and the processes of cultural transformation associated therewith (Joas 2013: 85–96, 2017: 426). This is because the articulation of self-transcendent experiences as well as associated practices that are guided by values are themselves situational, creative modes of action. New articulations can thus break with previous patterns of interpretation or can unearth or revive previously idle potential inherent in such patterns. We can then see that experiences of self-transcendence and their articulation are not limited to collectives alone, as the Durkheimians or *collégiens* suggest; rather, such a perspective directs our attention to individual experiences of the sacred and their articulation as well. Joas's action theory of situational creativity is closely linked with the pragmatist

theory of the constitution of the self. One might say that his theory of the *Creativity of Action* elaborates the social-theoretical and anthropological conditions of the possibility of sacralization (Joas 2017: 424–438).

(3) According to Joas (2017: 437), an action-theoretical perspective systematically incorporates the interplay and the tensions between the three dimensions: values, practices, and institutions. Sacralization and cultural change can originate in each:

> Institutionalization, in the sense of legal codification, can be the starting point. In my assessment, the West-German Basic Law preceded the establishment of democratic culture in Germany. Values can be the starting point as well: an intellectual debate over what can be justified as good can have chronological priority; the same, however, is true for practices. [...] What the precise constellation in a specific process of sacralization turns out to be is ultimately a purely empirical question.
>
> (Joas 2012: 155–156, my translation)[27]

The tension between these three dimensions does not unfold in empty space but in a field marked by institutions; this field and the interactions that characterize it are in turn "influenced by interests and power relations" (Joas 2013: 86). Although the *collégiens* had already called attention to the close connection between sacralization and power (cf. Moebius 2006a: 164–167), their considerations in this respect remained rather rudimentary and unsystematic. Some—Caillois, for instance—saw authoritarian power and the sacred as something to be politically utilized, whereas Bataille viewed authoritarian power as that which was above all to be fought against. Joas's considerations help us better understand the connection between sacralization and power. As he argues in his book *Die Macht des Heiligen* (*The Power of the Sacred*, Joas 2017), sacralization does not occur in a space devoid of power. One act of sacralization is faced with other acts of sacralization and with people who have an interest in these acts of sacralization and expanding or monopolizing them (Joas 2017: 441). Processes of sacralization must thus be analyzed empirically in terms of their relation to other processes of sacralization (e.g., collective acts of self-sacralization, such as the sacralization of the nation or of a religious community, or the sacralization of an authoritarian ruler, or of certain conceptions of the individual, such as the *homo economicus*), whether this relation involves alliances, conflicts, or indifference. In short, sacralization occurs in specific historical and culturally dynamic circumstances that involve constellations of power and specific interactions between different dimensions (values, practices, institutions) in each particular case. How these constellations unfold or what is sacralized in the process cannot be predicted and remains contingent (Joas 2017: 445). If we seek to understand and explain the dynamics of sacralization processes, we must think of the processes of power formation involved in sacralization not as the workings of anonymous forces—as, for instance, Michel Foucault did—but as a "phenomenon of action" (Joas 2017: 442), which is to say that we must take a more rigorous look at the social bearers of power and their forms of organization. Only then can we make an utterly convincing case—also one against the widespread thesis of the disenchantment of the world—that current processes of sacralization are not simply responses to an assumed comprehensive rationalization or secularization of the world, but that sacralization and the revitalization of past sacralization have always been an inherent part of human history to the present day. "The relation between sacredness and power, religion and politics remains one of tension that brings forth ever new resolutions but never disappears as such" (Joas 2017: 446, my translation).

Notes

1. The following contribution builds on ideas developed in my study *Die Zauberlehrlinge: Soziologiegeschichte des Collège de Sociologie* (Moebius 2006a), a study in the history of sociology on the cognitive, social, and discursive dimensions of the Collège. A key source for this research on the Collège de Sociologie was the collection of presentations and texts by members of the Collège edited by Denis Hollier (1988). I wish to cordially thank Hans Joas, Andreas Pettenkofer, and Frithjof Nungesser for their valuable comments on this text.
2. The close connections between Durkheim, the Durkheimians, and the Collège de Sociologie have been shown by Richman (1990, 2002, 2003), Ramp (2003), Kurasawa (2003), Jamin (1980: 20–24), Pearce (2001), Marroquín (2005), Riley (1999, 2005), and Moebius (2006a). These studies have served as my guideposts in the following considerations.
3. Among the participants in these seminars were Pierre Klossowski, Raymond Aron, Georges Bataille, Jacques Lacan, and, less regularly, André Breton, Maurice Merleau-Ponty, Jean-Paul Sartre, Pater Fessard, Raymond Queneau (who published the Kojève lectures in 1947 under the title *Introduction à la lecture de Hegel*), Eric Weil, and Emmanuel Lévinas.
4. Of course, this description of the "French school" also applies to Lévi-Strauss himself who was deeply influenced by the Durkheim school early in his career; for a detailed analysis of this influence, see Moebius and Nungesser (2013a, 2013b). On the controversy between Lévi-Strauss and Caillois, see Moebius (2018b). For a general account of the significance of the Durkheim school during the interwar period, see Moebius (2006a: 73–115), and for Bataille's view, Bataille ([1946] 1994: 104, 110).
5. The term "self-transcendence" is not a concept used by the Collège; I have adopted it from Hans Joas's studies on the genesis of values (Joas 2000).
6. An impressive example is Michel Leiris's autoethnobiography *L'âge de l'homme* (1939).
7. However, the members of the Collège did not always agree whether society was in a postsacred state or, in the light of fascism, witnessed an unparalleled intensification of the right sacred.
8. For a more detailed discussion on this, see the inspiring study by Joas (2013) and the conclusion to this contribution.
9. On Durkheim's equation of "the sacred = society," see also Pickering (1984: 120).
10. Note that the world of the sacred is subdivided into a pure and an impure world of the sacred (more on this in the section on Hertz; see also Riley 1999). This also means that collective effervescence does not invariably involve positive experiences of the sacred (see also Pettenkofer 2010: 232–234; Joas 2014: 102–115).
11. To demonstrate that his interest was not confined to analyzing archaic peoples, Durkheim referred to examples such as the Crusades or the French Revolution in his analysis.
12. Leiris's criticism seems strange since it was he who had abandoned the methodology of the Durkheim school in favor of his methodology of autoethnography, which drew sharp criticism from Mauss (cf. Fournier 1994: 610; Hand 2002: 54–55).

13. The *collégiens* also neither collaborated with representatives of academic sociology nor did they publish in social science journals but primarily in the literary-style *Nouvelle Revue Française*.
14. Krampus is the name of the "dark" companion in Austria, Slovenia, or Croatia; in other countries, there are other names such as Knecht Ruprecht in Germany, Schmutzli in Switzerland, or Zwarte Peit in the Netherlands.
15. On this lecture, see also Moebius (2006a: 308–310, 430). The lecture provides a good illustration of Leiris's autoethnographic methodology (cf. Hand 2002: 62–63). It was published in *Nouvelle Revue Française* in 1938 alongside Bataille's *L'apprenti sorcier* and Caillois's *Le vent d'hiver*.
16. Caillois's lecture ([1938] 1995) is not contained in the English edition edited by Hollier (1988). This is why I cite the French edition (Hollier 1995) here.
17. On Mauss and the Collège, see Moebius (2006b); on Mauss's life, work, influences, and impact, see Fournier (1994) and Moebius (2006c).
18. Mauss's pioneering work (cf. Moebius 2012) by no means belittles Durkheim's achievements in the sociology of religion. Yet it is obvious that these influences on Durkheim have largely been neglected to date in the reception of Durkheim's sociology of religion and that typically Durkheim's approach has been at the center of attention.
19. In regard to the following, I would like to point out the instructive introduction to Mauss by Heinz Mürmel (1997: 214), who also directs attention to the significance of Mauss, Hubert, and Hertz for the Collège.
20. On Caillois's thesis of war being the modern substitute for the archaic festival, see Joas and Knöbl (2012: 159).
21. As numerous researches have shown, the peaked forms of the *potlatch* are the result of colonial processes since the nineteenth century; see Hénaff (2002: 160–161).
22. This equation of Bergson and Heidegger is of course problematic. On Bergson's political beliefs (Bergson was also an ambassador to the United Nations), see Soulez (1989).
23. To some extent, this applies to some of Edward Shils's (1958: 156) assumptions as well, although the *collégiens* with their focus on experience would not agree with his functional thesis that need for order is the driver of sacralization.
24. On the application of this insight, see my analysis of the secret society *Acéphale*, which was associated with the Collège, in Moebius (2006a: 253–277) as well as Bataille (1999).
25. In this context, I shall mention only his major works. Joas has elaborated his perspective on sacralization processes in various articles in more detail, most of which are currently available only in German.
26. In *The Sacredness of the Person* (Joas 2013: 55) he writes: "We spontaneously ascribe the quality 'sacredness' to objects when we have an experience so intense that it constitutes or transforms our entire worldview and self-understanding. The components of the experiential situation are associated with the cause of this intensity. Sacred objects 'infect' other objects, thus spreading sacredness […]."
27. Joas (2013: 85–96) demonstrates what an analysis building on these dimensions might look like by referring to the example of the antislavery movement.

References

Albers, Irene, and Stephan Moebius. 2012. "Nachwort." In *Das Collège de Sociologie*, edited by Denis Hollier, 757–828. Berlin: Suhrkamp.

Bataille, Georges. (1933/34) 1979. "The Psychological Structure of Fascism." *New German Critique* 16 (Winter): 64–87.
Bataille, Georges. (1933) 1985. "The Notion of Expenditure." In Georges Bataille, *Visions of Excess: Selected Writings, 1927–1939*, edited by Allan Stoekl, 116–129. Minneapolis: University of Minnesota Press.
Bataille, Georges. (1937) 1988a. "Sacred Sociology and the Relationships between 'Society,' 'Organism,' and 'Being.'" In *The College of Sociology (1937–39)*, edited by Denis Hollier, 73–84. Minneapolis: University of Minnesota Press.
Bataille, Georges. (1938) 1988b. "Attraction and Repulsion II: Social Structure." In *The College of Sociology (1937–39)*, edited by Denis Hollier, 113–124. Minneapolis: University of Minnesota Press.
Bataille, Georges. 1989. *Theory of Religion*. Translated by Robert Hurley. New York: Zone Books.
Bataille, Georges. (1946) 1994. "The Moral Meaning of Sociology." In Georges Bataille, *The Absence of Myth: Writings on Surrealism*, edited and translated by Michael Richardson, 103–112. London: Verso.
Bataille, Georges. 1999. *L'apprenti sorcier: Textes, lettres et documents (1932–1939)*. Edited by Marina Galletti. Paris: La Différence.
Bataille, Georges, and Roger Caillois. (1938) 1988. "Sacred Sociology of the Contemporary World." In *The College of Sociology (1937–39)*, edited by Denis Hollier, 157–158. Minneapolis: University of Minnesota Press.
Bürger, Peter. 1984. *Theory of the Avant-Garde*. Manchester, UK: Manchester University Press.
Caillois, Roger. (1939) 1988. "Festival." In *The College of Sociology (1937–39)*, edited by Denis Hollier, 279–303. Minneapolis: University of Minnesota Press.
Caillois, Roger. (1938) 1995. "L'ambiguïté du sacré. Mardi 15 novembre 1938." In *Le Collège de Sociologie 1937–1939*, 2nd ed., edited by Denis Hollier, 364–402. Paris: Folio.
Caillois, Roger. (1939) 2001. *Man and the Sacred*. Translated by Meyer Barash. Urbana: University of Illinois Press.
Chiozzi, Paolo. 1983. "Marcel Mauss: Eine anthropologische Interpretation des Sozialismus." *Kölner Zeitschrift für Soziologie und Sozialpsychologie* 35: 655–679.
Clifford, James. 1988. "On Ethnographic Surrealism." In James Clifford, *The Predicament of Culture: Twentieth-Century Ethnography, Literature, and Art*, 117–151. Cambridge, MA: Harvard University Press.
Condominas, Georges. 1972a. "Marcel Mauss, père de l'ethnographie française. I. A l'ombre de Durkheim." *Critique. Revue générale des publications françaises et étrangères* 297: 118–139.
Condominas, Georges. 1972b. "Marcel Mauss, père de l'ethnographie française. II. Naissance d'une ethnologie religieuse." *Critique. Revue générale des publications françaises et étrangères* 301: 487–504.
Durkheim, Émile. (1898) 1973. "Individualism and the Intellectuals." In *Emile Durkheim: On Morality and Society*, edited by Robert N. Bellah, 43–57. Chicago: University of Chicago Press.
Durkheim, Émile. 1974. *Sociology and Philosophy*. Edited and translated by D. F. Pocock. New York: Free Press.
Durkheim, Émile. (1895) 1982. *The Rules of Sociological Method*. Translated by W. D. Halls. New York: Free Press.
Durkheim, Émile. (1912) 1995. *The Elementary Forms of Religious Life*. Translated by Karen E. Fields. New York: Free Press.
Dzimira, Sylvain. 2007. *Marcel Mauss, savant et politique*. Paris: La Découverte.
Falasca-Zamponi, Simonetta. 2011. *Rethinking the Political: The Sacred, Aesthetic Politics, and the Collège de Sociologie*. Montreal: McGill-Queen's University Press.

Fournier, Marcel. 1994. *Marcel Mauss*. Paris: Fayard.
Hand, Séan. 2002. *Michel Leiris: Writing the Self*. Cambridge: Cambridge University Press.
Hénaff, Marcel. 2002. *Le prix de la vérité. Le don, l'argent, la philosophie*. Paris: Seuil.
Hertz, Robert. (1907) 1960a. "A Contribution to the Study of the Collective Representation of Death." In Robert Hertz, *Death and the Right Hand*, translated by Claudia and Rodney Needham, 27–86. Glencoe, IL: Free Press.
Hertz, Robert. (1909) 1960b. "The Pre-Eminence of the Right Hand: A Study in Religious Polarity." In Robert Hertz, *Death and the Right Hand*, translated by Claudia and Rodney Needham, 89–113. Glencoe, IL: Free Press.
Hollier, Denis, ed. 1988. *The College of Sociology (1937–39)*. Minneapolis: University of Minnesota Press.
Hollier, Denis, ed. 1995. *Le Collège de Sociologie 1937–1939*. Textes de Bataille, Caillois, Guastalla, Klossowski, Kojève, Leiris, Lewitzky, Mayer, Paulhan, Wahl etc., 2nd ed. Paris: Folio.
Hubert, Henri, and Marcel Mauss. (1899) 1964. *Sacrifice: Its Nature and Functions*. Translated by W. D. Halls. Chicago: University of Chicago Press.
Jamin, Jean. 1980. "Un sacré collège ou les apprentis sorciers de la sociologie." *Cahiers internationaux de sociologie* 68: 5–30.
Joas, Hans. 1996. *The Creativity of Action*. Chicago: University of Chicago Press.
Joas, Hans. 2000. *The Genesis of Values*. Chicago: University of Chicago Press.
Joas, Hans. 2002. "On Articulation." *Constellations* 9 (4): 506–515.
Joas, Hans. 2008. *Do We Need Religion? On the Experience of Self-Transcendence*. Boulder, CO: Paradigm.
Joas, Hans. 2012. "Die Sakralität der Person." In *Hans Joas in der Diskussion. Kreativität—Selbsttranszendenz—Gewalt*, edited by Heinrich Wilhelm Schäfer, 147–165. Frankfurt am Main: Campus.
Joas, Hans. 2013. *The Sacredness of the Person: A New Genealogy of Human Rights*. Washington, DC: Georgetown University Press.
Joas, Hans. 2014. *Faith as an Option: Possible Futures for Christianity*. Stanford, CA: Stanford University Press.
Joas, Hans. 2016. "Sacralization and Desacralization: Political Domination and Religious Interpretation." *Journal of the Society of Christian Ethics* 36 (2): 25–42.
Joas, Hans. 2017. *Die Macht des Heiligen. Eine Alternative zur Geschichte von der Entzauberung*. Berlin: Suhrkamp.
Joas, Hans, and Wolfgang Knöbl. 2012. *War in Social Thought*. Princeton, NJ: Princeton University Press.
Kurasawa, Fuyuki. 2003. "Primitiveness and the Flight from Modernity: Sociology and the Avant-Garde in Inter-War France." *Economy and Society* 32 (1): 7–28.
Leiris, Michel. 1939. *L'âge de l'homme*. Paris: Gallimard.
Leiris, Michel. 1948. *La langue secrète des Dogons de Sanga*. Paris: Institut d'ethnologie.
Leiris, Michel. (1938) 1995. "Le sacré dans la vie quotidienne." In *Le Collège de Sociologie 1937–1939*, 2nd ed., edited by Denis Hollier, 94–118. Paris: Folio.
Lévi-Strauss, Claude. 1945. "French Sociology." In *Twentieth Century Sociology*, edited by Georges Gurvitch and Wilbert E. Moore, 503–537. New York: Philosophical Library.
Marcel, Jean-Christophe. 2003. "Bataille and Mauss: A Dialogue of the Deaf." *Economy and Society* 32 (1): 141–152.
Marroquín, Carlos. 2005. *Die Religionstheorie des Collège de Sociologie. Von den irrationalen Dimensionen der Moderne*. Berlin: Parerga.

Marroquín, Carlos, and Hubert Seiwert. 1996. "Das Collège de Sociologie. Skizze einer Religionstheorie moderner Gesellschaften." *Zeitschrift für Religionswissenschaft* 4 (2): 135–149.

Mauss, Marcel. (1925) 1966. *The Gift: Forms and Functions of Exchange in Archaic Societies*. Translated by Ian Cunnison. London: Cohen & West.

Mauss, Marcel. (1896) 1968. *Œuvres*, vol. 2: *Représentations collectives et diversité des civilisations*. Edited by Victor Karady. Paris: Minuit.

Mauss, Marcel. (1925) 1969. "In memoriam: L'œuvre inédite de Durkheim et ses collaborateurs." In Marcel Mauss, *Œuvres*, vol. 3: *Cohésion sociale et divisions de la sociologie*, edited by Victor Karady, 473–499. Paris: Minuit.

Mauss, Marcel. (1938) 1990. "Marcel Mauss et Heidegger. Une lettre inédite de Marcel Mauss à Roger Caillois du 22 juin 1938." Edited by Marcel Fournier. *Actes de la recherche en sciences sociales* 84: 87.

Mauss, Marcel. 1997. *Ecrits politiques*. Edited by Marcel Fournier. Paris: Fayard.

Mauss, Marcel, and Henri Beuchat. (1906) 2004. *Seasonal Variations of the Eskimo: A Study in Social Morphology*. Translated by James J. Fox. London: Routledge & Kegan Paul.

Mauss, Marcel, and Henri Hubert. (1903) 2001. *A General Theory of Magic*. Translated by Robert Brain. London: Routledge.

Moebius, Stephan. 2003. "Contre-Attaque. Eine politische Initiative französischer Intellektueller in den 30er Jahren." *Sozial.Geschichte. Zeitschrift für historische Analyse des 20. und 21. Jahrhunderts* 18 (2): 85–100.

Moebius, Stephan. 2006a. *Die Zauberlehrlinge. Soziologiegeschichte des Collège de Sociologie (1937–1939)*. Konstanz: UVK.

Moebius, Stephan. 2006b. "Die sozialen Funktionen des Sakralen. Marcel Mauss und das Collège de Sociologie." In *Gift: Marcel Mauss' Kulturtheorie der Gabe*, edited by Stephan Moebius and Christian Papilloud, 57–80. Wiesbaden: VS.

Moebius, Stephan. 2006c. *Marcel Mauss*. Konstanz: UVK.

Moebius, Stephan. 2006d. "Intellektuelle Kritik und Soziologie. Die politischen Schriften und Aktivitäten von Marcel Mauss." In *Soziologie als Gesellschaftskritik: Wider den Verlust einer aktuellen Tradition. Festschrift für Lothar Peter*, edited by Stephan Moebius and Gerhard Schäfer, 142–160. Hamburg: VSA.

Moebius, Stephan. 2009a. "Im Rausch der Revolution. Kunst und Politik bei André Masson und den surrealistischen Gruppierungen Contre-Attaque und Acéphale." In *Avantgarden und Politik. Künstlerischer Aktivismus von Dada bis zur Postmoderne*, edited by Stephan Moebius and Lutz Hieber, 89–110. Bielefeld: transcript.

Moebius, Stephan. 2009b. "Die elementaren (Fremd-)Erfahrungen der Gabe. Sozialtheoretische Implikationen von Marcel Mauss' Kultursoziologie der Besessenheit und des 'radikalen Durkheimismus' des Collège de Sociologie." *Berliner Journal für Soziologie* 19 (1): 104–126.

Moebius, Stephan. 2012. "Die Religionssoziologie von Marcel Mauss." In Marcel Mauss, *Schriften zur Religionssoziologie*, edited by Stephan Moebius, Frithjof Nungesser, and Christian Papilloud, 617–682. Berlin: Suhrkamp.

Moebius, Stephan. 2018a. "Die Sakralisierung des Individuums. Eine religions- und herrschaftssoziologische Konzeptionalisierung der Sozialfigur des Helden." In *Heroes—Repräsentationen des Heroischen in Geschichte, Literatur und Alltag*, edited by Johanna Rolshoven and Toni Krause, 41–65. Bielefeld: transcript.

Moebius, Stephan. 2018b. "Zur Konkurrenz im Gebiete des Geistigen. Die Kontroverse zwischen Roger Caillois und Claude Lévi-Strauss." In *Logik des Imaginären. Diagonale Wissenschaft nach Roger Caillois*, vol. 1: *Versuchungen durch Natur, Kultur und Imagination*, edited by Anne von der Heiden and Sarah Kolb, 213–229. Berlin: August.

Moebius, Stephan, and Frithjof Nungesser. 2013a. "'La filiation est directe': Der Einfluss von Marcel Mauss auf das Werk von Claude Lévi-Strauss." *European Journal of Sociology / Archives Européennes de Sociologie* 54 (2): 231–263.

Moebius, Stephan, and Frithjof Nungesser. 2013b. "Total Art: The Influence of the Durkheim School on Claude Lévi-Strauss's Reflections on Art and Classification." In *Durkheim, the Durkheimians, and the Arts*, edited by Alexander Riley, W. S. F. Pickering, and William Watts Miller, 178–201. Oxford: Berghahn Books.

Moebius, Stephan, and Christian Papilloud. 2007. "Einleitung in das Werk von Robert Hertz." In Robert Hertz, *Das Sakrale, die Sünde und der Tod. Religions-, kultur- und wissenssoziologische Untersuchungen*, edited by Stephan Moebius and Christian Papilloud, 15–64. Konstanz: UVK.

Mürmel, Heinz. 1997. "Marcel Mauss (1872–1950)." In *Klassiker der Religionswissenschaft. Von Friedrich Schleiermacher bis Mircea Eliade*, edited by Axel Michaels, 211–221. Munich: Beck.

Needham, Rodney. 1973. "Introduction." In *Right and Left: Essays on Dual Symbolic Classification*, edited by Rodney Needham, xi–xxxix. Chicago: University of Chicago Press.

Parkin, Robert. 1996. *The Dark Side of Humanity: The Work of Robert Hertz and Its Legacy*. Amsterdam: Harwood.

Pearce, Frank. 2001. *The Radical Durkheim*. 2nd ed. Toronto: Canadian Scholars' Press.

Pettenkofer, Andreas. 2010. *Radikaler Protest. Zur soziologischen Theorie politischer Bewegungen*. Frankfurt am Main: Campus.

Pickering, W. S. F. 1984. *Durkheim's Sociology of Religion: Themes and Theories*. Cambridge: James Clarke & Co.

Ramp, William. 2003. "Religion and the Dualism of the Social Condition in Durkheim and Bataille." *Economy and Society* 32 (1): 119–140.

Richman, Michèle H. 1990. "Anthropology and Modernism in France: From Durkheim to the Collège de Sociologie." In *Modernist Anthropology: From Fieldwork to Text*, edited by Marc Manganaro, 183–214. Princeton, NJ: Princeton University Press.

Richman, Michèle H. 2002. *Sacred Revolutions: Durkheim and the Collège de Sociologie*. Minneapolis: University of Minnesota Press.

Richman, Michèle H. 2003. "Myth, Power and the Sacred: Anti-Utilitarianism in the Collège de Sociologie 1937–9." *Economy and Society* 32 (1): 29–47.

Riley, Alexander. 1999. "Whence Durkheim's Nietzschean Grandchildren? A Closer Look at Robert Hertz's Place in the Durkheimian Genealogy." *European Journal of Sociology / Archives Européennes de Sociologie* 40 (2): 304–330.

Riley, Alexander. 2005. "'Renegade Durkheimianism' and the Transgressive Left Sacred." In *The Cambridge Companion to Durkheim*, edited by Jeffrey C. Alexander and Philip Smith, 274–301. Cambridge: Cambridge University Press.

Shils, Edward A. 1958. "Tradition and Liberty: Antinomy and Interdependence." *Ethics* 68 (3): 153–165.

Soulez, Philippe. 1989. *Bergson politique*. Paris: Presses universitaires de France.

Stallybrass, Peter. 1990. "Marx and Heterogeneity: Thinking the Lumpenproletariat." *Representations* 31: 69–95.

Tarot, Camille. 2008. *Le symbolique et le sacré. Théories de la religion*. Paris: La Découverte.

Tarot, Camille. 2009. "Emile Durkheim and After: The War over the Sacred in French Sociology in the 20th Century." *Distinktion. Scandinavian Journal of Social Theory* 10 (2): 11–30.

Wiechens, Peter. 1999. "L'homme du mythe. Batailles Abweichung von Durkheim." In *Georges Bataille: Vorreden zur Überschreitung*, edited by Andreas Hetzel and Peter Wiechens, 223–242. Würzburg: Königshausen & Neumann.

CHAPTER 24

LÉVI-STRAUSS'S CRITIQUE OF DURKHEIM

JING XIE

AMONG critiques of Durkheimian sociology, that of Lévi-Strauss is notable in two respects: it is highly theoretical, and it appears to be an internal critique within the French tradition of social anthropology (Clarke 1981). In this chapter, Lévi-Strauss's critique will be discussed with regard to these two aspects. What is its philosophical significance? What is its impact on French social anthropology? Regarding these two questions, an orthodox view, forged to a large extent by Lévi-Strauss himself, had first prevailed before severe objections were raised. Not only can reviewing this critique help shed light on the genuine purpose of Lévi-Strauss's structural anthropology, it also can help question a widespread, though oversimplified, understanding of Durkheim.

DURKHEIM'S THEORETICAL DIFFICULTIES ACCORDING TO LÉVI-STRAUSS: THREE ANTINOMIES

Lévi-Strauss's critique of Durkheim is of a philosophical nature. It relates to the way in which social reality is defined and social phenomena are explained. Lévi-Strauss reproaches Durkheim for making ontological and methodological mistakes. All of Lévi-Strauss's major arguments in this regard can be found in an early text on French sociology (Lévi-Strauss 1945), in which Durkheim's alleged mistakes are pointed out in terms of antinomies.

The Antinomy between the Historical Approach and the Functional Approach

Lévi-Strauss (1945: 516–517) considers Durkheim's sociology of religion to have a strong historical perspective since it aims to seek out the "most primitive and simple religion," whose explanation does not depend on "any element borrowed from an anterior religion." Indeed, when Durkheim wrote this in his Introduction of *The Elementary Forms of Religious Life* (hereinafter, *The Forms*), he suggested a typical historical and even evolutionary approach (which was common in anthropology at the time Durkheim wrote this book), that is, the idea that any complex form of religious life should be explained through reference to its anterior forms:

> [...] whenever we set out to explain something human at a specific moment in time—be it a religious belief, a moral rule, a legal principle, an aesthetic technique, or an economic system—we must begin by going back to its simplest and most primitive form. We must seek to account for the features that define it at that period of its existence and then show how it has gradually developed, gained in complexity, and become what it is at the moment under consideration.
>
> (Durkheim [1912] 1995: 3)

Later in the Introduction, Durkheim specifies that by looking for origins, he is actually aiming to find *efficient causes* (Durkheim [1912] 1995: 7–8). He explains the importance of efficient causes in *The Rules of Sociological Methods* (hereinafter, *The Rules*). After showing that seeking the efficient cause of a social phenomenon and seeking its function are to be understood as two distinct methods, Durkheim ([1895] 2013: 82) gives priority to the former for the sake of a social *science*: when a science takes its objects of study as real (and otherwise it would not be a science), it considers them ipso facto to be coming from something, that is, to be the effect of a cause. A social fact can exist through mere survival without serving any purpose, but it must have an efficient cause to be a fact ([1895] 2013: 79).

However, one of the main purposes of *The Forms* is to precisely contradict the view of social evolutionism which sees in "primitive" beliefs merely "delirium" or "illusion." For Durkheim, this kind of explanation has no scientific value at all. He thinks that the sociology of religion, so as to be a science, needs to consider primitive beliefs as *real* as any social fact, that is, to see that they respond to a certain need and thus play an objective role in social life. This is why functionalist sociology is considered to have originated from Durkheim's doctrine. One of the major theses of *The Forms* is that religions are expressions of collective reality and that they are necessary for sui generis realities to persist. It is indeed a thesis of a functionalist nature.

For Lévi-Strauss, these two methods are not only distinct but incompatible. Either we explain a social fact by its origin or efficient cause, which means that it can be seen as a residue without any actual function (which Durkheim himself admits in the *Rules*), or we explain that social fact by its function, meaning that its anterior form (if any) would be irrelevant and useless for sociological investigations. Further, since all forms of religious life, for Durkheim, together constitute a homogeneous type of fact, the same type of explanation should be applied to both elementary and complex forms. Hence, the functional explanation seems to prevail since there would always be one form—the most elementary—for which we can find no historical explanation. In contrast, within the functional approach, the study of one single religion (simple or not) will suffice to show the very essence of all religions.

The Antinomy between the Rejection of Finalism and the Requirement of Systematic Explanations

Not only does Durkheim's social realism make him waver between efficient causes and objective functions, it also leads to the rejection of any pre-established harmony or universal teleology of human life. While functional explanations can still be admitted as sociological explanations, teleological explanations cannot:

> We use the word "function" in preference to "end" or "goal" precisely because social phenomena generally do not exist for the usefulness of the results they produce. We must determine whether there is a correspondence between the fact being considered and the general needs of the social organism, and in what this correspondence consists, without seeking to know whether it was intentional or not. All such questions of intention are, moreover, too subjective to be dealt with scientifically.
>
> (Durkheim [1895] 2013: 81–82)

Meanwhile, if the core thesis of Durkheim's sociology of religion is the social realism of religious life, the second most important is without any doubt the systematic character of religious thought out of which the sciences are derived.

For Lévi-Strauss (1945: 518–520), the primacy of causal explanations conflicts with the systematic thesis. If religions, of which totemism is supposed to be the simplest form, derive from nonteleological facts, that is, collective effervescence, and if they are composed of symbols and emblems of those facts, then the reason why they do not form heterogeneous ensembles rather than structured systems would be a total mystery. In *Totemism*, Lévi-Strauss ([1962] 1963: 96) raises the same issue in a more detailed way: Durkheim, while showing totemism to be the most primitive symbolic thought, tries to prove two contradictory ideas. Believing that the sciences have their origins in religions, he postulates a coherent character of totemism which provides the most primitive systems of classification.[1] At the same time, according to his sociological thesis, which states the primacy of the social over the intellectual and of collective consciousness over individual consciousness, totems are considered as emblems of social reality. It is for assuring the persistence and solidarity of social groups, and not for representing physical reality, that emblems are needed. Originally, they are arbitrary signs. When *later on*, clans see in them animals and vegetables, this is only because of some graphic instinct. As a result, totems are twice arbitrary: first by appearing only as abstract symbols, second by being transformed into randomly chosen images of concrete and natural beings through some "instinctive tendency" (Lévi-Strauss [1962] 1963: 59–60, 70–71); this is why totems as symbols are primitive. But how can randomly chosen emblems form a coherent system of classification? To Lévi-Strauss ([1962] 1963: 95–96), the sociological thesis (the primacy of collective activities over intellectual ones) rendered the systematic thesis (the systematic and rational character of religious thought) completely baseless.

The Antinomy between Priorism and Empiricism, the Internal Point of View and the External Point of View

As Durkheim's first methodological rule prescribes, social facts should be considered as things; that is, they resist subjective and individual psychism (Durkheim [1895] 2013, preface to the second edition: I). It follows that sociological investigations must be realized through empirical and external observation of which the natural sciences provide the paradigm. This positivist position gives rise to the most well-known methodological dispute in classical sociology: social facts are to be *explained* according to Durkheimian sociologists but to be *understood* according to Weberian sociologists (Winch [1958] 1990). At the same time, social facts are representations: their existence is of a psychic nature. The fact that social facts resist subjective and individual psychism does not imply any materiality,[2] but rather means that "collective representations" are irreducible to "individual representations." This is not because these representations are two different substances but because they have distinctive properties and constitute two levels of reality (Durkheim [1953] 2010).

Although Durkheim works carefully to demonstrate that there is no contradiction in considering social facts as both things and representations, Lévi-Strauss (1945: 528–529) still raises two objections. First, if social facts ultimately rest on collective representations, then they will not differ from "objectivated systems of ideas," as Durkheim claims. Therefore, the relevant approach should be one of internal understanding. The systematic, logical, and rational features of collective representations that Durkheim himself stresses could only be grasped by understanding and not by observation. Second, if social facts rest on representations, then it would be difficult to draw the very distinction between the collective psychology that sociology is and individual psychology. The scientific autonomy of sociology that Durkheim tries to build on causal explanations seems to be rendered superficial by the psychic nature of sociological objects.

Lévi-Strauss's critique, due to its focuses on conceptual and methodological problems, appears to be objective and pertinent. However, it can also be questioned as to whether and to what extent it is pertinent (for instance, Lévi-Strauss sees no difference between historical and causal explanations whereas Durkheim does). But this is not the aim of this chapter. Durkheim's writing certainly contains postulates and requirements that apparently come into conflict. This was unavoidable at a time when a new science was to be constructed through the use of a deeply rooted metaphysical vocabulary, a vocabulary through which Durkheim and his collaborators received their education. Instead of finding weaknesses, we should rather consider Durkheim's philosophical contradictions as indicators of an original intellectual project for which the existing philosophical language was inadequate. As a result, any perceived philosophical problem within his work needs to be examined in relation to that project.

It is precisely that project that Lévi-Strauss intended to alter the direction of. What follows will show that, while criticizing Durkheim, Lévi-Strauss was not actually analyzing a theory as such but rather was putting forward his own discipline, that is, structural anthropology.

The Structuralist Reversal: Social Origin of Symbolism versus Symbolic Origin of Social Reality

Regarding Lévi-Strauss's genuine purpose, it is worth noting that his critique focuses essentially on Durkheim's sociology of religion—not as a theory of specific social institutions, as Durkheim defines it, but as a theory of symbolism in general. The reason is quite obvious: symbolism is the major, if not unique, topic of Lévi-Strauss's structural anthropology. (It will be shown later that not only classification and myth are approached by him as symbolism, i.e., semiological structures, but also kinship.) All the aforementioned reproaches seek to invalidate the core idea of Durkheim's sociology of religion, according to which symbolism arises from collective reality: all the antinomies show that the idea in question is logically defective. It leads to a vicious circle:

> Durkheim was strongly aware of the importance of symbolism, but probably not enough: "Without symbols, social feelings could have but a precarious existence." He could have said: no existence at all [...] he tries to deduce symbol from representation, and emblem from experience. For him, the objectivity of the symbol is only a translation, or an expression of this "outwardness" which is an inherent property of social facts. Society can not exist without symbolism, but instead of showing how the appearance of symbolic thought makes social life altogether possible and necessary, Durkheim tries the reverse, i.e. to make symbolism grow out of society. He does it with an ingenious theory of tattooing's origins [...] As a matter of fact, he sees it as nearly instinctive [...] But either tattooing must be considered in man as a true

instinct, and the whole argument breaks down, or it is a product of culture and we fall in a vicious circle.

(Lévi-Strauss 1945: 518)

In *Totemism*, the sociological thesis, that is, the thesis of the social origin of symbolism, once again becomes a target. As mentioned, Lévi-Strauss considers that totemism cannot be at the same time a system of classification and an expression of collective entities. He also considers the systematic thesis as "Durkheim at his best" (Lévi-Strauss [1962] 1963: 96). As a result, the contradiction between the systematic thesis and the sociological thesis, for Lévi-Strauss, reveals the fallacy of the sociological thesis. Trying to prove this thesis leads us into a vicious circle. This is particularly striking within Durkheim's explanation of graphic symbols. He claims that totemism as symbolism originates in collective reality, that is, the solidarity of a community, which needs to be expressed to perdure. But in the final analysis, he explains the need for primitive men to symbolize their clan affiliations through a kind of "instinct." In other words, he derives symbolism from affectivity. However, this affectivity, far from being spontaneous (otherwise the sociological thesis would fall apart), is itself an outcome of ritual activities. As a result, the collective origin of symbolism is established through a *petitio principii*: we cannot discern whether it is the symbolism, together with the affectivity, which guarantees the collective life, or if it is in fact the reverse (Lévi-Strauss [1962] 1963: 70–71).

From his early text on French sociology until his later writings gathered in *Structural Anthropology I* and *II*, Lévi-Strauss's critique of the sociological thesis remains a leitmotiv each time he discusses Durkheim and French sociology. Concerning the issue of symbolism, he claims that Durkheim and Durkheimian sociologists are going in the wrong direction by postulating the primacy of collective reality. The right direction can only be that of Lévi-Strauss's—the structuralist approach, which is to reverse the relation between the social and the symbolic. (How he realizes the structuralist approach will be discussed in detail in the third section.) Indeed, Lévi-Strauss's critique is systematically put forward together with his structural program. This is particularly apparent in his *Introduction to the Work of Marcel Mauss*, which is well-known for not presenting Mauss's thought but rather being a *manifesto* of structural anthropology. Mauss, according to Lévi-Strauss, differs from Durkheim in some quite positive respects. However, he is still seen to commit the Durkheimian mistake, especially in his early essay on magic and, more precisely, in his account of the notion of *mana*. "Analysing the notions of mana, wakan and orenda [...] Mauss anticipates by ten years the organisation and some of the conclusions of *Les Formes élémentaires de la vie religieuse*" (Lévi-Strauss [1950] 1987: 51). The same critique that we find in his article on "French sociology" and in *Totemism* is here raised against the Durkheimian Mauss, and it is raised as a *manifesto*: "Mauss still"—"still" means: like Durkheim—"thinks it possible to develop a sociological theory of symbolism, whereas it is obvious that what is needed is a symbolic origin of society" (Lévi-Strauss [1950] 1987: 21).

Was it the discovery of the Durkheimian mistake that drove Lévi-Strauss to the construction of his structural anthropology, as his critique suggests? His direct source of inspiration being American anthropology and, above all, Jakobson's phonology (the only Durkheimian research that has a significant influence on him is Granet's work on kinship in ancient China), the opposite is true: it is in order to put his own discipline onto the stage that he opposes himself to Durkheimian sociology. Lévi-Strauss's critique is neither an objective analysis of a specific theory for its own sake nor an account of the genesis of his own thought. It is a strategy. He focuses on Durkheim's theory of symbolism because he already considers symbolism to be the very topic of any social anthropology research. The systematic thesis is "Durkheim at his best" because it is Durkheim having an affinity with structuralism. Lévi-Strauss's critique and his own theory of symbolism are two sides of the same coin. An understanding of the one goes together with an understanding of the other. What does Lévi-Strauss mean by the symbolic origin of the social reality? How does he turn it into a new anthropological program?

The Fundamental Structures of the Human Mind

To answer these questions, we should notice how Lévi-Strauss explains Durkheim's methodological and ontological weaknesses via an empirical reason: if Durkheim was not able to surpass the (essentially neo-Kantian) philosophical framework of his time, this was because sociology, as a science under construction, still suffered from a lack of empirical knowledge. This apparently contradicts Lévi-Strauss's approval of Durkheim's theoretical focus at a time when anthropologists had already collected enough information but had not interpreted it correctly. Actually, according to Lévi-Strauss, it is not facts in general that Durkheim ignores but a single one, a linguistic discovery, that is, the structural nature of language. Lévi-Strauss stresses two features of linguistic activities. To give full account of them, it is Jakobson's phonology (the learning of which led Lévi-Strauss to become consciously structuralist) rather than Saussure's linguistics that we need to refer to.

Opposition as the Most Fundamental Principle of Any Linguistic Activity

To consider, as Saussure does, that in language there is only difference and that one sign signifies what other signs of the same language do not signify (claims which are usually taken to be the credo of all structuralist doctrines) will not suffice, for "difference" is a very vague relation. What Jakobson's phonology (Jakobson [1976] 1978) shows is that linguistic units, phonemes in his case, are made up of distinctive features. These features are the results of binary oppositions such as open and closed, nasal and nonnasal, round and unround. Hence, they are neither physical nor psychological but logical entities. Furthermore, the oppositions of phonemes are functional. They are necessarily associated with the oppositions of signifieds in order to create meaning. Signifieds are also bundles of distinctive features such as high and low, diurnal and nocturnal (Lévi-Strauss [1962] 1963: ch. IV). As a result, a system of signs as a whole is built on binary, logical, and oppositional features. Lévi-Strauss uses the concept of "structure" only in this very technical sense. Languages as structures, that is, meaningful wholes, turn out to be completely logical entities.

The Unconscious Character of Linguistic Activities

An understanding of the logical nature of language is a crucial turning point in linguistics (we can still find in Saussure's teaching a strong psychological tendency) and sheds light on the second feature stressed by Lévi-Strauss: that linguistic activities are unconscious. Although Lévi-Strauss's reference to Freud as a major inspiration could mislead readers here, and although he uses the unconscious qualification without fully explaining it, it follows from his understanding of the logical nature of language that his conception of the unconscious is distinct from the psychoanalytic one: it is not an autonomous psychic mechanism sharing our mental space with the consciousness and being in conflict with it. It is merely the way linguistic activities occur: when we talk, we are not aware of the grammatical and lexical rules we follow,[3] though following those rules is a sine qua non condition that renders our talking possible. Thus, the unconsciousness thesis does not only mean that in ordinary linguistic activities there is a part that we are not aware of, but also that that part, that is, following rules (the most basic one being the oppositional principle) is the fundamental part of these activities.

From Structure to Structural Anthropology

To get from the technical concept of structure to structural anthropology, that is, a social anthropology that takes structures as its object, there is one step left to take which constitutes the very originality of Lévi-Strauss's doctrine. Behind every social institution he examines, he finds the same kind of structures. His first object, kinship (Lévi-Strauss [1949] 1969), is reduced first to rules of the exchange of women and then to the principle of reciprocity—a typically binary relation based on the self/other opposition. In quite the same way, totemism is reduced to a system of signs having classification as its function (Lévi-Strauss [1962] 1963). It is not a distinct institution but one type of a group of signifiers among others. After turning institutions, which anthropologists usually take as playing a fundamental role in social life, into classification activities (Lévi-Strauss [1962] 1966), Lévi-Strauss ultimately chooses myths as his object. This is because their elaboration benefits from the advantage of being relatively free from material constraints of all kinds (economic, demographic, etc.). Hence, myths exhibit the semiological principles in a purer state. The only object of social anthropology then becomes the mental operation of binary oppositions, their combinations and transformations.

It is not difficult to discover that, in the writings of Lévi-Strauss, symbols and signs are synonyms. One example among many: in his article on the "Effectiveness of Symbols," Lévi-Strauss ([1958] 1963: 197–198) explains the healing power of shamanism as follows:

> [...] the relationship between germ and disease is external to the mind of the patient, for it is a cause-and-effect relationship; whereas the relationship between monster and disease is internal to his mind, whether conscious or unconscious: It is a relationship between symbol and thing symbolized, or, to use the terminology of linguists, between sign and meaning. The shaman provides the sick woman with a *language*, by means of which unexpressed, and otherwise inexpressible, psychic states can be immediately expressed.

For Lévi-Strauss, magico-religious symbols *are* what linguists call signs. They effectively heal because they provide a *language* and give *meaning* to chaotic psychic states. Hence, symbolism can be considered as a short name for "the fundamental structures of the human mind," that is, hidden (because unconscious) principles generating signs and meaningful wholes. We understand now the very program behind the slogan of "the symbolic origin of society": since semiological structures constitute the foundation of all social institutions, the account of our unconscious mental level and its semiological result should be taken as the genuine explanation of any social fact, and the only task of any social science.

The objectivity of Lévi-Strauss's account of different social institutions (such as the universality of the prohibition of incest) is not within the purview of this chapter, which instead focuses on a history of ideas. What does really happen in the history of French social anthropology (especially with regard to its philosophical element) when Lévi-Strauss reverses Durkheim's sociological thesis by prescribing research into unconscious sign-making and sociality-founding rules and procedures?

From Durkheim to Lévi-Strauss: An Orthodox History of French Social Anthropology

What does really happen in the structuralist reversal? At first, one might think that the answer lies in the question itself: what happens is a *reversal*. That reversal seems to bring with it progress: it remedies all Durkheim's aforementioned antinomies. Since social facts are now seen as semiological and mental facts, and the discovery of the logical nature of language can be ipso facto applied to social facts, the ontological dilemma between thing and representation is definitively overcome. Structures are neither things nor representations but unconscious and logical rules. Social facts are signs or symbols issued from those structures. As a result, the methodological dilemma existing between historical and functional explanations, between final cause (either in the sense of objective function or subjective purpose) and efficient cause, is also surpassed. Neither of them is appropriate for the social sciences. A social fact is neither a force nor a means but a sign or symbol. Its nature can neither be explained by its cause nor by its purpose. Its nature should be explained by its meaning and, in the final analysis, by a structure of meaning. For the same reason, the conflict between the internal point of view and the external point of view is rendered superficial. As structures and meanings are found in an unconscious level of our mind—which Lévi-Strauss names the intermediate level—there is no longer an absolute separation between individual and collective representations. Both of them are reducible to meaningful structures, that is to say, to logical products of unconscious mental activities. This common origin makes them immediately communicable. Lastly, now that social reality is seen to be fully symbolic, symbolism fully semiological, and semiological rules fully mental, the view that social reality is rendered possible by symbolic activities of the human mind can be established without risk of falling into a vicious circle.

By trying to remedy Durkheim's weakness, the structuralist reversal seems, to a certain degree, to be characterized by humility: its aim is to realize a Durkheimian project ("a forgotten part of the program")—the sociology of symbolism as a "formal psychology" (see Durkheim [1895] 2013: 12; Lévi-Strauss [1973] 1976: 24–25)—and one could say that this makes Lévi-Strauss a successor to French sociology. His critique would then be an internal correction that concerns concepts and methods, and not a fundamental problem. Structural anthropology and French sociology undertake the same task with different methods, the former being the most coherent and successful as it benefits from a crucial scientific discovery that the second did not have at its disposal. To establish this filiation, Lévi-Strauss presents Mauss as a member of an in-between generation who makes steps forward while working in the continuity of his uncle and master. On the one hand, he pays attention to the unconscious character of social phenomena; on the other hand, he sheds light on direct links between collective and individual psychology. Mauss would have been practicing structuralism without knowing it, "like Moses conducting his people all the way to a promised land whose splendour he would never behold" (Lévi-Strauss [1950] 1987: 45). Now we have the three generations in sight: Durkheim having the vision but not the intellectual tools, Mauss using them without realising it, and Lévi-Strauss being the real founder of the appropriate theory for the social sciences.

It was as a part of a continuous and progressing history that Lévi-Strauss's critique was accepted with enthusiasm. It did not take long for it to be turned into an orthodox history of the French social sciences, and it received philosophical consecration through Merleau-Ponty ([1960] 1964). After criticizing Durkheimian sociology in the same terms as Lévi-Strauss—regretting the contradictory qualification of social facts as both things and representations, the separation of individual and collective psychism, and the confusion of what is historically simple with what is logically essential—Merleau-Ponty saw in the structuralist anthropology not only a methodological innovation, overcoming the positivist/introspective dilemma, but also an ontological revolution.

Social facts were now to be grasped neither as things nor as ideas, but as signs within a structure—a meaningful system. They do not lie in any collective force or consciousness but in relations that provide them with their constitutive meaning. What is ontologically primary is now the logical and meaningful relations between facts, not facts themselves. By finally accounting for social reality in an appropriate way, structuralism frees us from the traditional substantialism (either in the materialist or the spiritualist form) and from atomism.

The Controversy: Were Durkheimian Sociologists and Lévi-Strauss Talking about the Same Symbolism and the Same Sociality?

By accepting this orthodox and very popular history, we put ourselves within Lévi-Strauss's perspective. It is Lévi-Strauss who makes symbolism the very focus of Durkheim. *The Forms* is "Durkheim at his best" because it contains the idea of a "formal psychology" which is, among Durkheimian ideas, the closest to the idea of the structural, that is, semiological anthropology. To what extent can we rely on Lévi-Strauss's account? Since the 1990s, some scholars began to question that account as well as the real significance of the structuralist turn within the social sciences. Descombes ([1995] 2001, [1996] 2014) points out a substantial difference between Durkheimian sociologists and Lévi-Strauss. According to Descombes, the former indeed suffer from a philosophical weakness that he calls "the illusion of collective individuals": conceptual difficulties prevent them from thinking about society as a whole being irreducible to the sum of its parts. In particular, the substantialism that lies behind their social ontology can only suggest a conflicting relation between society and its members, since it turns that relation into one between a "collective individual" and its members who are themselves individuals. This is not a relation between a *whole* and its *parts* (Descombes [1996] 2014: ch. 5.1). However, the solution Lévi-Strauss proposes is not a solution to social holism. To have structuralism as a solution to social holism, we need to show, through the concept of "structure," how social facts and social members constitute parts of meaningful wholes. Though he claims to do so, Lévi-Strauss's structuralism does not follow this path. Instead, it stops talking about the social as consisting of meaningful wholes, since he does not treat the social as being at the level of reality that Durkheim assumed.

The core argument of Descombes is that Lévi-Strauss's anthropology is a cognitivist and naturalist theory that completely dismisses the obligatory character of social facts, which is, however, the prime concern of Durkheimian sociology. For Durkheim, this obligatory character is the result, and evidence, of the emergence of a new level of reality. It proves the heterogeneity between collective ideas and individual ideas (without necessarily hypostasizing the two categories), between social facts (which are moral because they are obligatory) and physical or psychological facts. It is the sui generis character of social reality that justifies the autonomy of the social sciences. The holist thesis, the sui generis thesis, and the obligation thesis are inseparable. Yet Descombes considers that the unconscious structures by which Lévi-Strauss explains social facts actually play the role of efficient causes. In this way Lévi-Strauss changes obligations into causes, identifies "rules to be followed and laws to be discovered" (Descombes [1995] 2001: ch. 3, note 17), and moves from the intentional to the natural, from the ideological[4] to brutal facts, from deontic to physical necessity (Descombes [1996] 2014: 253–254). This naturalist theory runs counter to the autonomy requirement of Durkheimian sociology (the requirement of an autonomous social science treating a sui generis reality). In other words, Lévi-Strauss's structuralism, instead of being a solution to the Durkheimian question concerning the specific ontology of the social, dismisses the question itself through generating a general theory of mental necessity.

To demonstrate Lévi-Strauss's naturalism, Descombes refers to Dan Sperber's work ([1982] 1985). Sperber's work is one of the very first commentaries to draw attention to the cognitivist turn of Lévi-Strauss, especially when the latter moves his focus from kinship to totemism and myth. Indeed, Sperber gives an original account of Lévi-Strauss's anthropology by claiming that its real contribution does not lie in its analysis of varied social institutions but in its cognitivist position, according to which the true mission of anthropology, as a unified science, is to reveal how the human mind functions universally. Put differently, Lévi-Strauss's social anthropology is less a social theory than a theory of knowledge. Sperber regrets that Lévi-Strauss did not go further in this cognitivist direction but persisted in showing how institutions function as language.

Sperber is particularly convincing in one respect: what Lévi-Strauss really did was not to show what symbols, for example myths, "signify," that is, which linguistic and social meanings they have, but what they "display," that is, how the human mind is capable of knowing, classifying, and naming the world through structural operations (Sperber [1982] 1985: 83–84). Oppositions, combinations, and transformations of distinctive features of language are Lévi-Strauss's main interests. His investigations always move from given signs to original signifiers, whereas it is the opposite direction that we take when we try to discover a specific meaning. In Sperber's account, Lévi-Strauss himself becomes a Moses of the social sciences, setting up a new era of anthropology (the cognitivist era) yet believing himself to belong to a given tradition—the social symbolism tradition seeking the essence of social reality in the meaning of symbolism.

The naturalist and cognitivist qualification of Lévi-Strauss's anthropology is fully acceptable, since Lévi-Strauss has clearly asserted that the structures of social institutions build on the structures of the human mind. He has even suggested that behind the structures of the human mind lie the structures of the human brain. Thus, he claims that our mind is "a thing among things" (Lévi-Strauss [1964] 1986: 10). Yet he would have most likely responded to Descombes by saying that his naturalism and cognitivism are perfectly compatible with the other tradition of anthropology—the one that takes institutions as objects—and that by shedding light on "the fundamental structures of the human mind" he is precisely explaining how social institutions, that is, obligations, become possible. There is no discontinuity between the cognitive law by which our mind puts the whole world into a classified system (a meaningful whole) and the law (in a large sense which includes any normative rule) by which social life is organized. This is his technical conception of "rule" and "order" that Benoist (2003), in response to Descombes's critique, presents with great clarity. Benoist's debate with Descombes is of great importance for finding out what, from the point of view of social philosophy, really happens in the structuralist reversal.

To understand Benoist's position, we need to go back to Lévi-Strauss's theory on the prohibition of incest. Lévi-Strauss sees in the prohibition of incest, which constitutes the crossing point from nature to culture, the prototype of any human rule. The prohibition of incest "touches upon nature" because it is universal. (Its universality is questioned but our issue here is not its factual universality but Lévi-Strauss's concept of "rule" that it represents.) Nevertheless, this universality cannot be explained by natural instincts, such as horror or repugnance, or by utility, such as eugenic reasons (Lévi-Strauss [1949] 1969: ch. II), but only by the fundamental structures of the human mind, the first of which being "the exigency of the rule as a rule" (Lévi-Strauss [1949] 1969: ch. VII). At this point, as an innate foundation of mental activities, the prohibition carries a purely negative meaning—it is not allowed that a person takes just anyone else as spouse. The import of this is not that of concrete rules determining what are forbidden or permitted acts, but the very exigency of order and rules. Since this exigency results from the specificity of our mental activities, it is a physical necessity; thus, it is not yet an institutional norm. As an exigency, however, it is the emergent point of any institutional norm. Before turning into norms, it is as such normative and constitutes the beginning of the cultural and the social. Benoist tries to explain this complex conception of "normativity" and criticizes Descombes for having missed it.

The debate between Descombes and Benoist focuses on rules and normativity: Are there such things as rules to follow in Durkheimian sociology and Lévi-Strauss's anthropology? Has the latter given a genuine account of obligations at all? Indeed, that Lévi-Strauss betrayed French sociology by taking a naturalist position must appear to be a very controversial thesis. Benoist agrees with Descombes on one point: there is no such thing as an intentional act in Lévi-Strauss's structuralism. But contrary to Descombes, he takes this as evidence that Lévi-Strauss's specific conception of normativity allows him to achieve the aim of Durkheim's project: to treat social facts as things.

Whichever side we support, to participate in the debate means to acknowledge that the real divergence between Durkheim and Lévi-Strauss does not concern the relation between the social and the symbolic but their respective meanings. According to Descombes, Durkheimian sociologists see in social facts obligations and actions that social members effect by following rules, while Lévi-Strauss sees the results of mental operations obeying structural laws (in the sense both of laws to follow and laws to discover); the former see in collective entities a sui generis existence, while the latter turns out to be an individualist for whom the common structure of each single human mind is ontologically prior to their collective formation. The defenders of Lévi-Strauss, though showing there are accounts for norms and actions in Lévi-Strauss's thought, recognize that these accounts are quite special. Correspondingly, it is doubtful whether the semiological concept of symbolism would have satisfied Durkheimian sociology. It will be shown in the next section that it is for entirely opposite reasons that religious symbolism is chosen by both Durkheim and Lévi-Strauss as symbolism par excellence. As a consequence, they are not interested in the same phenomena when studying symbolism.

If Durkheim and Lévi-Strauss do not understand the same thing by social reality and symbolism, then they are simply not addressing the same problem, their disagreement is not internal to a shared tradition, and the history of French social anthropology will need to be revised. From Durkheim to Lévi-Strauss, there was not the continuity that the latter asserts, but rather a shift of direction and a change in the level of investigation. To consider the latter as a successor amounts to simplifying that history: simplifying this historical passage into a monodirectional progress and, in the same breath, simplifying Durkheim's sociology into a purely positive discipline, that is, neglecting the normative dimension of the social as its prime preoccupation.

Did Durkheim and Lévi-Strauss have comparable concepts of "rule" or "normativity" and, consequently, comparable concepts of symbolism and social reality? These questions can be elucidated particularly well from the point of view of action. By doing so, we no longer limit ourselves to what Durkheim explicitly said (as a matter of fact, "normativity" and "action" are used neither by Durkheim nor by Lévi-Strauss as chief concepts), but join a current focus of Durkheimian thought and thus discover its most living aspect.

From the Point of View of Action

Durkheim's claims on the subject of normativity are doubtlessly ambiguous. Social facts are *obligations*; meanwhile they need to be explained by *causes*. As collective consciousness, they are external to individuals, but they are so internalized that individuals do not always feel their weight. These seem to be pure contradictions that render Durkheim's normative theory very confusing. However, as we already suggested, instead of attempting to absorb the inner tension of a newborn discipline through a uniform solution, it would be more constructive to discover its genuine purpose. In fact, this purpose can be found explicitly in Durkheim's definition of "institution":

> The great difference between animal societies and human societies is that in the former, the individual creature is governed exclusively from *within itself*, by the instincts [...] On the other hand human societies present a new phenomenon of a special nature, which consists in the fact that certain ways of acting are imposed, or at least suggested *from outside* the individual and are added on his own nature: such is the character of the "institutions" (in the broad sense of the word), which the existence of language makes possible and of which language is itself an example.

They take on substance as individuals succeed each other without this succession destroying their continuity; their presence is the distinctive characteristic of human societies, and the specific object of sociology.

(Durkheim [1895] 2013: 190)[5]

The sui generis character of social reality is here explained by its institutionality, and institutions are given a specific definition: they are not churches or ministries but "ways of acting." (It is remarkable that Durkheim considers using language a way of acting, not merely a way of thinking or expressing.) Collective reality is irreducible to individual reality because, being made up of institutions, it is "imposed or at least suggested *from outside*," giving rise to a sui generis pragmatic dimension of human activities.

It follows from this conception of "institution" that a theory of action lies at the core of Durkheim's sociology. Its development can be found in the *Forms*, but in such an unexpected way that it can be easily missed. When Durkheim says that religions are institutions, that is, ways of acting, par excellence, we would intuitively think about their ritual dimension. In fact, it is through the other dimension, that of symbols, that Durkheim tries to establish the ways of acting that religious life brings about. In the Conclusion of the *Forms*, while showing that scientific and logical thought originates from one of the two elements of religious life—symbolism as a system of ideas (the other element being ritualism as a system of practices)—Durkheim argues that science and religious symbolism are composed of two different kinds of ideas. This is because knowledge and faith (of which symbols are expressions) are heterogenous. He explains this heterogeneity in terms of action:

[…] as important as these borrowings from the established sciences may be, they are in no way sufficient; faith is above all a spur to action, whereas science, no matter how advanced, always remains at a distance from action.

(Durkheim [1912] 1995: 432)

The difficulty for us to grasp religions and social institutions in general, such as they are defined in the Conclusion of the *Forms*—which is also the reason that the theory of action it implies has been neglected for a long time—is that by this theory Durkheim does not merely attempt to show specific actions that religions prescribe (just as rules do in explicit or implicit ways), but tries to unveil a whole new relation to actions that is rendered possible by the kind of ideas that religious symbols are (Karsenti 2012). Just like theoretical (scientific and logical) ideas, religious ideas are ideas because they establish abstract relations between different beings (that is, they classify, systematize, and categorize), and because they cannot be obtained by the generalization of sense impressions and mental images—they are in complete discontinuity with them. Only social experiences, as a new kind that is irreducible to individual experiences, can give rise to religious ideas. However (and this is the corollary of the social origin of symbolism which Lévi-Strauss pays no attention to while criticizing this genetic thesis), to believe that collective experiences give rise to religious symbols amounts to admitting that they do not create merely an intellectual capacity, but above all a sui generis psychism—the faith that religious symbols necessarily bring by carrying the idea of the sacred, that is, the very expression of collective experiences. Faith is not a spontaneous feeling but a constitutive part of the kind of ideas that religious symbols are. As such, it connects humans to actions in a specific way: it constitutes a specific mediation, one that differs from the immediate relation between individual psychism and spontaneous acts but also from two other kinds of mediated relations—that between theories and their application, and that between rules and the actions of following them. It makes intelligible what Durkheim calls "obligations": things that we do not intuitively do and do not have the physical or logical necessity to do, but that still appear as things that must be done.

A similar thesis can be found in an article on magic that Mauss cowrote with Hubert (Mauss [1950] 2001). Magical notions (the most prominent being *mana*) are called "practical ideas"[6] because Mauss ([1950] 2001: 119), as does Durkheim later in the *Forms* with regard to religious symbols, sees in these notions two constitutive components: "the adherence of all men to an idea, and consequently to a state of feeling, an act of will, and at the same time a phenomenon of ideation." At their foundations there is "a non-intellectualist psychology of man as a community," as ideas, however, they are fully rational.[7] A nonintellectualist rationalism appears at first sight to be paradoxical. In fact, just as in Durkheim's later analyses of faith, it means that, on the one hand, collective life creates a new type of idea and a rationalism which, like the scientific type, is in total discontinuity with the sense impressions experienced by singular individuals. On the other hand, being filled with sentiment and volition that only collective life can provoke, this rationalism differs from the scientific type—to use a more recent vocabulary, it is performative rather than merely descriptive, as is the scientific type. While Durkheim emphasizes the performative dimension by the idea of the sacred, Mauss sheds light on it via the sui generis efficacy of magic, which is irreducible to physical efficacy. In short, magical notions, as symbols, are a result of social reality, and as such, they are institutions, that is, ways of acting. But again we need to understand "ways of acting" not just as specific ways of doing things—this concept implies that a whole new pragmatic dimension is opened up by a specific kind of ideas that are rendered possible by our collective experience.

While remaining silent about Durkheim's pragmatic account of faith (and paying exclusive attention to the common origin of religion and science), Lévi-Strauss severely criticizes Mauss's pragmatic account of *mana* as being still too Durkheimian. He reproaches him for two reasons. First of all, Mauss lets himself become mystified by indigenous people. He accepts their interpretations of magic notions as scientific explanations, taking "a picture of indigenous theory" for "a theory of indigenous reality" (Lévi-Strauss [1950] 1987: 47–48). In this way he seems to go the opposite way of Durkheim, since he pays too much attention to individual consciousness. For Lévi-Strauss, it is for the same reason that sociologists pay excessive attention to either individual or collective consciousness: they ignore what happens at the unconscious level. That ignorance led them, in the case of Durkheim and Mauss, to seek sociological explanations in irrational and fortuitous psychism.

Secondly and consequently, Mauss misunderstands the real meaning of magic notions, which cannot be what indigenous people take them to be, that is, a specific force and efficacy. Lévi-Strauss agrees with Mauss that *mana* is a holist notion as much as the gift is a total social fact. But he explains its holist character in a semiological way. The *mana* is the "floating signifier" with "zero symbolic value" (Lévi-Strauss [1950] 1987: 63–64). Just as the prohibition of incest is the expression of the mental requirement of rules as such, *mana* is the expression of the mental requirement of meaning. "Rule" and "meaning" both refer to Lévi-Strauss's conception of "order" and, in the final analysis, to the same cognitive attitude: any order is better than the absence of order.[8]

However, to believe that Mauss intends to explain *mana* through individual interpretations is to miss his point, that is, the connection between *mana* and action, which as we have seen has a collective and not an individual basis. By claiming that the Melanesian people take *mana* as a magical force, and that this means that we should take it to be a magical force *to them*, Mauss suggests by no means that *mana* is an *interpretation*, but that it is a specific reason for acting that *they* have and *we* do not. He would not have accepted *machin* and *truc* as translations of *mana* into French (as Lévi-Strauss does) even if they could have the same reference. French people do not act for the reason of *machin* or *truc* as Melanesian people do for the reason of *mana*. Lévi-Strauss's critique is misleading. Instead of discussing the pragmatic dimension of *mana* and its relation to collective reality, he instead turns the whole issue into an intellectual one, identifying magic with cognitive activities.

It is for quite the same reason that Lévi-Strauss keeps silent about Durkheim's account of faith: he sees in religions merely cognitive activities of a "savage" state. His silence does not signify mere negligence but an attempt to remove the pragmatic dimension of religion in order to reduce religion to cognition. This is evident when he claims that religious studies are one of the essential parts of social anthropology insofar as religiosity is removed from what is studied, that is, insofar as religion as a sociological category is dissolved into the vast and homogenous field of classificatory thought: religions are not distinctive institutions but systems of classification among others.[9] This attempt goes together with his claim of a "formal psychology." The recognition or refusal of religions as distinctive institutions, and of collective psychology as autonomous science, amounts to the recognition or refusal of practical reasons and actions as irreducible to theoretical reasons and cognitive activities. Just as Mauss would not have accepted *machin* and *truc* as translations of *mana*, Durkheim would not have accepted the program of a formal psychology as the best part of his sociology and the future of social anthropology. He certainly tried to prove the religious origin of scientific thought, but this thesis on genesis, as we have noticed, contains a thesis on difference.

As a matter of fact, the theory of action has remained embryonic in Durkheim and Mauss's writings and has been given attention only in recent years. Yet the importance for the social sciences to recognize a specific practical rationalism that is different from theoretical rationalism has already been stressed by Bourdieu (1980, preface), precisely by means of a critique of Lévi-Strauss's intellectualism. According to Bourdieu, Lévi-Strauss's structuralism renders ethnographical studies fruitless in many cases. This is because it denies the existence of a specific logic which is irreducible to the intellectual one, since it does not put the world into ordered relations so that it can be known and talked about. Structuralist ethnographers would describe their objects as if what the indigenous people do was to construct perfectly coherent systems. For instance, the purpose for them to have a kinship nomenclature would be to know relatives *correctly* (so that they can exchange women *correctly*). However, ethnographical information often does not show this kind of coherence, not because indigenous people have a "savage mind" but simply because what they do is not to know or exchange people (as signs). Instead, they establish new relations, for instance, to marry people and make an alliance. And they do so always in order to create something: wealth, esteem, peace, and so on, something that "has *mana*," something that, socially speaking, makes sense. Something that is a social reality.

Conclusion

If we shift our focus to the normative and pragmatic dimension, Durkheimian sociology and its relation to Lévi-Strauss's structuralism appear in a new light and are seen to be more complicated than Lévi-Strauss suggests in his critique. We discovered that to question the relation between the social and the symbolic is one thing, but to modify their content is another; to doubt the historical approach is one thing, but to replace it with a semiological approach is another. What Lévi-Strauss claims to do is the former; what he truly does is the latter. By doing so, he does not, as many have believed and continue to believe, inherit Durkheim and Mauss at their best; instead, he steers French social anthropology toward a cognitivist direction that Durkheim and Mauss would not consider as their own. The genuine divergence between Durkheimian sociology and Lévi-Strauss's structuralism lies above all in the definition of the social and the symbolic. While Lévi-Strauss's definition, in a purely intellectualist perspective, reduces both of them to knowledge-making, Durkheim's definition acknowledges a genuine creativity in them. Collective experience gives rise to a sui generis reality because its normative dimension makes social members do things in sui generis ways, and it can be proved to do so only if symbolism, that is, expressions of that experience, is considered to create a sui generis psychic element—the faith of the sacred. In short, the divergence in question lies between two incompatible social philosophies: either we consider that there is no such thing as a sui generis social (nonphysical but institutional) reality, or we believe that this social reality makes us do things other than acquiring knowledge, and that (once we are inside social reality and symbolic thought) we continue to create social reality through symbolism and symbolism through social reality. What Lévi-Strauss saw as a vicious circle may just be one of the most alive aspects of Durkheimian sociology: a convincing account of the way that sociality becomes the main, if not unique, source of human actions.

Notes

1. For Durkheim's systematic thesis, see Durkheim and Mauss ([1903] 1963).
2. "Indeed, we do not say that social facts are material things, but that they are things just as are material things, although in a different way" (Durkheim [1895] 2013: 7).
3. "There is no need to be conscious of linguistic laws to be able to speak, nor of laws of logic to think. None the less, these laws exist, and the theoretician rightly strives to discover them" (Lévi-Strauss [1949] 1969: 177).
4. Here, "ideology" means a system of ideas and values, as defined by Louis Dumont (see Dumont [1966] 1981, Introduction).
5. This article was originally written as a remark on the article "society" in André Lalande's *Vocabulaire technique et critique de la philosophie*. Published in *Bulletin de la société française de philosophie* 15 (1917), and later published in Durkheim (1975: 71).
6. "Actions and representations are inseparable to such an extent that magic could be called a *practical idea*" (Mauss [1950] 2001: 112).
7. "Thanks to the idea of *mana*, magic—the domain of wish-fulfilment—is shown to have plenty of rationalism" (Mauss [1950] 2001: 156).
8. With regard to the function of the magic, Lévi-Strauss ([1962] 1966: 9) says: "The real question is [...] whether some initial order can be introduced into the universe by means of these groupings. Classifying, as opposed to not classifying, has a value of its own, whatever form the classification may take."
9. "Inasmuch as religious facts have their place in such a system, it can be seen that one aspect of our attempt consists in stripping them of their specificity" (Lévi-Strauss [1973] 1976: 66).

References

Benoist, Jocelyn. 2003. "Structures, causes et raisons. Sur le pouvoir causal de la structure." *Archives de philosophie* 66: 73–88.

Bourdieu, Pierre. 1980. *Le Sens pratique*. Paris: Minuit.

Clarke, Simon. 1981. *The Foundations of Structuralism: A Critique of Lévi-Strauss and the Structuralist Movement*. Brighton: The Harvester Press.

Descombes, Vincent. (1995) 2001. *The Mind's Provisions: A Critique of Cognitivism*. Translated by S. Schwartz. Princeton, NJ: Princeton University Press.

Descombes, Vincent. (1996) 2014. *The Institutions of Meaning: A Defense of Anthropological Holism*. Translated by S. Schwartz. Cambridge, MA: Harvard University Press.

Dumont, Louis. (1966) 1981. *Homo Hierarchicus: The Caste System and Its Implications*. Translated by M. Sainsbury. Chicago: University of Chicago Press.

Durkheim, Émile. (1895) 2013. *The Rules of Sociological Method and Selected Texts on Sociology and Its Method*. Translated by W. D. Halls. New York: The Free Press.

Durkheim, Émile. (1912) 1995. *The Elementary Forms of Religious Life*. Translated by K. E. Fields. New York: The Free Press.

Durkheim, Émile. (1953) 2010. "Individual and Collective Representations." In Émile Durkheim, *Sociology and Philosophy*, translated by D. F. Pocock, 1–34. London: Routledge.

Durkheim, Émile. 1975. "Une définition de la société." In *Textes 1: Éléments d'une théorie sociale*, 71. Paris: Minuit.

Durkheim, Émile, and Marcel Mauss. (1903) 1963. *Primitive Classification*. Translated by R. Needham. Chicago: University of Chicago Press.

Jakobson, Roman. (1976) 1978. *Six Lectures on Sound and Meaning*. Translated by J. Mepham. Cambridge, MA: MIT Press.

Karsenti, Bruno. 2012. "Sociology Face to Face with Pragmatism: Action, Concept, and Person." *Journal of Classical Sociology* 12, no. 3–4: 398–427.

Lévi-Strauss, Claude. 1945. "French Sociology." In *Twentieth Century Sociology*, edited by Georges Gurvitch and W. E. Moore, 513–545. New York: Philosophical Library.

Lévi-Strauss, Claude. (1949) 1969. *The Elementary Structures of Kinship*. Translated by J. H. Bell and J. R. von Sturmer. Boston: Beacon Press.

Lévi-Strauss, Claude. (1950) 1987. *Introduction to the Work of Marcel Mauss*. Translated by F. Baker. Routledge: London.

Lévi-Strauss, Claude. (1958) 1963. *Structural Anthropology*. Translated by C. Jacobson and B. G. Schoepf. New York: Basic Books.

Lévi-Strauss, Claude. (1962) 1963. *Totemism*. Translated by R. Needham. Boston: Beacon Press.

Lévi-Strauss, Claude. (1962) 1966. *The Savage Mind*. Translated by G. Weidenfeld. Chicago: University of Chicago Press.

Lévi-Strauss, Claude. (1964) 1986. *The Raw and the Cooked*. Translated by J. and D. Weightman. New York: Penguin.

Lévi-Strauss, Claude. (1973) 1976. *Structural Anthropology 2*. Translated by M. Layton. New York: Penguin.

Mauss, Marcel. 2001. *A General Theory of Magic*. Translated by R. Brain. London: Routledge.

Merleau-Ponty, Maurice. (1960) 1964. "From Mauss to Claude Lévi-Strauss." In *Signs*, translated by R. McCleary, 114–125. Evanston, IL: Northwestern University Press.

Sperber, Dan. (1982) 1985. *On Anthropological Knowledge: Three Essays*. Cambridge: Cambridge University Press.

Winch, Peter. (1958) 1990. *The Idea of a Social Science and Its Relation to Philosophy*. London: Routledge.

CHAPTER 25

ORDINARY RITUALS

Durkheim, Mead, Goffman

FRÉDÉRIC KECK

IN 1973, Pierre Bourdieu had some central works of Erving Goffman (1959, 1971) translated into French under the title *La mise en scène de la vie quotidienne* (Goffman 1973a, 1973b). Then, Goffman was portrayed as connecting the sociological tradition of Durkheim to the empirical discoveries of the Chicago School on the daily life of urban groups, and as revealing the logic of domination of total institutions (Goffman 1961) in the interactions between individuals (Boltanski 1973; Ditton 1980; Drew and Wotton 1988; Burns 1992). In recent years, however, Goffman has been read in relation with the pragmatist tradition of American philosophy (Joas 1993; Rawls 2005; Karsenti 2012). At the same time, the inspiration that Goffman found in ethology—the observation of animal behaviors—has resonated with recent investigations in social sciences on presymbolic forms of communication (Conein 1992; Despret 1996). This chapter, reading Goffman's *Interaction Ritual* (1967) together with Durkheim's *Elementary Forms of Religious Life* ([1912] 1995) and George Herbert Mead's *Mind, Self and Society* (1934), shows how taking his use of pragmatism and ethology into account establishes a more complex sociological genealogy from Durkheim to Goffman. Goffman transforms the Durkheimian conception of rite by linking extraordinary ceremonies of primitive groups to ordinary interactions between urban individuals. The concepts of the sacred and the symbolic that are at the heart of Durkheim's sociology are thus challenged through Goffman's concept of ordinary ritual; but despite Goffman's reference to pragmatism, he retains the formalist quality of Durkheim's concepts.

DURKHEIM: RELIGIOUS RITUALS AND SACRIFICE

Goffman's *Interaction Ritual* (1967) takes up the definition of ritual that Durkheim gives in *The Elementary Forms of Religious Life* ([1912] 1995). According to Durkheim, religion can be defined as a set of beliefs and rituals that concern sacred objects: "Religious phenomena fall into two basic categories: beliefs and rites. The first are states of opinion and consist of representations; the second are particular modes of action" (34). This definition assumes a distinction between theory and practice, or between representations and actions. Ritual is secondary to the full representation of the sacred, because it repeats its classifications at the level of action. But ritual is necessary because, without concrete actions on things, religion would be a collective delirium. The distinction between the sacred and the profane emerges through collective interaction in the operation of sacrifice, but then regulates ordinary interactions through categorization and classification. Ritual is thus superior to other types of practice because it relates the action of individuals to the representation of society through belief.

Rituals take place where the sacred is being manifested through a distinction from the profane. Their site is the temple or the church, which concentrates all social activity in this well-founded delirium that is the religious ceremony. For religion to exist, there must be a spatial distinction between the sacred, the place of the manifestation of society through worship, and the profane, the place of ordinary economic and domestic activities. It is in this sense that Durkheim, following Robertson Smith's work on holy places in Semitic societies (1889), compares them to totemic forms of organization: the place where the totem is collectively killed and eaten is surrounded by individual houses where the rest of the economic and domestic activity takes place. For Durkheim, who probably had the small villages of rural France in mind, the totemic community is the form of social organization from which all other forms of political and religious organization derive, progressively becoming more complex.

This totemic model implies a first divergence from the Chicago School of sociology. Durkheim's village is a social space that is organized in a concentric fashion, in which social life oscillates between moments of effervescence, when it occurs at the center of this space, and moments of relaxation, when it occurs on its margins (Pickering 1984). On the contrary, the city, as analyzed by the Chicago School, is a space without a center, where the smallest interaction can become an occasion for celebrating the social order, and the margins are no longer seen only as places of anomia but also as sites where new norms are being invented (Park 1915). The opposition between the center and the margins that organizes Durkheimian dualisms (religion/magic, politics/economy, public/private, collective/individual) leads him to devalue ordinary activities in favor of festive ceremonies:

> On ordinary days, the mind is chiefly occupied with utilitarian and individualistic affairs. Everyone goes about his own personal business; for most people, what is most important is to meet the demands of material life; the principal motive of economic activity has always been private interest. [...] On feast days, however, these concerns are overshadowed obligatorily; since they are in essence profane, they are shut out of sacred periods. What then occupies the mind are the beliefs held in common: the memories of great ancestors, the collective ideal the ancestors embody; in short, social things.
>
> (Durkheim [1912] 1995: 352)

Hence, the sacred is present in the minds through the memory of past sacrifices. Rituals inscribe the collective ideal in embodied actions by reiterating the separation between the sacred and the profane. Thus, rituals produce an ambivalent mixture of constraint and attachment which Durkheim calls "respect." Individuals do not choose collective representations—they are imposed on them—but they feel elevated by them to a superior state of being. Durkheim articulates this concept of respect through the concept of contagiousness of the sacred forged by Robertson Smith: the sacred attracts those who live in its margins but destroys those who approach it without precautions; hence the need for rituals to accommodate the presence of the sacred. Respect thus means a mixture of admiration and caution for the ambivalent sacred, considered as the source of social values. Radcliffe-Brown has taken up this Durkheimian definition of the sacred in order to describe how, through feelings that express the worth of collective life, individuals are integrated into a group: "There exists a ritual relationship whenever a society imposes on its members a certain attitude towards an object, which attitude involves some measure of respect expressed in a traditional mode of behavior with reference to this object" (Radcliffe-Brown 1952: 129, quoted in Goffman 1967: 57). Parsons, too, thought that society imposes its values on individuals through rituals: "Attitudes about final values, religious ideas, and forms of interaction are intertwined. [...] Rites occur whenever men take or are forced to take, because of the circumstances, an active attitude towards things that are not fully intelligible in empirical terms" (Parsons 1937: 430, quoted in Goffman 1967: 53). It is through these two Anglo-American mediations that Goffman inherits the Durkheimian definition of ritual: "Ritual is a perfunctory, conventionalized act through which an individual portrays his respect and regard for some object of ultimate value, to that object of ultimate value or to its stand-in" (Goffman 1971: 62).

Including acts of respect in the definition of ritual implies that rituals do not only refer to an object (society) but also constitute subjects, inscribing themselves into individuals in the form of affects. In order to describe this double movement of objectivation and subjectivation through rituals, Durkheim uses the concept of the moral personhood: rituals submit individuals to a moral personhood that is superior to them, in the sense that the aggregation of individuals in the effervescence of collective action constitutes a whole which is superior to the sum of its parts; but at the same time, rituals constitute individuals as moral persons who owe each other respect. This presupposes that individuals are persons only in so far as they participate, in their minds, in that true personhood which is constituted by society. This leads to the problem of understanding what *differentiates* persons. According to Durkheim, this principle of individuation is the body:

> Two sorts of elements produced the notion of person. One is essentially impersonal: it is the spiritual principle that serves as the soul of the community. That principle is the very substance of which individual souls are made. [...] From a different point of view, if there are to be separate personalities, some factor must intervene to fragment

and differentiate this principle: in other words, an element of individuation is necessary. The body plays this role.

(Durkheim [1912] 1995: 273)

According to Durkheim, all individuals have, within themselves, a segment of society that they have received and internalized through education, and this makes them not just individuals but persons, not just material bodies but bodies endowed with a soul, and therefore worthy of respect. However, this conception, which played a central role in the formation of the laicist morality of the Third Republic (Blais 2007), poses a certain number of theoretical problems because it starts by presupposing the moral personhood of society in order to deduce the individual persons, whom it treats as emanations of this social personhood (Karsenti 2006). Indeed, Durkheim, following Marcel Mauss, uses the Melanesian notion of *mana* to designate this suprapersonal force of society in which all individuals participate to different degrees. It is well-known that Lévi-Strauss has interpreted this notion as referring not to some substantial force of the social but rather to a symbolic function—to a set of differential relations that constitute the social order of culture (Lévi-Strauss [1950] 1987). But presupposing an already existing symbolic order means falling back on a speculative hypothesis and, in this sense, does not really help to explain how individuals become persons.

Mead: Animal Rituals and Symbolic Interaction

Goffman's sociology makes it possible to address this criticism to the Durkheimian tradition because it is based on a different conception of the symbolic which owes a lot to the social psychology of George Herbert Mead. Mead's philosophy makes it possible to reverse three dichotomies posited by Durkheim: the dichotomy between thought and action, that between man and animal, and that between society and the individual.

Mead, in the pragmatist tradition of Peirce, James, and Dewey, argues that an action cannot be explained as a translation, or application, of a preexisting idea; on the contrary, ideas can only be explained within the context constituted by an ongoing process of action. Action, not thought, is ontologically primary. In this framework, the relations between thought and action or between representation and ritual, as they are posited by Durkheim, are reversed: rituals do not translate a religious representation of society into a practical form; rather, the representation emerges in the course of a ritual activity which, at the outset, has no purpose beyond itself. Pragmatism is based on the principle that thought, far from being the culmination of action, or its climax of intensity (what Durkheim called "the collective ideal"), arises from a failure or an interruption of action. From this point of view, any religious representation is not, as it was for Durkheim, a trace of the collective ideal, but only a phase where ritual action turns on itself to understand the meaning of what it is doing.

To this pragmatist perspective, Mead (1934: 51) brings an essential contribution through his theory of imitation. According to him, action is not created through imitation; on the contrary, imitation is secondary to action. A child that imitates its parents does not learn to act but to look at itself imitating them, that is to say, to play the role of the parents. Reflection thus appears through imitation as a return of action onto itself. This theory of imitation allows Mead to rethink the relationship between humans and animals in the light of an original theory of the symbolic. If ritual, too, is a type of action that precedes thought instead of resulting from it, there is no reason to think, as Durkheim and Lévi-Strauss do, that religious representations are primary.

When Goffman refers to Durkheim to define ritual action, he adds a second source: ethology, the science of animal behavior. He notes: "The term 'ritualization' is widely used in ethology (following initial work by Julian Huxley) in a derivative sense to refer to a physically adaptive behaviour pattern that has become removed somewhat from its original function, rigidified as to form and given weight as a signal or 'releaser' to conspecifics" (Goffman 1971: 62n1). Indeed, according to Julian Huxley (1966), some animal behaviors can be defined as rituals—for example, the Great Crested Grebe's sexual parade—in the sense that these behaviors, which could first serve to reproduce the species or adapt it to its environment, have been deviated from this primary function and are now being exercised for pleasure, or to control the emotions of fear or desire they first aroused. According to Huxley what is a derivative function of ritual among animals becomes, among humans, a central function of communication, linked to the institutionalization of a language of symbols. This theory was anticipated by Mead: what in animal rituals, which are derived from reflex acts, functions as a trigger or a signal appears in human rituals as a symbol, that is, as a sign endowed with a value in the process of communication between humans, who recognize themselves through these symbols as rational persons.

This "symbolic interactionism" (Blumer 1969) enables Mead to articulate in a new way the relationship between society and individual. Mead does not start with society but with individuals who interact and, in the course of reciprocal imitation, achieve a presentation of themselves through signs. Hence, symbols are not representations of society but products of a dynamic process of interaction that constitutes the social experience that individuals have of others and of themselves. This process is described by Mead through the metaphor of the game: individuals play and take all the available social roles by representing themselves in various ways on the social scene:

> A striking illustration of play as distinct from the game is found in the myths and various of the plays which primitive people carry out, especially in religious pageants [...] That response finds its expression in taking the role of the other, playing at the expression of their gods and their heroes, going through certain rites which are the representation of what these individuals are supposed to be doing. The process is one which develops, to be sure, into a more or less determined technique, and is

controlled; and yet we can say that it has arisen out of situations similar to those in which children play at being a parent, at being a teacher—vague personalities that are about them, and which affect them, and on which they depend. These are personalities which they take, roles they play, and in so far control the development of their own personality.

(Mead 1934: 152–153)

For Mead, the evolution of social life gradually prescribes which role can be played in which situation. If symbolic interactionism provides arguments for criticizing social control because it limits human capacities, this theory nevertheless legitimates social control as necessary for the formation of a community of moral persons. Indeed, the role of education, according to Mead, is to teach the spirit of community without denying the freedom of individuals. But such a conception can be described as optimistic and normative, because it supposes that the evolution of society goes toward the production of well-integrated moral persons who have interiorized all the roles they have to play in different situations. Here, Durkheim's sociology enables Goffman to think of the possibility of a radical anomia in the production of moral persons: The "regulated game" through which moral persons are formed need not have a substantial purpose; it might be performed simply to maintain a social order which has no intrinsic justification. This game might be driven not by the willingness to cooperate but by the simple need not to be disturbed. It is possible that sentinels, those individuals who learn to play different roles at the margins of society, raise alarm when they could just lead a normal life. This is Goffman's fundamental objection to Mead:

> George Herbert Mead must be our guide. What the individual is for himself is not something that he invented. It is what his significant others have come to see he should be, what they come to treat him as being and what, in consequence, he must treat himself as being if he is to deal with their dealings with them. Mead was wrong only in thinking that the only other relevant others are ones who are concerned to give sustained and pointed attention to the individual. There are other others, namely those who are concerned to find in him someone unalarming whom they can disattend in order to be free to get on with other matters. So what the individual must come to be *for himself* is someone whose appearances are ones his others can see as normal.
>
> (Goffman 1971: 279)

Here, Goffman raises an essential point of Durkheim's sociology that breaks with evolutionist ontology (and hence also with the evolutionism that underlies Mead's symbolic interactionism): society is constituted sui generis without relying on biological tendencies, because its existence is fundamentally formal. It is of little importance *which* roles individuals play: what matters is that there *are* roles, and that everyone plays their role and makes the whole play meaningful. Goffman offers a formalist interpretation of the Durkheimian concept of the sacred as that which stabilizes a current of social forces by establishing a primary distinction between what makes sense and what doesn't. Goffman asserts that the person is sacred in the sense that, while having no meaning in itself, it acquires one through the social relations that produce respect. To put it in the Durkheimian language of representation, there might be nothing behind the person, it might be a pure representation without any object that is being represented. The moments when people appear abnormal are the moments of interaction where it becomes apparent that the norms are not founded on anything, and that the person is only a reassuring façade. Mead had seen this element of anomie when he wrote about the multiplicity of possible selves, but according to Mead, each of these selves emerges as a response to an interaction situation and to the rules of that situation:

> We realize in our everyday conduct and experience that the individual does not mean a great deal of what he is doing and saying. We frequently say that such an individual is not himself. [...] We carry on a whole series of different relationships to different people. We are one thing for one man, another thing to another. There are parts of the self which exist only for the self in relation to itself. We divide ourselves up in all sorts of different selves with reference to our acquaintances. We discuss politics with one and religion with the other. There are all sorts of different selves answering to all sorts of different social reactions. It is the social process that is responsible for the appearance of the self; it is not there as a self apart from this type of experience, the self does not exist. A multiple personality is in a certain sense normal.
>
> (Mead 1934: 142)

Goffman's sociology abandons the model according to which the multiplicity of personalities is necessarily absorbed into a unique "normal" personality, but he retains the concept of the self as a representation of oneself in a process of social interaction. With this, he returns to the analysis of the person developed by Marcel Mauss ([1938] 1985). Mauss noticed that in ancient Rome, the notion of *persona* referred to the mask that the individual shows to others; this is what Goffman, quoting the language of Chinese rituals, calls *face*. The risk of any face-to-face interaction is to lose face, to discover that behind the mask there is nothing but an anxious human animal. Rituals, then, are no longer the grand religious ceremonies through which society manifests itself to individuals, nor the children's games through which individuals, by taking all the roles, learn to become responsible persons; rather, they are theater stages onto which actors must jump as if into a vacuum.

Goffman: Stage Rituals and Identity Reserves

When studying the rites of everyday life through which individuals pay respect to each other—such as professional etiquette, politeness, greetings—Goffman refuses to lament the disappearance of the great rites of representation, because he discovers in these small rites of self-presentation a set of social ceremonies that engage the psychic energies of individuals just as much. This is clearly a Durkheimian move—even in individualistic societies, society operates through the respect that individuals pay to each other in interaction:

> In contemporary society, rituals performed to stand-ins for supernatural entities are everywhere in decay, as are extensive ceremonial agendas, involving long strings of obligatory rites. What remains are brief rituals one individual performs for and to another, attesting to the civility and goodwill on the performer's part and to the recipient's possession of a small patrimony of sacredness. What remains, in brief, are interpersonal rituals. These little pieties are a mean version of what anthropologists would look for in their paradise. But they are worth examining. Only our secular view of society prevents us from appreciating the ubiquitousness and strategy of their location, and, in turn, their role in the social organization.
>
> (Goffman 1971: 63)

By moving from collective representations to self-presentations, however, Goffman subverts the teleological schema according to which society will necessarily represent itself through the sovereign figure of the state. On the contrary, Goffman situates his analysis of rituals on the threshold from which society can always switch back to an order of purely animal relations—a threshold that individuals continually cross when they recognize each other, sometimes as foreigners or even as enemies, sometimes as partners within the same social scene. Therefore, Goffman is attentive to all those moments of rupture where social representations break down in embarrassment. The question Goffman asks is: How can actors survive these moments where their representations collapse? How can they rebound on the stage and assume a new role in a way that makes a new social representation possible?

Goffman's answer is that social actors have a reserve of identities which, for them, fulfils the role that the backstage fulfils for stage actors: while projecting themselves onto the social scene, they preserve a secret place to which they can return. The backstage is a site of solidarity between actors and their teams: it is the site that should not be seen by the public, but which enables actors not to be alone on the stage. According to Goffman, who takes up Georg Simmel's analysis of secret societies (Simmel 1906), all social actors have an interest in the existence of this reserve: this is the meaning of the tact they show toward each other, which respects not only the role that an actor plays but also the set of secret identifications that support this role.

Goffman discovered this backstage phenomenon during his fieldwork in a small hotel on the Shetland Islands, while observing the differences in the behavior of restaurant employees when they serve their customers and when they comment on the customers or receive instructions in the kitchen. Referring to Sartre's analysis of the *garçon de café* (Sartre 1956), Goffman showed that the waiter plays a waiter on the restaurant stage, but plays a different role on that other stage, the kitchen. However, this other stage is not, as for Sartre, the site of bad faith where an individual renounces freedom by choosing a role without justification, but the site of the secret identifications which determine the role that is being played on the official stage. When these secret identifications too strongly contradict the role played on stage, or when the individual must play contradictory roles, the actor is led to question the very conditions under which the staging takes place and to demand a reorganization of the roles and the setting up of a new scene. Therefore, the staging of everyday life that Goffman describes is fundamentally dynamic: it is not a static representation that is given once and for all, but a set of presentations and interactions linked in contingent and unpredictable ways. Hence, one should not say that "the world is a stage," which would suggest that a higher degree of reality could be reached by withdrawing into oneself, but rather that "every social world is a stage," which is an encouragement to project oneself into the social world in order to invent new roles and new games, since there are as many realities as there are social worlds.

Goffman may be said to hold a structural approach in the sense of Lévi-Strauss, because he considers rituals of everyday life as a universal language through which actors can perform possible behaviors while retaining a secret reserve of unrealized behaviors which, when put on the stage, overturn established structures by actualizing *other* virtual structures. This kind of analysis discovers structural constraints where subversion and radical novelty seem to reign:

> Just as one cannot learn a new language every time one makes or hears a different statement, so one cannot acquire a new ritual idiom every time one wants to change the alignments in a gathering or discover what alignments others present have taken up. It is a technical not an ethical argument to say that freedom to express is contingent on constraint in regard to the idiom of expression. Of course it is possible to break the ground rules for a particular mode of social intercourse, as when individuals attack institutional authority by publicly performing obscene gestures. But even here conventions reign. A particular set of understanding is violated, but the means of violation are themselves necessarily drawn from a wider vocabulary of ritual that is common to all. Revolutionaries of decorum must rely on the same idiom as those who would gently tiptoe through all their social occasions.
>
> (Goffman 1971: 237)

This dynamic aspect of the structural variations of the ritual idiom is due to the fundamentally unstable character of the elements that it combines. The "face"—the mask that social actors present to their interaction partners—is, like the sign according to Saussure's linguistics, an "opposing, relative and negative" entity (Saussure [1916] 1974: 119). But just as the combination of signs in language, according to Saussure, follows structural laws, so the "face-to-face" interaction, according to Goffman, follows a binding ritual idiom. The concept of face enables Goffman to go beyond the dramaturgical analysis of masks and roles toward a structural analysis of interaction: the concept of mask suggests that there is some deeper reality which is being concealed in the form of a secret interiority, whereas the concept of face compels its user to remain on the "surface" of social life in order to observe the meaning effects that emerge there. The structural dimension of Goffman's analysis of interactions thus leads us beyond the apparent superficiality of the theatrical metaphor, toward a kind of deeper superficiality, which makes it possible to analyze transformations of meanings, too.

However, Goffman has been criticized for restricting his analysis to one single level of interaction, that of reciprocal relations between equal partners who belong to the American middle classes, and for thus ignoring the effects of the violence that results from the domination of one class over another (Boltanski 1973). How can one describe these forms of unequal relations while focusing on ordinary rituals which, at first, always appear as relations between equals? Here, the reference to Durkheim opens the way for an analysis of the juridical forms of human practices and of the types of subjects that they create.

Back to Durkheim: Juridical Rituals and Mourning

Goffman borrows from Durkheim a distinction between two kinds of rituals: positive rituals based on obligations, such as sacrificial, mimetic, and commemorative practices, and negative rituals based on prohibitions, such as ascetic forms of mortification. Goffman translates this distinction into his own language: he calls positive rites "confirmatory exchanges" and negative rites "restorative exchanges":

> In his famous analysis of religion, Durkheim divided ritual into two classes: positive and negative. The negative kind involves interdiction, avoidance, staying away. It is what we consider when we look at the preserves of the self and the right to be let alone. Positive ritual consists of the ways in which homage can be paid through offerings of various kinds, these involving the doer coming close in some way to the recipient. The standard argument is that these positive rites affirm and support the social relationship between doer and recipient. Improper performance of positive rite is a slight; of negative rites, a violation.
>
> (Goffman 1971: 63)

Through confirmatory exchanges, the partners in a game show to each other that the exchange is well underway, and that both actors respect the roles they are playing. In this sense, they confirm that a social interaction is actually happening, and that this is not a scene of aggression. Two people who meet, even if they do not know each other, will engage in the following exchange: "Hello.—Hello.—How are you?—I'm fine, thanks. How are you?—I'm fine, thanks." They thus confirm that they consider each other as civil persons, paying discrete homage to the sacredness of the person. This exchange can be interrupted at this point because it is complete in itself; or it can be linked to another cycle of exchange, for example by respectfully asking for a service. Restorative exchanges, on the contrary, take place when a rule of civility has been violated; they repair the damage thus caused, returning to a situation of confirmative exchange. For example, someone bumping into someone else in the street says, "Excuse me," and the other answers, "It's ok."

In this way, confirmatory exchanges take a juridical form: they are tiny everyday lawsuits that social actors pursue against each other, sometimes taking the role of the victim and sometimes that of the accused. The rituals of everyday life are therefore not only a way of continually inventing something social through a reciprocal exchange of signs of respect; they are also soft forms of accusation through which actors judge each other daily. Hence, Goffman does not describe "social control" as a huge machine subjecting individuals to arbitrary rules received from above, but as a set of strategies operating within everyday interactions, continually reinventing the entire judicial cycle that leads from offense to reparation. The dramaturgical frontstage-backstage model with its blunt opposition of shadow and light is thus replaced by a structural analysis of the micro-practices of power that are performed in the game of reciprocal judgments.

Goffman distinguishes two types of restorative rituals. The first is the defense of the territories of the self, which consists of simply removing strangers from the territory on which they have encroached, be it the foot of the passerby or the private space of a house. One might say that this type of exchange is not really an exchange, since it pushes the interaction partner back into their own hermetically sealed territory. The second type is the reparation of the offense, which takes the offense as an occasion to establish an exchange between two actors, asking the offender to recognize the right of the victim to exist as a person:

> The job of the offender is to show that it was not a fair expression of his attitude, or, when it evidently was, to show that he has changed his attitude to the rule that was violated. In the latter case, his job is to show that, whatever happened before, he now has a right relationship—a pious attitude—to the rule in question, and that it is a matter of indicating a relationship, not compensating a loss.
>
> (Goffman 1971: 118)

The distinction between these two types is strictly Durkheimian: it takes up the distinction, made by Durkheim in *The Division of Labour*, between the repressive law of primitive societies, where the whole community unites in order to destroy the individual who has transgressed the rule, and the restitutive right of modern societies, where the sanction for the fault consists of re-establishing the situation as it was before the fault, thus preserving the social existence of the offender (Durkheim [1893] 1997). The whole evolution of law is thus recapitulated in every social interaction: actors can choose between a repressive ritual that removes everybody to their own territories, a restitutive ritual which repairs the offense and recognizes the existence of the rule of reciprocity, or a confirmatory ritual that establishes, from the outset, an exchange in which persons are respected.

However, there is one type of ritual that Goffman does not mention, even though it occupies a central position in Durkheim's sociology of religions, namely, piacular or mourning rites through which individuals express, with sadness and seriousness, the loss of a sacred object. These rituals, according to Durkheim, reveal the ambiguity of the sacred, since they force participants to rejoice in what should cause the greatest sadness. Neither positive nor negative, they show the ambivalence of the sacred. According to Durkheim, it was necessary for society to die so that social actors are born as separate persons: this is the origin of all the rites recalling the presence of society to itself at the time of its disappearance. Can we find this idea in Goffman's sociology? We can say that it was necessary for the person to die so that the social actors can be born as different characters, in the sense that it is only by bidding farewell to the idea of a person which is fully and absolutely present to itself that social interactions become possible in which actors assume a social character that excludes other possible roles. According to Goffman, the phenomenon of madness demonstrates that an individual who refuses to play the roles given to him does not at all return to some full and complete personality, but is affected by the deepest dereliction. Gradually breaking all ties, the individual that Goffman calls "the manic," at the very moment where he (or she) hopes to reconnect with that absolute object that a self unaltered by social relations would constitute, moves closer toward the void: "The manic gives up everything a person can be, and gives up too the everything we make out of jointly guarded dealings. His doing so, and doing so for any of a multitude of reasons, reminds us of what our everything is, and then reminds us that this everything is not very much" (Goffman 1971: 390).

Madness thus brings us back to that point where ritual activity fails because no role is possible anymore, and there remains only the void that a person in itself is. And yet, at this final stage, rituals of everyday life are still possible. Goffman analyzes in *Asylums* all the interactions that connect patients to each other or to the institution's staff, such as asking for a cigarette, playing a game, taking a walk with a companion of misfortune. While Goffman is undoubtedly very critical of "total institutions" such as asylums, convents, barracks, prisons, and concentration camps, he nevertheless shows that in these sites of domination, something like a relation between daily life and the law is being reinvented through the simplest rites of all, those through which nonpersons manage to become or remain persons. These asylum rituals are fundamental because they derive from the most extraordinary ritual, the one by which the manic agrees to enter the asylum. This ritual is a veritable confession that requires an admission of madness putting an end to all the ritual activities that the manic had refused so far, in order to initiate a new ritual cycle within the context of the asylum; but also a rite of passage through which the manic accepts to recognize himself as a nonperson, by identifying with his madness, in order to be able to become a person again: "And what is sought is an extraordinary thing indeed. If ritual work is a means of retaining a constancy of image in the face of deviations of behavior, then a self-admission that one is mentally ill is the biggest piece of ritual work of all, for this stance to one's conduct discounts the greatest deviations" (Goffman 1971: 366).

References

Blais, Marie-Claude. 2007. *La solidarité. Histoire d'une idée*. Paris: Gallimard.
Blumer, Herbert. 1969. *Symbolic Interactionism: Perspective and Method*. Englewood Cliffs, NJ: Prentice Hall.
Boltanski, Luc. 1973. "Erving Goffman et le temps du soupçon." *Information sur les sciences sociales* 12 (3): 127–147.
Burns, Tom. 1992. *Erving Goffman*. London: Routledge.
Conein, Bernard. 1992. "Éthologie et sociologie. Contribution de l'éthologie à la théorie de l'interaction sociale." *Revue française de sociologie* 33: 87–104.
Despret, Vinciane. 1996. *Naissance d'une théorie éthologique. La danse du cratérope écaillé*. Le Plessis-Robinson: Synthélabo.
Ditton, Jason, ed. 1980. *The View from Goffman*. London: Macmillan.
Drew, Paul, and Anthony Wootton, eds. 1988. *Erving Goffman: Exploring the Interaction Order*. Cambridge: Polity Press.
Durkheim, Émile. (1912) 1995. *The Elementary Forms of Religious Life*. Translated by Karen Fields. New York: Free Press.
Durkheim, Émile. (1893) 1997. *The Division of Labor in Society*. Translated by W. D. Halls. New York: Free Press.
Goffman, Erving. 1959. *The Presentation of Self in Everyday Life*. New York: Anchor.
Goffman, Erving. 1961. *Asylums: Essays on the Social Situation of Mental Patients and Other Inmates*. New York: Doubleday.
Goffman, Erving. 1967. *Interaction Ritual: Essays on Face-to-Face Behavior*. New York: Anchor.
Goffman, Erving. 1971. *Relations in Public: Microstudies of the Public Order*. New York: Harper.
Goffman, Erving. 1973a. *La mise en scène de la vie quotidienne*, vol 1: *La présentation de soi*. Paris: Minuit.
Goffman, Erving. 1973b. *La mise en scène de la vie quotidienne*, vol 2: *Les relations en public*. Paris: Minuit.
Huxley, Julian. 1966. *Ritualization of Behaviour in Animals and Me*. Paris: UNESCO Archives.
Joas, Hans. 1993. *Pragmatism and Social Theory*. Chicago: University of Chicago Press.
Karsenti, Bruno. 2006. *La société en personnes. Études durkheimiennes*. Paris: Economica.
Karsenti, Bruno. 2012. "Sociology Face to Face with Pragmatism: Action, Concept, and Person." *Journal of Classical Sociology* 12 (3–4): 398–427.
Lévi-Strauss, Claude. (1950) 1987. *Introduction to the Work of Marcel Mauss*. London: Routledge.
Mauss, Marcel. (1938) 1985. "A Category of the Human Mind: The Notion of Person; the Notion of Self." In *The Category of the Person: Anthropology, Philosophy, History*, edited by Michael Carrithers, Steven Collins, and Steven Lukes, 1–25. Cambridge: Cambridge University Press.
Mead, George Herbert. 1934. *Mind, Self and Society: From the Standpoint of a Social Behaviorist*. Chicago: University of Chicago Press.
Park, Robert E. 1915. "The City: Suggestions for the Investigation of Human Behavior in the City Environment." *American Journal of Sociology* 20, no 5: 577–612.
Parsons, Talcott. 1937. *The Structure of Social Action*. New York: McGraw-Hill.
Pickering, W. S. F. 1984. *Durkheim's Sociology of Religion*. London: Routledge.
Radcliffe-Brown, Alfred. 1952. *Structure and Function in Primitive Society*. Glencoe, IL: Free Press.

Rawls, Anne Warfield. 2005. *Epistemology and Practice, Durkheim's The Elementary Forms of Religious Life*. Cambridge: Cambridge University Press.

Robertson Smith, William. 1889. *Lectures on the Religion of the Semites: Fundamental Institutions. First Series*. London: Adam & Charles Black.

Sartre, Jean-Paul. 1956. *Being and Nothingness: An Essay on Phenomenological Ontology*. Oxford: Philosophical Library.

Saussure, Ferdinand de. (1916) 1974. *Course in General Linguistics*. Edited by Charles Bally and Albert Sechehaye. Translated by Jonathan Culler. London: Fontana.

Simmel, Georg. 1906. "The Sociology of Secrecy and of Secret Societies." *American Journal of Sociology* 11, no. 4: 441–498.

CHAPTER 26

DURKHEIM AND THE NEW SOCIOLOGY OF MORALITY

STEVEN LUKES

In sociology's early days, morality or ethics—*la morale* in France, *Ethik* in Germany—was the center of attention. The concern with this topic, or rather range of topics, was general and can be seen in the writings of Herbert Spencer, Edward Westermarck, Max Weber, Georg Simmel, Lucien Lévy-Bruhl, and Émile Durkheim. In France, in particular, the founders of the discipline were especially focused on morality and on their claim to study and reflect upon it, thereby challenging their close academic neighbors, the philosophers, who had long been its natural guardians. As for Durkheim himself, morality was, Georges Davy reported, "the center and end of his work" (Davy 1920: 71).[1] But in the course of the twentieth century, and for reasons worth exploring, morality faded into the margins of both sociology and social anthropology, at least as an explicit object of research and theory. This is now changing. The "science of morality" is increasingly reappearing across a range of disciplines.

In a recent survey article on "The New Sociology of Morality," in a section entitled "The Return of the Moral to Sociology," the following assessment is made:

> If the old sociology of morality was Durkheimian—seeing morality as a property of entire societies and binding its members together—then the new sociology of morality is more Weberian. Morality belongs more to cross-cutting groups and less to society as a whole. [...] recent sociological research shows that religions, occupations, generations, educational categories, organizations, and social movements can all have their own moralities. Moral sharing exists, but at many cross-cutting and competing levels. Moral motivation exists, but these motivations struggle with one another and with nonmoral concerns in their expression. Morality can bind groups together but it can also be the subject of negotiation, contestation, and exclusion. The new sociology of morality looks beyond just norms and values, casting a broader net that includes narratives, identities, institutions, symbolic boundaries, and cognitive schemas.
>
> (Hitlin and Vaisey 2013: 53–54)

This assessment merits some scrutiny. What *was* the "old sociology of morality"? Was it indeed "Durkheimian"? Does departing from, even discarding its assumptions and approach require rejecting Durkheim's thought and work as irrelevant, even an obstacle to addressing the topics and themes indicated? In what follows I shall, in the spirit of this volume, ask to what extent and in what ways Durkheim's thought remains of value in approaching morality and morals from a sociological standpoint.

Regarding the first two of these questions, it is plain that the authors do not have Durkheim specifically in mind: their target is rather Parsonian functionalist sociology. Thus, they write that within that perspective, with its "emphasis on internalization and compliance to norms and values," morality became "nearly synonymous with conformity." According to Parsons's theory of action, "situations provide the means and conditions of action, values motivate the pursuit of some ends rather than others, and norms limit the selection of means to achieve those ends" (Hitlin and Vaisey 2013: 53, 61, citing Parsons and Shils 1951: 2–6). But deep internalization is rare, the links between people's values and their actions are weak, people have conflicted inner lives and it is time, they argue, to reject "assumptions about universal internalization and unproblematic consensus that doomed functionalist theory" (Hitlin and Vaisey 2013: 53). We must, they say, look beyond values and norms and cast a broader net. Leaving aside the question of their fairness to Parsons, we should here simply observe that Durkheim was not Parsons.

It is worth noting that there has also been a recent "return of the moral" to anthropology (Lambek 2010; Fassin 2012; Fassin and Lézé 2014) (and it is also worth noting that for Durkheim and his contemporaries the very distinction between these disciplines would have seemed arbitrary and unjustified). And here too rejecting the legacy of Durkheim has played a role. Thus, James Laidlaw delivered the Malinowski Memorial Lecture in 2001, which was published the following year in a much-cited article entitled "For an Anthropology of Ethics and Freedom" in the *Journal of the Royal Anthropological Institute*. After commenting on the absence of an anthropology of ethics and the lack of "sustained theoretical reflection on ethics," despite "some individually brilliant discussions of morality by anthropologists," and lamenting the lack of a serious dialogue with moral philosophy, Laidlaw went straight to the source of the problem. "And then," he told his audience, "of course, there is Durkheim" (Laidlaw 2002: 312).

Anthropologists, Laidlaw urged, must abandon Durkheim's "peculiarly narrow conception of ethical life" (317), in particular his "equation of the moral with society" (314), where society is understood "to be based on moral obligation," and indeed defined as "being a system of moral facts" and where morals derive "directly from social collectivities." The result is a conception of the social that "so completely identifies the collective with the good that an independent understanding of ethics appears neither necessary nor possible" (312–313). Durkheim, he added, "wrote at times as if freedom were an insignificant practical issue," even advancing the "chilling" proposal of a "comprehensive system of modern guilds" to remedy the "assumed absence of ethics from commercial life," membership in which would be compulsory. This "vision of human life [...] simply lacks ethical complexity, dilemma, reasoning, decision, and doubt." Urging the abandonment of this vision, Laidlaw called instead for taking seriously, "as something requiring ethnographic description, the possibilities of human freedom" (315). In his book *The Subject of Virtue: An Anthropology of Ethics and Freedom* (Laidlaw 2014), Laidlaw has renewed and considerably elaborated on this call for an anthropology that links ethics to freedom and escapes from Durkheim—a call taken up by several others, among whom some see it as an inspiration for research into "ordinary ethics" (see Lambek 2010).

Taken together, these authors marshal a number of familiar ways in which Durkheim's sociological approach to morality has been criticized. I shall first set these out and consider to what extent they are justified and then turn to suggesting ways in which sociologists—and anthropologists—can continue to find value, indeed inspiration, from rereading and reconsidering Durkheim.

THE LIMITS OF DURKHEIM'S VIEW OF MORALITY

It is obviously true that Durkheim's focus was on morality as belonging to "society as a whole" and "binding its members together." It is also true that he wrote about morality in relation to groups and institutions—notably occupational groups or professions, the family and the school, and in *Suicide* about religious denominations—but he did not treat these as cross-cutting and competing (apart from the discussion of the countervailing power of "secondary groups" vis-à-vis the state in *Professional Ethics and Civic Morals* and the introduction to the second edition of *The Division of Labor*). One central reason, no doubt, for this "methodological nationalism" was his lifelong preoccupation with analyzing and his mission of contributing to the shaping of civic education in the French Third Republic: "Just as the priest is the interpreter of God," the school teacher is "the interpreter of the great moral ideas of his time and country" (Durkheim [1925] 1961: 155). It was indeed in his lectures published posthumously as *Moral Education* that Durkheim set out most clearly and systematically his sociological theory of morality.

The elements and also the limits of that theory, as set out in that text, are plain to see. First, morality is a set of obligations, a "system of rules of action that predetermine conduct" (24), which are "so many molds, with limiting boundaries, which shape our behavior" (26, translation modified). These can be recognized as distinct from legal rules in being diffusely rather than formally and authoritatively sanctioned and distinguished from technical rules by the "synthetic" nature of sanctions when they are violated: moral rules are subject to punishment because and insofar as they were violated. But second, going beyond this rigorous Kantian conception, Durkheim posited a second element of desirability, an intrinsic pleasure in doing our duty, which he called "attachment to social groups," arguing that "moral goals are those the object of which is a *society*. To act morally is to act in the light of a collective interest" (59, translation modified). For Durkheim duty and the good were inextricably united; fulfilling one's obligations yields the distinctive pleasures of "attachment." As Bruno Karsenti notes, this is an antifoundationalist conception of the co-penetration of these first two elements: "good is within duty and duty within good," as with sacredness which "represses inasmuch as it elevates, and elevates inasmuch as it constrains" (Karsenti 2012: 26–27).

The third element, autonomy, which only becomes a crucial element of morality with secularization and the advance of rationalism, invokes a very specific idea of freedom as "enlightened acceptance" (that recalls Saint Augustine and Spinoza). For modern individuals it is no longer enough "to respect discipline and to be attached to a group; beyond this we must, when deferring to a rule or devoting ourselves to a collective ideal, have as complete awareness as possible of the reasons for our conduct" (Durkheim [1925] 1961: 120, translation modified). For just as natural science enables us to adapt ourselves to natural facts we cannot change, and modify nature to the extent we can, so through empirical investigation, the sociology of morality, the "scientific study of the moral order," will enable us to grasp what moral rules and ideals are to be followed, pursued, and taught, for "It is never possible to desire a morality other than that required by the social conditions of a given time." This may require judgment when there are "changes that have occurred within the conditions of collective existence," and we confront "moral ideas that we know to be out of date and nothing more than survivals." In such cases we may "judge it our duty to combat" such ideas, and "the most effective way of doing this may appear to be the denial of these ideas, not only theoretically, but also in action" (Durkheim [1924] 1953: 38, 61, translation modified). In Durkheim's view this was the historical role of Christ and Socrates. It was also the way in which he justified his activism in support of Dreyfus during the Dreyfus Affair.

"Let us suppose," Durkheim wrote in *Moral Education*, that

> a science of morality is an accomplished fact. Our ascendancy has attained its goal. [...] It is no longer external to us, since from this point on it is represented through a system of clear and distinct ideas; and we understand all the relationships between these ideas. Now we are able to check on the extent to which the moral order is founded in the nature of things—that is in the nature of society—which is to say to what extent it is what it ought to be. In the degree that we see it as such, we can freely conform to it. For to wish that it be other than is implied by the natural constitution of the reality that it expresses would be to talk nonsense under the pretext of free will. We can also see to what extent it is not based on the order of things, for it is always possible that society may involve some abnormal elements. In this way we shall have available, thanks to the same sciences we are supposing established, the means of restoring it to a normal state. Thus, on condition of having adequate knowledge, of their causes and of their functions, we are in a position to conform to them, but consciously and knowing why. Such conformity is then unconstrained.
>
> (Durkheim [1925] 1961: 116–117, translation modified)

The limitations of this view of what a sociology of morality can deliver need little elaboration. True to Durkheim's doctrinal rejection of psychological explanation, it bypasses any consideration of the moral motivations of individuals and their conflicted inner lives: it gives no consideration to what Laidlaw misses, namely, "ethical complexity, dilemma, reasoning, decision, and doubt." The *judgments* that a sociological understanding enables us to make are about the "nature" of the "moral order"—about causes and functions. At most we are to assess what the moral order requires as distinct from what is anachronistic; and to make the judgment (but how and when?) to endorse what is emergent. In the absence of a fully realized scientific understanding, we must just do the best we can and make "reasoned evaluations" on as informed and scientific a basis as possible. But notice that such judgment is cognitive: a question of assessing "the extent to which the moral order is founded in the nature of things." Thus, moral disagreement disappears. So does the possibility of moral diversity in the sense of coexisting multiple moralities within a single society. And Durkheim, on this account, allows no room for Georg Simmel's idea that individuals contain multiple selves with multiple group affiliations; or for Max Weber's that individuals confront irreconcilable conflict among incompatible plural values.

Later Developments

Durkheim's thinking about morality did, to some extent, evolve beyond the account just outlined, which has been accepted, for the most part, as the standard or "official" version, by subsequent scholars, interpreters, sociologists, and anthropologists, whether friendly or critical. It is based on the first part of *Moral Education*, a strikingly lucid text compiled from the texts for various courses but unchanged after that of 1902/03. There are three subsequent texts focusing on the sociology of morality: two lectures addressed to philosophers, namely, "The Determination of Moral Facts" in 1906 and "Value Judgments and Judgments of Reality" in 1911; and his introduction to the major work he planned on *La morale*, on which he was working in the months before his death in 1917, but which is a mere fragment. According to Georges Davy, Durkheim intended this projected book to replace his existing publications on morality, and, according to Marcel Mauss, it was the book he "wanted to write," awaiting "an opportunity [...] to recast his whole theory" (both cited in Lukes 1972: 411). We cannot know how or to what extent he was aiming to do this or what directions his projected recasting might have taken. But there are a few clues.

The focus of his attention was gradually shifting from the obligatory to the "desirability" aspect of morality, and from the rules people follow to the moral beliefs expressed by the rules. Largely as a result of his new preoccupation with religion, he became more and more interested in the sociological explanation of *evaluation*: in the attribution of moral values. By 1906 he was characterizing society as "above all a composition of ideas, beliefs and sentiments of all sorts which realize themselves through individuals. Foremost of these ideas is the moral ideal which is its principal *raison d'être*," the existence of incommensurable secular values, a "separate world of *sui generis* representations," endowing certain things and ways of seeing with a "sacred quality which effects a solution of continuity between morality and economic and industrial techniques, etc." (Durkheim [1924] 1953: 59, 71). The ideal, he liked to say, was part of the real world and could be studied as such. In 1911 he described values as "*sui generis* realities" (81) corresponding to ideals which were "essentially dynamic, for behind them are [...] collective forces—that is, natural but at the same time moral forces [...]. The ideal itself is a force of this type and therefore subject to scientific investigation" (93, translation modified).

In 1917, in the planned introductory pages to *La morale*, he begins by observing that there are two senses in which the word *morale* is commonly understood. One is as "a set of judgments that people, individually or collectively, make about their own acts and those of others, with a view to attributing to them a very special value, which they judge to be incomparable to other human values"; this "incomparability of moral values suffices to establish that moral judgments occupy a place apart among human judgments." He then notes that these judgments are

> inscribed in the *consciences* of normal adults; we find them ready made within us, without being aware, for the most part, of having elaborated them in a reflective manner, either methodologically or scientifically. When faced with a moral or immoral act, a person reacts spontaneously, even unconsciously. This reaction seems to one to come from the depths of one's nature; we praise or we blame by a sort of instinct without it seeming possible to do otherwise. That is why we so often represent the moral conscience as a sort of voice that makes itself heard within us without our knowing for the most part what this voice is or whence its authority derives.
>
> (Durkheim [1917] 1975: 313–315)

The other sense of *morale*, which Durkheim rejects, is that of the "moralists" and philosophers, who devise general principles and elaborate universalistic doctrines in a "methodical and speculative" manner. Beginning with the first sense, Durkheim proposes its scientific study, noting that "the moral ideal is not immutable: it lives, evolves, ceaselessly transforms itself, despite the respect surrounding it" (316), in order to understand

> what are the causes that have generated the various states of mind, ideas, and sentiments that constitute morality. Why do human beings have this set of features, this unique attitude of mind and of will, unknown among animals, or that animals only exhibit in an indirect and analogous way? (326)

And, when describing this new science of morality, which is only "at its beginning, dating from yesterday," he suggests the need for a new distinction: between *morale* and *mœurs*, arguing that

> the morality (*morale*) of the time is doubtless to be found in the practices (*mœurs*), but in a degraded form, reducible to the level of human mediocrity. What they express is the way in which the average man applies moral rules, and he never

applies them without compromising and making reservations. The motives on which he acts are mixed; some are noble and pure but others are vulgar and base. Contrary to this, the science whose scope we are outlining seeks to attain moral precepts in their purity and their impersonality. It has as its subject matter morality itself, ideal morality, over and above human behavior, not the deformations it undergoes in being incarnated in current practices which can express it only imperfectly. (330)

There are several new ideas here that are relevant to currently live debates. First, Durkheim, in seeking to demarcate the moral by suggesting that moral judgments are incomparable or incommensurable and set apart from others foreshadows the claim made by Elliot Turiel and his colleagues that the distinction between the moral, on the one hand, and the conventional or customary, on the other, is not only present across social contexts but enacted by very small children who can distinguish between rules and orders that are authority dependent and those that are not (Turiel 2002). (How close is this to Durkheim's late distinction between *morale* and *mœurs*?) The question of whether indeed some such distinction, generating the difference between "what we do round here" and our basis for criticizing or endorsing what we do round here, is operative across cultures is indeed fascinating and open. Second, the suggestion that such judgments are "inscribed" in consciences, intuitive and spontaneous, even unconscious, recalls present-day discussions concerning dual-process thinking, contrasting fast (or spontaneous) with slow (or reflexive) judgments (Kahneman 2011), Bourdieu's notion of *habitus* and also the operation of moral schemas below the level of consciousness. The passing reference to morality as part of what makes humans unique among animals and the question of whether and in what ways what animals display is "indirect" and "analogous" clearly resonates with debates among a variety of present-day philosophers and scientists studying both humans and animals (De Waal 2006). And finally, and most deeply, Durkheim himself is here beginning to confront what some have called the "Durkheimian dilemma": how to relate the "external" description and explanation of what shapes or determines moral experience, judgment, and behavior with the "internal" actor's perspective, the objective and the subjective. The new science, he writes, is to study a "set of judgments that people, individually or collectively, make about their own acts and those of others." These constitute the "reality" it studies and they are plainly "phenomena of consciousness" and so, inevitably, they require the study of moral motivations of actors.

This last issue of the "Durkheimian dilemma" has been addressed, among others (e.g., Isambert 1992), by Bruno Karsenti. How are we to relate "descriptive studies of the mores and social constraints [moral facts] manifest" to "the properly subjective pole of morality, marked by the subject's relation to values and reflected [...] in moral acts and judgments that can be understood only by reconstituting their internal structure"? Karsenti claims that the later writings (and especially in the 1911 lecture) "cast a different light on his sociology, freeing it from the objectivism or conformism for which it is commonly criticized." Value judgments, he argues, have for Durkheim their own distinctive kind of objectivity that relies on distinguishing evaluation from "the process of formulating a preference." Thus, when making value judgments,

> the subject seems to note a dimension of the object that is independent of the way she perceives that object with her senses. However, while the object's value is not part of the relationship obtaining between it and the evaluating subject, that value does imply, by definition, the existence of such a relationship. Value does exist outside of myself, but only "in a way" [Durkheim's phrase]. Durkheim's restriction is decisive. A value judgment is not a judgment of reality because value does not exist the way a thing does; nonetheless, value does exist outside the subject, objectively [...]. Value does inhere in the thing. Its objectivity is reflected in the intrinsic communicability of a value judgment and in its justifiability, the fact that such a judgment can be legitimately affirmed only if it is demonstrated on the basis of impersonal reasons. In operations of justification—and here Durkheim strikingly anticipates the major problematic of contemporary sociology of action, at least if we make an effort not to think of him as prisoner to his "dilemma" (Boltanski and Thévenot [1991] 2006 is the primary reference here)—the subject is implicated impersonally.
>
> (Karsenti 2012: 21–22, 30–31)

Values are "added to things by the way the subject, in acting, relates to them" (33), and ideals involve an augmentation and indeed transformation of given reality. Values and ideals can be "naturalized" and "social valuing processes" can be studied empirically and indeed "measured and compared in terms of variations in intensity" as representations, which "possess a measurable, analyzable normative dimension." Thus, the "core of Durkheim's argument" is that values are indeed "within social things" but involve a "self-surpassing" (*autodépassement*) and "transfiguration" of nature (34). Ideals and values are "natural realities that can be grasped as things" (35). According to Karsenti, Durkheim offers new perspectives in sociology that the objectivism of his earlier works did not allow for: he did this by

> relating the concept of society to "social life" understood as the life in which individuals' lives are truly engaged and which, though irreducible to the lives of its individual components, can be accomplished only through those individuals, their ability to fuel society through constant innervation, a process attested to by value judgments and the moral acts commanded by those judgments. Durkheim's moral sociology is a sociology of moral facts, facts intrinsically linked to other types of facts, judgments, and acts, facts in which social subjects are actively implicated. If his sociology appears externalist, that is because he undertook to redefine the subjective status of social subjects, inscribing a split within the subject that is not resolved by that subject's integrating of moral norms, a split according to which a kind of being-outside-self becomes the very wellspring of internal moral tension, determined by the ever continuous, ever timely coexistence of good and duty in the structuring contradiction of their coexistence. Living socially does of course mean submitting to an external order. But the externality of that order, all the difficulty it involves, is to be found first within the subject, as one of the subject's own dimensions. (34–35)

Demarcating the Sociology of Morality

For Durkheim the very enterprise of embarking on the sociology of morality required defending it against other claimants to the territory: in particular, the philosophers and the psychologists. Today, too, it is the philosophers and the psychologists who lay claim to the study of morality. What light do the old battles shed on the new?

The Philosophers

Philosophy was the hegemonic academic discipline in nineteenth-century France. And the terms *moral* and *les sciences morales* carried a distinctive set of connotations, sustaining "the lineage of classical moral philosophy" and embodied in the Academy of Moral and Political Sciences, whose objective was to replace the revolutionary social scientific tradition, from Condorcet on with "a liberal view aimed at ensuring the stability of France's institutions" (Heilbron 2015: 21), and so the "social sciences" developed outside the Academy and were ignored by the academicians. Thus, Durkheim faced a double challenge: wresting the academic study of morality from its time-honored guardians, the philosophers, and presenting it as a topic for social scientific research that would give guidance to institutionalizing progressive civic morals, in his capacity as Professor of Pedagogy, in the schools of the young Third Republic.

After his death, as Johan Heilbron has shown, the Durkheimians were split into two groups with very distinct orientations. On the one hand, there were the university professors (notably Célestin Bouglé, George Davy, and Paul Fauconnet), who produced little original research and were "organized around the philosophical thrust and the social implications of Durkheim's sociology" (Heilbron 2015: 103). On the other were the research scholars (notably Marcel Mauss, Maurice Halbwachs, and Marcel Granet) whose work continues to be read and who were skeptical of oversimplified philosophizing and moralistic prescriptions. (Indeed, Mauss, most engagingly, wrote that it was "not particularly useful to philosophize about general sociology when we have so much to know in order to understand what we know" [Mauss 1969: 303].) It is interesting, given this background, that Bouglé published in 1924 a well-known collection of the master's relevant texts entitled *Sociologie et philosophie*, translated into English in 1953 and many other languages, with the aim of showing "how and to what degree sociology renews philosophy" (Durkheim 1953: xxxv, translation modified). The book reprints Durkheim's 1906 and 1911 lectures, but, significantly, Bouglé edited the subsequent discussion of Durkheim's lecture on "The Determination of Moral Facts" at the Société française de philosophie in such a way as to create, in Heilbron's words, "an impression quite different from what actually occurred" (Heilbron 2015: 104). So what did occur?

In essence, Durkheim displayed to his philosopher colleagues the same attitude that he once expressed, though more sharply, to a poor doctoral candidate, quoting his teacher Fustel de Coulanges: "to philosophize is to think what one wants" (cited in Lukes 1972: 644). To one interlocutor he comments that in the moral realm as in others, the reason of the individual can claim "no special privileges": what counts is "human, impersonal reason, which is only realized truly in science." Thus, it is "the science of moral facts that puts us in a position to correct, rectify and direct the course of the moral life." Such intervention substitutes "for the collective ideal of today, not an individual ideal, but an ideal no less collective, and one expressing not a particular personality, but the collectivity better understood." What matters is the "attitude of mind in the face of the questions of which we speak." The attitude of the scholar requires "extracting oneself from one's personal impressions and submitting oneself to *l'école des choses*" (Bulletin 1906: 174–175). Philosophers, he tells another, never aim

> to translate faithfully, without adding or subtracting anything, a determinate moral reality. The philosophers' ambition has much rather been to construct a new morality, different, sometimes on essential points, to that followed by their contemporaries or forebears. [...] Now the problem I pose is to know in what morality consists or has consisted, not that which this or that philosophical personality conceives or has conceived, but rather that which has been lived by human collectivities. From this point of view, the doctrines of the philosophers lose much of their value. (196)

He was not, he added, excluding these from consideration: they "inform us of what is occurring within the moral consciousness of an epoch; one must therefore take them into account." But, he insisted, "I only deny them that sort of prerogative and primacy that is so often accorded them" and "what I refuse to admit is that they express in a pre-eminent way moral truth, as physics or chemistry express the truth concerning facts of a physico-chemical order." And as for philosophers' claims to engage in the enterprise of "justifying, demonstrating and giving reasons" and in these ways "give a conscious, more reflective account than ordinary people do, of moral life," his comment was scathing: "In this respect they have been, in part, the precursors of this science of moral facts that we are seeking to develop, as alchemists were precursors of chemistry" (196–197). There has always been

> a moral reality beyond the awareness of philosophers who seek to express it. This morality is practiced by everyone, without our caring, for the most part, what reasons philosophers give to justify it. Proof of this is the embarrassment we would most often feel if asked for a solid and rational justification for the moral rules we observe. (199)

(Here Durkheim foreshadows what Jonathan Haidt calls "moral dumbfounding" [Haidt 2001, 2012].) How, then, should this moral reality be investigated? What are the relevant data? First, Durkheim answers: the vast number of ideas and moral maxims, often "condensed in juridical formulae"—"in the law, in much of domestic morality, in contractual morality, in the morality of obligations, all the great, basic duties that are there translated and reflected." Here is a little-explored field for observation, but beyond it there are "proverbs, popular maxims and non-codified customs," and also "literary works" and indeed

> the conceptions of philosophers and moralists (you see that I do not exclude them) [which] inform us of the aspirations that are just in the process of forming, allowing us to go deeper into the analysis of the *conscience commune* and reach the sources where obscure, still imperfectly conscious currents are elaborated.
>
> (Bulletin 1906: 199)

There are doubtless very few, if indeed any, practitioners of the new sociology of morality who would endorse Durkheim's aggressively positivist (and polemically overstated) view of philosophy as premature science. Most contemporary social scientists are, in different ways and to different degrees, receptive to some philosophical contributions. In work on morality, for instance, they explicitly draw on it, especially, for instance, on "experimental philosophy" (see Appiah 2008) and on moral philosophy (Abend 2008, 2010); and anthropologists writing about ethics draw considerably on Alasdair MacIntyre, Bernard Williams, and Michel Foucault. There has, moreover, increasingly been some reciprocal interest by some philosophers in the sociological study of morality as experienced and practiced by "ordinary people." A few have even tried their hands at ethnography (Brandt 1954; Ladd 1957; Lear 2008). But, for the most part, Durkheim's charge that philosophers express the moral consciousness of their epoch while seeking the form and basis of the one true morality (a suggestion most eloquently made by Nietzsche) remains essentially true and has even been echoed by some philosophers, notably by MacIntyre, David Wong (2006), and most recently by Owen Flanagan in his remarkable book *The Geography of Morals*. Durkheim would surely have warmed to MacIntyre's recent critique of the overall state of twentieth-century moral philosophy as

> seriously defective as a form of rational inquiry. How so? First, the study of moral philosophy has become divorced from the study of morality or rather of moralities and by so doing has distanced itself from practice. We do not expect serious work in the philosophy of physics from students who have never studied physics or on the philosophy of law from students who have never studied law. But there is not even a hint of a suggestion that courses in social and cultural anthropology and in certain areas of sociology and psychology should be a prerequisite for graduate work in moral philosophy. Yet without such courses no adequate sense of the varieties of moral possibility can be acquired. One remains imprisoned by one's upbringing.
>
> (MacIntyre 2013: 31)

And he would have also endorsed Flanagan's elaboration of this critique, agreeing that philosophers "operate only or mainly with the resources of their own traditions, but claim to speak transcendentally," so that "Anglophone moral philosophy sings the praises of the moral attitudes of the dominant educated classes." What, Flanagan asks, "does ordinary moral discourse assume about the existence of moral facts or moral objectivity, where 'ordinary' means what is spoken in Bloomsbury or Oxbridge or Sydney by people like ourselves, well-heeled, white, mostly male, folk." The point is that the

> standard philosophical picture of moral interaction and exchange is historically and ecologically unrealistic because it is transcendentally pretentious, conceiving the philosopher's vocation as identifying what is really good or right independently of history or culture.
>
> (Flanagan 2017: 13, 7)

The Psychologists

It was of course Durkheim who wrote in *The Rules of Sociological Method* that "every time a social phenomenon is directly explained by a psychological phenomenon, we may rest assured that the explanation is false" and that sociology and psychology are "as sharply distinct as two sciences can be" (Durkheim [1895/1901] 2013: 86, 11). By "psychology" he had four distinct targets in mind: "the science of the individual mind" or *conscience* (10), with its own laws; explanations in terms of what he called "organico-psychic" factors, that is, presocial features of the individual organism given at birth and independent of social influences; explanations in terms of particular individual situations rather than general social conditions; and explanations in terms of individual motivations, mental states, or dispositions. But with respect to all these, the core idea is the same: facts about and features of individuals in all these senses *underdetermine outcomes*. They facilitate outcomes but are "simply the indeterminate matter which the social factor fashions and transforms" (87). Thus, innate capacities are "malleable predispositions which of themselves could not assume the definite and complex forms which characterize social phenomena" and a "purely psychological explanation of social facts cannot therefore fail to miss completely all that is specific, that is, social, about them." Typically, Durkheim argued, what blinkered sociologists who failed to see this was

> that, taking the effect for the cause, they have very often highlighted as causal conditions for social phenomena certain psychical states, relatively well defined and specific, but which in reality are the consequence of the phenomena. Thus it has been held that a certain religiosity is innate in man, as is a certain minimum of sexual jealousy, filial piety or fatherly affection, etc., and it is in these that explanations have been sought for religion, marriage and the family.

But, Durkheim reasoned, far from these inclinations being "inherent in human nature," "these sentiments result from the collective organization and are far from being at the basis of it" (88).

What I have called Durkheim's core idea here—that facts about individuals, and, in particular, innate capacities, underdetermine outcomes—remains an assumption that is basic to the sociological (including anthropological) enterprise. What, I suggest, Durkheim was reaching for in the argument sketched earlier is the idea of *affordances*: the idea, which itself comes from psychology, of objective, natural features or properties that in combination with others offer diverse *possibilities of action* (as "a chair invites us to sit down").[2] They only exist *as* affordances relative to the properties of some *other* perceiving and acting entity. In the present context we can think of what Webb Keane has called "ethical affordances," referring to cognitive, emotional, and social capacities that research has found, in children, come to fruition only when prompted through interactions with other people. Thus understood, Keane writes, the concept of affordances leaves things more open-ended than the concept of "pre-conditions," "without, however, turning the infant into a tabula rasa." In this way, "the idea of affordances does a better job of illuminating links between the particularities of social and historical circumstances and the universal capacities on which ethical responses draw than do the more traditional versions of cultural construction" (Keane 2016: 31). Moreover, as a result of research by psychologists, we now know, as Durkheim did not, something substantial about those capacities that have an ethical potential and are thus relevant to the sociology of morality. These Keane summarizes as including

> a strong orientation toward other persons for their own sake, an ability to displace one's attention and feelings away from the self, helping and cooperating behavior, gut feelings of disgust or attraction, the motivation to engage in activity without instrumental goals beyond the activity itself, the propensity to evaluate persons and acts on other-than-utilitarian grounds, conformism, and norm-seeking. (63)

How these are actualized varies widely in the form of "empathy, intention-seeking, sharing, helping, conformity, discrimination, norm-seeking, and norm-enforcing" (31).

How, then, should contemporary sociologists of morality view the psychologists of our time? In place of Durkheim's forthright and polemically fueled rejection, the suggestion by Hitlin and Vaisey of bridge building across disciplines with quite distinct research agendas is far more promising. Sociology is, it is true, a latecomer to the scientific study of morality. In the vanguard have been evolutionary psychologists, child psychologists, moral psychologists, cognitive scientists, and neuroscientists. They have made major advances in hitherto uncharted territory. But for the most part, their research questions have focused on what are assumed to be *universal* features of moral judgment and behavior, on *individuals*—for instance, on the functioning of their brains in the face of moral dilemmas and on the hypothesized influence of dual-process brain systems on their moral judgments. They have also adopted a *narrow view of what counts as moral* (Abend 2013) that focuses on discrete one-shot decisions that concern highly artificial moral dilemmas and situations (notably the inescapable "trolley problem") that are typically framed in terms of thin rather than thick concepts (Abend 2011), avoiding larger and deeper questions about the meanings to differently situated actors of moral judgments, norms, and behavior and indeed about their very conceptions of the boundaries and content of what is moral. We should, accordingly, follow the advice of Hitlin and Vaisey: engage with the theories and research results of the psychologists but ask distinctively sociological questions about morality in the broadest sense (going beyond altruism and pro-social behavior), questions about "sources and consequences of variation in conceptions of morality" and "what is good and worthy" and about "organizations, groups, nations, and institutions" (Hitlin and Vaisey 2013: 54). In this way we may, as Keane suggests, "open up a more productive relationship between disciplines that stress diversity and change on a historical scale, on the one hand, and those that stress universality and change on an evolutionary scale, on the other" (Keane 2016: 31).

INFLUENCES AND REACTIONS

Let us turn, finally, to consider the impact of Durkheim's legacy on current work by sociologists on morality. Such impact can be discerned in two main ways: as positive direct influence, whether acknowledged or not; and as a negative response to what are seen as limitations of vision and an unpromising methodology and research agendas.

Most explicitly and straightforwardly Durkheimian is the earlier work of Robert Bellah. In *Habits of the Heart* (Bellah et al. 1985) and its successor *The Good Society* (Bellah et al. 1991), he and his colleagues shared Durkheim's earliest and central preoccupation with "social solidarity," addressing failures of integration at every level within American society, eroded by "individualism" in its various forms, centered on the pursuit of self-interest, and by the decline of biblical traditions, republicanism, and earlier American ideals of citizenship. But Bellah's most Durkheimian contribution was his celebrated essay on "Civil Religion in America," which generated an intense debate that reached its peak in the mid-1970s. Starting from the Durkheimian notion that every group has a religious dimension expressed in "beliefs, symbols, and rituals with respect to sacred things and institutionalized in a collectivity" (Bellah 1967: 8), Bellah's essay traced the course of its sacred symbolism, stressing the ways in which it reproduced biblical archetypes. These are, Bellah wrote, "powerful symbols of national solidarity" that are able to "mobilize deep levels of personal motivation for the attainment of national goals" (13). While aware that it "has often been used [...] as a cloak for petty interests and ugly passions," he nonetheless viewed it as a "living faith" in need of "continual reformation, of being measured by universal standards" (18–19). Other work by sociologists focusing on solidarity and shared moral meanings includes Christian Smith's study (Smith 1998) of how embattled evangelicals in the United States achieved numerical growth and organizational vitality.

Another major contribution that draws on Durkheim's thinking is Hans Joas's work on the genesis of values and on the development of "the sacralization of the person." In the former he draws on Durkheim's notion of "collective effervescences"—"immense experiences of self-loss and of a force which causes the everyday to vanish" (Joas

2000: 59)—in order to develop an account of the mechanism that both creates and restabilizes what Charles Taylor has called "strong evaluations" (Taylor 1985), where "we sense that something lies beyond our mere desires and interests, something which we cannot identify until we reflect on the grounds of our moral feelings" (Joas 2000: 129). In the latter he uses Durkheim's ideas about a specifically modern form of sacralization as the "religion of individualism" (most clearly set out in Durkheim [1898] 1969 in response to the Dreyfus Affair) in order to explain the emergence of the idea of human rights, which involves showing how such sacralization gets to be translated into formal rules, so that viewing every human being as sacred has been institutionalized into law (Joas 2013).

Hitlin and Vaisey write that the focus these days on "shared moral meanings is, relatively speaking, a less flourishing area of sociological inquiry" (Hitlin and Vaisey 2013: 60). But one major area in which this is not true is the study of punishment, where Durkheim's striking and counterintuitive theory of crime and punishment, according to which punishment is addressed to the law-abiding with solidarity-enhancing effects (thus linking crime and social health) is, in David Garland's words, "so thoroughly taken-for-granted in the punishment and society literature that it is sometimes rendered in exaggerated versions" (Garland 2013: 24). This has generated much interesting research and discussions exploring the different effects on solidarity of different kinds of punishment, ritual and symbolic aspects of punishment, different forms of solidarity, and the relations between collective sentiments and state punishment.

There are other prominent areas of sociological research into moral matters which, though not explicitly Durkheimian in inspiration, can be viewed as exemplifying his vision of how morality works. One example is the work on symbolic and social boundaries, which establish systems of classification invoking judgments of worth relating, for instance, to professions, class, and gender (Lamont 1992, 2000) and "separate people into groups and generate feelings of similarity and group membership" (Lamont and Molnár 2002: 168). These are, in Durkheim's words quoted earlier, a "system of rules of action that predetermine conduct," which are "so many molds, with limiting boundaries, which shape our behavior." Michèle Lamont, in particular, while strongly influenced by Pierre Bourdieu, argues that he "tends to minimize the importance of moral boundaries" (Lamont 1992: 186), that he "defines moral behavior rather narrowly" (185) and "allows no autonomy to moral discourse," presuming that "people stress moral values *only* with the goal of improving their social position" (184). She sees her work as complementing "neo-Durkheimian work that tends to focus on the content of cultural codes themselves without relating them to the structure of social groups that produce them," citing Robert Wuthnow's *Meaning and Moral Order* (1987) and Mary Douglas (1966, 1970), whose work "links the degree of elaboration of symbolic systems to group structure and cohesiveness" (279). Another example is the work on what is held to be sacred in secular life and how this can change over time (as when life insurance changed the meaning of the value of a human life, and when the moral value of children rose as the economic value of their labor declined), and in the relations (hostile or mutually involved) between purely economic interest-driven interactions and what people view as sacred and intimate—themes in the earlier and later work of Viviana Zelizer (1979, 1994, 2005; also Quinn 2008).

This chapter began by citing the observation of Hitlin and Vaisey that the new sociology of morality "looks beyond just norms and values, casting a broader net that includes narratives, identities, institutions, symbolic boundaries, and cognitive schemas." We should note, as they do, that the very concept of "the new sociology of morality" is a construct that is somewhat arbitrary, embracing heterogeneous research questions, levels of analysis and methods, and, indeed, differing conceptions of what counts as "moral," but we should add that it remains, in a general sense, Durkheimian in *scope*, focusing on normative structures that are viewed from above, so to speak, and understood as shaping, more or less determinedly, the properties and dispositions of actors. It encompasses all of the following and more: studies of moral traditions as overarching worldviews that shape attitudes in a variety of contexts (Hunter 2000; Starks and Robinson 2005; Davis and Robinson 2006), the impact on moral attitudes of social class (Sayer 2005; Svallfors 2006) and of religious tradition (Smith and Denton 2005), distinct traditions in the teaching and promotion of business ethics (Abend 2014), the role of moral entrepreneurs in struggles within social fields, studies that investigate the institutional arrangements that facilitate and promote altruism, and studies of what has been called "a new economy of moral judgment," in the new world of megadata where people are sorted into "categories of taste, riskiness or worth" and "outcomes are experienced as morally deserved positions based on prior good actions and good tastes" (Fourcade and Healy 2017: 9).

We should, however, also note what the "new sociology of morality" *excludes*. Why should it not include the entire and growing corpus of work by sociologists and experimental philosophers, much of it inspired by rational choice theory and/or exchange theory, that builds upward from microfoundations with the aim of explaining macrooutcomes as emerging from micro-level patterns and processes, focusing on the properties and propensities of actors—their dispositions, experiences, expectations, judgments, beliefs, and behavior—and their interactions? What, in particular, about all the studies of trust, collective action, and the evolution of social norms (see, for example, Gambetta 1988; Yamagishi et al. 1998; Ostrom 2000; Bicchieri 2005, 2017; Fehr and Gintis 2007; Habyarimana et al. 2007; Cook et al. 2009; Henrich et al. 2010; Yamagishi 2011; Brennan et al. 2013), some of which make use of experiments derived from game theory in natural settings to study reciprocity, group attachment, altruism, fairness, and punishment (see, for example, Baldassarri and Grossman 2012, 2013; Baldassarri 2015). The *object* of much of this work is, after all, thoroughly Durkheimian, namely, social solidarity, in its different aspects. It can be read as exploring what Durkheim understood as the noncontractual element in the contract, opening up the possibility of investigating the very mechanisms of solidarity within and across groups and whether mechanical or organic. Yet this literature is entirely distinct and distant from Durkheim and his legacy, since it focuses—as does the whole tradition of so-called analytical sociology—on interaction, including interdependencies and expectations, which Durkheim, preoccupied with rejecting the psychology of his time, never addressed.

Durkheim's concept of morality invoked a commonly assumed but questionable contrast between *morality* and *interests*. Morality, he wrote, "begins where disinterestedness and devotion begin" (Durkheim [1924] 1953: 52, translation modified), whereas "where interest alone reigns, as nothing arises to check the egoisms confronting one another, each self finds itself in relation to the other on a war footing" and "self-interest [...] can give rise only to transitory links and associations of a fleeting kind" (Durkheim [1893] 2014: 160–161). But the best of the literature referred to in the previous paragraph puts this framing of the issues into question by showing, through both analytical reasoning and experimental empirical research, the unrealism of this conception of individual motivation as exclusively self-regarding, and hence the inadequacy of this conception of interests. Thus, Ernst Fehr and Herbert Gintis argue that self-regarding and norm-regarding actors coexist and that the available action opportunities will determine which of these actor types dominates the aggregate level of social cooperation (Fehr and Gintis 2007). Lamont, as we have seen, criticizes Bourdieu for arguing that "all apparently disinterested acts, including the consumption of culture and the display of moral character traits, are in reality 'interested' because they are ultimately oriented toward the maximization of one's social position" (Lamont 1992: 184). And in a quite different tradition, Axel Honneth has argued (Fraser and Honneth 2003; Honneth 2014) that even the pursuit and defense of material self-interest is not independent of morality because it contains a normative core involving claims to social recognition.

What these last observations suggest is that the sociological study of morality is most likely to prosper by extending its scope, thereby overcoming exclusiveness on both sides of a gap we don't need: the Durkheimian exclusion of individualistic explanation and the corresponding exclusiveness of many of the latter's proponents.[3] This will require investigating "how interests are constructed in complex macro- and meso-social processes" (Spillman and Strand 2013: 98; see Swedberg 2005; Barbalet 2012) and ceasing to view the study of normative structures and that of interaction among individuals as distinct and unrelated traditions of inquiry.

NOTES

1. Unless otherwise indicated, translations are by the author.
2. The idea originated in the psychology of perception and has influenced developments in studies of situated cognition and in cultural psychology. It was defined by James J. Gibson as follows: "the affordance of anything is a specific combination of the properties of its substance and its surfaces" in the light of what it offers, provides, or furnishes for the animal that perceives it. Thus if "an object that rests on the ground has a surface that is itself sufficiently rigid, level, flat, and extended, and if this surface is raised approximately at the height of the knees of the human biped, then it affords sitting-on [...]. [But] knee-high for a child is not the same as knee-high for an adult" (Gibson 1977: 67–68). Keane, who cites this definition, comments that affordances are "objective features in contingent combinations" which

"only exist as affordances relative to the properties of some *other* perceiving and acting entity" (Keane 2016: 28).
3. Boltanski and Thévenot were making this very point when they noted a "reductive operation" practiced by "seemingly contrasting explanatory methodologies—one based on 'individual' behavior and one based on 'collective' behavior." On the one hand, there are economists studying "individuals who enter into relationships in a marketplace" and "question the reality of collective phenomena, which they view as human constructs": on the other are sociologists (they refer specifically to Durkheim's sociology) for whom collectivities constitute a "object that is as real as a specific person, and even more 'objective.' " The former fail to see individuals as "moral beings capable of distancing themselves from their own particularity and coming to terms over commonly identified goods on which their acquisitive desires have converged and reached agreement"; the latter achieve "reduction through the internalization of collective reality, a process that takes on the aspect of an unconscious" (Boltanski and Thévenot 2006: 27–30).

References

Abend, Gabriel. 2008. "Two Main Problems in the Sociology of Morality." *Theory and Society* 37 (2): 87–125.
Abend, Gabriel. 2010. "What's New and What's Old about the New Sociology of Morality." In *Handbook of the Sociology of Morality*, edited by Steven Hitlin and Stephen Vaisey, 561–584. New York: Springer.
Abend, Gabriel. 2011. "Thick Concepts and the Moral Brain." *European Journal of Sociology* 52 (1): 143–172.
Abend, Gabriel. 2013. "What the Science of Morality Doesn't Say about Morality." *Philosophy of the Social Sciences* 43 (2): 157–200.
Abend, Gabriel. 2014. *The Moral Background: An Inquiry into the History of Business Ethics*. Princeton, NJ: Princeton University Press.
Appiah, Kwame Anthony. 2008. *Experiments in Ethics*. Cambridge, MA: Harvard University Press.
Baldassarri, Delia. 2015. "Cooperative Networks: Altruism, Group Solidarity, Reciprocity, and Sanctioning in Ugandan Producer Organizations." *American Journal of Sociology* 121 (2): 355–395.
Baldassarri, Delia, and Guy Grossman. 2012. "The Impact of Elections on Cooperation: Evidence from a Lab-in-the-Field Experiment in Uganda." *American Journal of Political Science* 56 (4): 964–985.
Baldassarri, Delia, and Guy Grossman. 2013. "The Effect of Group Attachment and Social Position on Prosocial Behavior: Evidence from Lab-in-the-Field Experiments." *PLOS ONE* 8 (3).
Barbalet, Jack. 2012. "Self-Interest and the Theory of Action." *British Journal of Sociology* 63 (3): 412–429.
Bellah, Robert N. 1967. "Civil Religion in America." *Daedalus* 96 (1): 1–21.
Bellah, Robert N., Richard Madsen, William M. Sullivan, Ann Swidler, and Steven M. Tipton. 1985. *Habits of the Heart: Individualism and Commitment in American Life*. Berkeley: University of California Press.

Bellah, Robert N., Richard Madsen, William M. Sullivan, Ann Swidler, and Steven M. Tipton. 1991. *The Good Society*. New York: Knopf.

Bicchieri, Cristina. 2005. *The Grammar of Society: The Nature and Dynamics of Social Norms*. Cambridge: Cambridge University Press.

Bicchieri, Cristina. 2017. *Norms in the Wild: How to Diagnose, Measure, and Change Social Norms*. New York: Oxford University Press.

Boltanski, Luc, and Laurent Thévenot. (1991) 2006. *On Justification: Economies of Worth*. Princeton, NJ: Princeton University Press.

Brandt, Richard B. 1954. *Hopi Ethics: A Theoretical Analysis*. Chicago: University of Chicago Press.

Brennan, Geoffrey, Lina Eriksson, Robert E. Goodin, and Nicholas Southwood. 2013. *Explaining Norms*. Oxford: Oxford University Press.

Bulletin de la Société française de philosophie. 1906. Vol. 6 (4): Séances des 11 février et 22 mars 1906: 169–212.

Cook, Karen S., Margaret Levi, and Russell Hardin, eds. 2009. *Whom Can We Trust? How Groups, Networks, and Institutions Make Trust Possible*. New York: SAGE.

Davis, Nancy J., and Robert V. Robinson. 2006. "The Egalitarian Face of Islamic Orthodoxy: Support for Islamic Law and Economic Justice in Seven Muslim-Majority Nations." *American Sociological Review* 71 (2): 167–190.

Davy, Georges. 1920. "Durkheim: II — L'œuvre." *Revue de métaphysique et de morale* 27 (1): 71–112.

De Waal, Frans. 2006. *Primates and Philosophers: How Morality Evolved*. Princeton, NJ: Princeton University Press.

Douglas, Mary. 1966. *Purity and Danger: An Analysis of Concepts of Pollution and Taboo*. New York: Praeger.

Douglas, Mary. 1970. *Natural Symbols: Explorations in Cosmology*. London: Barrie and Rockliff.

Durkheim, Émile. (1924) 1953. *Sociology and Philosophy*. Edited and translated by D. F. Pocock. London: Cohen.

Durkheim, Émile. (1925) 1961. *Moral Education: A Study in the Theory and Application of the Sociology of Education*. Translated by E. K. Wilson and H. Schnurer. New York: Free Press.

Durkheim, Émile. (1898) 1969. "Individualism and the Intellectuals." Translated by S. and J. Lukes. *Political Studies* 17 (1): 14–30.

Durkheim, Émile. (1917) 1975. *Introduction à la morale*. In Émile Durkheim, *Textes*, vol. 2: *Religion, morale, anomie*, edited by Victor Karady, 313–331. Paris: Les Editions de Minuit.

Durkheim, Émile. (1895/1901) 2013. *The Rules of Sociological Method and Selected Texts on Sociology and Its Method*. Edited by Steven Lukes and translated by W. D. Halls. New York: Free Press.

Durkheim, Émile. (1893) 2014. *The Division of Labor in Society*. Edited by Steven Lukes and translated by W. D. Halls. New York: Free Press.

Fassin, Didier, ed. 2012. *A Companion to Moral Anthropology*. Chichester, UK: Wiley-Blackwell.

Fassin, Didier, and Samuel Lézé, eds. 2014. *Moral Anthropology: A Critical Reader*. London: Routledge.

Fehr, Ernst, and Herbert Gintis. 2007. "Human Motivation and Social Cooperation: Experimental and Analytical Foundations." *Annual Review of Sociology* 33: 43–64.

Flanagan, Owen. 2017. *The Geography of Morals: Varieties of Moral Possibility*. New York: Oxford University Press.

Fourcade, Marion, and Kieran Healy. 2017. "Seeing Like a Market." *Socio-Economic Review* 15 (1): 9–29.
Fraser, Nancy, and Axel Honneth. 2003. *Redistribution or Recognition: A Political-Philosophical Exchange*. London: Verso.
Gambetta, Diego. 1988. "Can We Trust Trust." In *Trust: Making and Breaking Cooperative Relations*, edited by Diego Gambetta, 213–237. Oxford: Blackwell.
Garland, David. 2013. "Punishment and Social Solidarity." In *The SAGE Handbook of Punishment and Society*, edited by Jonathan Simon and Richard Sparks, 23–39. New York: SAGE.
Gibson, James J. 1977. "The Theory of Affordances." In *Perceiving, Acting and Knowing: Toward an Ecological Psychology*, edited by Robert Shaw and John Bransford, 67–82. Hillsdale, NJ: Lawrence Erlbaum.
Habyarimana, James, Macartan Humphreys, Daniel N. Posner, and Jeremy M. Weinstein. 2007. "Why Does Ethnic Diversity Undermine Public Goods Provision?" *American Political Science Review* 101 (4): 709–725.
Haidt, Jonathan. 2001. "The Emotional Dog and Its Rational Tail: A Social Intuitionist Approach to Moral Judgment." *Psychological Review* 108: 814–834.
Haidt, Jonathan. 2012. *The Righteous Mind: Why Good People Are Divided by Politics and Religion*. New York: Pantheon.
Heilbron, Johan. 2015. *French Sociology*. Ithaca, NY: Cornell University Press.
Henrich, Joseph, Jean Ensminger, Richard McElreath, Abigail Barr, Clark Barrett, Alexander Bolyanatz, Juan Camilo Cardenas . . . John Ziker. 2010. "Markets, Religion, Community Size, and the Evolution of Fairness and Punishment." *Science* 327 (5972): 1480–1484.
Hitlin, Steven, and Stephen Vaisey. 2013. "The New Sociology of Morality." *Annual Review of Sociology* 39: 51–68.
Honneth, Axel. (2011) 2014. *Freedom's Right: The Social Foundations of Democratic Life*. New York: Columbia University Press.
Hunter, James D. 2000. *The Death of Character: Moral Education in an Age without Good or Evil*. New York: Basic Books.
Isambert, François-André. 1992. "Les avatars du 'fait moral.'" In François-André Isambert, *De la religion à l'éthique*, 358–393. Paris: Les Editions du Cerf.
Joas, Hans. (1997) 2000. *The Genesis of Values*. Chicago: University of Chicago Press.
Joas, Hans. (2011) 2013. *The Sacredness of the Person: A New Genealogy of Human Rights*. Washington, DC: Georgetown University Press.
Kahneman, Daniel. 2011. *Thinking, Fast and Slow*. New York: Farrar, Straus and Giroux.
Karsenti, Bruno. (2006) 2012. "Durkheim and the Moral Fact." In *A Companion to Moral Anthropology*, edited by Didier Fassin, 21–36. Chichester, UK: Wiley-Blackwell. (English translation of "Le 'dilemme durkheimien' en sociologie morale," in Bruno Karsenti, *La société en personnes. Études durkheimiennes*, 69–91. Paris: Economica.)
Keane, Webb. 2016. *Ethical Life: Its Natural and Social Histories*. Princeton, NJ: Princeton University Press.
Ladd, John. 1957. *The Structure of a Moral Code: A Philosophical Analysis of Ethical Discourse Applied to the Navaho Indians*. Cambridge, MA: Harvard University Press.
Laidlaw, James. 2002. "For an Anthropology of Ethics and Freedom." *Journal of the Royal Anthropological Institute* 8 (2): 311–332.
Laidlaw, James. 2014. *The Subject of Virtue: An Anthropology of Ethics and Freedom*. Cambridge: Cambridge University Press.

Lambek, Michael, ed. 2010. *Ordinary Ethics: Anthropology, Language, and Action.* New York: Fordham University Press.

Lamont, Michèle. 1992. *Money, Morals, and Manners: The Culture of the French and American Upper-Middle Class.* Chicago: University of Chicago Press.

Lamont, Michèle. 2000. *The Dignity of Working Men: Morality and the Boundaries of Race, Class, and Immigration.* Cambridge, MA: Harvard University Press.

Lamont, Michèle, and Virág Molnár. 2002. "The Study of Boundaries in the Social Sciences." *Annual Review of Sociology* 28: 167–195.

Lear, Jonathan. 2008. *Radical Hope: Ethics in the Face of Cultural Devastation.* Cambridge, MA: Harvard University Press.

Lukes, Steven. 1972. *Emile Durkheim: His Life and Work.* London: Allen Lane.

MacIntyre, Alasdair. 2013. "On Having Survived the Academic Moral Philosophy of the Twentieth Century." In *What Happened in and to Moral Philosophy in the Twentieth Century? Philosophical Essays in Honor of Alasdair MacIntyre*, edited by Fran O'Rourke, 17–34. Notre Dame: University of Notre Dame Press.

Mauss, Marcel. (1934) 1969. "Fragment d'un plan de sociologie générale descriptive." In *Marcel Mauss, Œuvres*, vol. 3: *Cohésion sociale et divisions de la sociologie*, edited by Victor Karady, 303–354. Paris: Les Editions de Minuit.

Ostrom, Elinor. 2000. "Collective Action and the Evolution of Social Norms." *Journal of Economic Perspectives* 14 (3): 137–158.

Parsons, Talcott, and Edward A. Shils, eds. 1951. *Toward a General Theory of Action.* Cambridge, MA: Harvard University Press.

Quinn, Sarah. 2008. "The Transformation of Morals in Markets: Death, Benefits, and the Exchange of Life Insurance Policies." *American Journal of Sociology* 114 (3): 738–780.

Sayer, Andrew. 2005. *The Moral Significance of Class.* Cambridge: Cambridge University Press.

Smith, Christian. 1998. *American Evangelicalism: Embattled and Thriving.* Chicago: University of Chicago Press.

Smith, Christian, and Melinda Lundquist Denton. 2005. *Soul Searching: The Religious and Spiritual Lives of American Teenagers.* New York: Oxford University Press.

Spillman, Lyn, and Michael Strand. 2013. "Interest-Oriented Action." *Annual Review of Sociology* 39: 85–104.

Starks, Brian, and Robert V. Robinson. 2005. "Who Values the Obedient Child Now? The Religious Factor in Adult Values for Children, 1986–2002." *Social Forces* 84 (1): 343–359.

Svallfors, Stefan. 2006. *The Moral Economy of Class: Class and Attitudes in Comparative Perspective.* Stanford, CA: Stanford University Press.

Swedberg, Richard. 2005. *Interest.* Maidenhead, UK: Open University Press.

Taylor, Charles. 1985. "What Is Human Agency?" In Charles Taylor, *Philosophical Papers*, vol. 1, 15–44. Cambridge: Cambridge University Press.

Turiel, Elliot. 2002. *The Culture of Morality: Social Development, Context, and Conflict.* Cambridge: Cambridge University Press.

Wong, David B. 2006. *Natural Moralities: A Defense of Pluralistic Relativism.* Oxford: Oxford University Press.

Wuthnow, Robert. 1987. *Meaning and Moral Order: Explorations in Cultural Analysis.* Berkeley: University of California Press.

Yamagishi, Toshio. 2011. *Trust: The Evolutionary Game of Mind and Society.* Tokyo: Springer.

Yamagishi, Toshio, Karen S. Cook, and Motoki Watabe. 1998. "Uncertainty, Trust, and Commitment Formation in the United States and Japan." *American Journal of Sociology* 104 (1): 165–194.

Zelizer, Viviana A. 1979. *Morals and Markets: The Development of Life Insurance in the United States*. New York: Columbia University Press.

Zelizer, Viviana A. 1994. *Pricing the Priceless Child: The Changing Social Value of Children*. Princeton, NJ: Princeton University Press.

Zelizer, Viviana A. 2005. *The Purchase of Intimacy*. Princeton, NJ: Princeton University Press.

Index

9/11 terrorist attacks, 249, 296n14

abolitionism, 399n27
Aboriginal Australians, 58–59
    Durkheim on, 68
    religions of, 294
    rituals of, 150
    social change among, 77n30
    totemism among, 268 (*see also* totemism)
    views of animals, 60–61
Académie française, 118, 189
Academy of Moral and Political Sciences, 446
Acéphale (secret society), 384, 399n24
Action française, 118, 137–138
activism. *See also* social movements
    for animal rights, 303–304 (*see also* animal rights)
    society and, 308
actor-network theory, 374–375
    animals and, 316
Adorno, Theodor W., 7
aesthetics, 8, 287
agency, 375
Alcan (publisher), 145, 150
Alexander, Jeffrey, 9, 273, 304, 308
Alsace, 117, 124
Ammon, Otto, 145
Andersen, Bjørn Schiermer, 15
animal rights
    activism for, 303–304
    in law, 328
    sacredness and, 304, 310
        (*see also* sacred, the)
animals
    Aboriginal views of, 60–61
    anthropism and, 326
    behavior of, 424
    classification among, 78n40

Durkheim on, 14, 320–324, 329n3, 330n8
    exclusion of, 327
    humans and, 310, 322–323, 327–329, 427–428
    in indigenous religions, 112, 235
    individual sacredness of, 310
        (*see also* sacred, the)
    learning in, 73
    legal status of, 328
    morality in, 444 (*see also* morality)
    in philosophy, 200 (*see also* philosophy)
    ritual behavior of, 428
    ritual sacrifice of, 115n1
    sacredness of, 321, 324 (*see also* sacred, the)
    sociology and, 316
    totemism and, 172, 316–318, 320–326, 407
Annales sociologiques, 151–152, 238, 272
Année sociologique, L' (journal), 12, 117, 134
    on the arts, 284–285, 287, 293
    Bergson and, 166
    contributors to, 149
    economics and, 229, 236
    on family, 351
    founding of, 145–146, 195
    historiography of, 265
    history and, 283
    influence of, 154
    Mauss and, 238
    publication of, 221
    publications in, 146–148
    reviews in, 196
    revival of, 151–152
    social morphology and, 334
    sociology of religion and, 264
    switch to book format, 150
anomie, 218, 289–290, 294, 302, 385, 430
    cities and, 339
    economic, 237
    social, 116, 126

Anscombe, Elizabeth, 91
anthropistic societies, 326–329
Anthropocene, 346
anthropocentrism
    anthropism and, 326
    of sociology, 175, 316
    totemism and, 324–325
anthropogeography, 334, 347n8
anthropology
    Bergsonianism and, 174, 176
    classification and, 65
    colonialism and, 155
    Durkheimian sociology and, 152
    in France, 404, 417
    goals of, 415
    historiography of, 417
    history of, 3
    Lévi-Strauss on, 412
    morality and, 439–440
    nonhumans and, 329n3
    philosophical, 34
    race and, 145
    of religion, 272
    of rituals, 10, 112
    of ritual sacrifice, 115n1
    structural, 64, 408–410
    views of Durkheim in, 7–8, 10
    views of totems, 104
anthroposociology, 145
anti-intellectualism, 191
antinomy, 41, 102, 139, 216–217, 290, 404–408, 412
Anti-Semitic Leagues, 118, 120
anti-Semitism
    Dreyfus Affair and, 117–122, 221
    Durkheim and, 12, 17n7, 118–120, 123–127, 248–249, 253, 257, 260, 265
"Anti-Semitism and Social Crisis" (Durkheim), 260
appropriation, of Durkheim's work, 7, 9
architecture, 336
Arendt, Hannah, 256
Ariès, Philippe, 352, 360n5
art
    Durkheim on, 14, 35, 285–289, 291–295
    in France, 284

science and, 26–27, 34–35, 288
society and, 291
sociology and, 283, 288–289, 294
Arunta people, 3, 58, 61, 103, 150, 284
    religious art of, 291
    rituals of, 108
asylums, 435
atheism, 250, 269
attachment, 31, 54, 55n7, 55n8
Aubin, Abel, 148, 156n4
Auden, W. H., 245, 259
Augustine of Hippo, 441
Australia, 3, 58, 77n30, 222–223
    ethnography in, 103, 105, 151
    indigenous religions of, 223–224, 320–321, 376
    religious art in, 291
Austria, 399n14
authoritarianism, 221, 225, 397
authority, of social rules, 86
autoethnography, 385, 398n6, 398n12, 399n15
Axial Age, 69–71, 77n31, 77n34, 274–277

Bangladesh, 248
Basic Law (West Germany), 397
Bataille, Georges, 129, 152, 154, 272, 295n9, 392, 398n3
    on authoritarianism, 395, 397
    on the sacred, 382, 386–390
bears, 329n4
Beckert, Jens, 240–241
Becquerel, Henri, 283
Begum, Shamima, 248, 258, 260n3
Bellah, Robert, 60, 64, 76n29
    on the Axial Age, 77n31
    on civil religion, 276, 277n3
    Durkheim and, 72–73, 76n28, 451
    on play, 71
    on religion, 68–70, 77n35, 274
    on ritual, 75n10
    on social evolution, 77n33
Benoist, Alain de, 416
Béra, Matthieu, 216
Berg, Alban, 284
Berger, Peter, 354

Bergson, Henri, 75n13, 130, 192n12, 393, 399n22
　critiques of, 167–169
　Durkheim and, 12, 164–173, 177, 182
　influence of, 175–177
　philosophy of, 170–171
　on pragmatism, 189–190, 192n8 (*see also* pragmatism)
　on religion, 139
　scholarship on, 165–166
　social theory, 172–175, 177
Bergsonism, 164–167, 172–177, 188
Berthelot, René, 187
Beuchat, Henri, 148, 156n4, 391
Bianconi, Antoine, 150, 156n4
biosphere, 346
Birnbaum, Pierre, 12
birth rates, 352
Blumer, Herbert, 379n2, 428
Bluntschli, Kaspar, 340
Bolivia, 328
Bologna, 187–188
Boltanski, Luc, 58, 64, 66–67, 72, 455n3
Bonald Law, 355
Bordeaux
　anti-Semitism in, 121
　Durkheim in, 11, 118–119, 350
Bordeaux, University of
　Durkheim's dissertation at, 39–41
　Durkheim's teaching at, 15, 50, 130, 229
　Durkheim's work at, 14, 116, 200, 214, 283, 285–286
　Gaston Richard at, 146, 151
Bororo people, 64, 76n22
Bouglé, Célestin, 49, 120, 137, 275
　L'Année sociologique and, 145–146, 148–149, 156n4, 208n17
　on Bergson, 167
　Durkheim and, 150–151, 236
　German sociology and, 202–204
　philosophy and, 130, 446
Bourdeau, Jean, 187
Bourdieu, Pierre, 8–9, 16n2, 17n16, 17n17
　on art, 283
　combat epistemology, 142
　critiques of, 67, 454
　on Durkheim, 72, 138, 155

Durkheimian sociology and, 64
on economics, 240
on family, 359
Goffman and, 424
influence of, 452
on Lévi-Strauss, 421
on marriage, 353
on morality, 444
on rationalism, 420
social theory, 346
structuralism and, 65–66
Bourgeois, Léon, 48–49
Bourgin, Gérard, 146, 148, 156n4
Bourgin, Hubert, 146, 148–149, 156n4
Boutroux, Émile, 132–133, 187, 200, 207, 218
Breen-Smyth, Marie, 249
British Centre for Durkheimian Studies, 153
Bronze Age, 70
Brunetière, Ferdinand, 121–122, 221
Brunschvicg, Léon, 139, 187, 189
Buchenwald (concentration camp), 152
Bücher, Karl, 45, 228
Buddha, 69
Buddhism, 266, 274
Buechler, Steven M., 299, 302
Buisson, Ferdinand, 132, 266, 269, 286
Butler, Judith, 6

Caillé, Alain, 241
Caillois, Roger, 152, 154, 272, 382, 384, 386–393, 397, 399n20
Callède, Jean-Paul, 287
Callegaro, Francesco, 11
Cambridge University, 151, 364, 378n1, 378n2
Canguilhem, Georges, 12, 113, 164, 170, 174, 177
capitalism, 45, 176, 241
Carls, Paul, 12, 156n12
Cartesianism, 165, 169–170, 174, 183, 374
Castoriadis, Cornelius, 12, 164, 172–173, 175–176
Catholicism. *See also* Christianity
　Durkheim and, 116, 250
　in France, 32
　French laws and, 271
　in French politics, 120, 122, 125–126, 265
　philosophy and, 139, 142n3
　sociology and, 137

Causes of Suicide, The (Halbwachs), 151
Cézanne, Paul, 284
Chagall, Marc, 284
Chantepie de la Saussaye, Pierre Daniel, 147
Chewong people, 321–322
Chicago School of sociology, 16n5, 154, 424–425
Chicago, University of, 154
childcare, evolution and, 69
children
    education of, 354
    role of, 352
    views of morality, 444
chimpanzees, 78n40
China
    divination in, 58, 60
    kinship in, 272, 410
    religion in, 275–276
    rituals in, 430
Christianity. *See also* Catholicism; Protestantism
    Durkheim on, 209n28, 270
    Judaism and, 117–118, 127
    morality and, 28, 386
    views of humans, 326
churinga, 103, 105, 108, 235
Cintron, Josefina, 14
Cité moderne, La (Izoulet), 47–48
cities, 339, 425
citizenship, 54
    individualism and, 260
    in the United Kingdom, 246–248, 251, 253–255, 257–259
civic morality, 54. *See also* morality
civil disobedience, 254, 303
civil religion, 276, 277n3
"Civil Religion in America" (Bellah), 451
civil society, in the United States, 9
Cladis, Mark S., 11, 156n12
clan societies, 338–339
class, 8, 105, 249
class conflict, 218
classification
    in Aboriginal societies, 60
    Bourdieu on, 66
    by chimpanzees, 78n40
    pragmatic theory of, 67

sociology of, 64–65
systems of, 58–59
taxonomic, 74n6
Clastres, Pierre, 164, 174, 176
Code civil (France), 232
collective
    definition of, 11, 86–89
    individual and, 92, 97
    morality and, 93
collective action, 302, 305–306
collective conscience, 122, 127, 307
collective consciousness, 41–42, 98
    criticism of, 82–83
    definition of, 83–84, 89, 94
    Durkheim and, 82–84, 88–90, 98–99
    solidarity and, 215
    totems and, 104
collective effervescence, 61–62, 234, 268, 284, 289, 294. *See also* effervescence
    Joas on, 71, 277, 451–452
    Lévi-Strauss on, 406
    Mauss and, 393
    religion and, 291, 387
    the sacred and, 273, 277, 291, 388, 398n7, 398n10
    social movements and, 299–300, 302–304, 306
collectivism, 49, 368–369
Collège de France, 48, 149, 288
    Bergson at, 167, 189
    Durkheim and, 204
    Durkheimians at, 151–152
Collège de Sociologie, 15, 272, 398n1, 398n12
    Durkheimian sociology and, 382–384, 388, 398n12
    founding of, 382
    history of, 383–384
    Mauss and, 382, 384, 390–392, 398n12
    politics of, 385, 392–393
    on the sacred, 388–389, 393, 398n7, 399n23
Collins, Randall, 9–10, 273, 305, 307
colonialism, 28, 155, 275
Combes, Émile, 192n7, 265, 270
communism, 238
Comte, Auguste, 33, 113, 131, 135–136, 201–203
    Durkheim and, 229
    on labor, 228, 230

positivism and, 284
on religion, 271
"Concerning the Definition of Religious Phenomena" (Durkheim), 147, 317, 324
Condorcet, Marquis de, 201, 203, 446
conformity, 368, 377, 439, 444
Confucius, 69
conjugal family, 352, 355–356, 358, 360n4
"Conjugal Family, The" (Durkheim lecture), 357
consciousness, 11, 91–95. *See also* collective consciousness
conservatism
  collective consciousness and, 82
  Durkheim and, 4, 23, 28, 32, 265, 306
  Durkheimian sociology and, 152
  philosophy and, 137–138
  sociology and, 137
  Tarde and, 366
constructivism, 377
consubstantiability, 319–320, 325
contracts, 232
Contre-Attaque (political group), 384
cooperation, as ritual, 9
Corroborree (Aboriginal gathering), 268
Cosmides, Leda, 73
cosmopolitanism, 343
Cotterrell, Roger, 154, 245–246, 250, 252, 258
Couat, Auguste, 121
Cousin, Victor, 131, 133, 142n1
Couturat, Louis, 187
coyotes, 329n4
Creative Evolution (Bergson), 171, 188
crime, 254–255
Cristi, Marcela, 37n1
critical legal studies, 154
critical theory, 376
Croatia, 399n14
Crossley, Nick, 299, 302–303
crowd, sociology of, 88–89, 366, 369–370, 379n6
Crusades, 62, 398n11
Cubism, 284
culture wars, 225
Curie, Marie, 283
Curie, Pierre, 283
"Current State of Sociological Studies in France, The" (Durkheim), 202
Cuvillier, Armand, 183, 191, 192n1

Darlu, Alphonse, 138–139
Darwin, Charles, 200, 329, 330n5
David, Maxime, 148, 150, 156n4
Davy, Georges, 137, 147–148, 150, 156n4, 186, 446
  Durkheim and, 141, 250, 438, 442
de Biran, Maine, 135
de Bonald, Louis, 17n6, 355
Debussy, Claude, 284
de Castro, Viveiros, 178n8
Declaration of the Rights of Man, 122–123
deductive approach, 27
"Defender of Children, The" (French agency), 360, 361n15
Défenseur des droits (France), 361n15
De Gaudemar, Paul, 193n13
Delacroix, Henri, 139
Deleuze, Gilles, 12, 164, 170–171, 173–175, 177n1, 325
Delitz, Heike, 12
democracy, 31–32, 36–37, 255, 259, 397
Department of Primary Education (France), 151
Deploige, Simon, 196, 205, 207, 208n20, 209n22, 209n25
Derrida, Jacques, 392
Descola, Phillippe, 77n36
Descombes, Vincent, 191, 414–416
De Singly, François, 15
desirability, moral facts and, 30–31
Des sociétés animales (Espinas), 200
"Determination of Moral Facts, The" (Durkheim), 29, 31–32, 442, 446
Deux vies, Les (Margueritte), 355–356
Dewey, John, 95–96, 182, 186, 190, 192n3, 193n14, 394, 427
Diaghilev, Sergei, 284
discipline, moral facts and, 31
discrimination, solidarity and, 43
distributive justice, 220
diversity, protection of, 36
divination, 58, 60
Division of Labour in Society, The (Durkheim), 2, 34, 39–44, 95, 130, 228, 230, 242
  on *anomie*, 289
  on art, 285, 287–288

Division of Labour in Society, The
(Durkheim) (*cont.*)
  on association, 55n4
  on attachment to groups, 54
  collective and, 98
  collective consciousness and, 83
  economics and, 242
  on gender, 353–354
  German scholarship and, 202
  Goffman and, 434
  impact of, 47–48
  on the individual, 13, 213–220, 224
  on individualism, 219
  on law, 245, 253, 256
  on modernity, 224–225, 337
  on philosophy, 131
  publication of, 116
  on religion, 270
  second edition of, 47, 51–52
  on social facts, 133
  on society, 120
  on solidarity, 217–218, 251–252
  Tarde on, 132, 365
divorce, 351, 355–356, 361n14
Donald, Merlin, 70, 76n29, 274
Douglas, Mary, 75n18, 317, 452
drag, 6
Dreyfus Affair
  beginning of, 116
  Durkheim and, 17n7, 117–119, 121–127, 196, 221, 266, 286, 441
  French-German academic ties and, 205
  French politics and, 192n7, 207, 225
  individualism and, 31–32, 271
  influence on Durkheim, 12, 17n7, 250, 253, 452
  morality and, 386
  sociologists and, 149
Dreyfus, Alfred, 32, 121–122, 126, 441
  arrest of, 116
  background of, 117
  Durkheim and, 118–122, 149, 207
  trial of, 119, 124–125, 250
Dreyfusards, 123, 221, 366
Dreyfus, Louise Julie, 288, 350, 353, 357, 360n7
Drumont, Edouard, 117, 122
Duclaux, Émile, 118–119

Dumont, Louis, 422n4
Durkheim, André, 151, 350–352, 356–359
Durkheim, Émile
  on Aboriginal societies, 58–61, 68–69, 77n30
  on animals, 14, 320–324, 329n3, 330n8
  L'Année sociologique and, 145–146, 148–150
  on *anomie*, 289–290
  anthropocentrism and, 316
  anti-Semitism and, 12, 17n7, 118–120, 123–127, 248–249, 253, 257, 260, 265
  on art, 14, 35, 285–289, 291–295
  on association, 55n4
  Benoist and, 416
  Bergson and, 12, 164–173, 177, 182
  on the Bororo, 75n15
  Bourdieu and, 66, 72, 138, 155
  on Christianity, 209n28, 270
  on classification, 62–64, 74n6
  collective consciousness and, 82–84, 88–90, 98–99
  Collège de Sociologie and, 384–385
  consciousness and, 95, 97
  critiques of, 76n28, 155, 174, 364, 439–440
  on the crowd, 369–370, 379n6
  cultural mediation and, 293
  definition of religion, 75n11, 266–267
  Deploige on, 209n22
  on desire and morality, 30–31
  dissertation of, 40–44, 55n1, 353
  on divorce, 355–356
  Dreyfus Affair and, 17n7, 117–119, 121–127, 196, 221, 266, 286, 441
  economics and, 27, 228–230, 233–236, 240–242
  on education, 126, 135, 271, 286, 290, 354
  on emotion, 305
  English influences and, 209n22
  evolution and, 73, 330n5
  on faith, 419–420
  on family, 350–353, 356, 358–359, 360n4, 360n5
  on French sociology, 203–205
  on generality, 85
  Germany and, 13, 195–200, 202, 204–207
  Goffman and, 424–425, 433–434
  on group attachment, 55n7

on history of sociology, 201–203
on humans, 22–25, 229, 234, 304, 330n8
on imitation, 371–372
on the individual, 156n12, 213, 215–221, 256–258, 260n1, 358, 426–427
on individualism, 4–5, 31–32, 122–123, 218–221, 256–259, 342–343, 386
influence of, 16, 152, 272–275, 378, 391, 451
influence on moral inquiry, 35–36
on institutions, 417–418
Joas and, 68, 71–73, 394–397
Judaism and, 116–117, 123–124, 250, 253, 265, 288
Kant and, 33–34, 75n13, 131, 196, 199, 208n12, 226n2
on labor, 13, 42–44, 213–220, 228, 230–233, 337, 340–342
Latour and, 364, 366, 376–377
on law, 14, 245–246, 249–251, 253–258
lectures by, 55n6
Lévi-Strauss and, 72–73, 138, 398n4, 404–410, 412–414, 417–418, 421
library loans of, 216
on *mana*, 427
on marriage, 353–354, 356–358, 361n14
Mauss and, 350–351, 357, 399n18
on modernity, 14, 224–225, 337–338, 340–342, 355
on morality, 14, 16, 33–37, 50–54, 250, 307–310, 438–446, 454
on moral science, 197–199
on nation-states, 340–341
on networks, 306
on normativity, 86
organicism and, 46–47
as outsider, 249–250
personality of, 360n7, 361n10
philosophy and, 12, 129–133, 135–138, 141–142, 156n12, 167, 192n2, 447–448
on philosophy of mind, 91–92
Pinker on, 78n38
political views of, 153, 214, 266, 270–271, 277n3, 385
postcolonial studies and, 155
pragmatism and, 13, 140–141, 182–185, 188–191, 192n12
psychology and, 90, 156n12, 420, 449–450, 453

on racism, 253
rationalism of, 185–187
Ratzel and, 346n1, 347n8
relational theory and, 311
on religion, 68, 77n35, 142n4, 266, 269–272, 304–305, 386–387, 405–406
reputation of, 1, 3, 7–10, 17n11, 17n15, 333
on ritual, 11–12, 61–62, 71, 111–113, 296n14, 425–426, 435
on the sacred, 6, 70, 106–108, 266–267, 269–270, 272, 347n9, 382, 387, 389–390
on sacrifice, 110–111
science of morality, 21–23, 28
Smith and, 74n5, 108–109, 294, 425–426
socialism and, 25, 153, 193n3, 201, 304, 385
social morphology and, 74n7, 333–336, 347n5
social movements and, 299–303
on social things, 109–111
on society, 1, 120, 222–223, 307, 335–339, 341–342, 368–369
sociology and, 1–3, 7–11, 16, 134, 140, 164–165, 283, 334, 347n7, 455n3
on sociology of knowledge, 57–58, 68, 74n2
on sociology of religion, 264–265
on solidarity, 39–43, 49–51, 54, 214–218, 251–252, 258–259, 350
on space, 344–346
on symbolism, 408
Tarde and, 365–366, 368–369, 371–375, 378n1, 378n2, 379n3, 379n4
teaching, 40, 360n1
on territory, 338–341, 346
theory of knowledge, 185
theory of the sacred, 273, 276–277
on things, 102–103
on Tönnies, 44–46
on totemism, 102–105, 112–114, 268, 317–321, 324–326
on truth, 13, 185–186
use of historical examples, 398n11
views of contracts, 232
views of cultures, 28–29
views of objects, 93
views of sociology, 1–4
vitalism and, 347n2
World War I and, 13, 205–206

Durkheim, Émile (*cont.*)
  writings of, 17n19
  writings on, 11–16, 17n8, 246, 265–266
  on xenophobia, 260
Durkheimian approach, 4, 13, 299. *See also* Durkheimian sociology
  Bergson and, 165
  Bourdieu and, 8
  economic sociology and, 14, 229, 236, 239–240, 242
  social movements and, 300, 306, 311
  structural anthropology and, 64
Durkheimian sociology, 5, 134
  activism and, 304, 311
  L'Année sociologique and, 150
  art and, 294
  authors of, 173
  Bergson and, 164, 168–169, 171, 175, 177
  Collège de Sociologie and, 382–384, 388, 398n12
  context of, 12
  critiques of, 102, 155, 364, 404, 413
  dynamism of, 28
  economics and, 229, 236–240
  ethnology and, 74n4
  factions of, 446
  Goffman and, 424
  history of, 12, 398n4
  on imitation, 371–372
  influence of, 151–154, 453
  Lévi-Strauss and, 64–66, 152, 409–410, 421
  Mauss and, 390
  modernization of, 296n17
  on morality, 438–439, 451–452
  philosophy and, 136
  pragmatism and, 191
  on reason, 183
  religion and, 147, 273–275, 277, 405, 408
  research and, 13
  on the sacred, 393
  social movements and, 299–301, 306–307
  Tarde and, 375
Durkheimian Studies (journal), 153, 287
Durkheim, Louise, 288, 350, 353, 357, 360n7
Durkheim, Mélanie, 351–352
Duvignaud, Jean, 290

Earth, society and, 336–337, 341–342
eclecticism, 131, 133, 142n1
Ecole normale supérieure, 117, 130–131, 167, 195, 242n1
  admission to, 214, 249
  Durkheimians at, 151
  Herr at, 133, 146
Ecole polytechnique, 117
economics
  Durkheim and, 27, 228–230, 233–236, 240–242
  Durkheimians and, 229, 236–240
  morality and, 36–37, 51, 455n3
  religion and, 235, 238–239
economic sociology, 13, 227–228
  Durkheim on, 233
  history of, 239–240, 242
ecosphere, 346
Écrits politiques (Mauss), 153
Ecuador, 328
education
  Durkheim on, 126, 135, 271, 286, 290, 354
  family and, 354, 359–360, 360n5
  of French philosophers, 132
  in Jewish community, 117
  morality and, 290, 446
  philosophy of, 136
effervescence
  Bergson and, 166, 168
  collective (*see* collective effervescence)
  creative, 223–224
  the crowd and, 379n6
  definition of, 140
  Durkheim on, 225, 425–426
  economics and, 237
  ideals and, 240
  imitation and, 372
  Latour on, 377
  religion and, 272, 387, 390–391
  the sacred and, 394, 396
egalitarianism, individualism and, 256
Eisenstadt, Shmuel N., 274
Elementary Forms of Religious Life, The (Durkheim), 2–3, 7, 9, 11, 14, 16n3, 222–224, 285
  on animals, 317

anthropology and, 106, 405
art and, 289–292
Bergson and, 166–168, 172
categories and, 113
on classification, 62
collective consciousness and, 83, 98
criticism of, 76n28, 269
definition of religion and, 267
Durkheim's collaborators and, 150
economics and, 228, 234–235, 238
on effervescence, 237, 240, 284
Goffman and, 424
Halbwachs on, 151
on ideals, 309
on the individual, 213
on institutions, 418
Kantianism and, 140
on law, 245
Mauss and, 150, 409
on mind, 92
on modern religion, 272
philosophy and, 137–138
on pragmatism, 182, 185
on reason and science, 35
on religious experience, 142n4
on ritual, 71
on the sacred, 383, 386–387
sacred things and, 103
on sacrifice, 109
social movements and, 299–300, 303
on society, 222–223, 376–377
on sociology of knowledge, 57–59, 63
on sociology of religion, 264
on solidarity, 258–259
on space, 344
on symbolism, 318
tensions in, 71–72
on things, 102
title of, 74n9
on totemism, 268
on the Zuñi, 75n13
Ellwood, Charles, 151
Emirbayer, Mustafa, 155, 304–306, 309
emotion
    crowds and, 370
    morality and, 355
    social movements and, 305

empiricism, 21, 27, 183, 186
emus, 112
England, 43, 209n22
Enlightenment, 126, 142n1, 256
environment, sociology and, 346
Epicureanism, 289
epistemology, social, 30
Espinas, Alfred, 130, 200–201, 203
ethnocentrism, 67–68, 72, 176
ethnography, 103, 105–106, 151
ethnology, 58, 74n4, 392
ethology, 73, 328, 424, 428
Études Durkheimiennes. See *Durkheimian Studies* (journal)
Europe
    classification in, 60
    family in, 15, 53, 360n4
    moral claims and, 28
    morality in, 23
    pragmatism in, 187–188
    secularization in, 4
    solidarism in, 40
Evangelicalism, 451
evolution
    Durkheim and, 73, 330n5
    human–animal relationship and, 329
    of humans, 69
evolutionary psychology, 73, 156n12
evolutionism, 65, 68, 405
    of Durkheim, 72
    in sociology, 3, 267–268
    theory of family, 352
Evolution of Educational Thought in France, The (Durkheim), 130, 134, 136–137
exchange theory, 453
expression, paradigm of, 93–94
Eyerman, Ron, 303, 308

Fabiani, Jean-Louis, 12, 186
family
    Durkheim on, 350–353, 356, 358–359, 360n4, 360n5
    morality and, 52–53
    nuclear, 59, 352
    sociology of, 15, 360
    state and, 359–360
fascism, 272, 382, 385, 389–390, 398n7

Fauconnet, Paul, 146–149, 151, 156n4, 446
    on Durkheim, 150
    influence of, 154
    on institutions, 230
Fauré, Gabriel, 284
Fehr, Ernst, 454
Felice, Philippe de, 148, 156n4
Ferry, Jules, 120, 135, 265
festivals, 391–392, 399n20
    of Arunta people, 61
Feuerhahn, Wolf, 13
Fields, Karen, 62, 284
Flanagan, Owen, 448–449
food, in rituals, 319–320
force, concepts of, 62
Foucault, Marcel, 148, 156n4
Foucault, Michel, 397, 448
    on Durkheim, 129
    on philosophy, 135
Fouillée, Alfred, 48, 187
Fournière, Eugène, 127
Fournier, Marcel, 12, 132, 153, 166, 287, 295n9
Franc (currency), 238
France
    academic debates in, 5
    anthropology in, 404, 417
    anti-Semitism in, 120, 122, 124, 126, 221, 248–249
    associations in, 52–53
    children's rights in, 359–360, 361n15
    civil religion in, 276, 277n3
    colonialism and, 155
    divorce laws in, 355–356, 361n14
    economics in, 228, 236, 240
    German academics and, 195
    history of, 213–214
    history of sociology in, 176–177, 265
    ideology in, 191
    individual dignity in, 32
    Jewish community in, 117, 120, 122, 124–125, 214, 248–249
    moral sociology in, 438
    nationalism in, 120–124
    philosophy in, 12, 129–133, 136, 139, 142n1, 166–167, 187–188, 446
    political values in, 241
    pragmatism in, 140, 184, 187–191
    rationalism in, 186–188, 193n14, 204
    religion in, 32, 270
    religious conflict in, 272
    republicanism in, 127, 136, 192n7
    science in, 207, 207n1, 283
    social sciences in, 413
    society of, 16n2
    sociology and philosophy in, 164, 166
    sociology in, 15, 45–46, 140, 142n2, 151, 202–206, 364–365
    sociology of religion in, 264, 273
    sociology of the crowd in, 369
    solidarism in, 40
    textbooks in, 16n3
    theories of society in, 172
    views of Germany in, 197
    villages in, 425
    World War I in, 266
France juive, La (Drumont), 117
Franco-Prussian War, 117
Frankfurt School, 7
Frazer, James George, 112, 268, 330n6
freedom, 439–441
Freemasons, 122
French Academy. See *Académie française*
French Revolution
    aftermath of, 213
    Durkheim on, 17n7, 122–123, 218–219, 224, 249, 301, 304, 398n11
    effervescence and, 223
    motto of, 216, 218
    religion and, 271–272
    sacredness and, 62
    values of, 121–122
Freud, Sigmund, 30, 108, 390, 411
functionalism
    criticism of, 246
    Durkheim and, 299
    moral sociology and, 439
functionalist discourse, 215–217, 219
Fustel de Coulanges, Numa Denis, 74n5, 265, 333, 447

Ganges River, 328
Garfinkel, Harold, 17n9, 75n18, 273
Garland, David, 254–255, 259, 452
Geertz, Clifford, 70

Gehlen, Arnold, 327
Gemeinschaft und Gesellschaft (Tönnies), 44–45
gender
   categorization and, 17n9
   labor and, 353–354, 361n9
   religion and, 105
   ritual and, 6
   sacralization and, 17n10
"General Theory of Magic, A" (Mauss), 147
geography, 334
geosociology, 346
German language, 196
German school of moral philosophy, 34
German school of sociology, 201–202, 204
Germany
   academic influence of, 195, 197, 283
   anti-Semitism in, 123–124
   associations in, 52
   democracy in, 397
   Dreyfus Affair and, 116, 120
   Durkheim and, 13, 195–200, 202, 204–207
   Durkheim in, 33, 130
   fascism in, 389
   folklore of, 399n14
   militarism in, 209n28
   political values in, 241
   pragmatism in, 184 (*see also* pragmatism)
   science in, 207
   sociology in, 45–46, 199–200, 203
"Germany above all" (Durkheim booklet), 196
Gernet, Louis, 148, 156n4, 275
Gestapo, 351
Gibson, James J., 454n2
gift-giving, 239, 241–242, 392–393
Gift, The (Mauss), 16n2, 64, 153, 391
   economics and, 236, 238–239
   publication of, 151
Gillen, Francis James, 103, 105, 108, 268, 285, 291, 294
Gilligan, Carol, 355, 361n11
Gintis, Herbert, 454
Girard, Alain, 353
globalization, 276, 343
Goffman, Erving, 9, 16, 273, 427–429
   Durkheim and, 424–426, 433–434
   on ritual, 424–426, 428, 430–435
   on the sacred, 424, 429–431
Goldberg, Chad Alan, 126, 253
Good Society, The (Bellah), 451
Goodwin, Jeff, 305–306
Granet, Marcel, 275, 410, 446
gray geese, 328
great crested grebe, 428
Greece, 275
Greek philosophy, 60, 69, 289
Grimaux, Edouard, 118
Gross, Neil, 155
Groundwork, The (Kant), 217–218
guaranteeism, 49
Guattari, Félix, 325
guilds. *See also* professional groups
   Durkheim on, 219
   morality and, 51–53
Gumplowicz, Ludwig, 199
Guyau, Jean-Marie, 266, 289–290, 295n12

Habermas, Jürgen, 156n12, 274
Habits of the Heart (Bellah), 451
habitus, 65–67
Haidt, Jonathan, 156n12, 447
Halbwachs, Maurice, 12–13, 130, 137, 152, 156n13, 446
   L'Année sociologique and, 147–148, 156n4, 236
   on art, 296n16
   Bergson and, 169, 177
   Durkheim and, 151, 155
   economics and, 229, 237–238, 242n1
   on roads, 347n4
   scholarship on, 154
   social morphology and, 333, 336
   on space, 346
Halévy, Elie, 130, 132, 187
Halphen, Marie, 351
Hamelin, Octave, 130
Hauriou, Maurice, 173
Hébert, Marcel, 187
Hegel, Georg Wilhelm Friedrich, 31, 78n38, 93, 195, 383
Hegelianism, 131
Heidegger, Martin, 393, 399n22
Heilbron, Johan, 134, 142n2, 192n2, 446
Heinroth, Oskar, 328

Hennion, Antoine, 285, 293–294, 295n3, 296n17
Herr, Lucien, 119, 133, 146, 149
Hertz, Robert, 12, 75n12, 147–148, 156n4, 383
    Bergson and, 168
    Collège de Sociologie and, 384, 387, 389–390
    Elementary Forms and, 150
    Joas on, 394
    on religion, 386
    on the sacred, 272, 293, 391
    scholarship on, 154
Hervieu-Léger, Danièle, 273
history
    Durkheim on, 343
    Simiand on, 154
Hitlin, Steve, 438–439, 450–453
Holleaux, Maurice, 361n10
Hollier, Denis, 398n1
homeland, morality and, 52–53
Home Office (UK), 248
Homo oeconomicus, 240
Honig, Bonnie, 258
Honneth, Axel, 454
Hourticq, Jean-Paul, 148, 156n4
Howell, Signe, 321–322
Hrdy, Sarah, 69
Hubert, Henri, 12, 109, 119, 122, 130, 137
    L'Année sociologique and, 146, 148–149, 151, 156n4, 284–285, 293, 295n1
    Bergson and, 168–169, 172, 177
    Collège de Sociologie and, 384, 391
    Elementary Forms and, 150
    on *mana*, 419
    on religion, 267
    on sacredness, 147, 272, 293
    on sacrifice, 115n1, 242–243n2, 296n14
human exceptionalism, 320, 326
humanism
    Durkheim on, 220
    reactionary, 316
humanities
    Durkheim and, 155
    teaching of, 137
humanity
    attachment to, 55n8
    morality and, 52–53
human rights, 14, 17n7
    attachment and, 55n8
    citizenship and, 247
    sacralization and, 395, 452
    states and, 256
    in the United Kingdom, 258
    women's rights and, 37n1
humans
    animals and, 310, 322–323, 327–329, 427–428
    art and, 295
    association and, 55n4
    Bergson on, 169–171
    dignity of, 32
    Durkheim's views of, 22–25, 229, 234, 304, 330n8
    games and, 287
    ideals and, 30
    ideas of, 22
    in indigenous religions, 321–323
    individualism and, 257
    minds of, 65
    nature of, 24, 28
    in religion, 326–327
    sacralization of, 31–32, 220–221, 271–272, 276, 386
    the sacred and, 385
    social life of, 213
    social relationships and, 52
    sociology and, 78n38, 316
    solidarism and, 48
    study of, 328–329
    Tarde on, 368
    totemism and, 317
Hume, David, 113
Huvelin, Paul, 154, 156n4
Huxley, Julian, 428

ideals, Durkheim on, 29–30
ideology, 7–8, 422n4
Ihering, Rudolph von, 198–199, 201–202
imagination, 288, 290
    role in science, 34
imitation, 364–366, 371–372, 375–376, 378n2
imitative rites, 323–324
immanent critique, 28, 32
immigration, 252, 254–255
Index of Forbidden Works, 188
India, 275, 328

indigenous peoples
  beliefs of, 65, 419
  classification systems in, 59
  concepts of force, 62
Indignados (Spain), 233
"Individual and Collective Representations" (Durkheim), 89, 93, 222
individualism
  Collège de Sociologie on, 386
  debates about, 120–123
  Durkheim on, 4–5, 31–32, 122–123, 218–221, 256–259, 342–343, 386
  in France, 197–198, 219
  Kant and, 122, 208n12
  morality and, 251, 254, 260, 310, 342–343
  politics and, 225
  sacralization and, 452
  socialism and, 214
  in the social sciences, 3–5
  Tarde and, 372–374
  Weberian, 373–375
"Individualism and the Intellectuals" (Durkheim), 31, 219–220, 253
individualization, of collective beliefs, 223
individuals
  the crowd and, 379n6
  Division of Labour on, 213, 224
  Durkheim on, 156n12, 213, 215–221, 256–258, 260n1, 358, 426–427
  family and, 352, 354
  groups and, 88–89
  Latour on, 376–377
  mind and, 57
  morality and, 442
  sacralization of, 14, 220–221, 256–258, 271–272, 310, 386, 395
  sanctity of, 256
  social norms and, 367–368
  society and, 369, 431
  solidarity and, 54
inductive approach, 27
In Memoriam (Mauss), 182
institutions, economic, 230, 232
integration, 51
Interaction Ritual (Goffman), 424–425
International Conference of Philosophy, 187–188

intichiuma (Arunta ritual), 11, 108, 110–111, 113–114, 268
Introduction à la morale (Durkheim), 23–27, 29, 442
"Introduction to the Sociology of the Family" (Durkheim lecture), 350
Inuit, 59, 75n10, 391
Irish people, in the United Kingdom, 249, 260n5
Iroquois people, 62, 105
IS (terrorist group), 248
Isambert, François, 168
Israel, 275
Italy, 203–204, 389
Izoulet, Jean, 47–48

J'accuse (Zola), 118, 149
Jacobsson, Kerstin, 14
Jainism, 266
Jakobson, Roman, 410–411
James, William, 90, 140, 142n4, 178n5, 394
  Bergson and, 188–189, 192n8, 192n12
  Durkheim on, 192n3
  pragmatism and, 182–187, 190–191, 427
  on religion, 269
Janet, Paul, 131–132
Janet, Pierre, 89
Jarry, Alfred, 284
Jasper, James, 305
Jaspers, Karl, 274
Jaurès, Jean, 130, 149, 356, 392
Jeanmaire, Henri, 148, 156n4
Jesus Christ, 441
Joas, Hans, 398n1
  on abolitionism, 399n27
  on the Axial Age, 77n31, 77n34
  Durkheim and, 68, 71–73, 256, 387, 394–397
  on *Elementary Forms*, 76n28
  on the individual, 225, 258
  on morality, 451–452
  on pragmatism, 184, 186
  on religion, 16n1, 277
  on the sacred, 15, 16n1, 70, 383, 394–398, 399n25, 399n26
  on sociology of religion, 64, 387
  on values, 398n5

Judaism
　　Christianity and, 117–118, 127
　　Dreyfus Affair and, 196, 207
　　Durkheim and, 116–117, 123–124, 250, 253, 265, 288
　　Durkheim on, 12, 125
　　in France, 117, 120, 122, 124–125, 214, 248–249

Kabyle Berbers, 16n2, 272
kangaroos, 112
Kantian displacement, 95
Kantian philosophy, 27, 199, 440
　　values of, 256, 258
Kant, Immanuel, 30–31
　　categories and, 75n13
　　Durkheim and, 33–34, 75n13, 131, 196, 199, 208n12, 226n2
　　on education, 135
　　individualism and, 122, 208n12
　　influence of, 136
　　influence on Durkheim, 216–218
　　on perception, 344
　　on understanding, 269
Karsenti, Bruno, 11–12, 17n6, 209n27, 378n1, 379n3, 441, 444–445
Keane, Webb, 450–451, 454–455n2
Keck, Frédéric, 16
Kejara (Bororo village), 64
Kellner, Hansfried, 354
kinship, in Aboriginal societies, 59
Kishinev pogrom, 123
knowledge
　　Durkheimian sociology of, 71–72
　　Durkheim on, 74n2
　　professional groups and, 233–234
　　sociology of, 11, 57–60, 63, 68–73, 74n2
Koenig, Matthias, 14
Kohlberg, Lawrence, 354–355
Kojève, Alexandre, 383–384
König, René, 334, 346
Krampus, 389, 399n14

labor
　　Comte on, 228, 230
　　Durkheim on, 13, 42–44, 213–220, 228, 230–233, 337, 340–342

　　gender and, 353–354, 361n9
labor, division of
　　anti-Semitism and, 123–124, 126
　　Durkheim on, 42–44, 213–220, 230–233, 337, 340–342
　　gender and, 353–354
　　gifts and, 242
　　individual and, 213–220
　　knowledge and, 138
　　publications on, 148
　　the sacred and, 385–386
　　social structures and, 5, 252, 340–342
　　sociology vs. philosophy, 26, 141
　　solidarity and, 252, 340, 350
　　study of, 142, 228
　　Tönnies on, 45
La Capra, Dominique, 166
Lachelier, Henri, 197
Lachelier, Jules, 139
Lacombe, Paul, 203
Lacroix, Bernand, 186
Lafitte, Jean-Paul, 148, 156n4
Laïcité, 264–266
　　Durkheim on, 270–271
Laidlaw, James, 439–440, 442
Lalande, André, 187, 422n5
Lalo, Charles, 148, 156n4, 284–285, 293, 295n2, 295n3
Lamanna, Mary Ann, 351
Lamont, Michèle, 452, 454
language, 410–412
Lapie, Paul, 146, 148–149, 151, 156n4
Lapoujade, David, 190
Latour, Bruno, 15, 16n2, 152, 193n14
　　on Durkheim, 364, 366, 376–377
　　reenactment of Durkheim-Tarde dispute, 378n1
　　on sacralization, 378
　　on social morphology, 347n5
　　Tarde and, 15, 364, 374–377, 378n1, 379n7
Laughter (Bergson), 172
law
　　animal rights in, 328
　　Durkheim on, 14, 245–246, 249–251, 253–258
　　religion and, 269
　　repressive, 42, 253–254, 337, 434

restitutive, 42, 74, 253–254, 270, 337
  sociology of, 249, 260
  solidarity and, 246, 250, 252–253, 258–260
Lawler, Lillian, 324
Laws of Imitation, The (Tarde), 134
League for the Defense of Human Rights, 221
League of Nations, 48
Le Bon, Gustave, 126, 190, 192n8, 369
  on activism, 302
  Bouglé and, 203
Le Bras, Gabriel, 273
Lectures on the Religion of the Semites (Robertson Smith), 108–109, 266
Leibniz, Gottfried Wilhelm, 374
Leiris, Michel, 151, 154, 382, 384–385, 388–390, 392
  autoethnography and, 385, 398n6, 398n12, 399n15
Léon, Xavier, 130, 132, 187, 207
Le Play, Frédéric, 142n3, 350–351
Leroi-Gourhan, André, 164, 174–175
Leroy-Beaulieu, Paul, 228
Le Roy, Edouard, 189–190
Lévi-Strauss, Claude, 16, 392, 414–416, 419–420
  Bergson and, 174
  on Bergson and Durkheim, 165–166
  on the Bororo, 76n22
  on classification, 422n8
  collective effervescence and, 406
  on the *Collège de Sociologie*, 384
  critiques of, 421
  Durkheim and, 72–73, 138, 398n4, 404–410, 412–414, 417–418, 421
  Durkheimian tradition and, 64–66, 152, 409–410, 421
  Goffman and, 432
  on language, 410–411
  on *mana*, 427
  on religion, 420, 422n9
  on ritual sacrifice, 115n1
  on society, 347n6
  on symbolism, 272, 408–410, 412–414
  on totemism, 114, 317–318, 406–407, 411
Lévi, Sylvain, 74n5, 147
Lévy-Bruhl, Henri, 152

Lévy-Bruhl, Lucien, 65, 106, 113, 145, 151–152, 172, 208n20, 438
Lévy, Emmanuel, 146, 154, 156n4
Lévy, Isidore, 147, 156n4
Liard, Louis, 132, 137, 207n4, 209n29
liberalism
  among sociologists, 149
  Dreyfus Affair and, 121
  Durkheim and, 4, 156n12
  education and, 137
  solidarism and, 49
libraries, 216
life
  Bergson on, 171–172
  Durkheim on, 27
life-style, 66
Ligue antisémite française, 118, 120
Ligue des droits de l'homme et du citoyen, 118, 120
Lindblom, Jonas, 300, 306
London University, 151
Lorenz, Konrad, 328
Loritja people, 150
Louis XVIII, 355
Louvain, University of, 205
Lukes, Steven, 16, 74n9
  on citizenship, 260
  on Durkheim, 152, 155, 166, 256
  on Durkheim's philosophy, 136–137, 141–142
  on law, 252, 254–255
Lycee de Sens, 214, 216

MacIntyre, Alasdair, 448
Mahler, Gustav, 284
Maillol, Aristide, 284
Malaysia, 321
Malinowski, Bronisław, 65
mana, 62, 105–106, 147, 150, 235, 268, 409, 419–421, 422n7, 427
Man and the Sacred (Callois), 390–391
Margueritte, Paul, 355–356
Margueritte, Victor, 355–356
Marion, Henri, 132
markets, USSR and, 238–239
marriage
  debates about, 351
  Durkheim on, 353–354, 356–358, 361n14
  history of, 352

Marxism, 149
  Bergsonianism and, 176
Marx, Jean, 148, 156n4
Marx, Karl, 27, 78n38, 240
  collective consciousness and, 82
  Durkheim's criticism of, 234
  on family, 352–353
Massis, Henri, 205
Mathiez, Albert, 265, 272
Matisse, Henri, 284
Matter and Memory (Bergson), 168–169, 174, 178n7
Maurras, Charles, 118, 136–138
Mauss, Marcel, 16n2, 105
  on Aboriginal societies, 60
  L'Année sociologique and, 146, 149–152, 236, 285, 295n1
  art and, 295n9
  Bergson and, 169, 177
  on the Bororo, 76n22
  Bourdieu and, 66
  on classification, 62–63, 74n6
  Collège de Sociologie and, 382, 384, 390–392, 398n12
  correspondence with Durkheim, 118–119, 234
  on Durkheim, 140, 182, 442
  Durkheim and, 105, 350–351, 357, 399n18
  on economics, 229, 238
  Elementary Forms and, 150, 409
  The Gift, 16n2, 64, 151, 153, 236, 238–239, 391
  on gifts, 241–242, 242–243n2
  on Hertz, 389
  on institutions, 230
  Joas on, 394
  Lévi-Strauss and, 409, 413
  on *mana*, 419, 422n7, 427
  on mechanical solidarity, 47
  philosophy and, 130, 446
  political views of, 149, 385, 392–393
  postcolonial studies and, 155
  on religion, 75n11, 267, 272, 277n1, 386, 390, 399n18
  on religious sociology, 270
  René Worms and, 46
  reputation of, 155
  on the sacred, 293, 383
  on sacrifice, 109, 115n1, 242–243n2, 296n14
  scholarship on, 153
  social morphology and, 333
  on social rhythms, 75n10
  on sociology of knowledge, 57–59
  on solidarism, 49
  on space, 346
Mead, George Herbert, 16, 354–355, 424, 430
  on imitation, 428
  pragmatism of, 427–428 (*see also* pragmatism)
Meillet, Antoine, 148, 156n4
Melanesia, 105
Melanesians, 268, 420
Menger, Pierre-Michel, 288–289
Merleau-Ponty, Maurice, 177n1, 398n3, 413
Merton, Robert, 61, 74n8
metaphysics, 131
Middle East, ancient history of, 70
Milhaud, Albert, 146, 156n4
Mill, J. S., 135
mind
  naturalization of, 97
  philosophy of, 91–92
  sociality of, 57
  views of, 73
Mind, Self, and Society (Mead), 424
Mitchell, Wesley C., 237
modernism, in sociology, 2
modernity
  anomie and, 290
  Durkheim on, 3, 14, 224–225, 337–338, 340–342, 355
  individuals and, 213, 224–225, 251
  religion and, 264, 271
  solidarity and, 214, 217–218, 220
modernization
  the sacred and, 393
  territory and, 346
  theory of, 2–3, 264, 337–338, 342, 346
modern order, 2
Moebius, Stephan, 15
moieties, 59–60
monadology, 373–376
Monadology and Sociology (Tarde), 373–375
money, 238, 240
Monnerot, Jules, 152
monotheism, 376–377

Montesquieu, 201–203, 333, 336–337
Moral Education (Durkheim)
    on art, 286, 288
    on attachment, 50, 52
    on family, 354
    philosophy and, 135
    social movements and, 14, 300–301, 307
    solidarity and, 40, 258–259
    theory of morality, 50, 440–442
moral facts, 21, 27–31
    Division of Labour on, 41
    religion and, 269
moral individualism, 342–343
morality
    in animals, 444
    beliefs about, 442–443
    civic, 54
    definition of, 25
    Durkheim on, 14, 16, 33–37, 50–54, 250, 307–310, 438–446, 454
    education and, 290, 446
    law and, 246, 255
    modernity and, 220
    philosophy and, 446–449
    rituals and, 304
    the sacred and, 31–32, 386, 441
    science of, 11, 21–24, 29, 33–35, 37, 197–199, 202, 443, 446, 450
    social facts and, 266
    social movements and, 306–311
    social rules and, 86–87
    society and, 41, 50, 52, 290–291, 343
    sociology of, 26–27, 438–439, 445–446, 451–454
moral pluralism, 36
moral reflexivity, 309–311
moral science, 11, 21–24, 29, 33–35, 37, 197–199, 202, 443, 446, 450
Moret, Alexandre, 148, 156n4
Morland, Jacques, 204
morphological effects, 6
Mosbah-Natanson, Sébastien, 198, 202
Mother Earth (Pacha Mama), 328
Muffang, Henri, 145–147, 156n4
music, 284
Muslims, in the United Kingdom, 247, 249, 260n5

Naquet Law, 355
nationalism
    of Durkheim, 207
    Durkheim on, 32, 127
    in France, 120–124
    in Germany, 206–207
    religion and, 264, 275–276
nationality, sociology and, 201–202
nation-states, 340–341, 343
naturalism, 415–416
naturalistic fallacy, 35
Natural Law, 24, 32
nature
    Aboriginal societies and, 60
    culture and, 77n36
    of humans, 24, 28
    ideals and, 30
    society and, 346
Nazism, 169, 393
Needham, Rodney, 74n6
neo-Durkheimian sociology, 310
neo-Kantianism
    Durkheim and, 12, 229
    in education, 141
neoliberalism, 4
neo-Thomism, 208n20
Netherlands, 399n14
New York City, 296n14
New Zealand, 328
Nietzsche, Friedrich, 154, 204, 448
Nisbet, Robert, 283
Nizan, Paul, 152
Nobel Peace Prize, 286
nonanthropocentric theory, 14
nonhumans, in sociology, 376–377. *See also* animals; plants
normality, Durkheim on, 5
normativity, 85–86
Norms and the Normal, The (Canguilhem), 174
Northern Ireland, 249
Notes critiques—Sciences sociales, 149
Nouvelliste, Le, 119, 121
Nungesser, Frithjof, 11, 398n1
Nye, Robert, 188

objectivism, 84
obligation, 30–31, 87

Occupy Wall Street movement, 233
On Prayer (Mauss), 150
"On Some Primitive Forms of Classification" (Durkheim/Mauss), 58–63, 105–106, 150
  on Aboriginal Australians, 77n30
  tensions in, 71–72
  on the Zuñi, 75n15
On Totemism (Durkheim), 317, 324
orenda (Iroquois principle of force), 62, 105
organicism, 46–47
Orléan, André, 240
otherness, 32
Oxford University, 153

paganism, 209n28
paleoanthropology, 69
Paoletti, Giovanni, 131, 139, 141, 216
Paretian approach, 239
Paris
  art in, 284, 288, 294
  Durkheim and Tarde's dispute in, 364, 378n1, 378n2, 379n3
  Durkheim in, 14, 214, 250, 285
  philosophers from, 133
  Tarde in, 366
  World War II in, 351
Paris Sociological Society, 46
Parodi, Dominique, 146–148, 156n4
Parsons, Talcott, 7, 16n5, 78n38, 299, 378n2, 426
  theory of action, 439
pars pro toto principle, 109–110
Passeron, Jean-Claude, 155, 359
Pasteur, Louis, 283
patriotism, 342–343
Paugam, Serge, 11
Peirce, Charles Sanders, 186, 192n3, 427
perception, of space, 344–345
personhood, of nonhumans, 328
Pettenkofer, Andreas, 17n18, 387, 398n1
Pham Minh Quang, 247
phenomenology
  of action, 95
  things and, 102
philosophy
  animals and, 200
  of Bergson, 164–165, 169–171, 177

  Durkheim and, 12, 129–133, 135–138, 141–142, 156n12, 167, 192n2, 447–448
  Durkheim on, 22, 25–26, 131, 167
  in France, 12, 129–133, 136, 139, 142n1, 166–167, 187–188, 446
  in Germany, 33–34
  morality and, 446–449
  pragmatism and, 183, 188–189 (*see also* pragmatism)
  religion and, 106, 139–140
  sociology and, 12, 26, 129, 134, 137–138, 141, 165–166
"Philosophy Lectures" (Durkheim), 17n19
phonology, 410–411
piacular rites, 292–293, 296n14, 435
Piaget, Jean, 354
Picasso, Pablo, 284
Pickering, W. S. F., 63, 153, 166, 225, 265, 288
Pinker, Steven, 78n38
Pinto, Louis, 166
Pius X (Pope), 188
plants
  Aboriginal views of, 60–61
  in indigenous religions, 321, 325–326
  legal status of, 328
Plato, 78n38, 200–201
Platonism, 183
play, as form of life, 71
pluralism, 36–37
Polanyi, Karl, 239, 241
political economy, 236, 240
political geography, 347n8
political science, sociology as, 99
"Politics of the Future, The" (Durkheim), 224–225
politics, ritual and, 9
"Positive Science of Morality in Germany" (Durkheim), 195
positivism
  Bergson and, 170, 174
  criticism of, 246
  of Durkheim, 448
  Durkheim and, 37, 125, 141, 249, 252–253, 265
  history of, 283
  law and, 251
postcolonial studies, 154–155
potlatch, 392, 399n21

Poulsen, Stephen, 305
power, sacredness and, 397–398
Prabhat, Devyani, 14
pragmatism
   consciousness and, 95–98
   debates about, 189–191
   Durkheim and, 13, 130, 140–141, 182–185, 188–191, 192n12
   Elementary Forms on, 182, 185
   in Europe, 187–188
   in France, 140, 184, 187–191
   in Germany, 184
   Goffman and, 424
   James and, 182–187, 190–191, 427
   Joas on, 184, 186
   of Mead, 427–428
   politics and, 192n9
   popularity of, 187–188
   socialism and, 193n13
Pragmatism and Sociology (Durkheim), 35, 140
   Bergson and, 168–169
primates, 78n40
primatology, 69
"Primitive Classification" (essay). *See* "On Some Primitive Forms of Classification"
Professional Ethics and Civic Morals (Durkheim), 36, 50–53
   collective and, 98
   on law, 245
   on nation-states, 340
   social movements and, 300
professional groups, 233–234, 301, 342. *See also* guilds
property, ritual sacrifice and, 110
prophets, Hebrew, 69
protest, theories of, 302
Protestantism. *See also* Christianity
   Durkheim on, 116, 270–271
   in France, 120–122, 127, 265
   in Germany, 195
Prussia, 195
Psychologie des foules (Le Bon), 369
psychology
   Durkheim and, 90, 156n12, 420, 449–450, 453
   morality and, 450–451
   sociology and, 127, 145, 203, 367, 369, 449–450

Public Assistance (France), 359
"Public Lectures on Social Science" (Durkheim), 40
Pudal, Romain, 13
Puritans, 288

Rabier, Elie, 132
race
   anthropology and, 145
   Durkheimian theory and, 6
   normality and, 5
racism
   Durkheim on, 253
   social networks and, 6–7
   solidarity and, 43
Radcliffe-Brown, Alfred, 7, 151
   reputation of, 155
   on the sacred, 426
Radical-Socialist Party (France), 48, 286
rational-actor model, 3, 10
rational art, 11
rational choice theory, 453
rationalism
   Durkheim and, 12–13, 131, 141, 185–187
   Durkheim on, 168, 183
   in France, 186–188, 193n14, 204
   French politics and, 191, 193n14
   Mauss and, 392–393
   neo-Kantian, 135
   philosophy and, 139
   pragmatism and, 189–190 (*see also* pragmatism)
   sociology and, 23, 167, 208n20
rationality, morality and, 22
rational moral art, 22–23, 28–29, 35–37
Ratzel, Friedrich, 148, 234, 333–335, 344, 346n1, 347n3, 347n8
Ravaisson, Félix, 187
Rawls, Anne, 185–186, 225, 323
Rawls, John, 86, 156n12
reactionary humanism, 316
reason, historicity of, 183
Rebérioux, Madeleine, 192n7
Reformation, 270
Reform Judaism, 265
regulation, 51

relativism
    Durkheim and, 28
    pragmatism and, 184 (*see also* pragmatism)
religion
    activism and, 303–304
    animals and, 112, 235
    art and, 291–292
    Collège de Sociologie on, 384–386
    definition of, 75n11, 266–267, 424–425
    in Durkheimian sociology, 147, 273–275, 277, 405, 408
    Durkheim on, 68, 77n35, 142n4, 266, 269–272, 304–305, 386–387, 405–406
    Durkheim's focus on, 228, 234–235
    economics and, 235, 238–239
    family and, 360n4
    individualism and, 219–220
    as institution, 418
    Lévi-Strauss on, 420, 422n9
    Mauss on, 75n11, 267, 272, 277n1, 386, 390, 399n18
    morality and, 31–32
    philosophy and, 106, 139–140
    politics and, 4
    property and, 110
    rituals and, 317
    sacredness and, 2–3
    sociology of, 14–15, 64, 70, 147, 264–266, 268–270, 272–277, 382–383, 386
    sociology of knowledge and, 69–73
    solidarity and, 117, 270
    space and, 347n9
    symbolism and, 419
    totemism and, 61, 105, 316–317
Religion in Human Evolution (Bellah), 69–70
Renan, Ernest, 195, 207n1
Renouvier, Charles, 33, 135, 209n23
    Elementary Forms and, 166
    influence of, 141
    Kant and, 218, 229, 266
    political views of, 136
representation
    Durkheim's use of, 92–94
    totems as, 104
repressive law, 42, 253–254, 337, 434
repressive sanctions, 250, 253

republicanism
    discourse of, 215–219
    Durkheim and, 366
    in France, 127, 136, 192n7
    philosophy and, 136, 138
    rationalism and, 187–188
restitutive law, 42, 74, 253–254, 270, 337
restitutive sanctions, 252
Revue bleue, 356
Revue de métaphysique et de morale, 130, 132–133, 136–137
    on pragmatism, 187
    reviews in, 146
Revue internationale de l'enseignement, 197
Revue internationale de sociologie, 46, 134
Revue philosophique, 130
    on pragmatism, 187–188
    sociology and, 137–138
Rey, Abel, 156n4, 187–188
Reynier, Jean-Pierre, 148, 156n4
Ribot, Théodule, 130, 187
Richard, Gaston, 151
    Bergson and, 168
    L'Année sociologique and, 145–146, 148, 156n4
Richet, Charles, 207
Riley, Alexander, 154, 166, 288
ritual
    activism and, 303–304
    animals and, 327, 428
    anthropology of, 10, 112
    Bellah on, 69
    classification and, 63
    Durkheim on, 11–12, 61–62, 71, 111–113, 296n14, 425–426, 435
    entertainment and, 291
    in everyday life, 431–433
    gender and, 6
    Goffman on, 424–426, 428, 430–435
    group membership and, 322
    imitation and, 364, 371–372
    Latour on, 377
    in modern society, 8–9
    social evolution and, 77n33
    social rhythms and, 75n10
    social things and, 103, 110–112
    sociology of, 16

symbolism and, 324–325
theory of, 317, 319
totemism and, 108, 111–112, 319–320, 323, 425
types of, 433–435
Rodin, Auguste, 284
Rogers, Juliette, 360
Rolland, Romain, 167
Rome, 265, 430
Rousseau, Jean-Jacques, 122, 198, 271, 276
Roussel, Pierre, 148, 156n4
royalism, 32
Royce, Josiah, 71, 394
Rules of Sociological Method, The (Durkheim)
    Bergson and, 167
    collective consciousness and, 94
    the crowd and, 369
    economics and, 230, 236
    German school and, 202
    on imitation, 372
    on law, 245
    normativity and, 85–88, 379n5
    on observation, 125
    on philosophy, 133
    positivism and, 246
    pragmatism and, 140–141 (*see also* pragmatism)
    on psychology, 203, 449
    publication of, 116
    on the social, 34, 366, 379n5
    on social science, 405
    on sociology of religion, 266
    on solidarity, 50
    Tarde and, 365
    on things, 102, 104
Russian Empire, anti-Semitism in, 123–124
Ryle, Gilbert, 91

sacralization
    Bourdieu on, 8
    Durkheim on, 8, 387
    gender and, 17n10
    of individuals, 14, 220–221, 256–258, 271–272, 310, 386, 395
    Joas on, 395–398, 399n25, 451–452
    of objects, 377–378
    order and, 399n23
    of people, 5, 23, 271–272

of places, 347n9
processes of, 277
theory of, 391
sacred, the
    ambiguity of, 75n12
    animal rights and, 304, 317
    animals and, 310, 321, 326
    art and, 288
    Collège de Sociologie on, 384–386, 388–389
    contagiousness of, 106–107, 112
    distinction from the profane, 61
    Durkheim on, 6, 70, 106–108, 266–267, 269–270, 272, 347n9, 382, 387, 389–390
    experience of, 104
    Goffman on, 424, 429–431
    ideas of, 70
    Joas on, 70, 383, 394–398, 399n25, 399n26
    Mauss on, 391
    modernization and, 393
    moral ideals and, 307–309
    morality and, 31–32, 386, 441
    plants and, 321
    ritual and, 426
    science and, 292
    sociology of, 2–3, 15, 268, 382–383
    theory of, 14, 272–273, 276
    types of, 62, 389–390, 398n10
    value and, 235
sacred things, 103–107, 110
"Sacrifice: Its Nature and Function" (Hubert/Mauss), 109, 147
sacrifice, ritual, 108–109, 111, 115n1, 391
Sadowa, Battle of, 195
Saint Nicholas, 389
Saint-Saëns, Camille, 284
San Francisco, 206
Sapir, Edward, 329n4
Sartre, Jean-Paul, 129, 398n3, 431–432
Sassoon, Joseph, 299
Saussure, Ferdinand de, 148, 410–411, 432
Savage Mind, The (Lévi-Strauss), 114
Say, Jean-Baptiste, 228
scandale, 284
Schäffle, Albert, 83, 198–201, 205, 208n7, 208n14, 228
Schiller, F. C. S., 185, 192n3
Schinz, Albert, 187, 192n9

Schmaus, Warren, 73, 75n13, 226n2
Schmoller, Gustav, 33, 198–199, 201, 205, 228, 333
Schoenberg, Arnold, 284
Schroer, Markus, 14–15
Schütz, Alfred, 70, 77n35
science
    art and, 26–27, 34–35, 288
    Collège de Sociologie and, 385–386, 388
    in France, 207, 207n1, 283
    imagination and, 34
    of morality, 11, 21–24, 29, 33–35, 37, 197–199, 202, 443, 446, 450
    religion and, 70
    the sacred and, 292
    sociology and, 167, 347n7
    views of humans, 328–329
"Science positive de la morale en Allemagne, La" (Durkheim), 33
Sciences sociales en Allemagne, Les (Bouglé), 145, 202–203
Scull, Andrew, 252, 254–256
Séailles, Gabriel, 132, 197
Searle, John, 155
Seasonal Variations of the Eskimo (Mauss/Beuchat), 75n10, 391
Second Empire (France), 213
secularism
    Durkheim and, 270–271
    in France, 265–266
    ritual and, 9
secularization, theories of, 3–4, 264, 270, 274, 276
Sedan, Battle of, 195
Segre, Sandro, 306
Sembel, Nicolas, 216
Sens, France, 130–131
Seyfert, Robert, 14
Shetland Islands, 431
Shils, Edward, 399n23
Shook, John R., 187
Simiand, François, 12–13, 151
    L'Année sociologique and, 146, 148–149, 156n4, 236
    economics and, 229, 236–238, 240, 242n1
    influence of, 154
    philosophy and, 130

Simmel, Georg, 131, 146, 148, 202, 204, 208n7, 208n17, 431, 438, 442
Simondon, Gilbert, 12, 164, 174–175, 177
Sioux people, 58, 60, 62, 64, 105
Slovenia, 399n14
Small, A. W., 150
Smelser, Neil, 302–303
Smith, Adam, 113, 228, 239
Smith, Christian, 451
Smith, William Robertson, 74n5, 106–108, 266
    definition of totemism, 319–320
    Durkheim and, 74n5, 108–109, 294, 425–426
    on ritual, 110–111
    on the sacred, 292, 389
    on sacrifice, 115n1
social, the, 34, 366, 379n5
    definition of, 85
    Durkheimian concept of, 87
social consciousness, collective consciousness and, 94
social Darwinism, 330n5
social democracy, 188
social facts, 102, 405, 407, 416
    Bergson on, 164
    critiques of, 170
    divorce and, 356
    materiality and, 336
    money as, 238
    morality and, 266
    norms and, 417
    philosophers on, 133
    scholarship on, 202
    symbolism and, 412–414
socialism
    among sociologists, 149
    Durkheim and, 25, 153, 193n3, 201, 304, 385
    in France, 219, 356
    individualism and, 214
    Mauss and, 392–393
    pragmatism and, 193n13 (*see also* pragmatism)
    Schäffle and, 208n14
social morphology, 14–15, 333–335, 344, 346, 347n5
social movements. *See also* activism
    Durkheim and, 299–303

Durkheimian sociology and, 299–301,
    306–307
  emotion and, 305
  morality and, 306–311
  society and, 307–308
  theory of, 304, 311
social physiology, 334, 336
social protest, 17n18
social psychology, 88–89
social reform, Durkheim on, 29
social sciences
  approaches to, 3
  Durkheim and, 155, 405
  ethics and, 21
  evolutionary psychology and, 73
  in Germany, 33
  historiography of, 413
  polities and, 16n4
  rationalism in, 420–421
  theoretical basis of, 229
social things, 102–103
  philosophy and, 129
  production of, 111
  religion and, 114–115
  totemism and, 105, 109–110
Société française de philosophie, 132, 139
society
  Durkheim on, 1, 120, 222–223, 307, 335–339,
    341–342, 368–369
  economics and, 230
  Latour on, 376
  Lévi-Strauss on, 347n6
  moral facts and, 27
  morality and, 41, 50, 52, 290–291, 343
  nature and, 346
  philosophers and, 25
  ritual and, 431
  spatial order and, 333, 335
  Tarde on, 375
  traditional vs. modern, 42
sociocentrism, 60
sociologists, philosophers and, 26
sociology
  anthropocentrism in, 175, 316
  of anti-Semitism, 127
  art and, 283, 288–289, 294
  Bergson and, 170–171, 174

  collective and, 83
  comparative, 275
  of the crowd, 88–89, 366, 369–370, 379n6
  definitions in, 84–85
  Division of Labour and, 39
  Durkheim and, 1–3, 7–11, 16, 134, 140, 164–
    165, 283, 334, 347n7, 455n3
  Durkheimian, 13, 71–72, 153
  Durkheim's views of, 200–202, 214, 354
  economic, 13, 227–228, 233, 239–240, 242
  of family, 15, 360
  founding of, 130, 134, 245
  in France, 15, 45–46, 140, 142n2, 151, 202–
    206, 364–365
  generalizations and, 131
  in Germany, 45–46, 199–200, 203
  history of, 16, 142n2, 200–202
  journals of, 145
  of knowledge, 11, 57–60, 63, 68–73, 74n2
  Lévi-Strauss on, 419
  Latour on, 364
  of law, 249, 260
  materiality and, 333–336
  of morality, 26–27, 438–439, 445–446,
    451–454
  morality and, 22, 438–439, 441, 455n3
  natural rights theory and, 208n20
  nonhumans in, 376–377
  normality in, 5
  philosophy and, 12, 26, 129, 134, 137–138, 141,
    165–166
  politics and, 99, 135, 186
  pragmatism and, 141, 182–185 (*see also*
    pragmatism)
  psychology and, 127, 145, 203, 367, 369,
    449–450
  of religion, 14–15, 64, 70, 147, 264–266, 268–
    270, 272–277, 382–383, 386
  The Rules of Sociological Method and, 266,
    366–367
  schools of, 15
  science and, 167, 347n7
  of space, 333, 335, 337, 345–346
  Tarde and, 167, 373–374
  of totemism, 114, 321
Sociology and Philosophy (Durkheim), 7
Socrates, 441

soil, normality and, 5
solidarism, 39–40, 47–49
Solidarité (Bourgeois), 48
solidarity
    art and, 285, 295
    concepts of, 39–41, 45, 47–49, 54
    democracy and, 36–37
    discrimination and, 259
    Durkheim on, 11, 39–43, 49–51, 54, 214–218, 251–252, 258–259, 350
    economics and, 233
    in Jewish community, 117
    law and, 246, 250, 252–253, 258–260
    mechanical, 41, 44–45, 47, 49
    organic, 39–41, 44–47, 49, 231
    politics and, 241
    religion and, 117, 270
    social movements and, 299, 302–303
    types of, 214–215, 251–252, 337
Sorbonne, 46, 205
    Bergson and, 189
    Durkheim at, 130, 140, 145, 266–267, 285–286, 353–354
    Durkheimians at, 151
    Lalo at, 285
    Lévy-Bruhl at, 145
    philosophy at, 132
    spiritualists at, 200
Sorel, George, 187, 189–190, 193n13, 209n21
Soulié, Stéphan, 136
Sources of Religious Sentiment (Halbwachs), 151
Soury, Jules, 125
Soviet Union, 238–239
space
    Durkheim on, 344–346
    modernity and, 341
    perception of, 344–345
    religion and, 347n9
    society and, 15
    sociology of, 333, 335, 337, 345–346
Spain, 233
Spencer, Herbert, 55n4, 131, 271, 438
    Durkheim on, 167, 201, 203, 206, 266
    on economics, 231–232
    social Darwinism and, 330n5
    social morphology and, 333, 336
Spencer, Walter Baldwin, 103, 105, 108, 268, 285, 291, 294

Sperber, Dan, 415
Spinoza, Baruch, 173, 441
spiritualists (philosophy), 200
sports, 287
Sri Lanka, 275
standard social science model (SSSM), 73
Stapfer, Paul, 121
state
    Durkheim on, 340, 342
    family and, 359–360
    German and French views of, 198
    human rights and, 256
    origins of, 69
    society and, 431
    solidarism and, 49
Stedman Jones, Susan, 141, 166, 306
Steiner, Philippe, 13
Stoetzel, Jean, 152
Strasbourg University, 151
Stravinsky, Igor, 284
Strehlow, Carl, 150
structural anthropology, 64, 408–410
structuralism
    classification and, 64, 72
    critiques of, 421
    Durkheimian sociology and, 15–16, 152
    historiography of, 414, 416
    language and, 410
    Mauss and, 413
    things and, 102
    totemism and, 114
suicide
    Durkheim on, 250
    economics and, 233
    rates of, 13, 116, 356
Suicide: A Study in Sociology (Durkheim), 2, 30, 34
    on *anomie*, 289–290
    on anti-Semitism, 125–127
    collective consciousness and, 84
    economics and, 237
    on imitation, 372
    on individualism, 219–220
    law and, 245, 255, 257–258
    on morality, 440
    on objects, 93
    publication of, 116–117
    on religion, 270
    reviews of, 146

on society, 368
sociology and, 133
on solidarity, 40, 50–51, 54
Tarde and, 365
western focus of, 58
surrealism, 385, 388
Swiss Constitution, 328
Switzerland, 399n14
symbolic property, 109
symbolism
    animals and, 327
    communication and, 324
    Mead on, 428–429
    theories of, 408–410, 412, 415, 417
    totemism and, 317–320, 324–326
sympathetic magic, 112
Syria, 247–248, 255

Takelma people, 329n4
Talence, France, 350
Tarde, Gabriel
    on anti-Semitism, 126
    Bouglé and, 203
    criticism of Durkheim, 88, 205
    on *The Division of Labour*, 132, 365
    Durkheim and, 15, 365–366, 368–369, 371–375, 378n1, 378n2, 379n3, 379n4
    Durkheim on, 134, 204
    on imitation, 82, 371, 375
    individual and, 190, 372–375
    influence of, 378, 379n2
    Latour and, 15, 364, 374–377, 378n1, 379n7
    sociology and, 167, 373–374
Taylor, Charles, 71, 270, 275, 394, 396, 452
territory, 338–341, 346
terrorism, 247–248, 252
theater, 290
theoretic culture, 70, 77n33
Thévenot, Laurent, 58, 64, 66–67, 72, 455n3
things, social. *See* social things
Third Republic (France)
    academics in, 283
    civil religion in, 277n3
    divorce laws in, 355
    Durkheim's views of, 130–131, 267
    founding of, 214
    Germany and, 195
    ideals of, 23, 53
    individualism and, 271

    morality and, 427
    motto of, 216
    rationalism and, 130–131, 188
    religious conflict in, 265–266, 270
Thomas Aquinas, 205, 208n20
Tiktaalik (prehistoric fish), 329
Tilly, Charles, 155, 302, 304
time, perception of, 345
Tiryakian, Edward, 14, 16
Tooby, John, 73, 78n38
Tönnies, Ferdinand, 41, 44–46, 201, 208n7
Topalov, Christian, 156n13
totemism, 14, 61, 113, 406, 409
    animals and, 172, 316–318, 320–326, 407
    in Arunta religion, 108
    in Australia, 223–224
    Bergson on, 172–173
    definition of religion and, 266
    Durkheim on, 102–105, 112–114, 268, 317–321, 324–326
    economics and, 235, 330n6
    evolution and, 329
    Lévi-Strauss on, 114, 317–318, 406–407, 411
    phases of, 324–327
    ritual and, 108, 111–112, 319–320, 323, 425
    sacrifice and, 109
    theories of, 114, 284, 317–320
    transformation in, 322–323
totems, 8, 59
traditional order, 2
Traugott, Mark, 299, 302–303
Travaux de L'Annee sociologique, 150
Treitschke, Heinrich von, 206–207
tribal societies, 68–69
Troeltsch, Ernst, 267, 277, 394
Troyes, France, 130
truth, Durkheim on, 13, 183–186
Tunisia, 290
Turiel, Elliot, 444
Turkey, 275–276
Turner, Victor, 6, 75n10
"Two Laws of Penal Evolution" (Durkheim), 256
Two Sources of Morality and Religion, The (Bergson), 166, 169–170, 172–173
Tyrell, Hartmann, 209n28

Ubu roi (play), 284
United Kingdom
    anthropology in, 106, 112–113

United Kingdom (*cont.*)
    citizenship in, 246–248, 251, 253–255, 257–259
    discrimination in, 260n5
    Durkheimian sociology in, 151
    moral science in, 198–199
    sociology in, 14
United Nations, 254
United States
    anthropology in, 410
    civil religion in, 276
    Durkheimian sociology and, 151
    Durkheim's reputation in, 299
    economic protests in, 233
    individualism in, 241
    philosophy in, 140
    politics of, 9
    prisons in, 247
    religion in, 451
    sociology in, 379n2
    totemism in, 105
Universal Reason, 32
Unreligion of the Future, The (Guyau), 289–290
Unter den Naturvölkern Zentral-Brasiliens (Among the Indigenous Peoples of Central Brazil) (von den Steinen), 320
"Useful Durkheim" (Emirbayer), 155, 304
"Useless Durkheim" (Tilly), 155, 302
utilitarianism, 34, 122, 198–199
    pragmatism and, 185–186

Vacher de Lapouge, Georges, 145
Vaisey, Stephen, 438–439, 450–453
value, theories of, 240
"Value Judgments and Judgments of Reality" (Durkheim), 92, 442
Van Gogh, Vincent, 284
Veblen, Thorstein, 237, 240
Vietnam, 247
virtue theory, 30
vitalism, 174, 189, 347n2
Vogt, Paul, 152, 192n9
von den Steinen, Karl, 320–322

Wacquant, Loïc, 66
wages, 237
Wagner, Adolph, 198–199, 201–202, 205
Wahl, Jean, 177n1, 187

Wakan (Sioux concept), 105
Walbiri people, 275
Wallaschek, Richard, 284
Wanganui River, 328
Warramunga people, 223
Watts Miller, William, 13, 249, 292
Weberian tradition, 14, 240, 267, 274, 373–375, 407, 438
Weber, Max, 27, 78n38, 367, 374, 378n2, 438, 442
    influence of, 152, 274–275, 277
    on meaning, 141
    on religion, 264, 267, 276
    on social relationships, 41
welfare state, 49
West Germany, 397
Wilbois, Joseph, 178n6
Williams, Bernard, 448
Wilson, David Sloan, 156n12
Wittgenstein, Ludwig, 86, 91
women's rights, Durkheim on, 37n1
Wong, David, 448
worker's rights, 67
World War I
    Durkheim and, 13, 205–206
    Durkheim family and, 357
    Durkheimian sociology and, 150, 293
    French politics and, 266
    marriage and, 352
    pragmatism and, 187
    sociology and, 130
World War II, 12, 351, 383
Worms, René, 46, 134, 166, 378n1
Wundt, Wilhelm, 33–34, 198–200, 209n24
Wuthnow, Robert, 452

xenophobia, 127, 260
Xie Jing, 15–16

Yale Center for Cultural Sociology, 9
Yale University, 17n15
Yamuna River, 328

Zelizer, Viviana, 453
Zola, Émile, 118
Zolberg, Vera, 283
Zoroaster, 69
Zuñi people, 58, 60, 64, 75n15